SOVIET INDUSTRIALIZATION, 1928–1952

Soviet Industrialization

1928-1952

Naum Jasny

 THE UNIVERSITY OF CHICAGO PRESS

Library of Congress Catalog Number: 61–5605
The University of Chicago Press, Chicago 37
The University of Toronto Press, Toronto 5, Canada
© *1961 by The University of Chicago. Published 1961.*
Printed in the U.S.A.

To

VLADIMIR GUSTAVOVICH GROMAN

the planner, the fighter, the great man

The idea of dedicating to V. G. Groman the best writing that I could master is one of long standing. It was difficult to realize because I thought the task could be properly accomplished only with a monograph on planning. I started on a two-volume book on Soviet planning; but circumstances beyond my control prevented its completion. (A small part of it, covering long- and medium-range planning, makes up "Perspective Planning" in *Essays on the Soviet Economy,* to be released about simultaneously with this volume.) Since this work is probably one of my last major efforts, it must serve as a substitute. A short note on Groman is included (see Appendix A). It was previously published in the *Russian Review* (this publication has graciously given me permission to reprint it in this book), because of the possibility that anything worthy to be so dedicated might not be completed. It is important to secure the widest possible circulation of this little note, because of the violent and highly successful efforts of the Soviets to tear out a glorious page from their own history by eliminating every memory of a great generation of Russian intelligentsia (see chapter 3, note 5, for a few other names).

This volume covers the period of Stalin's great drive for industrialization from 1928 to his death. The period from the October Revolution to 1927, inclusive, is handled in an introductory manner in chapter 2. While Stalin died in March, 1953, for statistical reasons the presentation terminates with the end of 1952.

The publication of this book represents the culmination of more than a dozen years of studies concentrated exclusively on the development of the Soviet economy V. The writer's background, which has given him an approach to the problems of Soviet industrialization rather different from that of other analysts, is one of prolonged studies of the agricultural economy of various countries, including Russia, studies which were begun in pre-revolutionary Russia. Work limited to Soviet agriculture was largely completed and published in *The Socialized Agriculture of the USSR* (Stanford University, 1949).

This writer was for a long time caught in the trap of accepting the official subdivisions of the Great Industrialization Drive into five-year-plan periods. Once having realized the error, he proceeded to establish a subdivision of this era into economically relevant stages. The subdivision suggested by the writer is the foundation and the essence of this book. It is hoped that it will ultimately be accepted. The work on the economic stages in turn brought the need for year-to-year analysis. The task is far from being completed, but something along this line seems to have been accomplished here.

There is an obvious lack of proportion among the different parts of this book. Fully in agreement with my ideas, Dr. Colin Clark pointed out (*Encounter* [London], 1955, pp. 43–44) that "the most fundamental problems of the people's well-being in the USSR are now receiving less attention in the Western World, and especially in the United States, than are some of the minute problems of heavy industry." He gave, as an apparently hypothetical example, a study on the output of sulfuric acid. In the United States alone have been published a book on Soviet industry, another on labor productivity in Soviet industry, still others on Soviet steel, petroleum, electric power, and so on. Before long there will be two or three books on Soviet transportation (one exists already), but only one article has been published in the United States, in addition to this writer's sketchy works, on consumption levels of the population. The text which follows shows that holding down private consumption levels lower than anybody could have believed possible was the key to the economic growth of the Soviet economy during the quarter-century of Stalin's complete rule.

Real income of wage earners and peasants, supplies of farm products and industrial consumers' goods, and retail trade—everything related to the consumption levels of the population—all receive as much attention as possible in this book. So far as peasant incomes in particular are concerned, this writer tried his hand in his volume on agriculture, but had to withdraw the analysis as unsatisfactory.

He repeatedly returned to the subject and now has worked out an analysis which seems to be more conclusive. Only the findings are incorporated here. (This makes up one of *Essays on the Soviet Economy,* mentioned above.)

A further disproportion in the book is that in discussing the opposition to Stalin's economic planning in the early years, the non-Party opponents are given considerable attention, while the opposition within the Party is hardly mentioned. This occurs partly because I am so tired of reading Stalin and his followers that I have not studied carefully the writings of Bukharin, Preobrazhenskii, and others. These authors are also better known in the West than the non-Party opposition. The Soviets have succeeded in burying the names of Groman, Ginzburg, and many others who were active in the economic field in the 1920's. N. D. Kondratiev is the only one of this group known in the West. However, he is not known for his important work on the Soviet economy, but for his *Long Waves of Conjecture.* The Communists active in the Gosplan and the VSNKh (Krzhizhanovskii, Strumilin, Kuibyshev, and Kovalevskii) have not been disregarded.

My earlier work contained a significant error in the subdivision of the growth of industrial output into those of producers' and consumers' goods. This item was straightened out with the help of the important findings of Dr. Donald Hodgman.

The writer is over 77 years of age. He has only his pencil as an assistant. For these reasons, the reader will recognize that a full documentation is not possible, and that small errors are unavoidable (large errors are, of course, inexcusable). The writer will appreciate it if his attention is drawn to them.

Together with the *Essays* mentioned above, this volume was started in 1951/52 and was first finished in 1955. It was then reworked and finally completed in the summer of 1958. The manuscript was given brief goings-over in the summer of 1959 and again in the spring of 1960. No full rewriting was attempted. Important new material or similar new findings were just worked in. Most of the additions made in the spring of 1960 are in the form of asterisk notes to the text. The retaining of some material which no longer seems correct, has the advantage that it permits the reader to see, first, the difficulties encountered by the analyst in dealing with the Soviet type of statistics and, second, the degree to which hard work enables penetration behind the Iron Curtain even with regard to such items for which no, or only distorted, official statistics are available. No changes in appraisals were needed. The only changes which might have been made would have been such that the quite substantial revelations of the past in the Soviet statistics published since the completion of the manuscript made unnecessary some of the reservations and restraint believed needed in view of deficient evidence.

The draft completed in 1955 was edited by Mr. Hans Frankel in Dr. Colin Clark's Institute in Oxford, England, with the active participation of the latter. While substantial changes were later made in the book, much of the original text was preserved. The second version was edited by Mr. Will Klump and (first chapter) Mrs. Marlene and Mr. Lester Tanzer.

The various phases involved in Soviet postwar agricultural development were almost endlessly talked over with Mrs. Luba Richter of the U.S. State Department, so that it is impossible to keep apart what is hers and what is mine. This statement pertains also to my other more recent publications on the subject.

Mrs. Martha Bargar, Mrs. Claire Friday, Mrs. Elizabeth Foulger, Mrs. Irene Glass, and Mr. Walter Pintner should also be mentioned. To all of them, and to others unmentioned here, my heartiest thanks are extended.

My work would have been greatly handicapped if the United States Department of Agriculture Library had not let me have books on permanent loan.

With great appreciation I acknowledge assistance in the research and for publication made available under the program for Slavic and East European Studies of the Joint Committee on Slavic Studies of the American Council of Learned Societies and Social Science Research Council.

N. J.

Washington, D.C., June, 1960

CONTENTS

1. Introduction and Summary   1

    The Aims   2
    Over-all Results   5
    Major Stages of the Great Industrialization Drive   11
    Over-all Results Re-examined   21
    The USSR and the USA   24
    Planning   25
    Price Developments   27
    The Background for a Forecast   28
    A Note on a New Index of Soviet Industrial Production   31

2. The First Assault and the Respite   34

    Introduction   34
    The Assault   37
    The Breathing Spell   40

PART A. THE PRE–WORLD WAR II PERIOD

3. The Warming-up Period   51

    Introduction   51
    The "Extinguishing Curve"   53
    Equilibrium   59
    Widening of "Socialism"   62
    Reality and the Targets of the First FYP   64
    Conclusion   69

4. All-out Drive I   70

    Introduction   70
    Bacchanalian Planning   73
    Deflation-Inflation   80
    Investment   81
    On the "Socialist" Front   92
    Greatly Increased Output or Control   93

5. All-out Drive II   96

    Agriculture   96
    All-out Industrialization   97
    Transportation   100
    Retail Trade   101
    Output per Man   104
    Incomes   109
    National Income   114
    The Soviet Economy Grounded   114
    Conclusion   117

6. The Three "Good" Years I   119

    Introduction   119
    The Main Features of the Upswing   122
    Planning   125
    Investment   133
    Agriculture   139
    Industry   142
    Construction   144
    Transportation   146
    Output per Man   146

7. The Three "Good" Years II: The Private Sector   149

    Targets, Boasts, and Reality   149
    Prices of Consumers' Goods   151
    Supplies of Farm Products   156
    Retail Trade   158
    A Note on the Consumption Level of the Population in 1937   161
    Real Incomes   167
    National Income   176

8. The Purge Era I   177

    Introduction   177
    Planning   183
    Investment   187
    Agriculture   195

Industry 198
Transportation 202
Output per Man 204

9. The Purge Era II: The Private Sector 206

Retail Trade 206
The Attack on the Peasants' Economy and the Needs of the
    Population 222
Personal Incomes 223
National Income 231

PART B. THE POST–WORLD WAR II PERIOD

10. Stalin Has Everything His Way 235

Introduction 235
Population 243
Factors Operating toward Recovery 245
Planning 247

11. Inflation-Deflation 257

Introduction 257
Inflation Goes On 260
Deflation 267
Nominal Wages 282
The Price Structure 284

12. Investment 297

Investment as a Whole 297
Investment by Sector 303
Unfinished Investment 305
Concluding Remarks 307

13. Agriculture I: Conditions 308

Introduction 308
Production Factors 310
Enterprises of the Kolkhozniki 317
Payments of Kolkhozy to Kolkhozniki 320
Collectivization in the New Territories 322
Amalgamation Campaign 323
The Picture as a Whole 326

14. Agriculture II: Output; Marketings 331

Output 331
The Various Producers 334
Marketings 355

15. Industry; Transportation; Output per Man   **359**

    Industry   359
    Transportation   376
    Output per Man   380

16. Retail Trade   **387**

    Introduction   387
    Official Trade   390
    Kolkhoz Trade   401

17. Personal Incomes: National Income   **407**

    Personal Incomes   407
    National Income   425
Postscript   **431**

Appendix A.

    Vladimir Gustavovich Groman   435

Appendix B.

    Table I: USSR Net National Product or Income, Selected
       Years   444
    Table II: Real Wages and Real Incomes of the Peasants, Spe-
       cified Years   446
    Table III: Personal Incomes in Specified Years   447

Appendix C.

    The Concept of Kolkhoz Trade   448

Appendix D.

    Glossary and Abbreviations   450

Appendix E.

    Frequently Cited Publications, with Abbreviations 452

Index   **457**

1. The End of Realistic Planning: Planned Rates of Growth of Gross Production of Large-scale Industry in Successive Drafts of the First FYP   57

2. Bacchanalian Five-year Planning   75

3. *All-out Drive:* Fixed Investment Spent and Put into Operation   89

4. *All-out Drive:* Fixed Investment of the Socialized Sector by Major Sector   89

5. *All-out Drive:* Gross Farm Output, 1928–32   97

6. *All-out Drive:* Output of Selected Industrial Goods   99

7. *All-out Drive:* Production and Labor in the Timber Industry   106

8. *Three "Good" Years:* Industrial Production, Specified Targets and Fulfilments, 1935 and 1936   130

9. *Three "Good" Years:* Fixed Investment and Other Important Indicators   134

10. *Three "Good" Years:* Fixed Investment of the State by Sector   137

11. *Three "Good" Years:* Gross Agricultural Production, 1933–36   140

12. *Three "Good" Years:* Output of Industrial Goods, 1932–36   143

13. *Three "Good" Years* versus *All-out Drive:* Railway Operations   147

14. Consumption of Certain Foods by the Non-farm Population in 1937   163

15. *Purge Era:* Fixed Investment in the Socialized Sector   188

16. *Purge Era:* Fixed Investment of the State by Sector   192

17. *Purge Era:* Putting Industrial Capacities in Operation and Utilization of Capacities   193

18. Putting Industrial Capacities in Operation in Specified Periods   194

19. *Purge Era:* Agricultural Production   196

20. *Purge Era:* Industrial Output   199

21. *Purge Era* versus *Three "Good" Years:* Indicators in Railway Operation   203
22. Prices in Kolkhoz Markets in 1950 and 1955   277
23. Investment, 1940 and 1945–52   298
24. Fixed Investment of the State by Sector, FYP Periods   304
25. Sown Acreages: 1940 and Selected Postwar Years   332
26. Output of Major Farm Products: Pre–World War II and Selected Postwar Years   337
27. Sown Acreages, by Type of Producer, 1940, 1945, 1950, and 1953   345
28. Livestock: 1941 and Selected Postwar Years by Type of Producer   346
29. Kolkhozy, 1940 and 1950–53   351
30. Kolkhozy and MTS. RSFSR, 1940, 1950, and 1952   353
31. State Farms, 1940 and Selected Postwar Years   354
32. Marketings and State Procurements of Farm Products: Selected Years 356
33. Industrial Production, 1928, 1932, 1937, 1940, and 1945–53   368
34. Output of Pig Iron by Region   373
35. Output of Crude Petroleum by Region   374
36. Freight Traffic in 1940 and 1945–53   376
37. Rates of Growth of Freight Traffic by Various Carriers in Specified Years   377
38. Rates of Growth of Passenger Traffic by Various Carriers in Specified Years   379
39. Changes in Output per Man in Industry by Branch, 1940–50, and 1951 and 1952   383
40. Retail Trade, 1940–55   389
41. Retail Turnover and Sales Taxes, 1940 and 1944–56   394
42. Volume of Official Retail Trade by Commodities in 1950 and 1952   396
43. Distributions to Kolkhozniki per *Trudoden* in Moscow Oblast, 1948–56 422

1. Growth of Soviet National Income and Its Components, 1928–52   2
2. Major Stages: Three Principal Indicators, 1928–56   13
3. Major Stages: Specified Indicators, 1928–56   18
4. Major Stages: Utilization of Steel Capacities   19
5. Targets of the First FYP   61
6. Targets and Fulfilments of the First FYP   67
7. Investment in Construction vs. Output of Building Materials, 1928–33   87
8. Official Retail Trade, 1932: Specified Commodities   103
9. The End of Bacchanalian Planning: Targets of Annual Plans, 1931–33   120
10. Propaganda and Realistic Planning: Output of Cotton Fabrics   132
11. Investment in Construction and Installation vs. Output of Building Materials, 1932–37   145
12. Official Retail Trade, 1937: Specified Commodities   159
13. *Purge Era:* Five-year Targets and Three-year Fulfilments   186
14. Investment in Construction and Installation vs. Output of Building Materials, 1936–40   189
15. Increases in Sales vs. Increases in Prices in Official Trade from 1937 to 1940   210
16. Official Retail Trade, 1940: Specified Commodities   211
17. Priorities during the Postwar Recovery Period   240
18. Retail Prices in Official Trade, 1945–58   268
19. Retail Prices in Official Trade: Specified Commodities, 1947 (last quarter), 1950, and 1955   271
20. Prices in Official and Kolkhoz Trade, 1945–58   275
21. Investment in Construction vs. Ouput of Building Materials, Selected Years   299

22. Investment in Construction vs. Output of Building Materials, 1936, 1940, 1945–50   301

23. Livestock Herds of the Peasants, 1938, 1941, 1951, and 1953   319

24. Livestock Herds, 1941–54   333

25. Vodka Helps: Sales in Eating Places at Current Prices, 1940, 1950, and 1955   399

CHAPTER 1

INTRODUCTION AND SUMMARY

The quarter of a century covered in this monograph was one of truly great events, including a full-scale revolution. It was a great event that a backward agricultural country was converted into an industrial nation in so short a time and in spite of immense handicaps. Another great event was that an indifferently armed country became one of the best-armed countries in the world. The most striking event of all was that industrialization was accomplished without its normal concomitant—the improvement of the living standards of the population.

The Bolsheviks came on the scene as fighters for socialism and against exploitation, for a great improvement in the well-being of everybody. What they achieved was a great increase in the rate of exploitation, reducing the people's share of the national income to an extent nobody had believed possible. This strangulation of consumption put such large funds in the hands of the state as to permit extensive industrialization and even greater militarization, despite loss and waste of every kind caused by wars, internal strife, mismanagement, and so on.

If one looks for figures as evidence of this revolution, there are probably no better ones than these: While the total personal income (calculated at constant prices) of the expanded population increased by about one-third from 1928 to 1952, the real value of the funds in the hands of the state for investment, military and other expenses, grew almost eightfold. This transformation must be considered a financial, economic, and social revolution. Whether one would agree that it is a transformation into a socialist state is another matter (Chart 1).

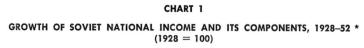

CHART 1

GROWTH OF SOVIET NATIONAL INCOME AND ITS COMPONENTS, 1928–52 *
(1928 = 100)

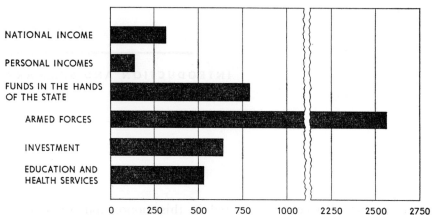

* At real 1926/27 prices. Only the index for total national income is presumably strongly affected by the selection of the weights.

The Aims

By about 1927 the economy of the USSR had recovered from the devastation of wars fought with internal and external enemies, and from Lenin's experiment in introducing communism based on grain confiscated from the peasants. Without any further delays, the Party embarked on a drive aiming at quickly converting Russia from an agrarian into an industrial country. Moreover, the whole economy was to become socialized simultaneously. This new policy meant the end of the NEP (New Economic Policy) which, starting in 1921, had produced the economic recovery, largely with the help of independent and, to a considerable extent, self-sufficient peasants. The inauguration of the post-NEP policies was proclaimed at the Fifteenth Party Congress in December of 1927, which was officially baptized the Congress of Industrialization. The period since this Congress may be properly designated the Great Industrialization Drive.[1]

[1] Approximately the same period was called the Plan Era, meaning the Era of the Five-Year Plans (FYP's), in this writer's *The Soviet Economy during the Plan Era,* published in 1951. The assignment of so much importance to the FYP's was soon recognized as a deeply regrettable error.

The aim of the Great Industrialization Drive was formulated by Stalin with the greatest clarity in summing up the results of the operation of the first FYP: "The basic task of the FYP's was to create such an industry in our country as to be able to rearm and reorganize not only industry as a whole, but also transportation and agriculture—on the basis of socialism." [2]

The super-rapid industrialization, which was made the basic aim, was obviously equivalent to a rate of expansion of industry considerably more rapid than that of the economy as a whole. Within industry, the production of producers' goods, or of "industries A," as they are called in Russia, was to expand at a more rapid, indeed much more rapid, rate than the production of consumers' goods ("industries B"). Such a large rate of industrial expansion necessarily called for a correspondingly rapid growth of investment. Consequently, investment was to expand at a greater rate than national income, while private consumption was to rise more slowly than the latter.

For years, indeed for the whole period covered in this monograph, almost the whole economy was geared to produce ever more steel for the construction of ever more steel and other heavy-industry factories, as well as for the output of ever more armaments. While Joseph Dugashvili probably picked his Party name ("Stalin" comes from *stal'*, the Russian word for "steel") for other reasons, it fitted him extremely well in this sense. The obstacle, obviously deplored by Stalin, was that expanding production of steel and construction of steel factories could not proceed without enlarging the output of building materials and transportation facilities. Nor could much expansion take place without producing at least some consumers' goods and housing for those operating and constructing the steel factories, and these were the least desired items. The principle that the share of investment in national income grows more rapidly than national income itself became so characteristic of the Soviet economy that the years and periods when this was not achieved were definitely marked down as unfavorable, indeed, as times of great disturbance.

The disproportionately rapid expansion of heavy industry remained the basic principle of the Soviet economy, one of its basic "laws," until the death of Stalin. In his comments on Stalin's *Economic Problems of Socialism in the USSR*, the last work by Stalin, E. Lokshin, an official interpreter, wrote:

Of decisive importance for insuring the expanding reproduction is the establishment of correct relationships between the output of means

[2] *Problems of Leninism* (11th ed.; Moscow, 1947), p. 369.

of production and the output of consumers' goods. The principal peculiarity of these proportions, determined by the needs of expanding reproduction, is the greater growth of output of the means of production.[3]

The idea of priority for heavy industry was temporarily abandoned under Malenkov. Even this occurred only in actions, not pronouncements.[4] Khrushchev at once restored the "law" to its full rights. The new seven-year plan for 1959–65 is based on it. In actual practice, for several years beginning about 1949 heavy industry was hardly expanding more rapidly than light industry. In general this was brought about by the fact that the share of heavy industry in the total industrial output had become so large by that time that the Bolsheviks were satisfied to let light industry retain the small share to which it had been reduced. But specifically in 1956 and 1957 efforts to expand heavy industry more rapidly than light industry were frustrated by poor planning resulting in failure to complete investment projects, heavy industry having been primarily affected by this failure.

Industrialization was not simply the principal initial aim of the Drive; it was the only aim. Contrary to official and semiofficial assertions, "defense" was not a problem at the birth of the Great Industrialization Drive. Defense came up only after several years, in 1934 to be exact, but then it grew ever larger in importance, until at a later stage of the Drive defense may have assumed more significance than industrialization itself.

Strangulation of the production of consumers' goods may first have been a necessity. Without this the Industrialization Drive could not have got under way at the great rate desired. As industrialization gained more prominence and as limitless defense requirements came to the fore, the Soviets acquired a real taste for keeping down personal consumption. One might say that this had become almost an aim per se.

After 1949, the output of industrial consumers' goods expanded at the same, or almost the same, large rate as producers' goods, but the initial point having been very low, the output of consumers' goods remained small for years. Only recently have the large rates of growth of these goods started to represent respectable amounts. Also, a larger proportion of the building materials classed as pro-

[3] "The Law of Steady Growth of the National Economy of the USSR," *Communist*, 1952, No. 20, p. 76.

[4] See K. V. Ostrovityanov *et al.*, *Political Economy*, (official) textbook (Moscow, 1954), pp. 409–13. The text contains a special chapter, "Basic Economic Law of Socialism," in which the idea of priority of heavy industry is expounded at length.

ducers' goods have recently begun going into housing, a durable consumer good. But all this is so recent (indeed almost all of it is in the future) that it cannot be covered here.

Over-all Results

The aim of full socialization was attained, if we class as socialism the state ownership of means of production of every kind, including the collective farm (kolkhoz), maintained by sheer force. For that matter, Soviet "socialism" in non-farm pursuits, realized to an even greater extent than in farming, has also been based, not on the economic superiority of socialist enterprise, but on prohibitions[5] and severe taxation.[6]

Industrialization was achieved, but the price in lowered living conditions was great. The rates of industrialization attained did not satisfy those in power, however, and they did not have any intention of disclosing the price paid. Large-scale falsification of statistics was resorted to in order to make the rates of growth seem much bigger than they really were and especially to conceal the fact that instead of rising greatly, as promised and claimed, the level of personal consumption had declined.

The immense rates of growth of industry and national income claimed by official Soviet statistics have been fully discredited. The efforts of pro-Soviet forces to propagandize these rates, which exist only on paper, are only empty gestures and not worthy of much attention. For we have a fair idea of the rates of growth actually attained in the USSR. Indeed, all estimates of the rates of growth of national income, and specifically of industrial output, made outside Russia that are worthy of attention are reasonably close to each other, particularly when compared with the officially claimed fantastic percentage rises. In some cases, there is even full agreement among the estimates of independent analysts. As compared with them, the official calculations of real incomes sound ludicrous.

All estimates presented below are of course only crude. They seem,

[5] Private trade was already fully prohibited in 1931. In 1957, a boy was put in jail for a week for peddling a book by Fenimore Cooper (obviously his own) in the street. Even this little act of trade is believed incompatible with the Soviet kind of socialism.

[6] A person engaged in one of the few permitted handicrafts and not employing hired labor has to pay taxes on an annual income of between 8,401 and 12,000 rubles amounting to 1,596 rubles on the first 8,401 rubles, plus 37.5 per cent on the balance. The rate charged for each additional ruble increases beyond 12,000 rubles per year until it reaches 81 per cent of the amount over 70,000 rubles per year. See decree of March 21, 1951, in *Reference Book of a Tax Officer* (Moscow: State Publishing Office for Finance, 1951), p. 119.

however, to be sufficiently reliable to permit broad appraisals of the significance for the Russian people of "the second revolution" (as the all-out collectivization drive was called by the Bolsheviks themselves) and other developments of the period.

National income by origin.—Gross industrial output appears to have expanded from 1928 to 1950 almost 4 times in size at United States prices and about 4.7 times at Soviet 1926/27 prices. But the Soviets were not after industrialization as such; they were after expansion of the output of producers' goods and this was enlarged about 8.8 times during 1928–50. Output of consumers' goods by industry was just about doubled during this period.

Construction increased about fivefold from 1928 to 1950.[7] The much smaller decline in the growth of construction—and, for that matter, net investment—than of output of producers' goods was due to the much greater growth in expenditures on the armed forces as well as to the great shrinkage of imports of machinery, which had been large in 1928.

Contrary to the high rates of growth of industry and construction, farm output appears to have practically stagnated over the same period. The increases in farm output from 1928 to 1950 (or 1953), within the territorial boundaries of the respective years (i.e., the figures were not adjusted to pertain to the same territory), was indeed no larger than the growth of the population, in spite of greatly increased needs. Furthermore, it is important to note that the output of cotton, which is the principal non-food farm product, was expanded greatly. Hence the production of food items makes an even poorer showing than the total farm output.

Recomputed to 1955, the following approximate indices are obtained, at 1926/27 prices (1928 equals 100):

Industry.................... 775
Construction[a]................ 782
Agriculture................. 150 or somewhat less

a The index was calculated for net investment.

Since agriculture played a very large part in the material production of 1928, the total increase in material production and national income was closer to that shown by agriculture than by industry. Measured at 1926/27 prices—which means that the results are considerably biased in favor of those goods whose output was expanding rapidly during the Great Industrialization Drive, national income

[7] The figure is for net investment implied in the data given in Appendix B, Table I. Construction proper may have increased somewhat less.

at factor cost appears to have grown 3.7 times in 1928–55.* Estimates in dollar prices by Colin Clark[8] (retail prices) and by Grossman and Shimkin[9] (factor cost) indicate a doubling of it in 1928–52 and 1928–50, respectively.[10]

National income by allocation.—Great as was the discrepancy between the expansion of industry, construction, and for that matter transportation, on the one hand, and the creeping growth of agriculture, on the other hand, the discrepancies among the various allocation components of national income were even greater. The almost exclusive attention, common in the West, to the growth of Soviet national income as a whole (this showed quite a large increase, even in per capita terms, during the Industrialization Drive) is likely to mislead. The divergent trends of the major components of national income are at least as important.

As Chart 1 shows, personal incomes increased by only about one-third from 1928 to 1952—a period of immense changes, including a trebling of the urban population. The funds which the state could appropriate for investment and the armed forces increased almost nine times, funds earmarked for expenditures on the armed forces alone about twenty-six times.

The fact that the real value of the funds in the hands of the state grew almost eightfold, while private incomes increased by only one-third cannot be overemphasized. It may be assumed with confidence that this phenomenon is entirely unique; simple comparisons of the growth in Soviet national income with those in other countries thus become rather meaningless.

Net investment increased more than sixfold in 1928–52 at the same time that national income was growing only a little more than

* Late in 1959, after the above was written, *Economy of the USSR in 1958,* the official statistical yearbook, brought fully revamped official estimates of farm production. For the period from 1928 to 1950 it implies a decline in per capita farm production of about 5 per cent, and for the same item in 1928–55 an increase of 5 per cent (*ibid.,* p. 350). The small differences between this writer's and the new official estimates may be partly due to the difference in the concept used. But also, when one tries hard not to picture the situation as gloomier than it actually was, one lands a little bit too high. Finally, it would be inadvisable to accept the new official indices as 100 per cent correct.

[8] Personal communication from Dr. Clark.

[9] "Mineral Consumption and Economic Development in the United States and the Soviet Union," supplement to D. B. Shimkin, "Minerals: A Key to Soviet Power" (Cambridge, Mass: Russian Research Center, Harvard University, 1952, mimeographed), p. 49.

[10] In *Konjunkturpolitik* (Berlin), 1956, No. 2, p. 80, the growth in Soviet national income in 1928–52 was calculated by the writer at 228 per cent at 1926/27 prices and at 159 per cent at 1952 prices. The geometric average for the two percentage rises is 189 (1928 equals 100).

threefold. This would be very important in itself in insuring great rates of economic growth. However, there were also shifts in the distribution of net investment that operated in the same direction. Investment in heavy industry increased at least twelvefold during the Industrialization Drive.

Accompanying these means of expanding plant capacity at high rates were measures taken to assure a plentiful supply of labor. Peasant women were forced into gainful employment by law; practically all other women also held jobs, because of the low income of the family or strong pressures, moral and otherwise. Sacrificed to the Moloch of industrialization were all interests of the wage earners, not only their incomes, but also the right to choose an occupation, to have a family, and the like. The fact that it would mean leaving her family was not considered an adequate excuse for a married woman to refuse a job.[11] Everything, especially planning, was adapted to the main goal of expansion. The targets of the plans were set, not simply to be fulfilled but also to be exceeded. Risks of disproportions were taken into the bargain. To the great benefit of industry, markets tend strongly to be sellers' markets in the USSR.

So far as growth in expenditures is concerned, military might seems to have had, at least until quite recently, an even greater claim than investment in heavy industry. Funds *earmarked* for military use increased, in real terms, about twenty-six fold, in 1928–52, about twice as much as investment in heavy industry. (This expansion continued after World War II on a grand scale, although nothing threatened the Soviet Union except the consequences of her own aggression.) In 1952, the last Stalin year, the funds *earmarked* for military expenditures were more than 60 per cent of net investment at 1926/27 rubles. Total military expenditures[12] may have been not very much smaller than the total net investment in that year.[13]

Against those immense rises in investment and in military expenditures was the increase in personal incomes by only one-third in real terms. Actually the situation was even worse than this over-all figure indicates. As in other poor agricultural countries, national income

[11] Compulsory transfers from one job to another and similar assignments of new jobs were in force from 1940 to about 1953. Since then, the practice seems to have been limited to former students who have to accept jobs assigned them as payment for the tuition and the stipend they were getting while at school.

[12] In addition to expenditures earmarked in the budget for the military ministries, expenditures of a military nature are found also in budgetary appropriations for fixed investment, education, and so on.

[13] The two items (investment and total military expenditures) should not be added in view of a certain amount of duplication.

per capita of the non-farm population was much larger than that of the farm population in the USSR before the Great Industrialization Drive. According to official estimates, the former was 2.7 times as large as the latter in 1927/28.[14] The non-farm population in 1955 showed a growth to about 3.6 times its 1928 size, raising its share from about 25 per cent to substantially more than half of the total population. Under such conditions, an income of the total population in 1952 only moderately below that in 1928, if calculated per capita on the basis of the whole population, implied a large decline in per capita consumption of both the farm and the non-farm population. The increase of total personal incomes by about one-third from 1928 to 1952, as shown in Appendix B, Table I, actually represented a decline of about 25 per cent in real per capita income for the wage-earning population and a decline of about 40 per cent in real per capita income for the rural population. The calculations in this volume, which, it is hoped, are fairly reliable, indicate that even a level of real per capita income equal to 75 per cent of that in 1928 was exceeded only after 1951 (1952–58) for the non-farm population and only in about five years for the farm population (1937 and 1955–58).[15] In some non-war years real per capita income, calculated separately for the rural and the urban population, may have been less than half that of 1928.

A development may not have been fully considered in those figures. During the period analyzed, a great shift occurred from an economy largely based on consumption of home-produced goods to one based much more on purchases. In 1927/28, the income in kind [16] of the farm population was about 58 per cent of its total income and close to one-third of the income of the whole population. By 1938 income in kind was only about 30 per cent and less than 10 per cent, respectively. Operations of the transportation system and trade, as well as the national income, were boosted by this shift in the economy, without any effect on actual consumption. The transfer of much processing from homes, where it is not registered statistically, to industry, where it is so registered, is in itself an advantage to the consumer, but the volume of consumption is

---

[14] The average per capita income was estimated at 313.8 rubles for the non-farm population and at 116.8 rubles for the farm population. See *1st FYP*, I, 137. The difference was actually not as large as the data indicate in view of the differences in prices at which the incomes of the two great population groups were calculated, but it was large even at equal prices.

[15] Real incomes were presumably above the 75 per cent mark for both population groups also in 1929 and 1930. It took time to press the consumption level down from that predating the Industrialization Drive to a level more typical of the Drive era.

[16] Including barter, wages in kind, etc.

not necessarily affected by it; and where, as in the USSR, the transfer of processing is largely forced on the consumer, the value to him of the advantage may be only a fraction of its cost.[17]

Even in a dictatorship as strong as that of Stalin, it was not easy to hold private consumption at the described low level. The task may have become impossible after Stalin's death. If at the same time the state desired to maintain the growth rates of the rest of the economy, there may not have been any other choice for Stalin's heirs but to reduce or at least stabilize military expenditures. The recent sudden interest of the Soviet government in "peace" may be due to a certain or large extent to this necessity.

Rate of exploitation.—The immense shift in the distribution of national income during the Great Industrialization Drive may also be arrived at in another way. Output per man in industry increased presumably by more than 100 per cent over the period 1928–55. Since labor productivity in construction was particularly low in 1928, the increase in it may have been larger than that in industry. Labor productivity in railway transportation just about quadrupled in this period. It increased by at least 35 per cent even in agriculture. Yet real wages in 1952 were less than three-quarters of those in 1928 and per capita peasant incomes were equal to only three-fifths of the respective level.

The rate of exploitation, or, as Marx called it, the surplus product, was small in 1928. But the subsequent rise in exploitation was huge. The surplus value became much greater than the original share of the worker in the total newly produced value.

The figures quoted indicate a worsening of the incomes of the peasants relative to those of wage and salary earners, although they were already particularly low before the start of the Great Industrialization Drive. Small as the total personal incomes were, there was an immense stratification among wage and salary earners and, to a smaller extent, among peasants. The lower strata of the working people, very broad strata at that, were reduced to the position of paupers. Again, if this was socialism, it was a very peculiar form of socialism.

Appraisals.—The Soviets and the pro-Soviet forces consider the results of the Great Industrialization Drive amazing—in the form, of course, in which these results appear in the falsified Soviet indices. Looking at the correct figures, one can only be amazed at the strength

---

[17] Colin Clark and Julius Wyler avoided dealing with the effect of the commercialization of consumption and of the transfer of production on the rates of growth of national income by calculating the consumption of households uniformly at retail prices.

of the dictatorship, which persisted in holding down personal consumption to such astoundingly low levels. This done, the rest appears modest. The real value of the funds in the hands of the state having been increased almost eightfold through 1952 and all the concerted effort made toward industrialization considered, there is no wonder that industrial output, originally small, could have expanded almost six times in 1928–52. With full justification, one could say that the actual attainment was much smaller than it looks at first glance.

At least a partial answer to the question of why an economy which per se is heavily geared to expansion shows only a relatively small *over-all* growth is found by a more careful consideration of the stages through which the Great Industrialization Drive passed after its initiation late in 1927.

Major Stages of the Great Industrialization Drive

The ascertainment of the rates of growth during the Great Industrialization Drive as a whole, while of considerable importance, is not all that is needed. The Soviets continually proclaim that their socialist economy is developing smoothly and proportionately according to plan (there is even said to be a law of such development). That there is a huge disproportion between the farm and non-farm sectors of the economy was shown above in the discussion of national income by origin. There are many other important areas where smoothness of "socialist" economic development exists only in the Soviet imagination. The Drive actually consisted of stages with quite different rates of growth. These stages lose at least some of their characteristics when combined into the rates for the period as a whole. This remains true even if World War II and the recovery from this war are excluded from the period considered.

The great differences in the rates of growth during the various stages of the Great Industrialization Drive have thus far not been given enough attention by analysts. This lack has prevented a full realization of what has happened in the USSR in the past and, even more important, of what may happen there in the future.

The insufficient attention paid to the various stages has been due partly to the state of the evidence with which the analyst has had to deal and—to a much smaller degree—still has to deal. Five dates stand out in the research on the Soviet economy thus far done, i.e., 1927/28 [18] or 1928 (these dates differ only by three months), 1937, 1940, 1950, and 1955. The initial date of practically all research is 1927/28 or 1928. The periods covered are mainly 1929–37, 1938–40,

[18] Fiscal year October–September; the fiscal year was abolished at the end of 1930.

1940–50, and 1951–55—or combinations of these periods. These dates and periods were selected not because they had some specific meaning but simply because statistical data for them were accessible.

This great accessibility was to a large extent due to the fact that the dates and periods were those connected with the operation of the FYP's. The period 1928/29 to 1937 was that of the operation of the first two FYP's, while the period 1938–40 was the time in which the third FYP operated (the third FYP discontinued operating after World War II had started). The fourth FYP was in force in 1946–50, but except where it was advantageous to depart from this principle, the official comparisons for this FYP period were based on the period from 1940 to 1950. The period 1951–55 is that of the so-called fifth FYP. The period most thoroughly analyzed thus far is 1928–37, and again not because of some features which would stamp it as of particular significance but because the data are more plentiful, or were until recently the only plentiful data.

The Soviets are very proud of their planning. It is supposed to be an inseparable part of the "socialist" economy and applicable nowhere else. The planning takes the form of quarterly, annual, and five-year plans.[19] The importance assigned to each type of plan in official pronouncements increases directly with the length of the plan.

The successive FYP's make very convenient stages of development for the official Soviet economic history. Deliberately—to force on the student the FYP periods as the major stages of the Soviet economic development—or not deliberately, statistical data are most ample for the periods of the FYP. Practically no data, for example, existed until recently for 1939, but there was a certain amount of data for 1940.

My examination, to be printed as an essay, "Perspective Planning," leads to the conclusion that the FYP's are largely façade, not playing the role in the economy ascribed to them, but serving principally as propaganda. A specific advantage of the use of the FYP's as major stages of economic development is that, if the Soviets did not subdivide their economic history since 1928/29 into FYP periods, they would have to subdivide it into other periods which might permit an undesirably closer insight into Soviet reality than that permitted by the FYP periods.

As soon as one realizes that the FYP periods are not really significant periods of Soviet economic history and are largely façades, the situation becomes clear, and the subdivision of Soviet economic

---

[19] By order of May, 1955, the idea of planning for a period of ten to fifteen years (the general plan) has been revived. According to the announcement of October, 1957, the Soviet Union will have a seven-year plan in 1959–65.

the factors leading to the slowdown probably started to operate as far back as the period *Stalin Has Everything His Way*. For some reasons not clear to this writer (possibly the moral disintegration of the dictatorship) new construction projects were started in numbers far exceeding the ability to complete them. Unfinished construction gradually reached such huge proportions and new capacities entering production became so few that a substantial retardation in the rate of economic growth ensued. A large part of this mismanagement may have originated in 1951 and 1952, the years of the Korean War. The five Great Stalin Constructions of Communism, inaugurated in the second half of 1950, may have been the starting point. Nothing was done in the first *Post-Stalin* years to bring the situation under control.

The rates of growth of the Soviet economy during the various stages will be analyzed in greater detail in the subsequent chapters. It is sufficient here to say that the rates of growth of industry and investment in the *Three "Good" Years* and during the periods of *Stalin Has Everything His Way* and *Post-Stalin* were very large. The effects of the very considerable share of investment in national income and of the dominating role of heavy industry in the large total investment reveal themselves with the greatest force in these periods. The slowdown in 1952 shown by the statistics of industrial output and investment was due not only to the fact that the recovery was already a matter of the past but also to the rapid expansion of military expenditures. Taking into consideration these factors and the stagnation in agricultural production, the rate of over-all growth in this year still appears very large.

On the other hand, more than half of the thirteen-year period from 1928 to 1940, namely, about three years of the *All-out Drive* and four years of the *Purge Era*, was extremely bad. The average rates of growth of industry and transportation in these periods were several times lower than during the *Three "Good" Years* and *Stalin Has Everything His Way*. There is no trace of the effect of the large share of investment, especially in heavy industry, in total national income on the over-all growth during these periods. Part of these investments simply went to waste. Otherwise the expanding capacities served to offset the declining utilization of capacities previously accumulated. Real national income was actually declining for the greater part of the *All-out Drive*.

The *All-out Drive* and the *Purge Era* obviously contributed greatly to the fact that the rates of growth during the whole Industrialization Drive, especially during its prewar period, turned out so much lower than during the periods favorable to the Soviets. The

history into really relevant periods forces itself directly on the analyst. The only difficulties arise from the fact that the effects of certain policies continued to operate for some time after the policies themselves had been discarded, and one is, therefore, uncertain whether to consider a certain period as starting with the inauguration of the respective policies or with the time when they had begun to show their effects. Furthermore, in order not to complicate the statistical analysis more than is absolutely necessary, one wishes to limit oneself to whole years (actually calendar years), but neither the discontinuation of certain policies nor the start of the operation of new policies necessarily occurs on January 1 of a given year.

CHART 2

MAJOR STAGES: THREE PRINCIPAL INDICATORS,* 1928–56
(Year-to-year rises, in per cent)

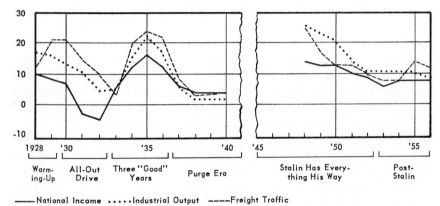

——National Income   ·····Industrial Output   ----Freight Traffic

* Indices of national income and industrial output as calculated by this writer at 1926/27 prices. The figure for national income shown under 1928 pertains to 1927/28. Data for freight traffic in ton-kilometers are official but are here mostly taken from the material of Dr. Holland Hunter.

The Soviet economy passed two stages, the War Communism and the New Economic Policy (NEP), before it embarked on the Great Industrialization Drive. The era here analyzed begins with a short period of less than two years, designated the *Warming-up* period (Chart 2). The period was characterized primarily by the maturing of ideology, which permitted the Great Industrialization Drive to get into full stride, an ideology fundamentally different from that of the NEP. Actions along these lines, departing more and more from those appropriate under the NEP, were secondary. Farm output stagnated as the result of the fight against the *kulaki* (larger peasant farms), already in progress, while private retail trade was rapidly shrinking for similar reasons. As stated above, the Party Congress of December, 1927, is taken as the starting point of the whole era. It is also the starting point of the *Warming-up* period.[20]

The *Warming-up* period ends and a new period begins with the start of the All-out Collectivization Drive in the autumn of 1929. The publication of Stalin's famous "The Year of the Great Turn" in *Pravda* of November 7, 1929, is taken as the specific date when the period started. It was characterized not only by the All-out Collectivization Drive itself but also by a similar drive to industrialize almost overnight, which was associated with immense appropriations for investment, and, last but not least, with wildly unrealistic planning. These additional features justify the more general designation of the period as *All-out Drive*, rather than the narrower All-out or Full-scale Collectivization Drive.

Declining farm production; declining rates of growth in industry and transportation, which finally ended in complete stagnation and possibly even in a decline; immense declines in consumption levels; and, at the end, decline also in real national income—these are the features of the *All-out Drive*. Ideologically the period ended with the acceptance of the 1933 annual plan early in January of 1933. But the catastrophe brought about by the *All-out Drive* lasted all through the winter of 1932/33. In our statistical presentation, the period ends with the expiration of the calendar year 1932.

While the first half of 1933 was disastrous, the second half of the year showed recovery features. Hence, the whole of 1933 lacks any definite face and is left outside of the subdivision suggested here.

The Soviets enjoyed a period of rapid expansion, which is assumed to have started at the beginning of 1934 and to have lasted until the end of 1936—the *Three "Good" Years*. (Quotation marks are used here to qualify "good" because the rapidity of the recovery was to a considerable extent assured by keeping consumption levels very low for two years and only relaxing the pressure moderately in the third year.)

The four years 1937–40 constitute the *Purge Era*. While the purges were over by the middle of 1938, their paralyzing effect on the economy lasted until the end of 1940. The insistence of the government that an upturn had started in the second half of 1940 seems not to be in accordance with facts.

An appropriate name for the postwar period until Stalin's death

---

[20] In the summer of 1927, the almost endless upward revisions of the targets set in the draft of the first FYP, known as the *Perspectives*, began (see Table 1, p. 57). This time might have been another suitable data as the starting point of the *Warming-up* period and the Great Industrialization Drive as a whole.

seems to be "Stalin Has Everything His Heart Wanted" *Has Everything His Way*. The characterization of the Grea trialization Drive as the striving for steel and almost not steel pertains with particular force to this period. The pa followed was already set early in 1946, but the crop failure prevented Stalin's wishes from moving into high gear b second half of 1947. Thus the features of the period are parent only in the developments of its last five years, if w only with full years.

The period *Stalin Has Everything His Way* was charact the rapid, indeed super-rapid, growth of industry, con transportation, and national income, in spite of the un effects of the Korean War and, what is even more imp spite of the slow growth in farm output, which in the last t years stagnated, or possibly declined.

The rates of economic growth during *Stalin Has Every Way*, which would be large anyway, were considerably a by the fact that it was a recovery period, as well as by so factors. At first glance, it would seem that the recovery peri be counted only until the time the level of the 1940 o reached, an event which occurred in 1948 for the non-farm But it seems more accurate to regard as the end of the recov the time when the economy achieved the *productive cap* had been reached by 1940 (and even later) but was not ful in that year because of the effect of the purges. Until this reached, rates of growth could well be substantially larg normal years. For some sectors of the economy this po recovery was not reached before 1951.

It is of immense importance, considering the present st world, that *Stalin Has Everything His Way*, a period fav the Soviets, was not followed by a period unfavorable fc was the case before World War II.[21] The year of Stal (1953) caused some temporary retardation in the rate of growth, but the subsequent years until 1956 were on the w favorable. Moreover, they were healthier than the years of *Everything His Way*, because after 1954 expansion had although not in a very satisfactory way, to agriculture as

A certain slowdown in the economic growth took pla and became considerably stronger in 1957. Strange as this

---

[21] Peter Wiles of Oxford wants to treat the prewar segment of th analyzed as a preliminary stage, with postwar the mature stage. This v to accept this subdivision. But Wiles's suggestion contains the relevant the substantial difference between the prewar and postwar economy.

unworkable kolkhoz system, the great amount of over-all irrationality and inefficiency, the squandering of immense resources on propaganda, and Stalin's plans for changing the climate of Russia, specifically forest-belt plantings on millions of hectares—all these were factors tending to reduce further the over-all results. But it may be argued that the Soviet system has advantages over the capitalist system, which may have largely offset the effect of these additional disadvantages.

The disasters of the *All-out Drive* and the *Purge Era* followed upon the more or less favorable periods. The moment there was some improvement, the Soviets came up with something tremendously wasteful. The restoration of the pre–World War I level in agriculture by about 1926, for example, led to increased pressure on the kulaks and soon thereafter to the "second revolution," with "annihilation of the kulaks as a class" as its battle cry. The restoration of the industrial output to pre–World War I capacity brought about the *All-out Drive*.

The three favorable years, 1934–36, were immediately followed by the immense wastefulness of the *Purge Era*. In agriculture the recovery by 1937 to the production levels which had prevailed before the All-out Collectivization Drive brought an attack on the peasants consisting in encroachment on the small concessions made to them, in the form of plots of private garden land and permission for limited livestock holdings. These were the very concessions which had made possible the *Three "Good" Years*. The attack on the private economy of the kolkhoz peasants, which began in 1938, has never ceased. It was only relaxed somewhat during World War II.

After World War II, recovery to prewar levels was followed by the Korean War, associated with great military expenses, Khrushchevshina (amalgamation of the kolkhozy, agro-cities, etc.), and ultimately by the wasteful practice of starting too many investment projects. Whatever gains there were, the Soviets seemed to be unable to avoid wasting part of them. But the negative effects of all these practices on the rest of the economy in the postwar years were very much smaller than during the *All-out Drive* and the *Purge Era*.

The stages illustrated.—Chart 2 shows the rates of growth in three important indicators (national income, industrial output, and transportation). Chart 3 adds the rate of growth of steel, as representative of the output of heavy industry; cotton fabrics, as representative of the output of consumers' goods; and farm output. Chart 4 shows how the stages of the Great Industrialization Drive were reflected even in the development of production techniques.

Farm output has already been discussed. Steel output reflects

CHART 3

MAJOR STAGES: SPECIFIED INDICATORS, 1928–56 *
(Steel in millions of tons; cotton goods in billions of meters; farm output in billions of rubles)

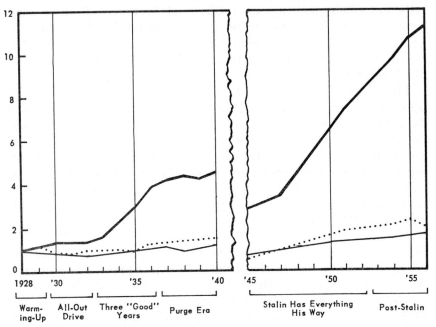

Steel ····· Cotton Fabrics ———— Farm Output

* Data for steel and cotton fabrics from *Industry of the USSR,* 1957, pp. 106, 329; and *Economy of the USSR in 1956,* pp. 69, 90. Data on farm output (volume available for sale and consumption in the farm home) in pre–World War II years from *Soc. Agri.,* p. 676, with small adjustments; the 1940 figure pertains to pre-1939 territory; the estimates for postwar years also were made by this writer.

clearly the relevant steps of economic growth; rapid growth in the *Warming-up* period, including 1930, stagnation during the *All-out Drive* (not including 1930), rapid growth during the *Three "Good" Years,* and renewed stagnation during the *Purge Era. Stalin Has Everything His Way* and *Post-Stalin* show an uninterrupted strong rise in steel output until 1956. Stalin's death did cause a small slowdown of the rate of steel output. More important was the slowdown in 1956 and 1957.

The doubling in the output of cotton fabrics in 1928–56, as against an almost elevenfold increase in steel output, characterizes the Great Industrialization Drive perfectly. It is also very relevant that the output of cotton fabrics was smaller in 1935 than in 1928, in spite of the great increase in urban population, with its much larger per capita consumption in value terms.

CHART 4

MAJOR STAGES: UTILIZATION OF STEEL CAPACITIES *

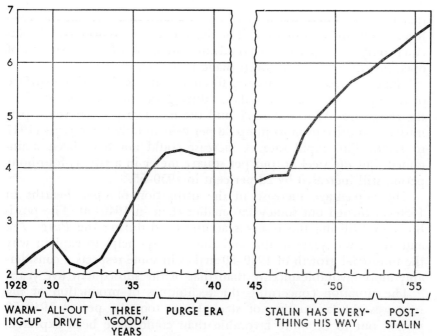

* Steel output per square meter of capacity of open hearths in tons in 24 hours. See *Economy of the USSR in 1956*, p. 68.

The helplessness of those in power under the conditions of the *Purge Era* is clearly reflected in the fact that the slowdown in the rate of growth in output of cotton fabrics was not as large as that of the badly needed and badly wanted steel.

It is of great interest that the stages of the Great Industrialization Drive are reflected with great force even in such technical factors as steel output per square meter of open hearths. While steel output increased 10.5 times in size from 1928 to 1955, the number of open hearths was little more than doubled. The latter increased from 222 in October of 1928 to 489 on January 1, 1956. This drastic misproportion was made possible by the fact that the surface of the hearths was enlarged on the average by 63 per cent and the output of steel per square meter of the open hearths rose 3.2 times during the period.[22] But these great enlargements and improvements did not occur at anything like a uniform rate (Chart 4).

The average output of steel per square meter in a twenty-four-

[22] *Industry of the USSR*, 1957, pp. 122, 124.

hour period increased by 21 per cent from 1928 to 1930, but was back almost at the 1928 level in 1932. Then came a jump of 74 per cent in the *Three "Good" Years* to a level by 1936 almost double that in 1928. There was a small increase also in 1937, but the 1940 level was below that of 1937. The decline during World War II was equal only to 11 per cent. No advance to speak of in utilization of open hearths could have been made in 1946 and 1947.

The great reserve of capacity to enlarge utilization of the surface of the open hearths, accumulated during the decade comprised of the *Purge Era,* World War II, and the first two postwar years, permitted this utilization to jump 38 per cent in only three years (1947 to 1950). This rapid rate of increase could not have been maintained, but the steel output per square meter in a twenty-four-hour period still increased by 22 per cent in 1950–55.

The percentage increase in the utilization of open hearths in 1950–55 turned out somewhat smaller than in 1940–50. The possibility of utilizing the reserves accumulated during the *Purge Era* and in the war years in this and similar ways helps to explain why the industrial growth of 1940–50 makes in some respects a considerably more favorable picture than that of the subsequent five years.

The situation concerning the techniques of production of pig iron was similar to that of steel. Here, too, the period 1940–50 turned out to be more favorable than could have been expected, owing to such a phenomenon as considerable unused capacities in 1940. The output of pig iron was enlarged by 29 per cent in 1940–50. The number of blast furnaces, however, went down from 99 to 92, while the cubic volume of all of them remained unchanged.[23] Thus the total increase in the output of pig iron in 1940–50 was attained by a more intensive utilization of the volume of the blast furnaces.

Data such as those for open hearths and blast furnaces could be multiplied greatly. All of them reflect the major stages of Soviet economic development during the Great Industrialization Drive with about as great a force as the data for output. Any departures had special reasons. For example, labor productivity on railways continued to stagnate through 1934 (a growth of 0.3 per cent per year in 1932–34), but then it increased by 45 per cent in three years (1934–37). The behavior of labor productivity on railways in 1933 and 1934 merely reflected the lagging recovery of all rail transportation from the *All-out Drive.* After a rapid growth in 1935–37, the

[23] *Ibid.,* p. 120.

rise in labor productivity on railways was again equivalent only to exactly 3.3 per cent during the last three years of the *Purge Era.*[24]

Over-all Results Re-examined

With the greatly divergent rates of growth during the various stages of the Great Industrialization Drive established, one can return to the question of why all the great sacrifices had produced relatively little.

To begin with, one has to deduct from the total period of the Great Industrialization Drive about seven years for World War II and the postwar recovery of output. Even less time would have been needed for this recovery than was actually spent if the Soviets had demobilized properly after the end of World War II. Actually, they continued to expend tremendous amounts on the armed forces all through the period *Stalin Has Everything His Way.* In spite of the handicap of large military expenses recovery was rapid and the annual rates of growth remained very large until 1951. During the whole prewar period of thirteen years, from 1928 to 1940, we find only about five years, of which three were made up of the *Three "Good" Years,* really favorable from the Soviets' point of view. For agriculture, the *Three "Good" Years* were merely part of the recovery from former losses. Agricultural output stagnated in the remaining two of the five years.

But this also stands out clearly: In those periods when the Soviet machine operated with a reasonable smoothness, when major disturbances were absent, or when the Soviets succeeded in reducing the harmful effects of those disturbances, the large sector of the economy consisting of heavy industry, investment, and transportation made big strides ahead. It could not be otherwise in an economy powerfully geared to expansion by the large share of net investment in national income, the distribution of investment so as to foster particularly rapid expansion of the economic potential, and in view of all the other factors operating toward expansion. In these favorable periods even real national income as a whole expanded greatly, in spite of the lagging of farming and, consequently, of personal incomes.

Relevant stages versus FYP periods.—As is obvious from the preceding presentation, the proposed subdivision of the Great Industrialization Drive into stages has some features in common with the FYP periods. But these similarities are overshadowed by the differ-

[24] Data from A. A. Chertkova, *Labor Productivity on the Railway Transportation of the USSR* (1957), p. 50.

ences. The *Warming-up* period started almost a year before the first FYP period (one and one-quarter years ahead of approval of the FYP) and ended after the first FYP had been in operation for about one year (but only a few months after its approval).[25] The culmination of the *All-out Drive* period coincides, at the end of 1932, with the termination of the first FYP period, but only because the operation of this FYP was discontinued nine months ahead of schedule. Those in power may have been anxious to set a landmark to indicate the end of the abhorrent situation into which their previous policies had plunged the country's economy. The period of the *Three "Good" Years* excludes the first and last years of the second FYP period. The *Purge Era* starts in 1937 rather than in 1938, the first year of the third FYP. The period of *Stalin Has Everything His Way* extends for two years beyond the fourth FYP period. But there actually were no approved FYP's in final form during the *Post-Stalin* period. There will be none until at least 1966.

Even the official subdivision of the Great Industrialization Drive into FYP periods does not support the Soviet claim that the Soviet "socialist" economy operates according to the law of proportionate expansion according to plan. The period of the first FYP was disastrous, that of the second FYP favorable. Output per man in large-scale industry, for example, declined by 8 per cent during the first FYP, according to Donald Hodgman, but increased by 68 per cent during the period of the second FYP.[26] The official third FYP period was again unfavorable, while those of the fourth and fifth FYP's were favorable.

But the actual fluctuations were even more dramatic. The far less favorable developments in 1933 and again in 1937 as compared with those during the *Three "Good" Years* are buried in the period of the second FYP, being partly smoothed out by the high rates during the *Three "Good" Years,* 1934–36. In Soviet practice the first and second FYP periods are usually combined into one period (unfortunately this practice is common also in the research of private students outside the USSR) and thus the disaster of a large part of the first FYP period is concealed entirely. The decline of the rates of growth during the third FYP period, if acknowledged by official sources at all, has been explained by the effect of war preparations. In spite of the obvious evidence to the contrary, this unjustified explanation has been accepted also by many foreign analysts.

[25] The time of approval is actually considerably more important for the appraisal of the targets set in the FYP than the official date the FYP was supposed to have come into effect.

[26] *Soviet Industrial Production, 1928–51* (Cambridge, Mass.: Harvard University Press, 1954), p. 113.

The period 1928–37, the one best covered thus far by foreign analysts, was indeed the least uniform period of the Great Industrialization Drive—without a significant beginning or a significant end. It actually consisted of two periods distinguished here—the *All-out Drive* and the *Three "Good" Years*—and of portions of the *Warming-up* period and of the *Purge Era*. Moreover, the period 1928–37 is largely history. The whole economic setup of the country has changed so fundamentally since then that hardly any reliable conclusions can be drawn for the future from the rates of growth in that period.

The rates of growth during the third FYP period (1938–40) differed little from those of the *Purge Era* (1937–40); the former were slightly more unfavorable than the latter. The main fact in this case is that the years 1938 through 1940 must be clearly marked as belonging to the *Purge Era* rather than as having been the period of the third FYP. The fact that the third FYP is supposed to have operated during those years lacks any economic significance.

The fourth FYP period was just an abbreviated *Stalin Has Everything His Way*. The basically unchanged attitude toward farming in 1951 and 1952, the last two years of *Stalin Has Everything His Way*, makes it preferable to deal with this period rather than with the period of the fourth FYP. The other changes brought about by Stalin's death also make it advisable to deal with the periods *Stalin Has Everything His Way* and *Post-Stalin,* rather than with the periods of the fourth and fifth FYP's.[27]

Neglect of relevant stages illustrated.—David Granik's *Management of the Industrial Firm in the USSR* (Columbia University Press, 1954) contains a great deal of interesting material, but it suffers from insufficient realization of, or insufficient discrimination among, the various relevant stages of Soviet economic development. The development from 1934 to 1941, i.e., in substance from the *Three "Good" Years* with their enormous rates of growth to the *Purge Era* with its near stagnation, is described (*ibid.*, p. 55) as movement to "a more stable industrial economy." On pages 73–74, Mr. Granik says: "There has . . . been considerable unexplained idleness of plants." In support, the "glaring case" of the cement industry in 1936–40 is cited. Practically full use of capacities is one of the most important features of the Soviet economy in normal periods. The glaring amount of unused capacities in 1940 and the immediately preceding years in the cement and other important

---

[27] Actually the Soviets also operate with the *Post-Stalin* period, only they do not call it this, and more frequently use 1953 rather than 1952 as the base year for comparisons.

industries was brought about by the paralyzing effect of the purges on the economy (see "Unfinished Investment" in chap. 12).

It may be an impossible task for an analyst to distinguish in all cases between phenomena which are more or less typical and those brought about by exceptional conditions, between phenomena which represent gradual maturing and those which are departures in the opposite or another direction. But the realization of the great differences between the individual stages of Soviet economic development helps much to place things in their proper perspective.

The USSR and the USA

The first thing reporters have usually wanted to know is how the USSR compares with the USA in gross national product (GNP). They have been disappointed when I have told them that I do not cover this topic. This is not exactly the truth. The truth is that comparisons of the Soviet and American GNP have been greatly misused and it could be dangerous to pass the evidence on to inexperienced hands.

The comparison of the economic potential of such greatly divergent countries as the USSR and the USA cannot be expressed in one relevant figure. Yet this is what is wanted and what is usually done. Industrial and farm output of the USSR was about 40 and 60 per cent, respectively, of those of the USA in 1955. USSR construction in that year was probably equal to 60 per cent or more of that of the USA and freight traffic was half as large. But the USSR had more teachers, physicians, and, most notably, soldiers than the USA, although their average quality was presumably not as good.

According to a calculation of Allen Dulles, head of the Central Intelligence Agency, rather widely used in the USA, the gross national product of the USSR was slightly greater than one-third of that of the USA (the calculation presumably pertains to 1955). The estimate has frequently been reproduced in a form even more favorable to the USA.* The estimates of *material* production underlying Dulles' calculation hardly differ significantly from those given above. The figure given by Dulles for the Soviet GNP was so low as compared to that for the USA because he estimated *services* in the USSR (by implication) at only 15 to 16 per cent of those in the USA.

This low evaluation of the relationship in the production of services is not obtained by comparing the *services rendered*. This is hardly possible, and would not have been so unfavorable for the USSR if it were possible. The low relationship in services is ob-

---

* I am happy to say that Mr. Dulles abandoned this calculation recently, but it had a very undesirable effect on American thinking for years.

338.0947   J311

c.1

tained by comparing their *cost* in terms of goods (services are re-duced to goods) in the two countries. The unfavorable showing of the USSR in services is simply due to the low earnings of teachers, physicians, and soldiers in that country. (White-collar workers par-ticularly are discriminated against in salaries in the USSR.)

It is obvious that the calculation "The United States may be producing currently about three times as much goods and services as the Soviet Union" [28] substantially underestimates the economic potential of the USSR. It is especially unusable for comparing the military potential of the two countries.[29] The output of armaments may have been no smaller in the USSR than the USA. Their large output would have been compensated for by such factors as the production in the USSR in 1955 of only 1.5 passenger automobiles for each 100 produced in the USA. Comparisons in terms of the GNP and similar material lead to embarrassment such as that caused by the appearance of the Sputniks.

Planning

It has already been mentioned that the FYP's were to a considerable extent just a façade. The Soviets acted as though the FYP's were the basic centralized single plans; the annual single plans were sup-posed to have been segments of the corresponding FYP's, and the quarterly single plans, segments of the annual plans.[30] Only the last assertion is correct.

[28] *Soviet Economic Growth: A Comparison with the United States,* a study prepared for the Subcommittee on Foreign Economic Policy of the Joint Economic Committee of the U.S. Congress by the Legislative Reference Service of the Library of Congress (Washington, 1957), p. 132.

[29] Such use was widespread in this country. See, for example, the paper of Edward Kershaw presented at the meeting of the American Economic Association in Chicago in December, 1950, *Papers and Proceedings, American Economic Review,* May, 1951. This writer has objected on several occasions to the comparisons of the GNP in the USSR and the USA in the form in which they usually are made. Discussing Kershaw's paper in the meeting just mentioned, I said, "The important factors seem not to have been considered that in the United States the pay and upkeep of a soldier costs several times as much in goods and services as in the USSR." *Papers and Proceedings,* p. 486. See also *Essay I,* p. 14.

Comparison of national income is not the only item liable to create confusion. G. Warren Nutter, head of research on the Soviet economy in the National Bureau of Economic Research, calculated for a great number of industrial commodities the number of years by which the USSR is behind the USA (*U.S. News and World Report,* March 1, 1957). It is a strange array of figures. The USSR was likely to reach the USA in coal output in 1958, yet in Professor Nutter's calculations, the USSR in 1955 was forty-seven years behind the USA in coal production. These and similar figures (fifty-four years for paper, sixty-nine years for railroad freight cars, and sixty-nine years for woolen and worsted fabrics) simply do not make sense for a country that more than doubled its industrial output in seven years, from 1949 to 1956. And where are the Sputniks in Professor Nutter's list?

[30] A single plan is a plan which covers the whole economy.

The lengthy preparations of the first FYP started on the premise that a real operational plan was being produced. But in the course of the preparations, contact with reality grew ever more remote, and in its final form the FYP could as well be called an instrument of propaganda. The FYP's continued largely to play this role until their end (the statement does not apply fully to the recently accepted seven-year plan [SYP]).

The important problem of the FYP's or centralized planning as a whole, cannot be discussed here in detail. The very facts that the second FYP, which was to start operating on January 1, 1933, was not finally approved until November of 1934, and that the first discussion of the Directives to the fifth FYP, which was to begin operating on January 1, 1951, did not take place before October of 1952, indicate that the Soviet economy did not operate on the basis of FYP's. The years 1956–58 were years entirely without a five-year plan. Ironically, the fourth FYP was the only one which was delayed for only a short period—about three months. But this FYP was passed under disturbed economic conditions, when the future could not be foreseen with any degree of accuracy, and hence when a proper FYP could not have been worked out at all. The task was easy under such circumstances. As for the third FYP, no trouble was taken to complete the formality of having the draft which had been accepted by the Eighteenth Party Congress stamped by the government. A document entitled "Directives of the Party to the Fifth FYP," and so treated at the Nineteenth Party Congress, which had approved it, later became, without any formal action, the final fifth FYP.

There were no FYP's which did not fail in at least some important individual targets. The first and third FYP's failed completely. The targets of the Directives to the sixth FYP were set so badly that this FYP was discarded even before it was approved.

It may be argued with considerable justification that the targets of the first three FYP's for the whole area of private consumption, including agriculture and trade, were never intended to be realized. The targets affecting private consumption of the fourth FYP (farm output, output of consumers' goods by industry and retail trade) also were missed although by smaller margins than previously. The targets of the so-called fifth FYP for increase in farm output were fulfilled only about 40 per cent.

The primary function of the FYP's as a means of propaganda does not preclude the fact that whatever long-range plans for individual sectors or branches—such as electric power and specifically hydro-electric power, railway traction, and some others—existed at the time of preparation of the respective FYP, they were incorporated in it with at least superficial linking among the individual parts. This gave the FYP's the appearance of solidity. But just about everything would probably have developed in the same way even if the FYP's had not existed.

The Soviet economy can hardly be operated without plans, specifically without centralized single plans. As far as the latter are concerned, the function of planning is carried out in the first place by the annual centralized single plans and their segments, the quarterly or half-yearly plans. The Soviet experience shows that it is quite possible to plan for the next year in a centralized manner, although planning as a whole suffers from overcentralization and, until recently, from overdrive, too. The second, third, and fourth annual plans of the early years (they were called Control Figures for 1926/27 through 1928/29) functioned reasonably well after the initial stage (Control Figures for 1925/26) had been passed. The situation would have been even better, if the Party had not tried to get more from the economy than this could yield. These excessive demands passed into circulation by way of the Control Figures and, in failing, discredited the latter. The annual and quarterly plans operated with reasonable smoothness during the *Three "Good" Years* and presumably were so operating (except probably for agriculture and some other items) during *Stalin Has Everything His Way* and later.

The annual plans did not fare so well during periods unfavorable to the development of the Soviet economy. During the *All-out Drive* the Bolsheviks made the sky the limit in their annual plans too. The unrealistic planning of that time was an important factor contributing toward the development which culminated in the disaster of the winter of 1932/33. During the *Purge Era,* the targets of the annual and quarterly plans were on the whole smaller than those during the *Three "Good" Years,* yet even these failed almost throughout. The annual plans thus again lost their contact with reality. Little is known of the operation of the annual plans in the years after World War II. Until 1956 only one (that for 1947) was published and even this in an extract. The annual plans of recent years have not functioned very well, but they have functioned.

Price Developments

In its forty years of existence the Soviet Union has passed through two incomplete major inflation-deflation waves of immense proportions. The first inflation-deflation wave was almost completed before the start of the Great Industrialization Drive. The latter began when the deflation which started early in the twenties was still alive, so far as producers' goods were concerned. With reference to consumers' goods, the deflation was over. Prices of consumers' goods started to rise again in 1928, simultaneously with the Great Industrialization Drive. Producers' goods followed suit in about mid-1930. The new inflation swing lasted almost two decades. It was only natural that World War II and its aftereffects accelerated this development to a considerable extent. From the end of 1947 for consumers' goods and from the end of 1949 for the producers' goods, a new deflation swing was in progress which may not have ended by 1958. The kolkhoz trade was the only exception in that it reached the peak of the second inflation in 1943.

The most important phenomenon in this area was the disproportionate development of prices. The prices of consumers' goods at their highest point were about thirty-five times higher than 1928 prices. The highest point reached by the prices of producers' goods was only six times the 1928 level. Although the price decline of consumers' goods from its highest point to 1958 was much greater than that of producers' goods (about 55 per cent for the former and perhaps one-third for the latter), the prices of consumers' goods in 1958 were almost fifteen times higher than in 1928, while the prices of producers' goods were only four times higher.

Thus an immense shift in price relationships took place. Producers' goods had become much cheaper relative to consumers' goods. While in 1928 the price relationship in the USSR was much less favorable for farm products than in the USA, the reverse has become true since then.

The inflations and deflations and even more the shifts in price relationships have, of course, been of great importance. They are discussed in various parts of this volume. Let it be stated right here that the great shift in price relationships implies immense difficulties for economic analysis. Indices computed in prices of any one year, whether initial, ultimate, or even intermediate, are obviously more or less defective. More refined methods are needed, but these are beyond the power of an analyst working without clerical assistance.

The Background for a Forecast

It has been shown that the smooth development of the Soviet economy according to plan existed only in official and semiofficial pronouncements. Actually, during the prewar years, short periods of high rates of expansion were followed by short periods of low rates of expansion and even by stagnation or an occasional decline. Only the postwar period shows strong uninterrupted expansion, with a certain slowdown of the rates of growth in the most recent years. These ups and downs may seem to make it advisable to base forecasts for the future, if made at all, on average rates of growth over the longer past—with necessary adjustments, of course. But this is hardly correct.

In dealing with periods showing more or less typical business cycles, the use of average rates during whole cycles is the only reasonable procedure. However, while the Soviet development displays ups and downs comparable in strength with those of the business cycles of the capitalist countries, the situation is vastly different. Under capitalism the ups and downs of the business cycles have their causes in the economic system itself. Each period of prosperity bears the seeds of the next depression, and vice versa. The Soviet economic system, as such, does not produce a regular recurrence of slowdowns. Whatever economic slumps had occurred had purely or largely political causes.[31] However, the Soviet dictatorship, on which economic development depends, has few elements of stability in itself. One can, therefore, with considerable justification, take the position that the great dependence of the Soviet economy on the political power, and the nature of this power, makes recurrence of economic disturbances so likely that it is inadvisable to neglect them in any forecast.

It is obvious that the introduction of the political factor immensely complicates the task of forecasting. The assumption that in the future the disturbances will be of about the same strength as in bygone days seems too simple. Observation of the developments during *Stalin Has Everything His Way* persuades one that the Soviets are learning from their own mistakes. It seems certain that the blunders of the *All-out Drive* are not going to be repeated in full strength. Purges also have acquired a form which thus far has been much less harmful to the economy than were the consequences of the *Purge Era*. It must be granted that *Stalin Has Everything His Way* had its own big blunders in the continual wrong handling of agriculture and in starting an immense accumulation of unfinished investment projects. But the negative effects on the economy were mild as compared with those of the *All-out Drive* and the *Purge Era*.

While the basing of forecasts on periods which have included mass purges or all-out drives is not without justification (wars and recoveries from wars must in any case be excluded; the forecast of

---

[31] The only exception may be the most recent slowdown which started in 1956, although even this may have been caused by the deterioration and weakening of the dictatorship during the last Stalin years and after his death.

future Soviet economic development aims first to estimate the economic strength of the USSR as of the time it may enter a major war), it seems more accurate to base the forecast on the assumption that the Soviets will be able to avoid major economic disturbances. If the assumption turns out to be wrong, the predicted rate of growth will just be too high. There is probably less harm in an occasional overestimate than in being persistently on the low side.

If the forecast is made for conditions excluding major economic disturbances, the outstanding factor to be considered seems to be that the Soviet economy is geared to great expansion rates. However, the specific conditions of the period for which the forecast is to be made introduce some relevant modifications.

To put the forecast on firm ground, it must be based on rates attained in the past. But it should not be a long past. To use the rates of growth of the Soviet economy since 1913 and specifically to compare them with those in the United States would keep the Western world in the dark concerning the Soviet potential. For various reasons the Soviet Union did not reach the 1913 level of production again before 1927. These thirteen years were lost entirely, and their inclusion in the calculation of the rates of Soviet economic growth as an indicator of possible development in the future is an artificial means of minimizing the Soviet threat.

The use of the periods 1928–37 or 1928–40 as guides for forecasts of the Soviet future is still standard in the United States. It may be wiser to agree with Peter Wiles, who considers the whole pre–World War II period a preliminary phase in Soviet economic growth.

Various attempts have been made to base an analysis on the rates of growth since 1937. This the writer has always regretted. The Sputniks, let us hope, have opened the eyes of many. The period 1937–55 consisted of three years of the *Purge Era,* four years of World War II, three years of recovery, and about eight years following the recovery. The post-recovery period was less than half of the total period, which lasted eighteen years.

With the proviso that major disturbances will not be considered, the period to be used as a basis for forecast naturally becomes the *Post-Stalin* period. The period of *Stalin Has Everything His Way* was largely one of recovery. Adjustments of the extra-large rates of growth in this period to arrive at "normals" would not be easy.

For the non-farm economy the five-year period 1952–56, inclusive, seems to be the most suitable starting point for forecasts. National income was growing at little less than 9 per cent per year in that period. The annual rate of industrial growth during this period was presumably about 11 per cent. The rate of growth of construction probably differed only little from that of industry. Farm output grew in the five years, 1952–56, inclusive, at about 5 per cent per year, or close to this.* All major adjustments needed to adapt the rate to the future (greatly declining availability of labor; shifting of satellite countries from assets to liabilities; help to underdeveloped countries; the complications arising from an excessive number of investment projects in process of construction; last but not least, the necessity to do more for the domestic consumers) will be in the direction of reducing rather than increasing the future rates of growth. The rate of economic growth in the USSR in 1951–55, or 1952–56, will probably remain unsurpassed except for *Stalin Has Everything His Way*, a period of recovery, and the *Three "Good" Years*, in a sense also a recovery period.

The Control Figures for 1959–65, released after the above was written, set the probable rise of national income in 1958–65 at 7.1 to 7.4 per cent per year as against the official rate of annual growth of over 11 per cent and the here-accepted rate of close to 9 per cent in 1950–55 or 1951–56. The official forecast does not substantially differ from that visualized by this writer. Large military expenditures would prove a handicap in reaching the goal set in the Control Figures.

**A Note on a New Index
of Soviet Industrial Production**

The June, 1960, issue of the *American Economic Review* (pp. 295–318) contains a new index of Soviet industrial production by N. M. Kaplan and R. M. Moorsteen of the RAND Corporation. Although this index is at least the sixth such attempt, it certainly serves a useful purpose in substantiating previous findings and bringing something new. This writer welcomes this addition to the armory of American research on the Soviet economy by authors one of whom did not welcome this writer's work (see p. 222 above).

The fact that the authors seem to have covered the subject thoroughly, that in particular they made a special extensive study, as yet unpublished, of the Soviet machinery industry, and yet did not believe it possible to cover the whole industry, imbues confidence in their work. Not covered are the very important armament industry, and also the non-ferrous industries, the chemistry industry, the whole sewing industry, bread and bakery products, etc. The omis-

---

* The most recent official estimates in *Economy of the USSR in 1958* (p. 350) imply an annual rate of growth of about 8 per cent in this period (48.5 per cent in five years), but the rate seems to be exaggerated.

sions certainly affected the findings substantially and must be kept permanently in mind in using the data.

Like some others, the index attempts to establish the trend in net output. A peculiarity of the index shared only with one other is that it uses a late year—1950—as the base. This feature must tend to make the rates of growth appear smaller than if an early year were used as the base.

The index is calculated year by year from 1950 to 1958. Only some years are covered for the period 1927/28 to 1950, i.e., the period studied in this volume. Moreover, the selected years are not those which marked the relevant stages of the eventful pre–World War II period (as such the years 1927, 1930, 1933, 1936, and 1940 would seem appropriate), but the standard years of investigations on the Soviet economy (1927/28, 1932, 1937, 1940), which unfortunately (by necessity) play an excessive role also in this volume (see for example, Appendix B, Tables I–III).

The over-all growth of Soviet industry during the period 1927/28 to 1950 in the new index is moderately smaller than in some other indices (the index shows a growth of 270 per cent over the period stated as against 335 of Shimkin-Leedy and 370 of this writer),[32] but the difference is caused, at least to a large extent, by the incompleteness of the new index. It seems, on the other hand, certain that this writer did not minimize the Soviet economic growth, as he rather widely was suspected to have done.

The most interesting finding of Kaplan and Moorsteen seems to be their calculations of the output per man. The findings, if they are in any way correct, are most disheartening for the Soviets. Fortunately the data are given for the industry minus machinery, i.e., with exclusion of the most uncertain part. Only manual workers were considered in the calculation, resulting in a certain exaggerating effect on the calculated rates of growth. The data are as follows (1950 equals 100):[33]

Year	Producers' Goods Other Than Machinery	Consumers' Goods	Total[a]
1927/28	68.7	86.7	79.3
1932	74.1	89.6	80.8
1937	112.5	98.8	105.8
1940	103.8	100.8	102.4

[a] The method of weighing is puzzling. In view of the producers' goods other than machinery being given much greater weight than consumers' goods in the total output (the weights used by the authors are stated on p. 296), one expects the weighted average, for example in 1927/28, to be much nearer to 68.7 than 86.7, but the reverse is shown by the data in the tabulation above. My count, for what it is worth, indicates a weighted figure for that year of 73.3 rather than 79.3 as shown in the source.

[32] *Op. cit.*, p. 301.
[33] *Ibid.*, p. 314.

All the growth in output per man in the industries specified which was attained in the twenty-two-year period from 1927/28 to 1950, was limited to 26 per cent, according to Kaplan-Moorsteen (36 per cent according to this writer's recount of the authors' data). The period 1932–37 was the only one with growth in any way substantial in output per man during the period mentioned. (Most of this increase certainly occurred in the three years 1934–36.) If the years 1931 and 1932, i.e., the main part of the *All-out Drive,* were taken out of the period 1927/28 to 1932, those years would have shown a substantial decline.

Output per man declined also during the 1937–40 period, the main part of the *Purge Era* (it is odd that the purges are not mentioned by the authors in the discussion of this period; only preparations for war are brought up, although there is no reason why these preparations should have reduced more than slightly the rate of growth in output per man observed in the *Three "Good" Years* in the industry specified. The output per man in 1950 was measurably smaller not only than that of 1940, but even more than that of 1937.

The growth in output per man in the machinery industry during the period specified was much greater than that shown by the total industry, less machinery. But the fact remains that all the industrial growth (other than that in the machinery output) in 1937–50 and more than this, was attained by sheer numbers of labor force, drawn from agriculture without regard to the adverse effect on the agricultural output and the well-being of the population. There is little so unfavorable for the Stalin era in this whole volume as the findings of Kaplan and Moorsteen on the output per man in industry.

CHAPTER 2

THE FIRST ASSAULT

AND THE RESPITE

Introduction

When Lenin's Party took power in 1917, Russia was a very poor, backward, agricultural country, much closer to Asia than to the more advanced countries of Europe or to the United States. Familiarity with these facts did not affect Lenin's actions when he got the chance to act.[1]   In 1928, when the situation was, in many respects, little different from that immediately before the Revolution, a farm population in the USSR[2] of over 100 million produced only 58 per cent of the farm products turned out by the United States with a farm population of thirty million.[3] The industrial output of the USSR amounted to 10.5 per cent of that of the United States in the same year.[4] The real national income of the USSR, as a whole, was 30 per cent of that in the United States in 1928, according to Colin Clark.[5]

[1] Lenin described the extremely low levels of peasant consumption in chapter 12 of his *Development of Capitalism in Russia.*

[2] CSO, *Statistical Handbook of the USSR for 1928* (Moscow, 1929), p. 42, gave for 1926/27 a farm population of 112.7 million out of a total of 148.1 million.

[3] The percentage for output, certainly exaggerated, is from *The USSR and the Capitalist Countries, Statistical Handbook*, compiled by Y. A. Joffe and L. M. Tsirlin (Moscow and Leningrad, 1939), p. 9. Farm population in the United States is from *Statistical Abstract of the United States, 1936*, p. 8.

[4] Rolf Wagenführ, *Die Industriewirtschaft* (Institut für Konjunkturforschung, 1933), p. 42. The estimate was accepted officially in the USSR by the Institute for Current Economic Research (Konjunktur Institut) of the Gosplan USSR, *The USSR and the Capitalist World* (Moscow and Leningrad, 1934), p. 28.

[5] Private communication.

The reorganization in agriculture brought about by the Revolution must have, *ceteris paribus,* proved a handicap to rapid economic progress, particularly to rapid industrialization. Not only were the large estates abolished but also the larger, more efficient peasant farms which, together with the estate owners, had a large share in the total marketings of farm products—these being the foundation of any non-farm economic activity. Little stratification remained in the village after the Revolution. The great emphasis on the riches of the "kulaks" (literally "fists," a term used maliciously for the more affluent peasants) was almost wholly a propaganda trick. Around 1926 total farm output was restored to the prewar level, yet marketings of farm products were far below this. The countryside in general presented one gray mass of largely self-sufficient peasants.[6] In 1927/28, the total value of farm products available for sale plus consumption by the farm homes and increase in livestock, was close to 10 billion rubles. Of these only 2.7 billion rubles' worth, or little more than one-quarter, was sold outside the village.[7] Of the approximately 7 billion rubles' worth of products which remained in the village, 2.3 billion were listed as sold within the village, but part of this was barter.

Before and after the Revolution, the peasants were largely vegetarians. Their diet included only very little fat (perhaps 2 kilograms of vegetable oil per person per year and some pork fat) and consisted almost exclusively of carbohydrates. In the northwest, it was grain products and potatoes; in the rest of the country, mainly grain products. The consumption of grain products by the peasants (in terms of grain) exceeded the very high figure of 250 kilograms per capita per year. On the other hand, an annual average of only 18.7 kilograms of meat (including pork fat), 183 liters of milk (including dairy products), and 46 eggs were consumed per capita.[8]

Since sales of farm products outside the village were small, the peasants had little to spend on non-farm goods. In 1927/28, at the then prevailing high prices for manufactured consumers' goods,[9] the rural population had only 27.4 rubles per capita per year for purchases of non-farm goods.[10] which at that time included sugar,

[6] See *Soc. Agri.,* chapter 8, especially Chart 11. As on many other occasions, foreigners go beyond the most baseless propaganda assertions in Soviet Russia itself. According to Paul Sweezy of Harvard (*Socialism* [New York, 1949], p. 19), ". . . before the end of the NEP such [farm] surpluses as there were had come largely under the control of the kulaks." Stalin himself seems not to have said anything so drastic.

[7] *Control Figures for 1929/30,* p. 478, and other official sources.

[8] *Soc. Agri.,* pp. 85, 92, 95, 778. All data on consumption are for 1927/28 but are roughly valid also for 1913.

[9] A pair of boots cost about fifteen rubles, a pair of shoes about nine rubles.

[10] *1st FYP,* II, Part 2, 74, and I, 105.

tea, vegetable oil, and the indispensable vodka. On the average, they could buy only one pair of footwear (of any kind) per person every four years.

The average living standards of the urban population, while very low, were higher than those of the rural population. The urban population consumed almost three times as much meat and twice as many eggs per capita as the rural population. It had 104.5 rubles per capita to spend on industrial consumers' goods (the population depending on wages had 127.8 rubles per capita for this purpose). This sector of the population consumed about twice as much textiles and about four times as much footwear per capita as the rural population.[11]

These much higher consumption levels of the urban population were to play havoc with the Party bosses, when their policies brought about a great increase in the proportion of urban population in the total population. They were unable to maintain the supplies of many important consumers' goods even at the national average per capita, let alone assure the urban and rural populations their respective former consumption levels.

Russia, like many other backward countries, had a large birth rate and a rapid population growth, which, per se, were handicaps to rapid economic growth, especially for a country relying heavily on agriculture. But these features proved an advantage for communist and socialist experimenting, because the excessive deaths and reduced birth rates caused by such experimenting did not matter so much as they would have under other conditions. Both Lenin and Stalin made the greatest use of this opportunity, but many of those in favor of a smaller population growth in Russia would have preferred birth control to the Lenin-Stalin methods of introducing communism at the cost of millions of lives.

In 1918, when Lenin started his attempt to introduce communism overnight, the economic situation was even worse than that in 1927/28 or 1913, described above. First, the economy of the country had been adversely affected, though not as much as is sometimes supposed, by World War I and, much more severely, by the developments since the Revolution of February, 1917. Second, as soon became apparent, that section of industry and trade which had been socialized shortly after the Revolution turned out to be a less efficient, and consequently a more expensive, producer and trade intermediary than it had been under free enterprise before the revolution. The non-socialized portions of industry and trade also operated less efficiently than before. All this must inevitably have occurred at the

---

[11] See source in note 10 above as well as *1st FYP*, II, Part 2, 81.

expense of the peasants and adversely affected their output, especially the marketed portion of it. Here was the nucleus of the disproportion between the Soviet non-farm and farm economy which plagued the Soviets at least until very recently.

The Assault

Before the abortive revolution of 1905, the Bolsheviks—as other Marxists—believed that the proletariat would be the creator of socialism and that socialism would therefore be introduced first in highly industrialized countries. They changed their minds when they saw a chance to come to power. In retrospect, it was found that backwardness is a factor favoring the introduction of socialism.[12]

Actually, when the chance offered itself, Lenin at once went all the way and tried to establish communism rather than socialism. The fact that the country had just gone through World War I and was involved in civil and other wars did not deter him.

The communism Lenin wanted to establish was of a peculiar type. It was to be limited to cities. Lenin showed little concern for the social order in the villages as long as these fulfilled the function assigned to them in his scheme, of providing, without any real payment in exchange, the grain through the distribution of which he expected to establish communism in the cities.

The experiment lasted only about three years. In March, 1921, Lenin was compelled to proclaim a retreat. But the short time which had passed was sufficient to bring the economy to a virtual stop. In 1921/22 gross farm output was equivalent to only about 55 per cent of that in 1913.[13] Under the generally precarious conditions of a poor, backward country, such an output level implied starvation for almost the whole country and death for millions. The "proud builders of communism" were compelled to let the despised American capitalists feed the starving objects of experimentation. Large-scale industry and public means of transportation were almost entirely paralyzed. The output of the former, compared with 1913, amounted to only 15 and 13 per cent in 1919 and 1920, respectively.

---

[12] This opinion gained acceptance even in highly scholarly places. Abram Bergson wrote, for example, under the auspices of the American Economic Association: "My impression, based on the Soviet experience, is that a most favorable moment for the socialist revolution is at an early stage of capitalist development . . ." ("Socialist Economics," in *A Survey of Contemporary Economics,* ed. M. S. Ellis [Philadelphia and Toronto, 1949], p. 440). This writer is unwilling to forget that the introduction of socialism at an early stage of capitalist development in the USSR was associated with millions of deaths by starvation, with mass purges, concentration camps, and plain slavery.

[13] *1st FYP,* I, 15.

Whole industries came to a standstill; the public transportation system almost completely stopped.

The following data demonstrate the "effectiveness" of the economy under Lenin's communism. Large-scale industry, whose output in 1920 was equivalent to 13.1 per cent of that in 1913, employed 51.6 per cent of the number of wage earners in the latter year, and net monthly earnings in real terms were equivalent to 26.4 per cent of those in 1913. Freight traffic by railway decreased 75.6 per cent, but the needed personnel more than doubled (an increase of 106.5 per cent, to be exact).[14] Thus, the effectiveness of transportation operations per wage earner declined to not much more than one-tenth of its prewar level.

The standing official version of the reasons for the measures taken to introduce communism was as follows:

This whole system of measures, brought about exclusively by the difficult conditions of defense of the country, having been of a temporary nature, was called War Communism.[15]

We have Lenin's authentic acknowledgment that War Communism was a *deliberate voluntary attempt* at introducing communism in cities based on grain obtained by force from the peasants and distributed by rationing. Moreover, he was frank enough to give this attempt as the reason for the disaster into which Russia plunged in those days. In a speech at the second All-Union Congress of Political Enlightenment in October of 1921, he said:

On the economic front, with the attempt at transition to communism, by the spring of 1921 we had suffered a defeat more serious than any from Kolchak, Denikin, or Pilsutskii.[16]

And also:

In the beginning of 1918 . . . we made this mistake that we decided to effect a direct transition to communist production and distribution. We had decided that the peasants would give us in the way of *razverstka* [requisitioning of all surpluses and more than this] the amount of grain we needed and that we would then apportion this among the factories and we would have communist production and distribution.[17]

---

[14] "Basic Indicators of the Dynamics of the National Economy during Ten Years of the Revolution," *Planned Economy*, 1927, No. 11, pp. 261–63.

[15] *Short History of the Communist Party* (approved by the Party in 1938), p. 219 of the Russian edition (Moscow, 1946).

[16] *Lenin's Works* (Moscow), XVII (1935), 40.

[17] *Ibid.* Several weeks after the speech quoted, in December of 1921, the Eleventh Party Conference, in a resolution passed on the report of the same Lenin (*VKP(b) in Resolutions and Decisions* [2d ed.; Moscow, 1932], I, 482), spoke of "the methods

A few million tons of grain deliveries more, and the ambitious goal of paradise on earth would have been reached.

Planning.—There was quite a bit of talk of national economic planning at that time. At Lenin's instigation a group of engineers even produced a State Plan for the Electrification of Russia (GOELRO), which also included targets for some other sectors of the economy. But only the immense propaganda ability of the Kremlin succeeded in presenting this plan as more than a lure to capture the support of the people, the only purpose Lenin himself intended it to have.[18] * It had not yet been realized at that time by those in power that economic planning was not a job which could be done by engineers alone.[19] Years passed after the end of the period of War Communism before planning started in earnest.

---

in the realm of national economy, which were used in the preceding period and were brought about by the special conditions of raging civil war." A few pages later (p. 486) the resolution even claimed that the basic principles of the New Economic Policy "were laid down in the spring of 1918." Later, the Party consistently disregarded Lenin's October, 1921, statement and insisted on the interpretation in the December, 1921, resolution.

[18] In the letter to Krzhizhanovskii, the future president of the GOELRO and of the Gosplan, Lenin, ordering the preparation of the plan which was to become the GOELRO, wrote: "It must be prepared at once to show clearly, understandably to the masses; . . . it must draw a clear and brilliant (basically fully scientific) perspective 'To work, and in ten to twenty years we will make all Russia, industrial and agricultural, electric'" (see G. M. Krzhizhanovskii, *Works*, Vol. I: *Electrification* [Moscow, 1933], p. 66). In 1952, a volume was published, *On the History of the Plan for the Electrification of the Soviet Country* ("Collection of Documents and Materials 1918–20," ed. I. A. Gladkov [Moscow]). The above-mentioned letter from Lenin, the most important among the documents pertaining to the GOELRO, was wisely omitted from the collection.

* Columbia University is in possession of very valuable Memoirs (in manuscript) of N. V. Valentinov, who was editor of the VSNKh, *Trade-Industrial Gazette* (Moscow), in 1922–27. With the gracious permission of Mr. Valentinov, I got access to the Memoirs, but only in 1960. One of the important items I drew from the Memoirs was that Lenin had obtained the idea of the GOELRO from a book, *Postwar Perspectives of Russian Industry*, by a Moscow professor of engineering, V. I. Grinevetskii. The book was published in Kharkov in 1919. The GOELRO turns out to be largely an elaboration of Grinevetskii's brilliant ideas. Lenin's wrong opinion that planning is to be done by engineers seems also to have had its origin, at least partly, in the fact that such an exciting book was produced by an engineer. The success in concealing the real father of the GOELRO would have been 100 per cent, if not for the Memoirs, at least so far as this writer is concerned. The fact that Grinevetskii turns out to be the father of the GOELRO does not change the credit given to Groman in note 19 below for having been first to propagandize the idea of a single economic plan. Grinevetskii can be considered the father, if at all, only of the long-range plan, the least important form of planning. Moreover, it is unlikely that Grinevetskii did not hear of Groman's "Single Plan of Regulating the National Economy and Labor."

[19] John Jewkes (*Ordeal by Planning* [New York, 1948], pp. 2–3) said, incorrectly, that Lenin "is believed to have been the first in the USSR to speak of planning." V. G. Groman started to propagandize the single economic plan as far back as March, 1917. At that time Lenin's ideas went along anarcho-syndicalist lines (workers' control inside the enterprises, the latter remaining fully independent from the outside).

The Breathing Spell

The basic principle.—Lenin turned to the NEP (New Economic Policy) to heal the wounds inflicted by the wars with domestic and foreign enemies and by the experiment with communism. "Exchange of goods is recognized as the basic lever of the new economic policy," stated a resolution of the Tenth Party Conference.[20] The resolution of the Eleventh Party Conference on the report of Lenin spoke of "starting from the existence of the market and accepting its laws," and "of alleviating and expanding the exchange between towns and villages." It also demanded that the economic services of the state be paid for.[21] The measure itself (the introduction of the NEP) was decided by the Tenth Party Congress (March 8–16, 1921) on the report of Lenin and A. Tsuryupa.[22]

The proclamation of the exchange of goods as the basic lever and the emphasis on the existence of the market and its laws as the foundation, the basic point of the party's economic policies, are understandable only if we remember that in the last stage of War Communism distribution in the cities was by rationing *without* the use of, even without appraisal in, money. This form was believed to be the realization of the communist ideal. Nor was there actually any exchange between the city and the village, the latter delivering its products in the way of *razverstka*. It was irrelevant that the goods were paid for in money, because money was worthless.

Under the NEP, exchange of goods was to be the way in which wage earners were to obtain the goods they needed. But the cornerstone of the system was to be the *exchange* between the cities and the peasants. Thus, the NEP was to be primarily a combination of socialized large-scale industry with small-scale peasant farming, the latter largely liberated from the fetters of War Communism.

The course of events.—If the idea of expanding socialization was dormant at all, it was so for only a short time, possibly a few months, after the introduction of the NEP. Wholesale trade and, especially, large-scale industry were almost fully socialized even before the introduction of the NEP. In large-scale industry, for example, private enterprises employed only 2.7 per cent of all industrial workers employed in 1923/24.[23] The share of the private sector in

[20] *VKP(b) in Resolutions and Decisions* (2d ed.; Moscow, 1932) I, 469.

[21] *Ibid.*, p. 482. The abolishing of these payments a short time previously was the crowning gesture of the introduction of communism.

[22] *Ibid.*, pp. 418, 460–61.

[23] *Control Figures for 1926/27*, pp. 204–5.

wholesale trade was somewhat larger than this, but still very small. In 1925/26 it amounted to 7.3 per cent of the total.[24]

Private small-scale industry and private retail trade were at first favored. Later, private small-scale industry was just tolerated, while private retail trade was pressed hard by taxation and other measures.[25] In 1926/27, the share of private owners in small-scale industrial production still amounted to 82.1 per cent of the total.[26] The share of private owners in retail trade, which in 1923/24 made up 57.7 per cent of the total,[27] declined to 37.4 per cent in 1926/27.[28]

Only in the realm of agriculture was no progress made at all in the direction of socialization during the NEP. The Party was satisfied to leave the peasants alone, as long as they were rapidly expanding their output. The collective farms were favored in various ways, but there was no compulsion to join them. To the disappointment of the Communists, the number of collective farms and of their members even declined during the NEP. On June 1, 1927, less than 1 per cent of all peasant households was collectivized; the number of collectivized horses and cows amounted to only 0.2 and 0.1 per cent of their respective totals.[29]

The results in output.—In spite of the unfavorable price relation between farm products and industrial goods, the peasantry responded to liberation from the fetters of "communism" with a rapid increase in output. The recovery of agriculture carried in its wake a corresponding recovery of industry, transportation, and living standards.

The Party, certainly with considerable reluctance, acknowledged the leading role of agriculture. The following passage from the resolution of the Thirteenth Party Conference, January, 1924, is of particular interest in this connection, because it emphasized an idea later declared to be a crime (there was, it is true, an abundance of such ideas). The passage is as follows:

[24] *Control Figures for 1929/30*, pp. 442–43.
[25] According to computations of the Commissariat of Finance, a private trader in Moscow had to pay 15 to 20 per cent of his gross turnover in taxes (*Yearbook of the Economic Press, 1924/25* [published by *Planned Economy*, Moscow and Leningrad, 1926], I, 224). In 1928, S. G. Strumilin wrote: "In the interests of socialization we established *different prices* and other conditions *for the same commodities* sold to the private trader and the cooperatives, different freight rates for the private and socialized sector, and so on" ("The Process of Price Formation in the USSR," *Planned Economy* [1928], No. 5, p. 47).
[26] *Control Figures for 1929/30*, pp. 442–43.
[27] *Socialist Construction of the USSR, 1936*, p. 607.
[28] *Control Figures for 1929/30*, pp. 442–43.
[29] *Soc. Agri.*, p. 299.

The Twelfth Party Congress [April, 1923], in its resolution on the organization of industry, specifically put forward and emphasized the opinion that the rate of development of our state industry is restricted by objective limits, determined by the state of the peasant economy, and that a painstaking harmonization of the whole economic policy with the level of development of the peasant economy is an important task, the incorrect fulfilment of which inevitably brings about pernicious results not only in the economic, but also in the political sphere.[30]

The realization of the leading role of agriculture was still alive in the resolution of the Fourteenth Party Conference (April, 1925),[31] but it was mentioned as relating only to the first years of the NEP in the resolution of the Central Committee of the Party of April, 1926.[32]

Since the recovery of industry began from a very low level in 1921, the rates of growth were very large. The growth seems to have been particularly strong after the industrial machine was again in operation. In the two years 1925 and 1926, for example, industrial output increased by 138 per cent.

The output of industrial consumers' goods was growing more strongly than the output of producers' goods in those years. Large-scale industry showed the following rates of increase (in per cent of the preceding year):[33]

Year	Total	Consumers' Goods	Producers' Goods
1924	16.4	22.8	9.7
1925	66.1	71.9	59.3
1926	43.2	41.6	45.2
1927	14.4	14.1	14.8
1928	24.8	26.6	22.5

Total construction, as an index of investment, was expanding at very adequate rates in those years. The rates of growth of non-rural construction were, indeed, so large that everybody should have been satisfied. This is obvious from the following data at 1926/27 prices (increases in per cent of the preceding year):[34]

Year	Total Construction	Non-rural Construction
1926/27	25.9	43.9
1927/28	19.8	35.0

[30] See *VKP(b) in Resolutions and Decisions* (2d ed.; Moscow, 1932), I, 654.

[31] *VKP(b) in Resolutions and Decisions* (5th ed.; Moscow, 1936), II, 43.

[32] *Ibid.*, I, 95.

[33] Without forestry and fishing and at 1926/27 prices. See *Socialist Construction of the USSR*, 1935, p. xli.

[34] *Control Figures for 1929/30*, pp. 422–27.

Official statistics, shown below, indicate that the gross agricultural output and gross industrial output moderately exceeded the prewar level by 1927/28, but on a per capita basis there was still a slight deficit in both farm output and national income:[35]

Item	1913	1927/28	Increase from 1913 to 1927/28 (in per cent)
Population (million).................	139.7	151.3	8.3
Agriculture (billion rubles at pre-Revolution prices).................	10.5	11.0	4.8
Industry (billion rubles at 1913 prices)...	8.4	10.1	20.2
National income (billion rubles at 1913 prices).........................	14.0	15.0	7.1

As far as industry is concerned, the situation was actually not quite as favorable as the above data show because industrial statistics did not take into consideration the deterioration in the quality of output since prewar days.[36] This overvaluation of the post-Revolution industrial output was, of course, transferred to the national-income account.

Unhealthiness of the situation.—While the recovery from the depths brought about by War Communism was rapid, the situation was very unhealthy even after the restoration of the prewar production levels. The peasant economy remained largely self-sufficient. While during the recovery the peasants were in a hurry to restore their food consumption and also to obtain the means of purchasing the most indispensable industrial goods, there could not be any reason to expect that expansion of farm production would continue after the prewar level was approximately reached. There was particularly little elbowroom, with the existing price relationships and the discrimination against the more well-to-do peasants, for an expansion of the farm output *for the market,* even at a moderately rapid rate.

The socialized enterprises—in industry and even more in construction—were very expensive operators. Savings from the practical elimination of interest charges, and from smaller profits, were more than offset by inefficiency and high operating costs. The high production costs in industry were clearly reflected in the price indices. In 1927/28 the wholesale price index of industrial goods stood at 187.7 (1913 equals 100), while the same index of farm products was only 156.7.[37] Actually, the difference was even greater, because the

---

[35] *1st FYP,* I, 15, 144–46.

[36] Testimony of L. B. Kafengaus, who was in charge of the statistics of the VSNKh. See *Industry in the USSR in 1925/26,* p. 22. See also A. Dezen, in *Economic Review,* 1927, No. 5, p. 69.

[37] *Control Figures for 1929/30,* p. 578.

deterioration in the quality of industrial output was not reflected in the price index.

Private industry (mostly small-scale), hampered by inadequate supplies of raw materials and high taxation, had still higher costs than state-owned industry. The inefficient socialized trade could operate only at high margins, and these margins were still higher in private trade.[38] Owing to this, the retail price indices (1913 equals 100) were higher than the respective wholesale price indices for industrial goods (198 compared with 187.7) and especially for farm products (194 compared with 156.7).[39] Construction, which was to be the basic instrument of the Great Industrialization Drive, was the weakest point of the socialized economy, the index of construction cost having been equivalent to 247 (1913 equals 100) in 1927/28.

The increased production costs in industry were partly due to relatively higher labor costs.[40] The 8-hour working day replaced the 9.92-hour day after the Revolution of February, 1917, i.e., even before October Revolution.[41] The workers were supposed to have been the victors in the October Revolution, and it was felt that they had to be rewarded.[42] There was no disagreement over wage levels between the Communists and the Groman-Bazarov group, which had a great influence on current planning at that time. Only the Narodnik or Neo-Narodnik group, the ideological representatives of the peasantry, led by N. K. Kondratiev, objected.[43] But only manual workers in industry profited from these policies.

According to the Gosplan, real wages of manual workers in large-scale industry were 11 per cent higher in 1927/28 than in 1913.[44]

---

[38] On the trade margins, see *Control Figures for 1928/29*, p. 321. For a comparison with prewar years, see *Materials* (see note to Table 1 for full title), p. 27.

[39] *Control Figures for 1929/30, loc. cit.* The inefficiency of the trade apparatus is also demonstrated by the fact that, in spite of a reduced volume of trade, the share of trade in national income increased from 8.3 per cent in 1913 (see Dezen, *op. cit.*, p. 68) to 11.1 per cent in 1927/28 (*1st FYP*, I, 158).

[40] See Sh. Ya. Turetskii, "The Problem of Production Costs in Price Formation," *Planned Economy*, 1928, No. 11, pp. 171–202. Also see Albert Vainstein in *Economic Bulletin of the Institute for Current Economic Research*, 1927, No. 11–12, p. 13.

[41] The figure for 1913 is from *Socialist Construction of the USSR, 1936*, p. 529. Pre-Revolution data by I. M. Kuzminyuch-Lanin (*The Workday and the Workyear in Moscow Oblast* [Moscow, 1912] indicates a substantially smaller average workday (for Moscow oblast) in 1908 than the average for the country as a whole given in official post-Revolution sources.

[42] The savings (as one of the means of expanding the fixed capital) are not to occur "at the expense of the vital interests of the working class" (Fifteenth Party Conference [October 26 to November 3, 1926]). See *VKP(b) in Resolutions and Decisions* (5th ed.; Moscow, 1936), II, 133.

[43] See, for example, Vainstein, *op. cit.*

[44] The real wages (paid-out wage; yearly basis, i.e., without consideration of the curtailed workday) of these wage earners in 1925/26 were 8.7 per cent below those of 1913 (*Control Figures for 1926/27*, p. 92). A 22 per cent increase in real wages of all

The opinion seems to have been general at that time that wages in large-scale industry were relatively the highest.[45] Even the 1927 index for all wage and salary earners in large-scale industry was lower than the index for manual workers given above. This was in line with the position of large-scale industry as the citadel of the proletarian dictatorship and of the workers in large-scale industry as the selected group of the proletariat. Railway workers were probably second best in income. The index of real wages of railway wage and salary earners was equal to 88 (1913 equals 100) in 1927/28.[46] Real wages of other categories of working people (education, medical personnel, administration, etc.) are unlikely to have reached 60 per cent of the prewar wages on the average, according to Vainstein, cited in footnote 40 above. He concluded by saying that real wages of a certain group of teachers were only 24 to 32 per cent of their prewar level.[47]

While the paid-out real wage was only moderately higher in 1927/28 than in 1913 (even this was probably true only for the manual workers in large-scale industry), labor costs to the state as an entrepreneur were substantially higher (social insurance payments and especially the shorter workday). It was not only the larger expense for labor, however, but also the inability to get a reasonable amount of work from the wage earners or to utilize this work efficiently which led to the expensiveness of the socialized enterprises. This inefficiency was particularly pronounced in construction.[48]

The unsatisfactory operation of the non-farm economy adversely affected the relationship between prices paid to the peasants and prices paid by them. In the tabulation below are presented the unique but rarely utilized peasant indices of the Kondratiev's Institute for Current Economic Research. In these indices was calculated the relationship between the prices the peasants had received for the products they sold to the prices of goods they had bought. The calculation was made for 1913 and the postwar years. Then the thus

---

wage and salary earners in large-scale industry from 1925/26 to 1927/28 is implied in the Gosplan's data (*Control Figures for 1927/28*, pp. 535–37, and *Control Figures for 1929/30*, pp. 489, 578).

[45] Vainstein, *op. cit.*, p. 4.

[46] Calculated in the same manner as the earnings of manual workers in large-scale industry (see n. 44 above). The index of real wage for them was equal to 73.8 in 1925/26 (1913 equals 100). The wages of this group increased, with consideration of changes in living costs, by 20 per cent from 1925/26 to 1927/28.

[47] Vainstein, *op. cit.*, p. 4.

[48] "The greatest inefficiency and disorganization still reigns in the realm of construction," stated the resolution of the Fourteenth Party Conference, April, 1925 (*VKP(b)* in *Resolutions and Decisions* [5th ed.; Moscow, 1936], II, 25). In 1925/26 the index of constructions costs (1913 equals 100) was as high as 269. The subsequent decline to 247 in 1927/28 was very inadequate.

calculated price relationships for postwar years were related to those in 1913, which were assumed to equal 100.[49]

Type of Farm	October 1, 1925	October 1, 1926	October 1, 1927
Potato	68	65	79
Flax	76	70	76
Sugar beets	76	61	61
Wheat, Ukraine	76	63	82
Wheat, RSFSR	76	60	74
Dairy, Urals	76	66	69
Dairy, West Siberia	76	67	86

As the above figures show, the price relationships declined quite substantially from their prewar level for all major groups of farm producers, to the disadvantage of the latter, of course.

Since output per man in industry was increasing rather rapidly in those years (there was ample room for such an increase in the then existing low level of this output), non-rural employment and urban population as a whole were rising at a relatively slow rate. The latter grew by only about six million in the five years from 1922/23 to 1927/28. The growth of the rural population was more than double this number. At the rates of growth of the non-farm economy in those years there was no prospect for holding back the accumulation of surplus labor in the villages. The strange phenomenon could, indeed, be observed that, in spite of the rapid growth of output in industry, the number of registered unemployed increased from 846,000 in 1924/25 to 1,255,700 in 1926/27,[50] and continued to grow in later years.

It is by no means a great achievement to enlarge industrial output, even by leaps and bounds, if sales are assured and, moreover, if the increase in output occurs with no regard to costs and quality of the product. Great perils lie ahead if only the ability to expand is considered and if the accompanying adverse developments are minimized or overlooked entirely. But this was exactly what happened. In spite of the adverse phenomena which accompanied the expansion of industry, the Stalin Communists saw only the expansion and were greatly elated. Already in 1926, i.e., before the prewar output level of industry was restored and at a time when the output per man in industry was still greatly below the very low prewar level, the Party proclaimed in a resolution of the Fifteenth Party Conference (October 23, 1926): "It is necessary to strive to reach, and then to exceed,

[49] *Economic Bulletin of the Institute for Current Economic Research,* 1927, No. 10, p. 16.

[50] "Labor in the Fiscal Year 1926/27," *Economic Bulletin of the Institute for Current Economic Research,* 1927, No. 11–12, p. 86.

the level of industrial development of the capitalist countries." [51]

Planning.—Economic planning was begun during the NEP era, first by organizing the collection and working-up of indispensable statistics, and then by working on individual projects, of the type also planned in other countries. Attempts at planning whole economic sectors were unsuccessful, except for agriculture. By 1925, the Gosplan, organized in April of 1921, succeeded in starting the planning of the whole economy (*single* economic plan) in the form of its famous annual Control Figures. Three issues for the years 1925/26 through 1927/28 were released during the NEP under the leadership of V. G. Groman (to whom this volume is dedicated).

The task was huge. Under the specific conditions prevailing in the USSR the difficulties could not be overcome. As far as the planners themselves are concerned, their wishes and ideas were along the lines of realistic planning. But the Party asked more from the economy than could be realized. These demands were, perforce, incorporated into the plans and weakened them. Expanding investment, advancing the living standards of hired workers, yet reducing production costs in industry, construction costs and prices, and, on top of this, increasing the rate of socialization without regard to its efficiency or inefficiency—all this at very high rates and in almost no time—was just too much for the economy and for the smooth functioning of planning. If any sound planning developed at all, it was because Stalin was still busy fighting his enemies inside the Party and could devote only relatively little attention to "guiding" economic planning.

Work also proceeded during the NEP period on a five-year plan and a general plan (of about fifteen years' duration), but the completion of the first and the discontinuation of the work on the second belong to later periods.

[51] *VKP(b) in Resolutions and Decisions* (5th ed.; Moscow, 1936), II, 131.

THE
PRE-WORLD WAR II
PERIOD

CHAPTER 3

THE WARMING-UP PERIOD

Introduction

In retrospect, the NEP period seems to have been only a relatively short breathing spell. But at the time, it was regarded by everybody as practically permanent. Did not Lenin himself proclaim that the NEP had been introduced in earnest and for a long time? In the spring of 1927, N. A. Kovalevskii, an official very high up in the Gosplan's hierarchy,[1] spoke of the NEP as likely to continue for several more five-year periods.[2] Little more than a year later, the July plenary meeting of the Central Committee of the Party denied in a typically Stalin manner that NEP was on the way out, "decidedly sweeping away the counter-revolutionary blabber about the abolition of the NEP." [3] Yet Oscar Lange[4] completely disregarded these denials of his friends when he expressed the opinion, accepted by the present writer, that the NEP had ended in December, 1927, at the Fifteenth Party Congress, which was later officially named the Industrialization Congress. The decisions of the Congress to step up the rates of industrialization and of collectivization of peasant farming—the latter associated with increased pressure on the "kulaks"—were certainly a milestone in Soviet economic development.

[1] Kovalevskii was *inter alia* editor of *Planned Economy*, the Gosplan's journal. At that time he also was, or a few months later had been made, responsible for the long-range planning of the Gosplan.

[2] *Planned Economy*, 1927, No. 5, p. 22.

[3] Quoted from *The Ways of Agriculture*, 1928, No. 7, p. 6.

[4] *The Working Principles of the Soviet Economy* (New York, 1943), p. 16. Oscar Lange, at that time professor at the University of Chicago, soon relinquished his American citizenship and became Polish ambassador to the United States.

A speed-up of industrialization was incompatible with the preservation of the village setup on which the NEP was based. This was all the more true because, at the time, the increased rate of industrialization had not yet been visualized without a proportionate rise in the living standards of the wage earners, which in turn was impossible without a corresponding expansion of the marketings of farm products. The peasants had to be deprived of the right to dispose of their produce, and, in the opinion of Stalin, this was attainable only by way of collectivization. Increased pressure on the "kulaks," which was decided upon at the Fifteenth Party Congress in December, 1927, and the next step, "the liquidation of the kulaks as a class," which accompanied the All-out Collectivization Drive, were merely cloaks to cover up the attack on the peasantry as such.

There is no doubt that the All-out Collectivization Drive, accompanied by a similar drive to industrialize Russia in no time at all, totally disregarding the sacrifices of the population, initiated a new period in the economic development of the USSR. The Bolsheviks spoke of the start of this period as the second revolution. The most tempestuous part of it, which ended with a breakdown in the winter of 1932/33, is here designated as the *All-out Drive.* The day of November 7, 1929, on which Stalin released, in *Pravda,* his eventful article, "The Year of the Great Turn," seems to be the appropriate date to be considered the beginning of this period.

Since it is accepted that the NEP ended in December, 1927, and that the *All-out Drive* began in November, 1929, the period of twenty-two to twenty-three months which was of a transitional nature is, therefore, designated here as the *Warming-up* period. Its main characteristics may be considered as having consisted not so much of fundamental changes in the economy itself as of changes in the ideas on how the economy had to be developed.

There were two main issues around which ideological war was waged within the Party and, even more, between the Party and the opposition groups, mostly Mensheviks, Neo-Narodniki, and persons close to them, none officially members of any party. The two issues were the rate of industrialization and the extent of socialization. The fight went on all during the NEP but ended during the *Warming-up* period with the defeat of the opposition.[5]

[5] The Soviets have been quite successful in having the names of the persons involved erased from history, although these can easily be found in the publications of that time. V. P. Milyutin, president of the Central Statistical Office, in a speech before the Agrarian Institute of the Communist Academy, enumerated the following persons as wreckers with the details as stated: "[V. G.] Groman was a member of the Presidium of the Gosplan, [N. D.] Kondratiev for a long time played an important role in the Commissariats of Finance and Agriculture, [N. N.] Sukhanov for a long time occupied an

The "Extinguishing Curve"

The fight concerning the rate of industrial growth was largely concentrated around the idea of the "extinguishing curve," for which Groman and certain others were made solely responsible at a later time but which earlier had been accepted by everybody.

In his report to the Nineteenth Party Congress in October, 1952, on the Directives to the fifth FYP, M. Z. Saburov, president of the Gosplan, stated that the rates of industrial growth had been higher during the fourth FYP period than those which were scheduled for the fifth FYP period in the Directives to the fifth FYP and submitted for the approval of the Congress. "The smaller rates of growth of industry during the fifth FYP period are due . . . to the discontinuation of reconstruction work in industry, when a rapid expansion was attained by putting into operation rehabilitated enterprises," he stated.[6] Not a single dissenting voice seems to have been raised. Exactly the same issue was treated quite differently in the late twenties.

---

important position in the Commissariats of Trade and Agriculture, [N. P.] Makarov occupied an important position in the Commissariat of Agriculture, [P.] Sadyrin was a member of the Central Executive Committee, [L. N.] Yurovskii was at the top level in the Commissariat of Finance and was a member of the Presidium of this Commissariat—so that they held a great number of our most important positions in the USSR." See *Kondratievshchina*, a collection of speeches delivered at the Agrarian Institute of the Communist Academy (Moscow, 1930), p. 7. Many prominent non-Communists (V. A. Bazarov among them, of course) were mentioned as wreckers or hirelings of capitalism in other speeches in the meeting of the above-mentioned Agrarian Institute and in similar meetings of other top-ranking economic institutes, which, among others, *Planned Economy,* 1930, especially in No. 1 and No. 10–11, reported in detail.

V. G. Groman, to whom the volume is dedicated, was the leader of the non-Communist forces in the Gosplan. Specifically, he was responsible for *Control Figures for 1925/26, for 1926/27,* and *for 1927/28.* L. N. Yurovskii was primarily responsible for the stabilization of the Soviet ruble in the early twenties. The draft of the FYP of the VSNKh, quoted above and below under the abbreviation *Materials,* was known for years as the Ginzburg FYP (for the Menshevik, A. M. Ginzburg). There were many others. There is no point in trying, as Dobb does (*Soviet Economic Development since 1917* [New York, 1928], p. 327), to make Groman look stupid. At that time the Bolsheviks readily acknowledged that the more gifted, the better-educated people were in the anti-Bolshevik camp. The positions of the Groman-Bazarov group in the Gosplan, and of the Kondratiev group in the Commissariats of Agriculture and Finance in particular, were well defined and argued. Those who believe that the Bolsheviks have succeeded in building socialism will consider those positions wrong. Those who think that freedom is an indispensable component of real socialism and that the Bolsheviks have largely succeeded in building a great concentration camp, will draw the conclusion that history has vindicated the Groman-Bazarovs and Kondratievs. Specifically, the results of the *All-out Drive,* which culminated in the starvation deaths of millions and in a great slowdown of the economic growth of the USSR, fully justify Groman's persistent emphasis on equilibrium. It makes his urgings to preserve this indispensable economic prerequisite prophetic.

[6] *Pravda,* October 10, 1952.

Until about the middle of 1927, everybody, indeed everybody, expected a substantial slowdown in the rates of economic development, especially in industry, after the 1913 level of output was restored. This anticipated slowdown was named the "extinguishing curve." The Fifteenth Party Conference (October 26 to March 3, 1926) proclaimed:

The national economy is entering the stage where the rate of its expansion must greatly slow down as compared with the preceding years. . . . The expansion of industry on the basis of enlargement of fixed capital (new capital construction) could never and cannot proceed at the same speed with which industry has been expanding in the period of recovery of the last few years. But the specific conditions of the Soviet State assure industry of a more rapid growth than the conditions of a capitalist state.[7]

Then suddenly the order came out: the operation of the "extinguishing curve" will not be tolerated. Stalin was greatly helped in this attitude by the fact that at first the curve did not operate as expected. Gross industrial output, after having risen by 17.2 per cent in 1926/27 (in terms of 1926/27 prices), did not slow down its growth considerably in the following year as expected, but actually expanded by as much as 19.0 per cent.[8]

Nobody but Bazarov, one of the staunch adherents of the "extinguishing curve" idea, was eager to recognize the error and to point out the reason for it. He correctly saw this reason in the fact, which had not been realized previously (by either anti-Communists or Communists), that industry had reached the prewar *output,* but not the prewar *capacity.* Moreover, under Soviet conditions capacity of industry could be utilized much more fully than under capitalism. Owing to the simplification of the goods produced, and the worsening of their quality, and, last but not least, owing to the assured markets, an easily attainable capacity may indeed under Soviet conditions have been larger than the full *prewar capacity.* Speaking in mid-1928, Bazarov said that even then there still was an unused industrial capacity of about 30 per cent.[9]

Bazarov's estimate turned out to be correct. According to official estimates, the output of large-scale industry (excluding timber) rose by about 22 and 24 per cent (at 1926/27 prices) in 1928 and 1929,

[7] *VKP(b) in Resolutions and Decisions* (5th ed.; Moscow, 1936), II, 131.

[8] Official estimates; see *Control Figures for 1929/30,* pp. 422–23.

[9] Discussion "On the Methodology of General Plan" in *Planned Economy,* 1928, No. 6, p. 153.

respectively, as against 17 per cent in 1927.[10] The output per man was also advancing satisfactorily (by 12 and 13 per cent in 1928 and 1929, respectively), and the same was the case with production costs (a decline of 5.6 and 5.3 per cent in large-scale industry in 1927/28 and 1928/29, respectively).

The indices quoted may not be entirely correct. This is especially true of the index of production costs in industry. But even more precise data would probably not have disclosed any trace of an "extinguishing curve." Moreover, the official indices were not doubted, and the Kremlin certainly acted on the basis of them.

The expansion in industrial output during the period involved was, it is true, primarily quantitative. As far as production costs are concerned, a large share in their reduction came from fuller utilization of capacities. According to obviously official data, the expansion of output, as such, was responsible for 39.6 per cent of the total cost reduction in 1928/29. A further deterioration in the quality of produce also took place in the same year.[11] On the other hand, the share of the so-called rationalization factors in the reduction of production costs was equivalent to only 23 per cent of the total.

The situation in agriculture and, indeed, in the whole consumption sector was obviously threatening, although the real peril was only in preparation. Crop production, which increased by 4.5 per cent in 1928, declined by 3.6 per cent in 1929.[12] The output of grain, which was badly needed, showed a definite downward trend with the result that the "extraordinary measures," already mentioned above, directed toward obtaining grain for the urban population by force, had to be resorted to in the spring of 1928 and later. Meat consumption was temporarily helped by the "windfall" of excessive slaugh-

[10] *Economy of the USSR, 1932,* p. 4. According to *Stat. Handb.,* 1956, p. 45, the output of large-scale industry increased by 24 and 25 per cent in 1928 and 1929 as against 13 per cent in 1927. We will still prefer the unrevised figures.

Insufficient utilization of capacities and more or less full utilization of previously incomplete utilized capacities during different periods were also going to be of great importance under "socialism." Capacities were not fully utilized during the *All-out Drive* or during the *Purge Era.* The second FYP period and the two postwar periods showed the opposite nature.

[11] Sh. Ya. Turetskii, "The Struggle for the Quality Factors of the Plan," *Planned Economy,* 1930, No. 9, p. 77. In a special article on "Quality of Goods of Mass Consumption" (*Economic Review,* 1929, No. 10, p. 28), I. Z. Kaganov mentioned that the galoshes produced in 1928/29 lasted only four to five months as against eight to nine months for the galoshes produced in 1913. *Control Figures for 1929/30,* p. 26, states of the development in the preceding year that "one of the most negative factors among the results of industrial production was the deterioration of the quality of the goods."

[12] *Control Figures for 1929/30,* pp. 424–25, and *Planned Economy,* 1930, No. 12, p. 362.

tering. The dangerous situation which obtained at that time in agriculture is evident from the changes in the value of livestock herds (at constant prices). This increased by 549 million and 598 million rubles in 1925/26 and 1926/27, respectively. The increase was smaller in 1927/28 (427 million rubles).[13] Then in 1929, there occurred a drop of not less than 910.8 million rubles, equivalent to about 10 per cent of the total value of the livestock.[14]

The rate of growth of real personal incomes declined sharply in 1928/29, instead of increasing as provided in the first FYP. But those in power saw only that the "extinguishing curve" failed to appear in industry. Actually, the rapid skyrocketing of ideas on the possible rates of growth in industry, which are discussed below, had already started in mid-1927, i.e., *before* the failure of the "extinguishing curve" to materialize *at the erroneously expected time* and, for that matter, before the Fifteenth Party Congress of December of the same year.

Rather than quote pronouncements, let us operate with figures. They speak volumes (see Table 1).

The second part of Table 1 shows the ascending rates of growth of large-scale industrial production planned for the period of the first FYP (from the year preceding the start of the operation of the plan to its terminal year) in the successive drafts of the FYP. The period during which this revising occurred extended from mid-1927 to April, 1929, i.e., less than two years.[15]

Early in 1927 both the Gosplan commission under S. Strumilin and the committee of the VSNKh, headed by A. Ginzburg, expected a rate of growth of about 80 per cent in five years for large-scale industry controlled by the VSNKh—certainly a satisfactory goal to try for.[16] By rapid successive increases this rate was more than doubled in little more than two years.

---

[13] *Control Figures for 1929/30*, p. 448.

[14] Implied in data in *Planned Economy*, 1930, No. 12, p. 362.

[15] Work on the first FYP was conducted simultaneously by the Gosplan and the VSNKh (the Supreme Soviet of the National Economy). It started in 1925, but the earliest draft of the Gosplan, compiled in 1926, is disregarded here as too immature (the VSNKh was not able to produce even such an immature draft at that early time). The VSNKh had one set of goals in all its drafts. The Gosplan, however, introduced, late in 1927, the system of two sets of targets (in the form of a basic and an optimum variant of the FYP). While it is hard to believe that the Gosplan itself fully believed in the targets of the basic variant of the final draft of the first FYP, one is justified in assuming that the optimum variant of the FYP was definitely forced upon it. With reference to grain production, for example, the Gosplan was bound by a special decree of the Central Executive Committee to attain a rise in per acre yields by 35 per cent in five years (*1st FYP*, I, 9, and II, Part 2, 290). The *optimum* variant of the final Gosplan draft became the first FYP.

[16] Strumilin's preface to *Perspectives* was dated March 21, 1927. The *Materials* were completed a little later.

TABLE 1

The End of Realistic Planning: Planned Rates of Growth of Gross Production
of Large-scale Industry in Successive Drafts of the First FYP*
(In per cent)

A. Annual Rates of Growth

Draft	1926/27	1927/28	1928/29	1929/30	1930/31	1931/32	1932/33
1. Spring, 1927, Gosplan, *Perspectives*	19.1	13.2	10.6	9.9	9.2	...	...
2. Mid-1927, VSNKh, *Materials*	...	16.3	13.1	13.7	10.5	10.0	...
3. End of 1927, VSNKh	...	18.1	16.6	17.6	13.8	12.8	...
4. End of 1927, Gosplan, "Perspective Orientation":							
Basic variant	...	16.4	14.0	14.1	12.9	12.3	...
Optimum variant	...	18.1	16.6	17.6	13.8	12.8	...
5. August, 1928, VSNKh	...	...	19.7	17.3	17.7	17.5	14.4
6. November, 1928, VSNKh	...	...	19.2	18.9	18.1	19.4	17.6
7. December, 1928, VSNKh	...	...	21.9	20.2	21.8	22.6	22.4
8. Early 1929, first FYP:							
Basic variant	...	...	21.4	18.8	17.5	18.1	17.4
Optimum variant (became law)	...	...	21.4	21.5	22.1	23.2	25.2

B. Five-year Rates of Growth

Plan	1925/26 to 1930/31	1926/27 to 1931/32	1927/28 to 1932/33
1. Spring, 1927, Gosplan, *Perspectives*	79.5	...	...
2. Mid-1927, VSNKh, *Materials*	...	82.0	...
3. End of 1927, VSNKh	...	108.0	...
4. End of 1927, Gosplan, "Perspective Orientation":			
Basic variant	...	92.0	...
Optimum variant	...	108.0	...
5. August, 1928, VSNKh	...	...	121
6. November, 1928, VSNKh	...	...	135
7. December, 1928, VSNKh	...	...	167.7
8. Early 1929, first FYP:			
Basic variant	...	...	135
Optimum variant (became law)	...	...	179

* Large-scale industry controlled by the VSNKh. Data for (1) from Gosplan USSR, *Perspectives of Unfolding of the National Economy of the USSR in 1926/27 to 1930/31*, p. 124; for (4) from "Summarized Table of Indicators of the National Economy of the USSR for 1925/26 to 1931/32," *Planned Economy*, 1927, No. 11, pp. 269–75. (Yearly data for the optimum variant are from Sabsovich, cited below); for (8) from *1st FYP*, I, 131; the balance of the data is from M. Sabsovich, "Hypothesis of Scales of Output of Basic Branches of the National Economy during the Period of the General Plan," *Planned Economy*, 1929, No. 1, pp. 58–59. The source abbreviated to *Materials* is VSNKh, *Materials for the Five-Year Plan for the Development of the Industry of the USSR, 1927/28 to 1931/32* (Moscow, 1927). The other VSNKh drafts were called Control Figures. Some of the figures from which the percentages were calculated were in terms of pre–World War I prices and some in terms of 1926/27 prices.

The first part of Table 1 shows the gradual elimination of the "extinguishing curve" in the minds of those in power. By December of 1928, it was fully disposed of. In the approved version of the first FYP, the curve even became an ascending one. As the result of this transformation, the rate of growth of industry in the terminal year, which, according to the Gosplan draft of early 1927, was to have been equal to 9.2 per cent, was raised to 25.2 per cent in the approved version of the first FYP.

Possibly even more fantastic was the fact that the rate of growth in output per man in industry, besides having been planned immensely high, was to increase, in only three years, from 14.0 per cent in 1929/30 to 21.7 per cent in 1932/33 [17]—a rise in output per man of 21.7 per cent in only one year!

As already mentioned, all this exuberance of planning originated, to a large extent, from the fact that the "extinguishing curve" delayed its appearance. But it did not delay its appearance for too long. It was clearly there, as far as output per man was concerned, one year after the approval of the first FYP and only several months after Stalin's "Year of the Great Turn." Even the doubtful official index of output per man at "unchangeable 1926/27 prices" shows this reversal in the trend (1927/28 equals 100): [18]

1928/29:
1st quarter	106.7
2d quarter	112.2
3d quarter	119.5
4th quarter	122.1

1929/30:
1st quarter	127.9
2d quarter	134.9
3d quarter	133.7
4th quarter	126.3

The peak was reached in the first quarter of the calendar year of 1930. The second quarter still held its own, but afterward, the trend was definitely downward. Under other conditions, these figures would have been more than adequate to teach a lesson in planning. Not for Stalin. All the terrific developments of the *All-out Drive* were needed to make him change his course.

[17] The percentages here were obtained by the crude method of dividing the scheduled percentage increases in output of industry controlled by the VSNKh (*1st FYP*, I, 164–65) by the scheduled percentage increases in the total labor force of the respective industries (*ibid.*, II, Part 2, 206–27).

[18] *Economy of the USSR, 1932*, pp. 16–17. Although the yearbook was published in 1932, the quoted data significantly end with the last quarter of 1929/30.

Equilibrium

The idea of the "extinguishing curve" did not play a great role in Groman's pronouncements. His central idea was undoubtedly the necessity of equilibrium between the various economic sectors. The idea of the "extinguishing curve" was implied in this general thesis. But under Soviet conditions the fate of the idea of equilibrium was fundamentally different from that of the "extinguishing curve."

Groman did not tire of harping on the idea of equilibrium. On one occasion he said:

The criteria [which will permit finding objective appraisals for characterizing the situations, for establishing the role of each economic branch, and for appraising their relative needs] were formulated by comrade Bazarov in this way: "The optimum combination for growth of production powers; increase in well-being of the working masses; and development of socialist forms of the economy." I always add to this— simultaneously taking care to preserve the dynamic equilibrium of the national economy which requires proportionality in the development of its individual parts.[19]

Groman's almost endless emphasizing of the idea of economic equilibrium, extremely elementary per se, is not understandable unless one takes into consideration the tendency of those dominating the Party and the country to industrialize and, therefore, to expand investment beyond the means of the country and without regard for proportionate development in the other sectors of the economy. The consequences of this policy became fully apparent during the *All-out Drive*. The idea of equilibrium was originally stressed because of the demands of the Party for industrialization at rates unrestrained by considerations of agriculture's ability to expand. But Groman also felt compelled to emphasize such simple things as there being no reason to plan investment for which building materials could not be provided.[20]

The stand taken by the first FYP, the most important economic document of the *Warming-up* period, with reference to equilibrium, is of particular interest. The almost endless upward revisions of the targets for industrial output described in the preceding section made it obviously difficult to preserve proportionality among the various

[19] "Towards an Appraisal of the Economic Situation in the USSR," *Planned Economy*, 1927, No. 7, p. 137. Note that Bazarov put the development of socialist forms in the last place. This ranking was, of course, not to the taste of Stalin Communists.

[20] See, for example, *Planned Economy*, 1928, No. 7, p. 127. Bukharin was accused for having issued the same warning. See *Kondratievshchina*, p. 69.

economic sectors. Yet the creators of the first FYP stuck staunchly
to the idea of equilibrium and succeeded in having the FYP, based
on this idea, approved.

This recognition of the principle of proportionality in the first
FYP even included the retention of the idea that the population
should have a considerable share in the expanding wealth. When,
by applying the principle of equilibrium, all targets were brought
into line with the extremely high rates for heavy industry decided
in advance, the outcome was a phantom, an assembly of fantastic
goals for everything, goals which had not the smallest chance of
approaching fulfilment.

All targets of the final draft of the first FYP were so obviously
unrealistic that it was believed necessary to draw upon the assistance
of even the weather god by basing the targets on weather conditions
much more favorable than normal.

The "quality" factors in industry were to show a similar rosy
picture. Output per man in the industry planned by the VSNKh
was to rise by 110 per cent in five years, and production costs in it
were to decline by not less than 35 per cent.

The more than doubling of the originally desired rates of growth
of large-scale industry naturally required a more than proportionate
boost of the investment goals. The targets for fixed investment of
the state in all five years of the FYP period are shown below (in
billions of rubles at current prices): [21]

Perspectives (plan to operate between 1926/27 and 1930/31, inclusive)............   15.9
1st FYP (plan to operate between 1928/29 and 1932/33, inclusive).............   34.2

The fact that the first FYP, as approved, was scheduled to operate
during a period later by two years than the plan embodied in
Perspectives, takes off about 30 per cent of the very large increase in
the investment scheduled by it. Part of the needed discount was,
however, offset by the fact that the costs involved in investment were
scheduled to be substantially lower in the first FYP than in *Perspectives.*

An increase of 55 per cent was planned for agricultural output
in the first FYP—a fantastic rate for this branch of the economy.
The marketing of farm products to buyers other than farm producers was to rise by as much as 106 per cent!

All this was topped by the target of raising non-rural real wages

[21] They are given in this form by the sources; *Perspectives*, text, p. 32 (see note to
Table 1, above, for full title); *1st FYP*, I, 154–55. Investment in education, health, and
administration has been excluded to make the data of the *1st FYP* comparable with
those of *Perspectives.*

by 76.8 per cent and almost as high targets for increasing incomes of the other population groups.[22]

With reference to weather conditions, even the basic variant of the first FYP, dismissed as too low, provided only for "the possibility of one partial crop failure during the five-year period," although the assumption of one crop failure and one partial crop failure in five years would have been more in line with the Russian climate. The approved variant of the FYP was based on the "absence of a crop failure in any way serious during the five-year period." [23]

As the result of all the planning, the targets of the optimum variant of the FYP, which had become the first FYP, for 1932/33 in per cent of the actual performance in 1927/28 were as shown in Chart 5.

In contrast to Groman's other ideas, the idea of equilibrium survived. It was indeed destined to become a component of the

CHART 5

TARGETS OF THE FIRST FYP *

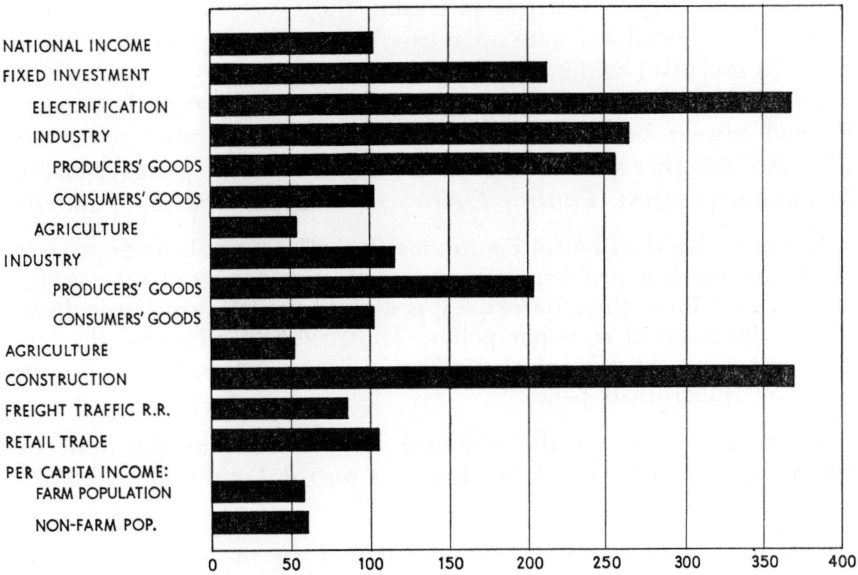

* Percentage rises from 1927/28 to 1932/33 at constant prices, except for freight traffic, for which the data are in ton-kilometers. See *1st FYP*, I, 129–34, and II, Part 1, 444. For retail trade the percentage rise shown *ibid.*, II, Part 2, 156–57, at current prices was deflated with the price index given *ibid.*, I, 135.

[22] *1st FYP*, I, 85, 137. Paul Baran (*A Survey of Contemporary Economics* [1952], p. 293) speaks of a target of raising wages by 40 per cent. This was the target at current prices, which were scheduled to decline sharply during the first FYP.

[23] *1st FYP*, I, 11.

"basic law of socialist economic development," formulated by Stalin himself. The replacement of the word "equilibrium" in the formula of this law by the word "proportionate" is irrelevant. The claim of proportionate development was, of course, made with full disregard for reality. It joined other claims put up the more vigorously, the greater their lack of conformity with the factual situation.

Widening of "Socialism"

Chapter 2 showed that, except in farming, the successful fight for socialization, which had been temporarily lost with the introduction of the NEP, continued all during this period. But it was not won without considerable opposition. The disagreement was not on socialization as a principle. The Mensheviks of that time were as much in favor of socialization as the Bolsheviks of all shades.[24] Part of the Neo-Narodniki, possibly a large part, may have been less enthusiastic about it, but it seems unlikely that many were definitely antisocialist. The issue at stake, however, was not socialization as a principle, but immediate socialization, a do-or-die socialization, without any regard for the fact that those activities which had already been socialized were operating badly. The opposition wanted as much socialism as the circumstances warranted.

Groman's attack was particularly effective in this regard, because he had always been a Marxist and, as such, operated with the Marxian idea that growth of productive powers is the primary factor in human progress. *Control Figures for 1926/27* (pp. 5–6) stated:

In computing the Control Figures for 1926/27, we put before ourselves the following basic problems: Are the productive powers of the country rising . . . ? From these [principles] is derived the following basic directive in the realm of economic policy: *To develop by all means the productive powers* [main issue], *strengthening in this process the position of socialism* [subordinate issue].

If there is one specific sentence that caused the downfall of Groman, it may be the following in *Control Figures for 1927/28* (p. 28):

It must . . . be decisively emphasized that for the coming year the solving of the most difficult task of raising the quality of the operation of the whole socialized sector [quality of operation embraced such factors as output per man, production costs, and quality of the produce] is infinitely more important than the scheduled shifts in the relative positions

[24] The phrase "of that time" is emphasized. Experience with socialization in the USSR and, for that matter, in other countries has considerably cooled off the still surviving remnants of this party.

of the social sectors [i.e., the quantitative increase in the share of the socialized sector in the economy].[25]

S. G. Strumilin, the Gosplan's most prominent Communist in those days, recognized early the danger of the idea of an "expansion of productive powers without regard to where this development leads." [26] Stalin settled the issue with reference to Groman's idea by stating in April, 1929:

We do not need just any growth of productivity of the people's labor. We need a *definite* growth of productivity of the people's labor, namely, the growth which insures a *systematic preponderance* of the socialist sector of the economy over the capitalist sector.[27]

While the ideological war went on, socialization proceeded at a considerably accelerated pace during the *Warming-up* period. This was partly because the advocates of socialization were in power and partly, also, because in the unhealthy atmosphere of that time private enterprise, especially private trade, could operate only at a high cost to the community. The share of the private sector in wholesale trade, small as it was, was cut to less than one-half in only one year (from 4.6 per cent in 1926/27 to 1.9 per cent in 1927/28).[28] Its share in retail trade was slashed to little more than 10 per cent in only two and a quarter years (from 36.9 per cent in 1926/27 to 13.5 per cent in 1929).[29]

Privately owned small-scale industry was the only non-farm activity which the first FYP did not schedule for practical elimination.[30] Yet its share in the total small-scale industry went down from 82.1 per cent in 1926/27 to 62.1 per cent in 1928/29.[31]

In comparison with the preceding stagnation, the collectivization of peasant farming made very rapid progress during the *Warming-up* period, more than quadrupling in only two years. However, the total scope of collectivization remained small (on June 1, 1929, 3.9 per cent of all peasant households were collectivized as against 0.8 per cent on June 1, 1927). Even more than in the case of small-scale industry, the first FYP exerted restraint in planning socialization of

[25] See also V. A. Bazarov, in *Planned Economy*, February, 1928, pp. 42–43.
[26] "On the Plan Front," *Planned Economy*, 1925, No. 1, p. 32. See also E. Quiring, another Gosplan Communist who also devoted space to an attack on Groman's idea on the role of the rise of productive powers in human progress in his important paper, "The Economic Position of the Party before the XVth Congress," *Planned Economy*, 1927, No. 10, p. 9.
[27] *Problems of Leninism* (11th ed.), p. 253.
[28] *Control Figures for 1929/30*, pp. 442–43.
[29] *Socialist Construction of the USSR, 1936*, p. 607.
[30] *1st FYP*, I, 150–51.
[31] *Control Figures for 1929/30*, pp. 442–43.

agriculture. Although the FYP provided for a great speed-up in the rate of collectivization (without pointing out any reasons for expecting the peasants to change their attitude toward collectivization), the individual households were still to amount to 89.6 per cent of the total number of peasant households in 1932/33 and to 85.4 per cent in 1933/34.[32] The signal for the All-out Collectivization Drive had not yet been given, but one would not have long to wait for it.

It was a phenomenon of a distinctly transitory nature that, in view of the obvious impossibility of assuring much more collectivization on a volunteer basis and the decision not yet having been made to go ahead with forced collectivization, an attempt, the final one, was made in the 1928/29 crop season to insure the needed supplies of farm products from independent peasants (but with emphasis on middle and small peasants) by quite substantially raising the procurement prices of certain farm products, mainly grain. Consequently, the index of all procurement farm prices rose from 141.4 in 1927/28 to 157.3 in 1928/29.[33] This measure was thought of as a great sacrifice. It might have had more effect had it come a year or two earlier. It was as good as useless in 1928/29, when it was accompanied by the strengthening of the pressure on the "kulaks" and by the "extraordinary measures" taken in the spring of 1928 and repeated in the next crop year to obtain "surpluses" from the peasants by force.[34] Moreover, the greatest effect of the measure would not have satisfied Stalin, whose appetite for coercion was growing almost hourly at that time.

Reality and the Targets of the First FYP

Even Communists do not pretend, now, that there is a possibility of very rapid industrialization without sacrifices in current consumption. A plan like the Soviet first FYP, which sought to expand the non-farm sector greatly and, simultaneously, to make everybody almost rich in only five years, would be impossible now. The question is, did anyone take the first FYP seriously at the time of its adoption? Could anyone take seriously, for example, the target to expand the generally slow-moving farm output by 55 per cent in

[32] *1st FYP*, II, Part 1, 328–29. The year 1933/34 was of course already beyond the period during which the first FYP was to operate. The introduction of the year 1933/34 here is a clear indication of the restraint of the planners on this point.

[33] 1911–14 equals 100. *Control Figures for 1929–30*, p. 580.

[34] The utilization of force and the fact that this led to dissatisfaction in the "upper groups of the middle peasants" was officially recognized. See *VKP(b) in Resolutions and Decisions* (5th ed.; Moscow, 1936), II, 273–74. There actually was not enough stratification in the Soviet village to permit the distinguishing between upper and middle groups of middle peasants.

only five years, a target adopted in the face of stagnation in this output at that very time? For that matter, could anyone have taken seriously the target of the first FYP to enlarge real wages by 77 per cent, although it had already been necessary to resort to rationing in the autumn of 1928, i.e., about half a year before the approval of the FYP? Moreover, since there was not enough food in the hands of the state to supply everyone in need of it, rationing was first introduced only in large industrial centers. For other reasons, rationing was also to operate on a class principle (manual workers were the most favored, salaried men received less, and the rest of the population received nothing on rations). Even this setup did not function well.[35]

With reference to the second and succeeding FYP's there is no doubt that they were drawn up almost exclusively for propaganda purposes and were never intended to play any real role in the direction of the national economy. Strumilin, who headed the work on the first FYP in the Gosplan, may have taken his work seriously (even this is doubtful), but he may also have gone far in drafting what he did not believe in, to preserve his position and the principles of planning as he understood them. It is, however, doubtful whether the real bosses, or the real boss, saw anything but propaganda in the first FYP.

If, or insofar as, the first FYP can be taken seriously, it seems reasonable to assume that certain very important portions of it were disposed of right in the document pertaining to the FYP itself. The basic aims of the FYP were laid down in the introduction, which probably was not written by the authors of the FYP itself. These basic aims are found in the very beginning of the introduction in the section entitled "Basic Positions" (*1st FYP*, p. 9) , as follows:

The Fifteenth Congress of the VKP(b) [December, 1927] gave exhaustive political and economic directives for the setting-up of the Five-Year Plan, from the viewpoint of the *general course toward the industrialization of the USSR, toward the socialist reorganization of the village, toward the overcoming of the capitalist elements and the consistent strengthening of the socialist elements in the economic system of the country.*

There is nothing on personal incomes in this "exhaustive" list, and, indeed, nothing is said of them until the end of "Basic Posi-

---

[35] *Soviet Trade* (weekly), 1929, No. 45–46, p. 30. The resolution of the plenary meeting of the Central Committee (November 16–24, 1928) acknowledged disorganization, queues, poor provision for bread, etc. See *VKP(b) in Resolutions and Decisions* (5th ed.; Moscow, 1936), II, 297.

tions," although personal incomes played a great role in the FYP itself. This cannot be simply an oversight.

That the first FYP was never accepted as anything that could actually be realized is also indicated by the annual plans, worked out by the same organization which produced the first FYP at the same time. While the first FYP wanted urban real wages enlarged by 77 per cent in five years, *Control Figures for 1928/29*, i.e., the plan for the first year of the same FYP period, scheduled an increase of only 5.2 per cent.[36] Moreover, at the time of approval of the first FYP in April, 1929, it must have been clear that the respective modest targets of the *Control Figures for 1928/29* would not be fulfilled.

Control Figures for 1929/30, worked out only a few months after the approval of the first FYP, openly broke with the idea of equilibrium and of adequate participation of the population in the expanding output. Special tables of the *Control Figures* (pp. 428–35) compared their goals for 1929/30 with those of the respective year in the first FYP. The targets for gross industrial output in 1929/30 was raised in *Control Figures for 1929/30*, as compared with the target of the first FYP for the same year, by 12.2 per cent; that for industry planned by the VSNKh by 13.1 per cent, which included raising the target for output of producers' goods by 26.2 per cent and that for output of consumers' goods only by 2 per cent (everything in terms of 1926/27 prices). The 1929/30 target for capital investment of the socialized sector was boosted as compared with the first FYP, by not less than 38 per cent (at current prices).[37] The situation in agriculture was so discouraging that, without any effort to be realistic, *Control Figures for 1929/30* cut the goal for farm output in 1929/30 by 6.8 per cent as compared with the target of the first FYP for that year. The target for the average *nominal* wage at current prices was raised by barely 1 per cent in the face of incipient inflation. There was nothing in those tables either on real incomes of wage and salary earners or incomes, whether nominal or real, of the rest of the population.[38]

[36] See S. G. Strumilin, "The Control Figures for 1929/30," *Planned Economy*, 1929, No. 9, p. 20.

[37] Maurice Dobb said: "We have seen, moreover, that the upward revision of targets which started at the end of 1929 was not ungrounded on the evidence of successful achievement to date" (*Soviet Economic Development since 1917* [New York, 1949], p. 245). The present writer is not among those who are able to see this. The lessons of the *All-out Drive* were lost on Professor Dobb.

[38] The targets of *Control Figures for 1929/30* for the real incomes of the population were not included in the main tables, obviously because these targets alone or, even more, in combination with the small attainments in 1928/29, which may have existed only on paper, fell far short of the corresponding targets of the first FYP. Data from a less conspicuous place in *Control Figures for 1929/30*, p. 178, indicate

Further increases in the targets of the first FYP for industrial output and especially for investment were decided upon in 1930. It is obvious that even if all the good intentions of the first FYP with reference to the operation to the other sectors of the economy and especially of the quality factors (productivity per man, production costs, etc.) had been fulfilled, the additional appropriations for investment could have been made only at the expense of personal consumption, including real wages. But who, at that time, cared for equilibrium and, in particular, for personal incomes including real wages? Certainly not those who had the power of making the decisions.

What actually happened to the targets of the first FYP can be observed from the data in Chart 6.

CHART 6

TARGETS AND FULFILMENTS OF THE FIRST FYP *
(Rise or decline, in per cent)

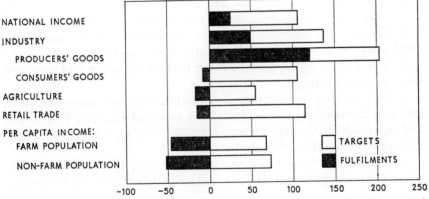

* Targets are for 1932/33 in terms of 1927/28; fulfilments are for 1932 in terms of 1928. For targets see note to Chart 5. Fulfilments are estimates of the writer. Fulfilment for incomes of the non-farm population is based exclusively on changes in real wages.

The data showing fulfilments are simply from a world different from that to which the targets belong. Instead of the tremendous

that per capita real income of the whole population increased by 4.0 per cent in 1928/29; for 1929/30 an increase of 8.4 per cent from the 1928/29 level was scheduled. Even if this target had been fulfilled, the total rise in two years would have been only 12.7 per cent. But it is impossible to take seriously a combination of a target to increase real incomes of the whole population by 8.4 per cent in one year with rationing based strictly on the class principle. Actually the "Control Figures" showed a certain concern only for insuring an improvement in providing the manual wage earners with basic foodstuffs (*ibid.*, p. 16). Stalin disregarded even this modest aim when he decided to go ahead with full collectivization at the very time the Control Figures for 1929/30 were to begin operating.

progress represented by the targets, in reality, the whole private sector, including even output of consumers' goods by industry, shows a decline. As far as personal incomes are concerned, instead of the great prosperity provided for in the FYP, starvation prevailed at the end of the operation of the first FYP, curtailed by nine months in view of its "successful fulfilment." Even the target for raising the output of producers' goods, for the sake of which all sacrifices were made, was fulfilled only to little more than one-half.

The official insistence that the first FYP was fulfilled [39] implies of course that the FYP actually operated. The Soviets and their friends pretend this to have been the case. They are justified in doing so by the fact that their assurances are still frequently accepted as trustworthy.

The propaganda value of a document like the first FYP in the hands of such skilful propagandists as the men in the Kremlin is evidenced by the fact that it was possible to write in 1952, under the auspices of the American Economic Association,[40] that the increase of consumption levels scheduled by the first FYP "did not materialize in view of the unexpected difficulties associated mainly with the peasants' resistance to collectivization." [41] This short statement contains at least three departures from the facts:

a) The targets of the first FYP for real wages never had any connection with reality.

b) Any minute connection with reality they may originally have had was removed in the introductory pages of the first FYP itself, and especially in *Control Figures for 1929/30,* i.e., before the All-out Collectivization Drive got under way.

c) Stalin must have foreseen (and did!) that the peasants would not accept compulsory full-scale collectivization without resistance.

---

[39] The Soviets' refined techniques for dealing with the results of the FYP's were developed already at that early time (with reference to annual plans this had been achieved still earlier). The most common procedure in comparing the fulfilments with the targets is to have fulfilment at higher prices than the targets. For industrial goods the higher prices were the "unchangeable 1926/27 prices" of the *last* year of the FYP period, while the targets were in the lower "unchangeable 1926/27 prices" of five years earlier. For investment and some other items, even retail trade, fulfilment in *current* prices of the last year of the plan period was compared with the target in lower *current* prices of five years earlier. Many other techniques are resorted to, e.g., targets missed are simply disregarded in the analysis of the results of the fulfilment of the plan. With reference specifically to the first FYP it is noteworthy that, except for the rate of collectivization, the subsequent upward revisions of the targets were neglected in comparisons with the fulfilment figures.

[40] *A Survey of Contemporary Economics,* ed. B. F. Haley (Homewood, Ill., 1952), p. 293.

[41] The statement quoted is standard for a certain type of publication. Maurice Dobb has it too, but instead of "unexpected" resistance he has the more cautious "which scarcely could be foreseen." See his *Soviet Economic Development since 1917,* p. 237.

Incidentally, it is misleading to speak simply of non-fulfilment of the target for real wages (which for urban workers were to rise by 76.8 per cent in real terms during the first FYP period) in the face of their decline during this period to about one-half of their previous level (Chart 6).

The "operation" of the first FYP proceeded fully during the *All-out Drive*, the next stage of the Great Industrialization Drive. There will be a lot to say on it in the next two chapters.

Conclusion

In the Menshevik trial of March 1–9, 1931, V. G. Groman, the star among the accused, confessed to the following "wrecking" activities carried out by himself and his colleagues in the Gosplan:

> Putting into the control figures and into the surveys of current business [of the Gosplan] planning ideas and deliberately distorted appraisals, antagonistic to the general Party line (lowering the rates of the expansion of socialist construction, distorting the class approach, exaggerating the difficulties), stressing the signs of an impending catastrophe (Groman) or, what is close to this, assigning a negligible chance of success to the Party line directed toward the socialist attack (Bazarov, Gukhman), putting the genetic point of view over the teleological point of view in working out long-range plans (Groman) or placing both points of view on the same level (Bazarov). . . .[42]

The worst apprehensions of Stalin's adversaries were exceeded during the *All-out Drive*. The foresight of these men is dramatically underscored by the fact that their "crimes" were "committed" not in 1931 or 1930 but years before. The disastrous effects of Stalin's policies were already operating with great force at the time the trials took place.[43]

---

[42] *The Trial of the Counter-Revolutionary Organization of the Mensheviks*, official, supposed to be a stenographic transcript (Moscow, 1931), p. 37.

[43] While the Menshevik trial did not take place until 1931, Groman had already lost his position in the Gosplan in 1929. His important work, the Control Figures, had already been taken from him late in 1927. Kondratiev was removed from the Institute for Current Economic Research (Konjunktur Institut) in the same year. Somewhat more "flexible" or less prominent persons kept their positions a year or so more.

CHAPTER 4

Introduction

Since the decision of the Fifteenth Party Congress in December, 1927, to increase the pressure on the peasants and the "extraordinary measures" resorted to in 1927/28 and 1928/29 for obtaining farm products left no room for a healthy peasant economy, it may have seemed advisable to have the collectivization of the peasants over in one stroke. Stalin announced this drive on November 7, 1929, in his famous "Year of the Great Turn" under the battle cry, "Annihilation of the kulaks as a class," meaning, of course, annihilation of the independent peasantry, as such. The actual drive started a few weeks prior to the publication of the article.[1]

[1] The idea that, once it had been decided to proceed with the compulsory collectivization of peasant farming and the liquidation of the "kulaks" as a class, it might have been advantageous to do it as quickly as possible, may have been behind the statement by N. P. Makarov, one of the most prominent leaders of the Neo-Narodniki group. He is supposed to have made this statement during the "cleaning" of the Commissariat of Agriculture in December, 1929 (see *Kondratievshchina*, a symposium, Communist Academy, Agrar-Institute [Moscow, 1930], pp. 116–19). Makarov allegedly said: "Two years ago I gave warning and very freely said that the attack [on the "kulaks"] was unnecessary, because we need their marketable output. Now the situation has changed fundamentally. They have no marketable output. They are only creating social and political unrest, and, hence, it is necessary to wind up the process of socialized construction. . . . I, one of the first, said about two months ago that it is necessary to take some measures to bring the speed of socialization almost to 100 per cent right away, because the process of socialization is a means of maintaining the productive powers of agriculture at a certain level and of stimulating its further development. I said that delay in this respect would have very negative results." The writer, who knew Makarov personally, is sickened by such statements attributed to him—that he was one of the first, etc. Makarov's deplorable assertions cannot possibly be taken for anything but bowing before crushing power. Those who may be

The big collectivization drive, and all that went with it, has been repeatedly described and must be assumed to be well known, in spite of the efforts of the Party to eliminate from history such facts as the freezing to death of "kulaks" being taken into exile in mid-winter in unheated freight cars or the starvation deaths of many hundreds of thousands, possibly more than a million, in the winter of 1932/33.[2] Dr. R. Schlesinger delicately called all this "birth pangs." [3]

Little attention is paid to the fact that the All-out Collectivization Drive was paralleled by similar developments in all other sectors of the national economy, or, more correctly, the All-out Collectivization Drive was only part of one big drive—the *All-out Drive.*

A decline in farm production during the mass collectivization and a few years thereafter was inevitable. This must have been foreseen, and policies in the other sectors of the economy must have been shaped in accordance with these prospects. A sensible policy would have called for much lower rates of industrialization than those which might have been believed possible under favorable conditions, in this case the very favorable conditions visualized in the first FYP. A reduction in investment targets was also needed, and, moreover, the desired fundamental reorganization of agriculture at one stroke required a much greater investment in it than otherwise would have been needed. Hence, it may have been necessary to redistribute the curtailed total investment. In other words, industrialization, for the sake of which the collectivization drive was undertaken, needed to

---

in the mood for throwing bricks at Makarov and many others who "confessed," may be reminded that Makarov voluntarily returned from the West to Russia in 1923, because he believed that he would have a better opportunity to serve the Russian people there than by lecturing in the United States.

[2] Among others, this writer dealt with the All-out Collectivization Drive in *Soc. Agri.,* chapter 13. A very interesting document turned up after the publication of *Soc. Agri.* Its significance is that it pertains to a time when the *All-out Drive* had already ended and the Stalin hordes were in retreat. We have in mind the secret instructions to all Party-Soviet workers and all offices of the OGPU, courts, and attorneys, devoted to the new methods of conducting class war in the villages, dated May 8, 1933, and signed by Stalin and Molotov (reproduced in *Socialist Courier,* February–March, 1955, pp. 50–52). The "Instructions" acknowledged arrests without the least justification, arrests by everybody, including those who did not have any right to such actions. The document, the authenticity of which seems beyond doubt (it was obtained by the invading Germans in the Smolensk Party Center), contained the important detail that the fight against the "kulaks" and *podkulachniki* (the word is derived from *kulak* and designates a lower category of relatively well-to-do peasants), which started in 1929, was intensified as late as 1932. While the document was quite frank, it did not go so far as to state the number involved in the mass deportations. But it mentioned that at the time it was issued there were requests by the local officials for deportation of about 100,000 peasant families. The number of persons under arrest, excluding those in all kinds of camps, was given at 800,000.

[3] See his "Some Problems of Present Kolkhoz Organization," *Soviet Studies* (Glasgow), April, 1951, p. 351.

be largely postponed. The later development showed that all this was inevitable and, of course, should have been foreseen. Yet the drive to collectivize in one stroke was accompanied by a drive to industrialize at very high rates. Large sums were appropriated for investment in general and especially for it in heavy industry—in addition to those scheduled in the first FYP. The targets for investment were not reached, it is true, even in nominal terms. Another portion of them was swept away by monetary inflation. But even that part of the investment goals that was fulfilled was very large.

The adverse effect of the burdensome investment was augmented by its improper use. Part of the effected investment was simply waste. A substantial number of very large plants which had been started during the *All-out Drive* were not completed before this period had ended. For the rest, utilization of capacities was declining owing to an ever growing disorganization of industry itself, to the disorganization of the transportation system, the great shortage of skilled labor, the impossibility of feeding the workers adequately, and so on. Instead of increasing by 110 per cent in five years, as foreseen in the first FYP, output per man in industry declined by perhaps 25 per cent in the last three years of its operation. Only the very large decline in real wages may have prevented an increase in production costs in industry (in real terms).

Thus the drive for full collectivization was expanded to the *All-out Drive,* which embraced the whole economy and culminated in the disaster of the winter of 1932/33, when, in spite of immense investments, industrial output started actually to decline and masses died from starvation. The birth rate of the whole population fell from 45.0 per 1,000 in 1928 to 32.4 in 1933 and 30.1 in 1934 and was not re-established to a level reasonable for the conditions of that time before 1937 or 1938. Frank Lorimer's hypothesis of the decline and recovery in the annual rate of growth of the Soviet population is possibly even more illuminating: [4]

Year	Increase (in millions)	Year	Increase (in millions)
1928	2.9	1934	1.0
1929	2.8	1935	0.9
1930	2.1	1936	1.2
1931	1.8	1937	2.1
1932	1.4	1938	3.5
1933	0.1	1939	3.5

The transformation of a country with a 1928 population growth of close to three million into one with practically no growth what-

[4] Estimates by Frank Lorimer, *The Population of the Soviet Union: History and Prospects* (Geneva: United Nations, 1946), p. 135.

soever in 1933 is positive indication of earthquake-like developments. That this happened in only four years is also sufficient explanation of why even Stalin retreated. The remarkable drop in population growth during the *All-out Drive* was caused partly by a rapid decline in the birth rate. There is, however, hardly any doubt that in 1933 alone many more than a million died unnecessarily of starvation.

There is a Russian saying which calls a man's most unreasonable actions "what my left leg wants." Planning during the early thirties depended almost entirely on what Stalin's left leg wanted. This type of planning was the natural concomitant to all the other drives. Such planning could not have been in the hands of people who knew anything about it. Even such willing tools as Party members G. M. Krzhizhanovskii, president of the Gosplan, and S. G. Strumilin, who had been primarily responsible for the first FYP, were removed (apparently in 1930 or somewhat earlier) to less prominent positions. Planning had become a plaything of demagogy of the worst kind. "Bacchanalian" seems an appropriate designation for this type of activity.

Bacchanalian Planning

Bacchanalian planning[5] in its fully developed form embraced the Control Figures for the so-called special quarter, i.e., October–December, 1930, the annual plans for 1931 and 1932, and the long-term planning of the respective period. The first step toward it was the upward revision of many targets of the first FYP for 1929/30 in the respective annual plan made in the fall of 1929, a few months after the passing of the first FYP. Revisions of the first FYP, revisions of the draft of the general plan not discussed here, fantastic annual plans, and a similar preparatory draft of the second FYP followed in rapid succession.

A good demonstration of the manner in which planning was done in those years is the following outburst of oratory, delivered by Stalin on the occasion of the discussion of the 1931 Plan:

> Our production program is realistic already because its fulfilment depends exclusively on us ourselves, on our ability and our desire to utilize the richest resources which are at our disposal.[6]

[5] It may seem unnecessary to spend seven or eight pages on a subject like this. The unreality of planning during the *All-out Drive* period can be made sufficiently clear by one or two examples. The justification for the space used is that not one word about this phenomenon can be found in the pertinent Soviet literature. Since nothing seems to have been published in the Western literature either, the Soviet desire to bury those inglorious activities is well on its way to realization.

[6] Stalin, *Problems of Leninism* (11th ed.), p. 349.

Bacchanalian five-year planning.—So far as FYP's are concerned, the first FYP, inherited from the preceding *Warming-up* period, was first to be fulfilled, or disposed of, during the *All-out Drive*. They tried to overcome the too "moderate" targets of this FYP by the slogan, "The FYP in Four Years." [7]

The revision of the target of the first FYP for Stalin's metal was even more significant. The last draft of the first FYP scheduled the output of pig iron in 1932/33 at 8.0 million tons (basic variant) and 10.0 million tons (the ultimately approved optimum variant).[8] The very next year, i.e., in 1930, the Party gave the directive to produce 17 million tons of pig iron in 1933.[9] Only 7.1 million tons were turned out in that year.[10]

But the real image of the *All-out Drive* period was completely revealed when its own FYP was drafted, i.e., the second FYP.

As early as the beginning of 1931, V. V. Kuibyshev, who had recently become president of the Gosplan, in a report to the plenary meeting of the Gosplan entitled "On the Organization of Planning and Accounting," [11] demanded an output of not less than 60 million tons of pig iron in 1937, the last year of the second FYP (actual fulfilment in this year—14.5 million tons), and the doubling of housing in urban and rural areas during this period (actually urban housing increased little more than 10 per cent, while rural housing probably declined).

The Party did not go the full way with Kuibyshev, but it went far enough. It started very early and was already busying itself with the second FYP in the beginning of February, 1932, at the Seventeenth Party Conference. The Conference accepted the Directives for the Preparation of the Second FYP on the reports of Molotov and Kuibyshev. The theses and reports of these gentlemen, as well as the resolution of the Conference on this subject, were rather brief, containing much verbiage and very few figures, and some of their targets were rather indefinite. Molotov and the resolution of the Conference, for example, said that per capita consumption was to increase threefold in the five years until 1937,[12] but Kuibyshev first declared that "consumption rates are to increase two- to threefold," and later in the same report he spoke of not less than a two- to threefold increase.[13] Whatever figures on the targets of the Directives for

---

[7] *History of the VKP(b), Short Course* (Moscow, 1946), pp. 296–97.

[8] *1st FYP*, II, Part 1, 248–49 (large-scale industry only).

[9] V. Levin, "Industry in the Plan for 1931," *Planned Economy*, 1930, No. 12, p. 150.

[10] *Socialist Construction of the USSR, 1936*, p. 80.

[11] *Planned Economy*, 1931, No. 4, p. 12.

[12] *Pravda*, January 30, 1932.

[13] *Pravda*, February 8, 1932.

1937 could be extracted from the sources are compiled in Table 2
with some comparisons.

TABLE 2

BACCHANALIAN FIVE-YEAR PLANNING*

ITEM	1932 FULFIL-MENTS	TARGETS OF THE SECOND FYP FOR 1937		1937 FULFIL-MENTS	YEARS WHEN TARGETS OF 1932 DIRECTIVES WERE REACHED
		1932 Party Directives	1934 Final		
Electric power (billion kw-h.).......	13.4	Not less than 100	38.0	36.2	1951
Coal (million tons)......	64.3	250	152.5	128.0	1950
Pig iron (million tons)...	6.2	22.0	16.0	14.5	1952
Crude petroleum (million tons)ᵃ........	22.3	80–90	46.8	30.5	1955
Machinery (percentage rise)......	...	200–250	107.2	...	...
Trucks and automobiles (thousands)..........	23.9	300–400	200	199.9	1950
Sown acreage (million hectares).....	134.4	160–170	139.7	135.3	1955
Grain (million tons).....	66.4	130	105	96	1956
Sugar beets (million tons)	6.6	19.8	27.6	21.9	1937
Seed cotton (thousand tons).......	1,271	2,542	2,125	2,582	1937
Flax fiber (thousand tons)	498	996	800	570	not reached by 1958
New railways (thousand km.)ᵇ......	...	not less than 25–30,000	10,700	3,380	probably not reached by 1958ᶜ
Gross fixed investment (billion rubles at current prices)ᵇ.......	50.5	140–150	133.4	115	...

* Except as noted, the targets of the 1932 Directives for the Preparation of the Second FYP are from the resolution of the Seventeenth Party Conference on the respective reports of V. Molotov and V. Kuibyshev (*Pravda*, February 5, 1932). Targets for crude petroleum, sown acreages, and investment are from V. Kuibyshev's report to the Seventeenth Conference (*Pravda*, February 8, 1932). Targets of the second FYP as approved in 1934, are from *2d FYP*, I, *passim*. Fulfilments in 1932 and 1937 as well as data in the last column are, except as noted, from *Economy of the USSR in 1956* and other similar sources. Data on farm output in 1932 and 1937 from *Soc. Agri.*, p. 792. Data for railways are from *Transport and Communications of the USSR*, 1957, p. 28.
   ᵃ Including gas.
   ᵇ FYP periods. "Fulfilment of the 2d FYP," from *3d FYP*, draft, p. 197.
   ᶜ In 1933–55, a total of 20,101 kilometers of new railways were constructed (*Attainments*, p. 212). There was an increase in railways in 1956 of only 400 kilometers (*Transport and Communications*, p. 28).

The crucial point of the Directives, according to those who
reported on the Directives at the Conference, was the target for
electric power. This output of electric power for 1937 was set at the
round figure of 100 billion kilowatt hours. This was scaled down
in 1934 in the final text of the second FYP, worked out after the

end of the *All-out Drive,* to one-third and actually fulfilled. The 1937 target of the Directives of February, 1932, for output of electric power was not reached until 1951.

Of the targets of the 1932 Directives, specified in Table 2, only the targets for cotton and sugar beets were reached on time (for sugar beets, because of the exceptionally good weather). The rest were missed. Some of the targets were not fulfilled before 1956 or later, i.e., after the end of the fifth FYP period. The delay in fulfilment of the targets of the Party Directives was smallest for investment. This occurred because the targets for investment were on a lower level than many production targets. The Directives actually wanted production without providing anything like an adequate amount of capacities to accomplish it. But nobody would of course expect proper tie-ins in such a product as the Directives of the Seventeenth Conference for the Preparation of the Second FYP. A huge disproportion, for example, also existed between the relatively modest targets for some farm products, on the one hand, and the output of consumers' goods and per capita consumption of goods processed from those farm products, on the other.

Although most targets of the Directives were either unfulfilled until thirteen to nineteen years after the year for which they were planned, or have still not been fulfilled, Stalin made the following declaration at the same 1932 Conference:

The Five-Year Plan is accepted by us as a minimum. We will also have control figures [for annual plans] which will expand the Five-Year Plan from year to year. We will also have counterplans which likewise will lead to a further expansion of the Five-Year Plan.[14]

Possibly even better than this was Kuibyshev's declaration: "With reference to consumption the Soviet Union will be the most advanced country of the world [by the end of the second FYP]." [15] He wanted to forestall the need for N. S. Khrushchev's efforts.

Work on the second FYP had actually proceeded after the Seventeenth Conference along the phantom lines called Directives for the Preparation of the Second FYP. On an order of the Sovnarkhom, the first draft of the FYP was to be completed by the Gosplan by

[14] *Izvestiya,* February 7, 1932. Counterplans were an institution which grew out of converting planning into demagogy. The guiding principle was: "From the center down to each [man at the] lathe and from each lathe up to the center." Under the conditions prevailing at that time the results of this climbing down and climbing up again could have been only that the large targets originally accepted at the top level grew larger and larger as they passed down and up the ladder.

[15] *Pravda,* February 8, 1932.

November 15, 1932, the final draft by January 15, 1933.[16] According to I. Smilga, who reported on the second FYP in 1932, the first draft was actually nearing completion.[17] The same issue of *Planned Economy* which carried Smilga's article contained three more on the second FYP, all strictly along the lines of the Directives. Smilga said: "The decision of the Seventeenth Conference is the basic political document, organizing and directing the work on the preparation of the second FYP."[18] It did this until the plenary meeting of the Party Central Committee in January, 1933, which gave directives of its own for the preparation of the second FYP and did not even mention the 1932 Directives or the work done in accordance with them.

Bacchanalian annual plans.—The annual plans accepted during the *All-out Drive* were in some ways even more fantastic than the targets of the FYP's. It would have been more pardonable to go astray with hopes for the more distant future than to approve in December, 1930, unrealistic goals for the year immediately following. Most absurd in this respect were the targets for the last quarter of 1930, approved when the quarter had already started.

Steel was, of course, king with Stalin. The targets of the annual plans for steel output in 1931–33, with the corresponding fulfilment figures, were as follows (in millions of tons): [19]

Year	Target	Fulfilment
1929/30	6.1	5.8[a]
1931	8.8	5.6
1932	9.5	5.9

[a] 1930.

Thus, for 1931 an increase in steel output of three million tons had been planned but, instead, a decline of 0.2 million tons occurred. Not impressed by this, the planners raised the target for the *increase* in output of steel in 1932 from 3.0 million to 3.9 million tons, but the total increase realized amounted only to 0.3 million tons. Therefore, all that the fantastic planning, all that "we ourselves, our ability and our desires" could yield, was a 2 per cent rise in steel output from 1929/30 to 1932.

[16] See I. Smilga, "On the Methodology of Preparing the 2d FYP," *Planned Economy*, 1932, No. 3, p. 17.

[17] The exact date of Smilga's writing is, unfortunately, not ascertainable. The journal was dated August, 1932.

[18] Smilga, *loc. cit.*

[19] Targets from *Control Figures for 1929/30*, pp. 436–37; *Planned Economy*, 1930, No. 12, p. 343; and *Bulletin of Financial-Economic Legislation*, 1932, No. 1, pp. 4–8. Fulfilments from *Socialist Construction of the USSR, 1936*, p. 134.

The following "target" is interesting in connection with steel. S. Ordzhonikidze, the commissar for heavy industry, reported to the Seventeenth Party Conference in February, 1932, that the target for putting blast furnaces in operation in that year was 7.5 million tons of yearly output capacity.[20] The total pig-iron capacity put in operation during the whole first FYP period, including 1932, was 4.5 million tons.[21]

Steel, however, was not an isolated item in which they let themselves go. All targets of the annual plans of that era were of the same "unbelievable" type. The output of industrial producers' goods was to be expanded by not less than 58.4 per cent according to the 1931 Plan. Although 1930 was a favorable year weatherwise, crop production was planned to increase by 24.7 per cent in 1931. Output per man in the industry controlled by the VSNKh was to rise by 28 per cent, that of the People's Commissariat of Supplies by as much as 35 per cent. The sky was not the limit: It was overshot with a target to expand national income by 38.3 per cent in *one* year (1931).[22]

It seems impossible to select the most unrealistic target of the era of bacchanalian planning. Again and again one stumbles on another, even more farfetched. But possibly this would qualify: the plenary session of the Central Committee of the Party in June, 1931, decided that the output of farm machinery in 1932 should insure the harvesting by machinery of at least 50 per cent of the cotton, flax, and sugar beets in 1933.[23] In 1956, 23 per cent of the flax was harvested mechanically.[24] The percentage of cotton acreage harvested mechanically was still so small in 1956 that the official statistical handbook withheld the information. Only in the case of sugar beets could the target established for 1933 have been reached sometime after World War II. Even this is uncertain.[25]

The 1931 Plan foresaw a growth of national income of 38.3 per cent. This meant doubling the national income in little more than two years, quadrupling it in little more than four years, and so in

[20] *Pravda*, February 3, 1932.

[21] *Attainments*, p. 212. The corresponding figures for open hearths: target for the year of 1932, 4.6 million tons; fulfilment in four and a quarter years, including 1932, 2.8 million tons.

[22] All data from "Basic Indicators of the National Economic Plan for 1931," *Planned Economy*, 1930, No. 12, pp. 336–37.

[23] See editorial in *Planned Economy*, 1931, No. 5–6, p. 5.

[24] See *Economy of the USSR in 1956*, p. 152.

[25] Only 43 per cent of the sugar-beet acreage was harvested by the sugar-beet combine in 1956 (*Economy of the USSR in 1956*, p. 152), but the plenary session, if it gave any thought to the method of harvesting, possibly thought of lifting the beets with a plow, a much simpler operation than harvesting by the combine.

geometric progression. Did anyone at least smile when presenting these figures in meetings or when putting them on paper?

No smile can be detected in the article by V. Kats, commenting in detail on the target of the 1931 Plan for national income,[26] i.e., on the scheduled increase in it of over 38 per cent in only one year. On the contrary, he at least pretended to be serious when he insisted that, owing to statistical reasons, the target set for agriculture appeared somewhat too low. Kats also attacked the wreckers who had tried to underestimate "the statistical reflection of our successes in industrializing the country." [27]

There is also no smile in the editorial of the same issue of *Planned Economy,* entitled "The Year of Direct Construction of Socialism and the Planning Work," which proclaimed that planning had entered a new stage:

Now we can exert a *direct* planning influence on all branches of the economy. . . . The possibility of doing this will lead to a new acceleration of socialist industrialization. . . . It represents a new reserve in our attack. . . . The transition from "Control Figures" to the national economic plan, which is the direct result of the present period, i.e., the completion of laying the foundation of a socialist economy, cannot but lead to a fundamental change in the character of planning work, in its volume, methods, and rates of growth.[28]

It must be granted that there was a fundamental change from the Control Figures of the NEP to the plans of the *All-out Drive,* but the change consisted of a vast deterioration. Instead of helping to "accelerate industrialization," the new form of planning had become a contributing factor to the general disorganization.

Concluding remark.—Although the FYP's as a whole were recognized as largely propaganda, certain parts of them had considerable operational significance. All those gigantic targets for output of steel and the other Stalin favorites, and the appropriations for them, were in the plans. They were not properly tied in with one another even in these. Much more disruption came from unequal priorities in the fulfilment stage, steel, of course, having the top priority. Thus the FYP had become a major contributory factor to the prevailing chaos.

The same is even more true of the annual plans of the *All-out Drive* because the Soviet economy can hardly be run without any plans. Plans like the Control Figures for the special quarter of 1930

[26] "National Income of the USSR in a New Stage," *Planned Economy,* 1931, No. 1, pp. 67–87.
[27] *Ibid.,* p. 75.
[28] *Planned Economy,* 1931, No. 1, p. 5.

or the annual plans for 1931 and 1932 could have led only to a catastrophe.

One must give credit to the Kremlin's immense propaganda ability, which has succeeded in having the planning activities of those years accepted as something besides the actions of madmen.

Deflation-Inflation

The first FYP was permeated by deflationary policies. These were an inheritance from a time long before the *Warming-up* period. The fact that farm prices were much too low was recognized, but the gap was to be closed by cutting down all prices other than farm prices. The relatively moderate increase of farm prices for 1928/29 and later crop years was made merely because the campaign for reducing prices of other goods, as well as the costs involved in investment, yielded only very inadequate results.

Based, as elsewhere, on perfectionism, i.e., on rates of increase which could be attained only on paper, the first FYP went out for deflation in a big way. The cost of industrial construction was to be almost halved in the five years from 1927/28 to 1932/33 (the scheduled decline amounted to 45 per cent), and the planned cost cuts in other types of construction were not much less. Wholesale prices of producers' goods were to go down by 30 per cent. Since procurement prices of farm products were to decline by only 5 per cent, a reduction of "only" 18 per cent could be scheduled for the wholesale prices of industrial consumers' goods.[29] The first FYP was similarly optimistic about the development of retail prices.

The claimed "successful" fulfilment of the first FYP did not include fulfilment of its targets for the development of prices—to put it mildly. The very unsatisfactory situation in the consumers'-goods markets, and especially in the food markets, necessarily led to inflation which had begun during the *Warming-up* period. In private trade, inflation started early in 1928, i.e., shortly after the beginning of the *Warming-up* period and a considerable time before acceptance of the first FYP. In April, 1929, when the first FYP was approved, retail prices of food in private trade were almost twice as high as in state trade.[30]

The inflation in private consumers'-goods markets necessarily affected the rest of the economy. The ascertainment of the exact time when deflation was superseded by inflation all along the line is impossible because of the discontinuation of the publication of price statistics. But this discontinuation occurred in the second

[29] *1st FYP*, I, 135.
[30] *Soc. Agri.*, p. 784.

quarter of 1930, and it may reasonably be assumed that this was the time when the price trend was reversed. Contrary to the slow deflationary process of the preceding years, inflation proceeded rapidly. Even rationed-food prices doubled from 1928 to 1932,[31] while by March, 1933, bread prices in the free markets had reached a level of perhaps fifty times that of 1928.[32]

Investment

The Soviets call the All-out Collectivization Drive the Second Revolution. With no less justification, this term could be applied to investment in the non-farm economy. The rise in this investment during the *All-out Drive* period was enormous, indeed, too enormous. Together with misdirection of investment, it ultimately caused, or greatly contributed to, the disaster with which the *All-out Drive* culminated. The rate of growth of investment during this period, great as it was, appears much larger in official data, and it is not easy to reduce these to the real proportions.

According to one of the most important official Soviet statistical sources of the 1930's, gross fixed investment of the socialized sector jumped at current prices from 4.1 billion rubles in 1928 to 20.1 billion in 1932, i.e., about fivefold.[33] Construction (including installation) is supposed to have grown even somewhat more than this, namely, from 2.6 billion rubles in 1928 to 13.4 billion rubles in 1932.[34] The jump in investment of the socialized sector appears very large (close to fourfold) even if the rise in investment costs of about 25 per cent over the period is considered.[35]

The *All-out Drive* period was revolutionary, not only in the size of investment and other things, but in the rapid deterioration of all statistics and specifically those of investment. Since losses were huge during the *All-out Drive,* the first thing to do was to drop from the data on investment those on net investment,[36] in spite of the fact

---

[31] See S. N. Prokopovicz, *Russlands Volkswirtschaft unter den Sowiets* (Zurich and New York, 1944), p. 306.

[32] See below, pp. 113–14.

[33] *Socialist Construction of the USSR, 1936,* pp. 384–85. The source, as usual in the USSR, does not specify the data as "gross." But at that time data for fixed investment undoubtedly involved gross investment. This is apparent, for example, from a comparison of data in *Control Figures for 1929/30,* pp. 446–53, with *ibid.,* pp. 456–61.

[34] *Ibid.,* p. 407.

[35] Twenty-five per cent is a semiofficial Soviet estimate, but it is roughly in line with the findings in *Essay III,* pp. 99–100, and others.

[36] *Control Figures for 1929/30* apparently gives statistics for the last time on fixed investment for both gross and net (see pp. 46–53). M. Ragolskii, who presented a detailed paper on accumulation of basic funds in the Institute of the Economic Investigations of the Gosplan in 1932, was after all not strictly official. See his "Results of Accumulation during the 1st FYP Period," *Planned Economy,* 1932, No. 3, p. 142.

that for some important items net investment was growing more rapidly than gross investment. Next, data of investment, or more correctly, "disinvestment," in livestock were scuttled.

Since the *All-out Drive* was the period of rapid socialization with a rapid growth of the investment of the socialized sector, while private investment, still large in 1928, turned into a negative asset, the official statistics on fixed investments have become restricted to those of the socialized sector.[37] It was in a way a great "achievement" to claim very large investments in agriculture at exactly the time when tens of millions of head of livestock owned by individual peasants were being destroyed and other forms of peasant capital worth billions of rubles were disappearing in one way or another.

As if this were not enough, something not easy to explain happened even to the data on gross investment of the socialized sector. The gross fixed investment of the socialized sector at the prices of the respective years, according to two different issues of the same official statistical handbook, were as follows (in millions of rubles):

Year	Socialist Construction, 1934 (pp. 300–302)	Socialist Construction, 1936 (pp. 384–85)
1928	4,088	4,083
1929	5,873	5,885
1930	9,250	9,786
1931	14,914	15,681
1932	19,000	20,086

The difference between the two sources in data specifically on investment in agriculture was huge (see p. 84 below).

The period as a whole.—The total gross fixed investment of the socialized sector not including that of the kolkhozy during the four and a quarter years of the first FYP period was given at 50.5 billion rubles at current prices.[38] The investment of the kolkhozy during the same period is stated to have been equal to 3.0 billion rubles, but at prices of July 1, 1955.[39] A substantial portion of these investments disappears, if the losses during the same period are deducted.

To get an idea of the losses sustained by the private sector during the *All-out Drive,* let us glance at what the private sector had in 1927/28. The total funds in agriculture at the end of 1927/28 were officially estimated at prices of 1925/26 as follows (in millions of rubles):[40]

---

[37] The data on fixed investment included the private sector for the last time in *National Economy of the USSR, 1932,* pp. 294–96.

[38] *2d FYP,* I, 442.

[39] *Attainments,* p. 207.

[40] *1st FYP,* II, Part 2, 60–64.

Total	28,741
Of this:	
Machinery, including means of transportation	3,280
Buildings	5,734
Livestock	8,001
Irrigation and other improvements	893
Housing	10,833

Practically all these funds, namely, 27,328 million rubles' worth, were privately owned.

In addition to funds in agriculture at the end of 1927/28, the private sector owned funds in industry equal to 763 million rubles and in urban housing valued at 5,047 million rubles. The total fixed property of the private sector thus amounted to 33 billion rubles, of which almost 16 billion rubles were in housing.[41]

Private housing remained on the whole intact during the *All-out Drive,* except that conditions were very unfavorable even for the most indispensable repairs, and hence there must have been a considerable decline in the value of the housing. The same pertains to the investment in irrigation and other improvements which passed to the kolkhozy and sovkhozy, but which certainly did not get proper care. Close to half of the livestock (total livestock, not that owned individually) disappeared from 1928 to 1932 at a loss equal to perhaps 3.5 billion rubles. A large part of the buildings for production purposes, owned in 1927/28 by the peasants, later collectivized, were not needed later on and must have been destroyed (burned for fuel, decayed, etc.). The same must have been true of privately owned farm machinery including wagons. Only part of these passed to the kolkhozy, and part of those obtained by the kolkhozy also disappeared, the kolkhozy having no use for many of them. In addition to their great losses of fixed investment, the individual peasants, former or still continuing in this capacity, lost most of their variable capital in the form of seed, feed, etc.

On the whole, through collectivization the loss in investment previously owned by individual peasants must have been stupendous, even after considering what had passed to the kolkhozy and was used by them. When these losses are considered, the increase in investment during the *All-out Drive* period becomes substantially less than officially calculated for the socialized sector by at least 20 per cent, probably by considerably more.

According to *Attainments* (p. 209), fixed investment of the socialized sector in agriculture without that of the kolkhozy amounted to 9 billion rubles during the first FYP period at prices of July 1, 1955. In addition the kolkhozy, as was mentioned, are supposed to

[41] *Ibid.*

have invested 3.0 billion rubles at the same prices and during the same time.[42] The prices of July 1, 1955, were, of course, very much higher than those of 1927/28. Whatever the official Soviet statistics may show, all funds in all agriculture at the end of 1932 were much below those at the end of 1927/28.

Great losses must have been sustained, not only in agriculture and not only by the private sector. With the "planning" and the directing of the economy characteristic of that period, construction projects certainly were started and never completed. Some others were substantially altered, possibly more than once. All or most of those losses are not reflected in the official calculations, and it is impossible for a private analyst to estimate them.

1932 versus 1928.—For purposes of our analysis, we must turn specifically to the changes in investment in 1928 and 1932. It was pointed out above that a substantial discrepancy exists between *Socialist Construction, 1934,* and *Socialist Construction, 1936* in the estimate of fixed investment of the socialized sector in agriculture. *Socialist Construction, 1934* pp. 300–301) gave this investment in 1932 at only 605.6 million rubles.[43] In *Socialist Construction, 1936* (pp. 384–85), the same item was stated as having been not less than 3,820 million rubles.[44]

Losses in peasant agriculture were heavy also specifically in 1932. More than two million peasant households were collectivized in this year,[45] and this meant, of course, additional destruction of the peasant property. Total livestock declined from the spring of 1931 to the springs of 1932 and 1933 as follows (in millions):[46]

Type of Livestock	1931	1932	1933
Horses	26.2	19.6	16.6
Cattle	47.9	40.7	38.6
Hogs	14.4	11.6	12.1
Sheep and goats	77.7	52.1	50.6

It may be easily overlooked that, while the statistics of fixed investment in the statistical handbooks for 1934 through 1936 did

---

[42] *Attainments,* p. 207.

[43] Without the value of the livestock.

[44] All data without consideration of the livestock. The figure of the later source implies a more than tenfold growth since 1928 (the investment for this item in 1928 is given by the same source at 379 million rubles). The figure of *Socialist Construction, 1936* for gross fixed investment in agriculture in 1932 contains as one of its components 515 million rubles for the item "resources and labor of the kolkhozniki," but this new item, the legitimacy of inclusion of which is doubtful, explains only part of the discrepancy between the two statistical handbooks.

[45] The percentage of all households collectivized increased from 52.7 on July 1, 1931, to 61.5 on July 1, 1932. See *Economy of the USSR in 1956,* p. 105.

[46] *Socialist Construction, 1934,* p. 226.

not consider livestock and gave data only for gross investment and at current prices, better data on the same item ("better" does not mean "good") may be found in the sections of the same handbooks devoted to agriculture. The data are of two different kinds: (*a*) the cost of the basic funds of the socialist sector including the kolkhozy, with consideration of depreciation, at 1926/27 prices; and (*b*) gross fixed investment for the same sector at current prices.

Socialist Construction of the USSR, 1935 (pp. 283–90) gives the gross fixed investment of the socialized sector in agriculture in 1932 at 4,432 million rubles, but the increase in the basic funds of the same enterprises with consideration of depreciation and at constant prices amounted only to 1,192 million rubles in the same year, according to the same source. The difference between the two figures is certainly large, in spite of the fact that the cited increase in basic funds is probably still exaggerated. It shows that one cannot be too cautious in using Soviet data on gross investment, especially at prices of the respective years.

The losses of the private sector in agriculture in 1932 certainly were larger than the 1.2 billion rubles officially calculated as the net increase in funds of the socialist sector in agriculture in that year. The probable exaggeration of the increase in the later funds must also be considered.

With agriculture excluded, the cited official calculations of gross fixed investment of the socialized sector as stated in *Socialist Construction of the USSR, 1936,* indicates an increase from 3.7 billion rubles in 1928 to 16.3 billion rubles in 1932, i.e., a rise of about 4.4 times in current prices or about 3.4 times at constant prices. The growth in the *net* investment in the items covered by the above estimates must have been larger than this, because depreciation charges were increasing at a slower rate than gross investment or gross construction.[47]

The net fixed investment in the non-farm economy in 1927/28 amounted to 70.4 per cent of the total net fixed investment.[48] Assuming that investment in agriculture was the same in both 1927/28 and 1932 and disregarding the decline in private non-farm economy, total fixed investment during the period of the first FYP appears to have risen to a level 2.4 times what it had been at the beginning of the period. The increase in net fixed investment (thus far only agriculture was calculated on this basis) must have been measurably larger. The consideration of the losses sustained by the

[47] See the analysis by Ragolskii, "Results of Accumulation during the 1st FYP Period," *Planned Economy,* 1932, No. 3, p. 42.

[48] *Control Figures for 1928/29,* pp. 446–53.

economy through misdirection of investment and its bad management, on the other hand, would have pressed that figure down.

As shown in Appendix B, Table I, net investment in 1937 at 1926/27 prices is estimated at 18 billion rubles. The increase in it in 1932–37 is roughly estimated in chapter 6 at 50 per cent. These estimates in conjunction with the estimate of investment in 1927/28 in Appendix B, Table I, imply a net investment at constant prices in 1932 amounting to 2.3 times the level of 1927/28.

It is hardly necessary to emphasize that even such an increase in net investment in the whole economy in only four or four and a quarter years must be considered very large, especially if the immense losses of the economy during the period needed to be covered are taken into account. Moreover, the fact must be kept in mind that the net fixed investment in the non-farm economy may have grown close to, or even fully, 3.5 times its earlier level.

In concluding the analysis of the growth in investment during the first FYP period, we must again emphasize its tentative nature. Even the by no means lucid presentation given above is the result of almost endless reworking stretched out over a period of about six years.

The great jump in investment of the socialized sector during the *All-out Drive* was of course impossible without a really great effort. For 1931 the Party was already aiming at a gross fixed (capital) investment of the socialized sector (at that time this investment included capital repairs) equivalent to not less than 35 per cent of the national income.[49] The stated percentage share would obviously have been considerably larger still, if Kuibyshev, president of the Gosplan at that time, had considered the other forms of investment.

The target for gross fixed investment of the socialized sector in 1931 was 17.1 billion rubles.[50] The actual investment at current prices amounted to 15.7 billion rubles. With consideration of increased costs of investment (by perhaps 15 per cent), the target was underfulfilled by about 22 per cent. The corresponding figures for 1932 were: target at 1931 prices—22.6 billion rubles; fulfilment at the higher 1932 prices—20.1 billion rubles.[51] At 1931 prices the 1932 realized investment amounted to about 17.0 billion rubles, i.e., about 25 per cent short of the target. Large as the failures to attain the targets for investment were, they seem to have been much

[49] V. Kuibyshev, "The Plan of Socialist Construction in 1931," *Planned Economy,* 1930, No. 12, p. 37. Kuibyshev related the target for capital investments as planned for 1931 at current prices to the target for national income at 1926/27 prices, but this did not cause much distortion at that time.

[50] *Planned Economy,* 1930, No. 12, p. 338.

[51] Target from Ragolskii, *loc. cit.* Fulfilment from *Socialist Construction, 1936,* p. 384.

smaller than those for many other items, such as, for example, steel output. While everything was not achieved, the accomplishments in investment were more than the economy could stand without a great deal of harm.

Construction.—The year-by-year estimates of fixed investment of the socialized sector at prices of July 1, 1955, presented for the first time in *Stat. Handb.*, 1956 (pp. 158–59), contain in addition to data for the totals, separate estimates for investment in construction and installation. Chart 7 compares these estimates for 1928–33 with the

CHART 7

INVESTMENT IN CONSTRUCTION VS. OUTPUT OF BUILDING MATERIALS, 1928–33 *
(1928 = 100)

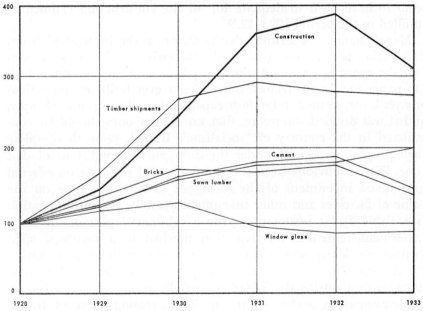

* Investment in construction, which includes installation, of the socialized sector at prices of July 1, 1955, in 1929–33, from *Stat. Handb.*, 1956, p. 158. The respective figure for 1928 is approximately calculated from another official source. Data on output of building materials from *Industry of the USSR*, 1957, *passim*. It must be considered that the data for output cover the total output, while construction and installation of the socialized sector represented a rapidly rising percentage of the total.

official data on the output of building materials in the same years.

The almost fourfold increase in construction at constant prices claimed officially for the period from 1928 to 1932 seems to be rather large as compared with the increase in output of building materials. It would seem that the expansion in the latter could more likely support only about a doubling in construction. The output of window glass could, of course, not support any increase in it at all. The utilization of building materials was, however, rather wasteful in the preceding years, and some building materials produced by state industry in 1928 were sold to non-state customers. The official calculation of investment in construction will not be dismissed as incorrect, but will just be held under suspicion.

The data for 1930–32 in Chart 7 are of particular interest. According to them, the value of construction and installation at constant prices increased by 61 per cent in those years. At the same time, the outputs of bricks, cement, and industrial timber were practically stagnant (increases of 4, 16, and 3 per cent, respectively). There was a precipitous decline in the output of window glass.[52]

The rates of growth of output and of imports of machinery also seem to have been inadequate for all the construction claimed as fulfilled in the period 1928–32.[53]

Megalomania.—A serious adverse factor on the investment front, in addition to the excessiveness of appropriations for constructions and the growing general futility of all efforts was "megalomania." On paper the largest factories, the largest ever built or larger than any yet built, seemed to be those capable of producing most cheaply, and it was decided, therefore, that no smaller ones should be constructed in the country of "socialism." It took years to complete such projects, especially under the disorganized conditions of that time. This is obvious from the comparison of the data on effected gross fixed investment of the socialized sector with those on the value of factories and other investment actually put into operation (see Table 3). At least temporarily a substantial part of the large investment remained inactive in unfinished blast furnaces, open hearths, etc. Many giants, which tied up badly needed capital during the *All-out Drive,* became active only after conditions had become more sensible during the *Three "Good" Years.*

Investment by sector.—The rapidly increasing share of investment in national income was in agreement with the desires of the

[52] This writer wrestled with the great discrepancy between the claimed growth of investment and those of output of building materials in *Essay III.* In Appendix Table XIII, p. 163, of that essay, official data are reproduced showing the utilization of building materials per million rubles' worth of *Glavstroiprom* constructions in 1930–34. They indicate such immense declines in the use of individual materials per million rubles' worth of construction that these cannot possibly be fully explained by increased costs and rationalization. Deterioration of the quality of construction, which was certainly present to a considerable extent, was offered as an additional explanation for the reduced utilization of building materials (see *Essay III,* p. 101). But was this enough?

[53] On machinery output, see data in Table 6 (see p. 99, below); on imports of machinery, see *Socialist Construction of the USSR, 1936,* pp. 692–93.

TABLE 3

All-out Drive: FIXED INVESTMENT SPENT AND PUT INTO OPERATION*
(In millions of rubles)

Year (1)	Invested (2)	Put into Operation (3)	Column (3) in per cent of Column (2) (4)
1928......	4,083	3,393	82.9
1929......	5,885	4,788	81.4
1930......	9,786	8,194	81.7
1931......	15,681	11,697	74.6
1932......	20,086	15,085	75.1
1933......	18,432	17,551	95.2
1934......	23,832	22,053	92.6

* *Socialist Construction of the USSR, 1936*, pp. 384–85, 390–91.

Communists. But this was only part of the story. Expansion, not just of industry, but, specifically, of heavy industry was the thing aimed at and correspondingly the share of fixed investment in heavy industry in total investment of this kind rose rapidly until it was absorbing a very large part of the total fixed investment. This process started before the *All-out Drive* but made great progress during this period (see Table 4).

TABLE 4

All-out Drive: FIXED INVESTMENT OF THE SOCIALIZED SECTOR BY MAJOR SECTOR*
(In millions of rubles)

YEAR	TOTAL	INDUSTRY			AGRICULTURE	TRANS- PORTATION	EDUCATION	HEALTH SERVICES
		Total	Producers' Goods	Consumers' Goods				
1928..	4,083	1,880	1,444	436	379[a]	905	130	99
1929..	5,885	2,615	2,127	488	840	1,259	221	116
1930..	9,786	4,115	3,425	690	2,590	1,780	241	128
1931..	15,681	7,407	6,513	894	3,645	2,874	239	141
1932..	20,086	10,431	9,080	1,351	3,820	3,692	250	148

* *Socialist Construction of the USSR, 1936*, pp. 384–85.
[a] Total investment in agriculture in this year was estimated at 2,376 million rubles. See *National Economy of the USSR, 1932*, p. xxx.

In 1924/25, gross fixed investment in heavy industry, including electric power which was then listed separately in the statistics of investment, was equivalent to 364 million rubles, representing 29.9 per cent of total gross fixed investment of the socialized sector. It rose almost fourfold in the subsequent three and a quarter years (somewhat more if the decline in construction costs is allowed for), representing 35.4 per cent of the total gross fixed investment of the socialized sector in 1928. But fixed investment other than that of the socialized sector, almost nothing of which went into heavy industry, was still large in those years, and hence the stated percentages considerably exaggerate the share of heavy industry in total fixed investment.

The growth of fixed investment in heavy industry in the following four years is shown below at current prices:[54]

Year	Fixed Investment in Heavy Industry (in million rubles)	Rates of Growth (in per cent of the preceding year)	Investment in Heavy Industry (per cent of total fixed investment of the socialized sector)
1928........	1,444	...	35.4
1929........	2,127	47	36.1
1930........	3,425	61	35.0
1931........	6,513	90	41.5
1932........	9,080	39	45.2

The very large rate of growth of investment in heavy industry between 1924/25 and 1928 could not have been accelerated much more in the succeeding years. Taking inflation into account, the 584 per cent increase in this investment in four years (1928–32) was hardly much greater, relatively, than the rise of about 300 per cent in the preceding three and a quarter years (1924/25 to 1928). But even the maintaining of such a tempestuous rate of growth, at the much higher level reached, was very significant. The share of heavy industry in total fixed investment of the socialized sector continued its rise in 1928–32 as well. In 1932 it made up almost half of the latter. The share of this investment in *total* investment increased even more, because private investment, practically none of which had been channeled into heavy industry, disappeared almost entirely by 1932.

Collectivization, especially since it was associated with the loss of more than half of all horses (between 1928 and 1934), made a fundamental reorganization of farm techniques indispensable. The agricultural economy was transformed from one operating with horsepower and small implements to one which should have been largely operated with tractors and large implements. In addition to a mass of machinery, the newly created collective farms and MTS (machine-tractor stations) also required an immense amount of new construction. Relative to these requirements, the gross fixed investment in agriculture was very inadequate. Stalin needed the investment funds for construction of steel factories.

[54] *Socialist Construction of the USSR, 1936*, pp. 384–85.

While total gross investment of the socialized sector in nominal terms rose almost fivefold from 1928 to 1932, and gross investment in heavy industry increased more than sixfold, total investment in agriculture, i.e., including that of the peasants, in 1932 (see Table 4 and especially note "a") was only 61 per cent greater than in 1928— also in nominal terms. About half of this increase was probably due to rising costs.

The Soviets do not distinguish between investment which is intended for expansion of previously existing capacity and that which is intended merely as compensation for losses caused by all kinds of plights, such as wars, external and internal, bad policies, etc. In view of the fact that farm output (in 1939 boundaries) increased little from 1928 to, say, 1953,* one wonders how small the total net investment in agriculture during this long period would have been if expenses for compensating previous losses had not been counted as investment.

The connection between heavy industry and the transportation system is extremely close. Five products of heavy industry (coal, petroleum, steel, timber, and cement) alone accounted for 52 per cent of the total tonnage carried by the railways in 1932.[55] Yet the relation of fixed investment in the transportation system to the fixed investment of the socialized sector in heavy industry was rapidly declining:[56]

Year	Per Cent
1928	62.7
1929	59.3
1930	52.0
1931	44.1
1932	40.7

Such large disproportions do not occur in the economy without severe penalty. This came in the form of great disruption in the transportation system, which continued to be a great bottleneck for a considerable time after the *All-out Drive* had ended.

Investment in education services at current prices increased little from 1929 to 1932 and may have declined somewhat, if the inflation is considered. Investment in health services did not grow in those years at constant prices either, although, in view of the great deterioration of the diet, the need for them must have increased greatly.

* It is implied in *Economy of the USSR in 1958,* p. 350, that in comparable boundaries the 1953 farm output was somewhat smaller than that of 1928.

[55] James Blackman in *Symposium,* p. 145.

[56] *Socialist Construction of the USSR, 1936,* pp. 384–85.

On the "Socialist" Front

The course of the All-out Collectivization Drive, which affected
more than half of the peasant households in a matter of weeks during the winter of 1929/30, the great violence on the part of the
government which accompanied it, the temporary retreat proclaimed in Stalin's notorious "Dizziness from Successes" in *Pravda*
of March 2, 1930, and the final victory of collectivization were
described in some detail in *Soc. Agri.*[57] "Dizziness from Successes,"
intended to take the responsibility for the crimes from Stalin and
put it on those who were only his tools, led to a precipitous exodus
from the kolkhozy, but the sheep, which had wandered away, were
soon brought back into the fold. April 1, 1932, saw 61.5 per cent of
all peasant households and 77.6 per cent of the acreage sown by
peasants collectivized.[58] As far as livestock is concerned, however,
the holdings of the collective farms in 1933, expressed as percentages
of the combined holdings of peasants and collective farms in 1928,
were only: horses, 30 per cent; cattle and hogs, 12 to 13 per cent of
each kind; and sheep and goats, 8 per cent.[59] The rest either remained in the hands of the collectivized and non-collectivized peasants or (very large numbers) were annihilated.

With respect to private enterprise in economic sectors other than
agriculture, not much more than mopping up was left to be done
during the *All-out Drive*. Only 0.2 per cent of large-scale and 28.7
per cent of small-scale industry remained private in 1930.[60] All private trade, even direct sales by the producers of farm products to the
consumers, was prohibited in 1930. Private trade by intermediaries
remained prohibited for good. Sales of farm products by producers
to consumers were legalized only shortly before the expiration of the
All-out Drive, and, even then, only direct sales to consumers were
permitted.[61]

The resolution of the Seventeenth Party Congress on the second
FYP in February, 1934, proclaimed:

[57] See chapter 13.
[58] *Socialist Construction of the USSR, 1936*, p. 278. Sown acreage excludes fallow.
[59] *Soc. Agri.*, pp. 789, 796.
[60] *Economy of the USSR, 1932*, pp. xlvi–xlvii.
[61] The so-called kolkhoz markets, where the producers (kolkhoz and individual peasants and the kolkhozy themselves) could sell their products directly to the consumers, were permitted by the order of May 6, 1932, but many restrictions, especially
with reference to the sales of grain and potatoes, were imposed (see *Soc. Agri.*, pp.
383–84). Sales of farm products by producers and also by private traders, of course,
also took place before the stated date. There certainly were even statistical data collected about these sales. But the trade was illegal and nothing was published. See, for
example, the blanks under private trade in the years since 1931 in *Socialist Construction of the USSR, 1936*, p. 607.

By the heroic struggle of the working class [i.e., Stalin] the foundations of the socialist economy were already laid during the period of the first five-year plan. Destroyed was the last capitalist class—the kulaks. . . . The USSR had definitely established itself on the socialist path.[62]

The price of victory on the farm front was a substantial decline in farm production, specifically the destruction of more than half of the total livestock, and an almost proportionate drop in output of animal products (see beginning of next chapter). Since the victory insured the control of the state over the supplies of farm products, procurements increased greatly, in the face of the decline in output, with a resultant large reduction in consumption by the farm population and, ultimately, the death by starvation of hundreds of thousands, perhaps more than a million, of peasants in the winter of 1932/33.

As far as human life is concerned, the Soviet government and its friends in the West continue their efforts to erase the memory of the huge losses of 1932/33. The merciless figures of population estimates before and after the collectivization drive and, in particular, the estimates of the changes in population from 1931 to 1934 presented above (see p. 72) leave, however, no doubt on this point. There is, moreover, excellent supporting evidence in the fantastic prices paid in kolkhoz markets.

Greatly Increased Output or Control

Paul Sweezy wrote in 1949: "The purpose of collectivization was not so much to increase aggregate production as to bring agriculture under control. . . ."[63] The obvious conclusion from this assumption is: control was assured; hence, collectivization was a success. Fortunately, a moderate increase in grain output could also be "proved" by comparing production in 1934 in "biological" terms with the production in 1913 and 1926/27 in "barn" or real terms.[64] (The official estimate of the 1934 crop was too high in relation to that of 1913 and 1926/27 by about 20 per cent according to *Soc. Agri.* [p. 544]. It appears that the one million people who died of starvation died without a cause.)

[62] *2d FYP*, I, v.

[63] *Socialism* (New York, 1949), p. 30. See also the review of this writer's book on Soviet agriculture by Joseph Kershaw of the RAND Corporation in *American Economic Review*, March, 1950.

[64] Sweezy, *op. cit.*, p. 21. N. Khrushchev harshly attacked G. Malenkov for the use of "biological" as "barn" crops. See *Pravda*, December 16, 1958. By implication he attacked Paul Sweezy and Dr. Rudolf Schlesinger of Glasgow, from whom Sweezy borrowed his data. To an objective observer it was clear from the very introduction of the estimating of grain crops in "biological" terms in 1933 that this had been done to mislead.

When the present writer argued that Soviet statistics were falsified, the reaction was an outburst of indignation. Yet Sweezy's and Kershaw's position implies an amount of hypocrisy and deceit on the part of the Soviets greater than the present writer has ever ascribed to them.

As good Marxists, the Bolsheviks, Lenin not excepted, had always adhered strongly to the idea that in farming, as elsewhere, large-scale enterprise is much superior to small-scale enterprise. Bolshevik pronouncements, before, during, and after the *All-out Drive,* are all in unison on this score. The agricultural targets of the first FYP were certainly based on this idea. The average yield of grain, for example, was planned for 1932/33 at 11.28 quintals per hectare for the collective farms and at "only" 9.22 quintals per hectare for the individual peasants, an excess of 22.3 per cent in favor of the former.[65]

In the experience of the world, it is true, the family farm has successfully held its own, and even gained, on the large farm. Nor did the operations of the collective farms in the USSR in the 1920's justify any enthusiasm for large farms. The Bolsheviks' belief in the great advantages of large-scale farming may, therefore, seem to have been unjustified. But we face fanatics for whom economic science reached its peak in Marx's *Capital.* Why doubt the belief of the Bolsheviks in the superiority of the large farm, when moderate social-democrats like Karl Kautsky still held it? [66]

Mr. Sweezy is, however, right in emphasizing the great importance for the Soviets of getting control over farm supplies. It may indeed be argued with great justification that the *All-out Drive* would have taken place even if the Bolsheviks had fully realized in advance that farm output would be unfavorably affected by collectivization. Fanatics as they were, the desire to go ahead with the Industrialization Drive anyway may have suppressed any doubts which might possibly have existed in the minds of some of them about the superiority of large-scale farm enterprise. They wanted control. The Marxian ideas on the superiority of large-scale enterprises in agriculture fitted in admirably with their wishes, and they stuck to these ideas. Wishful thinking of this type is quite common, indeed it might almost be said to be the rule under such conditions, and not only among Bolsheviks.

Contrary to the position of Sweezy *et al.,* the Bolsheviks must probably be granted some degree of sincerity with regard to the

---

[65] *1st FYP,* II, Part 1, 328–29.

[66] Kautsky's *Agrarfrage* (Stuttgart, 1902) accepted Marx's position on the problem of the large versus the small farm.

problem of the large versus the small farm, but only prior to the Drive. When their optimistic expectations with reference to raising the farm output did not materialize, they did not reverse their policies. Indeed, they never conceded the error, but forged statistics to prove their case.[67]

By now even non-economists realize that collectivization of peasant farming is a means of industrialization by way of obtaining farm products from the producers without adequate pay. Wilhelm Starlinger, a doctor of medicine, speculated on the future of China:

> Should China have to rely on Soviet Russia for a long time to come and without any prospect of making an agreement with America, she would be compelled "to become large by hunger," i.e., to industrialize at the expense of the peasants, and this means to collectivize. . . .[68]

But this was written in 1954, a quarter of a century after Stalin made his decision to go ahead with full-scale collectivization.

[67] The problem is discussed in greater detail in *Soc. Agri.*, pp. 23–26.
[68] *Grenzen der Sowiet Macht* (Wurzburg, Germany, 1955), p. 116.

CHAPTER 5

Agriculture

Agriculture during the *All-out Drive* and other stages has been dealt with in such great detail in *Soc. Agri.* that it seems unnecessary to repeat the material here. (The acreages and yields per hectare are shown in *Soc. Agri.,* Appendix Chart Tables 25 and 27, the livestock herds in Appendix Chart Table 37.)

While acreages were expanded during the first FYP period, there was a great deterioration in yields per hectare. The yield of grain, less sensitive to disorganization than some other crops, went down from an average of 7.7 quintals per hectare in 1927 and 1928 to an average of 6.5 quintals per hectare in 1931 and 1932. The yield of the more sensitive sugar beets fell to less than half that before collectivization. Livestock herds showed the following enormous losses (June figures in millions):[1]

Year	Horses	Cattle	Hogs	Sheep and Goats
1928.......	33.5	70.5	26.0	146.7
1932.......	19.6	40.7	11.6	52.1
1933.......	16.6	38.4	12.1	50.2

By June of 1933 only cattle herds had declined less than 50 per cent, but not much less.

[1] See *Socialist Construction of the USSR, 1936,* pp. 354–55. The losses in livestock herds were concealed for years—to be ultimately disclosed by Stalin in 1934 at the Seventeenth Party Congress. Hence the two-volume draft of the second FYP, released a short while before this Congress, did not contain any data on livestock. They were incorporated in the final version of the FYP after their disclosure by Stalin.

TABLE 5

All-out Drive: GROSS FARM OUTPUT, 1928–32

Item	1928	1929	1930	1931	1932
Gross farm output (billion rubles at 1926/27 prices)[a]............	15.5	14.7	14.0	13.9	13.1[b]
Gross crop production (billion rubles at 1926/27 prices)[a]......	9.5	9.1	9.6	9.9	9.8[c]
Of this:[d]					
Grain (million tons)...........	73.3	71.7	83.5	66.1	66.4
Potatoes (million tons).........	46.4	45.6	49.4	44.8	43.2
Sugar beet (million tons).......	10.1	6.2	14.0	12.0	6.6
Sunflower seed (million tons)...	2.1	1.8	1.6	2.5	2.3
Seed cotton (thousand tons)....	821	864	1,113	1,290	1,271
Hay (million tons)............	78.8	70.1	61.3	75.3	65.3
Gross animal production (billion rubles at 1926/27 prices)[e]......	6.0	5.7	4.4	4.1	3.3
Of this:[f]					
Meat (thousand tons).........	3,611	3,940	4,473	n.a.	2,138
Milk (thousand tons)..........	30,106	30,709	27,969	24,806	19,620
Eggs (billion units)...........	10.5	10.2	n.a.	n.a.	4.2[g]

[a] Official figures for 1929–32 from *Socialist Construction of the USSR, 1936*, pp. 232–33. Data for 1928 and 1932 from *Soc. Agri.*, pp. 673, 669.

[b] According to the estimate of this writer, 12.0 billion rubles(see *Soc. Agri.*, p. 775).

[c] According to the estimates of this writer, 8.7 billion rubles (see *Soc. Agri.*, p. 775).

[d] *Soc. Agri.*, p. 792.

[e] Data for 1928 from *Soc. Agri.*, p. 671; data for 1929–32 from *Socialist Construction of the USSR, 1936*, pp. 232–33.

[f] *Soc. Agri.*, p. 798. All data, except for 1932, are for the fiscal year; for example, 1927/28 instead of 1928.

[g] Eggs for consumption only.

Table 5 gives a summarized picture of developments in agriculture year by year. According to official calculations, crop production increased by a few per cent from 1928 to 1932. This writer's estimates indicate a decline in it of almost 10 per cent. Animal production went down to little more than 50 per cent in the same years. Altogether there was a decline in gross farm output of about 15 per cent (official estimate), or of somewhat more than 20 per cent (this writer's estimate). If this writer's estimate is right, the USSR produced in 1932 half of what was scheduled in the first FYP for 1932/33. Quite a difference!

All-out Industrialization

Instead of converting the Soviet Union into an industrial state almost overnight, the Soviets suffered the humiliation of having brought about the operation of the same "extinguishing curve," for which Groman, Ginzburg, and others were tried in March, 1931. Indeed, the "extinguishing curve" was already in operation when the trial took place, and the total decline in the rate of growth of industrial output turned out much stronger than any "wrecker" had ever forecast. That decline was actually so great that even Stalin found its recognition unavoidable.[2]

The decline in the rates of industrial growth was not at first very marked. According to Hodgman, it went down from 20 per cent in 1928/29 to 15.6 per cent in 1929/30 and 18 per cent in the last quarter of 1930 and in 1931. But in 1932 further growth, according to him, amounted only to 5.2 per cent.[3] This figure, even as it stands, and without consideration of the deterioration in quality of the products, was considerably smaller than that contemplated by Ginzburg for the last year of *his* FYP. With the needed adjustments (Hodgman's index for those years covers large-scale industry only) and with due consideration for the deterioration of quality, 1932 industrial production was certainly smaller than that of 1931.[4]

The development in industrial output during the first FYP period as a whole obviously had nothing in common with the targets of the FYP. Industry, the output of which was planned by the VSNKh, was to increase by 90 per cent in the three years from 1929/30 to 1932/33.[5] The growth should have exceeded 100 per cent in three and a quarter years. According to Hodgman, large-scale industrial output was enlarged by 44 per cent in the three and a quarter years from 1928/29 to 1932. But timber procurement, which is not included in Hodgman's index, increased by only about 30 per cent, so total large-scale industry grew by about 40 per cent rather than the more than 100 per cent planned.

[2] He tried to bypass the issue by insisting that one should not limit oneself to the analysis of percentage rates of growth, but should pay attention to the growing absolute amounts represented by each succeeding percentage (see Stalin's report on the fulfilment of the first FYP, *Pravda,* January 10, 1933)—as if this had not already been obvious at the time when the FYP was drafted and approved. There were, moreover, in many cases, no growing absolute amounts, during the first FYP period.

The way in which the most meaningless assertions are made in the USSR can be explained only by the 100 per cent monopoly which the Kremlin enjoys on the spoken, written, and broadcast word. In the discussion of the 1954 budget Mikoyan said (*Pravda,* April 27, 1954) that the procurement plan for meat in the first half of 1954 was not fulfilled because the owners preferred to fatten their livestock in the summer in order to sell in the autumn. This seasonal phenomenon has repeated itself since time immemorial. The great seasonal decline in the marketing of cattle and sheep in the spring and summer should obviously have been foreseen and taken care of in the plan. The truth is that the plan for meat procurements in the first half of 1954 was based, not on the probable deliveries of animals by the producers, but on the promises of meat to the consumers.

[3] *Symposium,* p. 232.

[4] Data on freight traffic fully support the findings. The rate of growth in freight shipped by railways (in tons) declined from 27.6 per cent in 1930 to 8.2 jer cent in 1931 and 3.6 per cent in 1932. See *Transport and Communications* (Moscow, 1957), p. 32.

[5] *1st FYP,* II, Part 1, 252–53.

The deplorable picture shown by the industrial production during the first FYP period is apparent with even greater certainty in data for individual commodities (Table 6).

TABLE 6

All-out Drive: OUTPUT OF SELECTED INDUSTRIAL GOODS*

Commodity	1930	1931	1932	1933
Coal (million tons).................	47.8	56.8	64.4	76.3
Petroleum (million tons)............	18.5	22.4	21.4	21.5
Electric power (billion kw-h.).......	8.4	10.7	13.5	16.4
Steel (million tons).................	5.8	5.6	5.9	6.9
Iron and steel (million dollars)......	263	268	308	353
Machinery (million dollars).........	427	532	535	603
Cement (thousand tons)............	3,006	3,336	3,478	2,709
Industrial timber, shipped from forest (million cubic meters)............	96.7	104.1	99.4	98.0
Paper (thousand tons)..............	495	505	471	506
Cotton fabric (million meters).......	2,351	2,242	2,694	2,732
Footwear (million pairs)............	75.4	86.7	84.7[a]	80.2[a]
Meat (thousand tons)[b]............	550	692	458	411

* Except as noted, the data are from *Industry of the USSR, 1957, passim.* Data for machinery, at 1939 dollar prices, from Alexander Gerschenkron, *A Dollar Index of Soviet Machinery Output, 1927/28 to 1937* (Santa Monica, Calif., 1951), p. 25. Data for iron and steel in 1939 dollar prices from Gerschenkron's "Soviet Heavy Industry: A Dollar Index of Output, 1927/28 to 1937," *Review of Economics and Statistics,* May, 1955, p. 123. The source for meat is *Socialist Construction of the USSR, 1936.*

[a] Data from *Socialist Construction of the USSR, 1936. Industry of the USSR,* 1957, p. 351., has 86.9 million pairs for 1932 and 90.3 million pairs for 1933.

[b] *Socialist Construction of the USSR, 1936.*

The stagnation in output of steel during the *All-out Drive* has been discussed in chapter 4. Even the maintaining of the steel output at the previous level was achieved only by deterioration of what are called in the USSR the quality factors:

Indicator	1929	1930	1931	1932	1933
Coefficient of utilization of blast furnaces in terms of calendar time[a]....................	1.78	1.69	1.88	1.75	1.71
Stoppages of blast furnaces for repairs in per cent of calendar time[a]....................	3.5	3.8	5.8	6.1	7.3
Kilograms of ore charged per ton of pig iron[b]............	...	1,656	1,675	1,737	1,843
Output of steel per square meter of open hearths in tons[c].....	2.39	2.63	2.22	2.12	2.29
Stoppages of open hearths in per cent of calendar time[c].......	28.8	24.2	32.7	34.7	32.6

[a] *Industry of the USSR,* 1957, p. 118.
[b] Gardner Clark, *The Economics of Soviet Steel,* p. 145.
[c] *Industry of the USSR,* 1957, p. 122.

As the data in Chart 7 show, in output of building materials, the last years of the first FYP period were characterized not just by retardation in the rate of growth, or even stagnation, but by actual decline.

Consumers' goods did not, of course, matter at all. So far as sugar is concerned, the standard Soviet statistics normally carry only data for output of crystal sugar. But the consumers want most of their sugar in the form of lump sugar, a refined product made from crystal sugar which is not fully refined. The Soviets successfully managed to conceal for almost twenty years the fact that in 1930, when, owing to an excellent harvest of sugar beets, the output of crystal sugar almost doubled (an increase of 83.1 per cent from the 1929 level), the output of lump sugar dropped by 59 per cent.[6] While in 1929 the output of lump sugar amounted to 63.5 per cent of that of crystal sugar, the percentage slumped to only 14.3 per cent in 1930. The cost of refining is small and the fact that already in 1930 it had been decided to neglect the desires of the consumers by not processing more than a small quantity of crystal to lump sugar may possibly be the most vivid testimonial of the real attitude toward the consumer, apparent as early in the *All-out Drive* as the end of 1929, when the decision must have been made not to process to lump sugar more than very small quantities (possibly only such demand as that of the armed forces was to be covered).

Another interesting feature of industrial output during the *All-out Drive* is the following: Here were people rapidly approaching starvation, but the socialist state uses its monopolistic position for a more than fivefold enlargement of the output of confections (from 99,000 tons in 1928 to 511,000 tons in 1932).[7] Output of alimentary pastes also increased fourfold during the period.[8] Such a thing as consumers' choice obviously did not exist. Otherwise the people would have bought bread, and more bread.

Transportation

A bottleneck in the transportation system had already started to develop in the last quarter of 1930. It increased greatly in subsequent years, and remained a great obstacle to recovery after the end of the *All-out Drive*. All this is described well and in great detail in Hunter's monumental volume.[9]

[6] *Industry of the USSR*, 1957, p. 373.
[7] *Ibid.*, p. 401.
[8] *Ibid.*, p. 403. The situation with sausage and meat was similar.
[9] *Soviet Transportation Policy* (Cambridge, Mass.: Harvard University Press, 1957).

The deterioration in the operation of the transportation system is clearly revealed by the following data (year-to-year growth in freight traffic in per cent):[10]

Year	Five Carriers (ton-kilometers)	Railways (tons shipped)	Railways (ton-kilometers)
1929.........	20.2	20.1	20.9
1930.........	20.6	27.2	18.7
1931.........	15.0	8.2	13.6
1932.........	10.1	3.6	11.3
1933.........	3.0	0.4	0.1

The transitional year of 1933 was the worst, so far as freight traffic is concerned. Shipments of freight on the railways did not increase at all in that year. It was not the "extinguishing curve" which had been forecast by the "enemies" of the country. The curve shown for railway traffic was fully extinguished.

The growth in the backlog of freight awaiting shipment by the railways is a much stronger indicator of the rapidly increasing disorganization than the decline in the rate of growth of shipments. The tabulation below shows the relation of the backlog to monthly shipments (in per cent):[11]

March, 1928....................	22.3
September, 1929...............	61.7
December, 1932................	90.9
December, 1933...............	114.2
December, 1934...............	57.0

The situation was at its worst as late as the end of 1933. Pakhomov (Gorkii oblast) reported to the Seventeenth Party Congress early in 1934 that 23,000 freight cars were expecting transportation on the short Kotelnits line; some of them had been waiting for about two years.[12]

Retail Trade

According to official data, total retail trade, i.e., official trade, including sales in eating places, and private trade, increased from 15.4 billion rubles in 1928 to 40.4 billion rubles in 1932, or by 162 per cent. Official retail trade grew from 11.4 billion to 40.4 billion rubles, or by 254 per cent, during the same years.[13] This is at current prices. While an index of retail prices for 1932 is not available,

[10] Holland Hunter's data.
[11] Holland Hunter's data.
[12] *Pravda*, February 8, 1934.
[13] *Soviet Trade*, stat. handb., 1956, pp. 14, 20.

the increase in these prices was so large that doubts can exist only with reference to the rate of *decline* in the volume of total retail trade during the period.[14] The turnover of official trade alone may have increased moderately.

While trade turnover as a whole declined from 1928 to 1932, sales in eating places were growing rapidly. The rations were very inadequate and many did not get any rations at all. The eating places were very popular, although they were probably not open to those who did not get rations, and the food was extremely poor. At current prices, sales in eating places increased twelvefold from 1928 to 1932.[15] An index of prices charged in eating places is unfortunately not available, but the average prices must have grown substantially less than in stores. Assuming about a twofold increase over the period, a sixfold expansion in sales in eating places at constant prices is indicated.[16] Since the turnover in eating places was enlarged greatly, the decline in retail trade proper, i.e., without the eating places, was even greater than that for total retail trade including eating places.

One of the main features of retail trade during the *All-out Drive* was that it was dominated by the sale of vodka. As now disclosed in *Soviet Trade,* stat. handb., 1956, the sale of vodka was a big item in financing the building of "socialism" and in making the Party "the victors." [17] There was not enough grain to make bread from. All the grain needed to make vodka was available.[18] The first FYP foresaw a 31 per cent decline in vodka sales in physical terms from 1927/28 to 1932/33;[19] output of vodka and other strong liquor increased by 30 per cent in 1928–32 in the same terms.[20]

Together with other alcoholic and non-alcoholic beverages, the sale of vodka made up almost one-fifth (exactly 19.4 per cent) of the total retail trade and more than one-fifth (exactly 20.8 per cent) of the retail trade proper in 1932.[21] The sale of beverages amounted

[14] Retail sales in 1937 are calculated below at only about 10 per cent above the figure for 1928. An increase of at least 30 per cent from 1932 to 1937 seems certain and this implies a decline in total retail trade from 1928 to 1932 of about 15 per cent.

[15] *Soviet Trade,* stat. handb., 1956, p. 20.

[16] *Ibid.,* p. 74, contains data on the number of courses served in eating places, but only since 1932. There was an increase of 22 per cent from 1932 to 1933, implying the probability that capacity to serve was a large limiting factor in 1932.

[17] Concerning crowning "the victors," see below, p. 117.

[18] The output of vodka and other hard liquor by industry increased from 55.5 million dekaliters in 1928 to 72.0 million dekaliters in 1932; see *Industry of the USSR*, 1957, p. 372.

[19] *1st FYP,* II, Part 2, 46.

[20] See note 18 above.

[21] *Soviet Trade,* stat. handb., 1956, pp. 45, 53.

to more than one-third of all food sales in the total official retail trade (somewhat more than 40 per cent of the food sales in the official retail trade proper). (See also Chart 8.)

CHART 8

OFFICIAL RETAIL TRADE, 1932: SPECIFIED COMMODITIES *
(In billions of rubles)

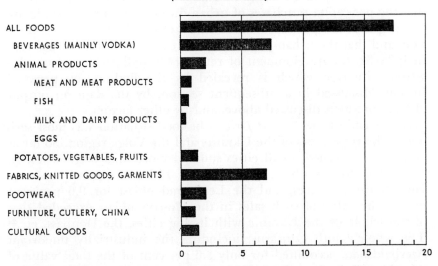

* Not including turnover in eating places. Sales of flour, bread, and other grain products amounted to 1.9 billion rubles in 1932. *Soviet Trade*, stat. handb., 1956, pp. 48–51.

The sale of beverages in eating places made up only about 9 per cent of their total sales in 1932. At that time the people went into eating places to eat. The idea that these places might be made into chiefly drinking places is the product of later years, of the height of Stalin's era.

Production of lump sugar, desired by the population, declined from 656,000 tons in 1928 to 438,000 tons in 1932. As mentioned above, the output of confections, not desired by the population, increased fivefold during the same period.[22] This development was reflected in turnover in official trade in that the sales of sugar increased (at current prices) by only 18 per cent, but those of confections expanded more than 4.7 times.[23] Candy, a minor item in production and sales in 1928, had become a major item in both during exactly the same period when personal incomes were declining rapidly.

[22] *Industry of the USSR.*, 1957, pp. 372–73.
[23] *Soviet Trade*, stat. handb., 1956, p. 41.

In a similar way, the sales of fabrics grew by 40 per cent *at current prices* from 1928 to 1932, i.e., they actually declined greatly, but the sales of garments jumped to 6.9 times the previous level.

This analysis could be continued but it is clear anyway that while the volume of retail trade declined by perhaps 15 per cent over the period, the real reduction in sales of things to eat and to wear was greatly in excess of this. If it is considered, furthermore, that the per capita purchases of urban dwellers from retail trade are a multiple of the per capita amounts purchased by the rural population, and that the urban population increased by almost 50 per cent in 1928–32, the development of retail trade indicates the same disastrous situation which is revealed by the findings on personal incomes discussed in a subsequent section, by the data on output of farm products discussed above, and by other factors.

At the end of the *All-out Drive,* the food situation was most serious in the rural areas of the Ukraine and the Volga region. So far as cities are concerned, small cities suffered more than large cities. In 1933, the Moscow oblast accounted for 15.1 per cent of the total sales in eating places, and the Leningrad oblast for 9.6 per cent more. The value of such sales in the Moscow oblast exceeded that of the whole of the Ukraine with its big cities, the Donbass, etc.[24] The whole South Caucasus, including the industrially important Azerbaidzhan, accounted for only 3.6 per cent of the total value of sales in eating places in 1933.

Output per Man

The increase in large-scale industry output of perhaps 35 to 40 per cent in three years from 1929 to 1932 [25] was accompanied by an increase in the labor force of 89 per cent,[26] implying a decline in output per man of over 30 per cent. The decline remains large after a discount is made for the fact that the increase in output involved primarily heavy industry, in which the share of labor costs is higher than the average in industry as a whole. Since the computation above refers to output per work year, a discount may also possibly be needed for the curtailment of the number of work hours per year with the transition from the eight-hour to the seven-hour workday[27] (an increase in labor productivity per hour was expected from this measure, however). Moreover, this transition must have been offset,

[24] *Socialist Construction of the USSR, 1935,* pp. 562–63.

[25] Hodgman's *Soviet Industrial Production, 1928–51,* p. 73. This is without consideration of the deterioration in quality of the product.

[26] *Socialist Construction of the USSR, 1936,* p. 508.

[27] The average workday in large-scale industry went down from 7.8 hours in 1928 to 7.0 hours in 1934.

or overcompensated for, by the deterioration of the quality of output which was not properly considered in establishing the volume of production.[28]

The immense deterioration in labor productivity in large-scale industry during the *All-out Drive* period is revealed with particular force in the year-by-year data (increases in per cent of the preceding year):

Year	Output[a]	Number of Wage and Salary Earners[b]
1928/29	20.0	. . .
1929	. . .	8.7
1929/30	15.6	. . .
1930	. . .	26.7
1931 as compared with 1929/30	18.0	. . .
1931	. . .	28.6
1932	5.2	18.1

[a] Large-scale industry. Hodgman, *Symposium*, p. 232.
[b] Large-scale Industry. Implied in data in *Socialist Construction of the USSR, 1936*, p. 508.

Labor productivity was the first to react to the start of the *All-out Drive*. After a satisfactory rise in 1929, it showed the large decline of almost 10 per cent in 1930. The year of 1931 was much worse, and that of 1932, when output per man again declined by more than 10 per cent, was as bad. The picture shown by the data in the tabulation above may be supplemented by the evidence on the targets for raising output per man, incorporated in the annual plans which were supposed to be "accelerating socialist industrialization"; they are shown below (targets in per cent):

4th quarter of 1930, compared with the average fulfilment in 1929/30	31.2
1931	28.0
1932	22.0

Thus there was at least a 10 per cent decline per year in the face of plans demanding increases of 22 to 31 per cent. Galenson's data on the output per man in individual large-scale industries from 1930 to 1932 are as follows (decline in per cent):[29]

[28] Official Soviet statistics succeeded in calculating an increase of 21.1 per cent in output per man in large-scale industry in the same three years, from 1929 to 1932. It seems unwise to reproduce these unrealistic figures, even with the comment that they were based on an index of industrial output that tended to exaggerate the rate of growth (see Walter Galenson in *Symposium*, p. 195).

[29] Walter Galenson, *Labor Productivity in Soviet and American Industry* (New York: Columbia University Press, 1955), p. 234. The data for cotton spinning and weaving are from a Soviet source, quoted by Galenson, p. 196. The use of Alexander Gerschenkron's data for output in 1939 dollars (*Review of Economics and Statistics,* May, 1955, p. 123), in conjunction with Galenson's employment data, indicates twice as large a decline in output per man in 1930–32 for coal as Galenson's figures, a smaller decline in labor productivity in iron and steel, and the same decline in petroleum.

Coal...........................	6
Iron ore.......................	14
Petroleum.....................	13
Iron and steel.................	19
Cotton spinning................	10
Cotton weaving................	11
Shoes.........................	23

The timber industry, where the decline of labor productivity was especially large, was not included in Galenson's computations. On the basis of official statistics, the decline in output per man in this industry appears to have been of tremendous dimensions. As Table 7 shows, total procurements of timber (including firewood) rose by

TABLE 7

All-out Drive: Production and Labor in the Timber Industry[*]

YEAR	Shipment from Forests[a]		Sawn Timber	Wage and Salary Earners in Timber Industry (thousands)
	Total	Industrial		
	(million cubic meters)			
1929.......	95.5 (139.8)	60.0 (85.1)	16.6	415
1930.......	147.2 (170.2)	96.7 (112.2)	21.9	611
1931.......	159.8 (199.5)	104.1 (128.9)	23.8	857
1932.......	164.7 (176.1)	99.4 (103.5)	24.4	1,140
1933.......	173.3 (178.7)	98.0 (98.9)	27.3	1,193

[*] *Socialist Construction of the USSR, 1936*, pp. 187, 190, and 508–9.
[a] The figures in parentheses are for the amounts procured in forests.

26 per cent from 1929 to 1932, but the number of wage earners increased by not less than 175 per cent.[30] Output per man consequently declined to less than half the previous level. The situation was not so bad on the basis of timber shipped from the forests, but it still was very serious.

Output per man in construction showed a picture similar to that in industry. Construction and installation of the socialized sector, with part of the investment financed from the budget and other sources (on this investment see note 33 in chapter 4), increased by 169 per cent from 1929 to 1932. The labor force in construction was enlarged by 242 per cent,[31] implying a reduction in output per man of 27 per cent. The great deterioration in the quality of construction[32] was an additional factor.

[30] It must be emphasized that the evidence on the labor force is not on a seasonal but on an all-year basis.

[31] *Socialist Construction of the USSR, 1936*, pp. 508–9.

[32] See above, p. 88. On deterioration in quality, specifically of housing, see *Essay III*, pp. 112–13, 116.

Railway transportation showed certain peculiarities with reference to performance per man. The decline in this seems to have been smaller than in all other economic branches, the great disorganization having been mainly reflected in the deterioration of service. Furthermore, there was some lag in the effect of the disorganization on the performance per man in transportation, the worst having come when the *All-out Drive* was already over.

According to official data, cited by Holland Hunter, the number of cumulative ton-kilometers per operational worker increased by 21 per cent from 1930 to 1932. It declined slightly in 1933 and increased almost insignificantly in 1934. The total increase in 1932–34 amounted to 2 per cent.

It is questionable, however, whether the calculations per operational worker fit the conditions of that particular time adequately. Thanks to the disorganization, the need for repairs must have grown considerably, and in calculating the performance of railway personnel, it would seem correct to consider the additional staff required to make the repairs.

Based on the total number of those employed by the railways, performance per man on them increased by only 7 per cent from 1930 to 1932. The total length of railway track was enlarged only by about 6 per cent in those years; the proportion of bulky commodities and the crowding of passenger trains grew considerably, and there was also a small increase in the average length of freight hauls. All these factors combined imply a substantial decline in performance per man of the railway personnel.[33]

It would seem that the decline in output per man in the timber industry could not be surpassed. Yet this appears to have been the case, and, moreover, of all sectors, in trade, although this seems to be true only with reference to retail trade proper. But the decline in performance per man was also very large in the eating places.

The number of wage and salary earners in official retail trade proper about trebled from 1928 to 1932 (an increase from 471,100 in 1928 to 1,410,800 in 1932).[34] Even according to official calculations, the volume of total official trade, i.e., including the greatly expanded sales in eating places, increased only by 34 per cent (at 1940 prices),[35] and the same trade minus eating places increased substantially less than this. Sales per man in official trade proper

[33] The increase in freight transported by railways in those two years (in percentage terms) was ten times as large as the increase in the length of track, and this factor alone overcompensated for the increase in cumulative ton-kilometers per worker by 7 per cent.

[34] *Socialist Construction of the USSR, 1935*, pp. 476–77.

[35] Implied by data in *Questions of Economics*, 1957, No. 10, p. 131.

declined to much less than one-half, according to those data. Actually, the volume of official retail trade proper may not have increased at all, and the sales per man in it were reduced to only about one-third during the four-year period.

The main calamity probably occurred in the last two years of the period. The turnover in official retail trade proper at current prices exactly doubled in those years. The weighted prices of all sales in official trade may likewise have been doubled or nearly doubled. Yet the number of persons employed in this trade was enlarged by 73 per cent,[36] and sales in real terms per man may consequently have declined by as much as 40 per cent in only two years.

The development of sales in eating places in those years is shown in the tabulation below:

Year	Turnover (billion rubles at current prices)[a]	Wage and Salary Earners (thousands)[b]
1928	0.4	37.4[c]
1929	0.6	73.5
1930	1.3	180.2
1931	2.7	364.6
1932	4.9	515.1

[a] *Soviet Trade*, stat. handb., 1956, p. 20.
[b] *Socialist Construction of the USSR, 1935*, pp. 476–77.
[c] 1927/28.

Already in 1929, the number of persons employed in eating places was increasing more rapidly than even the sales in them at current prices. Over the whole period of four years, there was a decline of about 10 per cent in sales in eating places per employed person. But this was at current prices. While the rate of increase in prices in public eating places in the period stated is unknown, a very large decline in sales per employed person in real terms over the period is indicated.[37]

Among the factors which tended to reduce output per man in all sectors of trade in those dark days, a strongly pronounced tendency to foster socialized trade, whatever the cost, was in evidence. The number of enterprises in state trade proper was increased almost threefold (a growth of 193 per cent) from 1928 to 1932. Of the 48,100 enterprises added to it during this period, 33,400 were added in the one year of 1932,[38] although there were certainly no more goods for sale in that specific year than in 1931. As compared with the huge

---

[36] *Socialist Construction of the USSR, 1935*, pp. 476–77.

[37] It may have been a factor, though, that the proportion of items prepared by the eating places tremselves may have increased, and that the average meal became poorer and, therefore, at constant prices, cheaper. All this required more labor per ruble at constant prices.

[38] *Soviet Trade*, stat. handb., 1956, p. 140.

increase in enterprises in state trade proper, the percentage increase in them in co-operative trade in 1928–32 seems almost small, although there were even fewer goods for sale in rural than in urban areas. On the whole, the personnel in official retail trade seems to have been largely employed in guarding empty shelves at the end of the *All-out Drive* period.[39]

The almost fourfold increase in the number of eating places in 1928–32 does not seem excessive in the face of the large increase in sales, but there were 23,600 eating enterprises in rural areas at the end of 1932, as against 32,200 such enterprises in urban areas,[40] although the sales of the former were only one-sixth of those of the latter.[41] The state and co-operative enterprises—to be effective at all—should not operate on a very small scale. Yet the eating places in rural areas had an average turnover of not quite 29,600 rubles per year in 1932.[42]

The Russian people themselves, of course, had to pay for all this experimenting. This was all fully in line with Stalin's doctrine that socialism was to be introduced even if it cost more to operate it than private enterprises.

Incomes

In his report on the fulfilment of the first FYP, Stalin claimed "a fundamental improvement in the material well-being of the toilers." [43] Nobody was permitted to claim less than this, but everybody was welcome to claim more. "A gigantic rise in the material-culture levels of the toilers of the USSR during the first FYP period" was proclaimed in a paper, "Real Wages of the Proletariat of the USSR during the second FYP," published in *Plan,* the periodical of the Gosplan and the Central Statistical Office. One of the authors of the article was Kleinman, a well-known Soviet expert on labor-wage problems.[44]

Somehow, the conclusions about the trend of private incomes during the *All-out Drive* seem different, depending on the approach, although everything points to an enormous decline. The difference

[39] The unhealthiness of this development is evident also from the fact that the rapid growth in the number of retail shops and their personnel during the *All-out Drive* was brought to a full stop with the end of the period. While the number of retail shops in official trade increased from 184,700 at the end of 1930 to 225,100 and 284,400 at the end of 1931 and 1932, respectively, the increases during 1933 and 1934 amounted only to 1,000 and 800 units, respectively (*Soviet Trade,* stat. handb., 1956, p. 137).

[40] *Ibid.,* p. 145.

[41] *Ibid.,* p. 23.

[42] *Ibid.,* pp. 23, 145.

[43] *Problems of Leninism* (11th ed.), p. 385.

[44] See *Plan,* 1934, No. 1, p. 48.

is only in degree. In Table II in Appendix B the average real non-farm wage in 1937 is estimated at 60 per cent of that in 1928.[45] The rise from 1932 to 1937 is unlikely to have been much less than 25 per cent.[46] Hence, a real wage of less than half of that in 1928 is indicated for 1932. If the rise from 1932 to 1937 was equal to exactly 25 per cent, a real wage of 49 per cent of that in 1928 is implied for 1932. The number of dependents per wage and salary earner declined from 1928 to 1932. But the decline was less than 10 per cent (for the wage and salary earners including the dependents per wage and salary earner), and hence in 1932 the real income, even on a per capita basis of the wage and salary earners' families, may have been not very much larger than half of that in 1928.

The data on peasant incomes around 1932, which the writer was able to bring together, are presented and discussed in a study of peasant incomes which, owing to its length, could not be incorporated into this volume. As in the case of wages, it was necessary to carry the analysis back from 1937, for which year the evidence is much better than for 1932. The prices of goods purchased by peasants were probably substantially lower in 1932 than in 1937. But the average per capita money income of the peasants in nominal terms in 1932 is calculated in the study mentioned at only about 40 per cent of that in 1937.

Specifically, the peasants had very little to sell in kolkhoz trade in 1932,[47] in spite of the very high prices prevailing in it and the peasants' very urgent need for a minimum amount of manufactured goods. It seems unlikely that more than a small part of the disadvantage caused by the lower money income was offset in the earlier year by the more favorable price relationship to the goods which the peasants bought. The evidence on the hundreds of thousands,

---

[45] After deducting taxes and bond purchases. The difference as compared with "before deducting taxes and bond purchases" was only small at the time here analyzed. The distinction between "before . . ." and "after deducting . . ." was dropped after the Soviets wiped out the whole indebtedness to the population on loans in 1957. The calculation of the real wage in 1937 in terms of 1928, checked and cross-checked with other factors, is one of the most secure among the estimates of real incomes found in this volume.

[46] A smaller difference in the average real wage between 1932 and 1937 would imply a *decline* in the average real wage from 1932 to 1935, and this seems not very probable. The official claim is that real wages increased by 101 per cent from 1932 to 1937. See, for example, Ya. Kronrod, "People's Consumption under Socialism," *Communist*, 1953, No. 16, p. 46.

[47] These markets operated only during part of 1932. All that was sold in kolkhoz markets in 1933, when the sales were substantially larger than in 1932, was, for example, 120,000 tons of meat, 424 million eggs, 1,200,000 tons of potatoes (cited from a Soviet source in *Soviet Studies*, April, 1956, p. 390). Remember that there were more than 100 million theoretical sellers and 50 million theoretical buyers at that time. Each consumer could buy on the average just about 2 kilograms of meat per year!

perhaps more than a million, who died in the winter of 1932/33, and other demographic data, reinforces this conclusion.

A picture not quite so disastrous for the population as that presented above is obtained by the approach via total supplies of farm products available per capita. The volume available for sale and consumption in the farm home in 1932 has been calculated by this writer at 1926/27 prices at 20 per cent below that in 1927/28.[48] Total population grew by about 7 per cent in the same period,[49] but urban population presumably increased by more than 40 per cent. In order to maintain the previous consumption levels of the rural and the urban population, an increase of about 15 per cent in the total supply of farm products would have been needed. Hence, the supplies of farm products on a per capita basis of the rural and the urban population probably declined by about 30 per cent from 1928 to 1932.[50] Since the estimate of incomes in real terms points to a greater decline than this, an overestimate of the 1932 farm output by the official statistics seems to be indicated.[51] But a certain discrepancy between the two approaches could also have occurred owing to an increase in the utilization of farm products by state organizations and enterprises.

Considerable deterioration of the diet over the short span of four years from 1928 to 1932 is also revealed by the analysis of data for individual products. Fish, potatoes, and possibly vegetables were the only products with moderate increases in per capita supplies in 1932 compared with 1927/28. The possibly too high estimate of 209 kilograms of grain consumed per person in 1932, made by this writer previously, implied a decline of about 10 per cent in per capita consumption of grain products, apart from the great deterioration of the quality of the consumed products.[52] Per capita consumption of sugar and milk went down by more than one-third, of meat by more than one-half, and of eggs by about two-thirds.[53] All these estimates, except that for grain, were based on official statistics, in spite of a certain skepticism toward these. Further studies made since then have rendered the present writer even more skeptical

[48] See *Soc. Agri.,* p. 676.

[49] Lorimer, *The Population of the Soviet Union,* p. 134.

[50] The formula "per capita of the rural and the urban population" could be replaced by "per capita in terms of the consumption level of the rural population," with the consumption level of the urban population recalculated to this basis.

[51] The estimate of the volume available for sales and consumption in the farm home in 1932 in *Soc. Agri.* was entirely based on these statistics.

[52] See *Soc. Agri.,* pp. 88, 551–55, 751. Little more than 5 per cent of the wheat and rye ground commercially was made into reasonably white flour. See *Socialist Construction of the USSR, 1936,* p. 208.

[53] *Soc. Agri.,* pp. 71, 89, 798.

about Soviet statistics on farm output during this crucial period.[54]

The uneven distribution of the small supplies of farm products certainly aggravated the situation. While in the Ukraine and the Volga region, peasants were dying from starvation in the winter of 1932/33 (they were already starving before that winter),[55] the peasants of some other areas may have raised their bread consumption to compensate for the decreased amounts of other available food.

A certain idea of specifically urban consumption in 1932 can be obtained from official estimates of the total marketing of farm products, although the accuracy of the estimates is uncertain. The figures involved are as follows (in thousands of tons):[56]

Grain and grain products	19,855
Potatoes	8,984
Vegetables	4,187
Meat	935
Dairy products (in terms of milk)	4,088

The urban population at the end of 1932 was estimated in the second FYP (the figure is probably too high) at 46.1 million. On the obviously incorrect assumption that none of the marketed supplies of meat and dairy products were sold to the rural population and also disregarding the small output of farm products by the urban population, it was computed in *Soc. Agri.* (pp. 777–78) that meat consumption in urban areas declined from 46.3 or 49.1 kilograms in

[54] The official estimate of milk yields in 1932, even the one established after the results of the first FYP were officially appraised, i.e., after the particularly urgent need of high figures had passed, together with the official data on cow numbers and milk yields per cow on the state and co-operative farms (see *2d FYP*, I, 475) imply practically the same yields of milk per cow owned by the peasants in 1932 as in 1927/28. In view of the general disorganization and the disappearance of the "kulak" households, with their better economy, and in spite of the fact that on the average the preceding decline in the number of cows was greater in areas with lower milk yields than in areas with higher milk yields, one would expect a decline in the average yield of milk from peasants' cows of at least a few per cent from 1928 to 1932. An obvious manipulation in the computation of the amounts of milk available for food of the population in 1932 may be found in *2d FYP*, I, 466 and 390. Only 1,680,000 tons of milk were allowed there for the feeding of calves, for producing export butter, and for waste. A fair allowance for these needs would have been 2,800,000 tons, of which 800,000 tons would have been for milk from which the exported butter was produced.

[55] This is indicated by the fact that in June of 1932, the price of rye bread in the kolkhoz markets of Dnepropetrovsk, Ukraine, was more than threefold that in Moscow. See I. Malyshev in *Planned Economy*, 1936, No. 4, p. 114. No similar data for the Lower-Volga region seems to have been made available. The price was equal to 5.5 rubles per kilogram there in March of 1933, according to Malyshev, i.e., much more than the average daily earnings of those employed for pay.

[56] *2d FYP*, I, 529.

1927/28 to 21.8 kilograms in 1932 and the consumption of dairy products dropped from 193 or 218 to 85 kilograms. After allowing for the milk used in the preparation of butter and sour cream, the latter being a popular food in Russia, the average daily utilization of fresh milk per capita of the urban population in 1932 emerges at one-tenth of a quart or less in a country with a high proportion of children in its total population.

Data on sales in retail trade indicate an even poorer situation than that implied in the official estimates of the total marketings. Sales of meat (including sausage) in the official retail trade proper, i.e., other than in eating places, amounted to 852 million rubles in 1932. The ration price of meat was 2.12 rubles per kilogram according to S. N. Prokopovicz.[57] Hence, about 400,000 tons of meat were sold. If all this meat was distributed on rations, the rations may have amounted to one kilogram per capita and per month, but an unspecified part of the meat sold consisted of sausage. Data in the same source indicate sales in official trade of only about 30,000 tons of butter in 1932 (less than this if some butter sold at higher than the ration price) or perhaps 65 grams (2.5 ounces) per person per month.

Considerable differences in consumption by various groups of the urban population were due not only to differences in earnings but also to the application of the "class" principle in rationing. Unfortunately, no data on the amounts distributed on rations in 1932 are available.

The fantastic prices paid in the kolkhoz markets after their legalization in May of 1932 can serve as evidence of the food situation in urban areas. In the last few months of 1932 these prices were as follows (in rubles per kilogram): [58]

PRODUCT	OFFICIAL TRADE Ration Prices in Moscow	KOLKHOZ MARKETS Moscow	Gorkii	Dnepropetrovsk
Coarse rye bread......	0.08–0.09 to 0.125	3.5	2.5	5.0
Potatoes.............	...	1.5	1.75	2.25
Beef.................	2.12	13.5	11.0ᵃ	9.0
Butter (melted).......	4.66	35.0	35.0ᵇ	24.0

ᵃ Sverdlovsk. The substitution here and in note "b" are from the source.
ᵇ Stalingrad.

Thus, in 1932 the price of unrationed bread was twenty to forty times as high as the price of rationed bread. In the Dnepropetrovsk

[57] *Russlands Volkswirtschaft unter den Sowiets* (Zurich and New York, 1944), p. 305.
[58] The prices in kolkhoz markets are from the charts in I. Malyshev, "Problems of Development of Kolkhoz Market Trade," *Planned Economy*, 1936, No. 4, pp. 114–16. The ration prices are from Prokopovicz, *op. cit.*, p. 305.

kolkhoz markets (in the Ukraine) course rye bread cost, in March of 1933, twelve rubles per kilogram, about 100 times the rationed price and about 135 times the 1928 open market price. As is natural under starvation conditions, the prices of bread went up considerably more than those of meat and butter, although bread was relatively more plentiful, while meat and butter were the goods in shortest supply. Who can think of butter if an average week's wage, or more, must be given for one kilogram of it? [59] For that matter, the price of a kilogram of bread in Dnepropetrovsk in March of 1933 was almost three times higher than the average daily wage of all wage earners in the USSR.

National Income

Contrary to what was claimed, the laying of the foundation of socialism during the *All-out Drive* was accompanied first by a complete stoppage in the growth of real national income and then by its decline. While investment and output of the favorite industries continued to grow, although at greatly declining rates, the gains were presumably more than compensated for by the declines in agriculture, trade, and private enterprises. As the data in Chart 2 in chapter 1 indicate, the total national income rose only several per cent during the whole period from 1928 to 1932. The figures for this period are acknowledgedly crude, but they are unlikely to be wrong by significant margins.

The Soviet Economy Grounded

The downward movement of the rates of growth in everything during the *All-out Drive* is obvious from the statistical data available. The whole year of 1932 was poor, and by the winter of 1932/33 the Soviet economy had completely run aground.

Farm output declined by 6.3 per cent in 1932 as compared with 1931, even according to official estimates at "unchangeable 1926/27 prices." In Soviet pronouncements poor weather was held responsible, but the decline was man-made. As compared with 1928, there was a decline in farm output of about 20 per cent.

Hodgman's index for large-scale industry (excluding timber) shows a rise of only 5.2 per cent in 1932. Since procurements of timber declined and the output of small-scale industry at best remained unchanged, the rise in total industrial output was equivalent to only about 4 per cent, according to Hodgman's data. Consideration of the further deterioration of the quality of the produce would make this rate a negative value.

[59] The average weekly wage of all wage earners was about 30 rubles in 1933.

Gerschenkron's index for the output of the great favorites (electric power, coal, iron and steel, petroleum, and machinery) showed a decline in the rate of growth from 22 per cent in 1930 to 17 per cent in 1931 and to 6 per cent in 1932.[60]

Construction by the socialized sector increased at current prices from 10.1 billion rubles in 1931 to 13.4 billion rubles in 1932, i.e., by about 33 per cent.[61] But the construction-cost index of even the principal construction organization showed a rise of about 27 per cent. The cost index for all socialized construction probably rose more than this and the deterioration in quality was particularly pronounced in this field,[62] having been caused by the cumulative effect of the great shortage and poor quality of building materials, and the poor construction work itself.

Tonnage shipped on railways rose by only 3.7 per cent in 1932,[63] while freight transportation on interior waterways and by sea declined.[64]

But the real catastrophe was that the decline in industrial output and construction, which had undoubtedly occurred when the deterioration in the quality of the products is taken into account, took place in the face of a huge increase in the labor force. The total number of wage and salary earners jumped almost four million (20.8 per cent) in 1932 after having increased by over four million (30.7 per cent) in 1931.

A comparison of the small increases, or even actual declines, in output in the various economic sectors from 1931 to 1932, shown above, with the large increases in the labor force, as shown in the tabulation below, suffices to show that no economic sector was spared from a large decline in output per man: [65]

	Per Cent
Total wage earners	20.8
Large-scale industry	18.2
Timber	33.0
Construction	22.6
Transportation	15.3
Railway	15.6
Interior waterways	10.5
Other	16.3

The decline in output per man in industry and construction in 1932 was equivalent to more than 10 per cent, possibly as much as

[60] *Review of Economics and Statistics*, May, 1955, p. 123.
[61] *Socialist Construction of the USSR, 1936*, p. 407.
[62] See *Essay III*, p. 100.
[63] *Socialist Construction of the USSR, 1936*, pp. 416–17.
[64] *Socialist Construction of the USSR, 1934*, pp. 279, 282.
[65] *Socialist Construction of the USSR, 1936*, p. 508.

15 per cent, even without allowance for the deterioration in the quality of products. Transportation showed almost as large a decline in service per man, apart from deterioration of the service. Again it was the timber industry which reflected the political atmosphere in Moscow with particular force. The number of wage and salary earners in this industry jumped by 33 per cent in the face of a decline of shipments of timber from the forest of 5 per cent—with a resulting curtailment in output per man of fully one-third in only one year.

Real national income, which could have still increased moderately in 1930, declined in both 1931 and 1932, in the latter year presumably more than in the former.

The bottom was reached in the winter of 1932/33 when the industrial machine, after stalling for a time, started to move backward in spite of all pushing. According to official data at "unchangeable 1926/27 prices," gross output of large-scale industry in the crop year of 1932/33 showed the following deplorable situation (in per cent of the corresponding month of the preceding year): [66]

Month	Percentage	Month	Percentage
July	107.4	January	95.2
August	100.0	February	99.5
September	101.0	March	99.5
October	100.3	April	101.1
November	98.4	May	106.8
December	101.1	June	108.7

Data in physical terms, free of the bias of "unchangeable 1926/27 prices," display a considerably poorer situation. They point, moreover, to the fact that the mainstays of communism—steel, coal, and the like—were not spared catastrophe. Electric power was the only exception. In January of 1932 and 1933, the output of certain specified products was as follows (in thousands of tons; millions of kilowatt-hours for electric power):[67]

Product	1932	1933	Increase or Decline (in per cent)
Electric power	766	916	+19.6
Coal	5,941	5,591	−5.9
Coke	705	685	−2.8
Iron ore	1,041	1,003	−3.7
Pig iron	489	464	−5.1
Steel	540	479	−11.3
Rolled steel	420	356	−15.3
Petroleum	1,937	1,538	−20.6

[66] *Planned Economy*, I (1937), 213.
[67] *Socialist Construction of the USSR, 1936*, pp. 79–81.

The monthly 1933 output figures continued to run behind those of 1932 for a few months more after January 1, 1933; for petroleum, even through July of 1933. The winter of 1932/33 probably also marked the low point in the immense decline of the consumption levels of the whole population.

This was the state into which the country had to plunge before Stalin could be induced to say "stop." There is a good parallel between January of 1933, when Stalin finally said "stop," and March of 1921, when Lenin announced the end of his experiment to introduce communism. Lenin acknowledged the failure, but not Stalin. The first FYP was declared a great success, a great victory.

It was fitting that the Seventeenth Party Congress early in 1934, the foremost job of which was to appraise the operation of the first FYP and to approve the second FYP, entered communist history as "The Meeting of the Victors." The baptizing took place either before or during the congress.[68]

Conclusion

The foregoing presentation has shown the heavy price the Russian people paid for industrialization and for making "socialism" complete by extending it to peasant farming. The situation is frequently described quite differently, even by sources commanding the highest prestige.

For example, in 1950, the Pakistan government, the Food and Agriculture Organization of the United Nations, and the International Bank for Reconstruction and Development arranged a course of lectures by persons said to be Western experts, with the ambitious aim of helping underdeveloped countries develop.[69] The first lecture (or lectures) dealt with "Development Projects as Part of National Development Programs" and chapter 6 dealt with "The Initial Fund for Development." This started prominently with "The Case of Russia" (p. 32). All the enthusiasm shown there for Russia's "very successful planning" need not be reproduced here. The author begins by saying that "quite often in the course of the economic history of particular countries, you can point to a certain thing that happened to raise these countries to this minimum level where the cumulative development process begins." Further on, after much rhetoric, the reader is informed that "in 1920 they [the Russians] had a job to keep themselves alive; they were starving. In 1926, they had got into a position that they could start planning for

[68] *Great Soviet Encyclopedia*, 1948, p. xxxv.
[69] *Formulation and Economic Appraisal of Development Projects* ("United Nations Publications," II, B.4, 1951), Vol. I.

economic development." Then comes the rhetorical question: "Now what happened between 1920 and 1926?" The triumphant answer is: "What happened, I think, was the collectivization of agriculture in Russia." In a letter to this writer, the lecturer subsequently admitted that this statement was "a mistake." To make an error of eight years in dating collectivization is bad enough, but the lecturer really goes too far when he gives credit to collectivization for the recovery from Lenin's War Communism and the restoration of food surpluses, which were restored only *because of the efforts of the individual peasant.* Thus, the fact is concealed that collectivization, when it was introduced, led to a considerable decline in farm output, to a fall in real wages of some 50 per cent, and, ultimately, to the death of millions by starvation. To the United Nations representative this was just "a mistake" (acknowledged in a private letter).

CHAPTER 6

THE THREE "GOOD" YEARS I

Introduction

The ideological abandonment of the *All-out Drive* may be confidently placed in January of 1933.[1] The 1933 Plan approved by the combined session of the Party's Central Committee and Central Control Commission on January 10 of that year, certainly was a milestone. It must indeed be regarded as a definite announcement of a retreat.

The death by starvation of perhaps a million, or at least hundreds of thousands, of peasants in the winter of 1932/33 is unlikely to have moved Stalin. But he must have been impressed by the fact that in the last months of 1932 industrial output was falling behind the corresponding monthly figures of the previous year. Stalin certainly was particularly aggrieved by the fact that the declines in output involved even such goods as steel and coal, so dear to his heart.

As far as planning is concerned, the retreat was fundamental: from setting up wild, unfulfillable goals, from plain shooting into the sky, to something incomparably more sound, although by no means fully on the level of realistic planning. Outside of planning, the retreat consisted in at least the partial elimination of the immense abuses which were characteristic of the *All-out Drive*. It was a consolidation to positions which permitted progress with, of course, preservation of all dictatorial pressures, instead of the regression which had occurred despite all those pressures.

[1] The legalization of the kolkhoz markets in May of 1932 may be considered the first retreat from the policies of the *All-out Drive*. But one swallow does not make a summer.

119

The fundamental change in planning is apparent from a comparison of some major targets of the 1933 Plan with those of the 1931 and 1932 Plans. The figures in Chart 9 are never mentioned by more recent Soviet sources, although, of course, they can be looked up in the documents of the respective years. The crucial point obviously was the lowering of the planned rate of growth in output of state industry from 42 per cent in 1931 and 36 per cent in 1932 to 16.5 per cent in 1933.

CHART 9

THE END OF BACCHANALIAN PLANNING: TARGETS OF ANNUAL PLANS, 1931–33 *
(Planned rise as compared with preceding year, in per cent)

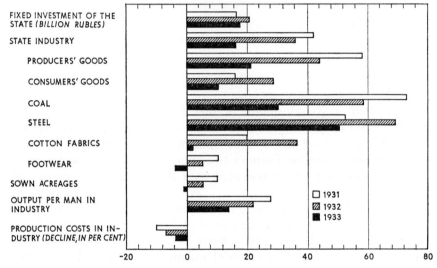

* *Planned Economy,* 1930, No. 12, pp. 336–59 (the figures for industry pertain to that part of it the output of which was planned by the VSNKh) and *Bulletin of Financial-Economic Legislation,* 1932, No. 1, pp. 4–8, and 1933, No. 4, pp. 8–14. The data for acreages represent spring crops of the respective year plus winter crops of the next year.

While, in nominal terms, the target for fixed investment appears to have declined by only about 15 per cent in 1933, the cut from 21.1 billion rubles in the 1932 Plan to 18.0 billion rubles in the 1933 Plan actually implied a decline in real terms by about 25 per cent.[2] This substantial reduction, as well as all others, had only one explanation: the realization that striving for the impossible, instead of stimulating growth, leads to disaster.

The sobering-up from plan-drunkenness was also very marked in respect to long-range planning. The same decision of the combined

[2] Construction costs alone rose by about 22 per cent during 1932.

session of the Central Committee and Central Control Commission of the Party which approved the 1933 Plan ordered that, in preparing the second FYP, the average yearly growth of state industry during the operation of the FYP be planned at about 13 to 14 per cent "compared with the 21 to 22 per cent during the first FYP period"[3] and the even much higher rates demanded in the 1931 and 1932 Plans. "The main emphasis should be not on the quantitative growth of production, but on improvement of the quality of the produce and on the growth of output per man; not on expansion of acreages, but on increase of yields and improvement of work in agriculture," stated the resolution.[4]

The usual practice of postponing the sensible things to later years, however, was not given up. This is revealed in the very fact that the same decision which for the second FYP period as a whole wanted an average yearly growth of 13 to 14 per cent in state industry ordered its expansion to 16.5 per cent for 1933. One would have expected that the opposite would have had more chance of materializing, because rates of growth usually rise more rapidly after a beginning has been made in overcoming the various bottlenecks. The locomotive starts very slowly and gradually accumulates speed.[5]

It must be granted, however, that nothing basic was given up. Only the great excesses were eliminated. The retreat was to positions which could be held. While the target for investment, for example, was reduced in 1933, the level to which investment was to be held was greatly above that at the beginning of the *All-out Drive.*

With reference to agriculture, the retreat consisted merely in that the Party, having proclaimed a drive to combine individual peasants into *arteli,* a form of co-operative permitting the collectivized peasants to have their own small private enterprises, and having at once embarked on a policy excluding these private enterprises, finally conceded them to the peasants. When on February 19, 1933, Stalin had solemnly given his Bolshevist word that in a year or two no kolkhoznik would be without a cow,[6] he only reaffirmed the kolkhoznik's right which had existed in the Kolkhoz Statute all the time. The solemn promise was never to be fulfilled, by the way.

The secret instructions of May 8, 1933, quoted in chapter 4, while

[3] The rise of 21 to 22 per cent per year during the first FYP existed, of course, only in Soviet "statistics."

[4] *VKB (b) in Resolutions and Decisions* (2d ed.; Moscow, 1936), II, 521–22.

[5] The postponement of the reasonable things to a later time was reflected even more in the not too sensible timing of the growth in investment from year to year as scheduled by the second FYP (see below), as well as in numerous other items.

[6] *Problems of Leninism* (11th ed.), p. 420.

proclaiming the discontinuation "in general" of mass deportations from, and sharp reprisals in, the village, stressed simultaneously that the principle of individual farming had been overcome and that the kolkhozy had become the predominant form of peasant farming. They also emphasized that the class struggle in the village was to be intensified in order to insure the final victory of this system.

An analogy was found above between the War Communism period and the period of laying the foundation of socialism, in that both ended in starvation of the masses and uncounted deaths. There is, however, a great difference between the two periods; Lenin frankly acknowledged the retreat (see above, p. 38), while under the leadership of Stalin the greatest efforts were made to deny anything of this sort. In his speech to the combined session of the Party's Central Committee and Central Control Commission, Molotov attacked Zinoviev for having spoken, although in a disapproving manner, of the idea of a retreat, which "takes possession of a great proportion of Party members." Even more violently did Molotov wage war against Trotsky, who, from abroad, had suggested that the operation of the first FYP be extended to the end of 1933; [7] and, for similar crimes, against the *Socialist Courier*, the Menshevik journal then published in Berlin.[8] How could Molotov recognize even a trace of retreat in addressing "the victors"? [9] Victors do not retreat; they forge ahead.

It must, of course, be granted that Lenin was compelled to give up his attempt at introducing communism, while Stalin succeeded in retaining the basic principles of the Great Industrialization Drive, giving up only, or mainly, the abuses. The fact remains, however, that both Lenin's War Communism and Stalin's *All-out Drive* led to a catastrophe. Lenin acknowledged this, while Stalin openly recognized only immense successes.

The Main Features of the Upswing

The peasants saw themselves compelled to accept the kolkhozy, partly because of starvation and partly owing to the assurance that their rights to small private enterprises, granted to them by the artel form of the collective farm, would be honored to a certain extent. The very low real incomes of the population made large funds available for investment, in spite of the per se small national income. Bacchanalian planning was discontinued. Weather conditions greatly

[7] Originally it was scheduled to end on September 30, 1933. But it was later decided to discontinue its operation with the end of 1932.

[8] *Izvestiya,* January 8, 1933.

[9] The Seventeenth Party Congress was so baptized in recognition of the achievements during the first FYP.

favored the 1933 crop.* All this combined to permit the Soviet economy to enter a period of great industrial upswing after the realization of the 1933 crop.

But the calendar year 1933 as a whole turned out to be rather mediocre in spite of the revisions in policies and the relatively good crop. Whatever progress was made in the second half of 1933 served merely to offset the losses of the first months of the year. For transportation, 1933 was even worse than 1932.

Rapid industrial growth started early in 1934 and went on for three years, 1934–36, and would probably have lasted longer if it had not been for the entirely external factor of the great purges.[10] The principal features of this great upswing were:

a) Industrial production was expanding at great rates.

b) Agricultural output was recovering, although not very rapidly.

c) Investment was kept at very high, but bearable, levels; it was distributed more wisely; the gigantic factories, the construction of which started during the *All-out Drive,* were ultimately completed and the considerable lag between funds invested and plants actually entering operation was eliminated.

d) Consumption levels of the population were permitted to rise only very slowly—mainly, or even exclusively, in the third year of the period, after heavy industry and its attributes, such as transportation, had already made considerable progress.

e) In spite of the continuation of deplorably low living standards, output per man rose rapidly as the prevailing chaos was gradually liquidated and the mass of new workers, recruited during the *All-out Drive,* acquired at least some skills. The Stakhanovite movement, which plainly meant still greater stratification of wages, may have helped.

f) While expenditures on the armed forces had been rapidly rising since 1934, their level, greatly reduced (in real terms) in the preceding period, remained relatively low and, even at the end of the period, had hardly become a major factor in determining economic development.

Investment continued to be heavily concentrated on the task of

---

* The newly revised agricultural statistics in *Economy of the USSR in 1958,* p. 350, shows a decline in crop production from 1932 to 1933 of 3 per cent instead of the increase of 13 per cent announced earlier (*Socialist Construction of the USSR, 1935,* p. 360). The previous statistics turn out to have been falsified. This writer was to some extent misled. The decided upturn from the disastrous *All-out Drive* to the, in many ways prosperous, *Three "Good" Years* occurred in spite of the poorer crop production—a further condemnation of the policies of the "victors." (The increase in the all-important grain production from 1932 to 1933 shown in *Soc. Agri.,* p. 792, still stands, though.)

[10] External for the economy.

expanding the output of producers' goods. This insistence was so great as to lead to absurdities, as was, for example, the case with the timing of the targets of the second FYP for investment of the socialized sector in heavy industry. The rates of growth for this investment in the individual years of the period were set as follows (in per cent of the preceding year):[11]

1934................	26.6
1935................	6.3
1936................	2.8
1937................	−1.1

One sees the hand of Stalin in such timing. Those who worked on the first FYP, and disappeared later, would not have planned for investment in the most important sector of the economy to expand by 26.6 per cent in one year and by only 7.9 per cent in the subsequent three years taken together.

Correspondingly, satisfying consumers' needs was postponed in the second FYP to better times. Fixed investment in the consumers'-goods industries, in housing, and in sociocultural needs other than housing were to grow rapidly during this FYP period; but, and this is the main point, they were to be very low in the initial years. The fixed investment of the state in total social needs, including housing, was to amount to 3,515 million rubles, or 19.2 per cent of the total investment of the socialized sector in 1933. By 1937, it was to reach 9,061 million rubles and represent 28.3 per cent of the respective total expenditure.[12] Expenditure specifically on housing was to rise from 1,475 million rubles in 1933 to 3,724 million rubles in 1937.[13]

The scheduled investment in consumers'-goods industries was odd also in that the rapid growth was to continue only through 1936. The year 1937 was then to show a substantial decline in this investment. The data are as follows (in millions of rubles):[14]

1933................	1,630
1934................	2,344
1935................	4,059
1936................	4,418
1937................	3,652

[11] *2d FYP,* I, 715–16 (in prices of the 1933 Plan). The year 1933 is omitted because it was already a part of the past when the second FYP was approved. The figure for investment (and for all other items) in 1933, given among the targets of the second FYP, was that of the actual performance in that year. The 1934 target in the second FYP was the target of the 1934 annual plan for that year.

[12] *2d FYP,* I, 715–16 (in prices of the 1933 Plan).

[13] *2d FYP,* draft, I, 434. The data are not to be found in the final text of the FYP, but the targets for house construction, as for all investment, remained unchanged from the draft. The figures do not include housing constructed by state enterprises and institutions for their personnel.

[14] *2d FYP,* I, 715 (in prices of the 1933 Plan).

The great priority of heavy industry and the subordinate position of consumers' goods were also revealed in the fact that when the Seventeenth Party Congress (January–February of 1934) felt that the targets of the Gosplan's draft of the second FYP were on too high a level, the 1937 targets for the output of consumers' goods were cut considerably more (from 54.44 billion rubles to 47.2 billion rubles) than the targets for the output of producers' goods (from 48.4 billion rubles to 45.5 billion rubles). The targets for investment were left fully intact.

The targets of the second FYP for investment in heavy industry were corrected in the fulfilment stage to make its growth much more rapid than was provided in the FYP. On the other hand, the scheduled steep rise of investment in the consumer'-goods industries and in housing did not materialize. A postponement following upon a postponement! Or, more probably, the respective provisions of the second FYP, as many others, were ignored.

The very moderate degree of the permitted recovery of living standards and the postponement to the last year of the three-year period of whatever recovery did occur are the reasons why the word "good" in the *Three "Good" Years* is put in quotation marks. It is, indeed, fully justifiable to accept the view that full advantage was taken of the immense decline in consumption levels during the *All-out Drive,* in order to permit rapid expansion in the output of producers' goods, of steel primarily, in the subsequent period. These low consumption levels absorbed so little, even from a moderate national income, that they left a great deal for investment; in other words, they permitted the formation of "The Initial Fund for Development," the kind described by the United Nations speaker referred to above (end of chap. 5).

Planning

Both the first FYP, and the annual plans for the last two and a quarter years of the respective period, were unrealistic to an extreme degree. The annual plans, a distinct product of the *All-out Drive* itself, actually were much more unrealistic than the original first FYP, which had belonged to an early phase of the planning madness, when the ideas of the *All-out Drive* were still in the infant stage.

The *Three "Good" Years* brought about a fundamental separation, in function and in character, of the FYP from the annual plans. The FYP retained its function as a means of propaganda. Such a function, especially under Soviet conditions, is, or at least was, incompatible with realism. The annual plans, on the other hand, started—only for a short while, it is true—to perform the function intended for the planning in the 1920's, namely, to be a guide in economic development. What need the Soviet economy had for planning was satisfied by them.

The second FYP.—The two-volume publication on the second FYP is impressive only if one does not look into it too carefully. Many items in the FYP are ridiculously unrealistic and would have been a serious handicap if the FYP had been intended for the important role of guiding the economy rather than for propaganda. The absurdity of the timing of the fixed investment of the socialized sector in heavy industry and of some other items has already been shown above. This absurdity also may be found in the timing of the fixed investment of the socialized sector as a whole.[15] The rates of growth scheduled for it in the second FYP were as follows (in per cent of the preceding year at the prices of the 1933 Plan): [16]

1934................	39.6
1935................	11.5
1936................	8.3
1937................	5.6

This timing simply does not make sense, especially for a planned economy. The boast is that the Soviet socialist economy is expanding smoothly according to plan. The figures above show no trace of smoothness—even in intentions. So far as a decline in the rates of growth was to be expected, it should have been planned to be gradual rather than precipitous. The burden of investment is obviously heavier, the smaller the national income and the lower the incomes of the population. Yet investment was to be raised right in the first year after the retreat by almost exactly 40 per cent. Since national income was to rise by 24.1 per cent,[17] the share of fixed investment in it was to increase substantially. On the other hand, much more rapid enlargements of national income were scheduled for the years 1935–37 than the planned percentage increases in capital investments, and hence a decline of the share of investment in national income was actually planned for the last three years of the second FYP period, although this was in full contradiction of the basic aim of the Party. Whether this was realized or not, the increase in total investment during the whole period of the second

[15] It would probably be preferable in this case to speak of great helplessness.

[16] *2d FYP*, I, 715–16.

[17] Target of the 1934 annual plan, taken over into the second FYP. The figure (a wild figure, for that matter) is taken here from 1935 Plan (2d ed.), p. 441. It is certainly not accidental that, among a mass of year-to-year targets found in the second FYP, the year-to-year targets for national income are missing.

FYP (1933–37) as scheduled in the FYP must also have been smaller than that of national income.

The second FYP contained, furthermore, obvious manipulations, which would have been unlikely if the FYP had been intended for operation. The manipulations in setting the targets for the unspecified animal products and for milk, both mentioned below in this chapter,[18] may serve as examples. The second FYP appears to have operated satisfactorily only if one follows the Soviet practice of disregarding failure to reach certain important targets by wide margins in the fulfilment stage.

The year 1937 belongs to an era different from that of the other four years of the second FYP period. Hence, if one wants to see how the second FYP operated, it seems appropriate to compare the actual performance in 1936 with the targets of the second FYP for the same year. Such a comparison is, of course, only valid for the operation of the FYP during three years, because for 1933 the second FYP had performance figures rather than targets.[19]

The targets of the second FYP for 1936 were most nearly fulfilled in the output of producers' goods (Table 8). Nevertheless, in the petroleum industry, one of the mainstays of the Soviet economy, only 29.2 million tons of petroleum (including gas) were produced, although 40.5 million tons were scheduled by the second FYP for this year. A serious discrepancy may be observed in super-phosphates. Some shortfalls also occurred in round timber and lumber (sawn timber).

As far as output of consumers' goods was concerned, the targets of the second FYP for 1936 were missed all along the line, some by great margins. An exception was bread, for which the target was exceeded.[20] But this "happy" event had nothing to do with improvement of consumption levels. It was the result of a much greater "success" than anticipated by the second FYP in commercialization of consumption, specifically in discouragement of home baking.

[18] The highly unrealistic dealings of the planners with retail prices (they wanted to reverse the trend) are described in the subsection on consumers' prices in the next chapter.

[19] As examples may be cited (million tons):

Product	Target of the 1933 Plan	Actually Produced in 1933, *Socialist Construction of the USSR*, 1935, pp. xx–xxi	1933 Target of *2d FYP*, I, 690
Steel	8.95	6.84	6.85
Coal	84.20	76.00	76.70

[20] A reorganization of the baking industry makes the comparison difficult. The target of the second FYP was to raise the output of bread produced by the Tsentrosoyuz from 7 million tons in 1932 to 10.5 million tons in 1937 (*2d FYP*, I, 462). In only two years, 1935 and 1936, bread output by all organizations was expanded by 6.2 million tons (*1936 Plan*, pp. 432–33; *1937 Plan*, p. 103).

The fulfilment of the targets of the second FYP for the so-called quality factors shows a varied picture. The targets for the principal category, namely those for the output per man, faired well. The target for increase in performance per operational worker on railways during the plan period was 45 per cent.[21] An increase of 48.6 per cent in those years is claimed [22]—an excellent piece of planning. The targets for raising productivity in industry (65 per cent) and construction (75 per cent) also seem to have been fulfilled or exceeded. However, the targets for length of the average haul and for eliminating overly long hauls and counterhauls on railways failed.

The target of the second FYP for total freight traffic in 1937 (in ton-kilometers) was just met in spite of the shortfall in material production. This occurred because the target for tons shipped was underfulfilled, while the target for the average haul was exceeded.

Of the individual carriers, the target for freight traffic on railways was exceeded by 18.2 per cent; there was a large shortfall of the target for freight traffic on the sea (27.9 per cent) and an immense shortfall in that for freight traffic on rivers (47.5 per cent). The second FYP foresaw an unchanged length of haul on railways (*2d FYP*, I, 476). This actually grew by 8.5 per cent.[23]

Not only did the planned conversion of inflation into a great deflation fail to materialize (retail prices of consumers' goods were to go down by 35 per cent from the 1933 level according to the second FYP), but inflation made considerable further progress during the preparation and execution of the FYP.[24]

Scrutiny of the second FYP reveals not only its unrealistic nature —a feature observed already in the first FYP. The first FYP was unrealistic, but it may have been taken seriously, at least by those who drafted it. It may have been decided from the start by those in power that the first FYP would remain a piece of paper as far as reality was concerned, but the piece of paper was at least left intact. The Party went much further in dealing with the second FYP.

The Gosplan draft of the second FYP was revised by the Seventeenth Party Congress by rule of thumb, and the Gosplan was left to work in the changes decided upon as best it could. It did not do a

---

[21] Year-to-year targets for output per man were apparently not set and in any case not released.

[22] A. A. Chertkova, *Labor Productivity on Railways and Ways To Raise It* (Moscow, 1957), p. 50.

[23] Implied in data by Holland Hunter, *Soviet Transportation Policy*, p. 331. Mimeographed material by Hunter circulated prior to the publication of his book was used extensively by this writer.

[24] The deflation targets of the second FYP are discussed in greater detail in the subsection on prices of consumers' goods in the next chapter.

good job of it, as a more thorough analysis of the final text by the present writer, as yet not printed, clearly shows.[25] It just did not matter.

A general remark seems appropriate here. Possibly it should have been put in a more conspicuous place. Economists, especially statistical economists, naturally stick to economics and specifically to statistics. This is also a procedure generally followed by the present writer. But the ignoring of the political situation, especially under Soviet conditions, frequently makes the analysis defective. Those economists who insisted that Soviet statistics were not falsified apparently did not take into account the fact that the disputed statistics were those of Stalin—the same Stalin who made his long-time Party friends Bukharin, Rykov, and thousands more "confess" that they betrayed the USSR and Russia. It suffices to put before oneself this question: Could an apparatus from which all sensible persons were eliminated during 1928–31, which produced the bacchanalian planning of the *All-out Drive* and "enjoyed" the highly demoralizing leadership of a Kuibyshev, produce such a refined product as a FYP, especially when the *All-out Drive* had ended less than a year before? Only those who believe in miracles might answer in the affirmative.

The annual plans.—The data in Table 8 show that in a year favorable for the Soviets it was possible, if an adequate effort was made, to forecast with considerable certainty the course of events in the next year,[26] at least with reference to such things as industrial output. This is true of both 1935 and 1936.[27]

One of the greatest shortfalls of the 1935 Plan, that in bricks, was by only 6.5 per cent. A relatively significant shortfall was that the 1935 Plan scheduled an 87-million-meter increase in output of cotton cloth, but there was, instead, a decline of 137 million meters.

[25] Here is only one of many examples. To bring the value of total agricultural production in 1937 to the figure prescribed by the Party Congress, the target for the output of unspecified animal products (mainly eggs and wool) in 1937 was set at 1,472 million rubles, an increase since 1932 to a level 4.5 times higher, in the face of only a doubling of the output of the animal products specified in the Plan (*2d FYP*, I, 464–65). This item was selected for a particularly large manipulation, because in the Gosplan draft of the second FYP only the total for the output of animal products was given. The manipulation is, therefore, not immediately obvious.

[26] Actually, the targets were forecast in the beginning of the year for the remaining months, because the annual plans were not completed before the start of the planned year itself.

[27] The time at the end of 1933 or early in 1934 was too close to the bacchanalian planning of the *All-out Drive* for good planning. The targets of the 1934 Plan for industrial production were missed practically all along the line. While the shortfalls were mostly small, they were large in the case of most building materials: cement by 18 per cent, bricks by 23 per cent (see *1935 Plan* [2d ed.], pp. 506–49). There still was a world of difference in degree between the shortfalls of the 1934 Plan and those of the annual plans of the *All-out Drive*.

TABLE 8

Three "Good" Years: Industrial Production, Specified Targets and Fulfilments, 1935 and 1936

Item	1935				1936			
	2d FYP, Draft[a]	2d FYP, Final[b]	Annual Plan[c]	Actual[d]	2d FYP, Draft[a]	2d FYP, Final[b]	Annual Plan[c]	Actual[d]
Producers' goods:								
Electric power (billion kw-h.)	24.0	24.0	24.9	26.3	30.0	30.0	32.0	32.8
Coal (million tons)	110.0	110.0	112.2	109.6	126.6	126.6	135.8	126.8
Crude petroleum including gas (million tons)	35.0	35.0	27.8	26.8	40.5	40.5	30.0	29.2
Steel (million tons)	12.0	12.1	11.8	12.6	15.5	14.8	16.0	16.4
Tractors (thousand 15 h.p. units)	125.9	113.3	126.7	155.5	132.8	145.9	154.0	173.2
Superphosphates (14 per cent)[f] (thousand tons)	1,624	1,466	1,200	1,460	2,822	2,297	1,688	1,671
Cement (million tons)	5.0	5.0	4.4	4.5	5.9	6.0	6.5	5.9
Industrial timber shipped from the forests (million cubic meters)	132	131	116	117	152	149	139	128
Sawn timber (million cubic meters)	30.3	30.3	27.4	27.6	35.8	35.8	33.9	32.9
Paper (thousand tons)	655	655	628	640.8	740	740	787	763.5
Consumers' goods:								
Cotton fabrics (million meters)	3,650	3,475	2,800	2,640	4,800	4,215	3,215	3,270
Socks and stockings (million pairs)	…	325	…	341	…	475	420	359
Footwear, large-scale industry (million pairs)	75	86	77	85.5	85	128	122[e,h]	120[e,h]
Rubber footwear (million pairs)	75	75	75	76	85	85	85	82
Cigarettes (billion units)	90	85	75	79	110	100	89	…
Bread (million tons)[h]	…	…	13.9	14.4	…	…	14.8	16.1
Meat (thousand tons)	625	600	460	586	850	850	650	773
Fish (thousand tons)	1,600	1,550	1,550	1,520	1,750	1,660	1,636	1,631
Crystal sugar (thousand tons)	1,700	1,650	1,450	2,032	2,100	2,000	2,500	1,998
Vegetable oil (thousand tons)	…	…	400	426	…	…	480	451
Soap (thousand tons)	600	555	482	479	850	750	581	557

a 2d FYP, I, draft, 446-57.

b 2d FYP, I, 69-705.

c National Economic Plan for 1935 (2d ed.), pp. 444-45 and passim.

d Data from Industry of the USSR, 1957, passim, except for electric power, petroleum, sawn lumber, footwear, bread, meat, cigarettes, soap, and vegetable oil, which are from 1937 Plan, passim. The previous estimates are likely to be more in line with the targets of the plans than the revised ones. The 1936 data are marked as preliminary in 1937 Plan.

e National Economic Plan for 1936 (2d ed.), pp. 410-32.

f Includes other phosphatic fertilizer, except raw phosphates.

g Total industry, see 1937 Plan, pp. 100-101.

h No comparable data in 2d FYP.

Several targets of the 1935 Plan were even exceeded, but the Soviets did not consider exceeding a target a shortcoming. The overfulfilments were small, moreover, except for tractors and sugar. The great excess in sugar production was due to exceptionally good weather (an unforeseeable occurrence).

The year 1936 also was satisfactory as far as fulfilment of the targets of the annual plan for industrial output was concerned, although the targets for cement, crystal sugar, and timber turned out to have been too high.

Some targets of the annual plans of 1935 and 1936 involving the delicate matter of quality factors likewise were fulfilled almost exactly. This was, for example, the case with the target for the output per man in large-scale industry. But it proved impossible to hold wages within the plan. In 1936, for example, the target for output of large-scale industry per man was exceeded (in terms of "unchangeable 1926/27 prices") by 4.9 per cent (actually there may not have been any excess) but the target for the average paid-out wage was surpassed by 12.0 per cent.[28] The plan may have been too stingy, though.

Gross agricultural production in 1935 was estimated officially at 16.1 billion rubles as against a target of 17.0 billion, although the weather was very favorable in that year. The target for agricultural production in 1936 displayed the feature common to Soviet targets for farm output in years following those with good weather, namely, that no allowance was made for this factor in setting the target for crop production for the next year. In this case it was the good weather in 1935 which was neglected. The 1936 target for farm production became 19.7 million rubles, an increase of 17.1 per cent over the good figure for 1935.[29] Actually, gross farm output in 1936 turned out to be lower than that of 1935. The Soviet government apparently never released its estimate of the actual 1936 farm output; this writer's estimate implies a decline of 8 per cent (see Table 11, p. 140).*

The target of the 1936 Plan for fixed investment in the socialized sector was missed by 12.6 per cent even in nominal terms.[30] The shortfalls were even greater for the partial items. In the case of fixed investment in postal services (admittedly a small item), the 1936 target for the total of such investment was missed by 17.2 per cent

[28] *1937 Plan,* pp. 44–45. The aim, a reasonable one, was to have wages rise less than gross output.

[29] *1936 Plan* (2d ed.), p. 433.

* *National Economy of the USSR in 1958* (p. 350), not available when the above was written, gives the same percentage decline.

[30] *1937 Plan,* pp. 142–43.

and the target for putting plant and equipment in this item into operation, by 23 per cent.[31]

The second FYP and the annual plans.—It may be useful, in conclusion, to follow up the fate of an important consumers' good from the draft of the second FYP to actual performance through the final text of the second FYP and the annual plans. For this purpose cotton fabrics, the most important non-food consumers' good, is chosen. The respective data are shown in Chart 10.

CHART 10

PROPAGANDA AND REALISTIC PLANNING: OUTPUT OF COTTON FABRICS *
(In billions of meters)

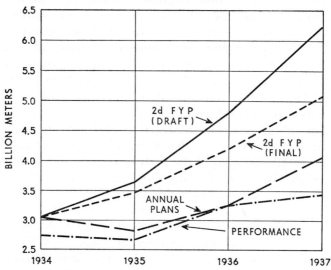

* The targets of the second FYP are from *2d FYP*, draft, I, 454–55; and *2d FYP*, I, 702–3. The targets of the annual plans are from *Bulletin of Financial-Economic Legislation*, various issues. Fulfilments are from *Industry of the USSR*, 1957, p. 328. The year 1933 was omitted because the second FYP was not passed by the Party before February of 1934 and by the government before November of 1934.

First, the Seventeenth Party Congress cut the Gosplan 1937 target for cotton fabrics from 6,250 million to 5,100 million meters. In no year was any attention paid to the targets of the second FYP in setting the targets of the annual plans. In 1936, the target for the output of cotton fabrics was 65 per cent of that set in the draft of the second FYP and little more than three-quarters of that which had been provided in the final draft of the FYP. The increase in output of cotton fabrics in two years from 1934 to 1936 was little more than half that scheduled by the second FYP. On the other

[31] *Ibid.*, pp. 140–41.

hand, the targets of the annual plans for output of cotton fabrics were fulfilled exactly in 1936 and missed by only a relatively small margin in 1935.

Chart 10 is also useful in showing the big change in planning and plan fulfilment which was brought about by the *Purge Era* right from its beginning. Contrary to the practice in preceding years, the annual plan for 1937 demanded a large increase in the output of cotton fabrics, by 814 million meters to be specific. But the actual increase was less than one-quarter of that planned.

Investment

Total.—It has already been shown above (p. 126) that, after moderation had been exerted in scheduling gross fixed investment of the socialized sector in 1933, the 1934 Plan, incorporated into the second FYP, asked for an increase in this investment of almost 40 per cent. For the subsequent years, however, only small or relatively small further advances were planned by the FYP.

The original 1934 target for gross fixed investment was later reduced from 25.1 to 23.5 billion rubles.[32] This still very large target appears to have been nearly fulfilled, on the basis of this writer's calculations.[33] After having attained this, it was only natural to set up considerably higher targets for investment in the years after 1934, with complete disregard for the second FYP. A particularly great appetite was displayed in respect to 1936 investment, but this only enlarged the extent to which the target was missed. The actual increase in investment in 1936 was not larger than in 1935.

As Table 9 shows, gross fixed investment of the socialized sector increased in the *Three "Good" Years* by 96 per cent at nominal costs and by nearly 70 per cent at costs adjusted for inflation. Although real national income must have been rising at a very good clip during the *Three "Good" Years* (see p. 176, below), the rate of expansion of fixed investment, in real terms, appears to have been materially larger than that of national income. It seems that the

[32] Compare *2d FYP*, I, 717, and *1935 Plan*, p. 441.

[33] The phrase "on the basis of this writer's calculations" is emphasized. The possibility of a 30 per cent expansion of investment in real terms in 1934, when the chaos of the *All-out Drive* was far from being fully overcome, especially when a great bottleneck in transportation facilities still existed, seems difficult to visualize.

But these doubts with reference to the growth of investment in 1934 may be unjustified. They are based on consideration of the great handicaps to progress still remaining. The appraisal possibly should be primarily based on consideration of how much conditions have improved as compared with the terrible situation which had prevailed in the years immediately preceding. Moreover, a certain potential accumulated during 1933. The 1934 investment level is not extremely high as compared with 1932.

TABLE 9

Three "Good" Years: Fixed Investment and Other Important Indicators
(Year-to-year increases in per cent, except as noted)

YEAR	Gross Fixed Investment of the Socialized Sector			Large-Scale Production	Output of Machinery		Mineral Consumption Shimkin[f]	Freight Traffic[g]	
	Current Costs[a] (billion rubles)	1932 Costs[b] (billion rubles)	Per Cent Increase or Decrease at 1932 Costs	Hodgman's Value-added Index[c]	Gerschenkron[d]	Hodgman[e]		Five Carriers	Railways
1932	19.1	19.1	...	5	0	10	...	10	11
1933	18.1	17.2	−10	11	13	26	...	2	0
1934	23.6	22.3	+30	19	21	12	48[h]	19	21
1935	27.2	25.0	+12	29	27	57	...	22	26
1936	35.5	29.1	+16	17	7	10	...	22	25
1937	33.2	25.5	−12	8	7	0	45[i]	8	10
1933–36	...	...	+69	79	84	142	...	78	91
1932–37	...	...	+34	116	98	142	109	97	110

[a] Data from Kaplan, RAND RM-735, Table XIII, but the investment of 1932 was reduced from 19.4 to 19.1 billion rubles. Investments of the kolkhozy from their own resources were not included throughout, because they presumably had a much lower purchasing power than the investment of the state, and the present writer sees no way of estimating, even very crudely, this purchasing power. *Stat. Handb.*, 1956, p. 158, shows an increase in fixed investment of the kolkhozy from 0.7 billion rubles (at prices of July 1, 1955) in 1932 and 1.1 billion rubles in 1933 to 2.3 billion and 2.7 billion in 1936 and 1937, respectively, implying an almost fourfold increase in 1932–37 and more than a doubling in 1933–36.

[b] The conversion was made with the help of the following price index: 1932 = 100; 1933 and 1934, 105; 1935, 109; 1936, 122; and 1937, 130. The price index is based on the material in *Essay III, passim* (esp. pp. 139, 165).

[c] Hodgman, *Soviet Industrial Production*, p. 73.

[d] At 1939 prices in the United States. See Alexander Gerschenkron, *A Dollar Index of Soviet Machinery Output in 1927/28 to 1937* (Santa Monica, Calif., 1951), p. 31.

[e] Hodgman, *op. cit.*, p. 72. Hodgman's index is for "metal working," which should have shown smaller rises than an index for machinery output proper.

[f] Dmitrii Shimkin, *Minerals—A Key to Soviet Power*, here quoted from Gregory Grossman and D. B. Shimkin, "Mineral Consumption and Economic Development in the United States and the Soviet Union" (mimeographed, supplement to *Minerals*, Harvard, Apr., 1952), p. 45.

[g] In ton-kilometers. Data from James Blackman in *Symposium*, p. 128.

[h] 1933 and 1934.

[i] 1935 through 1937.

concession made in respect to the share of fixed investment in national income in 1933 was fully made up by 1936, and the relation of fixed investment to total material production (the Soviet concept of national income) was about the same in 1936 as in 1932, at a level some 50 per cent higher for both items, in absolute terms.

Since fixed investment in the socialized sector in real terms declined in both 1933 and 1937, its rate of growth during the entire second FYP period appears relatively small (about 34 per cent according to this writer's calculations). It seems certain that real national income rose more in comparison. This is one of the many phenomena which are likely to lead to incorrect conclusions if the analysis is restricted to the official FYP periods.

The calculations in Table 9 were made prior to publication of *Stat. Handb.*, 1956. The calculations of gross fixed investment of the socialized sector at constant prices in the latter source compared as follows with those of the present writer:

| Year | STAT. HANDB., 1956[a] | | THIS WRITER | |
	Billions of Rubles at July 1, 1955, Prices	Year-to-year Rises or Declines (in per cent)	Billions of Rubles at 1932 Prices	Year-to-year Rises or Declines (in per cent)
1932	21.6	...	19.1	...
1933	18.0	−16.7	17.2	−10
1934	23.7	+31.7	22.3	+30
1935	27.8	+17.3	25.0	+12
1936	38.1	+37.1	29.1	+16
1937	33.8	−11.3	25.5	−12
1933–36	...	+112[b]	...	+69[b]
1932–37	...	+56[b]	...	+34[b]

[a] *Stat. Handb.*, 1956, p. 158.
[b] Rise during the period.

The broad picture in both calculations is similar, but the official index shows an increase of 112 per cent in 1933–36, while this writer has only 69 per cent. The increases in 1932–37 are 56 per cent (official) and 34 per cent (this writer). The greatest individual difference is in the estimates for 1936: the official index figure is more than double that of this writer. This writer is not inclined to revise his calculations.

The year-to-year data on gross fixed investment in 1932–37 show great variations: three years with great increases and two years with substantial declines. According to official calculations the declines were equivalent to 16.7 and 11.3 per cent in 1933 and 1937, respectively. The great variations observed make a joke of the officially claimed law that the Soviet economy is growing smoothly according to plan.[34] The contradictory data stare one in the eye in official yearbooks, but this fact is simply ignored in the USSR. Attention to it is not drawn even by a passing explanation that the period analyzed here was exceptional for Soviet conditions, which it was not. The significant phenomenon of the great year-to-year variations in gross fixed investment also is not given attention in the Western literature. The operation with FYP periods both helps the Soviets and impedes Western analysis.

The year-to-year variations in gross fixed investment are even more pronounced in construction, which constitutes the major part of the fixed investment.[35]

Total investment probably increased substantially more during the second FYP period than gross fixed investment of the state. For that matter total *net* fixed investment may have grown more than the corresponding gross investment. According to an official estimate at prices of July 1, 1955, investment of the kolkhozy grew from 0.7 billion rubles in 1932 to 2.7 billion rubles in 1937,[36] i.e., amost four-fold. While the calculation cannot be checked, a great increase in this investment is beyond doubt, especially since the 1937 crops were excellent and there was also a certain increase in kolkhoz live-stock. While the investment of the individual and kolkhoz peasants went down substantially in 1932, there was a considerable enlarge-ment in the latter in 1937, again partly owing to the excellent har-vest. The grain distributions by the kolkhozy to the kolkhozniki from the 1937 crops set a record never to be approached again. The livestock herds of the kolkhozniki also were considerably expanded. Only the variable capital of the state enterprises did not increase at all from 1932 to 1937.[37]

Total net investment in 1937 was estimated in *Essay I* (p. 85) at 22 billion rubles (1926/27 prices). This was cut to 20 billion in the "Corrigenda Sheet," because in the essay itself the depreciation charge on the gross investment was not deducted (most items in the total were gross rather than net). The deduction of the depreciation charge, however, was made on the basis of the officially prescribed

[34] The year 1937 showed both a decline and a development opposite to that provided in the plan. The decline in gross fixed investment in 1933 was according to plan, but, of course, any decline does not fit into the formula of smooth growth according to plan. The very fact that, to overcome the various bottlenecks of the *All-out Drive*, it was necessary to plan for a decline in gross fixed investment, contradicts the formula.

[35] See below, pp. 145–46.

[36] *Stat. Handb.*, 1956, p. 156.

[37] According to *2d FYP*, I, 541, 4.1 billion rubles were spent on this item from the budget in 1932. The total increase in the variable capital may have been somewhat larger than this. The increase in the variable capital of the state enterprises in 1937 was estimated at 5 billion rubles in *Essay I*, p. 108. The 1937 ruble was of course cheaper than the 1932 ruble.

rates. But since the essay was published, it has been made absolutely clear in Soviet publications that the prescribed rates of depreciation are vastly inadequate. If now the total net investment in 1937 is estimated at 18 billion rubles, this still may be too favorable.

Eighteen billion rubles, as the total net investment in 1937, exceed the estimate for 1928 in Appendix B, Table I about 3.5 times and that for 1932 in chapter 4 by about 50 per cent. This is certainly not too low considering that in 1933 and 1937 there were reversals in the biggest item, the fixed investment of the state, and that the large gains in the three "good" years, 1934–36, had to make up for these reverses.

By sector.—The wise part of the investment operations during the *Three "Good" Years* was that the Soviets were, on the whole, satisfied to keep investment in heavy industry at the high level reached previously (by 1933). Consequently, the share of heavy industry in total investment of the socialized sector declined from over 40 per cent in 1933 to approximately 30 per cent in 1936 (Table 10).

TABLE 10

Three "Good" Years: Fixed Investment of the State by Sector*
(In millions of rubles at current costs)

YEAR	INDUSTRY			AGRICULTURE[a]	TRANSPORTATION AND COMMUNICATIONS	HOUSING
	Total	Heavy Industry	Light and Food Industries			
1932....	10,403	8,505	1,257	2,942	3,658	1,591
1933....	9,475	7,420	1,432	2,390	3,283	1,343
1934....	11,244	8,458	1,563	2,831	4,905	1,729
1935....	11,789	8,959	1,572	2,155[b]	5,973[b]	1,930
1936....	13,412	9,300	2,150	2,562[b]	7,914[b]	2,400[b]
1937[c]....	13,146	8,667	2,376	2,614	7,979	2,425

* Data from Kaplan, RAND RM-735, Table X and Table 14. Kaplan's Table X gives data broken down by ministries. Hence, data for heavy, light, and food industries include only the investment of the respective Union and Republican ministries, but not those of the local industries. Housing, which is shown separately, is also included in the investment of the other sectors.
[a] Investment of the collective farms out of their own funds is not included. This column has been prepared to show what the government spent on agriculture out of the state funds. Second, the money spent by the collective farms must have had a much lower purchasing power than that of the state.
[b] Preliminary.
[c] Plan.

The Soviet government was not in a hurry to utilize funds in its possession to bring farm output to a level needed to fulfil even the substantially curtailed targets of the second FYP for the output of consumers' goods. It was somewhat more generous in appropriations for agriculture so long as it hoped to solve the farm problem by expanding state-owned farming, then the only real socialist form of enterprise from its point of view. But by 1933 the great venture with state farming was already as good as dead. The potential scope of operations of the existing state farms was actually curtailed, part of the land in their possession having been turned over to the collective farms. Except for the support of the remaining state farms and the expansion of the state-owned machine-tractor stations (MTS), agriculture was largely left to recover by its own power.

While the era of bacchanalian planning on the whole ended in the beginning of 1933, one feature of this era—namely, the failure to realize that industrial output and investment cannot be expanded without providing the facilities for transporting the goods involved —survived for another full year. A rapid rise of investment in transportation facilities did not start until 1934. In 1935, Lazar Kaganovich, one of the ablest Soviet trouble shooters, was delegated to put transportation in order. Apparently, one of his principal achievements was to persuade Stalin and the others of the need for appropriate investments in these facilities. While in 1933 investment in transportation and communications was equal to 44 per cent of that in heavy industry, it was 85 per cent of the latter in 1936.[38]

It has already been shown (see p. 124) that whatever the Soviets wanted to do for the consumer was to be postponed until a later date. In only four years, according to the second FYP, investment in consumers'-goods industries was to rise 2.7 times from the very low level of 1933. When the time came to realize this promise, action was postponed again and again. Even in nominal terms, investment in light and food industries in 1936 (2.15 billion rubles) was less than half of that scheduled in the second FYP (4.42 billion rubles).[39] In real terms, only little more than one-third of the goal was realized. The inadequacy of investment in light and food industries was indeed so marked that in the later years of the second FYP period the textile industry was unable to process all the cotton produced.[40]

In a similar way, the targets of the second FYP for residential construction were missed by more and more with the passing of time. House construction in 1936 fell short of the target by 29 per cent in nominal terms but by close to 50 per cent in real terms.[41]

---

[38] These figures again show that rather than proceeding at a smooth proportionate pace, the Soviet economy was advancing in jerks. It was characterized by "campaigns."

[39] The prices of the 1933 Plan, in which the investment target was expressed, presumably were about 8.5 per cent lower than the actual prices at the end of 1932.

[40] See Molotov's report on the third FYP to the Eighteenth Party Congress in *Problems of Economics*, 1939, No. 3, p. 53.

[41] The cost of house construction seems to have grown more in the years under review than those of other construction. House construction in physical terms during the second FYP amounted to only 38.5 per cent of the target (*Essay III*, p. 113). In nominal terms, however, the expenditures were more than two-thirds of those planned.

Agriculture

Farm output during the *Three "Good" Years* was amazingly small when compared with that needed to realize the ideas on the indispensable relationship of the various economic sectors, as visualized in the 1920's. Indeed, the merits of the *All-out Drive,* from the point of view of the Soviets, were that such ideas had been dispensed with for good.

As was shown above (Table 10), agriculture, which lost about half of its animal draft power and was also greatly disorganized by the *All-out Drive,* received little financial help from the state in the form of investment. One of the principal factors which stimulated the agricultural recovery was that the collectivized peasants ultimately were assured of the right to have small private plots and some private livestock.

The recovery of the output of potatoes and vegetables, and especially of animal products, for the needs of the peasants and for the urban population was, indeed, largely achieved by the kolkhoz peasants themselves rather than by the kolkhozy.[42] The recovery of the output of the other crops, grown almost exclusively by the kolkhozy and sovkhozy, was helped by the less belligerent attitude of the peasants toward the collective system.

The data on crop production discussed below do not give a correct picture of the trend, because 1933 was a good year and 1936 a very poor year, weatherwise. As Table 11 shows, crop production actually declined between 1933 and 1936, although the trend was rising. The value of the animal production increased by fully 50 per cent in the same years. For the major farm products, we have the following approximate increases (+) or declines (−) in output from 1933 to 1936 (in per cent):[43]

Grain	−9
Potatoes	+4
Sugar beet	+87
Sunflower seed	−37
Cotton	+86
Meat	+45
Milk	+21

[42] In 1938, the kolkhoz peasants had almost as large an acreage in potatoes as the kolkhozy, and about 44 per cent of their and the kolkhozy's acreage, combined, in vegetables (*Sown Acreages of the USSR, 1938, passim*). The per hectare yields of vegetables may, moreover, have been higher on the kolkhozniki's plots than in the fields of the kolkhozy (no data seem to have been released on the yields as obtained by the different owner groups in those years). In 1936, the kolkhozniki had 61, 70, and 56 per cent of the cattle, hogs, and sheep and goats, respectively, of the totals owned by them and the kolkhozy together. The role of the kolkhoz peasants in supplying the urban population with potatoes was particularly large because the state used the potatoes delivered to it, largely, for the output of alcohol and starch.

[43] Data from *Soc. Agri.,* pp. 792, 798.

TABLE 11

Three "Good" Years: GROSS AGRICULTURAL PRODUCTION, 1933–36*
(Values at 1926/27 prices in per cent of preceding year)

Year	Crops		Animal Products		Total[a]	
1933.........	113.0[a]	(97)	90.0	(87)	107.2[a]	(94)
1934.........	102.3	(104)	110.0	(110)	104.1	(105)
1935[b]........	107.8	(110)	118.9	(119)	110.3	(112)
1936[c]........	85.0	(85)	115.0	(112)	92.0	(92)
1933–36[d].....	94.0	(97)	150.0	(148)	106.0	(108)

* Official data for 1933–35 from *Socialist Construction of the USSR, 1936*, pp. 232–33.
   As this book was going to press, the figures in parentheses were inserted from *Economy of the USSR in 1958*, p. 350, top. The official figures are given at constant, but unspecified, prices. A comparison of the older data with the new figures shows that the transition to the "biological" crops and other manipulations affected, in the first place, the comparability of the 1933 crop data with those of 1932.
   [a] The increase of this year is exaggerated because, since 1933, grain crops have been estimated in the field rather than in the barn.
   [b] Preliminary.
   [c] Official estimates withheld. Rough estimates on the basis of output figures for individual products. *Soc. Agri.*, pp. 792, 798.
   [d] This writer's estimates.

As was stated, the crop supply situation during the *Three "Good" Years* was not so bad as is implied by Table 11 and the tabulation above. The non-farm economic activities during a given calendar year depend on the harvest of the preceding year to about the same extent that they depend on the harvest of the same year. Hence, to appraise the actual rise in supplies in 1933–36, it is necessary to relate the average of the 1935 and 1936 crop production to the average of 1932 and 1933. The outcome of such a computation is an increase in crop production of about 8 per cent, rather than a decline of 6 per cent, on the basis of the crops harvested in each calendar year. Even the corrected figure was of course nothing to be happy about. The gains were, indeed, pitiful.

Contrary to the situation with regard to crops, the development of supplies of animal products available for consumption was not as favorable as the changes in the value of animal production shown in Table 11 indicate. The large increase in animal production in terms of values was, to a considerable extent, due to the fact that a declining trend in livestock herds until about 1933 was replaced by a rising trend in the subsequent years. While the data on the value of total output of animal products in 1933–36 show an increase of about 50 per cent, the same data for four specified major items (milk, meat, hides, and wool) point to a rise of not much more than 20 per cent.[44]

[44] *Socialist Construction of the USSR, 1936*, pp. 232–33, and other official data.

The by no means favorable situation of the total supply of farm products would not have permitted a rapid expansion of non-farm activities had not the consumption of the peasants been held down drastically by large increases in procurements at very low prices. The year-to-year rises in all marketings of the four major products were as follows in those years (in per cent of the preceding year):[45]

Commodity	1933	1934	1935	1936 (Plan)[a]
Grain......................	122.6	113.0	105.5	119.1
Potatoes....................	114.0	108.0	141.7	120.9
Meat.......................	89.0	122.5	117.5	119.6
Milk and dairy products.......	127.6	122.1	108.8	123.1

[a] The yearly plans normally contained the targets for the year in question and the preliminary fulfilment data for the preceding year. Since it was apparently not desired to disclose the marketings of farm products in 1936, the whole section on marketings of farm products was omitted from the *1937 Plan.*

With the exception of meat in one year (1933), marketings of all specified farm products rose from year to year in practical disregard of the changes in output and with the result that their share in total output increased substantially during the short period analyzed here. Specifically for grain, Malyshev's data, certainly official, indicate a rise in marketings of 46 per cent in only three years from 1932 to 1935—in the face of an increase in output of only 15 per cent.[46] The cynicism of proclaiming these great increases in marketings, and in the share of these marketings in total production, which occurred largely at the expense of the consumption of the peasants, as a specific advantage of socialist organization of agriculture[47] would be astounding if one had not already stopped being surprised at anything in that realm of "socialism."

The much greater increase in marketings than in output went a long way toward explaining the great discrepancy between the growth in total supplies of farm products, only about 9 per cent in 1933–36, and the increase in production of consumers' goods by perhaps 40 to 50 per cent in the same years. Additional processing, stimulated by charging relatively higher prices for goods in lower stages of processing, was a further factor tending to raise the rate of growth of industrial production of consumers' goods above the rate of growth of total farm output. We find the following chain of events for the period from 1932 to 1936: grain production, prac-

[45] I. Malyshev, "Problems of the Kolkhoz Trade," *Planned Economy,* 1936, No. 4, p. 111.

[46] *Soc. Agri.,* p. 792.

[47] See, for example, Stalin's report to the Eighteenth Party Congress in 1939—the first Congress after completion of the second FYP period (*Problems of Leninism* [11th ed.], p. 583).

tically unchanged; marketings of grain, increased by perhaps 70 per cent; commercial bread output more than doubled.[48]

Industry

Industry expanded at very rapid rates during the *Three "Good" Years*. The official index, which, for one reason or another, involved a relatively small degree of exaggeration in those years,[49] showed a rise of 88 per cent for total gross industrial production, with the output of industries "A" rising by 107 per cent and that of industries "B" by 66 per cent.[50] Hodgman's value-added index in large-scale industry indicates a rise of 79 per cent.[51] Production of small-scale industry, even according to official data, was enlarged only by 35 per cent.[52] Hodgman's index, adjusted to apply to all industry, implies an increase of close to 70 per cent in the three years, or a yearly rate of growth of not much less than 20 per cent.[53]

Of the *Three "Good" Years* the middle year was the best. It was the first year when all disturbances of the *All-out Drive,* including those in transportation, were overcome (see Chart 2 in chapter 1).

Of the individual products (Table 12), steel finally came to its "rights" by showing a 140 per cent increase in output in only three years. Output of electric power nearly doubled, while coal mining expanded by two-thirds. The output of petroleum, however, could have been increased only by 30 per cent. The long-awaited expansion of the output of cement finally arrived, but the gain since 1933 appears particularly large owing to the considerable decline in output from 1932 to 1933. The disappointing picture in shipments of timber and especially its sawing was mentioned above.

The output of manufactured foods showed a satisfactory development—a clear testimony to the effectiveness of the procurement system but also to the disastrous situation at the beginning of the period and to the plight of the kolkhoz peasants during the whole period. The doubling of the output of bread in only three years has

[48] Great increases in output of such products, the 1926/27 prices of which consisted largely of tax (beer, cigarettes, *makhorka*), were also a factor in the expansion of the output of consumers' goods during the period analyzed.

[49] The tendency of Soviet statistics to be more reliable in years favorable to the Soviets is discussed by the writer in *International Affairs,* January, 1959.

[50] *Stat. Handb.,* 1956, p. 46.

[51] *Symposium,* p. 232.

[52] Assuming 3.7 billion rubles in 1933 (*1935 Plan,* p. 443) and 5 billion rubles in 1936 (*Planned Economy,* 1937, No. 1, p. 5).

[53] The wage bill used by Hodgman as weights must tend to show greater rates of growth in output than are shown in any other index computed for Soviet industry, official or private.

TABLE 12

Three "Good" Years: OUTPUT OF INDUSTRIAL GOODS, 1932–36*

Commodity	1932	1933	1934	1935	1936
Producers' goods:					
Electric power (billion kw-h.)........	13.5	16.4	21.0	26.3	32.8
Coal (million tons).................	64.4	76.3	94.2	109.6	126.8
Petroleum (million tons).............	21.4	21.5	24.2	25.2	27.4
Steel (million tons).................	5.9	6.9	9.7	12.6	16.4
Tractors (thousand h.p.).............	762	1,200	1,771	2,333	2,598
Commercial fertilizer (thousand tons)..	921	1,034	1,398	2,323	2,839
Cement (thousand tons).............	3,478	2,709	3,536	4,488	5,872
Industrial timber shipped from the forests (million cubic meters).........	99.4	98.0	99.7	117.0	128.1
Sawn timber (million cubic meters)...	24.4	27.3	30.6	35.7	40.9
Paper (thousand tons)..............	471	506	566	641	763
Consumers' goods:					
Bread[a] (million tons)..............	7.0	8.1	10.3	14.4	16.1
Meat (million tons).................	458	411	496	586	773
Fish (thousand tons)...............	1,333	1,303	1,547	1,520	1,631
Crystal sugar (thousand tons).......	828	995	1,404	2,032	1,998
Vegetable oil (thousand tons)........	490	321	422	492	503
Vodka and other strong liquor (million dekaliters).....................	72.0	...	...	...	89.7 (1937)
Beer (thousand tons)..............	414	431	457	519	744
Cigarettes (billion units)............	57.9	62.7	67.8	78.6	85.9
Makhorka (thousand cases).........	3,219	2,514	2,898	3,776	5,021
Cotton fabrics (million meters).......	2,694	2,733	2,733	2,640	3,270
Socks and stockings (million pairs)....	208	251	323	341	359
Knitted goods (million units).........	27	36	54	63	86
Footwear, "leather"[b] (million pairs)...	87	90	85	104	143
Rubber footwear (million pairs)......	65	62	65	76	82

* Data from *Industry of the USSR, 1957, passim,* except for meat, cigarettes, *makhorka,* the data for which are from earlier sources (*Socialist Construction of the USSR, 1936,* and *1937 Plan*). The other exceptions are mentioned in special notes.

a Data for 1933 and 1934 refer to the output of all organizations concerned (*Socialist Construction of the USSR, 1936,* p. 214). The figure for 1932 is presumably comparable with them, although *2d FYP,* I, 462, gave it as produced by the Tsentrosoyuz alone. Data for 1935 and 1936 are given in *1937 Plan,* pp. 102–3, as the output of the food industry. These too appear comparable with the rest.

b Statistical data on the output of leather footwear are generally in a confused state. Some of them pertain to large-scale industry only. See the different output series in Walter Galenson, *op. cit.,* p. 27. The data presented here are from *Industry of the USSR, 1957,* p. 351.

already been commented upon. A substantial part of the additional output of bread consisted of a transfer, from peasant homes especially, to commercial enterprises. Such a transfer also took place in the case of all other important processed foods, except sugar, of course.

The catch of fish, a food but not a farm product, showed a relatively moderate increase of 23 per cent in the three-year period.

The showing of non-food consumers' goods was poor by comparison. Output of cotton fabrics rose by only 16 per cent (the increase in cotton fabrics was equal to about 20 per cent, if the great expansion of output of socks, stockings, knitted goods, sweaters, and similar goods is considered); all this increase occurred in the last year of the three-year period. The increase in output of footwear was relatively large. This increase was probably attained exclusively, or almost exclusively, by the use of all kinds of substitutes for leather, and may also have included transfer of footwear production by artisans in the homes of the peasants to industry (the out-worker not being accounted for properly in official industrial statistics).

How starved the market was in the beginning and how ready it still was to absorb everything at the end of the period is well illustrated by the fact that the output of such poor stuff as *makhorka*[54] was doubled during the years under observation.

Construction

In analyzing the *All-out Drive* period, it was found that even those rates of growth of construction (including installation) which it seemed advisable to accept, may have been larger than those permitted by the growth in output of building materials. The situation was more favorable in this respect in the *Three "Good" Years* (Chart 11).

The comparison of the rate of growth in construction with that of output of building materials for the period dealt with here is particularly valid in view of the certainty that all possible savings on building materials had already been effected prior to the start of the period and that no significant carry-over of building materials was inherited. But this validity is one-sided. It is not impossible that stockpiles of building materials were larger at the end than at the beginning of the period.

The estimates of *Stat. Handb.*, 1956, shown in Chart 11, imply a growth in construction in 1933–36 of 136 per cent. Output of window glass showed an increase much larger than this. The increase in shipments and sawing of timber, on the other hand, was much smaller than the latter, but there was a relatively close agreement between the growth in construction and the output of the principal building materials such as bricks and cement.

The year-to-year variations in construction including installation

[54] A very poor tobacco smoked by peasants and low-income urban dwellers.

CHART 11

INVESTMENT IN CONSTRUCTION AND INSTALLATION VS. OUTPUT OF BUILDING
MATERIALS, 1932–37 *
(1932 = 100)

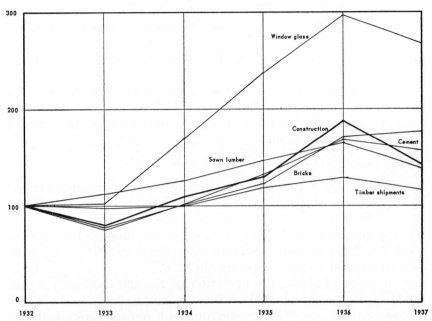

* Data for construction and installation of the socialized sector at prices of July 1, 1955, from *Stat. Handb.*, 1956, p. 158. Data for output of building materials from *Industry of the USSR*, 1957, *passim*.

of the socialized sector during 1932–37 were of immense proportions (annual rises or declines in per cent):

Year	Total Investment	Construction, Including Installation
1933	−16.7	−20.4
1934	+31.7	+35.9
1935	+17.3	+12.7
1936	+37.1	+45.7
1937	−11.3	−23.8

An increase in construction of 45.7 per cent is claimed for the one year of 1936. Such a jump could have existed only in statistics, and moreover statistics produced by fear of Stalin's henchmen.[55] But even the increase actually attained in that year was probably large. The increases in construction were large also in 1934 and 1935

[55] See *Socialist Construction of the USSR, 1935*, pp. 474–75.

according to official data. Correspondingly these data showed the large declines in construction of 20.4 and 23.8 per cent in 1933 and 1937, respectively.

Everything said above about the Soviet law of smooth growth of the Soviet economy according to plan in its relation to gross fixed investment pertains even more to the investment in construction. Both the increases and declines in construction as shown officially may be exaggerated but there is no trace of anything resembling smoothness in any case.

The number of persons employed in construction declined by as much as 1,013,800 from 1932 to 1936.[56] Yet absence of unemployment is claimed. In full measure, this exists only in statistics, which do not have such an item.

Transportation

Freight traffic by five carriers (in terms of tons originated) increased by 81 per cent in the three years from 1933 to 1936—certainly a great performance, indicating beyond any doubt great rates of overall economic growth. It must be considered, though, that not all goods needing transportation were transported in 1933, while probably no such handicap was present in 1936.

As mentioned above, the operation of the transportation system reached its worst state in 1933. The economic recovery in the *Three "Good" Years* proceeded for some time with transportation still very disorganized. This situation was not fully remedied before sometime in 1935.[57] The immense differences in the effectiveness of the operation of the railway system between the *Three "Good" Years* and the three years of the *All-out Drive* are so conspicuous (see Table 13) that comments seem unnecessary.

Output per Man

In contrast to the *All-out Drive,* the expansion during the *Three "Good" Years* was accompanied by a large increase in output per man. In construction a greatly expanded amount of work was done even by a reduced number of wage earners. While the output of large-scale industry increased by perhaps 65 per cent in 1933–36, the number of wage earners was enlarged by only 23.8 per cent.[58] Thus, an increase in output per man of over 30 per cent in three years, or about 9 per cent per year, is implied.

[56] But the decline was equal only to 249,000 in 1933–36. The end of the *All-out Drive* was particularly marked in this item.

[57] For details the reader is referred to Holland Hunter's book.

[58] On the basis of data in *Socialist Construction of the USSR, 1936,* pp. 508–9, and *1937 Plan,* p. 145.

TABLE 13

Three "Good" Years VERSUS *All-out Drive:* RAILWAY OPERATIONS*
(Increase or decline in per cent)

Item	1929–32	1933–36
Tons originated..	+42.8	+80.2
Cumulated ton-kilometers[a] per operational worker........	+12.6[b]	+36.4
Freight-car turnaround in days.........................	−6.1	−29.0
Gross ton-kilometers per freight-train hour..............	+16.7	+60.1
Locomotive-kilometers per locomotive day..............	+7.9	+42.1

* Three-year periods. Courtesy of Dr. Holland Hunter.
a Ton-kilometers plus passenger-kilometers.
b Based on data for all workers instead of operational workers only.

Hodgman has an increase in output per man in large-scale industry in the *Three "Good" Years* of not less than 43 per cent.[59] Galenson's computations for increase in output per man in individual large-scale industries in the same period are (in per cent):[60]

Coal.........................	45
Iron ore.....................	110
Petroleum....................	8[a]
Iron and steel.................	115
Tractors......................	75
Farm machinery...............	76
Cotton yarn..................	14[b]
Cotton weaving...............	21[b]
Footwear....................	46[c]
Sugar.......................	30[d]

a From 1933 to 1935.
b From 1932 to 1936.
c From 1933 to 1937.
d Weather: 1933 good, 1936 poor.

It was shown in the preceding section devoted to transportation that work per operational worker on railways increased by 36.4 per cent in 1933–36.

The performance per man in construction, implied in official data, shows too good a picture to be true. According to *Economy of the USSR in 1956* (p. 181), output per man in construction advanced by 86 per cent in 1932–37. This percentage is well in line with the official claims for expansion of construction (43 per cent including installation)[61] and decline in the number employed in it of 31 per cent.[62] But the official calculation of increase in construction and installation seems to be too high. So must be the official calculation

[59] Hodgman, *Soviet Industrial Production, 1928–51*, p. 113.
[60] Walter Galenson, *Labor Productivity in Soviet and American Industry*, p. 234.
[61] *Economy of the USSR in 1956*, p. 172.
[62] *Ibid.*, pp. 204–5.

in output per man in construction. Nevertheless, even this writer's calculations of investment indicate a substantial rise in total construction, and this, in conjunction with the large decline in the labor force, points to a very large increase in construction work per person engaged in it. It is, indeed, not improbable that output per man in construction, which was very low to begin with in 1928 and made practically no progress until 1932 (even official calculations claimed only an increase of 4 per cent), showed a greater advance during the *Three "Good" Years* than labor productivity in railway transportation and even than that in industry.

Output per man in retail trade is a puzzle. The number of persons employed in official retail trade proper increased by 48 per cent in 1932–37. The number of those engaged by eating places went down by 26 per cent. The total personnel in retail trade showed an increase of 17 per cent.[63] These data, in conjunction with the present writer's estimate of change in the volume of retail trade, indicate very little improvement in performance per man. The performance per man in eating places, whose operations were drastically curtailed with the end of rationing,[64] may have even declined.[65]

[63] *Soviet Trade,* stat. handb., 1956, p. 113.

[64] The number of courses served declined from 9.6 billion in 1932 to 4.2 billion in 1937 (*ibid.,* p. 74). The number of eating places went down by only 8.8 per cent during the period (*ibid.,* p. 144).

[65] Retail trade seems to have been a completely neglected area, even so far as output per man is concerned. The then existing technical backwardness of Soviet trade is simply unbelievable. The 1956 statistical handbook on trade does not give such data before 1950. There were 487,500 various trade enterprises in 1955 (*ibid.,* p. 137). Altogether, they had 132,100 scales of the type common in the United States. In addition there were 166,800 scales with weights, and about 100,000 enterprises had no scales (*ibid.,* p. 162). Less than half of the state shops dealing in perishable foods had any kind of cooling appliance in 1955 (*ibid.,* p. 166).

CHAPTER 7

THE THREE "GOOD" YEARS II

THE PRIVATE SECTOR

Targets, Boasts, and Reality

After a downward revision from an even higher target in the Gosplan draft (this, too, was approved by the Party and the government), real wages were to have been doubled, according to the second FYP in its final form.[1] Moreover, they actually "spoke" of doubling,[2] or nearly doubling, the per capita purchasing power for *goods,* rather than of mysterious items on which many claims for raising real wages of the workers and employees and real incomes of the peasants were, and still are, based. The following statement leaves no doubt on this account:

> The index of physical volume of food consumption of workers and employees (in unchangeable prices of 1932) will amount to 202.2 per cent of the 1932 level. The index of physical volume of consumption of goods of mass use will amount to 207.6 per cent of the 1932 level.[3]

What exactness! Even decimals. Moreover, those in power claimed fulfilment of the target or even more. V. Molotov in his concluding remarks in the discussion of the third FYP at the Eighteenth Party Congress (Molotov was the reporter on the subject) claimed an increase in real wages during the second FYP by 101 per cent (not

---

[1] *2d FYP,* I, 340.

[2] The word "spoke" is used advisedly. Nobody knows what they really were thinking about.

[3] *2d FYP,* I, 340. The phrase "goods of mass use" was used to mean consumers' goods other than food.

just 100, note, but 101 per cent).[4] The Gosplan summed up the respective results of the second FYP in this way:

The non-fulfilment of the target of the second FYP for the reduction of retail prices of mass consumption was overcompensated by a much greater rise of the wages of workers and employees than was provided by the FYP, as well as by the substantial rise of the money incomes of the collective farms and collective peasants.[5]

The targets of the second FYP for real wages and the claims of having achieved, or even exceeded, these targets do not merit attention, as they are nothing but propaganda. If the consumption levels during the *Three "Good" Years*, nevertheless, deserve detailed analysis, it is because, although this seems at first glance unbelievable, the acknowledged big improvement in non-farm activities during the *Three "Good" Years* was achieved, especially in 1934 and 1935, with a consumption not much above the starvation levels existing at the end of the *All-out Drive*. This writer reconciled himself to this idea only very reluctantly after repeated examination of the material.

Reputable authors have reached extremely pessimistic conclusions with reference to living conditions during the *Three "Good" Years*. Solomon Schwarz, for example, in his book *Labor in the Soviet Union* (New York: Praeger, 1952, p. 163) wrote: ". . . the living standards of labor at the end of 1935, after derationing, cannot have been much lower than at the end of the First Five-Year Plan," i.e., at the end of 1932. Prokopovicz' calculations, quoted below, are even less favorable to claims of an increase in real wages during the *Three "Good" Years*. With the statistics available to Prokopovicz and Schwarz, it was probably impossible to reach more accurate results. Moreover, exaggerated official claims such as those cited above almost inevitably tend toward the opposite extreme.[6] Concealment of evidence tends to produce the same effect.

Evidence on the problem dealt with is still in a confused state, and this makes a discussion of it both lengthy and less lucid than would be desirable. It seems best to start with prices. Familiarity with prices makes the data on retail trade and incomes more easily understandable. But the developments on the price front are also of great

[4] Here quoted from *Problems of Economics*, 1939, No. 3, p. 41.
[5] *3d FYP*, draft, p. 12.
[6] There was a specific reason for the possibility that those authors may have painted an even darker picture than that which actually existed. They were naturally interested in the first place in the real earnings of *low-wage* groups, and, as will be shown, these groups were discriminated against considerably more than the high-wage earners and more also than the hired force as a whole.

interest in themselves. After prices, the supplies of farm products and retail trade are dealt with, and in conclusion consumption and real wages are taken up.

Prices of Consumers' Goods

Prices of consumers' goods remained in a chaotic state during most of the *Three "Good" Years*. In January of 1932, bread was still distributed on rations at the pre-collectivization price. All rationed foods cost the wage earners about twice as much in 1932 as in state and co-operative trade in 1928. Rationed non-food products were apparently sold to wage and salary earners at relatively still higher prices. In addition, there were sales of non-food goods in state commercial trade without rationing at prices many times higher. The peasants apparently were charged higher prices in co-operative trade than the wage and salary earners were charged in state trade (there was no state trade in rural areas).

It was the first concession to the inevitable, when on May 20, 1932, the government legalized the peasant markets which had become known as the "kolkhoz markets," where farm products were sold by the producers to the consumers at free prices. With some other sales of the producers other than to the state, the kolkhoz markets formed the so-called kolkhoz trade. The prices in kolkhoz trade naturally were many times higher than in official trade at the time discussed. Attracted by the high prices realized in kolkhoz trade, and having some "surpluses" from the procurements not fully used for distribution on rations, the state immediately entered the high-price market with sales of food in its so-called commercial stores without rations, at prices not much lower than those in kolkhoz trade, and sometimes not lower at all. In 1932 *weighted* average prices of all state and co-operative trade are likely to have been about threefold those in 1928.

The subsequent development was one of rapid rise of the ration prices, with a simultaneous decline in the prices in kolkhoz and commercial state trade, but not before kolkhoz-market prices reached a peak early in 1933. The first increase of the bread prices on rations came even before the legalization of kolkhoz trade, namely, on February 1, 1932. Since the share of state commercial trade in total state and co-operative trade was never very large even in nominal terms[7] and its share in physical terms was several times smaller than this, the price declines in commercial state trade could compensate only for

[7] It was equivalent to little more than one-seventh of the total in 1933 and not quite one-quarter of this in 1934. Data from G. Ya. Naiman, *Domestic Trade in the USSR* (Moscow, 1935), p. 80.

a small part of the rapid rise of ration prices. There resulted, therefore, a rapid rise of the *weighted prices* of all or most individual as well as of all consumers' goods together in all state and co-operative trade. This process continued until bread was derationed on January 1, 1935, at a price which in Moscow was 12.5 times that of 1928 or of January, 1932. Most other goods were derationed on October 1, 1935, at prices which, although very high as compared with the prices in either 1928 or 1932, were on the average not quite as high, relatively, as the bread prices.

The price development observed in official trade during those years is also found in total, i.e., official and kolkhoz, trade, but in a much milder form. Still, the weighted prices of all trade presumably about doubled from 1932 to 1935.

Official writers discussing price developments in those years usually speak only of the price declines in kolkhoz and state commercial trade, neglecting the rises in ration prices, and also in the weighted average prices. They are even not disinclined to quote a few high prices in the kolkhoz markets and state commercial trade to show the generosity of the government in reducing them in state commercial trade, or forcing them down in kolkhoz trade. This evidence is very useful for the Western analyst.

The large decline of prices in kolkhoz and state commercial trade before derationing was to serve as proof of the care for a rapid improvement in consumption levels. The process was, however, much more complicated. Actually, the rapid rise of prices of rationed goods was absorbing the purchasing power of the population to such an extent that the expanding supplies in kolkhoz and state commercial trade could find buyers only at gradually reduced prices.

The ability of the state to put on the market the moderate supplies of food for sale in its commercial stores had obviously little to do with the general supply situation and general consumption levels. It reflected in the first place merely the efficiency of the procurement system, the smallness of the rations, the limited number of those entitled to rations, and, finally, the great stratification of earnings.

The decline of unrationed prices, from the top level presumably reached in kolkhoz trade in the spring of 1933 to the free prices after derationing, was, in general, the larger, the greater the previous rise. This rise in turn depended little upon the supply situation of the individual commodities, and more on the degree to which each of them could be dispensed with. Bread, the most essential food, was also the relatively most expensive product in those years, although it was not as scarce as some other necessities. Only vegetable oil, which was in extremely short supply and was also purchased in minute quantities, commanded about as high prices, relatively, as bread in 1934.[8] But at the highest point (in the spring of 1933) the bread price in those markets was about 50 to 60 times the price in 1928 (and in the Ukraine bread reached a level nearly 150 times the price in 1928).[9] Vegetable oil is unlikely to have been so immensely expensive. The prices of rye flour in kolkhoz trade were even higher in 1933, relatively, than those of bread.[10]

On the other hand, the highest price reached by meat and butter —goods in very short supply—in kolkhoz trade was about 25 times that of 1928. Sugar, another item in very short supply, occupied an intermediate position between bread and meat.

The official price established for unrationed bread effective January 1, 1935,[11] was about half the price in state commercial and kolkhoz trade at the beginning of 1934, but 4 times the rationed price of the same time and double the rationed price immediately before derationing. Thus, the meeting of the "low" rationed prices and the high unrationed prices at derationing—the official assertion —occurred nearer to the high prices in state commercial trade and kolkhoz trade than to the price on rations.[12] Bread did not occupy an isolated position in this respect.

Although the price of butter after derationing was 7 times the price in 1928, it represented a decline from the price in commercial trade in 1934 of only about 40 per cent. Not many could afford even these "moderate" prices.[13]

The changes in the price relationship of butter and bread in those years were as follows: the price of butter in state trade was about 30 times that of bread in 1928 (close to the normal situation), about 11 times higher at the highest level in 1933 in kolkhoz trade (extremely abnormal) and about 20 times higher after derationing on October 1, 1935 (less abnormal).

[8] Naiman (*op. cit.*, p. 293) cited a price of vegetable oil in state commercial trade of 35 rubles per kilogram in April, 1934, and of 24 rubles at the end of the same year. In 1928, the retail price of vegetable oil was 50 to 56 kopeks per kilogram in Moscow state stores, but it cost more than 1 ruble in private trade. Bread was selling in the same months of 1934 in the state commercial and kolkhoz trade at a price about 25 times that in co-operative trade in 1928 (and the relationship was not much less when compared with the private markets in 1928).

[9] I. Malyshev, "Problems of Development of Kolkhoz Trade," *Planned Economy,* 1936, No. 4, p. 114.

[10] See *ibid.*, p. 121.

[11] The price of coarse rye bread is used in this analysis.

[12] The doubling of the bread price effective June 20, 1934, may have been made with the special aim of reducing the great difference between the ration price and the price after derationing. There were many other such actions.

[13] Prices in commercial trade from Malyshev, *op. cit.*, p. 119. Prices in state trade in Prokopovicz, *Russlands Volkswirtschaft unter den Sowiets*, p. 305. In 1934, only 1,273 tons of butter, or less than 1 pound per capita, was sold in the kolkhoz markets of Moscow. See Malyshev, p. 124.

While this was going on in the world of reality, curious things were in progress in the world of fiction. These things still are called planning (this is done obligatorily in the USSR, but on a voluntary basis outside the USSR). The reference is to the reaching of another "milestone" of Soviet economic planning—the work on the prices of consumers' goods in the second FYP.

It may seem unbelievable, considering conditions in the country, but the planners scheduled, nevertheless, a great rise in the purchasing power of the consumers' ruble during the second FYP period. By 1937, the prices of consumers' goods in state and co-operative trade were to decline by 40 per cent, according to the draft of the second FYP;[14] and by 35 per cent, according to its final version.[15] It is true that the target was based, not on the prices of 1932, the normal base of the targets of the second FYP (it is easy to be misled on this score) but on the higher prices of 1933, and, moreover, on "weighted prices" of that year. This implied, although it was carefully left unmentioned, that the high prices in commercial state trade also were considered in the computation of the base prices. While sales in commercial state trade were less than one-sixth of total state and co-operative sales at current prices in 1933, the "weighted prices" were boosted by its inclusion. Thus, the price level used as a base in the second FYP was quite high. Nevertheless, any plan to cut back these prices in the existing atmosphere of rapid inflation would have been nothing but unrealistic wishful thinking, if it had been in earnest.

The target of a 40 per cent decline in average retail prices for state and co-operative trade in the draft of the second FYP was reduced to 35 per cent in the approved version, but one has to be extremely careless to be misled into believing that serious consideration was given to this whole issue. As is easily established by reading the dailies of that time and studying the draft and final texts of the second FYP, the scheduled reduction of the weighted prices of consumers' goods from 40 per cent in the Gosplan draft to 35 per cent in the final version was decided by a committee of the Seventeenth Party Congress by collective rule of thumb and later apportioned by the Gosplan in the crudest manner possible.

Actually, steps had been taken which precluded fulfilment of the target of the second FYP for the prices of consumers' goods even before the preparation of the FYP had started in earnest. Further such steps were still being taken during the very preparation of the FYP. The outcome turned out to be not a large decrease of the aver-

[14] *2d FYP,* draft, I, 437.
[15] *2d FYP,* I, 530–31.

age prices of consumers' goods from their 1933 level as prescribed by the second FYP, but a considerable rise. The timing of the announcements of the second FYP target for reducing the prices of consumers' goods is best reproduced here together with the timing of the bread-price increases in those eventful years:[16]

1932, February 1, ration bread price raised more than 50 per cent.

1933, August 20, ration bread price raised to 25 kopeks per kilogram, double the previous price in Moscow.

1933, second half, the Gosplan accepts the target of reducing the weighted 1933 retail prices of consumers' goods in 1933–37 by 40 per cent.

1934, February 1, the Seventeenth Party Congress accepts the target of reducing the weighted 1933 retail prices of consumers' goods by 35 per cent in 1933–37.

1934, June 20, ration bread price raised to 50 kopeks per kilogram, double the previous level.

1934, November 17, the government approves the second FYP, which included the target of reducing the weighted 1933 prices of consumers' goods by 35 per cent in 1933–37.

1934, December 7, bread price raised to 1 ruble per kilogram double the previous level, to be effective after derationing from January 1, 1935.

The synchronizing could not be more perfect!

It is not quite clear when it was definitely decided to deration at a very high price level, but probably not even a thought was given to operating toward deflation in earnest. The doubling of the ration price of bread on August 20, 1933, should have made the continuation of the drafting of the second FYP, along the lines in which this was presented to the Seventeenth Party Congress, senseless. The government was, in any case, very deceitful when it approved the second FYP in November, 1934, after having raised the ration price of common rye bread to 50 kopeks per kilogram beginning June 20, 1934, and only about twenty days before establishing the retail bread price beginning January 1, 1935 (after derationing), at 1 ruble per kilogram.

While it is uncertain *when* the decision as to the desired derationing price level was definitely made, it seems perfectly clear *why* the one and not the other solution was chosen. Farm output was much too small for deflation, the economic system was not adequately organized, the dictatorship was not sufficiently strong. Under the then prevailing conditions, it would have been impossible to deration

[16] The data on bread prices (in Moscow) from *Bulletin for Grain Business,* 1932, No. 14; 1933, No. 26; and 1934, No. 16. Only the dates since the wholesale price of flour was raised were stated in the sources for 1933 and 1934. But bread prices must have gone up on the same dates.

without raising the former ration prices, even if wages had remained stable, but the reverse was true. Consumption was to be kept at very low levels, and high prices are the easiest way toward this end.

It does not really matter by how much the target for reducing the prices of consumers' goods was missed. But the weighted prices of 1933, on which this target was based, and those of 1937, which was the year when the target was to be reached, are of immense interest in themselves. Unfortunately, the problem can only be treated very crudely. State and co-operative retail trade (including eating places) in 1933 is given officially at 49.8 billion rubles, as against 15.4 billion rubles in 1928 and 125.9 billion rubles in 1937.[17] The latter figure, recalculated to 1928 prices, is equivalent to about 16.8 billion rubles (see footnote 20, below, concerning this recalculation). If the 1937 retail trade amounted to 16.8 billion rubles at 1928 prices, that of 1933 is unlikely to have been much larger than perhaps 13 billion rubles at the same prices, and, hence, an increase in the weighted prices in state and co-operative trade from 1928 to 1933 of almost 300 per cent is indicated. A reduction of the 1933 price level by 35 per cent, to be achieved by 1937 according to the second FYP, would have brought the prices of that year to a level about 2.7 times that of 1928. The prices of consumers' goods actually rose about 7.5 times from 1928 to 1937. The retail prices in official trade in 1937 turned out to be about 2.8 times those scheduled for that year by the second FYP.

For the purpose of the subsequent analysis, it would be important to ascertain, at least crudely, the development in prices in state and co-operative trade (with and without consideration of commercial state trade) from 1933 to 1937 for wage earners and peasants separately. While the evidence at hand is very limited, it seems certain that around 1932 on the average the peasants had to pay higher prices than the wage and salary earners in this trade. In August of 1932, for example, soap was sold at 3 to 5 rubles per kilogram in the cities and at 4.0 to 7.2 rubles in rural areas (the 1928 retail price was 38 to 65 kopeks per kilogram). On the other hand, commercial state trade operated only in urban areas. Still, since there was little difference between the prices in rural and urban areas in 1937, the increase in weighted prices of consumers' goods in 1933–37 is likely to have been somewhat larger for wage earners than for peasants.

Supplies of Farm Products

It was mentioned above (see p. 140) that, as far as crop production is concerned, the supplies of products for immediate use in each

---

[17] *Soviet Trade,* stat. handb., 1956, pp. 14, 20. The 1928 figure includes private trade.

calendar year depend partly on the harvest of the preceding year. Computed on the crude assumption that each calendar year utilizes half of the preceding year's crop and half of the crop of the same year, the supplies of farm produce available for immediate use increased from 1933 to 1936 by the following percentages:[18]

Crop production..............	8
Grain (cereals).............	3[a]
Potatoes...................	31
Sunflower seed..............	−26
Sugar beet.................	112
Seed cotton................	61
Flax.......................	8
Animal products..............	29[b]
Meat.....................	45
Milk......................	21

[a] Based on estimates in *Soc. Agri.*, pp. 792, 798, and *passim*.

[b] In addition to meat and milk, eggs, hides, and wool are considered. The percentage here is slightly out of line with that computed above (Table 11) for the four major animal products, because the computation there was based on official data at 1926/27 prices while farm prices in 1928 are used here.

The amounts of farm products available for sale and consumption in the farm home appear to have increased from 1933 to 1936 by slightly more than 15 per cent. According to estimates by Dr. Lorimer,[19] the population grew by 2.7 per cent from the beginning of 1934 to the end of 1936. (The fact that the country, which only a short while before boasted a population growth of over 2 per cent per year, had such a small rate of population growth during the recovery period is in itself indicative of the fact that, as far as consumption was concerned, a disastrous situation continued to exist.) A further small adjustment is needed to account for the fact that perhaps two-thirds of the additional population was urban, with its much greater per head consumption of farm products in value terms than that of the rural population. Considering the greater consumption of farm products per head of the urban population, there was a small increase in supplies per head of the total population of somewhat more than 10 per cent over the period.

The *composition* of the additional supplies of farm products was unfavorable. Food was the item primarily needed, yet the all-important grain did not show any increase per head whatsoever. The output of cotton, on the other hand, increased greatly. There was, it is true, a partial offsetting factor in the almost negligible increase in the output of flax. The utilization of the additional supplies of cot-

[18] The average of crop production, but not animal production, in 1935 and 1936 is related to the average of 1932 and 1933.

[19] Frank Lorimer, *The Population of the Soviet Union: History and Prospects* (Geneva: United Nations, 1946), p. 135.

ton was, moreover, handicapped by the fact that the facilities for its processing had become inadequate. And, finally, consumption of textiles other than for private use (armed forces, professional uniforms) was increasing rapidly.

The dismal picture of the total supplies of farm products is indicative of consumption levels of the whole population. The big increase in marketings and, based on this, the great increase in consumers' goods produced by industry (see above) are relevant primarily insofar as the distribution of the total supplies between the rural and urban populations is concerned.

Retail Trade

While the official retail trade during the *Three "Good" Years* had many interesting features, the most illuminating one was the fact of its very slow growth in real terms in the face of the rapid expansion of heavy industry. The turnover in kolkhoz trade was increasing much more vigorously, but this development could not have had a large effect on the growth in total retail trade during this period.

Official trade.—Official retail trade more than trebled at current prices from 1932 to 1937. It more than doubled from 1933 to 1936. These rises were not all due to inflation, but were largely due to it. The 1937 retail sales at constant prices are estimated at about 10 per cent above those of 1928.[20] Hence, although this may seem unexpected in view of the great economic transformation of the USSR, the volume of official retail trade in 1928 had apparently not yet been restored by the year 1936 (official trade includes private trade as long as this lasted). This is another justification for putting the word "good" in the *Three "Good" Years* in quotation marks. While, in the absence of a price index, the rise in volume of the official retail trade from 1932 or 1933 to 1936 cannot be established exactly, it was amazingly small as compared with the growth of heavy industry.[21]

[20] In *Essay I* (p. 28) a factor of 8 was used for deflating 1937 retail prices to those of 1926/27 or 1928. Mrs. Chapman's calculations indicate a factor of 7.68 (in the *Review of Economics and Statistics,* May, 1954, p. 143). Both indices were based on the composition of purchases of wage earners in 1926/27 or 1928, respectively. The goods purchased by peasants must have increased in price almost as much as those purchased by the wage earners. If a factor of 7.5 is used for deflating the 1937 retail trade to 1928 prices, this trade becomes equivalent to 16.8 billion rubles at 1928 prices or exceeds the retail trade of 1928 as given in *Soviet Trade,* stat. handb., 1956, by roughly 10 per cent. In the recalculations of the 1928 to 1937 retail prices by Mrs. Chapman and me, adjustments were made for the higher 1928 prices in private than in official trade.

[21] Official retail trade in 1933 was estimated above at 13 billion rubles and that of 1937 at 16.8 billion rubles (in both cases at 1926/27 prices). This implies an increase of about 30 per cent. But retail trade grew by about 18 per cent from 1936 to 1937 at constant prices (see chapter 9) and hence an increase of only about 10 per cent remains for the *Three "Good" Years,* if no change in sales from 1932 to 1933 is assumed.

It has been shown that at the end of the *All-out Drive* official retail trade was dominated by vodka. This means of getting the consumers' purchasing power by giving very little in exchange (the price of vodka is almost entirely tax) was largely exhausted by 1932. A serious handicap to further expansion in sales of vodka through the official trade probably was that bootleg distilling reached very large proportions. So sales of beverages were not quite doubled from 1932 to 1937 in terms of current prices. Under the conditions of the time, this was not nearly enough to satisfy the state's growing need for funds. Indeed, the share of beverages in total official retail trade declined from 19.4 per cent in 1932 to 11.5 per cent in 1937.[22]

As retail sales during the *All-out Drive* were dominated by vodka, the official retail trade of the *Three "Good" Years* was dominated by bread. It seems on first glance unbelievable, but total sales of bread increased not less than twenty-one fold at current prices from 1932 to 1937, according to official data.[23] More than one-fifth (21.7 per cent) of the official trade in 1937 was made up of sales of grain products, predominantly bread. The deplorable composition of retail sales in 1937 is revealed even more clearly by the fact that the *sales of*

CHART 12

OFFICIAL RETAIL TRADE, 1937: SPECIFIED COMMODITIES *

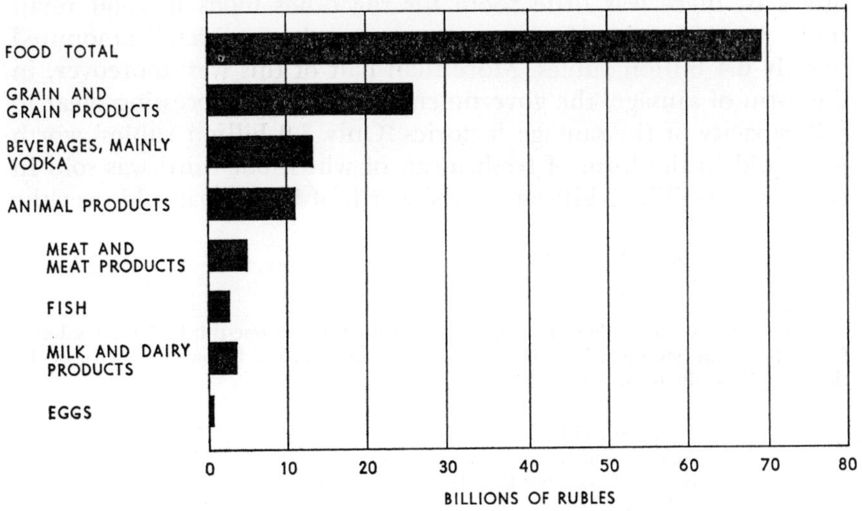

* Not including turnover in eating places. *Soviet Trade*, stat. handb., 1956, pp. 48–51.

[22] *Soviet Trade*, stat. handb., 1956, p. 45.

[23] *Ibid.*, p. 41. In discussing details of retail trade, and many other items as well, it is necessary to operate mostly with the periods 1928–32 and 1932–37, because no evidence is available for the years between these dates.

bread amounted to fully one-third of all sales of food other than beverages.[24] This is a role which even vodka could not have performed (see also Chart 12).

Sales of bread in official retail trade amounted to only 1 billion rubles in 1932. In 1933, the very next year, commercial trade in bread alone returned 2.2 billion rubles, and then jumped to 5.1 billion rubles in 1934.[25] These 1934 bread sales in commercial state trade were equivalent to possibly two million tons—an immense quantity to sell at a price about 25 times that of 1928, with wages having risen little more than 2.5 times. It may come as a surprise that commercial trade in food in 1933 and 1934 actually consisted primarily in sales of bread. The 5.1 billion rubles' worth of such sales in 1934 were almost three-quarters of the total commercial trade in food, which amounted to 6.9 billion rubles in that year.[26] The share of all sales of bread in total official trade was presumably as large in 1934 as in 1937.[27]

In 1932, certainly a bad year for consumers, sales of grain products and beverages amounted to 46 per cent of the total official trade in food (Soviet concept of food). The same foods made up 53 per cent of the respective total in 1937—a better year than 1932, but one with particularly high bread prices.

Since retail food sales were dominated by bread and other grain products, there was little room for the other foods in total retail trade. In 1937, sales of meat and meat products at retail amounted to only 6.4 billion rubles. More than half of this was, moreover, in the form of sausage, the government insisting on processing meat to full capacity of the sausage factories. Only 3.0 billion rubles' worth were sold in the form of fresh meat, of which one-third was sold in eating places. The 2 billion rubles' worth of fresh meat sold over the

---

[24] Implied in *Soviet Trade*, stat. handb., 1956, pp. 40–41.

[25] Malyshev, *op. cit.*, p. 119.

[26] *Ibid.*

[27] The sales of bread alone may have represented about one-third of total sales of food other than beverages in 1934. This is apparent from the following rough calculations for 1934 (in billions of rubles):

Total official trade[a]	61.8
Sales of food[a]	38.5
Sales of food other than beverages	28.6[b]
Sales of bread:	
State commercial trade	5.1
On rations	5.0[c]
Total	10.1

[a] *Socialist Construction of the USSR, 1936*, p. 612.
[b] *Estimated.*
[c] Ration prices of bread increased about fivefold from 1932 to 1934.

counter in official trade in 1937 represented about 250,000 tons or around 5 kilograms per head of the urban population.[28]

The discussion of trade in chapter 5 showed the great expansion, during the *All-out Drive,* of the turnover in eating places, which were selling food at about ration prices. When rationing was abolished in October of 1935, the attraction of these otherwise unattractive eating places was destroyed. The number of courses served in them dropped precipitously from 11.7 billion in 1933 to 4.9 billion in 1936.

Kolkhoz trade.—The turnover in kolkhoz trade[29] looks very small as soon as one turns from billions of rubles to physical quantities. The sales in kolkhoz trade were, moreover, not additional, because peasants' markets also existed before the Great Industrialization Drive and, in an unlegalized form, afterward as well, but sales in this trade were not registered by the official statistics, or if registered, not disclosed. The sales in kolkhoz trade during the *Three "Good" Years* were (in thousands of tons):[30]

Product	1933	1934	1935	1936
Grain	2,480	950	1,580	...
Meat	120	180	250	380
Milk and dairy products	1,600	1,870	2,330	2,400
Eggs (million units)	424	493	860	1,150
Potatoes	1,200	2,000	2,900	3,400
Vegetables, melons	600	750	1,070	1,550

While the quantities sold in kolkhoz trade were very small in 1933, their expansion was rapid, indeed much faster than that of sales in official trade. According to Dadugin and Kagarlitskii, total sales in kolkhoz trade increased by 98 per cent from 1933 to 1936 at constant prices. The role of kolkhoz trade in supplying the non-farm population in 1936 and the preceding years will be further clarified in the next section, which deals mainly with consumption levels of the non-farm population in 1937.

A Note on the Consumption Level of the Population in 1937

Certain foods.—In Table 14 an attempt is made to calculate the consumption of certain foods by the non-farm population in 1937. The calculation is restricted to the non-farm population and to 1937,

[28] Data on retail trade from *Soviet Trade,* stat. handb., 1956, pp. 40, 48, 59. S. N. Prokopovicz (*op. cit.*), gave as the Moscow retail price of beef and mutton, 7.60 rubles per kilogram. Pork certainly sold for more.

[29] See Appendix C for a statement concerning the concept of kolkhoz trade.

[30] Data for 1933–35 from a Soviet source cited by John Whitman in "The Kolkhoz Markets," *Soviet Studies,* April, 1956, p. 390. Data for 1936 were calculated from a chart in A. P. Dadugin and P. G. Kagarlitskii, *Organization and Techniques of Kolkhoz Market Trade* (1949), p. 6.

owing to limitations of available evidence. This factor also determines the selection of the analyzed goods.

The use of data for 1937 results in a substantially more favorable picture than if the calculation had been made for 1936. In 1937 crops were excellent. Sales in official trade were also expanded owing to the purges. Official trade was enlarged by close to 20 per cent at constant prices. The turnover in kolkhoz trade, it is true, remained almost unchanged.[31]

There is an intriguing feature in using 1937 for the analysis. This very year was described by Professor Abram Bergson, adviser to the RAND Corporation, as a year in which, according to some indications, living standards may have surpassed those of 1928.

The calculations in Table 14 are based on the assumption that only the non-farm population bought foodstuffs from official trade. That this should also be the case with reference to kolkhoz trade is implied in the concept of this trade. But actually the farm population bought some amounts of the products dealt with in Table 14 from official trade. Small, possibly negligible, quantities may also have been purchased by it in city kolkhoz markets (there seems to be no provision for excluding such purchases in the statistics). The probable purchases of the farm population from official and kolkhoz trade compensated, possibly only in part, for the supplies in the hands of the state which were distributed to the non-farm population, mainly the armed forces, through channels other than official trade.[32] There is obviously a certain inexactness brought in by the distributions by the state other than through official trade. Difficulty furthermore is encountered in converting meat and meat products from value to physical terms. The supplies available for the consumption of the non-farm population, other than official and kolkhoz trade, can likewise be determined only crudely. In spite of all these uncertainties, the data in Table 14 seem to provide a fair picture, if handled cautiously.

Milk, including dairy products in terms of milk, shows, relatively, the most favorable picture among animal products, with per capita consumption of the non-farm population in 1937 about two-thirds of that in 1927/28. Consumption of eggs appears to have declined by exactly one-half, while that of meat went down even more.[33]

[31] According to Dadugin and Kagarlitskii (*op. cit.*, p. 5), the volume of kolkhoz trade increased at constant prices by 4 per cent in 1937.

[32] The population receiving these supplies is not excluded in the calculations in Table 14.

[33] This writer has estimated the per capita consumption of milk and meat by the *urban* population in 1937 previously and by another procedure. The estimates obtained were moderately higher than those calculated presently. (For the previous estimates, see *Soc. Agri.*, pp. 777–78.)

TABLE 14

Consumption of Certain Foods by the Non-farm Population in 1937*

Product	Official Trade: Millions of Rubles	Approximate Price (rubles per kilogram or unit)	Thousands of Tons	Kolkhoz Trade: Thousands of Tons	Individual Net Production: Thousands of Tons	Total: Thousands of Tons	Per Capita Kilogram or Unit: 1937	1927/28	Strumilin's Suggestions
Milk:									
Milk and dairy products	1,442	1.60	900	2,400	3,416[a]	...	...	...	...
Butter	2,525	18.00	140	...	3,416[a]	...	...	...	...
Milk, total	3,967	...	3,980[b]	2,400		9,796	132	218 (193)	540
Meat:									
Meat and poultry	3,038	7.50	405	...	...	...	...	...	...
Sausage	3,325	8.00[c]	416	...	...	...	...	...	...
Meat, total	6,363	...	821	370	360[d]	1,551	21.0	49.1 (46.3)	89 (including fish)
Eggs, million units	490	0.55	890	1,375	1,000	3,265	44.1 (units)	90.7 (units)	350 (units)
Potatoes	1,005	0.40	2,500	5,000	3,000[e]	10,500	142	...	255 (including vegetables)

* *Official trade:* Sales in rubles from *Soviet Trade, 1956,* pp. 41–42. Prices from *Monthly Labor Review,* November, 1939, and other issues; but a lower price for meat is used than that indicated by this source.

Kolkhoz trade: Data for 1935 from a Soviet source, quoted in *Soviet Studies,* April, 1956, p. 390, were adjusted with use of a chart in A. P. Dadugin and P. G. Kagarlitskii, *Organization and Technique of Kolkhoz Market Trade* (1949), p. 8.

Individual production of the non-farm population: The official estimate was used as guide that in 1937 the gross farm output of all wage earners was equivalent to 4.8 per cent of the value of total gross agricultural production (see *Socialist Agriculture of the USSR, 1939,* p. 87). This implies a value of 960 million rubles at 1926/27 prices.

Non-farm population in 1937 is assumed to have been equivalent to 74 million.

The calculations for 1937 do not take into consideration the consumption of the armed forces and others supplied from state resources through channels other than retail trade. Stockpiling by the state belongs in the same category.

Estimates of consumption of the non-farm population in 1927/28 are from the Gosplan's *1st FYP,* I, 106. The figures in parentheses are those of the CSO (see *Soc. agri.* pp. 777–78).

Academician S. Strumilin believes his suggestions correspond to the requirements of hygiene (see *Courier of Statistics,* 1954, No. 5, p. 27).

[a] Wage earners owned 4,238,000 cows on January 1, 1938, and of these the wage earners in rural areas had 2,465,000. One-third of these cows are assumed to have been owned by the wage earners of the state farms and MTS. The remaining 3,416,000 cows are assumed to have yielded 1,000 liters of milk per year (net of use as feed).

[b] Butter converted to milk at a ratio of 22 to 1.

[c] One kilogram of sausage is assumed to have cost little more than one kilogram of meat.

[d] The potato acreage of all wage earners was equal to 660,000 hectares in 1938 (*Sown Acreages of the USSR, 1938,* p. 121). The acreage of the non-farm population was assumed to have been equivalent in 1937 to 500,000 hectares. These may have yielded 3 million tons of potatoes for consumption.

A very interesting feature of the data for meat and milk in Table 14 is that the state had only a small share in providing the population with fresh milk and fresh meat. The non-farm population itself produced about as much fresh meat as it obtained from the state and bought roughly the same quantity in kolkhoz trade. More than half of all the meat procured by the state for the private consumers was processed into sausage in 1937 (the output of sausage was almost negligible in 1928).[34] Thus, the consumers were not even permitted to choose the form in which they obtained the small amounts of meat available to them in socialist trade.

The role of the state was even much smaller in supplying the population with fresh milk, because the state processed almost all the milk it obtained into butter.[35] If people wanted fresh milk for their babies and could not get it from kolkhoz trade, owning a cow was the only resort in the Soviet state.

The supplies of potatoes available for consumption by the non-farm population in 1937 were relatively ample, but it was exactly this item which particularly reflected the excellent crop of that year. A reliable estimate for potato consumption by the non-farm population in 1927/28 seems not to be available, but the 1937 figure is probably the higher of the two.

However, potatoes were the only important food product which may have shown an increase in per capita consumption from 1928 to 1937. A certain increase also possibly occurred in fat, but fat consumption had been, and remained, very small.

One arrives at an incorrect conclusion in analyzing the trend in sugar consumption by the use of data on the *output* of crystal sugar.[36] The sales of sugar in official trade in 1937 returned 5.7 billion rubles.[37] The price in Moscow was 3.80 and 4.10 rubles per kilogram of crystal and lump sugar, respectively. This indicates sales of about 1,420,000 tons, or 8.5 kilograms per capita. The per capita consumption in 1927/28 was equal to 7.7 kilograms,[38] but the consumption of the urban population was 3.6 times that of the rural population in that year.[39] This implies a large decline in per capita

---

[34] *Soc. Agri.*, pp. 642–43.

[35] The small quantities (about 900,000 tons) of milk shown in Table 14 as sold by the state in 1937 included milk processed into cheese, sour cream, etc. (everything except batter).

[36] *Soc. Agri.*, pp. 89–90.

[37] *Soviet Trade*, stat. handb., 1956, p. 41.

[38] *1st FYP*, I, 104; II, Part 2, 81.

[39] *Ibid.*

consumption of the urban, the rural, or both populations from 1928 to 1937, because of the large increase in the urban population.

Textiles and footwear.—A veil has been lifted from an important item—the utilization of footwear by the population. The statistics on industrial output of textiles did not leave the smallest doubt that, considering the much larger per capita utilization by the urban population, the growth of total population, the large increase in urban population, and the large increase in the utilization of professional uniforms, the per capita utilization of textiles by the farm and non-farm population had declined considerably from 1928 to 1937. The situation was not so clear with reference to footwear, the second major non-food consumers' item.

The official data on the industrial output of what is officially called "leather footwear" have shown a great increase since 1928. According to *Stat. Handb.*, 1956 (p. 87), the increase was from 58 million pairs in 1928 to 182.9 million pairs in 1937. It has been known for a long time that the official statistics of leather footwear included fabric and combination footwear. But the data for this non-leather footwear was scarce and the likelihood remained of an increase in per capita utilization of real leather footwear. The possibility of a large decline in the utilization of such footwear, which would have been in line with the decline in real per capita incomes, seemed to be excluded in any case.

This issue is settled now. Footwear shared the fate of other consumers' goods. New evidence has made it certain that the output of footwear in 1937 (and other years of the Great Industrialization Drive) consisted, to a considerable extent, of something which, while footwear, could not be compared with the footwear produced in 1928. No doubt can exist that per capita utilization of footwear actually declined, perhaps greatly, from 1928 to 1937.

The 1937 output of footwear by the industry is given in *Stat. Handb.*, 1956 (pp. 58–59), at 182.9 million pairs of leather footwear and at 13.4 million pairs of felt footwear, a total of 196.3 million pairs.[40] Let it be assumed that of that number 175 million pairs were sold by the retail trade. The new evidence not previously available, at least to this writer, is that the total return for footwear of the stated categories, i.e., all footwear except rubber footwear, in official trade, was 4,025 million rubles, or an average of only 23 rubles per pair in 1937 (*Soviet Trade*, stat. handb., 1956, p. 42). Mrs. Janet

---

[40] Leather and felt footwear must be combined here because the returns from sales in retail trade in 1937 are given only for both types of footwear together.

Chapman gave the following prices from official sources in 1937 in official trade (in rubles per pair):[41]

Women's leather shoes......................	128.70
Men's leather shoes........................	138.23
Men's rubber-soled leather shoes.............	41.46
Fabric and rubber shoes....................	33.37
Sneakers................................	26.69
Felt boots...............................	75.00

The United States embassy reported the price of women's common shoes to be 48 rubles in January–March, 1937, and 60 rubles for the rest of the year. Leather *boots,* greatly preferred by the peasants and also by many urban workers, cost about 150 rubles per pair in 1937. Unfortunately, neither Mrs. Chapman nor the embassy gave the prices of children's shoes, which are cheap in the USSR; but, as revealed by official data for 1957, the proportion of children's shoes to the total footwear output was small. With ordinary shoes costing 41 rubles (men's), and about 50 rubles (women's), and felt boots 75 rubles, what kind of a mixture had been represented by the footwear sold in 1937 at retail prices in the official trade, which returned an average price of only 23.0 rubles per pair? Even sneakers cost more than this.

Children's shoes, although relatively cheap, and house shoes were not given gratis. The above average return per pair sold and the available retail prices indicate that street footwear for adults is unlikely to have amounted even to one-half of the total amount of footwear sold.[42] This implies a great decline in per capita utilization of footwear by the farm and non-farm population since 1928.

The problem can also be approached from another angle. This writer calculated a price index of footwear in 1937 (1928 equals 100) of 849.[43] Mrs. Chapman's index is 751.[44] Private trade in footwear may still have been large in 1928. Yet the official trade showed a return from footwear other than rubber of 449 million rubles in that year.[45] With Mrs. Chapman's price index, the above amount would have been equivalent to 3,472 million rubles at 1937 prices. Hence,

[41] Mrs. Chapman has kindly granted permission to this writer to use this unpublished data.

[42] The whole return for all footwear sold (leather, fabric, combination, and felt), namely, 4 billion rubles, could buy only about 90 million pairs of such shoes, if the rest were given gratis.

[43] *Essay I,* p. 111.

[44] *Op. cit.,* p. 141. Both Mrs. Chapman's and this writer's price indices include prices of rubber shoes, which increased in price much less than leather footwear during the period analyzed.

[45] This figure, in conjunction with the retail prices and roughly estimated numbers of footwear sold in official trade in that year, indicate that most of the footwear sold in official trade consisted of leather street shoes for adults in that year.

at constant prices, retail trade in footwear in 1937, which in this year was the only such trade in these goods, was only 16 per cent larger than the sales in official trade in 1928 reconverted to 1937 prices, which represented only part of such trade. With the non-farm population, which, in 1928, had a per capita utilization of footwear more than 3.5 times that of the farm population,[46] almost doubling during the period, the above calculation again implies a large decline in per capita utilization of footwear by both the urban and the rural population from 1928 to 1937.

Real Incomes

Wage earners.—The average nominal earnings of all wage earners rose by 77 per cent in 1933–36; from 1932 to 1936 the increase was equivalent to 94 per cent.[47] This rise remained far behind the increase in the prices of consumers' goods, if ration prices are used for the years before derationing. The large rise of the ration prices for bread during this period has already been discussed above. S. N. Prokopovicz[48] compared the cost of food of a worker's family in Moscow in various years, based almost exclusively on the ration prices in those years in which food happened to have been rationed, with the increase in the average wage in all of the USSR. Thus, his index of food costs for 1932 and 1934 is at ration prices and that for October 1, 1935, by which time almost all rationing had been abolished is at practically open-market prices in state and co-operative trade; for 1936 it is entirely at the open-market prices.[49]

Prokopovicz' index of food costs in 1932 and 1934–36 related to the average wage is as follows:[50]

Year	Average Yearly Wage		Cost-of-food Index
	Rubles	Index	
1932.......	1,385	100	100
1933.......	1,513	109	...ᵃ
1934.......	1,768	128	182
1935ᵇ......	2,224	161	401
1936.......	2,856	206	412

ᵃ Prokopovicz, unfortunately, has no figure for 1933.

ᵇ The food cost is as of October 1. The average wage at this date was presumably somewhat higher than the average yearly wage shown in the tabulation.

[46] According to *1st FYP*, II, Part 2, 81, the per capita utilization of footwear in 1927/28 was equal to 0.26 pair for the farm population, and to 0.95 pair for the non-farm population.

[47] *Socialist Construction of the USSR, 1936* pp. 508–11; and *1937 Plan*, pp. 144–45.

[48] *Op. cit.*, pp. 303–6.

[49] It is unfortunate that Prokopovicz used his index as one representing the food costs of the workers. The purchases of wage earners in kolkhoz trade and in commercial state stores, where the prices were several times higher than the ration prices, cannot be entirely ignored in constructing such an index.

[50] Prokopovicz, pp. 303–6. In a later study, Prokopovicz revised the estimates for

Comparison of the trend in the average wage and in food costs as calculated by Prokopovicz shows the astounding result that in 1936, in terms of nominal wages, food obtainable in state and co-operative trade was roughly twice as expensive as food obtained from this trade on rations in the famine year of 1932.[51]

However, Prokopovicz' index was based on ration prices. Sales of food other than beverages in official trade in 1932 amounted to 14.4 billion rubles. State commercial trade of food had not yet been introduced and the sales of food in official trade may have roughly represented sales on rations or, in any case, at approximately ration prices. Turnover in kolkhoz trade in 1932 during the months the kolkhoz markets were permitted (this occurred in May, 1932) was officially estimated at 7.5 billion rubles. The sales in kolkhoz trade during the whole year of 1932 were probably not very much smaller than the official trade in food other than beverages. Since the *volume* of the sales in kolkhoz trade was very small, the weighted prices of all food sales were close to double the ration prices. Hence a food-cost index based exclusively on ration prices was not representative.

It was shown that there were two different tendencies after 1932. On the one hand, the share of sales at high prices in total sales of food was on the increase, because sales in kolkhoz trade were growing much more rapidly than those in official trade and because to sales at high prices in kolkhoz trade were added similar sales in state commercial trade.[52] On the other hand, the spread between the high-price markets and ration prices, after expanding for some time, started to contract, owing to the simultaneous rise in ration prices and the decline in prices in kolkhoz and commercial trade. The development culminated in the abolition of rationing, beginning January 1, 1935, for grain products and October 1, 1935, for almost all other products.

The assumption is made here that in 1937 the prices in kolkhoz trade were 10 per cent lower than in official trade. This was certainly not true of 1935 and 1936. But the excess of prices in kolkhoz trade

---

1932 and 1936 and omitted those for 1933–35. The revised indices for 1936 (1932 equals 100) are: nominal wage—193.4; food costs—438 (see his *National Economy of the USSR*, II, in Russian [New York, 1952], 121).

[51] Correspondingly, Prokopovicz' computation of the number of food baskets purchasable for the average weekly wage shows a decline from 4.8 in 1932 to 3.4 in 1934 and to 2.4 in 1936, or to exactly one-half during the four-year period from 1932 to 1936; 5.6 baskets could have been purchased for an average weekly wage in 1928. The revised numbers of baskets are 5.00 in 1932 and 2.24 in 1936.

[52] State commercial trade was equal to 24 per cent of the total retail trade of the state and co-operatives in 1934, according to Rubinstein *et al.*, *Economics of Soviet Trade* (1950), p. 88.

over the prices in official trade in 1936 was probably only a fraction of the corresponding excess in preceding years.

While the average prices of all sales of food can be assumed to have been close to double the ration prices in 1932, the weighted average prices of all foods sold probably exceeded the open-market prices in official trade by only a few percentage points immediately after derationing.[53]

Thus, Prokopovicz' calculations, which, for 1932, represented ration prices almost exclusively, were, for 1936, very close to the average price of all food. To make the index figures comparable, the one for 1932 would have to be almost doubled. If this were done, the rise in average food prices in 1932–36 becomes roughly equivalent to the rise in the average nominal wage.

Even a correctly computed food-price index is, of course, not a cost-of-living index. The price of vodka, which is included with food in Soviet statistics, but was not considered above, was increasing, after 1932, much more slowly, if at all, than Prokopovicz' food-cost index.[54] Indeed, vodka had become much cheaper in relation to nominal wages during the period.

The cost of most services was likewise rising slowly at this time. The importance of this factor was not large, though, because all services, including housing, accounted for only about 13 per cent of the expenses of a worker's family in 1928[55] and for even less in 1932 and 1933.

The price movement of non-food consumers' goods during the period analyzed is an enigma. The share of these goods in the urban retail trade of the state and co-operative trade, including eating places, declined from 42.3 per cent in 1932 to 37.2 per cent in 1933 and to 30.5 per cent in 1935.[56] This makes a smaller rise in weighted prices of non-food goods than that in food goods likely in those years. The fact that the small amounts of food purchased in cities in 1935 made up 70 per cent of all purchases from official retail trade in that year indicates, of course, by itself, a very precarious situation, but we are interested in ascertaining the changes

---

[53] The sales in kolkhoz trade amounted to 15.6 billion rubles in 1936, sales of food other than beverages in official trade to perhaps 50 billion rubles in the same year. If the prices in kolkhoz trade exceeded those in official trade by 30 per cent, the average of all food prices exceeded those in official trade by 7 per cent.

[54] Sales of beverages in official trade increased at current prices by 84.7 per cent in 1932–37 as against an almost quadrupling for food proper. See *Soviet Trade*, stat. handb., 1956, pp. 40–41.

[55] *Essay I*, p. 102.

[56] *Socialist Construction of the USSR, 1936*, p. 612. The percentage was equal to 50.8 in 1928.

in the rate of precariousness from 1932 and 1933 to 1935 and 1936.[57]

All in all, the total cost-of-living index rose at a slower rate after 1932 than the food-cost index calculated by Prokopovicz and, indeed, possibly not quite as much as the rise in nominal wages.

Thus far we have operated with averages—average increases in wages and average increases in prices. There is, however, frequently serious untruth, or at least serious one-sidedness, in such a procedure. The vital point is that the low-income groups of consumers could afford to buy only negligible amounts at the high prices in kolkhoz trade and state commercial trade during rationing. In kolkhoz trade, a low-wage worker would have to give up two weeks' wages for 2.2 pounds of butter in the beginning of 1934 and not much less than a day's wage for 2.2 pounds of coarse rye bread. Thus, the decline in the prices in kolkhoz trade and state commercial trade during the *Three "Good" Years,* as well as the ultimate elimination of the latter, almost exclusively benefited the high-wage group. *The burden of the great rise in the prices of rationed food in the first place fell on the low-wage worker.*

And this is not all. The various wage groups were affected differently by the differences in the rates of increase in prices of the various foods.

Expenditure for bread always takes up a particularly large proportion of the income of the low-wage groups.[58] This proportion must have been especially large in the period discussed. Hence, the fact that coarse rye bread cost 12.0 kopeks per kilogram (on rations) in 1932, but its price was 1 ruble in January–September, 1935, and 85 kopeks beginning with October of 1935, was a matter of immense significance for these groups (the nominal wage of these groups probably increased by little more than 100 per cent from 1933 to 1936).

The discrimination of the price development against the low-wage groups was so great that it was felt that some action had to be taken. On those two occasions when wages were raised directly to compensate for the rises in prices of food, namely, in May of 1934 and January of 1935, the low-wage groups were the main beneficiaries, but the benefits were inadequate.

[57] No data seem to be available on the share of non-food consumers' goods in official retail trade in 1936. Data for 1937 (but only for the total, and not specifically urban, trade) indicate a small recovery for the share of non-food goods in total official trade from 33.8 per cent in 1935 (*Socialist Construction of the USSR, 1936,* p. 272) to 36.9 per cent in 1937 (*Soviet Trade,* stat. handb., 1956, p. 39).

[58] Sales of bread and other grain products accounted for fully 46 per cent of all sales of food other than beverages in official trade in 1937. They obviously comprised much more than one-half (perhaps two-thirds) of the food purchases from this trade by the low-wage groups.

In the May, 1934, wage increase only low-wage earners participated (about 9 million out of a total number of 23 million wage earners). The average increase in wages for them may have amounted to somewhat more than 10 per cent (the total rise comprised only about 3 per cent of the total wage bill of all wage earners).[59]

The wage increase, effective January 1, 1935, raised the total wage bill by about 10 per cent, but it was granted only to certain occupational groups. The low-wage manual workers in these groups received the same increase *in rubles* as the high-wage manual workers (low- and medium-salaried employees were discriminated against), and this implied a substantially greater wage rise for them in percentage terms.

While exact calculations are impossible, it seems unlikely that the favorable treatment of the low-wage earners in the wage raises came close to compensating for the discrimination against them arising from the price development.*

A minor favorable factor during the *Three "Good" Years* was the expanded output by the urban dwellers of farm products, mainly potatoes, vegetables, and milk. Presumably, low-paid wage and salary earners made a more extensive use of this opportunity than high-paid wage and salary earners, although the size of the city also was an important factor.[60]

As has been shown, the total per capita supplies of farm products appear to have increased only a little more than 10 per cent in 1933–36. Since there was a relatively large increase in real wages in 1936, a decline in real wages from 1933 to 1934 and/or 1935 is indicated, unless the whole burden of the inadequate food supplies was borne by the peasants. The rapid growth of procurements of farm products may be supporting evidence toward the latter conclusion.

[59] Solomon Schwarz, *Labor in the Soviet Union* (New York, 1952), p. 156.

* The phenomenon of the high-wage groups profiting from the disappearance of a great differential between prices in kolkhoz trade and ration prices in official trade was repeated in the 1940's. Long after this book had been completed, this writer succeeded in obtaining an interesting calculation of the effect of this disappearance on the incomes of the various income groups in the 1940's (see "The Summit of Falsehood" in the collection of essays to be published separately). With the same techniques, the terrific injustice to the low-wage groups in the 1930's could possibly be clarified better than is done here.

[60] The opportunity to buy meals at low prices in canteens, which was a certain advantage during rationing, disappeared after derationing. However, the prices in canteens followed the rises in prices of rationed food as long as rationing lasted. The prices in eating places also participated in the jump from rationed to open-market conditions after derationing. Hence, there must have been a parallel development of prices in canteens and in retail trade, first on rations and afterward without them. For this reason, the disappearance of the advantage of the relatively cheap food available in canteens after derationing is not considered an independent aggravating factor here.

The situation in 1934 and 1935 appears even worse on the basis of the data on changes in prices compared with nominal wages in the individual years of the three-year period. It is impossible for this writer to compute the changes in living costs from 1935 to 1936, because all major goods, except for grain products, were still rationed in January–September, 1935. However, a measurable rise in living costs in 1936 seems unlikely. The important grain products declined in price by about 7.5 per cent. A reduction in prices of 16.7 per cent was calculated for the kolkhoz trade.[61] But should no large increase in living costs have occurred in 1936, the large rise in nominal wages (22 per cent) must have been reflected, fully or largely, in the real wage. The greater the improvement in 1936, the worse must have been the real-wage situation in 1934 and 1935. The improvement in 1936 seems, indeed, to have been greater than that during the whole three-year period. Solomon Schwarz's conclusion that "the living standards of labor at the end of 1935, after derationing, cannot have been much lower than at the close of the 1st FYP" [62] may not have been too far from the facts.

Even to suggest for 1935, when industry had already advanced greatly, that real wages could not have been much lower than at the close of the first FYP period, shows the immense change since that time, not very long before, when the Fifteenth Party Conference proclaimed in 1926 that industrialization could not take place at the expense of the workers.

The index of real wages of non-farm labor, as shown in Appendix B, Table II for 1937, is estimated at 60 (1928 equals 100). The corresponding figure for 1936 is about 55 to 56.[63] In chapter 5 above, the real non-farm wage in 1932 has been arbitrarily set at 20 per cent below that of 1937, i.e., at about half that of 1928. The figure may be assumed to apply roughly to the whole period of 1932–35. It then implies an increase from 1933 to 1936 of only about 10 per cent. While all this is inexact, it is the best this writer can do at the moment.

The official claims, including that of Molotov, then chairman of the Council of Ministers, of a more than 100 per cent increase in

[61] Implied in Dadugin and Kagarlitskii, *Organization and Technique of Kolkhoz Market Trade,* p. 5. While the evidence of the authors is used here for all years exclusive of 1938 and 1940 (see pp. 216–20), the responsibility must rest entirely with them.

[62] Schwarz, *op. cit.,* p. 163.

[63] The average nominal wage increased by 9.7 per cent in 1937. Effective June 1 and July 1, 1937, the prices of many non-food consumers' goods were reduced by percentages mostly ranging from 5 to 10. If 20 per cent of the workers' spending was affected to the extent of 7 per cent during six to seven months, the saving from those price reductions was equal to less than 1 per cent of the workers' budget.

wages in real terms in 1932 to 1937 turn out to be immense distortions. Molotov and the others thought nothing of this. It was done for the sake of Communism.

Peasants.—The average real income of the non-farm wage earners in 1937 has been estimated above at about 60 per cent of that in 1928. It was equal to about 65 per cent of the 1928 level on a per capita basis. In the writer's special study of peasant incomes (scheduled to be published about the same time as the present volume) peasant incomes in the same year and on the same basis are calculated to have been 81 per cent of those in 1928. In 1936, wage earners' real incomes were not quite 10 per cent less than in 1937, say 60 per cent of 1928 on a per capita basis. But the difference between 1937 and 1936 incomes was much greater for peasants. Real per capita peasant income in 1938 is estimated in the special study at 64 per cent of that in 1928, and the year 1936 was probably worse for them than 1938. In the absence of reliable data, it may possibly involve not too great an error to assume about the same relative level of real income for 1936 on a per capita basis for both wage earners and peasants, i.e., about 60 per cent of 1928.*

It seems possible that during the *Three "Good" Years* the real incomes of the peasants did not show even the slight improvement assumed for the real incomes of the wage earners. This implies that, in spite of the acute starvation of millions of peasants in the winter of 1932/33, the whole of the peasantry may have been somewhat better off (on a relative and per capita basis) in 1933 than the wage earners. Because the real income of the peasants in 1928 (at equal prices for all groups of the population) was only about 60 per cent as high per capita as that of the wage earners, it may have been impossible during the *All-out Drive*—despite Stalin's wishes—to cut the peasants' real income as much as that of the wage earners.

The rapid enlargement of procurements from a slowly increasing output of farm products during the *Three "Good" Years* seems not to have left much room for an increase in farm income in kind in the latter part of this short period.

As far as the peasants' nominal money income is concerned, each year from 1933 to 1936 brought a substantial improvement. There was, however, the great advantage in favor of the earlier years of the

---

* Again and again it must be emphasized that the estimate of the real incomes of the peasants in 1937 at 81 per cent of those in 1928 does not exclude the possibility that the percentage might actually have been 80, 82, or some other. The figure of 81 is given because this is the result of itemized calculations. All that is hoped for in this estimate, as most others, is that the real incomes of the peasants in 1937 turn out to have been moderately below those in 1928.

period that, although in 1933 the peasants parted with only about 28 per cent as many goods for the kolkhoz trade as they sold in it in 1936, they received, nevertheless, about 75 per cent as much money.[64] It is not very likely that about one-third more money could have bought as many goods for the peasants in 1936 as in 1933. Thus, the outcome is that about *3.6 times as many farm products sold in kolkhoz trade may have bought less in things the peasants needed to buy in 1936 than they bought in 1933 with the money they received for their products in kolkhoz trade.*[65]

Rural and urban population.—Data on official retail trade on the surface seem not to support the idea that real incomes of the peasants were improving less during the *Three "Good" Years* than those of the wage earners. According to official statistics, retail trade (in nominal terms) increased 2.2 times in rural areas from 1933 to 1936 as against 2.1 times in urban areas.[66] This occurred even though the population was about stable in villages and continued to grow in urban areas. Also, the average price increase of consumers' goods from 1933 to 1936 may have been smaller for the rural than for the urban population. Official data on per capita purchases of individual consumers' goods by the rural population even indicated a great improvement in the well-being of this large group. However, these official data turned out to be a falsification.[67] When they are used for what they really are, i.e., as amounts *at current prices,* the per capita *spending* of the rural population increased from 1933 to 1936 by only 88 per cent for cotton fabrics and by only 59 per cent for footwear. While the increases in prices to the rural consumers in those years are unknown, they must have been substantial; and

[64] Calculations of Dadugin and Kagarlitskii, *op. cit.,* p. 5.

[65] The artistry, not to use a harsher word, is amazing with which the Soviet writers bypass the simple idea that the reduction of the prices in kolkhoz trade, so profitable for the purchasers, implied an equal loss to the sellers. The techniques acquired in the middle 1930's came in handy in the late 1940's, when the Soviet Union again entered a prolonged period of declining prices in kolkhoz trade.

[66] *Soviet Trade,* stat. handb., 1956, p. 21.

[67] *Socialist Agriculture of the USSR,* stat. handb., 1939, p. 101. The data, showing per capita utilization of a number of important consumers' goods by the kolkhozniki from 1933 to 1939, year by year, were deliberately presented in such form as to create the impression that they were in physical terms. M. M. Lifits, Deputy Minister of Trade, reproduced the data with a few chosen comments, referring to them as data on "quantities" sold (see his pamphlet, *Soviet Trade* [Moscow, 1948], pp. 84–85). The present writer must confess that for at least five years he considered "quantity" in the above statistics to mean physical quantity. Knowing the small utilization of industrial goods by the peasants in 1937 and 1938, he was compelled to draw even much more pessimistic conclusions about peasant utilization in 1933 and 1934 than was actually the case. Then, suddenly (this happened on October 21, 1954), he realized that "quantities" in those statistics were measured in rapidly rising nominal (current) rubles paid for the goods. This interpretation fits the evidence beautifully.

little, if any, room is left in those data for increase in the *quantities* of cotton fabrics sold per capita by official trade in rural areas;[68] respective sales of footwear certainly declined, probably considerably.

The somewhat larger increase in retail trade in rural than in urban areas may have been brought about by such factors as greatly increased sales of bread and, to some extent, of producers' goods.[69] The very large increase in purchases of bread from the co-operative trade in rural areas (state trade did not operate there) was pointed out in discussing retail trade. It is also reflected in the very large growth of industrial bread production. One can be certain that per capita purchases of bread by the peasants at current prices increased several times more than the purchases of some of the goods officially advertised as a demonstration of rapid growth in the well-being of this population. If bread was not included among the goods for which such data were presented, this was because, as everyone knew, peasants' bread purchases were not a sign of well-being under Russian conditions.

The assumptions that the indices of per capita income of the urban and the rural populations (1928 equals 100) were about the same in 1936 and that the improvement in 1933–36 may have been smaller in rural than in urban areas imply that the decline in real incomes in 1928–33 was not quite as huge in rural areas as it was in urban areas.

While the writer intends to stick to the idea that, on a relative basis, the peasants on the average were somewhat better off than the urban wage earners' families in 1932–34, the evidence is by no means conclusive. It would, indeed, possibly be more advisable to assume the same rate of decline in real incomes for the rural as for the urban population from 1928 to 1932–34.

Whether real incomes of the wage earners and peasants were a little higher or a little lower in 1932 and 1933 (their immensely low incomes in 1936 are certain), it is beyond doubt that the improvement in consumption levels of both major population groups during the *Three "Good" Years* was amazingly small, permitting the great increases in investment in spite of the manifold increase in spending on the armed forces.

[68] A decline in sales of cotton fabrics to the kolkhozniki is indicated by the fact that the total output of these goods by the industry increased only by 19.7 per cent in 1933–36. See *Industry of the USSR*, 1957, p. 329.

[69] Rural official retail trade includes sales of machinery and building materials purchased almost exclusively by the kolkhozy.

National Income

Since all economic sectors, except for agriculture and private consumption, showed a more or less rapid expansion during the *Three "Good" Years,* national income was also enlarged substantially. We have the following rough rates of growth in the components of national income over the three years (in per cent):

By origin:
Industry.   65
Construction. . . . .   69[a]
Agriculture.   6
By allocation:
Investment. . . . .   69[b]
Defense ministries, probably at least. . . . .   400[c]
Personal consumption.   25

[a] Assumed to have been the same as investment.
[b] Gross fixed investment of the state.
[c] The expenditures rose 10.5 times in nominal terms. In Appendix B, Table I, these expenditures are assumed to have grown 7.1 times from 1928 to 1937 in real terms.

An increase of national income by perhaps 45 per cent or slightly more during the three years and by about 13 per cent per year on an average seems likely.

Of the *Three "Good" Years,* the year 1935 was certainly the best. The growth of national income in this year is estimated (see Chart 2 in chapter 1) at 16 per cent, while that in 1934 and 1936 is taken to have been equal to 12–13 per cent each. The difference may have been even somewhat larger than this.

CHAPTER 8

THE PURGE ERA I

Introduction

The evidence presented below shows that for at least three and a half years, from 1937 to mid-1940, the Soviet economy, in spite of all efforts, was unable to make substantial progress. It is, indeed, probable that this paralyzed status lasted for fully four years, until the end of 1940. All endeavors at expansion, particularly of investment, proved futile; in fact, there was even a decline in the latter. It is even more significant that the continued large investment failed to yield anything like adequate results in enlarging industrial output or in anything else. Almost overnight the huge rates of growth during the *Three "Good" Years* were succeeded by a snail-like crawl, stagnation, and even actual declines.

Electric power, coal, non-ferrous metals, and armaments seem to have been the only important producers' goods, the output of which continued to advance more or less substantially. Output of steel, the need for which had become particularly urgent in the last year and a half of the *Purge Era* (for war preparations), practically stagnated. It increased by only 12 per cent in four years; the increase amounted to only 1.5 per cent in the last two years of the period. The output of rolled steel increased by only 4 per cent in the four years from 1936 to 1940. The output of building materials registered a decline all along the line, without exception.

The expansion of agriculture, which had not been rapid in the preceding years, ceased, or practically ceased, after 1937. The rise in freight traffic slowed down to such an extent that it must be considered as having become stagnant for an expanding economy such as that of the Soviets. All so-called quality factors, such as utilization of plant capacities, output per man, production costs, and so on, either displayed only small further improvements or showed deterioration. Completion of investment projects lagged badly. Continued inflation was inevitable under these conditions.

This great slowdown in economic expansion, indeed, the shift from very rapid rates of growth during the *Three "Good" Years* practically to stagnation, is often not fully realized. Insofar as the fact of a slowdown is accepted, the standard explanation is "war preparations." But war preparations mean, in the first place, steel, and more steel. The fact that in spite of large, ever rising investments in heavy industry, steel output, instead of increasing considerably, increased only from 18.1 million tons in 1938 to 18.3 million tons in 1940 excludes war preparations as a decisive factor in the economic development of those eventful years. The mobilization of men into the armed forces may have been a growth-retarding factor, but only a relatively minor one. If at all, it would primarily have affected agriculture.[1] Moreover, a great slowdown from the rates of growth during the *Three "Good" Years* had already occurred in 1937, when it was not yet possible to speak of serious war preparations.

One cannot but assign to the purges a large, and, indeed, a decisive role in the great change from very high rates of growth in 1934–36 to near-stagnation rates in 1937–40. The direct effect of the purges may have been small in agriculture, but here it was augmented by the adverse influence of the policy, initiated in 1938, of curtailing the private economy of the kolkhoz peasants, the same economy which had been, to a very considerable extent, responsible

---

[1] Norman Kaplan of the RAND Corporation spoke of "the rapid shift of resources to munitions production" as the cause of the great slowdown (*Symposium*, pp. 74–75). Kaplan neglected to draw the proper conclusions from his facts, that while the target of the third FYP for rolled steel output in 1938–42 was an annual increase of 10.1 per cent, the average annual rise turned out to be only 1.1 per cent in 1938–40. The third FYP was accepted in the spring of 1939, that is, before the start of World War II outside of the USSR. If the purges and their aftereffects had not prevented war preparations from having their proper effect on steel output, the output of steel would have been greater between the approval of the third FYP and the end of 1940 than that provided for in the FYP.

Donald Hodgman, likewise in 1952 (see the same *Symposium*, p. 241), based his forecast on the trend in Soviet industry in the next ten years on the rates of growth during 1938–40, to which he referred in the customary manner as peacetime years of the third FYP, with an upward adjustment of the rates of growth in these years for the slowing-down effect of military preparations.

The word "purges" seems not to have been pronounced at the conference in Arden, where Kaplan and Hodgman read their papers. Even less were these earthquake-like phenomena taken into consideration in appraising the development of the Soviet economy.

for the preceding recovery.[2] Moreover, the attack on the private peasant economy may have been still another outgrowth of the purges.

In discussing the reasons for the stagnation of those years, the Soviet commentators were expected to speak of everything which might have had the appearance of plausibility, rather than of the real causes of the disaster. In an important article, published as late as 1941 under the revealing title, "The Lagging of the Building Materials' Industry and Ways to Its Liquidation," G. Brodskii wrote:[3]

> The principal causes of the poor work in the building materials' industry were: poor organization of labor in many enterprises, lack of familiarity with the personnel [on the part of management, apparently], incorrect placement of labor, poor quality of the repairing of equipment, accidents, failure to adhere to [proper] technological processes of operation, neglected state of quarries, refuse in plants.[4]

This is, of course, nothing but talk!

As far as the future was concerned, optimism was obligatory: The activities of the NKVD had cleared, and would clear even more, the path to the upswing. This was the standard formula to be adhered to and to advance. The comments by A. Zelenevskii on the 1938 Program in the official journal devoted to planning were concluded in this challenging manner:

> Our glorious Soviet search apparatus has smashed the basic nests of the fascist spies, diversionists, and murderers and will completely destroy all their remnants. The task of the workers in the economic field and of the planners consists of liquidating at the quickest possible rate the consequences of wrecking in the national economy and of insuring the further mighty expansion of the total socialist national economy in the third Stalin FYP period.[5]

One has to work out for oneself the way in which the paralyzing of the economy by the purges actually occurred. Those who believe in such figures as 6 million, or more, persons in concentration camps in 1940 are likely to assign great importance to the removal of such huge numbers, mostly adult males, from the regular and

[2] It has already been pointed out that in addition to the direct effect on this recovery in the form of the enlarged output by the peasants themselves, especially of their output of animal products, the output of collective farms also was influenced favorably by the more satisfied, or less belligerent, state of mind of the kolkhoz peasants.

[3] *Planned Economy*, 1941, No. 3, pp. 87–100.

[4] *Ibid.*, p. 89.

[5] A. Zelenevskii, "Industry in the First Year of the Third FYP Period," *Planned Economy*, 1938, No. 5, p. 27.

productive work of free men to less productive work and, to a certain extent, simply to waste in camps. For most of the inmates of the camps must have been put there after 1936. The present writer estimated the number of camp inmates at the end of 1940 at the smaller figure of 3.5 million (on the basis of the 1941 Plan) [6] and, hence, assigns less significance to concentration camps as a direct cause of economic stagnation. The demoralizing effect of the purges on everybody, in and out of the camps, was presumably much more important. The supercentralization of the organization of the Soviet economy made the adverse effects of the purges particularly harmful.

In whatever way the purges may have affected the economy, the fact that the machine refused to operate effectively is clear from the official statistics. It was mentioned above that investment actually declined, in spite of all efforts to the contrary. But it continued large, and was heavily concentrated on producers' goods industries. The almost complete failure of big investment to become effective resulted from two factors: (*a*) putting capacities into operation which were unproportionately small as compared with the funds invested, and (*b*) reduced utilization of existing capacities, old and new. A good example of these phenomena was presented by no less a witness than Malenkov himself.[7] Cement was in extremely short supply all during the prewar years of the Great Industrialization Drive. Year in and year out, throughout the *Purge Era* and earlier, for that matter, plans demanded great enlargement of cement capacities and output.[8] Only a small part of scheduled capacities could have been completed. Still, the capacities for cement production were enlarged by 22 per cent in the four years of the *Purge Era*. Utilization of capacity, however, declined by 27 per cent, from 88 per cent in 1936 to 64 per cent in 1940, i.e., to such an extent that output was not maintained at the previous level.[9]

The phenomenon was not restricted to cement, however. It was general. But one had to wait for the evidence until the celebration of the Fortieth Anniversary of the Revolution at the end of 1957 (see below in this chapter).

Both the adverse phenomena which operated—(*a*) the splitting of the investment funds among too many projects and, consequently,

---

[6] "Labor and Output in Soviet Concentration Camps," *Journal of Political Economy*, October, 1951, p. 416.

[7] G. M. Malenkov, Report to the Eighteenth Party Conference, February, 1941. See *Planned Economy*, 1941, No. 3, p. 11.

[8] For example, *1937 Plan*, p. 92, asked for an increase in output of cement by 30 per cent. The 1941 plan even scheduled its output to rise by 38 per cent in one year. See Brodskii, *op. cit.*, p. 91.

[9] Malenkov, *op. cit.*, p. 11.

the small amount of capacities entering operation and (*b*) the reduced utilization of capacities—were probably traceable to the same factors. Few dared to make decisions, and this led to the slowdown in the utilization of capacities (the second phenomenon). Nobody in the know dared to object when irresponsible people decided to start more and more investment projects (the first phenomenon).

A feature of the *Purge Era* almost as noteworthy as the great slowdown of economic growth was the increase in the money incomes of the population. This is especially true of wage and salary earners. In only two years (1937 and 1938), the average nominal wage rose not much less than during the *Three "Good" Years*. While the share of private consumption in national income declined during the *Three "Good" Years,* it certainly increased in 1937 and 1938. Two factors may have been the cause for this phenomenon: (*a*) some weakening of the regime, and (*b*) a desire on its part to show that liquidation of the "wreckers" was in the best interests of the laborer. Both factors probably operated, with the first presumably having had the greater weight.

The great *Purge Era* of the late 1930's is here believed to have started in September of 1936, when the trial of L. Kamenev and others took place.[10] At what time the purges expanded to embrace economic organizations and when they started to affect economic progress adversely is difficult to ascertain. Stalin came out with his accusations against wrecking on the economic front in his speech of March 3, 1937. But he spoke of the purges not only as a matter of the future but also as a matter of the *past*.[11] For convenience in handling the statistical material, the *Purge Era* is taken to have started on January 1, 1937, on the economic front.

The full effect of the purges on the economy did not, naturally, come in full strength at once. There was much automatism in its operation. Although disorganization spread rapidly, it took some time. In the second half of 1937 the economy was also considerably helped by a bountiful harvest. So the whole year of 1937 turned out materially better than each of the three subsequent years of the *Purge Era.*

An upturn in industrial output is officially supposed to have

[10] There is reason to believe that the murder of Kirov, which occurred in 1934 and is ascribed by many to Stalin, was the first act of the *Purge Era*. This may be so, but it is difficult to see any strong effect on the national economy from this act, or from what immediately followed, before sometime late in 1936.

[11] See text of his speech in *Planned Economy*, 1937, No. 2. The preamble to the 1937 Plan, dated March 24, 1937 (*1937 Plan*, p. 1) said that the wrecking operations of the Japanese-German-Trotsky agents in industry and transportation had already been revealed in 1936.

occurred in the second half of 1940. However, the conspicuous absence of statistical data makes one suspicious. Such important sources as the major speech on the occasion of the anniversary of Lenin's death,[12] or an editorial in *Planned Economy*,[13] spoke of an upturn only in the coal and metallurgical industries. The resolution of the Eighteenth Party Conference on the 1941 Plan claimed, it is true, that "the rates of growth of industrial output were rising month by month during 1940." [14]

One cannot but acknowledge that, while the actual purges seem to have been discontinued in 1938, the economy was only able to start recovering from the prostration they caused after at least two more full years had passed. The year 1939 was a very poor year. It is particularly significant that the output of consumers' goods could have made some progress,[15] but output of producers' goods, so far as data are available, was completely stagnant.[16]

If the claimed upturn in industrial production in the second half of 1940 did occur, the reason, or one of the reasons, might have been the drastic measures introduced in that year to insure labor for the non-farm economy. By the law of June 26, 1940, the seven-hour workday was replaced by an eight-hour workday, the six-day week gave way to the seven-day week, and wage earners were prohibited from leaving their jobs. By a regulation following shortly afterward, specialists could even be transferred without their consent from one job or place to another. It seems not impossible that all these measures had, to some extent, a favorable effect on the output per man and, consequently, the volume of industrial and other activities. The greater the progress, if any, in the second half of 1940, however, the stronger was the effect of the purges on the economy in the first half of the year. The year 1940 as a whole showed nothing to brag about.

[12] *Planned Economy*, 1941, No. 1, p. 4.

[13] *Ibid.*, No. 5, p. 3.

[14] *Ibid.*, No. 3, p. 57.

[15] Cotton cloth, plus 8.8 per cent; wool cloth, plus 8.1 per cent; footwear, plus 6.6 per cent. But the catch of fish increased by only 1.5 per cent, while output of butter and crystal sugar declined by 4.0 and 27.5 per cent, respectively (the latter decline was due to unfavorable weather conditions). All data are from *Economy of the USSR in 1956*, pp. 89, 91, 93, 96–98.

[16] Declines were registered in pig iron, steel, rolled steel, tractors, cement, and paper; increases in output of electric power, coal, fertilizer, and in shipments of timber (see *Stat. Handb.*, 1956, pp. 62, 63, 65, 67, 71, 75, 78, 79, 81, 88). Tractors are, of course, not representative of all machinery. The official index for output of all machinery including other metal processing at "unchangeable 1926/27 prices" shows the immense growth of 75 per cent from 1937 to 1940 (see *Industry of the USSR*, 1957, p. 203), but little, if any, use can be made of this figure.

On technical considerations, the *Purge Era* is considered to have lasted from January 1, 1937, to the end of 1940.

Planning

The *Three "Good" Years* certainly yielded everything that Stalin may have wished. One of the features of the period in the realm of planning was that the annual plans did not display the usual immense discrepancies between targets and fulfilments. A number of annual-plan targets were actually exceeded. Stalin, with his lack of understanding of the practically attainable, did not ascribe target fulfilment to the good functioning of the economic system, including planning. On the contrary, he saw the reason for whatever fulfilment there was in the fact that the targets were too low, that "they [the planners] do not take into account the immense reserves and possibilities contained in our national economy. . . . It is necessary to smash and dispense with the . . . foul theory which declares that systematic fulfilment of the economic plans excludes wrecking. . . . If the wreckers had not been unmasked and expelled, the matter of plan fulfilment would have been in a much poorer state." [17]

No serious work could, of course, be expected in the way of planning in an atmosphere such as that of the *Purge Era,* especially from an organization which during a short period lost every responsible person.[18]

Even the formalities of planning could not have been fulfilled for years. The planners scrambled more or less successfully through the preparation of the third FYP, having it approved by the Party in April, 1939, that is, with a delay of over one and a quarter years. The FYP was never approved by the government nor was it ever published in final form. Possibly it was never put into such form.

[17] Stalin, Report to the Plenary Session of the Central Committee, delivered on March 3, 1937. See *Planned Economy,* 1937, No. 2, pp. xv–xvii.

[18] The writer wishes he had space to describe in some detail the tortures to which the planning and statistical organizations were subjected during the purges. On the occasion of the twentieth anniversary of the Gosplan in February, 1941, A. Zelenevskii wrote: "In the last three years fundamental changes have occurred in the work of the USSR Gosplan, which have great importance in principle. During this time, the personnel of the Gosplan was changed almost completely" ("Current Tasks of the Gosplan," *Planned Economy,* 1941, No. 2, p. 17). He should have said four rather than three years. Most of those at the top of the organizations involved had already disappeared in 1937. See also the lead article in *Planned Economy,* 1938, No. 2, pp. 18–30, entitled "The Work of the Gosplan to the Level of New Tasks."

The disorganization of the Gosplan by the purges was, *inter alia,* reflected in its monthly journal. The March, 1937, issue of *Planned Economy* (editors: Berilin, Gaister, Kraval, Nachalin, and Troitskii) got the imprimatur on May 5. For the April issue (editor: editorial board) the date of the imprimatur was June 29. A five-month delay occurred before the next issue, which was put out as the May-June issue (editor: M. A. Yampolskii), with the date of the imprimatur October 17.

The annual 1937 Plan was only approved on March 29, 1937.[19] Its size was not much more than one-tenth of that of the 1936 Plan. No single economic plan seems to have been released in 1938, 1939, or 1940.[20] One is, moreover, probably justified in believing that these plans did not actually exist as single economic plans, even in secrecy.[21] The fact is that when, in 1941, the government was able to work out a single annual plan without too much delay, the plan was publicly discussed at the Eighteenth Party Conference (February, 1941) as well as in the press.[22]

As far as plans for individual economic sectors were concluded in those years, some of them were released too late to be of much use.[23] There is no assurance that under the conditions prevailing during the *Purge Era* the various targets of plans worked out by different commissariats and agencies would have been mutually tied in, even if they had been worked out simultaneously and combined in a document having the name "National Economic Plan . . . in . . . Year." A proper tie-in was even less probable in plans which were concluded at different times.[24] The discrepancies in what was called

[19] See *1937 Plan*, p. 40.

[20] They are not to be found in *Bulletin of Financial-Economic Legislation*, the place where such documents were normally published in those years. For 1938, this publication contained a short preliminary program for centralized industry and freight traffic for the year 1938 and for the first quarter of the same year. It was released on November 30, 1937 (Nos. 32–33, pp. 2–3), and obviously implied that a comprehensive single plan would be worked out at some future time. However, only plans for individual industrial ministries (heavy, food, forestry, light industries) and for individual sectors (fixed investment of the state, animal husbandry) were issued from time to time in subsequent months.

If everything had been all right, the targets of the third FYP for 1939 would have served as the 1939 Plan, but the published document on the third FYP did not contain any year-to-year data and the source which mentioned the 1939 Plan (*Planned Economy*, 1939, No. 7, p. 3) was careful not to give a single figure of this plan.

[21] While a government order spoke of the preparation of the 1940 Plan (see below), the writer has found no mention of the completed plan.

[22] Large parts of two issues of *Planned Economy*, 1941, Nos. 3 and 4, were devoted to it. But the plan itself was not published. A copy marked "confidential" had become available to the Western world via the invading German army.

[23] The first mention of the 1938 Plan for fixed investment that this writer could discover is in *Planned Economy*, 1938, No. 6, pp. 31–41, released in July (the plan itself was apparently never released). By this time, most constructions had been under way for a long time. The issuing of an order, "On a State Plan of Development of Animal Husbandry in 1938," on June 16, 1938, made even less sense. By the time the order was passed down to the actual performers, the breeding of horses and cattle for that year had long been completed.

[24] Offhand, one would expect that a 1938 target for raising fixed investment of the state by more than 30 per cent (*Planned Economy*, 1938, No. 6, p. 62) would call for a much greater increase in railway loadings than 6 per cent, the 1938 target for these loadings (*ibid.*, p. 58). Most targets of the *Purge Era* were excessive. The extent of exaggeration is an arbitrary matter. Hence the extent of exaggeration allowed by the various commissariats in their respective plans must inevitably have differed widely. The Gosplan USSR was not in proper shape to correct this.

the 1939 Plan, or in what existed of the 1939 Plan, were so large that the Council of People's Commissars emphasized them and ordered that they should not be repeated in working out the 1940 Plan.[25] (This order throws an unfavorable light on the third FYP as a whole as well, because if everything went all right, the 1939 Plan would have been part of the third FYP.)

Quarterly plans still existed in 1938, but the plan for the second quarter apparently was not yet ready in mid-April.[26] These quarterly plans were almost as fragmentary as the Program for 1938 mentioned above. So far as the parts covered by the Program are involved, the quarterly plans were, indeed, probably based on it. The absence of *single* annual plans for 1939 and 1940 makes probable the absence of single quarterly plans, although quarterly plans for individual economic sectors may well have existed.

It must be granted that in the actual planning the planners did not, as they were supposed to do, calculate the activities of the NKVD as a factor stimulating economic growth. The targets for yearly performances accepted during the *Purge Era,* as far as they are known, not only did not exceed those of the *Three "Good" Years,* but actually called for smaller rates of growth than the latter.[27] But the rates of growth, if any, attained in any year of the *Purge Era* were so small that even less ambitious targets inevitably turned out to be vastly unrealistic.

The targets of the third FYP also might have been even larger, had it not been for the purges. It would be futile to speculate on this. The third FYP asked for plenty as it stands. Farm output, for example, was to rise 52 per cent over the output of 1937 with its excellent weather, but in 1940, not a bad year weatherwise, this output, on a most favorable estimate, was in the same territory only at the 1937 level.

The handling of the draft of the third FYP by the Eighteenth Party Congress (April, 1939) is simply a curiosity. In approving it, the Congress passed the "considered" decision to raise the targets for certain most important goods (all of them producers' goods except "leather" footwear), but mostly by small margins. A target of the Gosplan draft of the third FYP, to raise steel output from 1937

[25] *Planned Economy,* 1940, No. 3, p. 27.

[26] At least an article dealing with industry in the first quarter of the year in *Planned Economy,* 1938, No. 5, pp. 8–14, does not contain a trace of it.

[27] The targets of the 1938 Program, for example, by and large repeated those of the 1937 Plan (targets of the 1938 Program in A. Zelenevskii, "Industry in the First Year of the Third FYP Period," *Planned Economy,* 1938, No. 5, pp. 15–37; targets of the 1937 Plan in *1937 Plan*) and, thus, they were smaller than the latter by the portions fulfilled in 1937. Zelenevskii spoke of a plan rather than the Program, but he should not have been expected to be exact.

to 1942 by 56 per cent, under the circumstances of those years was nothing but a bad joke. Yet the Eighteenth Party Congress decided to raise the target by 2 percentage points (see Chart 13).[28] For cement we have: target of the draft of the third FYP, 10 million tons; target as approved by the Eighteenth Party Congress, 11 million tons; 1940 production in the pre-1939 territory, 5.2 million tons.

CHART 13

PURGE ERA: FIVE-YEAR TARGETS AND THREE-YEAR FULFILMENTS *
(Increases, in per cent)

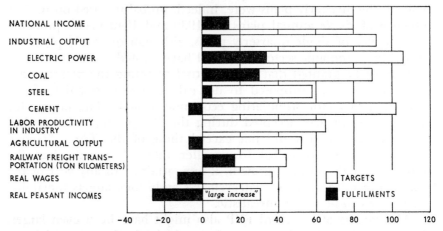

* The targets are those of the third FYP for 1942 as compared with 1937. Since they were not approved before April, 1939, and, furthermore, since the progress, if any, in 1938 and the first quarter of 1939 was but small, the targets should properly be treated as four-year targets. Fulfilment data are for 1940 in terms of 1937.

Railway freight is in ton-kilometers. Peasant incomes are per capita. The targets of the third FYP are from the resolution of the Eighteenth Party Congress, here quoted from *Problems of Economics*, 1939, No. 3, p. 92 and passim; otherwise they are from *3d FYP*, draft, *passim*. Fulfilment figures for industrial output in physical terms (except for cement) and for railway freight transportation are official. The other fulfilment figures are estimates by this writer. Labor productivity presumably did not increase.

A noteworthy command was included in the Program for 1938 and the first quarter of 1938 (see note 20, p. 184). It prohibited the raising of the set targets and the adding of the unfulfilled targets of past quarter-years to the targets of the current quarter-years. But the plans for the third and fourth quarters of 1938, evidence for which happens to be at hand, did exactly this. An editorial in *Planned Economy* (1938, No. 9, p. 9) stated that "in the fourth quarter a drastic improvement must be attained in the work of those sectors of the national economy which are behind in fulfilment of the

[28] Resolution of the Eighteenth Party Congress on the third FYP, here quoted from *Problems of Economics*, 1939, No. 3, p. 93.

annual plan." The target for industrial output in the fourth quarter of 1938 called for an increase of 21.1 per cent as compared with the fourth quarter of 1937. For the third quarter an increase of even 28 per cent over the corresponding period of the preceding year was ordered.[29] The annual Program provided for an increase of 17.2 per cent in output of state industry.[30]

The lack of understanding on the part of the "leadership" to which the planners were subjected, long after the end of the actual purges, is well characterized by the fact that in February, 1941, with the results of the purges not yet overcome and war imminent, there came, like a *deus ex machina,* an order of the Central Committee of the Party and of the government to the Gosplan USSR prescribing the commencement of work on a long-term, so-called general plan.[31] The idea must have come from Stalin, whom nobody dared to contradict in spite of the obvious absurdity of the undertaking.[32] Still, all that the journal of the Gosplan found to say about the project took only three paragraphs, one of which consisted of two lines.[33] This short comment was all the action that seems to have been taken in fulfilment of the order.

Investment

Total investment.—It would be futile to try to guess whether Stalin foresaw that his basic idea, his god, would have to be sacrificed in favor of the task of getting rid of his adversaries. But the fact is that investment, instead of rising more than anything else, remained stagnant during the *Purge Era*—albeit in the face of a slow rise in the national economy. Hence, the share of investment in the national economy was reduced, over the *Purge Era,* proportionately.

Fixed investment of the socialized sector is far the greatest part of the total investment in the USSR. Table 15 lists the existing estimates of this investment in 1936, 1937, and 1940. The estimates at the so-called prices and norms of 1936/37 should be relatively more reliable, because these estimates were used in the budget, a serious document. The difficulty with using the data at the prices and norms of 1936/37 is that various compensations and additions

[29] *Planned Economy,* 1938, No. 6, p. 26.

[30] *Ibid.,* No. 5, p. 20.

[31] *Pravda,* February 22, 1941.

[32] In the 1920's, the early days of planning, it was assumed that a long-term general plan must be the indispensable foundation of planning. The FYP's were to be merely segments of the general plan and the yearly plans segments of the FYP's. After several years of futile attempts to work out a general plan, the idea died in the first half of 1930 without even an announcement.

[33] *Planned Economy,* 1941, No. 2, p. 25.

TABLE 15

Purge Era: Fixed Investment in the Socialized Sector*
(In billions of rubles)

YEAR	Official 1936/37 Costs[a]	N. Voznesenskii, Current Costs[b]	Stat. Handb., 1956 (p. 158), Prices of July 1, 1955			Essay I,[c] Total Net Investment, 1926/27 Prices
			Total	Construction and Installation	Equipment	
1936.............	31.8	...	38.1	32.8	5.3	...
1937.............	29.5	30	33.8	25.0	8.8	20.0
1940.............	38.4	43	43.2	34.3	8.9	21.5
Percentage increase, 1937 to 1940.....	30.2	43.3	27.8	37.2	1.1	7.5

* The data cover practically only the pre-1939 territory.
  a Kaplan's data from RAND RM-735, Table III. They include capital repairs but do not include the invest-ment of the collective farms. Capital repairs were estimated as follows: for 1936, they were assumed to have been equal to those in 1937; for 1940, the estimates of capital repairs were made from the planned figure with a dis-count equivalent to the rate of underfulfilment of the plan for fixed investment as a whole.
  b *War Economy of the USSR during the Patriotic War,* 1948, p. 12.
  c See "Corrigenda Sheet," *Essay I,* p. 85.

to those prices and norms were permitted from time to time and that nobody took the trouble to incorporate the compensations and additions into the basic prices and norms. There is also a suspicion that the purges brought into existence some inflationary factors, which affected the value in these prices and costs and were not taken care of by the compensations and additions.

The estimates of the fixed investment in *Stat. Handb.,* 1956, allegedly at constant prices, cannot be taken seriously.[34] The esti-mates of the handbook imply almost the same prices after July 1, 1955, as at the end of the 1920's. The great inflations of the *All-out Drive* and of World War II appear in it as having been almost fully wiped out.* The year-to-year changes implied in the handbook's esti-mates for the specific period 1937–40 may still be correct and must be examined. It is fortunate that the source gave separate estimates for investment in construction (including installation) and in equip-ment.

According to official data, construction (including installation) in-creased by 37.2 per cent in 1937–40. From 1936 to 1940 the increase only amounted to 4.5 per cent, it is true, according to the same data.

In order to construct, building materials are needed. Data on the

[34] They are discussed in greater detail in *Commentary,* pp. 137–47.

* The decision to convert every 10 rubles into 1, effective January 1, 1961, is an official recognition of the great amount of inflation which occurred during the Great Industrialization Drive. Specifically, it officially stamps the series for fixed investment of the state since 1918, only published in 1956, and probably produced in 1955, as what it is, a great lie.

output of building materials in this period (Chart 14) show a decline from 1936 and 1937 to 1940 all along the line. Cement production went down by more than 10 per cent from 1936 to 1940, and an even greater reduction occurred in the output of bricks. A very large decline in output of soft roofing material and an astounding reduction in the output of window glass to less than one-half of the

CHART 14

**INVESTMENT IN CONSTRUCTION AND INSTALLATION VS.
OUTPUT OF BUILDING MATERIALS, 1936–40 ***

(1937 = 100)

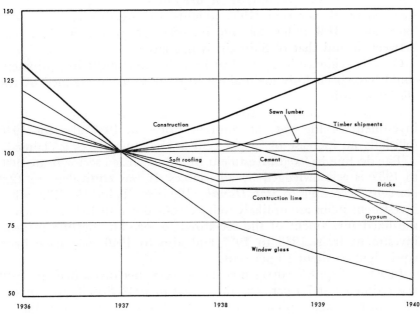

* Data for construction, which includes installation, of the socialized sector at prices of July 1, 1955, from *Stat. Handb.*, 1956, p. 158. Data for the industrial output of the various building materials from *Industry of the USSR*, 1957, *passim.*

The 1940 output figures exclude the Baltic States (data from *Industry of the USSR*, 1957). For cement the figure indicated for the pre–1939 territory was used. See note "b" to Table 20.

1936 level are officially reported. The only exception was a negligible increase in output of sawn lumber from 1937 to 1940 (from 1936 to 1940 a decline occurred even in this).

It was inevitable that, with the fall in output of building materials, construction in 1940 should show a decline as compared with 1937. Any stockpiles of building materials at the end of 1937 must have been practically exhausted before 1940.

The recent official calculations indicate the fantastic increase of

66 per cent in equipment used in investment (the figures for it include "other" investment) in only one year from 1936 to 1937 (Table 15). Thereafter there was no further increase for fully three years.

According to estimates by D. Shimkin and F. Leedy, output of all machinery, which is supposed to include armaments, declined by 2.7 per cent from 1937 to 1940; specifically the military end-items showed a substantial increase, while the output of the residual machinery went down by almost 20 per cent.[35] The calculations of the National Bureau of Economic Research, in general less reliable, point to a decline in output of machinery of 27 per cent (1928 weights) or 32 per cent (1955 weights) during the same period.[36] Since the NBER index does not include armaments, the difference between it and that of Shimkin is not large.

On this evidence it is not clear how the investment in equipment could have been fully maintained in those years, as claimed by the official statistics.

It is possibly only cowardice to assume the relatively large fixed investment of the state at constant prices in 1937 also for 1940 (officially an increase of 28 per cent at the same prices is claimed).

The decline in fixed investment in the socialized sector from 1936 to 1937 is acknowledged by all sources. It was equivalent to 12.8 per cent, according to *Stat. Handb.*, 1956 (see Table 15). The other investment items are unlikely to have gone down in 1937 as much as the fixed investment of the socialized sector. The decline in total investment from 1936 to 1937 and also to 1940 may have been equivalent to about 10 per cent.

In *Essay I* (p. 85, corrigenda sheet), total net investment in 1940 was estimated at 7.5 per cent above that in 1937. Specifically, investment in the fixed capital of the socialized sector was estimated at 17 per cent above (*Essay I*, p. 108). The estimate of total fixed investment of the state in 1940 is now cut, so that it equals that for 1937. The declines in investment in the working capital of state enterprises and in the investment of the kolkhozy (*ibid.*) are retained. But the increase in "others," which was estimated at only 0.6 billion rubles at 1926/27 prices, is raised by 0.9 billion rubles. Total net investment in 1940 is accepted as having been equal to that in 1937.

No year-to-year analysis of the data on investment during the

---

[35] See *Automotive Industries*, 1958, No. 1, Table I.

[36] The NBER calculations cover only civilian machinery. But this fact is all right for the situation presently discussed; all machinery which is used in construction and investment, even such of a military nature, is presumably classed as civilian in the USSR.

Purge Era will be undertaken here. It is, however, possible that the favorable effect of the bountiful 1937 crop, coupled with the setback in investment in the preceding year, permitted making up fully for the decline in the latter in 1937 by an increase in the following year. The year 1939, apparently, brought a renewed setback, and 1940, in spite of the recovery claimed for the second half, possibly just held its own, or also declined.[37] But the total net investment of 1940 probably exceeded those of the two preceding years, owing to the large stockpiling of consumers' goods (as reserves for the armed forces) attained by cuts in personal consumption.

The data in Chart 14 are, *inter alia,* another good illustration of the operation of "the law of the socialized economy expanding proportionately according to plan," discovered by Stalin and emphasized in his *The Economic Problems of Socialism in the USSR,* which was released about half a year before his death and was proclaimed a great enrichment of the Marx-Engels-Lenin theories. No trace of the operation of this law can, of course, be discovered in the data on investment in 1936–40. The existence of such a law is one of the many Stalin-Hitler types of "truth," put into circulation with the idea that the more frequently a lie is repeated, the more chance it has of being believed.

By sector.—Seeing the futility of their efforts to expand all fixed investment at the rates at which it had only recently been increasing, those in power concentrated their efforts on investment in heavy industry even more. Investment in this citadel of communism was to be enlarged, or at least maintained (in real terms), even at the expense of wrecking other economic sectors. The evidence for 1939 (Table 16) is particularly interesting in this connection. The drastic cuts of investment in agriculture, trade, and procurements, and even in transportation and communications[38] in that year were announced in Zverev's report on the 1939 budget at the end of May,[39] i.e., *before* the start of World War II outside of the USSR. This makes it probable that considerations of defense were not decisive in those cuts.

[37] These variations are indicated by official data at prices and norms of 1936/37.

[38] Investment in defense industries is mostly included under investment in industry. But some such investment is likely to have also been included in some of the items which make up the "balance" in Table 16. It is, therefore, noteworthy that this "balance" is the only item other than industry showing an increase in 1939 and 1940 compared with 1938. This increase was, moreover, quite substantial.

[39] A. G. Zverev, *State Budgets of the USSR, 1938–45* (Moscow, 1946), p. 49. The existence of a plan for fixed investment does not necessarily imply the existence of a single economic plan for that year. The Soviet budget cannot be completed without some plan for fixed investment.

TABLE 16

Purge Era: FIXED INVESTMENT OF THE STATE BY SECTOR*

(In billions of rubles)

Sector	1936	1937	1938	1939 Plan	1940 Plan	1941 Plan
Total......................	35.50	33.20	35.70	34.73	36.13	46.27
Industry......................	15.97	15.01	17.08	17.59	19.19	27.48
Agriculture......................	3.88	4.15	3.45	1.59	1.23	1.06
Transportation and communications	7.23	6.02	7.00	4.96	5.44	9.21
Trade and procurements..........	1.05	0.91	0.76	0.49	0.37	0.51
Balanceᵃ......................	7.37	7.11	7.41	10.10	9.90	8.01

* Kaplan, *op. cit.*, Table 6, p. 51. The data were presumably in prices and norms of 1936/37.

ᵃ In Kaplan's table these expenses are listed as "social-cultural services and administration." Actually, they consisted to a large extent of items unspecified in the official source and were presumably made up in the first place by constructions of the Defense Ministries, as well as those of the NKVD. In the 1939 budget, for example, the investments in house, communal, and social-cultural constructions were shown at 2,330 million rubles, and unspecified investments were to amount to 7,770 million rubles (see A. G. Zverev, *State Budgets of the USSR, 1938–45* [1946] p. 49).

Within industry, investment in consumers'-goods industries declined from 3,276 million rubles according to the 1936 Plan to 2,783 million rubles (fulfilment) in 1939, i.e., quite substantially, especially if the intermediate rise in investment costs is considered.

The largest increases in investment in 1939 were registered in coal, iron, metallurgy, building materials, and, especially, in petroleum.[40] It is important to note that the increase in investment appropriations in these items likewise occurred before World War II started outside the USSR. In view of the particularly strong efforts to enlarge the output of heavy industry by way of investment, the miserable results in increasing output of this very sector appear the more striking.

Putting capacities into operation and utilization of capacities.— Table 17 shows at a glance how big plans for increase in capacities and, for that matter, in output were reduced practically to nothing, or in any case melted greatly in reality, during the *Purge Era.* Strange as it may seem, capacities for the output of "leather" footwear, largely a consumers' good, made the best showing. The five-year targets for increase in them were one-half fulfilled in three and a half years and output increased more than capacities. Cement appears the worst among the items listed. Little more than 20 per cent of the planned increase in capacities was realized in the three and a half years of the operation of the third FYP, and what additional capacity was provided, and more, was made ineffective through reduced utilization of all capacities, old and new.

[40] Kaplan, RAND RM-735, Table 11.

TABLE 17

Purge Era: PUTTING INDUSTRIAL CAPACITIES IN OPERATION AND
UTILIZATION OF CAPACITIES

ITEM	PLANNED INCREASE IN CAPACITIES IN 5 YEARS[a]		PUTTING OF CAPACITIES IN OPERATION IN 3½ YEARS[b]	INCREASE IN OUTPUT IN 1937–40[c]	
	Quantities	Per Cent	Quantities	Quantities	Per Cent
Electric power (million kw.).........	9.1	112	2.8	. . .	33
Coal (million tons).......	120.0	64	54.0	38	30
Pig iron (million tons)....	8.7	53	2.8	0.4	3
Steel (million tons)......	10.0	49	3.5	0.6	3.3
Rolled steel (million tons)	7.0	44	2.2	0.1	0
Cement (million tons)....	4.3	59	0.9	decline	decline
Cotton mills, spindles (million units).........	3.6	46	1.15	. . .	15[d]
"Leather" footwear (million pairs).........	39	25	20	28	15

[a] From January 1, 1938, to January 1, 1943. See *3d FYP*, draft, p. 121. Since the third FYP was not approved before March, 1939, and the putting of capacities in operation in 1938 was very small, the targets for putting in operation of the third FYP were more nearly those of a four-year plan.

[b] *Attainments*, p. 212. There is a certain ambiguity in the source, but it is hoped that the meaning is grasped correctly here.

[c] *Economy of the USSR in 1956*, pp. 60–64. The figures for 1940 include part of output of the new territories. Cement is the only commodity to which this remark does not apply. The remark is of greater importance with reference to footwear and possibly spindles, than to the other commodities shown.

[d] Output of cotton fabrics.

But the developments in steel are the most instructive. Of the planned increase of 7 million tons in capacities for rolled steel during five years, a capacity equal to only 2.2 million tons was completed in three and a half years. This great shortfall was crowned with reduced utilization of all capacities for steel production and, as the outcome, output of rolled steel stagnated almost completely.

While the target for putting blast furnaces in operation failed by a great margin, capacities for a 2.8 million tons output were completed. But for some reason or other, a more than normal number of blast furnaces stopped operating during the *Purge Era*. The total number of operating blast furnaces consequently declined from 112 on January 1, 1938, to 99 on January 1, 1941. The total capacity of furnaces in operation increased only from 53,073 to 58,340 cubic meters.[41] In addition there was a deterioration in the utilization of capacities of the blast furnaces, the coefficient of utilization increasing from 1.11 in 1937 to 1.19 in 1940;[42] stoppages of blast furnaces also were enlarged moderately. The result was the same as with

[41] *Industry of the USSR*, 1957, p. 120.

[42] *Ibid.*, p. 118. The coefficient is measured in volume of blast furnaces per ton of produced pig iron. So an increase in the coefficient indicates a negative development.

steel: output of pig iron was rising only 1 per cent per year on the average at that crucial time for it.

No data are available on the increase in number of projects in process of construction. But the fact that this increase was unnecessarily large is obvious from the fact that the putting of capacities into operation was very large during World War II, relative to both the fixed investment in this period and the entering of capacities into operation during the third FYP. As is obvious from Table 18,

TABLE 18

Putting Industrial Capacities in Operation in Specified Periods*

Item	1st FYP Period	2d FYP Period	3½ Years of the 3d FYP Period	July 1, 1941, through End of 1945
Electric power (million kw.)..........	2.8	3.6	2.8	4.7
Coal (million tons)...................	57	78	54	111
Pig iron (million tons)...............	4.5	7.3	2.8	6.2
Steel (million tons)...................	2.8	7.6	3.5	8.7
Rolled steel (million tons)............	1.7	7.9	2.2	4.6
Cement (million tons)................	2.2	0.9	0.9	1.8
Spindles (thousand units).............	1,000	650	1,152	782
Footwear, leather (million pairs)......	25	44	20	50
Sugar, crystal, daily capacity (thousand quintals)	80	118	86	1,013

* *Attainments*, p. 212. The data in the last column pertain to a greatly varying territory.

showing the putting of capacities into operation in the various periods, the increase in steel capacities during World War II was 2.5 times the increase during the three and a half years of the third FYP period. It even surpassed the capacities put into operation during the second FYP period, clearly owing to accumulation of great numbers of unfinished capacities right before the start of war.

Table 18 also demonstrates the great inadequacy of capacities put into operation during the three and a half years of the third FYP as compared with those put into operation during the second and even during the first FYP. If the considerable expansion of the output level from 1932 to 1940 is taken into account, the *Purge Era* made a poor showing with reference to capacities put into operation even as compared with the disastrous *All-out Drive* period.

It is very significant that in an economy supposed to expand smoothly according to plan, capacities for output of footwear were enlarged during World War II more than in any preceding period.[43]

[43] The claims for the volume of fixed investment and capacities put into operation during World War II shown in Table 18 seem somewhat suspicious. The claim for new capacities for processing sugar beets during World War II is simply not understandable.

Agriculture

The attack on the kolkhozniki's economy.—The principal effect of the purges on agriculture may have been that the Party decided the time was ripe for an attack on the private economy of the kolkhoz peasants, which largely carried the preceding recovery in farm production. The analysis of consumption in chapter 7 clearly shows that the supplies of farm products made available to the population by the state by way of retail trade in 1937, i.e., in the year immediately preceding the attack on the peasants, were deplorable, and that specifically with reference to *fresh* milk and potatoes the state had practically nothing to offer (the situation was extremely unsatisfactory also with reference to fresh meat, vegetables, and fruits). But this was disregarded, although in general more attention was given to the consumers' needs in the first years of the purges than previously.

The drive against the private enterprises of the kolkhozniki started in 1938 with the livestock held by them.[44] The crop production of the kolkhozniki was attacked by the order of May 27, 1939, "On Measures toward Safeguarding Collectivized Land from Being Squandered." [45] From January 1, 1938, to January 1, 1941, the kolkhozniki lost more than a quarter of their cattle and hogs. Data released before World War II indicated that the loss of land by the kolkhozniki was small, but the evidence on the 1940 sown acreage in *Stat. Handb.*, 1956 (p. 108), points to a substantial decline in it from 1937.[46]

Output.—Rough calculations of the gross agricultural production of 1937 (an excellent year weatherwise) point to a jump of not less than 24 per cent as compared with 1936 (Table 19). The farm output in 1935, a good crop year, was surpassed by perhaps 15 per cent.

The pre-collectivization level of agricultural output would probably have been slightly exceeded in 1937, even had the weather been no better than normal. It would, however, be wrong to draw too optimistic conclusions from this fact. The previous level was just slightly enlarged, possibly because the most backward, most helpless enterprises were less numerous among the kolkhozy than among the individual peasants.[47] But, until very recently, the Bolsheviks proved themselves unable to surpass this slightly enlarged previous level.

---

[44] This is clearly reflected in the number of livestock they held; see *Soc. Agri.*, p. 789.

[45] *Soc. Agri.*, p. 341.

[46] See *Commentary*, p. 108.

[47] In 31.3 per cent of all peasant households in 1927, no workstock was owned. See *Soc. Agri.*, p. 781.

TABLE 19

Purge Era: Agricultural Production*

Item	1936	1937	1938	1939	1940
Gross agricultural production (billion rubles at 1926/27 prices)...........	14.8[a]	18.4	16.0[b]	17.0[c]	17.8[d]
Crop production (million tons):					
Grain[e]..........................	63.6	96.0	75.9	82.0	86.0
Potatoes.........................	51.5	65.6	42.0	...	...
Sunflower seed...................	1.49	2.08	1.67	...	...
Sugar beet.......................	16.8	21.9	16.7	21.0[f]	17.0[f,g]
Cotton...........................	2.39	2.58	2.48	2.66[f]	2.7[f]
Livestock products (million tons):					
Meat[h]...........................	2.5	2.4	3.3	3.0[i]	3.0[i]
Milk.............................	22.8	26.1	26.0	...	28[j]

* Pre-1939 territory. Largely based on *Soc. Agri.*, pp. 775, 792, 795–98.
[a] Estimate of this writer.
[b] Estimated at 17.4 billion rubles in *Soc. Agri.*, p. 775, under the assumption of average weather conditions.
[c] New rough estimate.
[d] Estimate of *Soc. Agri.*, under the assumption of normal weather conditions.
[e] *Soc. Agri.*, p. 792.
[f] "Biological" crops.
[g] *Economic Survey of Europe in 1953*, p. 269, estimates the losses in 1940 at 4 million tons, which are deducted here.
[h] Three principal kinds of meat, carcass weight. *Attainments*, p. 181, gives much higher figures, but its coverage is much wider.
[i] Average of 1937 and 1938 plus an allowance for the rising number of sheep.
[j] Revised downward from 30 million tons in *Soc. Agri.*, p. 798.

Had the purges not started full blast in the autumn of 1936, one could have thought that the relative abundance of farm products brought about by the good 1937 harvest was one of the factors making the Party leaders super-ambitious. But the Soviet leaders need little to skyrocket their ambitions. The purge wave may have been the outcome of the 1935 harvest, which, although much smaller than that of 1937, substantially exceeded those of the preceding disastrous years. There still may have been a certain connection between the excellent 1937 crops and the purges in that the better supply of farm products may have made possible an intensification and prolongation of the purge hurricane.

There is hardly any doubt that the beginning of the strangulation of the private economy of the peasants contributed to the fact that the trend in farm output, which was rising until 1937, came practically, or even fully, to a standstill.

The last prewar year, 1940, was, weatherwise, at least average and probably better than average. Under the assumption reached in *Soc. Agri.*, 1940 gross agricultural production in the pre-1939 territory amounted to 17.8 billion rubles, which was only about 3 per cent smaller than in 1937. With the weather factor eliminated, this estimate implied a certain rise in farm output from 1937 to

1940. As time passes, it becomes increasingly clear that this writer was not courageous enough in estimating the 1940 crop.*

Whether the rising trend of farm output continued to operate after 1937 or not, it seems certain that the non-farm economy of the *Purge Era* as a whole was based on a moderately larger farm output than that of the *Three "Good" Years*. Gross farm output may have averaged roughly 17 billion rubles in 1937–40 as against 15 billion rubles in 1934–36. The population in the pre-1939 territory averaged only a little over 5 per cent more in the later period.

Especially important was the improvement in grain output and supplies. The real grain crop in 1937–40 may have averaged 85 million tons as against 70 million in 1934–36, an increase of around 20 per cent.[48] This large addition permitted not only satisfying the

---

* After the manuscript was out of the hands of the writer (see Preface), *Economy USSR in 1958* (Moscow, 1959), with fundamental revisions of many official estimates of farm production, became available. It seems inadvisable to replace the data in Table 19 with the new official estimates. First, the latter are incomplete. Second, the writer has not yet decided that the new estimates are correct. And finally, most estimates in Table 19 are not the old enormously exaggerated official estimates now drastically revised. The data in Table 19 compare with the new official estimates (*ibid.*, pp. 350 top and 418–19) as follows:

	Table 19	New Official
Gross agricultural production (year-to-year increases in per cent):		
1937	24	23
1938	−13	−11
1939	6	1
1940	4	5[a]
1937–40	−3	−7[a]
Grain (million tons):		
1937	96.0	97.4
1940	86.0	95.5[b]
Potatoes (million tons):		
1937	65.6	58.7
Sunflower seed (million tons):		
1937	2.08	1.76
Cotton (million tons):		
1940	2.7	2.24

[a] Adjusted for the territory.
[b] Not adjusted for territory.

The comparison in the tabulation shows that, with a certain care, with some exceptions an analyst could avoid being misled by the old official statistics. The picture revealed by the new official data is just a shade gloomier than that in the text.

The exceptions mentioned are the data for potatoes and sunflower seed in Table 19. They, as well as the data for flax for the same years, turn out considerably lower after the recent revelations, as compared with the estimates released earlier. Since there was not even a hint of a possibility of distortions, the figures released earlier were used in Table 19. The 1940 figure for cotton in Table 19 also turns out too high.

[48] The comparison appears less favorable for the *Purge Era,* if it is considered that the first half of 1934 was favorably affected by the relatively good 1933 crop, while the first half of 1937 was adversely affected by the poor 1936 crop, and that consequently the supplies in 1934–36 were somewhat larger than the crops of those years.

moderate current requirements for grain but also stockpiling very considerable amounts.[49] There was also, perhaps, 25 per cent more meat during the *Purge Era* as compared with the *Three "Good" Years,* because of the doubtful blessing that, except for sheep, the livestock herds ceased to grow.

The weakening of dictatorial powers through the purges did not prevent the government from taking full advantage of the relatively large farm output in order to raise its procurements. Data on procurements in 1936 are unfortunately not at hand. As is implied in data shown in Table 19, net output of grain in a comparable territory declined considerably from 1937 to 1940, yet 1940 marketings of grain again reached the 1937 level.[50] The enlarged procurements of slaughter animals and oil seeds permitted state industry to expand its output of meat and vegetable oil by 50 and 48 per cent, respectively.[51] The better supplies of farm products in the hands of the state certainly were a big help to the Party in those critical days. But they may also have prolonged the purges.

Industry

Output.—Gross industrial output in 1940 (pre-1939 boundaries) was estimated at 15 per cent above that in 1937 in *Essay I* (p. 22). All other private analysts, including Colin Clark and Gregory Grossman, have lower figures. Shimkin *et al.,* have an increase of only 7.3 per cent in 1937–40.[52] The NBER found about the same percentage increase in its calculation with 1928 weights. In its calculation with 1955 weights, the Bureau even has a small decline in those years. As on many other occasions, with the little evidence at hand when *Essay I* was written, this writer was just too cautious. The increase in gross industrial output in the pre-1939 territory in 1937–40 will be assumed to have been equal to 10 per cent.

Industrial output may have grown in 1937 by about 6 per cent over the preceding year and the increase during the whole *Purge Era* works out to about 17 per cent. In spite of the absence of *adequate* data for the all-important machinery industry, including armaments, the estimate seems in any case not too low on the basis of the evidence on the output of individual commodities discussed below (see Table 20) and as handled by other Western investigators.

[49] The requirements are qualified by the small use of grain for feed; even the use of grain as food was restricted by the high prices of better-quality flour and bread. On stockpiles, see *Soc. Agri.,* p. 560.

[50] They amounted to 38.0 million tons in 1937 (*Soc. Agri.,* p. 78) and to 38.3 million tons in 1940 (*Attainments,* p. 154).

[51] *Stat. Handb.,* 1956, p. 59.

[52] *Automotive Industries,* January 1, 1958. The estimate of increase in armament production in those years implied in the calculations of the authors seems to be too low.

TABLE 20

Purge Era: INDUSTRIAL OUTPUT*

Commodity	1936	1937	1938	1939	1942 Target of the 3d FYP	1940	1941 Plan
Producers' goods:							
Electric power (billion kw-h.)..........	32.8	36.2	39.4	43.2	75.0	48.9	54.0
Coal (million tons)...................	126.8	128.0	133.3	146.2	230.0	165.9	190.8
Coke (million tons).................	19.9	20.0	19.6	20.2	29.0	21.1	23.8
Petroleum including gas (million tons)...	29.2	30.4	32.2	32.3	54.0	33.2	38.0
Iron ore (million tons)...............	27.8	27.8	26.6	26.9	43.5	29.9	34.0
Manganese ore (million tons).........	3.0	2.8	2.3	2.3	4.5	2.6	3.1
Steel (million tons)...................	16.4	17.7	18.1	17.6	28.0	18.3	22.4
Copper (thousand tons)..............	100.7	97.5	...	...	...	161.0	...
Machinery including other metal processing (billion rubles at "unchangeable 1926/27 prices")..................	24.7	27.5	...	...	63.0	48.1[a]	63.2
Cement (million tons)...............	5.9	5.5	5.7	5.2	11.0	5.2[b]	7.8
Industrial timber shipped from forests (million cubic meters).............	128.1	114.2	114.7	126.1	200.0	114.4	151.8
Sawn timber (million cubic meters).....	40.9	28.8	34.5	34.5	45.0	34.8	28.9
Paper (thousand tons)...............	763.3	831.6	832.8	799.8	1,500.0	781.4	970.0
Consumers' goods:							
Bread (million tons).................	16.1	19.1	16.6	...	21.3	...	22.1
Flour (million tons).................	...	15.1	...	...	18.5	...	18.8
Vodka and other hard liquor (million dekaliters).......................	...	89.7	...	...	...	92.5	95.0
Crystal sugar (thousand tons).........	1,998	2,421	2,520	1,826	3,500	2,102	2,650
Meat (thousand tons)................	773	797	1,140	...	1,600	1,150	1,240
Sausage (thousand tons)..............	244	369	395	...	650	391	382
Fish (million quintals)...............	16.2	16.1	15.4	15.7	22.5	13.8	16.7
Butter (thousand tons)..............	189	185	199	191	295	199.9	203
Vegetable oil (thousand tons).........	503	539	643	693	850	791.6	737
Soap in terms of 40 per cent fat (thousand tons)...................	557	495	...	...	925	708	746
Cotton fabric (million meters).........	3,270	3,448	3,460	3,763	4,900	3,924	4,338
Woolen fabric (million meters)........	101	108	113	122	177	117	122
Linen fabric (million meters).........	295	285	270	258	385	281	284
Socks and stockings (million pairs)......	359	409	451	457	716	485	538
Footwear (million pairs)..............	143	183	193	206.0	235	210	222
Rubber footwear (million pairs)........	82	85	86	80.0	...	68	80
Cigarettes (billion units)..............	86	102	96	...	140	100	110
Makhorka (thousand cases)............	5,021	5,300	...	...	...	4,600	5,600

* The data for 1936–40 are from *Industry of the USSR*, 1957, *passim.* So far as possible the output of the Baltic States as stated in this source was excluded from the 1940 figures. So far as the data were not found in the source cited, they are: for 1936 (preliminary) from *1937 Plan, passim;* for 1937 and 1942 (Plan) from *3d FYP,* draft, and *Problems of Economics,* 1939, No. 3; for 1938 (preliminary) from *Socialist Construction, 1933–38, passim.* The new series for meat already given in *Stat. Handb.,* 1956, p. 59, is not used because the data are not comparable with the targets of the third FYP and *1941 Plan.* The new series for meat as given in *Industry of the USSR,* 1957, p. 378, is as follows (in thousands of tons):

Year	Meat
1936.....................	995
1937.....................	1,002
1938.....................	1,447
1939.....................	1,639
1940.....................	1,418

The targets of the third FYP are, so far as available, from the resolution of the Eighteenth Party Congress; otherwise, from *3d FYP,* draft.

[a] Calculated from the 1937 figure with the index in *Industry of the USSR,* 1957, p. 203.

[b] The figure usually given is 5.8 million tons. But this includes the output of some of the new territories. The figure of 5.2 million tons is implied in the data given by Malenkov at the Eighteenth Party Conference in 1941. Data for the RSFSR, which were little affected by borderline changes, show a decline in output of cement from 4.0 million tons in 1936 and 3.7 million tons in 1937 to 3.6 million tons in 1940 (*National Economy of the RSFSR* stat. handb., 1957, p. 93).

From the point of view of the Party, the most significant failure was the fact that, in spite of the urgent need for steel for the production of armaments, particularly since mid-1939, and in spite of the rapidly rising investments in the steel industry, output, after a moderate increase (7.9 per cent) in 1937, practically stagnated in 1937–40 (an increase of 3.4 per cent in three years). The output of rolled steel increased by only 5.5 per cent in four years. Hence, if the recovery in steel claimed for the second half of 1940 really did take place, it was not big enough to offset the decline in 1939 and also possibly the one in the first half of 1940. It was a small compensation that the output of quality steel, which is of course included in the totals, increased from 2.4 million tons in 1937 to 3.2 million tons in 1940.[53] Mining of manganese ore, very important in the production of quality steel and certainly a very primitive operation in Russia, declined by 13.3 per cent from 1936 to 1940.

Electric power was one of the few brighter spots. While there was a certain slowdown as compared with the *Three "Good" Years,* the growth in capacities and output was large. Both were expanded by 47 per cent in 1936–40. Output in coal likewise continued to grow but at a much slower rate than that of the preceding years (an increase of 30 per cent in 1936–40). It is also significant that the output of the particularly important coke was enlarged by only 6 per cent in those four years.

The petroleum situation resembled the steel situation. Petroleum too was very important for war preparations and was also granted large increases in fixed investments, but the rise in output did not exceed 3.4 per cent per year.

The decline in the output of building materials has already been discussed. The reduction in the timber industry is of particular significance. Much concentration-camp labor was commonly used in timber procurements and the inflow of inmates certainly was large in those eventful years. Yet the amount of industrial timber shipped from the forests fell in 1937 and remained at this level until the end of the *Purge Era.*[54] The figures for shipments of industrial timber, insofar as they are available, are worth reproducing in some detail. In 1936, there were 128 million cubic meters shipped from the forests. But procurements in the forests were much larger, and, hence, a large stockpile of felled trees remained in the forests. The 1937 Plan scheduled an increase in shipments of 47.9 million cubic meters. In spite of the large stockpile in the forests, shipments

[53] Gardner Clark, *The Economics of Soviet Steel* (Cambridge, Mass.: Harvard University Press, 1956), p. 20.

[54] Industrial timber consists of all round timber other than firewood.

actually declined in 1937 by 14.0 million cubic meters. The shipments of industrial timber in 1940 were still considerably below the 1936 level, and the 1941 target for these shipments was below that of the 1937 Plan.

The official index for output of machinery, including other metal processing, in "unchangeable 1926/27 prices," indicates about a doubling in 1936–40 (for 1937–40 the increase is given at 82 per cent in *Industry of the USSR*, 1957, p. 203), but it cannot be taken seriously. The total increase in all these goods could not have been very large, because steel, the principal material, could only have been obtained for such an expansion through diversion from other relatively small uses.

Military goods, to which machinery production shifted during the period analyzed, were greatly overpriced in 1926/27 prices in relation to civilian machinery. The analysis of the official data on the output per man likewise shows the immense exaggeration in the index for output of machinery, including other metal processing, at "unchangeable 1926/27 prices." [55]

The analysis of the data for output of consumers' goods in Table 20 is handicapped by uncertainty on the extent to which the 1940 data also cover the output of the newly acquired territories, fully or in part. The data in Table 20 show a less dismal, even a favorable, picture only, or mainly, insofar as expansion in output was permitted by growth in state procurements of farm products and no complicated processing was involved. Industrial meat output increased by about 50 per cent. Vegetable oil showed a similar rise. Output of cotton fabrics, on the other hand, grew only little more than total industrial production (by 21.0 per cent in four years). The growth in output of socks and stockings slowed down greatly, amounting to 36 per cent in four years of the *Purge Era*.

The growth in output of footwear until 1937 reflected the recovery of the animal industry. A certain expansion in its output in subsequent years was brought about by the change from rapidly growing to stable livestock herds. The output of footwear in 1939 was given at 206 million pairs. The output of footwear in the enlarged territory in 1940 was usually stated as having been equal to 205 million pairs until the *Stat. Handb.*, 1956, raised this figure to 211 million. In any case, presumably there has been a quite sizable decline in output of footwear since 1938 in a comparable territory. The analysis of trade below indicates that the composition of re-

[55] The estimates of the machinery output by Western analysts, indicating a small increase for total machinery output and a large decline in the output of civilian machinery, was quoted above on p. 190.

tailed footwear deteriorated greatly from 1937 to 1940 and that the same may have been, to a smaller extent, the case with production of footwear. The output of rubber footwear went down presumably because of curtailment of rubber imports, of increased use of rubber for military purposes, or both. The catch of fish, which could not, like livestock and oil seeds, have been simply taken from the producers without regard to their own needs, declined absolutely.

Quality of the product.—Moderate as the total increase in industrial output during the *Purge Era* was, it was accompanied by a substantial deterioration of the quality of the goods produced. "The ash content of Donbass coal rose from 12.55 to 14.03 per cent and of Karaganda coal, from 16.54 to 19.16 per cent in the last three years," according to an editorial in *Planned Economy* (1940, No. 10, p. 5). The editorial also contains considerable other evidence of the unsatisfactory quality of industrial goods. As late as July 10, 1940, a special order was issued on this point, the very title of which discloses the situation: "On the Criminal Responsibility for Release of Unsatisfactory or Incomplete Products as Well as for Failure To Fulfil the Requirements of the Obligatory Standards." [56]

The editorial in *Planned Economy* with the data on the ash content in coal, which represented a comment on this order, after pointing out its main features, added, however: "It is necessary to remember that raising the quality of output will only serve to foster the economic and defensive might of the USSR, if it is associated with the struggle for unconditional fulfilment of the quantity targets of the national economic plan." [57] This obviously put the quality factor into the unpromising subordinate position which it had always occupied in the Soviet Union.

Transportation

The tabulation below shows the year-to-year development in freight traffic during the *Purge Era* (in billions of ton-kilometers):[58]

Year	Railways	River	Sea	Truck
1936	323.4	31.2	41.1	8.4
1937	354.8	33.0	36.4	8.7
1938	370.5	32.0	33.9	8.8
1939	392.0	34.6	...	8.8
1940	409.0	35.9	23.8	8.9

[56] See Malenkov's report to the Eighteenth Party Conference, February, 1941, in *Planned Economy*, 1941, No. 3, p. 17.

[57] *Planned Economy*, 1940, No. 10, p. 9.

[58] Holland Hunter, *Soviet Transportation Policy*, pp. 331, 335, 338, 342.

While total freight traffic increased by 81 per cent during the *Three "Good" Years,* the further increase in four years of the *Purge Era* was less than 20 per cent, of which almost half was the share of the year 1937. The distribution of the small increase in freight traffic among the individual carriers is also significant. Freight transportation by truck, which expanded 4.7 times in 1933–36, showed a further growth of only 6 per cent in 1936–40. It was certainly in line with the nature of the period that transportation by sea dropped to little more than half of the 1936 level by 1940.

The data in Table 21 give another good illustration of the law of proportionate expansion of the Soviet socialized economy according

TABLE 21

Purge Era VERSUS *Three "Good" Years:* INDICATORS IN RAILWAY OPERATION*
(Increase or decline, in per cent)

Item	1933–36	1936–40
Tons originated...	+80.2	+20.0
Cumulated ton-kilometers[a] per operational worker.........	+36.4	+12.5
Freight-car turnabout in days............................	−29.0	+8.6
Gross ton-kilometers per freight-train hour................	+60.1	+24.1
Locomotives, kilometers per locomotive day..............	+42.1	+9.8

* Data by courtesy of Dr. Holland Hunter.
[a] Ton-kilometers plus passenger-kilometers.

to plan. The average yearly increase in freight transported by railways declined more than fivefold from the *Three "Good" Years* to the four years of the *Purge Era.* The average annual rate of growth of shipments per operational worker went down about fourfold; freight-car turnabout, measured in days, instead of declining substantially as in 1933–36, increased during the *Purge Era;* and so forth.

Passenger transportation may be a minor item in the national economy, yet the great differences in the rates of growth of this item during each of the three periods—the *All-out Drive,* the *Three "Good" Years,* and the *Purge Era*—throw glaring light on the widely different all-around situations during these short periods, all of them squeezed into one decade. The number of transported passengers shows the following increases (in per cent):

All-out Drive................1929–32	164
Three "Good" Years.........1933–36	7
Purge Era..................1936–40	35

The period of forced collectivization, one-sided industrialization, bacchanalian planning, and general starvation was accompanied by an immense enlargement in the mobility of the people. Then came the relatively healthy *Three "Good" Years,* and the mobility of the population displayed a practical stability in the face of the rapid growth of the economy. In spite of the great decline in the rate of economic growth, the *Purge Era* brought a renewal of large movements of the population. The rate of growth of passenger traffic during the *Purge Era* was small as compared with that during the *All-out Drive,* but the much higher absolute level of passenger transportation reached by that time must be considered.

While the index of total traffic (in terms of cumulative ton-kilometers) per operational railway worker rose in three years (1928 equals 100) from 174.1 in 1933 to 237.6 in 1936 or by 36 per cent, it could increase only by 13 per cent in the next four years (1936–40).

Output per Man

It may be considered a success, as compared with the *All-out Drive,* that output per man did not decline during the *Purge Era,* but the change as compared with the *Three "Good" Years* was nevertheless great.

Railway transportation made possibly the best showing, with an increase in performance per man of about 3 per cent in 1937–40.[59] Performance per man declined slightly in river transportation and greatly (37 per cent) in transportation on the sea.[60]

The number of wage and salary earners in industry increased by 8 per cent in 1937–40.[61] This is approximately the percentage by which industrial output grew in those years according to the estimates of Western analysts.[62]

The official claim that output per man increased in industry by 33 per cent in 1937–40 (see *Stat. Handb.,* 1956, p. 52) is based on the fantastic claim of a 45 per cent increase in industrial output in the three years.[63] It was simply a curiosity when a 60 per cent increase was calculated in output per man in the machinery industry (including other metal processing) in 1937–40—a growth in output per man of 60 per cent in three years in a period like the *Purge*

[59] *Transport and Communications in the USSR,* 1957, p. 23.
[60] *Ibid.*
[61] *Economy of the USSR in 1956,* pp. 204–5.
[62] See above, p. 198.
[63] The labor force in industry in 1940 is given at 10,967,000 in *Stat. Handb.,* 1956, p. 190. For 1936, *1937 Plan,* p. 145, gave 9,677,000 for the same item.

Era! [64] Actually output per man in the machinery industry, at least in the production of civilian machinery, probably declined, in view of decline in output with less than proportionate reduction in the labor force.

An increase in output per man in construction in 1937–40 of 32 per cent is claimed officially (*Stat. Handb.*, 1956, p. 167). The officially calculated increase of 37.2 per cent in investment in construction and installation at prices of July 1, 1955, during the same period is fairly well tied in with this claim (the total labor force in construction remained unchanged).[65] Nevertheless, the claim does not make sense for the conditions of all-around stagnation during the *Purge Era*. Since it is unlikely that construction grew at all and may even have declined (see discussion above in the section on investment), an almost unchanged performance per man in it seems likely to have been the case.

Not having published an index of the official retail trade turnover at constant prices in 1936–40 or 1937–40 until late in 1957, *Soviet Trade,* stat. handb., 1956 (p. 114) literally smuggled in a calculation of performance per man in that sector in 1937 and some other years at 1940 prices. The calculation indicates for the period 1937–40 a 2 per cent decline in performance per man in retail trade proper, a 7 per cent increase in it in eating places, and a very small decline in performance per man in total trade. Even this result is not particularly favorable, but the analysis in the next chapter makes it probable that the official trade did not increase sharply at constant prices from 1937 to 1940 and that the 25 per cent increase in the labor force in this sector from 1937 to 1940 was accompanied by a significant decline in performance per man. Furthermore, retail trade was expanding in 1938 and 1939, but declined in 1940. Performance per man in official trade certainly went down markedly in the last year of the *Purge Era.*

[64] The figure mentioned in the text was never spelled out. *Industry of the USSR,* 1957, starts its more detailed data for output per man in the various industrial branches from 1940 (pp. 26–27 and *passim*). Data in *Economy of the USSR in 1956,* pp. 204 and 49, imply an increase of about 8 per cent in the number of wage earners in the machinery industry including metal processing in 1937–40. Officially there was an expansion in output of this industry of 82 per cent during these years.

[65] *Stat. Handb.*, 1956, p. 190. By exaggerating the growth in output of construction, the growth in output per man, which is calculated from the former, is simultaneously exaggerated.

CHAPTER 9

THE PURGE ERA II

THE PRIVATE SECTOR

Retail Trade

Quite recently, claims of enormous increases in per capita retail purchases and private consumption of two great groups (industrial manual workers and kolkhozniki) from the "prewar" year of 1940 to the postwar years were poured out.[1] The same claims were actually contained in the claims concerning real wages and real incomes of kolkhoz peasants in postwar years in terms of 1940 in the "Report on the Fulfilment of the 1949 Plan"; but the claims concerning real incomes, although carried over into subsequent years, remained the only claims of this kind for years. They were, moreover, so fantastic that their influence was probably nil. In the more recent claims concerning real incomes, fantasies are mixed with more or less correct data.

Retail trade was very small in 1940. Specifically, with reference to official trade its volume in 1940 was only slightly, if at all, higher than the level of 1937, in spite of the growth of the population. Moreover, there were large increases in retail sales of products which did not represent any real improvement in consumption, such as the increase in sales of grain products (nearly everybody was probably eating enough bread by 1937; the increases in sales of these

[1] *Stat. Handb.*, 1956, p. 208; *National Economy of the RSFSR,* 1957, p. 287; and *Courier of Statistics,* 1957, No. 1, pp. 86–87.

products must have been largely transfers to official trade from other categories), or represented increases in consumption of vodka and tobacco products. The enlarged sales of these products were accompanied by really painful decreases in sales and consumption of many vital commodities such as meat, sugar, cotton cloth, and footwear. In the second half of 1940, consumption was very close to starvation levels, and now Communist statistics are using the consumption levels in the "peacetime" or "prewar" year of 1940 as a basis for measuring postwar "successes."

The high prices in kolkhoz trade in 1940 were detrimental to purchasers in this trade. Yet, the sellers were not profiting from them in view of the impossibility of spending all the money realized on needed goods. There is, of course, nothing objectionable in the fact that the Soviet Union was preparing for imminent war. It was, and is, very objectionable to base claims of postwar improvements on 1940 retail sales and consumption, while concealing the real degree to which retail sales and personal consumption were reduced in that year. It is very objectionable to persist in calling the year 1940 a "prewar" or a "peace" year, because it was neither, especially insofar as retail sales and personal consumption are concerned.

The great official claims for the well-being of the population in postwar years, expressed in terms of 1940, make it advisable to subject the situation in that year to more detailed scrutiny.

Official trade.—Sales in official trade during the *Purge Era* were as follows (in billions of rubles at current prices):

Year	Billion Rubles
1936	106.8
1937	125.9
1938	140.0
1939	165.8
1940	175.1

A year-to-year price index for official trade in those years was never calculated. In *Monthly Labor Review* (November, 1939, p. 1276) the prices in official retail trade, weighted by an unspecified procedure, were calculated as having increased by 13 per cent from July 1, 1936, to July 1, 1939. An index of prices in official retail trade based on the composition of purchases of wage earners in 1926–27 showed an increase of 35.2 per cent from 1937 to 1940.[2] Of this, prices of food products increased 30 per cent, non-food commodities

[2] *Essay I*, p. 111.

50 per cent. The calculations in a French study indicate the following increases in prices or cost in per cent (July 1, 1938, equals 100):[3]

Item	July 1, 1939	July 1, 1940	January, 1941
Official retail trade (58 commodities, 1926/27 weights)	111	145	148
Cost of living (prices in official trade, 42 commodities, 1928 weights)	113	157	160
Cost of living (prices in official trade, 83 commodities, 1951 weights)	110	153	153

It is possible to visualize the price development in official retail trade during the *Purge Era* as follows: There may have been a small increase from 1936 to 1937, but this can possibly be disregarded.[4] The prices in official trade probably remained about unchanged in 1938 as well. Then came an increase of about 10 per cent in 1939 and of about 25 per cent in 1940.[5]

After these rough price estimates are applied to the sales at current prices, the following approximate index figures for sales in official retail trade during the *Purge Era* are obtained:

YEAR	CURRENT PRICES		CONSTANT PRICES	
	Year-to-year	Cumulative	Year-to-year	Cumulative
1936	...	100	...	100
1937	118	118	118	118
1938	111	131	111	131
1939	118	155	107	140
1940	106	164	82	115[a]

[a] *Soviet Trade*, stat. handb., pp. 113, 114, implies the following increases in the volume of official trade from 1937 to 1940 (in per cent):

Retail trade proper	7.15
Eating places	77
Total retail trade	13.3

The calculation was made from the official data on sales per employed person in 1940 prices and on the number of personnel in the state and co-operative trade in both years. In the particular conditions of that year, the use of 1940 prices in the calculation of the volume of sales per employed person must have produced a somewhat more favorable picture than would have been the case in a calculation at prices of an earlier year. Correspondingly, the rate of price inflation in 1937–40 turned out smaller in the official calculation than in that of the present writer. But even the calculation according to which official retail trade at constant prices increased by only 13 per cent in three years is a big concession, if one recalls Voznesenskii's assertions (at the Eighteenth Party Conference in 1941) that the targets of the third FYP were successfully fulfilled and overfulfilled (the third FYP called for an increase in official trade of 64 per cent, with prices unchanged, in five years; see *3d FYP*, draft, p. 233).

[3] *Études et Conjoncture* (Institut National de la Statistique et des Études Économiques), April, 1955, p. 343. The compilation of prices in this source is extensively used by this writer.

[4] From April–July of 1936 to April–July of 1937, the prices of such important items as grain products, sugar, most grades of beef, veal, fresh ham, all sausages, sugar and beverages, and tobacco products remained unchanged. On the whole, moderate price increases for some other products were more numerous than similar price reductions. See compilation of retail prices reported from Moscow in *Conference Board Bulletin*, March 7, 1938.

[5] It is not improbable that the over-all increase in prices in the two years 1939 and 1940 was so distributed that the increase in 1939 was slightly larger and that in 1940 slightly smaller than stated.

The large expansion of retail trade in 1937 must have been due partly to the excellent 1937 crop. But the desire to show the population that purging the "enemies of the country" was to its advantage is likely to have been a contributing factor. Any desire to maintain the rapid growth in official retail trade in subsequent years was frustrated by the small increases in available supplies in the hands of the state.

The great decline in the volume of official retail trade from 1939 to 1940 was clearly the result of feverish preparations for war, combined with only small increases in the output of industrial consumers' goods. Meanwhile, the quantity of consumers' goods which was not permitted to go into retail channels but was diverted for the needs of the greatly enlarged armed forces and especially for accumulation of stockpiles was apparently much larger than had ever been visualized.[6]

The monthly figures of the 1940 retail turnover, also apparently released for the first time in 1956,[7] fully support the United States embassy's reports from Moscow on the situation at that time.[8] In January–April of 1940, when prices were not much higher than in the corresponding months of 1939, retail sales in nominal terms were slightly below those of the corresponding months of 1939. But sales in those terms were about 14 per cent larger in September–December of 1940 than in the same months of 1939, after a large non-food-goods price raise went into effect on July 15, 1940. Greatly inadequate supplies to cover demand and, consequently, empty shelves in stores characterized the first half of the year, and prices too high for many and stores a little better stocked characterized the second half of "prewar" 1940.[9]

The situation in 1940 is further clarified by a comparison of the rise in sales at current prices with that in prices of individual commodities from 1937 to 1940 (Chart 15). As is obvious from the chart, there were more or less substantial increases in the volume of sales of grain products, beverages, tobacco products, milk (including dairy products other than butter) vegetable oil, and eggs. The increases in

---

[6] According to N. A. Voznesenskii (*War Economy of the USSR during the Patriotic War* [Moscow, 1948], p. 154), stockpiles increased in value by 3.5 billion rubles during 1940 and the first half of 1941. The amount seems small in relation to the official retail trade of 125 billion rubles in 1937, even if all sales taxes, which were very high in 1940, were deducted from the value of the stockpiled goods. Indeed, with the evidence on retail sales in 1940 now at hand, Voznesenskii's data strike one as a trap.

[7] *Soviet Trade,* stat. handb., 1956, p. 30.

[8] *Monthly Labor Review,* May, 1940, February, 1941, and other issues.

[9] An embassy report contained a list of over forty commodities still not on sale after July 1. The list included the better kinds of flour, macaroni, most meats, etc. See *Monthly Labor Review,* February, 1941, p. 475.

milk, eggs, and vegetable oil were from very low levels. The three items with significant increases in *volume* of sales were grain products, vodka, and tobacco products. There were, on the other hand, declines in the volume of sales of potatoes, meat, eggs, footwear,

CHART 15

INCREASES IN SALES VS. INCREASES IN PRICES IN OFFICIAL TRADE FROM 1937 TO 1940 *
(1937 = 100)

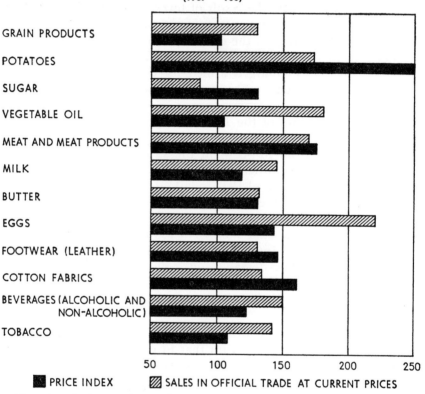

* Data for sales from *Soviet Trade,* stat. handb., 1956, pp. 40–43. Sales of milk include dairy products other than butter; sales of footwear include felt footwear.

Data for prices from *Essay I,* pp. 111–12. The price for meat pertains only to beef; the price of cotton fabrics is a simple average of prices of calico and satinet; the price of beverages is that of vodka only. The price of vodka was raised on August 12, 1940.

and cotton fabrics. It must not be forgotten that the comparisons are with 1937 and that retail sales increased in both 1938 and 1939. A comparison of 1940 with 1939 would be much more disheartening.

A vivid picture of the immensely miserable state of official trade in 1940 can also be obtained by just looking at the official data on

sales of certain commodities (Chart 16). More than half (52.4 per
cent) of all sales of "food" consisted of grain products and beverages,
mostly vodka.[10] Sales of animal products in all forms (including fish
and herring) did not quite come up to the sales of beverages. Sales of

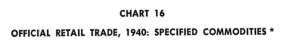

CHART 16

OFFICIAL RETAIL TRADE, 1940: SPECIFIED COMMODITIES *

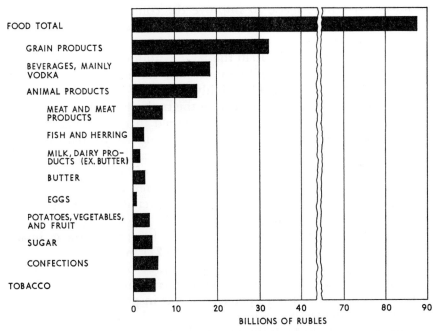

* Excluding turnover in eating places. Data from *Soviet Trade,* stat. handb., 1956, pp.
48–51.

eggs, milk, and dairy products other than butter were half as large
as sales of confections. Sales of eggs were one-fifth the sales of tobacco
products, and sales of fresh milk, cheese, sour cream, and other dairy
products except butter amounted to about 40 per cent of the sales
of these products.

The worst part of it was that so little essential food was sold. Less
than fifteen quarts of milk (in the form of fresh milk, cheese, sour
cream, and other milk products except butter), about a dozen eggs,
and less than 30 kilograms of potatoes per capita were sold to the

[10] The proportion of those goods was even larger, if cakes, waffles, cookies, and
similar goods are transferred from confections, in which they are included in the
official statistics, to grain products.

non-farm population through official trade in the whole year of 1940.[11]

It is claimed that the per capita sales of leather, fabric, and combination footwear to families of wage earners and kolkhoz peasants increased by 42 and 65 per cent, respectively, in 1940–55. Sales of real leather footwear grew by 72 and 80 per cent, respectively, according to the source.[12] It would be a mistake to assume that serious efforts were made to improve the composition of footwear sold to the consumers after the war. The difference between the two sets of percentage increases quoted above was brought about simply by the fact that in 1940 the large withdrawal of footwear for the armed forces and stockpiling must have consisted almost entirely of real leather footwear. The highly treasured leather boots were probably completely withdrawn from the trade channels.

As was shown in chapter 7, footwear sold in retail trade in 1937 consisted only to a relatively small extent of leather footwear for adults that was suitable for wear on the street and at work, especially in the cold season. The balance was made up of fabric and combination footwear, children's footwear, and other cheap goods. The composition of footwear released for sale in retail trade in 1940 was even worse.

It has been mentioned that *Stat. Handb.*, 1956, raised the estimate for output of "leather" footwear in 1940 to 211 million pair. According to N. A. Voznesenskii (*op. cit.*, p. 126), 21 per cent of the total output of "leather" footwear was withdrawn from retail sale. If this is true and if Voznesenskii's percentage was in physical terms, about 167 million pairs were sold in retail trade in that year.[13] The return for this footwear was 4.9 billion rubles,[14] an average of only 29 rubles per pair. The United States embassy in Moscow reported the following prices of footwear in the first and second half of 1940 (in rubles per pair):[15]

---

[11] These calculations had been concluded when this writer got access to data on the so-called market supplies, published by Pavlov, Minister of Trade, in *Soviet Trade* (daily), October 1, 1957. Market supplies seem to be equivalent to official retail trade except for changes in stocks in wholesale trade and for foreign trade. Pavlov's figures for 1940 are so low (655,000 tons of meat and meat products, 4,754,000 tons of milk and dairy products, 120,000 tons of vegetable oil, and 971,000 tons of sugar) that they indicate that the estimate of the sales of food in retail trade made in the text may be somewhat too high.

[12] *Courier of Statistics*, 1957, No. 1, p. 87.

[13] There is no need to include felt with "leather" footwear, as was done in the corresponding discussion in chapter 7, because *Soviet Trade*, stat. handb., 1956, does not include, for 1940, this type of footwear in its data on sales of "leather" footwear at current prices.

[14] *Soviet Trade*, stat. handb., 1956, p. 42.

[15] *Monthly Labor Review*, February, 1941, p. 476.

GRADE	MEN'S		WOMEN'S	
	1st half	2d half	1st half	2d half
Best..	. . .	510	. . .	478
All-leather shoes.........................	175	280	. . .	404
Rubber-soled for men, common for women...	75	180	85	160

It seems not difficult to visualize just what the footwear sold in 1940 consisted of, if the average price realized was only 29 rubles. At this average price probably only one-quarter of the footwear sold to the population was made up of adult leather shoes for street wear, i.e., the total sales of such footwear may have amounted to about 40 million pairs.[16]

The changes in retail sales of the major consumers' goods from 1937 to 1940 have had to be presented in a rather complicated form, because *Soviet Trade,* stat. handb., 1956, does not contain data on the amounts sold. It does, however, provide such data for the sales of so-called cultural goods in 1940, with comparable data for scattered preceding and succeeding years (p. 57). Data on the amounts of building materials sold in 1940 also are supplied, but the figures for the preceding years are lacking (p. 56).

In general, sales of the so-called cultural goods showed great declines from 1937 to 1940 (clocks and watches from 3.4 million to 2.5 million; sewing machines from 510,000 to 175,000; bicycles from 500,000 to 200,000). Cameras, the sales of which remained virtually unchanged, were the only exception.

The most striking figure among the retail sales figures for building materials in 1940 was the sale of only 14,000 tons of nails (official retail trade also served the kolkhozy, it should be remembered). The sales of roofing steel also amounted to only 10,000 tons; no automobiles were sold at retail in that year, while the sales of trucks were limited to 3,000. It can be correctly maintained that the population and the kolkhozy were practically cut off from metal products in 1940. This may be all right for the conditions of a year of feverish preparations for war. It is not all right for a "peaceful" or a "prewar" year.

In such an important journal as *Planned Economy,* Chernyavskii went out of his way to emphasize that in 1940 the increase in the purchasing power of the rural population for goods sold in official

[16] Something is odd about the sales of felt footwear in 1940 as well. *Stat. Handb.,* 1956 (p. 59), gave the output of this footwear in 1940 at 17.9 million pairs. Yet the total return for the sales of felt footwear in retail trade was only 419 million rubles. If the total output of this footwear was turned over to the retail trade, the average return for it was less than 25 rubles per pair. Does this mean that most of the output of felt footwear was withdrawn, or that a large part of the output was not real felt boots, the standard form of felt footwear, which cost 75 rubles in 1937 and probably much more than this in the second half of 1940?

retail trade had outstripped the increase in the purchasing power of the urban population.[17] One does not immediately realize that Chernyavskii measured purchasing power in nominal terms. Even after this idea had finally dawned on one, it still seemed, on the basis of the author's assertions, that the purchasing power of the peasants must have grown at least in current rubles. The data disclosed in *Soviet Trade,* stat. handb., 1956 (p. 21), came, therefore, as a surprise. It turned out that while there was a moderate increase in sales in the official retail trade *at current prices* in urban areas from 1939 to 1940 (from 114.3 billion to 123.5 billion rubles), trade in rural areas at the same prices stagnated completely, in spite of the fact that the prices of non-food products primarily needed by the peasants were raised more than the prices of food.[18]

That the supply of goods in official retail trade was least adequate in the village is also obvious from the data on the sales of individual products by the Tsentrosoyuz, which operates almost exclusively in rural areas.[19] Vodka and coarse rye bread were the only important products with which the village was supplied amply (vodka) or more or less adequately (coarse rye bread). Bread represented 16.1 per cent of the total Tsentrosoyuz trade, almost the same proportion as in the sales of bread in urban areas—a certainly abnormal phenomenon; the share of bread in 1940 sales of the Tsentrosoyuz was twice as large as that in 1950 and more than three times as large as that in 1955.[20] All beverages, mainly vodka, amounted to not less than 20.6 per cent of the Tsentrosoyuz sales in 1940.[21]

The Tsentrosoyuz sold 1,224 million rubles' worth of sugar in 1940.[22] The average price was close to 5 rubles per kilogram. This indicates sales of about 250,000 tons or, since there were more than 100 million prospective customers, less than 2.5 kilograms per

[17] See his "Money Incomes of the Population and the Retail Turnover," *Planned Economy,* 1941, No. 5, p. 84.

[18] Sales in rural areas are given at 51.5 billion rubles in 1939 and 51.6 billion rubles in 1940. See *Soviet Trade,* stat. handb., 1956, p. 21. It is not known how the sales in rural areas were calculated. The sales of the Tsentrosoyuz, which operated in rural areas, went down from 45.1 billion rubles in 1939 to 42.2 billion rubles in 1940 (*ibid.,* p. 27).

[19] *Soviet Trade,* stat. handb., 1956, pp. 62–63.

[20] It is possible that peasants may have bought bread as a safety measure (by eating purchased bread they saved whatever grain they had). Another reason may have been that the very high prices in kolkhoz trade made the official bread prices look low. This is the more probable, if M. Makarova, cited below, is correct in stating that 18 per cent of the grain marketed by the agricultural producers "on the eve of the Great Patriotic War was sold in kolkhoz markets."

[21] The percentages were actually somewhat higher, because most of the retail margin was not considered in this calculation.

[22] Implied in *Soviet Trade,* stat. handb., 1956, pp. 27, 63.

capita.[23] In 1927/28 the per capita consumption of sugar by the farm population was equal to 5.1 kilograms.[24]

Kolkhoz trade.—The released data on the sales and prices in kolkhoz trade are partly incorrect and contain immense contradictions (some general remarks on the turnover and prices in kolkhoz trade may be found in Appendix C). While an idea, it seems, can be formed, a sense of uncertainty remains. The sales in kolkhoz trade during the *Purge Era* were as follows (in billions of rubles at current prices):[25]

1936	15.6
1937	17.8
1938	24.4
1939	30.3
1940	41.2

The figure of 41.2 billion rubles for the 1940 sales given in the tabulation is that which appeared in Soviet publications for about ten years. Then, after a few years of silence, quite unexpectedly, the previously announced figure was scaled down to 29.1 billion rubles.[26] According to an official interpretation, the new figure, together with all estimates for postwar years, pertains to ex-village kolkhoz trade, defined as sales of farm products by producers to the non-farm population as well as to organizations—to both "at prices formed at the market." This must imply that the previous estimate of the 1940 sales in kolkhoz trade included also sales by the farm producers to the farm population at those prices.

The anniversary publication *Forty Years of Soviet Trade* (Moscow, 1957) treats the estimates of the sales in kolkhoz trade in 1933–40 as released but with the 1940 trade revised downward from 41.2 to 29.1 billion rubles (p. 112) and the estimate for 1950 (p. 115) as comparable. Since the latter is definitely defined as covering ex-village kolkhoz trade only, the data in the anniversary publication is a recognition (there are other recognitions) that the concept of "ex-village kolkhoz trade" already existed in pre-World War II years, and that only the previous estimate of the 1940 kolkhoz trade allegedly covered more than this.

[23] The figure is much smaller if the per capita purchases of sugar by the rural population in 1955 is calculated in the same manner as is done here, and the 1940 to 1955 increase of 177 per cent claimed for the kolkhozniki by the Soviet statisticians (see *Courier of Statistics*, 1957, No. 1, p. 87) is applied to the figure obtained.

[24] *1st FYP*, I, Part 2, 81.

[25] See, for example, M. M. Lifits, *Soviet Trade* (Moscow, 1948), p. 33. The figure for 1937 is in A. P. Dadugin and P. N. Fedorov, *Organization of Kolkhoz Market Trade* (1957), p. 9.

[26] *Soviet Trade*, stat. handb., 1956, p. 19, and other sources.

It is possible that in 1941 the Soviet rulers wanted to have a high figure for the 1940 sales in kolkhoz trade and so extended secretly the concept of this trade. After having cited the false estimate for about ten years, they may have disposed of it, because they wanted to have a low basis for the index of kolkhoz trade in postwar years with 1940 equal to 100. However, the decline in kolkhoz trade from 1939 to 1940 at current prices and the great increase in sales from 1940 to postwar years at constant prices—both implied in the revised figure for 1940—seem not to make much sense.

The official 1940 estimate of the kolkhoz trade which existed prior to the revision exceeded the 1937 sales by 131 per cent. This excess went down to 64 per cent after the revision. What does this mean in terms of quantities? Data by A. P. Dadugin and P. G. Kagarlitskii (*Organization and Techniques of Kolkhoz Market Trade* [1949], p. 5) imply that in 1937 the prices in kolkhoz trade were equal to 41.7 per cent of those in 1933. According to the same authors (*loc. cit.*), "from 1933 to 1940 the prices in kolkhoz trade went down more than twofold." [27] Both statements together imply that the prices in kolkhoz trade were less than 20 per cent higher in 1940 than in 1937.

Then, according to Dadugin and Kagarlitskii, who were the leading analysts in this field, there was an increase in sales from 1937 to 1940 in real terms of 40 per cent, even on the basis of the 1940 estimate revised downward. Dadugin and Kagarlitskii's data for 1938 through 1940 are as follows (in per cent of preceding year):

Year	Prices	Sales at Constant Prices
1938	−13	+57
1939	+30	−5
1940 (original estimate)	+5	+28
1940 (revised)	+5	−10

The price and amount data given by Dadugin and Kagarlitskii, however, immensely contradict the facts. Reliable evidence indicates that the 1940 prices in kolkhoz trade were nearly treble those in 1937,[28] a gigantic difference, of course. The decline in prices in 1938

---

[27] The same statement is repeated in Dadugin and Fedorov, *op. cit.*, p. 10.

[28] Data in *Soviet Trade*, stat. handb., 1956, pp. 133–34, in conjunction with official price indices for the official and kolkhoz trade, indicate that the prices of the products primarily sold in kolkhoz trade were in 1940 about 85 per cent higher than in official trade (for details, see chapter 11). Rather close to this is a statement by M. Eidelman in an article on the method of calculating the real wage (*Courier of Statistics*, 1956, No. 3, p. 42) that in 1940 the prices in kolkhoz trade exceeded those for the same products in official trade by 60 per cent. The scattered evidence on individual prices in kolkhoz markets in Moscow, reported by the United States

accompanied by a large increase in sales, in spite of the poor 1938 crops, is also improbable. An increase in prices in kolkhoz trade only of 5 per cent for such a year as 1940 would likewise have been a miracle. Of the data of the two authors, only the large rise in prices and the small reduction in sales in 1939 make sense. Even in this case the amounts sold appeared reasonable only in relation to those of 1938. The sales of this year and, for that matter, those of 1940, were distorted by the great exaggeration of the 1938 sales.[29]

With a 175 per cent rise of prices in kolkhoz trade from 1937 to 1940, a decline in the sales in this trade in real terms of about 15 per cent is implied for these years (on the basis of the 1940 official estimate of the turnover prior to revision) and a decline of fully 40 per cent on the basis of the estimate after its revision.[30] The prices in kolkhoz trade actually increased by about 60 per cent from 1939 to 1940. In conjunction with the revised official estimate of sales in kolkhoz trade in 1940, this price rise implies a decline in volume of trade of about 40 per cent, in spite of a considerably better crop (in the calendar year 1939 the kolkhoz trade was receiving its sup-plies from two poor crops, 1938 and 1939). Even the decrease in sales in real terms of 15 per cent, indicated by the estimate of the 1940 turnover prior to its revision in conjunction with the great jump in

---

embassy (see, for example, I. B. Kravis and Joseph Mintzes in *Review of Economics and Statistics,* May, 1950, p. 167) and others, point to even a much higher level of prices in this trade in 1940.

The prices of products primarily sold in kolkhoz trade (potatoes, vegetables, meat, milk, and eggs) increased in official trade by about 60 per cent from 1937 to 1940 (*Essay I,* pp. 11–12). The percentage goes down to about 50 after an allowance is made for grain.

This writer and Mrs. Janet Chapman assumed that in 1937 the prices in kolkhoz markets were about the same as in the official trade. Evidence compiled by Jerzy F. Karcz of the RAND Corporation indicates that the prices in kolkhoz markets were somewhat lower than in the official trade in the year stated. Thus, on the basis of all this material, the prices in kolkhoz trade in 1940 must have been close to threefold those in 1937. On the basis of Eidelman's statement, the excess of the 1940 prices in kolkhoz trade over those in 1937 was equal to about 165 per cent. (It is assumed in both calculations that in 1937 the prices in kolkhoz trade were 10 per cent below those in official trade.)

[29] The fact that Dadugin and Kagarlitskii distorted the prices of and sales in 1940 kolkhoz trade certainly points to the probability that something was to be concealed. Straight handling of the 1940 data is indeed not found in other sources released both prior to and after the revision of the 1940 sales. As was mentioned, *Forty Years of Soviet Trade* (p. 112) listed the sales in kolkhoz trade in 1933–40 year by year. The year 1939 was, however, omitted. This was obviously done to conceal the impossible fact that the 1940 estimate revised downward (29.1 billion rubles), given by the source for this year, turned out lower than that for 1939 (30.3 billion rubles), in spite of the better crops and much higher prices.

[30] Actually a threefold increase in prices in kolkhoz trade from 1937 to 1940 seems to be more correct. But here an earlier calculation of a 175 per cent rise is retained.

prices, points to immensely distorted conditions in this year, i.e., still before the entrance of the USSR into World War II.

A check of the 1940 turnover in kolkhoz trade may be attempted by comparisons with data for both 1939 and the postwar years. A Soviet source, here cited from *Soviet Studies,* 1956 (p. 370), contained data on sales of a number of products in kolkhoz trade in 1933 through 1935. These data can be extended to 1939 with the help of evidence given by Dadugin and Kagarlitskii, in percentage terms in the form of a chart (see *op. cit.,* p. 6). The approximate turnover obtained in this manner for 1939 is as follows (in thousands of tons):

Meat	575
Milk and dairy products	2,650
Eggs (million units)	1,600
Potatoes	4,350
Vegetables[a]	1,150

[a] Including melons.

Data recently supplied by M. Makarova, who presumably was a staff member of the statistical organization covering this item, indicate that the turnover in kolkhoz trade in 1940 in real terms, increased greatly from 1939. She reported that[31] "on the eve of the Great Patriotic War" (this always means 1940) the following large proportions of total marketings by agriculture were sold in kolkhoz trade: about 18 per cent of grain, more than 50 per cent of meat, and about 40 per cent of milk and dairy products. Data on total marketings of farm products in *Attainments* (p. 154) imply, on the basis of the percentages given by Makarova, the following approximate huge amounts as sold in kolkhoz trade in 1940: grain, 6.9 million tons, more than 945,000 tons of meat, and 4.3 million tons of milk and dairy products. Is it possible in view of these data that a decline in turnover in kolkhoz trade of 40 per cent in real terms occurred from 1939 to 1940? Even the decline of 15 per cent in real terms implied in the official estimate of 1940 kolkhoz trade prior to its revision seems too large.

Official data in physical terms are available for the sales of different products in the kolkhoz markets of 251 cities in 1950 and subsequent years (*Soviet Trade,* stat. handb., p. 185). The stated sales in 1955 are supposed to have been equivalent to 63.7 per cent of the total ex-village kolkhoz trade (see *ibid.,* pp. 19, 188). After the 1955 figures

[31] M. Makarova, *Soviet Trade and People's Consumption* (Moscow, 1954), p. 17.

for the 251 markets are adjusted accordingly, they can be brought to the level of 1940 with the official indices (see *ibid.*, p. 180). The following approximate amounts are then obtained for the 1940 kolkhoz trade (in thousands of tons; for eggs, in millions of units):[32]

Grain	345
Meat	361
Milk and dairy products[a]	705
Eggs	377
Potatoes	757
Vegetables[b]	850

[a] Including butter.
[b] Including melons.

Compare these figures with those implied for 1940 in Makarova's evidence or, for that matter, with those calculated above for 1939! Makarova's data indicate a turnover of grain in kolkhoz trade in 1940 of 6.9 million tons, when the turnover was equal only to about 350,000 tons on the basis of data in the recent official statistical handbook for trade.

The evidence on the turnover in kolkhoz trade in 1940 is certainly not fully conclusive, but it seems sufficient to reject the downward revision of the original estimate of 41.2 billion rubles, which with reasonably correct prices indicate a decline in the volume of turnover in kolkhoz trade of about 15 per cent from 1937 to 1940.

There remains to fill in the breach between 1937 and 1940. The turnover in kolkhoz trade in 1938 may be assumed on the basis of Dadugin and Kagarlitskii's data in physical terms to have been about 5 per cent larger than that in 1937. The turnover in kolkhoz trade in 1939 at constant prices declined by 5 per cent from 1938 to 1939, according to the same authors (p. 5; the data of their chart on p. 6 are roughly in agreement with this). Accepting their evidence and using the findings for 1940 previously obtained, we have the following changes in the volume of sales in kolkhoz trade since 1937 (from year to year):

Increase in 1938 of 5 per cent.
Decline in 1939 of about 5 per cent.
Decline in 1940 of about 15 per cent.

[32] The individual figures are inexact to the extent that the coefficient 63.7 to 100 used for converting the 1955 turnover in kolkhoz markets of 251 cities into the total ex-village kolkhoz trade applies only to the turnover as a whole rather than to individual products as it is used here

This series compares with that of Dadugin and Kagarlitskii as follows (year-to-year changes in per cent of preceding year at constant prices):

Year	Dadugin and Kagarlitskii	N.J.
1938	+58	+5
1939	−5	−5
1940 (original estimate)	+28	−15
1940 (revised estimate)	−10	...

From the combination of the data on sales at current and constant prices, the following year-to-year development of prices in kolkhoz trade since 1937 emerges:

> Increase in 1938 of about 30 per cent.
> Increase in 1939 of about 30 per cent.
> Increase in 1940 of about 60 per cent.

This year-to-year timing of sales and prices seems to make sense. The large rise in prices in the kolkhoz trade in 1938 even led to a small increase in sales in this trade in spite of the very poor crops in that year (however, the first half of the calendar year 1938 was the second half of the excellent 1937/38 crop year). The further strong rise in prices in kolkhoz trade in 1939 prevented more than a small decline in sales in spite of the repeated unsatisfactory crops. Ultimately, the better crops and even greater rise in prices than in each of the two preceding years could not prevent a certain decline in sales in kolkhoz trade in 1940. Without these two factors, the great disorganization which existed even prior to entrance of the USSR in World War II would have made the decline in sales large.

Thus the fact that in 1940 the prices in kolkhoz trade were 75 per cent higher (possibly even more) than those in official trade, a situation which seems to have come as a *deus ex machina,* actually represented the result of a prolonged development toward great scarcity. A large price differential between the kolkhoz trade and official trade had already developed in 1938, in spite of the fact that the first half of the calendar year was the second half of the excellent 1937 crop year. In the 1939 calendar year, in which two poor crop years were joined, this price differential rose to about 50 per cent. Then the further increase of the price differential to 75 per cent, or more, in 1940 seems natural, under the exceptional conditions of that year.[33]

[33] Data for Moscow kolkhoz markets indicate a larger price increase in 1939 and a considerably smaller increase in 1940 than those estimated for the total kolkhoz trade in the text. The repeated poor crop in 1939 and the start of World War II may well have had an even greater effect on the prices in kolkhoz trade in the second half of 1939 than is assumed here (see also p. 221, below).

In such disturbed conditions as those of the *Purge Era,* one would, of course, want to study the development of prices in kolkhoz trade in periods of less than a year, but as yet this writer has been unable to do this. The prices in the second half of 1937 certainly were substantially less than the average for the whole year. The prices in 1940 may well have been 3.5 times those in the second half of 1937. Quite an inflation!

On the occasion of the fortieth anniversary, this writer received a gift from the Finance Ministry of the USSR in the form of prices in urban kolkhoz markets in 1941–45 for every third month. The prices in 1941 were given in the source as follows (in per cent of average 1940 prices):[34]

January............	103
April..	95
July................	88
October............	112

It certainly came as a surprise that, rather than a seasonal rise, prices showed a decline in the second half of the 1940/41 crop year. Even more unexpected was the fact that the entrance of the USSR in World War II at first brought about only a small increase in the prices in kolkhoz trade. This whole price development was clearly the result of the fact that prices in kolkhoz trade were already high in 1940.

The opinion has been expressed in the West that the prices in kolkhoz trade were rising in 1940. This idea seems not to be supported by the new evidence. It is likely that after the prices of most non-food commodities in official trade were raised drastically, especially beginning with July 15, 1940, the purchasing power of the population was absorbed to such an extent that less was left than previously for purchases in kolkhoz trade. The realization of the relatively good 1940 crop also must have had a depressing effect on the prices in kolkhoz trade in the second half of 1940. The available evidence on the prices in kolkhoz markets of Moscow on January 1, 1940, likewise points to a price level early in the year above the yearly average. If those prices are in any way representative, there must have been a skyrocketing of prices in the second half of 1939, possibly caused by the beginning of World War II outside of the USSR. The prices may have doubled or nearly doubled during that year, possibly during a period of several months.

The fact that the USSR was one of the victors in World War II keeps one from realizing how precarious the situation in that country

[34] *Finances and Socialist Construction,* 1957, p. 39.

was and, specifically, to what an extent the country's economy was already disorganized even prior to its entrance into the war.[35] The almost endless designation of 1940, with its immense deprivations, as the "prewar" year by official sources certainly helps to mislead the rest of the world. One has to grant this. One also has to grant that only a totalitarian power with the Soviet Union's intensity (a totalitarian power of Italy's intensity would not have been powerful enough) could have held the country together during World War II, with the population starving and millions dying from this cause.

The Attack on the Peasants' Economy and the Needs of the Population

The attack on the private economy of the kolkhoz peasants, which started in 1938, was also an attack on the kolkhoz trade. It is therefore interesting to ascertain how the socialized economy was prepared to take over the supplying of the population with the foods primarily sold in kolkhoz trade.

The kolkhoz peasants, the principal sellers in kolkhoz trade, had no facilities for processing milk to make butter, even if this would have been profitable. In any case, of whatever butter there was for sale around 1938, practically all reached the consumers by way of the official trade. But all milk sales in this trade amounted to only about 900,000 tons in 1937 (see Table 14, p. 163). These sales, moreover, comprised certain amounts of cheese, sour cream, and other dairy products except butter. Furthermore, hospitals, schools, and eating places had the first claim on any milk available for sale in official retail trade. Part of the sales in this trade were, moreover, effected in rural areas.

The total consumption of fresh milk in urban areas was very small in 1937, and the share of the official trade in supplying these areas was negligible. Consumers had only two ways of providing a little milk for their children—to purchase it from the producers directly or to produce it themselves.

The state supplied only about one-third of the small amount of fresh meat consumed in 1937. It may, indeed, come as a surprise that the non-farm population produced almost as much fresh meat as was sold to it by official trade. A third portion of about equal size was obtained from kolkhoz trade.

[35] This disorganization, which must presumably be one of the aftereffects of the purges, may have been a contributing factor in the meteoric rise of the prices in kolkhoz trade in 1942 and in the first half of 1943. The subsequent decline in the second half of 1943, as well as in 1944, to less than half the level reached in April of 1943 may indicate that the 1942/43 price level in kolkhoz trade was higher than was justified by the supply situation.

About 2.5 million tons of potatoes were sold in official trade in 1937 in both urban and rural areas. The sales in kolkhoz trade were somewhat larger than this. It is unlikely that official trade supplied more than 25 per cent of the requirements of the urban population for this staple food.

The sale of eggs in official trade in 1937 did not even amount to 1 billion units, little more than a dozen eggs per capita of the non-farm population. Some 1,375 million units were sold in kolkhoz trade, and possibly a not much smaller number was produced by the non-farm population itself.

The role of kolkhoz trade was also rather important in vegetables.

Thus, the Soviet state declared war on the kolkhozniki's private enterprise and on the kolkhoz trade, although it supplied the urban population with no milk and the non-farm population with perhaps 35 kilograms of potatoes and 13 eggs per capita per year (a modest requirement is not much less than 150 kilograms of potatoes and at least 100 eggs a year per capita).

Personal Incomes

The neglect of personal incomes in United States research on the Soviet economy has been discussed in the Preface. An appendix note in my monograph published in 1951, a paper by Mrs. Chapman published in *Review of Economics and Statistics* in May, 1954, and a study on the subject published in France and neglected in the United States are all that have been done on this vital issue.[36] My calculations were made with 1928 weights (the Laspeure method). Mrs. Chapman's analysis made by the same method confirmed them fully, but she added a calculation with 1937 weights (the Paasche method) which yielded the obviously wrong result that real wages reached the 1928 level by 1952. This implied, of course, that the 1928 level of real wages was exceeded considerably in 1955 and even more in 1958. (It was not the Paasche method that was wrong, but the calculations made in using it.) The deplorable state of research in this field is revealed by the fact that Mrs. Chapman's incorrect findings by the Paasche method are constantly offered either as an alternative or in combination with her correct calculations by the Laspeure method (the latter is obviously spoiled by such use).

[36] An insight into what is going on in the field of research on the Soviet economy may be obtained from the memorandum of the RAND Corporation, "Arithmancy, Theomancy and the Research on the Soviet Economy," *Journal of Political Economy*, May, 1954; this writer's paper, "On the Wrong Track," *Soviet Studies* (Glasgow), 1956; RAND's letter and this writer's reply in consecutive issues of the same journal. It was this writer's research which was classed as "Theomancy" in RAND's paper, which, incidentally, was signed by Norman Kaplan.

The literature on the incomes of the nearly 100 million Soviet peasants is at present limited to the calculation of incomes in 1938 (1928 equals 100) in my book on Soviet agriculture, but that calculation was almost immediately withdrawn as incorrect.[37] An attempt to fill the breach is made in my "Peasant Incomes under Full-Scale Collectivization" (to be published together wth three other essays at about the same time as this volume).

While western European analysis was greatly inadequate, the previous blackout has been to some extent lifted by the recent publication of a number of official statistical handbooks, especially the one on Soviet trade. Before this, one could operate effectively almost exclusively with prices and nominal wages. This evidence, when applied to the evidence on retail trade in nominal terms, indicated more or less reduced consumption after 1928, but the findings were too general and indeed too uncertain. A careful analysis of the material in the official statistical handbook devoted to trade and published in 1956 permits considerable progress in clarifying the situation. Some use of this material has been made in various parts of this volume.

The analysis in chapter 7 of the amounts consumed by the non-farm population in 1937 showed an immense lag in the consumption of most foods as compared with the level of consumption before the start of the Great Industrialization Drive. Fat, the consumption of which remained very small, and potatoes were the only exceptions. There was also a lag in the utilization of textiles and footwear. The analysis of sales in the preceding portion of this chapter shows that the situation was worse in 1940 than in 1937.

Real Wages.—The only item reasonably settled with reference to the real wages in the period discussed seems to be the average real wage in 1937. It was estimated at 57.6 per cent of that in 1928 (1926/27 weights).[38] Mrs. Chapman obtained the same figure in her calculation for non-farm wage earners with the composition of expenditures in 1928 used as weights.[39] In this volume an index of 60 (a round figure) is used for that year.

The average nominal wage of all wage earners grew by 9.6 per cent from 1936 to 1937. The prices in official trade were assumed to have remained about unchanged. Calculations of Dadugin and Kagarlitskii indicate an increase in prices in kolkhoz trade of

---

[37] See "The Kolkhoz System, the Achilles Heel of Soviet Power," *Soviet Studies,* October, 1951.

[38] *Essay I,* p. 69.

[39] Mrs. Chapman has an index of 58 for real wages before bond purchases and taxes, and an index of 57 after bond purchases and taxes.

9.4 per cent.[40] The real wage in 1936 may be assumed to have been equal to 55 per cent of that in 1927, although this may be a slight downward stretch relative to the estimate of 60 per cent for 1937.

In 1938, the average nominal wage exceeded that of 1937 by 13.4 per cent. Prices in official trade are assumed to have remained unchanged, while prices in kolkhoz trade are calculated as having grown by about 30 per cent. The increase in the prices in kolkhoz trade must have swallowed up about half of the rise in nominal wages, and the average real wage of 1938 is assumed to have been equal to 64 per cent of that in 1928.

Since the number of those to be provided for from the wages, i.e., the wage earners themselves and their dependents, declined per wage earner by not quite 10 per cent from 1928 to 1938, the average real income per capita of the wage earners and their families in 1938 was about 70 per cent of that in 1928.[41]

The data for 1937 and 1938 show that a more or less substantial rise in nominal wages was permitted in the first two years of the *Purge Era;* and if not all these increases benefited the wage earners, it was because the state could not control the kolkhoz trade. There is, of course, the question of whether such a relatively large rise in nominal wages would have been permitted if the prices in kolkhoz trade had remained unchanged.

The relatively favorable trend in real wages during the first two years of the *Purge Era* occurred in the face of only a small increase in national income. Thus, the *Purge Era,* in this respect, too, went contrary to the basic aim of the Party, that private consumption must rise less rapidly than national income.

The difference in the behavior of real wages during the first two years of the *Three "Good" Years* compared with the first two years of the *Purge Era* is indeed striking. Real wages seem not to have grown at all in the first two years of the *Three "Good" Years* despite a rapid growth of national income during this period; but they rose relatively fast during the first two years of the *Purge Era,* with its low over-all rates of economic growth.

A further increase in the nominal wage of 9.8 per cent occurred from 1938 to 1939. But by 1938 an acute disproportion between expansion in total purchasing power of the population and the available supplies of consumers' goods began to develop. Prices in official trade are assumed to have grown in 1939 about as much as

[40] *Op. cit.,* p. 5.
[41] While the earnings of wives from gainful employment are considered in the calculation, the fact is not considered that this employment tends to raise family expenses.

nominal wages, although the increases in them may have been some-what larger. In mid-1939 when World War II started in western Europe, the need of the state for consumers' goods increased greatly (mainly for stockpiling), and this must have occurred almost entirely at the expense of private consumers. The report in *Monthly Labor Review* (November, 1939, p. 1277) described the conditions in July of 1939 as follows: "Bread lines and long lines for the purchase of various consumers' goods have been accompanied by an increase of underground private trade. . . ." Sugar, for example, was sold on the black market at twice the official price. The list of goods provided by the source—supposedly to be sold in state and co-operative stores, but actually not on sale in mid-1939—was very long indeed.

Prices in kolkhoz trade in 1939 again went up by about 30 per cent. The real wage was hardly much higher in 1939 than in 1937.

Recapitulating the development from 1937 to 1939 (this is neces-sary because the real wage in 1937 is established with reasonable certainty and because clarity on the development from 1937 to 1939 helps establish a proper background for the analysis of the compli-cated situation in 1940), we have: an increase in the nominal wage of 23 per cent; a rise in prices in official trade of 10 per cent, or somewhat more; and a price jump in kolkhoz trade of perhaps 70 per cent.

It must, however, be kept in mind that a yearly average for a year such as 1939 is not very illuminating. It seems certain that after the start of World War II, a great deal of disorganization set in at once, and the prices in kolkhoz trade began to rise by leaps and bounds. The only available evidence on the prices in kolkhoz trade at that time, that for Moscow markets on January 1, 1940, indicates a very high level of prices in this trade by the end of 1939. The prices in official trade were also higher at the end of 1939 than the average for the whole year. At that time the real wage was already quite measurably below that in 1937.

The following calculations of increases in living costs of wage earners, based on prices in official trade, have been made (in per cent):

1937 to 1940[a]. 35.6
July 1938, to July 1940 and January 1941[b].   53

[a] *Essay I*, p. 111.
[b] *Études et Conjoncture*, April, 1955, p. 343.

The two calculations for 1940 differ mainly because the first calcula-tion is based on average prices for 1940, while the second applies only to the second half of that year, when living costs were much higher than in the first half.

The average nominal wage rose by 6.5 per cent from 1939 to 1940 (a very small increase for the conditions of the time) for a total increase of 33 per cent since 1937. Thus, the rise in the nominal wage in 1937–40 had not quite offset even the increase in prices in official trade alone, if the calculation is on an annual basis. The compensation by way of rising nominal wages was certainly inadequate, if the price rise in the official trade is taken to the end of 1940. The French calculation, indeed, points to a 13 per cent real-wage decline from mid-1938 to the second half of 1940—again on the basis of prices in official trade only.

There is no way of estimating the people's difficulties resulting from shortages of goods in official trade, except those arising from the high prices charged in kolkhoz trade. But these difficulties were certainly large. The jump in number of courses served in official eating places from 5.6 billion in 1939 to 8.1 billion in 1940 is one of many indications of the rapidly increasing difficulties in obtaining food. But the great burden for the wage earners from the developments in the kolkhoz trade is obvious. Sales of food (other than beverages) in official trade amounted to 88.8 billion rubles in 1940.[42] The official estimate of sales in kolkhoz trade in that year was 41.2 billion rubles prior to the revision. The farm population certainly had a share several times larger in purchases of food (other than beverages) from official trade than it had in purchases from kolkhoz trade. Hence, it seems reasonably correct to assume that one-third of the food purchases (other than beverages) of the urban population was obtained from kolkhoz trade. It follows that the 75 per cent or more by which the prices in kolkhoz trade exceeded those in official trade were paid on about 20 per cent of the total workers' purchases.[43] This is equivalent to about 16 per cent, or more, of the workers' whole budget. Therefore, the real-wage index in 1940 was some 15 per cent below that in 1937 or, as unbelievable as it may seem, only a little more than 50 per cent of that in 1928.

In the second half of 1940 the real wage was still lower than the yearly average by about 10 per cent. Thus, if the calculations made here are at least reasonably correct, real wages already had slipped to below the disastrous level of the *All-out Drive* before the entrance of the USSR into World War II.

Peasant incomes.—In the special essay on "Peasant Incomes under

[42] Implied in *Soviet Trade*, stat. handb., 1956, pp. 40–41.
[43] Food took 54 per cent of the workers' budget in 1926/27. The percentage was considerably larger than this in 1940.

Full-Scale Collectivization," already mentioned (p. 224), per capita real income was calculated (in per cent) as follows (1928 equals 100):

1937................ 81
1938................ 64
1939................ 65
1940................ 66

Considerable time has been devoted to this essay during the past six or seven years, and the figure for 1940 incomes has been a part of this tabulation for years.[44] The procedure by which the 1937 and 1938 real peasant incomes were established seemed to assure a reasonably accurate result. Incomes in 1939–40 were determined by relating them to 1937. First there were to be considered the gross receipts of farm products in kind by the kolkhozniki from their own production and from distributions from their kolkhozy. The size of the 1937 receipts of the kolkhozniki from their kolkhozy made them outstanding in the history of collective farming. Grain is by far the predominant item among distributions in kind by the kolkhozy, and the 1937 grain distributions exceeded those of any other year by more than 10 million tons, or by more than one-third. The private production of the kolkhozniki in 1937 may likewise have surpassed that of any other year of the collectivization era.

The private production of the kolkhozniki declined sharply in 1938 and 1939. Part of the decline was recovered in 1940, provided the crops were harvested in a normal way (this is assumed here, although there were signs of serious disorganization). The distributions by the kolkhozy, which also went down sharply in 1938, did not display any signs of recovery in subsequent years.

All this was to the disadvantage of the peasants. A partial compensation seemed to be that for their sales in kolkhoz trade the kolkhoz peasants parted with only somewhat more supplies in 1938, with the same amount of supplies in 1939, and with even less supplies in 1940 (in all cases as compared with 1937); but received rapidly increasing amounts of money of the same (1938), or of moderately declining (1939), or of more strongly declining (1940) purchasing power in terms of prices in official trade. The 1940 returns from sales in kolkhoz trade represented an especially large purchasing power in terms of these prices.

[44] The topic was handled, although not quite successfully, in the book on agriculture published in 1949 (but completed in 1947). It seems that then the evidence did not permit exact conclusions. Some further improvements could, however, have been made even then by further probing. There was too much else to be taken care of.

The calculated 21 per cent decline in per capita incomes of the farm population from 1937 to 1938 seems to be fully justified by the great worsening all along the line, except for the return from sales in kolkhoz trade.

The distribution by the kolkhozy to the kolkhozniki in 1939 were probably somewhat smaller than in 1938.[45] Their own crop production may have increased somewhat, but this increase is likely to have been offset by the reduced output of animal products. All in all there may have been a small decline in gross receipts in kind, which was properly reflected in the decline in the volume of sales in kolkhoz trade. It is difficult to ascertain whether the net money receipts were larger or smaller in 1939 than in 1938. The change, if any, was hardly significant. Part of the considerably greater money return in kolkhoz trade was offset by the not yet strong rise in prices in official trade. The balance in money incomes may have been a net gain as compared with the preceding year.

In 1940, distributions by the kolkhozy in kind probably remained at the 1939 level; they did not, in any case, increase. The private output of the kolkhozniki should have increased with the better weather, provided nothing interfered with planting and harvesting.[46] The amounts of the products sold by the kolkhizniki in kolkhoz trade showed a greater decline in 1940 than in 1939. The prices at which these products were sold increased considerably more than the prices of industrial goods in official trade. There seemed to be sufficient reason to assume an increase in peasant real incomes from 1939 to 1940.

However, as revealed by *Soviet Trade,* stat. handb., 1956, the total rural population was only able to spend as many rubles in 1940 as in 1939 on purchases from official trade in rural areas, and if the purchases of the *rural non-farm population* were increased, as they may well have been, the spendings of the peasants may even have declined. The amount of goods obtained by the farm population from the official trade must have gone down by 25 per cent or more in that one year. On the evidence in the 1956 handbook on Soviet trade and other recent data, the real per capita income of the peasants is now estimated at 60 per cent of that in 1928, implying a decline of 7–9 per cent since 1938 and 1939 (for the estimates for 1938 and 1939 see tabulation above). Obviously, a certain, indeed quite substantial, amount of money was not spent at all in that year, and must have accumulated in the hands of the peasants. Later this accumulation was almost completely lost. There may already have been

[45] The distribution of grain declined by about 12 per cent. See *Soc. Agri.,* pp. 411, 695.
[46] Somehow one suspects that harvesting operations did not proceed normally in that year. But this writer has no evidence to support this suspicion.

some relatively large amounts of money carried over from 1939. There seems to be no clear-cut answer to the question of how those various pluses and minuses in peasant incomes add up. Specifically, should the money saved and later lost be counted at its full value at the end of 1940, or should all or part of it be written off in the calculation of the 1940 incomes? [47]

The trend in peasant incomes during the *Purge Era* as calculated above differed from that of the wage earners during the same period. It has been shown that real wages rose more or less substantially for two years (1937 and 1938) and then declined in 1940 by more than the total previous advance. By the end of 1940 wage earners' incomes were as low as at the catastrophic time at the end of the *All-out Drive*. Real incomes of the peasants, on the other hand, jumped strongly in 1937, then declined in a similar manner, but they were measurably better in 1940 than in 1932.

The difference was due to the fact that while wage levels were primarily determined by political decisions, peasant incomes were less influenced by them. The harvests affected peasant incomes much more than they did the real incomes of the wage earners.

In 1937 and again in 1940, the real incomes of the peasants were relatively higher than the real incomes of the wage earners. In 1937, this was brought about by the bountiful crops. The peasants profited more from them then than they would now. The grip of the state on the supplies of farm products was not yet so strong as it became later. In 1940, the higher relative level of peasant incomes was brought about by the inability of the state to control the prices in kolkhoz trade, which unfavorably affected real wages. High prices in this trade devalued real wages in 1938 and 1939 as well.

The total consumption of the populaton is obviously determined by the supplies of consumers' goods. Leeway exists only with

[47] Fantastic rises in the real incomes of the kolkhoz peasants from 1940 to 1948 and later years are claimed officially. The claim for 1952, the last Stalin year, when peasant incomes were extremely low, represents an increase over 1940 of 73 per cent (see chapter 17). No explanation whatsoever was ever given as to how this figure was arrived at. An immense overestimate of the so-called social wage in postwar years certainly played a great role in the overestimate of the postwar real incomes of the peasants as officially calculated. But this source alone is unlikely to have caused the total monstrous overestimate. The only other means of manipulation which occurs to this writer is the writing-off of all peasant money savings in the year 1940. Of course, the fact that no other means of manipulation occur to one does not mean that they did not exist.

The official claims for peasant incomes in post–World War II years in terms of 1940 mentioned above were dropped at the end of 1958, again without explanation. No standing official index for peasant incomes in 1952 exists. For 1950 the previous index was 145 (1940 equals 100); now it is 118 (implied in *Courier of Statistics*, 1960, No. 4, p. 91). But even the scaled-down index seems to be excessive.

reference to the distribution of the latter. It can be presumed that in 1940, and also somewhat earlier, the state was withdrawing all the goods it felt were needed for the armed forces and for stockpiling. The inability of the state to control the prices in kolkhoz trade gave the peasants more of what remained than was intended for them. It is impossible to decide to what extent this occurred. The experience of the late 1940's shows that, even when it was in a position to do so, the Stalin government granted very little to the peasants.

The great increase in prices effective July 15, 1940, of the most important non-food goods in official trade was one of the measures taken by the state to offset the effect of the high prices in kolkhoz trade, but it was too mild a measure to act against the hurricane-like developments in the kolkhoz trade.[48] The crude measure of just not providing the shops in rural areas with goods proved much more effective.

It still is possible that the *nominal* wages in 1939 and especially in 1940 would have been lower if it had not been for the high prices in kolkhoz trade, and, hence, that the peasants did not appropriate everything resulting from the high prices in kolkhoz trade.

National Income

According to Appendix B, Table I, national income is estimated to have increased in 1937–40 by about 10 per cent. This is probably a fairly accurate estimate, but it is not impossible that the estimate is slightly high. Net national income, less duplication, increased by 5.3 billion rubles (at real 1926/27 prices). The increase in the expenditure on the armed forces is estimated at 7.6 million rubles. Thus, net income, less the economically wasted expenditure on the armed forces, declined over the three-year period.

Net investment is estimated at the same figure for both 1937 and 1940; the estimate for 1940, while a drastic cut from official claims, may still be too favorable.

Total personal incomes for 1940 are estimated at 7.5 per cent below those in 1937. In this case, too, the 1940 estimate may be, relatively, somewhat too high.

[48] The French calculations (*Études et Conjoncture*, April, 1955, p. 342) show for the official trade an increase in food prices of 55 per cent and in non-food commodities of 75 per cent from July 1, 1938, to the second half of 1940.

THE
POST–WORLD WAR II
PERIOD

CHAPTER 10

STALIN HAS EVERYTHING HIS WAY

Introduction

In a sense, the entire Great Industrialization Drive era typified Stalin's "way." For Stalin to have everything his way, the individual peasant needed to be exterminated. Experience in the USSR prior to the Great Industrialization Drive, and recently reaffirmed by experiences in the satellite countries, showed that a collectivization drive must be implemented with force. Collective farming has no economic advantages to assure its rapid spread by the relatively mild means compatible with democracy. Moreover, Stalin needed full collectivization almost overnight, and this was impossible without the deprivations and sufferings of the full-scale Collectivization Drive.

For Stalin to have everything his way, suitable forms of planning had to be developed. Under the conditions of the full-scale Collectivization Drive, planning called for immense outputs as well as for appropriations for investment that far exceeded the country's capacities. It was to a considerable extent planning of this sort which, in little more than a year, so disorganized the economy that during 1931 and 1932 real national income, properly calculated, instead of increasing rapidly began to decrease. Even such keys to the Great Industrialization Drive as steel, coal, and petroleum did not escape the common fate of first stagnating and then (in the winter of 1932/33) declining.

Full-scale collectivization plus bacchanalian planning, plus many related features, added up to the *All-out Drive,* the second stage of the Great Industrialization Drive.

Just as Lenin needed the NEP (New Economic Policy) as a breathing space after his abortive attempt at introducing communism on the basis of grain taken by force from the peasants and distributed to the workers on rations via their factories, so Stalin needed a breathing space after the disaster of the *All-out Drive*. It came in the *Three "Good" Years*, the third of the stages into which the Great Industrialization Era is naturally subdivided. "Good" is in quotation marks because the immense lowering of consumption levels during the *All-out Drive* was made the basis of the subsequent recovery during those three years. Those very low consumption levels permitted investments of unprecedented dimensions out of a small national income—great investments which, in their turn, speeded up recovery. The "good" years were, indeed, years with extremely rapid rates of growth.

The NEP lasted almost seven years (almost nine years if *Warming-up,* the period of preparation for the Great Industrialization Drive, is included with the NEP). All that Stalin permitted in the way of a breathing space after the *All-out Drive* was three years. The "good" years were actually the *Three "Good" Years.*

To have everything his way, Stalin needed 100 per cent subordination, a grave-like country. The *Purge Era,* the fourth stage of the Great Industrialization Drive, which had begun in 1936, took care of this. The mass purges were discontinued sometime in 1938, but their paralyzing effect on the economy lasted until the end of 1940.[1]

The path was fully cleared for Stalin to have everything his way. The economy was socialized almost 100 per cent. Nor was there a need for further purges. Everybody behaved as if purged, anyway.[2]

When one reads Stalin's *Economic Problems of Socialism in the USSR* (released in the fall of 1952, about half a year before his death), and the almost endless comments on it, one would think that the path had been cleared for the realization of the law of proportionate expansion of the Soviet socialist economy according to plan. In actual fact, Stalin utilized his unlimited powers for fostering the production of steel. Military might was another favored item,

---

[1] No attempt has ever been made by this writer to study the situation in the first half of 1941. No easily accessible statistics are available, though something might possibly be found.

[2] A. A. Andreev, the Party agricultural boss in the early postwar years, was deprived of his powers, but not murdered or even completely dismissed, sometime in the late forties; he was rehabilitated late in 1955. N. A. Voznesenskii, the president of the Gosplan USSR, seems to have been the only person, on the top *economic* level, who disappeared without a trace in the postwar years (1948). It seems certain that he was murdered on Stalin's orders at that time and, moreover, possibly for opinions directly connected with his job. He is said to have advocated greater attention to agriculture in a meeting of the Politbureau.

but military might also consists primarily of steel. Such propaganda stunts as "Stalin changes the climate of Russia" by means of forest belts and artificial irrigation schemes rounded off the list of Stalin's favored projects. Everything else was largely neglected—the more so, the less it happened to be connected with steel. Although steel production was the aim of the Great Industrialization Drive, never before had there been such a concentrated effort in this direction.

Comparing the recovery after World War II with that after World War I is not very fruitful. The whole social setup had changed too much. It is much more illuminating to compare the recovery after World War II with the *Three "Good" Years,* the recovery period after the devastations of the *All-out Drive.* The situations were quite similar in the two periods. The aims and the means were the same. In particular, both periods were characterized by restraints on the recovery of consumption levels and use of the extremely low consumption levels at the end of the preceding period as the springboard for the recovery and expansion of the output of producers' goods, construction, and investment.

In view of these similarities, the fact of the ever greater concentration on steel, the basic aim of the Great Industrialization Drive during the post–World War II period, is most important. While past experience prevented a repetition of such absurdities as were committed in planning during the *All-out Drive,* this experience also showed the immense amount of pressure that the Soviets could apply, at least temporarily, on the people. Ample use was made of this type of experience in the *Stalin Has Everything His Way* period. The practices of the *Three "Good" Years* were, indeed, exceeded in all respects, partly owing to experience and partly owing to freedom even from the moderate restraint Stalin had been under during the earlier period. This may explain the difference in the manner in which each of the periods came to its end.

The end of the *Three "Good" Years,* as far as can be determined, came from outside the economy, from a purely political development. The end of *Stalin Has Everything His Way* was brought about, however, by internal weaknesses. Stalin's death may have shortened the period and simplified its end. The fact that the earlier period lasted only three years, while the later period lasted much longer, seems not to have had much to do with the different ways in which the two periods ended.

The first requirement for the attainment of Stalin's goal was large investment. Investment had been relatively large immediately after the end of World War II and was expanded after this, year after year, by leaps and bounds, until Stalin's death. The share of national income appropriated by the state for its needs (investment, armed forces, administration including the MVD, and education and health services) ultimately far exceeded the levels reached in the earlier periods of the Great Industrialization Drive. Correspondingly, real wages were much lower in 1948, the year when the prewar level of investment and industrial output was reached, than in 1939, the last prewar year before the 1940 decline.

There was an unprecedented increase in heavy industry's share in total investment during the *Stalin Has Everything His Way* period. By 1949, investment in heavy industry at constant prices was about one and a half times the prewar amount, and there was a continued high rate of increase after 1949. The needs of education and health services were neglected most of all. Even the transportation system was not provided for adequately, although it is closely linked to heavy industry.

While the share of agriculture in fixed investment had not been reduced since before the war, the investment funds allotted to agriculture were much too small considering the extensive destruction of farm machinery during World War II and the great deficiency of labor, especially the astounding shortage of adult males, in agriculture.[3] Those in power were so used to the idea that agriculture must provide all the labor needed for expansion of the non-farm economy, that no thought was given to the fact that the situation had changed fundamentally as compared with the 1930's. Last, but not least, while the *Three "Good" Years* were marked by a relatively benevolent attitude toward the private economy of the kolkhoz peasants, *Stalin Has Everything His Way* was characterized by a severe encroachment on it. This encroachment, indeed, far exceeded anything done in this respect during the *Purge Era*.

In the 1930's, the effort to reduce the private economy of the kolkhoz peasants did not start before 1938, i.e., before the modest pre-collectivization output level in agriculture was reached. In the 1940's the attack on the kolkhozniki's economy was renewed as soon as World War II was over, at a time when farm output was perhaps 40 per cent below that of 1940 and almost as much lower than in 1928 in a comparable territory. In 1950, i.e., at a time when the prewar level of farm production probably had still not been regained, the Party lashed out full blast against the peasants with Khrushchev's amalgamation-agro-cities campaign.

Smaller than prewar distributions by the collective farms to the

[3] The full extent of the phenomenon did not become known before the announcement of the census taken in January, 1959.

peasants (the result of unchanged or even increased deliveries to the state from a reduced output) and a curtailed output of the kolkhoz peasants themselves, as well as a manifold increase in taxation, combined to spell very small real incomes for the peasants—so small, indeed, that this factor became a decisive handicap to progress, even to progress in the Bolshevist sense.

The large total investment and its great concentration on heavy industry during the *Stalin Has Everything His Way* period did not fail to achieve very high rates of growth in industry, construction, and transportation. Even the 1951 and 1952 rates of growth, which were considerably smaller than those in the preceding three to four years, must be accepted as very large in view of the considerable expansion in military expenditure during these years in addition to full discontinuation of recovery features.

In spite of the great war devastation and the conversion of a large part of industry to armament production, the Soviets succeeded in reconverting industry to peaceful output and reaching the 1940 level of industrial production in about three years. By 1950, the 1940 level of industrial production had been exceeded by 40 per cent or somewhat more. It must be remembered, however, that industrial production in 1940 is not a good yardstick. Two factors easily escape attention. While the acknowledged large losses of the Soviets have been greatly exaggerated—even in this country—the considerable expansion of capacities in the eastern part of the USSR during World War II is ignored. Finally, the comparisons are normally with the 1940 *output*. But owing to the purges this output was substantially below the then existing *capacities*. The Soviets like to speak of inexhaustible reserves. The purges created substantial reserves in the form of unused capacities, which were then put to good use in the postwar recovery.[4]

While industry and the entire non-farm economy were rushing ahead with gigantic strides, desolation could be observed in agriculture. In agriculture, which had not been adequately provided with manpower and machinery, and where the policy of further "socialization" or "communization" was still continuing with great force, output did not even reach the prewar level by 1950 and possibly not even by the end of the *Stalin Has Everything His Way* period. It is, indeed, surprising that it came as close as it did.

The difference between the neglect of the transportation system and the neglect of agriculture in the postwar years was that agriculture was neglected to such an extent that this factor became a

[4] The capacity of blast furnaces, for example, was utilized better in 1948 than in 1940, to the extent of 13 per cent. See *Courier of Statistics*, 1958, No. 6, p. 9.

major obstacle to further progress by the end of the *Stalin Has Everything His Way* period. The transportation system, however, seems to have performed its function more or less adequately until the end of this period. Small defects in service occurred in 1952, it is true. A certain abatement of the dictatorship after Stalin's death sufficed to disclose that the transportation system, too, may have been inadequate for the needs of the economy. Also, the development of innovations, such as transportation by pipe, was totally neglected. Absence of innovations was a general feature of the period, though.

Neglect of agriculture was closely associated with neglect of the needs of the consumers. Real wages, and especially real peasant incomes, were below the prewar level in 1950.[5]

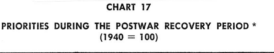

CHART 17

PRIORITIES DURING THE POSTWAR RECOVERY PERIOD *
(1940 = 100)

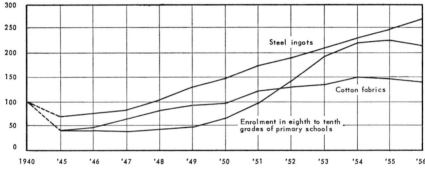

* Data for output of steel and cotton fabrics from *Economy of the USSR in 1956,* pp. 60, 64. Data for school enrolment from *Cultural Construction, USSR,* 1956, pp. 122–23, and *Economy of the USSR in 1956,* p. 246.

Chart 17, called "Priorities . . .," shows the *Stalin Has Everything His Way* period at a glance. The recovery of steel output began in 1946. By 1948, the prewar level of output was exceeded, in spite of the almost complete destruction of the steel industry in the Donbass, the principal steel area of the USSR, during World War II. The 1940 level of steel production was surpassed by 50 per cent in 1950. The recovery in the output of cotton fabrics also began in 1946, but from a much lower level than in the case of steel. The 1940 level had not quite been reached even by 1950. Any recovery of enrolment in the eighth to tenth grades of primary schools did not begin before 1948. In 1947, enrolment in the eighth to tenth grades of primary schools was indeed smaller than in 1945, which had had an

[5] "Prewar" here means prior to the 1940 cuts.

enrolment about 60 per cent below that of 1940. In 1950 enrolment in these grades was still less than two-thirds of that of 1940.

As during the *All-out Drive,* the great deficiency of useful consumers' goods in the early postwar years was to a large part made up by huge (in terms of money) sales of vodka. A large number of the state-owned and co-operative eating places, indeed, have largely become drinking places.

By the end of 1952, the *Stalin Has Everything His Way* period of rapid progress had lasted for about five and a half years,[6] i.e., almost twice the duration of the *Three "Good" Years.* Except for those who always see the dark side of everything, nobody seems to have discerned the full extent of the imminent danger. The situation, is was conceded, was obviously unsatisfactory in agriculture. But the fundamental changes in policies soon to come were not foreseen.[7]

The reports of Malenkov and Khrushchev in the summer of 1953 disclosed very serious deterioration in agriculture, exceeding anything visualized in the West. Yet these disclosures turned out to be only the beginning. The evidence has been given out only bit by bit. The fact that in 1952 all money distributions of the kolkhozy to the kolkhozniki amounted only to 12.4 billion rubles, or 1.4 rubles per *trudoden* earned, equivalent to about 2 rubles per average labor day, was not revealed until 1958. The even lower distributions in the preceding postwar years remain concealed. The situation in agriculture at the end of Stalin's day, indeed, turned out to be so precarious that serious measures to remedy it would have probably come soon, even if Stalin had not died early in 1953.

Thus, Stalin was not wise enough to set a pace which could be followed for a reasonable length of time. He misused his powers and brought the country to an impasse. One is presumably justified in asking whether the purges did not, after all, harm the regime. Without them, the concentration on heavy industry, on steel and ever more steel, and the neglect of agriculture might not have gone so far as they did during the *Stalin Has Everything His Way* period. The development during the *Three "Good" Years* was probably healthier, even from the point of view of the Bolsheviks themselves.

The Soviets do not tire of emphasizing the absence of business depressions, which thus far seem inevitable under capitalism. Actually, the Soviets had a severe crisis, indeed, a catastrophe, in

[6] Five and a half years are obtained by beginning the period with the realization of the 1947 crop. The poor crop of 1946 was a great handicap to rapid recovery.

[7] The failure to recognize the real extent of the disaster was at least partly due to the immense efforts of the Kremlin to conceal it.

1918–20, which was partly or largely brought about by an attempt to introduce communism almost overnight. The NEP was a recovery from this catastrophe. Then came the crisis of the *All-out Drive* period, followed by recovery in the *Three "Good" Years*. The *Purge Era* of the late 1930's was certainly akin to a depression. *Stalin Has Everything His Way* was a period of rapid growth, except in agriculture. Developments in agriculture during the *Post-Stalin* period certainly have important recovery features.

The similarity between certain vital Soviet economic developments and those of business cycles in capitalist countries even extends to post-depression recoveries at particularly high rates, partly at the expense of capacities accumulated during the depressions.

Cases of such an expansion are easily found in the USSR. Part of the growth during the *Three "Good" Years* was of this kind. There would probably have been more of it, had there not been a great deal of complete waste during the *All-out Drive*. The expansion of the non-farm economy during the *Stalin Has Everything His Way* period would have been slower, were it not for the capacities accumulated during the *Purge Era* but only inadequately used then owing to unfortunate conditions of this period. With the help of the previously unused capacities, not only was the prewar level of industrial output restored earlier than could have been expected, but the rate of industrial growth continued above what would have seemed normal for fully three years thereafter. The variations in the rates of growth of industrial output, in transportation, and in many other economic branches during the various stages reflect the phenomenon clearly.

For quite some time it seemed that agriculture and everything dependent on it was the only serious weakness of the *Stalin Has Everything His Way* period. Three years after Stalin's death, namely, in 1956, a moderate slowdown in the expansion of industrial production occurred. The slowdown gained momentum in 1957. The reason, not clear at first, was the insufficiency of new industrial capacities caused by spreading investment funds over too many projects and, consequently, a great accumulation of unfinished investment. Whether this phenomenon had already been in progress before 1951 cannot be ascertained. But it seems certain that the misdirection of investment funds operated on a large scale in the last two years of the *Stalin Has Everything His Way* period. Since under normal conditions it takes about four to five years to complete a large construction project, the effect of this mismanagement on the economic growth was not felt seriously until 1955 or 1956.

What appeared to be a dictatorial power of the highest order proved too weak to enforce proper action even from the ministries and their chief administrations right there in Moscow. The *Post-Stalin* period inherited this mess, and for years either nobody was able to do anything to remedy the situation, or nobody had enough sense to realize the incipient danger.

Population

This writer still feels uncomfortable over the fact that until the Soviets disclosed their estimates a short time ago, he accepted Western estimates of the Soviet population in postwar years, which were too high by more than 20 million. The Western figures could not possibly be fitted into the economic picture of those years—a clear-cut research weakness.

In May or June of 1956, after seventeen years of silence on the size of their population, the Soviets announced a population of 200.2 million for April 1, 1956. Data were also provided on the birth and death rates and the rate of net growth, starting with 1950.[8]

The claimed death rate is one of the lowest in the world. This rate may have been favorably affected by a particularly advantageous age composition which remained concealed. But it may also be the result of undercounting.[9]

The only evidence on population released officially in addition to that mentioned above was that in 1948 the death rate was 27 per cent less than in 1947 and 12 per cent less than in the last prewar year.[10] Fortunately this evidence includes, by implication, 1947, a year which probably marked the beginning of the end of acute want. The evidence implies for 1947 a death rate 20 per cent above that in the last prewar years, i.e., presumably substantially more than 20 per

[8] *Stat. Handb.*, 1956, pp. 18, 243. The new population figure was believed an under-estimate by some Western demographers (see, for example, W. Bracket in *American Statistician*, February, 1959, p. 16). In January, 1959, a population census was taken in the USSR, and it disclosed that the 1956 estimate was a small overestimate. The accuracy of the 1956 estimate is nevertheless simply amazing. The Soviets have shown that, when they want, they can produce excellent statistics.

[9] This writer has discussed the difficulty of bringing the claimed mortality .rate around 1955 into agreement with the crowded housing and poor diet (in *American Statistician*, October, 1957, pp. 18–21). Actually, however, while it is difficult to digest the claimed mortality rate of 8.2 and 7.7 per thousand in 1955 and 1956, a mortality rate of 9.6 per thousand, claimed for 1950, surprises one even more, because the diet was much worse in that year than five to six years later. Medical help and sanitary conditions also were much inferior.

Should the official estimates of the mortality rate turn out too low, the official rates of net growth of the population, used in the calculation below, may still be reasonably correct, if the birth rates are likewise underestimated in official statistics.

[10] *Pravda*, April 23, 1949.

thousand.[11] The birth rate is unlikely to have been much higher than this and may have been lower. Altogether, if there was an increase in the population in 1947, it was small, and there may not have been any increase.

The official figures for the population on April 1, 1956, and for the rates of net growth of the population in 1950–55 indicate a population of 180.2 million on January 1, 1950. This is more than 20 million less than the USSR in the present boundaries had in mid-1941 when it entered World War II. The evidence on the birth rates in 1947 and 1948 quoted above points to a large population growth in 1949 and a not so large, but quite substantial, growth in 1948. The 1948 population may have been equal to about 176 to 177 million and, if 1947 had no population growth to boast of, the level of the population around January of 1948 was about the lowest point. If there was an increase in the population in 1947, then the population at the beginning of 1947 was the bottom.

The loss in population from mid-1941 to the low in 1948 or 1947 is likely to have greatly exceeded 20 million. The bulk of the loss, of course, occurred during World War II in the armed forces, but the starving civilian population also showed huge losses, the latter both during and after the war.

The immense decline in the total population figure does not tell the whole story. A disproportionately great part of the population lost during this period consisted of males of the best working age. Contrary to the situation concerning the total population, information on the great losses specifically of males was available all the time. The 1959 population census only provided exact data on this score.

The revision of notions about the Soviet population is obviously of immense importance. The "achievement" of having restored the prewar level of industrial production by 1948 looms even greater if the tragic population conditions of the period are realized. Industry, primarily heavy industry, was expanding rapidly at the very time when the much smaller-than-prewar population was declining further because of starvation or near-starvation conditions. The plight of agriculture appears even greater in this light. The immense power wielded by the dictatorship and the ruthlessness with which it was used turned out to have been even greater than had been previously believed. It is a relatively minor matter that, because the population in postwar years was actually smaller than previously assumed, the *known* resources of food and other consumers' goods,

[11] The last prewar years of the official source may well have been 1940, for which a mortality rate of 18.3 per thousand is officially claimed.

produced and sold in retail trade, had to provide for fewer mouths than was supposed before the official population figure was announced in 1956.

Understanding of the situation in 1945–47 is immensely clarified by the new evidence on population. The country was scarcely alive when the victory came. Starvation rations were maintained until December 15, 1947. Output of other consumers' goods in 1945 did not much exceed the needs of the armed forces. The population was dwindling rapidly. Yet in the midst of this disaster came the words of the "beloved leader" (February, 1946) demanding the output of 60 million tons of steel and corresponding quantities of pig iron, coal, and petroleum.

Factors Operating toward Recovery

At first glance the speed of the Soviet recovery after World War II seems miraculous, or nearly so, especially since the Union, or Stalin, definitely refused to reconvert its armed forces fully to peacetime levels. The most important factor contributing to the rapid recovery of the USSR from war devastation was, of course, deprivation of the Soviet population. Much has been said on this score already, and more will be said later, especially in the analysis of retail trade and personal incomes. But along with this basic factor, there were numerous others, each lacking decisive significance in itself but very important in the aggregate. These factors are usually not given attention, and the Soviets themselves, of course, are making the greatest efforts to conceal them, while advertising their wartime losses *urbis et orbis*.

Additional factors which helped in the recovery were, for example, the utilization of productive capacities which lay idle in 1940, owing to the adverse effect of the purges on the economy, and the substantial productive capacities brought into existence in the eastern part of the USSR during World War II (concerning these factors, see chapter 12). In addition to these internal resources, the Soviets succeeded in getting substantial help from abroad in the form of material resources from the satellite countries and in the form of work done by German war prisoners.

The gains of the Soviets from the satellites after World War II cannot be calculated with any degree of exactness. What calculations of payments to the USSR are available were made from the point of view of those who paid. The paying country was justified in charging the whole cost of a plant taken over by the Soviets, but the latter usually took only the machinery, and part of this, apparently a large part in many cases, was used only as scrap. Furthermore, the estimates of payments by the satellites were calculated in dollars of 1938 purchasing power, and this writer is unable to recalculate these amounts to correspond with Soviet investment costs in the early postwar years. Whatever shaky suggestions are made below were arrived at with the help of Dr. Nicholas Spulber[12] and Mr. Victor Winston,[13] to whom I want to express my sincere gratitude.

Victor Winston calculated the annual payments and other benefits that the USSR had from the satellites for the period beginning in 1945 and ending in October of 1956 at 5 billion rubles per year. These payments and benefits probably were higher in the earlier years and less since 1953 or 1954. The calculations were made in 1938 dollars and then converted to rubles at the official Soviet exchange rate of 4 rubles to the dollar. But the dollar had a much higher value in rubles. How much more, I do not know.

The bulk of these payments came from Germany. As Dr. Spulber has informed me, the German payments are estimated at $609.6 million per year until 1950 (in 1938 dollars).

The official estimates of the fixed investment of the state in 1945 and 1946, however uncertain these figures may be, are 39.2 and 46.8 billion rubles, respectively, at prices of July 1, 1955.[14] Thus, the receipts from the satellites may have represented 10 per cent, perhaps more, of the total fixed investment of the state. This is, of course, nothing but a guess.

It seems preferable to leave the topic here. One can be certain, it would seem, that even part of the funds calculated as payment from the satellite countries was of considerable help in the recovery of the Soviet economy. This was particularly true at the beginning of the recovery, when the country, having suffered great losses, was in a very disorganized state and the population was starving.

The prisoners of war in the hands of the USSR consisted of German soldiers captured in the USSR as well as German civilians and soldiers taken in Germany. The total number of prisoners is not known, but there may well have been more than two million at one time. The average German was a much better worker than the average Russian, and the civilians taken in Germany, as is well known, were on the whole a select group, including specialists of

[12] Nicholas Spulber, *The Economics of Communist Eastern Europe* (New York, 1957).

[13] Victor Winston, "The Satellites—Economic Liability," *Problems of Communism,* January, 1958, pp. 14–20.

[14] *Economy of the USSR in 1956,* p. 173.

exceptional ability. The Soviets were certainly not in a hurry to release these war prisoners. The last groups did not leave the USSR before 1955 or 1956. This means that the USSR used men during their best working age for up to ten or eleven years (and this does not include the work of prisoners prior to the end of hostilities).

As was the case with the material resources obtained from the satellites, the number of prisoners was greatest in the early recovery years, and the work of each one of them was particularly important in those years, especially prior to full demobilization of the Soviet armed forces.

In 1945, two million war prisoners represented about 10 per cent of the total hired labor employed in material production. In addition, these prisoners were men with above-average qualifications.

Both the material resources obtained from the satellites and the German war prisoners were, of course, spread throughout the whole Soviet economy; but in a sense it can be assumed that practically all of them were used for investment purposes. The other economic sectors presumably could not be reduced below the level at which they actually were. Deprived of the resources from the satellites and of the war prisoners, the USSR would have had considerably fewer material resources and men to use for investment purposes than it actually had. With a much smaller investment, the economic recovery would have been much slower.

It will be shown that it was particularly difficult to get the economic machine started, especially in view of the poor 1946 harvest. The resources from the satellites and the war prisoners may have played a decisive role at this crucial stage.

Planning

Some analysts apparently think that there was a great difference between the planning "in the chaotic and experimental prewar period" and the planning after World War II.[15] The present writer does not share this view.

There is no doubt that the considerable amount of experience in planning gained during the prewar period was utilized in postwar years. But this experience involved only planning techniques, planning routine. Proper planning is not limited to techniques. It needs the application of imagination, of properly directed courage, and of real statesmanship. Who would expect such features under

[15] The quotation is from Peter Wiles, "Changing Economic Thought in Poland," *Oxford Economic Papers*, N.S., June, 1957, p. 205.

the deadening conditions of the Stalin regime at its height, i.e., at its worst.

Thought and statesmanship were absent from Soviet planning, not only during the whole period of *Stalin Has Everything His Way,* but also for almost four years of the *Post-Stalin period.* As concerns imagination, under Stalin it was of such a type that the USSR would have been much better off without it. Actually, even the merely routine revealed great shortcomings.

The absence of thought and statesmanship in planning during *Stalin Has Everything His Way* was not so apparent during the period of recovery, when in most cases it was cheapest and quickest to restore what had been available before World War II rather than to look for something new.

The negative effects of the absence of thought in planning became fully evident only at the end of *Stalin Has Everything His Way,* especially in the Directives to the fifth FYP, worked out in the second half of 1952, several months before Stalin's death.

In 1952 in the Directives to the fifth FYP an enlargement of the output of natural gas of only 0.9 billion cubic meters per year was planned, while the Control Figures for 1959–65 indicate a desired expansion of 15 billion cubic meters per year.[16]

Artificial fiber is another favorite of the Control Figures for 1959–65. The Directives to the fifth FYP scheduled bringing its output to a level 4.3 times higher over a five-year period, but even after reaching this target, fabrics made from artificial fiber would have amounted to only about 7 per cent of the total fabric production. Several more years passed before the Soviet planners realized that artificial fiber must be one of the major materials for fabrics.

And, of course, the Directives to the fifth FYP followed the old path on hydroelectric power, which was scheduled to treble in output during 1950–55, while that of all electric power was only to double. Planning just went on in the old way without real thought, not only during the *Stalin Has Everything His Way* period but for years thereafter.

The plenary session of the Central Committee of the Party of December, 1956, on the report of M. Z. Saburov, recognized existing planning as unrealistic. This appraisal fully applies also to the planning of the *Stalin Has Everything His Way* period. The Directives to the fifth FYP scheduled an increase in hired labor of about 15 per cent, i.e., of about 5.7 million workers and employees. The labor force grew by 7.1 million over the period. This is quite a

---

[16] Directives to the fifth FYP in *Pravda,* October 10, 1952; "Control Figures for 1959–65," in *Pravda,* February 8, 1959.

discrepancy, especially since the planners actually had to plan for only a little more than three years, rather than five years. But the plans of this period also contained items which did not have the smallest chance of being fulfilled and which were presumably included only out of the need to impress the populace.

N. D. Voznesenskii, president of the Gosplan USSR, was assassinated in 1948 on Stalin's orders, allegedly because he showed interest in the agricultural sector of the economy. There is no doubt that what Voznesenskii knew was known to his deputy, Saburov. Voznesenskii's fate would have been shared by Saburov if he had espoused the views of his former superior. So we see that the Directives to the fifth FYP prepared by Saburov called for an increase of farm output by 50 per cent in five years. With the implementation provided in the FYP, the increase would probably not have exceeded 10 per cent, and there might not have been any increase whatsoever. Saburov knew this, of course.

Imagination? Can a wilder product of the imagination exist than the idea that "Stalin is going to change the climate of Russia," the slogan particularly emphasized in 1948–50? Almost nothing of course came of this. Some of the measures taken for attaining "the change in climate" were part of the five Great Stalin Constructions of Communism—a highly ambitious assembly of projects. The great hydroelectric plants at Kuibyshev and Stalingrad now officially recognized as very great blunders, are almost the only parts of the constructions which have been fulfilled. A mystery surrounds the Kakhovka hydroelectric plant, also part of the Stalin Constructions of Communism. It was to be built under immensely difficult conditions (at the swampy mouth of the Dnepr River) with construction costs (per kilowatt of installed capacity) far exceeding those of the expensive Kuibyshev and Stalingrad plants. The partial completion of the plant was announced long ago. Yet the project is included among those to be completed in 1959–65 according to the Seven-Year Plan. I expected from the start, and now suspect even more, some incident such as the river changing its course.

The disorganization in the field of fixed investment, which was in progress in at least the last two Stalin years and which ultimately led to a slowdown of industrial growth in 1956–58, showed that even routine techniques did not operate well. Everyone shuddered before Stalin. Yet his ministers planned for many more constructions than could be completed in reasonable time, and his Gosplan was unable to impose moderation on these men.

The rapid rate of growth of the non-farm economy during the *Stalin Has Everything His Way* period can hardly be ascribed to good planning. Rather, planning was just not so bad as to become an important retarding factor in itself. There is a great deal of automatism in the Soviet economic machine. It requires wild planning like that of the *All-out Drive* to disrupt it seriously.

The Soviet government continued to pretend that the Soviet economy operated on the basis of the FYP's. Analysis of the actual situation during 1940–52 discloses the emptiness of the claim.

It may seem an indication of the great role of the FYP's that the disorganization of fixed investment, which brought about the slowdown of industrial output in 1956, and especially in 1957 and 1958, presumably started on a large scale in 1951 when there was no FYP at all—not even in the form of preliminary Party Directives. But the disorganization of fixed investment continued after a semblance of a FYP made its appearance late in 1952—in the form of Directives to the fifth FYP, which later were treated as the FYP itself.

Moreover, if the timing of the disorganization in fixed investment as suggested here is correct, there was a considerable amount of disorganization in planning and in the fulfilment of the plans at the very time when the Directives were being prepared. Yet, there seems to be nothing in them aiming at remedying the evil, although this would have been one of the most important tasks, if not the most important task, of this particular FYP, if it had been well designed.

The annual plans functioned more or less satisfactorily during the *Stalin Has Everything His Way* period. But there were substantial exceptions and, indeed, failures in exactly the areas where the devising of remedies was most important and most difficult to attain. The annual plans cannot be held responsible for the poor state of agriculture, since the rulers desired this state. But proper timing of construction is one of the most important functions of planning, and the annual plans were as responsible for the failure in this area as all the other plans.

Five-Year Plans.—The fourth FYP had the distinction of being approved with the least delay (less than three months) relative to the date it was scheduled to start operating.[17] But it was accepted at a date too near to the end of World War II—indeed, in the midst of an almost chaotic economic disorganization—to permit any long-range planning. There is no doubt, for example, that the costs associated with investment were unknown at that time. The government may not even have had a sufficiently exact knowledge of the

[17] The FYP was supposed to start operating on January 1, 1946; it was approved in March of 1946.

population. Most important of all, those who made the decisions were unable to foresee the speed with which recovery could be achieved; this may have been the reason, or one of the reasons, why the goals of the fourth FYP came closer to being realized than had been the case with the previous FYP.[18] The decision to come out with the FYP so soon after the end of the war was politically motivated. It was felt that the FYP was needed at once, so it was produced in what would have been too short a time even under entirely normal conditions.

The success of having prepared a FYP in a very short time and almost on time was attained by a simple device. The law on the fourth FYP was actually not a completed plan. An appendix to the law stated: "To assign to the Council of Ministers of the USSR the task of considering and approving the five-year economic plans by ministries and organizations of the USSR on the basis of the accepted five-year plan of restoration and development of the national economy of the USSR." More than a decade later it turned out that, in this work, certain targets of the law were changed.[19] No announcement was made of these changes at any time. The revised provisions of the FYP still remain unknown, and the plans by ministries and organizations were never announced either.

Timing of the developments during a FYP period should be considered an indispensable part of a good FYP. No trace of year-to-year targets can be found in the law on the fourth FYP. Specifically, they are not included among the assignments to the Council of Ministers of the USSR in the appendix to the law on the fourth FYP. One may be certain that year-to-year targets for the period of this FYP never existed. They were, it is true, absent from the third FYP also, but year-to-year breakdowns were given in the first two FYP's. On this score, the history of the FYP's was not one of increasing maturity.

Contrary to the usual assertions in the USSR, repeated in the West, many a target of the fourth FYP remained largely on paper. All announced targets for the private sector (agriculture, production of industrial consumers' goods, and retail trade) were underfulfilled by considerable margins. Even more significant from the Soviet point of view was the almost complete failure of the targets for output per man which necessitated a threefold overfulfilment of the targets for increasing the hired labor force.

[18] See N. J., "A Close-up of the Soviet Fourth Five-Year Plan," *Quarterly Journal of Economics,* May, 1952, pp. 139–71.
[19] See G. Sorokin, "Perspective Planning of the National Economy of the USSR," *Planned Economy,* 1956, No. 1, p. 33.

Any notion that the fourth FYP had started an era in which FYP's would be issued on time was shattered by the proceedings involving the fifth FYP. Only in October, 1952, i.e., twenty-one months after the FYP had to start operating, did the Nineteenth Party Congress approve the Directives to this FYP.[20] As is obvious from the concluding speech of M. Z. Saburov, then president of the Gosplan USSR, it was understood that the FYP would be worked out on the basis of these Directives in the future.[21] This did not, however, happen. The task was probably not considered important enough to be hurried. Then Stalin died. The Directives to the fifth FYP, based completely on his policies, died with him. It was also impossible to work out a new FYP based on the policies of the Malenkov government, because these were unclear even to Malenkov himself. The alternatives were to have no FYP at all or to approve the Directives, knowing they would not be used as a guide when they did not agree with the new policies. The second solution was chosen, but there was no formal approval of the Directives. They just started to treat the Directives as the final FYP. Since no date of approval of the FYP existed, they could pretend that it had been approved at the Nineteenth Party Congress in October of 1952.

Even if the Directives to the fifth FYP are accepted as the final FYP, it was, of course, only a three-year plan. The targets of this "plan" were fairly realistic for a great number of items, although as usual those for agricultural output were not.[22] Also unrealistic, although possibly to a lesser extent than in the prewar FYP's, were the targets for the size of the hired labor force, output per man, production costs, elimination of too-long hauls and counterhauls on railways, and some others.

It is obvious that, if the fifth FYP ever existed, Malenkov's policy of creating an "abundance of consumers' goods in two to three years" disposed of it, since the Directives to the fifth FYP were based on a

[20] The reasons for the delay of the fifth FYP are not clear. If there was a more or less serious reason, it must have been the Korean War, which had started exactly at the time when preparations of the fifth FYP should have been in progress. It might have been felt that the economic effects of the war, although it was waged abroad, prevented long-range planning in the USSR. The Soviets may, indeed, have believed World War III probable. The war preparations made by the Soviets were, in any case, very extensive. However, all this may be too complicated. Perhaps Stalin was just not interested in a FYP.

[21] *Pravda,* October 10, 1952.

[22] The assumption that many targets of the Directives for the non-farm sector were fairly realistic is, of course, very conjectural. With the provisions for such a big item as military expenses undisclosed, no reliable conclusions can be drawn with reference to many basic targets of the FYP or any other plan.

priority for heavy industry.[23] The fact that overfulfilment of targets is an even greater achievement than simple fulfilment, and that underfulfilments are customarily disregarded altogether, made it possible for the Soviets to act as though the fifth FYP stood unblemished.

In January of 1955, Malenkov's ideas were condemned by the Party and the return to the idea of priority for heavy industry was proclaimed. Less than a year remained of the fifth FYP period, yet it would be wrong to assume that the targets of the Directives started operating at long last; the Soviet economy actually operated on the basis of the 1955 annual plan in that year. The basic principle of the Soviet economic policies was thus changed twice in 1953–55, but the Directives to the fifth FYP stood up like a rock, because the FYP's were outside of real developments anyway.

A noteworthy occurrence in the way of planning during that period was Stalin's long-range scheme, which he presented as soon after the end of World War II as February 9, 1946; it was similar to the scheme with which he had come before the Eighteenth Party Congress in March of 1939.[24] Stalin's new long-range plan was as follows:

As concerns plans for a longer period, the Party intends to engineer a new mighty upswing of our national economy, which will enable us to raise the level of our industry, for example, to threefold the prewar level. We must make our industry able to produce yearly up to 50 million tons of pig iron, up to 60 million tons of steel, up to 50 million tons of coal, and up to 60 million tons of petroleum. . . . This will require, perhaps, three new five-year periods, if not more. . . .[25]

There are two interesting features in this "plan" of Stalin's. While he mentioned industry as such, the essence of his planning was goals for definite quantities of only three commodities—pig iron and steel,[26] coal, and petroleum. It included no provisions for agriculture or consumers' goods. Subsequently, the fact that Stalin also

[23] Before the shift in January of 1955, when the emphasis was still on consumers' goods, it was claimed, for example, that the target of the fifth FYP for output of consumers' goods would be fulfilled in four years. That this was to occur at the expense of investment and the armed forces was, of course, recognized though not made clear. The plans which were operating in 1953 and 1954 were just not those which would have been in line with the Directives, although these Directives had been approved only a few months before the beginning of 1953.

[24] The assignment of working out a general plan (see p. 187), given to the Gosplan in February, 1941, was a step toward converting this scheme into something resembling a plan.

[25] Here quoted from *Planned Economy*, 1946, No. 1, p. 10.

[26] Pig iron and steel may be considered as one commodity.

wanted industrial output trebled was neglected entirely, and only the demand for pig iron and steel, coal, and petroleum was mentioned. The narrowing of the scope of long-range planning since the early 1920's, even since the late 1920's, was certainly fundamental.

The other interesting feature of Stalin's long-range plan was the moderation in the timing of the targets. One might seem to be justified in seeing in this a sobering-up in comparison with the prewar years, especially, of course, in comparison with the *All-out Drive*. But the fact may also have been important that the very precarious situation existing at the time when Stalin's "plan" was set up made it difficult to anticipate the attainable speed of recovery. There is in this respect some similarity between Stalin's long-range planning and planning activities soon after World War I, when the approved and some of the unapproved targets of the GOELRO turned out to be easily attainable. As stated above, the same factor may have brought about, or contributed to, the fact that the targets of the fourth FYP were less excessive than usual. However, it seems certain that, except as concerns agriculture, the inhabitants of the Kremlin were gradually learning.

Annual plans.—Through 1956 only one annual plan (even this merely in an excerpt) had been released after World War II. This was the plan for 1947.[27] Apart from this release, there were only reports on *fulfilment* of the unknown annual and other short-term plans, and they contained mainly data on progress during the respective period, with inadequate reference to targets of the plans.[28] Data on target fulfilment were restricted to industry and transportation, and these data for industry were only by ministries, in one figure for each, and did not adequately reflect the results attained toward fulfilling the targets for various individual commodities.

Although the targets of the 1947 Plan for pig iron, steel, and rolled steel showed substantial shortfalls in the plan-fulfilment stage, the Ministry of Ferrous Metallurgy calculated in the record for this year a 1 per cent overfulfilment of its goal. The Ministry of Non-Ferrous Metallurgy boasted an excess of not less than 7 per cent, in spite of the miss in copper. The Ministry of Tractor and Automotive Transport managed to show a shortfall of only 2 per cent, in spite of a great shortfall in output of tractors. The Ministry of Building Materials exceeded its target by 1 per cent, in spite of the

---

[27] *Pravda*, March 1, 1947.

[28] For a number of years the reports on plan fulfilment were released for the year concerned and for three quarters of a year each, but starting in 1953 this was changed, apparently without announcement, to an annual report and a report for the first half of each year.

shortfall in cement. As far as coal is concerned, the Ministry for the Western Areas underfulfilled its target by 5 per cent, while the Ministry for the Eastern Areas hit the bull's eye.

Also, the fulfilment percentages sometimes referred not to the original but to the subsequently revised targets of the respective plans. These revisions were rarely announced.

Data in the reports on the fulfilment of plans for industrial output by commodities were in percentages of output of the preceding year. The commodities were not the same each time. Particularly unfavorable items would disappear from the list of commodities for which data were given, and particularly favorable commodities would as suddenly make their appearance.

The data on the fulfilment of the 1947 Plan show that the planning was not functioning too well even in regard to output of producers' goods, although this was the area for which planning is relatively easy. Below are a few examples (data in per cent of previous year's performance):[29]

Item	Plan	Fulfilment
Coal	116	112
Petroleum	118	119
Electric power	116	115
Steel	119	109
Copper	117	109
Tractors	287	209
Automobiles	157	130
Timber from forests	147	126
Cement	171	140
Window glass	142	119

The differences in plan fulfilment between the claims of ministries and the above figures for commodities were to a large extent explained by the usual malady in the operation of Soviet enterprises, i.e., shortfalls in some commodities were offset by overfulfilment in others. Time and again, the shortfalls involved the goods that were the most urgently needed.[30]

The difference in plan fulfilment between the eastern and western coal areas in 1947 reflected the greater ease with which targets could be set and fulfilled where nothing abnormal had happened. The fulfilment of the plan for coal output in the western territories de-

[29] *Pravda*, January 18, 1948.

[30] This was one of the major complaints voiced by N. Bulganin in his report to the plenary session of the Central Committee of the Party in July of 1955 ("On the Tasks for Further Enlargement of Industry, Technical Progress, and Improvement in the Organization of Production," *Pravda*, July 14, 1955).

pended largely on the restoration of capacities in the Donbass and the Moscow coal basin, damaged during World War II.

Shortfalls in fulfilment of the 1947 targets were frequently larger with respect to items other than industrial goods. The target of the 1947 Plan for freight car turnabout, for example, was 8.8 days—a scheduled reduction from 1946 of 0.81 of a day. The actual reduction amounted to only 0.46 of a day. It may be observed, however, that the situation was by no means easy for drafting the plan at the end of 1946, in the midst of a starvation and rehabilitation after the war. Hence, the shortcomings of the 1947 Plan did not necessarily need to be present in the more normal years that followed.

The fact that nothing but an occasional figure was revealed on plans other than the one for 1947 does not necessarily indicate that the plans operated poorly. Those in power had gradually become accustomed to the comfort of not releasing information.

Fairly effective operation of the annual, semiannual, and quarterly plans after 1947 and until the end of the period analyzed seems not improbable—as always, excepting farm output.[31] A similarity to the corresponding situation during the *Three "Good" Years* is likely, although the political "air" was worse during the *Stalin Has Everything His Way* period than in the middle 1930's. In this connection it is very interesting that the FYP's, i.e., the plans which were inaccurate, were released, while the more accurate short-range plans were not. There is certainly logic in this. The FYP's served largely, or at least primarily, as propaganda. Keeping them secret would have frustrated their primary aim. The short-range plans were almost entirely limited to operational functions, where too close a view would have revealed shortcomings.

[31] And possibly also excepting the poor management of the investment projects, for which the annual plans of the last years of the period were as much responsible as the FYP's.

CHAPTER 11

INFLATION—DEFLATION

Introduction

Among the few attainments of the *Stalin Has Everything His Way* period, was the realization of the long-time desire for deflation.[1] The Soviet Union was so plagued by strong prolonged inflation—in 1917–21 and again for almost twenty years from 1928 to 1930 until 1947 to 1949—that enthusiasm for deflation was understandable. As far as wages were concerned, the Soviets went even further than they had previously wanted to go—they nearly stabilized nominal wages.

The development of the various price categories since 1930 or somewhat earlier (in substance, during the Great Industrialization Drive) showed great variations. Two categories of prices, namely, nominal wages and the prices paid by the state to producers for farm products, rose in one ascending curve. Another pair of price categories, retail prices of consumers' goods in official trade and wholesale prices of producers' goods (changes in costs involved in investment, in railway transportation, and in some other areas were largely a variation of the wholesale prices of producers' goods) had one, possibly somewhat incomplete, cycle. The unorganized trade in food (since 1932 the kolkhoz trade) had two cycles, of which the

[1] In view of divergent timing of the trends of the various price categories, it seems preferable to discuss here the post–World War II period as a whole. The discussion in this chapter actually starts with the period beginning about 1930.

second is likely to turn out somewhat incomplete. Finally, farm prices show three cycles, the third probably incomplete.[2]

Inflation in kolkhoz trade had reached its second and last peak by 1943 (the first peak presumably occurred in 1933). In 1949 the highest prices (or costs) of producers' goods, railway freights, and investment were attained. Retail prices of consumers' goods in official trade were at their highest two years earlier, i.e., in 1947. Nominal wages and the prices paid by the state to producers for farm products, i.e., prices with only half a cycle, naturally are at their peak at this writing. Nominal wages will probably continue climbing and are unlikely ever to display a cyclical movement. But the Party expects that the prices paid by the state for farm products will go down from the level established on July 1, 1958. With reference to prices received by farm producers, the highest of the three peaks may have been that during World War II (the first peak was probably in 1933, the last in 1958).

The different price categories varied greatly in the levels to which they climbed and in the strength of their descents. The peak for the index of prices in kolkhoz trade (1928 equals 100) was several times higher than those of the other price types. The indices of prices of producers' goods, rates charged on railway freight, and investment costs were those with the smallest rises. The indices of prices of consumers' goods in official trade, nominal wages, farm prices, and prices paid by the state for farm products occupied intermediate positions. The level of the index of nominal wages in 1958 (1928 equals 100) was moderately below the level of the index of prices of consumers' goods in official trade in this year. The index of the prices paid by the state for farm products was in 1958 above the level of prices of consumers' goods in official trade in this year. The same may have been true of the farm prices.

The prices in kolkhoz trade declined to less than one-fourteenth their highest point in 1943. As compared with this reduction, the decline of the prices of consumers' goods in official trade to less than one-half of their highest level seems almost minute, but of course it is not. The prices of producers' goods showed the smallest decline from their top. These prices, nevertheless, are those with far the lowest rate of increase since 1928.

While nominal wages and the prices paid by the state for farm

---

[2] As many as three cycles can be observed with reference to farm prices, because these are a combination of two other price categories—the prices paid by the state to producers for farm products and the prices in kolkhoz markets—with greatly differing curves.

products were grouped together as those with only half a curve, there was a great difference in the shape of their curves, reflecting the difference in the attitude toward the two great classes of workers, wage earners and kolkhozniki. Wages rose strongly so long as the prices of consumers' goods in official trade continued to rise, although mostly not as strongly as the latter. The increase in nominal wages was nearly halted after 1947, when the inflation of official prices of consumers' goods was turned into a deflation. Contrary to this, the prices paid by the state for most staple farm products (grain, meat, and some others) remained almost unchanged for fully twenty-four years, from 1928/29 to 1952/53, and the rise was but small in all such prices weighted during this long period. Large increases in these prices have taken place only in the past few years.

While the Soviets are very proud of the deflation as a whole, the reduction in prices of consumers' goods is propagandized with particular force. Counting on short memories, the Soviets have even proclaimed deflation an inseparable part of socialism.[3]

It may be thought that it would have been preferable to have stable prices rather than deflation; nevertheless, the latter should be classed as a victory for Stalin. In this respect the *Stalin Has Everything His Way* period differs fundamentally from the prewar experience. Then, too, by April of 1936 most prices in the organized market were brought to a level at which it was hoped they could at least be held, if not reduced, later. But the *Purge Era* was launched a few months afterward with furious vigor, and the idea of stopping inflation had to be forsaken in favor of combating "the enemies of the people" within the Party.

Purges continued also after World War II, but they did not lead to such acute phenomena as great inflations. Deflation, indeed, once started, proceeded in the postwar years at a much stronger rate than this writer, at least, had foreseen. Only a small part of the great deflation was caused by the fact that inflation had been permitted to reach a level higher than that made necessary by circumstances, and no great difficulty was involved in getting rid of the part of the inflation not justified by the conditions.

A few words on the prices paid by the state for farm products may be found in chapter 13. Only weak attempts have been made to calculate the weighted farm prices and there is nothing to be found on this score in this work, except for the few words above. The whole topic needs to be studied anew and thoroughly.

[3] See the basic text on economics, *Political Economy*, by K. V. Ostrovityanov *et al.* (Moscow: Academy of Sciences of the USSR, Institute of Economics, 1954), p. 478.

Inflation Goes On

Before World War II.—The moderate deflation in the middle 1920's and the subsequent strong inflation during the *All-out Drive* were described in chapter 4. Inflation continued at a much slower rate during the *Three "Good" Years* as well. It has been shown (p. 146) that the average output per man in large-scale industry increased by somewhat more than 30 per cent in those three years. The average nominal wage, however, rose by 72 per cent.[4] Hence, even if the whole increase in output per man were fully reflected in wages, a rise in the cost of labor of about 30 per cent would have been inevitable. Actually, a large increase in nominal wages was accompanied by about as strong an advance in the prices of consumers' goods. In contrast to the price development of consumers' goods, the government maintained its efforts toward the deflation, or at least the stability, of the prices of producers' goods. It yielded only in 1936, when, effective April 1, the prices of all producers' goods were increased in one thrust by more than 50 per cent.[5] Freight rates on railways were raised simultaneously by about the same percentage.[6]

Inflation continued during the *Purge Era* as well, but the attitude toward the different types of prices was at first reversed. The prices of a small number of consumers' goods were actually reduced as of June 1, 1936. A serious rise in the retail prices of consumers' goods did not, apparently, start before World War II had begun outside the USSR, in mid-1939. But, once it started, this category of prices advanced very quickly. By the end of 1940, the 1937 level of retail prices of consumers' goods in state and co-operative trade had been exceeded by about 60 per cent. The advance of prices in kolkhoz trade started even earlier than in organized trade and was much stronger than that of the latter.

The prices of producers' goods, on the other hand, continued their advance once the prolonged policy of keeping them stable had been broken in 1936. The prices of some non-ferrous metals had already been raised on April 1, 1938; and the prices of coal, on February 1, 1939. Railway freight rates were increased on April 1,

---

[4] *Socialist Construction of the USSR, 1936,* pp. 512–13, and *1937 Plan,* pp. 145–46.

[5] *Essay III,* p. 15 and *passim.* According to Abram Bergson *et al.* ("Prices of Basic Industrial Products in the USSR, 1928–50," *Journal of Political Economy,* August, 1956, p. 322), the prices of basic industrial products, not including machinery and crude petroleum, increased by 70 per cent from 1935 to 1937. Civilian machinery advanced in price by less than 50 per cent, according to my calculations.

[6] *Essay III,* p. 15.

1939,[7] i.e., before the start of World War II outside the USSR. While the rise of steel prices, in effect as of January 1, 1940, and of some other producers' goods, occurred after World War II had begun outside of Russia, these actions apparently were not connected with the war. The increase in the fuel prices (other than petroleum) by about 50 per cent in effect as of February 1, 1939, and the advance of freight rates by about 20 per cent in effect as of April 1, 1939, as well as increases in wages, made price increases of some other goods necessary because the state did not want to return to the policy of subsidies on a large scale.[8]

At the time the USSR entered World War II, in mid-1941, the over-all price increase since 1937, or even 1936, was already much more marked in consumers' than in producers' goods, and the fate of both groups of prices was to be quite different for fully seven and one-half years.

Since World War II.—The population, receiving food and other goods on rations during World War II, paid the prices which existed at the outbreak of the war.[9] The retail prices of the small amounts of consumers' goods sold by the co-operative trade in the rural areas were about doubled as early as April of 1942. There were also sharp price increases in liquor and tobacco products during World War II. As in the first half of the 1930's, state commercial shops, selling without requiring ration coupons and at prices many times higher than the ration prices, made their appearance in 1944. This obviously raised the weighted retail prices for the official trade as a whole. A large increase in ration prices occurred a considerable time after the end of World War II, namely, effective September 16, 1946.[10] Similarly to the experience in 1935, the derationing of consumers' goods which took place as of December 16, 1947, was effected on the basis of prices greatly above the high prices existing at the outbreak of World War II.

[7] *Ibid.*, pp. 15, 38, 151.

[8] The decision to abolish subsidies to enterprises operating with losses since 1937 was never realized in full. According to Bergson *et al.* (*loc. cit.*), the basic industrial products, other than petroleum, increased in price by 32 per cent from 1937 to 1940. The increase in prices of civilian machinery during this period was roughly estimated at not quite 20 per cent. *Essay III*, p. 15.

[9] These prices are referred to in the USSR as prewar prices. This is greatly misleading in view of the large price rises in anticipation of war.

[10] The price of the cheapest bread jumped from 1 ruble per kilogram to 3.4 rubles. Yet the action was officially called "a certain raise of ration prices." The use of the adjective "certain" in this connection had become practically obligatory. Finance Minister A. G. Zverev adhered to this abominable practice eleven years later, after the celebration of forty years of the Revolution (see his *Problems of National Income and Finances of the USSR* [Moscow, 1958], p. 211).

262 The Post-World War II Period

Soviet writers, discussing the price development of consumers' goods, stress the price declines in commercial state trade in the last year of the war and thereafter until derationing. Not until it was possible to calculate the retail price level in those years did it become clear that *in total official trade,* including the commercial state trade with its declining prices, inflation continued right up to the time of derationing (December 16, 1947), i.e., right up to the time when deflation started. The prices in official trade were, indeed, growing at an accelerated rate at least in 1946. The level reached by the retail prices of consumers' goods in official trade in 1947 was more than threefold the average 1940 prices.

The price rise in official trade during the war and early postwar years, large though it was, was very small when compared with the developments in kolkhoz trade. After a slow start, prices in this trade went up like a rocket during the early part of World War II, reaching a level in 1943 about fourteen fold that in 1940. But contrary to all other price groups, the 1943 prices in kolkhoz trade were the peak. This occurred more than four years before the end of inflation in the retail prices of consumers' goods in official trade and more than six years ahead of the end of inflation of the prices of producers' goods. The development of the prices in urban kolkhoz markets during World War II was as follows (1940 equals 100):[11]

Year	January	April	July	October
1941............	103	95	88	112
1942............	268	636	693	886
1943............	1,440	1,602	1,467	1,077
1944............	1,317	1,488	1,160	758
1945............	754	737	590	417

The real level of prices in the kolkhoz trade during World War II becomes clear only after the very high 1940 level of prices in this trade is realized. If the prices in kolkhoz trade in 1940 are assumed to have been 85 per cent higher than the corresponding prices in official trade in that year (see pp. 216–17), the prices in kolkhoz trade in 1943 were about twenty-six times the latter. And, of course, these are merely averages. Private reports from individual localities

[11] *Finances and Socialist Construction,* a symposium (Moscow, 1957), p. 39. This was the first time that any prices for this trade in those years were made known. N. A. Voznesenskii in his *War Economy during the Patriotic War* (Moscow, 1948), p. 129, gave the prices of crops and animal products in kolkhoz markets in 1943 (at 12.6 times and 13.2 times those in 1940, respectively) in 1948. He also stated that these prices had declined 2.3 times from 1943 to 1945. But it seems impossible to make a full picture out of such isolated bits of evidence. The 1940 prices, which had been used as the basis of the calculation, were still not known in 1948 and much later.

pointed to one hundred fold and even one hundred and fifty fold increases in prices of bread.

The year when the prices were highest in kolkhoz trade (1943/44) was, weatherwise, a poor year. The effect of unfavorable weather conditions was augmented by great disorganization. In 1942/43 this disorganization was probably even larger than in 1943/44, and this may possibly explain the fact that the prices in kolkhoz markets were substantially higher in 1942/43 than in 1944/45.[12]

The peculiarities in the movement of kolkhoz-market prices continued also after the end of World War II: their preceding strong decline was suddenly arrested. In 1947 the prices in kolkhoz trade were somewhat above the level of October, 1945, i.e., somewhat more than fourfold those in 1940 and almost eightfold the prices in official trade in this year.

As far as civilian producers' goods are concerned, beginning about mid-1940 the USSR again embarked on a policy of price stability. The analogy with the first half of the 1930's is obvious. This time, the practice of maintaining the prices of producers' goods at an unchanged level remained in force for fully seven and a half years, until the end of 1948.[13]

Munitions occupied a separate place. Their prices were *reduced* by more than one-half during World War II, it is claimed (see *Essay I*, pp. 52–53), and these sharply cut prices were probably still in force in 1948. The ability to reduce munition prices during World War II was officially explained by mass production. The recently released data on subsidies (see below) indicate that if munitions required greater subsidies than other producers' goods after their price reduction during World War II, the additional amounts were not large.

The weighted prices of *all* producers' goods, including armaments, must have declined substantially during the war. They started to grow after the end of the war as the proportion of munitions in the total output of producers' goods began to decline.

While the prices of basic producers' goods were held stable in the postwar years until the end of 1948, the inflationary features in

[12] Note that the peak in the tabulation above was reached in April of 1943, which, of course, belonged to the 1942/43 crop year.

[13] According to Bergson *et al.* (*loc. cit.*), the weighted prices of basic industrial products other than petroleum went up by about 4 per cent from 1941 to 1945 and then remained fully stable through 1947. The prices of some building materials not considered by Bergson were slightly raised in 1947. Increases in the prices of some types of machinery also occurred in the early postwar years (see *Essay III*, p. 20), but all these price increases were minor departures from the principle of price stability. Bergson's index does not, of course, include munitions.

the economy brought about an uninterrupted, and by no means insignificant, increase in production costs in industry (1945–47), or at least in the prices paid by industry for goods (1948). This is obvious from the following official data, which show the year-by-year changes in production costs of comparable industrial production (in per cent) at both current and constant prices:[14]

Year	Current Prices	Constant Prices
1945............	+0.9	+0.9
1946............	+4.7	+0.7
1947............	+5.8	−2.0
1948............	−2.5	−8.6

Thus, while at constant prices production costs would have declined by about 9 per cent in 1945–48, they actually increased by about the same percentage when calculated at current prices.[15]

The development in prices of producers' goods, including munitions, in conjunction with rising production costs and expanding production necessarily led to mounting subsidies. The recently released data on this score are as follows (in billions of rubles):[16]

Year	Total	To Industry
1943...........	4.6	3.4
1944...........	8.1	6.5
1945...........	13.9	11.7
1946...........	25.8	22.4
1947...........	34.1	29.1
1948...........	41.2	35.3

Not a hint was given of the share devoted to munitions. But the fact that subsidies to industry almost doubled in 1946, a year when output was shifting from munitions to civilian production and total industrial production declined, points to the probability that the subsidies to industries producing munitions were not larger—and may have been smaller—than those to the rest of industry. Six and one-half billion rubles of subsidies to industry in 1944 was, of course, a great deal of money, but not all of it went to the munitions industries. Indeed, the subsidies to industry were quite substantial even in 1940, and all of them during that year went to industries other than those producing munitions.[17]

[14] *Industry of the USSR,* 1957, p. 29.

[15] The great decline in production costs in industry in 1948 of 8.6 per cent at constant prices vis-à-vis the unfavorable figures for the preceding years points to an extremely favorable effect of derationing at the end of 1947, provided the calculation may be fully trusted.

[16] Zverev, *op. cit.,* p. 212.

[17] The Commissariat of Forestry alone incurred a loss of over 700 million rubles in 1940 (implied in D. D. Kondrashev, *Price Formation in Industry of the USSR*

The official index of construction costs (1940 equals 100) was 136 in 1948.[18] Calculations in *Essay III* (p. 20) indicate a growth of construction costs of 64 per cent during this period.

As in the middle 1930's, the prices of producers' goods were drastically raised in one sweep, effective January 1, 1949.[19] The prices of all industrial goods went up by more than 50 per cent. Excluding machinery, prices rose by 80 per cent; machinery prices alone rose by 30 per cent.[20] No hint exists of what happened to the prices of munitions.[21]

Construction costs increased by 31 per cent from 1948 to 1949, according to official calculations.[22] Calculations of the present writer in *Essay III* (p. 165) point to an increase of 58 per cent.[23] The index figures of construction costs, official and calculated by this writer, are as follows for 1940–49:

Year	Official	N.J.
1940	100	100
1948	136	164
1949	178	258

The official index of construction costs for the years following World War II in terms of 1940, believed to be too low here, has a counterpart in the exaggeration of the likewise official calculation of investment in postwar years in terms of 1940, discussed in the next chapter (see also *Commentary*, pp. 137–48).

[Moscow, 1956], p. 118, and *1941 Plan*, p. 11); the loss of the whole forestry industry must have far exceeded 1 billion rubles in that year (for the share of the Commissariat of Forestry in the whole forestry industry see *1941 Plan*, pp. 67–69). The coal industry suffered a loss of about 400 million rubles in 1940, and there were other civilian industries which had to be subsidized.

We speak, of course, of direct subsidies to munition industries. Subsidies to industries producing raw materials for munitions must be charged to the munition industries in the final analysis.

[18] Implied in data in *Economy of the USSR in 1956*, p. 184.

[19] *Essay III*, p. 15.

[20] *Finances and Socialist Construction*, p. 49. Bergson *et al.* have the very large increase of 164 per cent from 1948 to 1949 for the basic industrial products included in their sample, which was apparently not very representative. The lower estimate of this writer (*Essay III*, p. 15) also turned out too high.

[21] Subsidies were not entirely eliminated by the sweeping increases in prices, effective January 1, 1949. In 1949, they amounted to 6.0 billion rubles, of which 2.9 billion rubles went to industry (Zverev, *op. cit.*, p. 213). But the subsidies did not necessarily involve munitions. The new prices of certain industrial products other than munitions, notably of timber and lumber, and coal, remained below production costs.

[22] *Economy of the USSR in 1956*, p. 184.

[23] The costs of building materials used in construction advanced by 137 per cent from 1945 to 1949 (see *Essay III*, p. 165). All freight rates on railways were raised by about 78 per cent in 1949. The charges for freight transportation by truck almost doubled (*ibid.*, p. 89). Only wages increased a little, if at all; the *cost* of labor may even have declined somewhat. But even a smaller cost of labor hardly made the increase in total construction costs from 1948 to 1949 as small as 31 per cent.

The index of production costs for the comparable industrial output showed a jump of 18.8 per cent from 1948 to 1949, although at constant prices a decline of 6.8 per cent should have taken place.[24] The effect of the boost in prices of producers' goods on production costs was thus quite substantial.

An interesting picture of the course of inflation in a great sector of the economy is revealed by the average per-kilometer rate on freight and average per-kilometer cost to the railways, with the resulting profit or loss shown in per cent of the cost. These data are as follows:[25]

Year	Average Unit Rate (kopeks per ton-kilometer)	Average Unit Cost (kopeks per ton-kilometer)	Profit (+) or Loss (−) (per cent of cost)
1939	3.010	2.414	+24.6
1940	3.162	2.566	+23.3
1941	3.272	2.676	+22.7
1942	3.356	3.668	−8.0
1943	4.199	4.287	−2.0
1944	4.144	4.715	−12.2
1945	3.865	4.360	−20.3
1946	3.360	4.870	−21.0
1947	3.420	5.157	−34.0
1948	3.380	4.505	−25.0
1949	6.012	5.053	+18.5

The entrance of the USSR into World War II in mid-1941 did not immediately cause any substantial disturbances in costs of railway transportation and profits therefrom in 1941. But the first full year of war brought such a rise in costs in 1942 that large profits were at once converted into losses. In 1944, when the highest transportation costs of the war years were attained, the unit cost of freight transportation to the railways was almost exactly double that in 1939. With certain ups and downs in the subsequent years, the unit cost in 1948 was about 80 per cent above that in 1939, causing a 25 per cent loss (in 1947 the loss was fully one-third of the cost). Then came the great sweep. Effective January 1, 1949, freight rates were raised by about 78 per cent on the average.[26] When this occurred, a level somewhat more than 4.5 times that in 1926/27 was reached by the average freight rate.

The great boost in prices of producers' goods, effective January 1, 1949, brought about an increase in the average unit cost of freight transportation of little more than 10 per cent from 1948 to 1949. Moreover, this was not the highest level reached by the unit cost.

[24] *Industry of the USSR,* 1957, p. 29.
[25] A. Arkhangelskii and A. Kreinin, in *Questions of Economics,* 1957, No. 11, p. 113.
[26] The increase was estimated at 62 per cent in *Essay III,* p. 15.

The peak level was attained in 1947, when the average unit cost of freight transportation was 4.9 times that in 1926/27.[27]

The several times greater percentage rise in the unit rate of freight transportation on railways as compared with the rise in the unit cost in 1949 converted the 25 per cent loss on the 1948 operations into a 18.5 per cent gain in 1949.

Deflation

Consumers' goods in official trade.—Through 1954, the retail prices of consumers' goods in official trade were reduced each year— effective from April 10, 1948, from March 1, 1949–51, and from April 1, 1952–54. The greatest cut was effected in 1950 (about 20 per cent), possibly in order to make a better showing in the last year of the fourth FYP. The price reductions were also quite substantial (about 15 per cent) in 1953, the year of Stalin's death—another case when it was particularly desired to show great benevolence.[28]

Publication of an index of retail prices in official trade (1940 equals 100) was started in 1956 but only the index figures since 1950 have been released.[29] By using the data in *Stat. Handb.*, 1956 (p. 211), as well as the percentages by which retail sales are supposed to have grown year by year at constant prices, in conjunction with the data on official trade at current prices, the official price index can be extended backward to 1945 (see Chart 18).

As the other evidence on trade in *Stat. Handb.*, 1956, and *Soviet Trade*, stat. handb., 1956, the official index of retail prices includes all beverages, even hard liquor, with food.[30] The prices of hard liquor were raised much more than those of the other goods after

[27] The lower unit cost in 1949 as compared to 1947, in spite of the higher prices the railways had to pay in the later year, was presumably brought about by the much greater traffic during 1949.

[28] Thereafter only minor price changes occurred. In 1956 prices were reduced on certain types of garments, fabrics, aluminum hardware, and radios; in 1957, price reductions were effected on pork, some kinds of canned goods, and medicinal goods. The total saving from the reductions in those two years is supposed to have exceeded 5 billion rubles. All these cuts were substantially overcompensated by increases in the prices of alcoholic beverages, automobiles, motorcycles, and machine-made carpets early in 1958 (see *Pravda*, January 2, 1958). The additional cost to the consumers was, of course, not announced.

[29] *Stat. Handb.*, 1956 (p. 210), and its successors. *Soviet Trade*, stat. handb., 1956, p. 131, gave the same index in greater detail. Before publication of the *Stat. Handb.*, 1956, the index of retail prices in state and co-operative trade was calculated for a great number of years, including the postwar years, starting with December 16, 1947, by the Institut National de la Statistique et des Études Économiques (Paris) in its journal *Études et Conjoncture*, April, 1955.

[30] At least one Soviet statistician believes that the inclusion of liquor with food in price indices is methodologically incorrect. See N. Ryauzov in *Problems of Economics*, 1957, No. 3, p. 135.

CHART 18

RETAIL PRICES IN OFFICIAL TRADE, 1945–58 *
(1940 = 100)

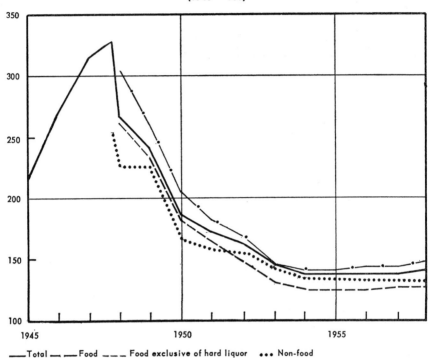

_____Total ___ ___Food ___ ___ Food exclusive of hard liquor ••• Non-food

* Data for 1950–55 from *Soviet Trade*, stat. handb., 1956, p. 131. Data for the last quarter of 1947 to 1949 were calculated with the help of other evidence in the volume, specifically on p. 132. Data for 1945–47 were calculated from the data on the increase in retail sales at current prices (*ibid.*, p. 21) and constant prices (from reports on the fulfilment of annual plans). Data for 1956 to 1958 are from *Economy of the USSR in 1958*, p. 770.

The share of hard liquor in official retail trade was assumed to have been 15 per cent or somewhat less. For 1958 the official index was used, which implies a share of sales of hard liquor in total food sales of 13.7 per cent. Prices of hard liquor are not indicated in the above chart. The index figures for them are given below (1940 equals 100):

Year	Index	Year	Index
1947 (last quarter)	719	1953	271
1948	590	1954	264
1949	430	1955	264
1950	338	1956	264
1951	302	1957	264
1952	298	1958	317

1940. Since the share of hard liquor in total retail trade was large, the trend of food prices and its relation to the index of non-food prices appear quite different, whether hard liquor, primarily vodka, is included with food or not. The index for the retail food prices is, therefore, shown in Chart 18, inclusive and exclusive of hard liquor.

As Chart 18 shows, the weighted retail prices in official trade in 1945 were 2.15 times those in 1940; the further increase until 1947 brought the price level to 3.1 times that of 1940. With an index of 328 (1940 equals 100) in the last quarter of 1947, a price level more than 60 times that in 1913 was reached. This adequately explains the tender feelings of the Soviets toward deflation. It also is the reason for their normally counting the deflation of retail prices from the last quarter of 1947.

It was certainly a great success to go down from a retail price index of 328 (1940 equals 100) in the last quarter of 1947 to an index of 138 in 1955. A wiser, although less spectacular, policy would probably have been to go down from 215 (the 1945 price index) more or less gradually to 138 in 1954, avoiding the great jump of the index to 328 in the last quarter of 1947. It is not clear that the great boost in prices in the early postwar years was absolutely necessitated by the circumstances.

In the last quarter of 1947, the price index for food (1940 equals 100) was substantially higher than that for non-food goods even with hard liquor excluded. But, since the prices of non-food goods were raised more than those of food in 1940, the prices of non-food goods may still have been relatively higher in the last quarter of 1947 than in either 1939 or 1938.

The decline of prices since the last quarter of 1947 was stronger for food than for non-food goods. In 1955, specifically, the index of prices for non-food goods (1940 equals 100) was about 8 per cent higher than that of food (excluding hard liquor). This 8 per cent adds to the gain which the prices of non-food goods made in 1940. There seems to have been no good reason for keeping food prices at a lower level in 1955 than the prices of non-food goods. On the contrary, the Soviets were and are in a better position to cover the demand for non-food goods than that for food. Discrimination against the peasants seems the only explanation of the higher prices for non-food goods.[31]

The success of the USSR in promoting study and research in science is now emphasized almost endlessly in the United States. But this writer deals not with science in the English or American sense of the word, but specifically with social science. And in this field

[31] They buy, of course, much more non-food goods than food.

shouting and, indeed, moral prostration are almost unavoidable for scholars in the USSR. Sh. Turetskii, a well-known professor of economics, boasted: "The Soviet price policies assured accessibility of white bread, butter, and wine." [32]

These "policies" consisted in making white bread, butter, and wine relatively cheaper than black bread, fat back, vegetable oil, vodka, and beer, all these being products consumed by the masses. While the index for better bread stood at 96 in 1955 (1940 equals 100), the index for whole-grain bread was 147. In 1955 vegetable oil, the fat used by the poor in Russia, cost about 60 per cent as much as butter, the fat used by the well-to-do. In 1913, the price of vegetable oil was little more than one-quarter of that of butter.

While the price policies stressed by Turetskii were equal to discrimination against all poor, the discrimination against the peasants was pronounced. With the exception of kerosene and vegetable oil, which had been very expensive prior to World War II, the price indices for all major commodities purchased by the peasants were considerably higher in postwar years than the index for all goods sold by the state retail trade. Here are, for example, the indices for 1955 (1940 equals 100):

Total index..................	138
Cotton fabrics.....................	176
"Leather" footwear................	163
Hard liquor......................	264

Chart 19 lists the price indices (1940 equals 100) of many consumers' goods in the last quarter of 1947, as well as in 1950 and 1955, in order from high to low. So far as the price indices for the last quarter of 1947 are concerned, the prices were in general higher, the more indispensable the goods were. Rubber footwear (because of a deficit of raw rubber, then almost exclusively an imported good) and hard liquor were the only exceptions. The price of salt was relatively lower than only that of rubber footwear. By 1955 the need to squeeze the consumer by all means was less urgent and salt was already among the relatively cheaper goods.

There were many indications of neglect of the demand conditions, deliberate and through oversight in setting prices. The demand for meat certainly remained unsatisfied to a much greater extent than the demand for fish, yet the price index for meat stood at 108 (1940 equals 100) in 1955, while that for fish was equal to 137. The output of "silk" (almost exclusively rayon) fabrics increased almost sevenfold from 1940 to 1955, while the output of cotton fabrics was expanded

[32] *Soviet Trade* (monthly), 1957, No. 1, p. 18.

CHART 19

**RETAIL PRICES IN OFFICIAL TRADE: SPECIFIED COMMODITIES, 1947
(LAST QUARTER), 1950, AND 1955 ***
(1940 = 100)

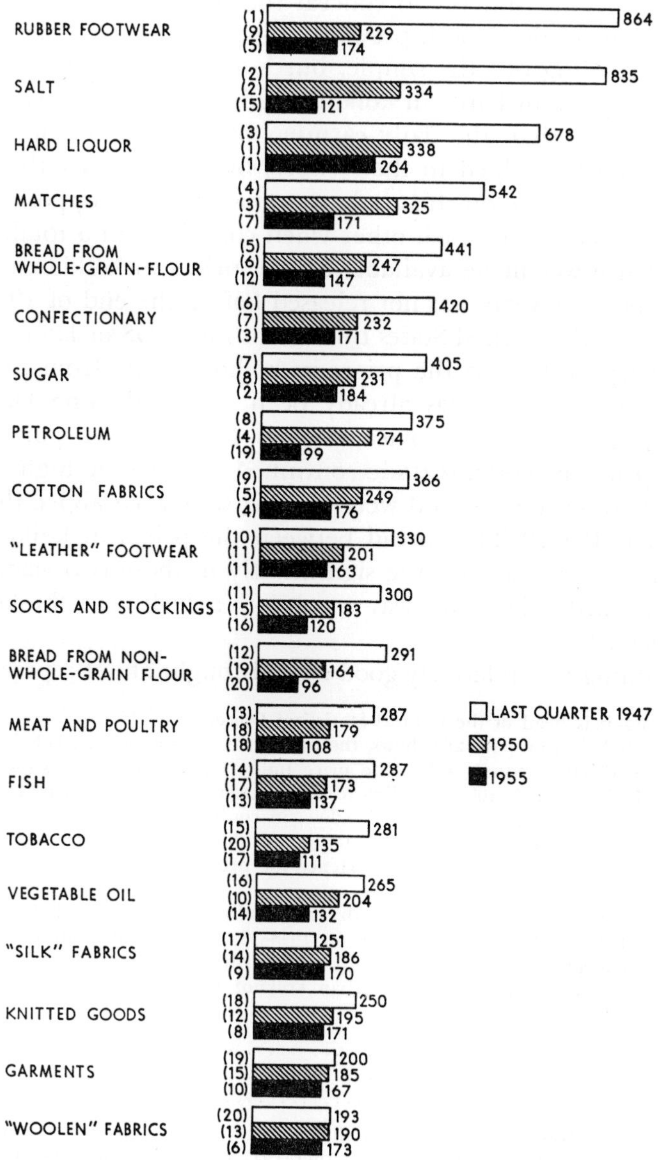

Commodity		1947	1950	1955
RUBBER FOOTWEAR	(1)(9)(5)	864	229	174
SALT	(2)(2)(15)	835	334	121
HARD LIQUOR	(3)(1)(1)	678	338	264
MATCHES	(4)(3)(7)	542	325	171
BREAD FROM WHOLE-GRAIN-FLOUR	(5)(6)(12)	441	247	147
CONFECTIONARY	(6)(7)(3)	420	232	171
SUGAR	(7)(8)(2)	405	231	184
PETROLEUM	(8)(4)(19)	375	274	99
COTTON FABRICS	(9)(5)(4)	366	249	176
"LEATHER" FOOTWEAR	(10)(11)(11)	330	201	163
SOCKS AND STOCKINGS	(11)(15)(16)	300	183	120
BREAD FROM NON-WHOLE-GRAIN FLOUR	(12)(19)(20)	291	164	96
MEAT AND POULTRY	(13)(18)(18)	287	179	108
FISH	(14)(17)(13)	287	173	137
TOBACCO	(15)(20)(17)	281	135	111
VEGETABLE OIL	(16)(10)(14)	265	204	132
"SILK" FABRICS	(17)(14)(9)	251	186	170
KNITTED GOODS	(18)(12)(8)	250	195	171
GARMENTS	(19)(15)(10)	200	185	167
"WOOLEN" FABRICS	(20)(13)(6)	193	190	173

□ LAST QUARTER 1947
▨ 1950
■ 1955

* Figures in parentheses show the order of the respective price (from high to low)
in the respective year.
 Data for 1950 and 1955 are from *Soviet Trade,* stat. handb., 1956, p. 131. The prices
in the last quarter of 1947 are calculated from *ibid.,* pp. 131, 132. Indices for 1947–
50, *ibid.,* p. 132, have only one set of data for all kinds of bread. So the indices for
the bread prices in the last quarter of 1947, shown in the chart, may be inexact.

by only 59 per cent. Yet the prices of cotton fabrics had increased since 1940 even somewhat more than those of "silk" goods.

Kolkhoz trade.—Mr. Starovskii's[33] men worked hard not to omit the kolkhoz trade and yet to conceal the immensely distorted conditions in this trade in both prewar and postwar years. They did not dream of spelling out the simple, but horrifying, fact that in 1955 the average price of fruits in kolkhoz trade was about 12 rubles per kilogram, more than the daily earnings of a low-paid worker. The statisticians were helped in their efforts by the fact that the distortions of the evidence on this trade were partly in the opposite direction and thus canceled each other when combined in a total. Whatever evidence was made available on the prices in kolkhoz trade in the early postwar years was not released before the end of 1957. For the analyst in the United States this means mid-1958 or later.

The sharp decline in the prices in kolkhoz trade from their top level in 1943 to 1945 has already been discussed. The fact, very surprising in view of the Soviet writings, has also been pointed out that the prices in kolkhoz trade continued close to the high level of 1945 for two more years and were in 1947 somewhat above the level of October, 1945.[34] The spread between the prices in kolkhoz and official trade went down quite significantly in those two years. As is obvious from the data, this was not due to a decline in the kolkhoz-trade prices.[35]

Derationing and relatively good crops brought about a precipitous

[33] V. Starovskii is head of the Central Statistical Office.

[34] As the tabulation on page 262 shows, the price index in kolkhoz markets in October of 1945 was 417 (1940 equals 100). The price index for the whole kolkhoz trade in 1950 was 104 (1940 equals 100) according to official calculations. The official evidence in *Forty Years of Soviet Trade* reproduced below, in conjunction with the index for the total kolkhoz trade for 1950 (1940 equals 100), shows for 1947 a price level in kolkhoz markets 4.17 times that in 1950. Hence the prices in 1947 were 4.3 times those in 1940.

[35] While on the occasion of the fortieth anniversary the indices of kolkhoz-market prices in 1941–45 (1940 equals 100) and in 1948–50 (1947 equals 100) were at long last disclosed, a gap, 1946, was left unfilled. According to *Soviet Trade* (monthly), 1956, No. 9, pp. 14–15, the prices in urban kolkhoz markets declined from 1946 to 1950 by the following percentages:

Potatoes. 73
Beef. 67
Milk. 69

With the corresponding index figures shown below, these percentages imply lower prices in kolkhoz trade in 1946 than in either 1947 or the end of 1945. The potato prices appear to have been in 1946 little more than half those in 1947 on this evidence. This seems unlikely, considering the poor 1946 crop. The question of the kolkhoz-market prices in 1946 is better left open.

price decline in kolkhoz trade in 1948. *Forty Years of Soviet Trade* supplied the following extremely valuable data on the prices in kolkhoz markets of seventy-one large cities during 1948–50:[36]

	1947	1948	1949	1950
All products......................	100	36	25	24
Grain products..................	100	22	14	13
Potatoes........................	100	21	13	15
Vegetables......................	100	37	26	25
Fruits...........................	100	45	35	36
Meat and meat products..........	100	44	31	27
Milk............................	100	37	29	26
Butter..........................	100	39	29	23
Eggs............................	100	50	33	29

With rationing over, there was naturally a rapid narrowing of the gap between the prices in kolkhoz trade and those in official trade in these years. While the prices in official trade went down 17 per cent from the last quarter of 1947 to 1948, the prices in kolkhoz markets declined by almost fully two-thirds from 1947 to 1948. From 1948 to 1949 the prices in official trade decreased by 12 per cent, while the kolkhoz-market prices went down by 31 per cent. The rare phenomenon could have been observed that prices in kolkhoz markets and probably also in the whole kolkhoz trade in this year were less than those of official trade.[37]

In the tabulation above, showing the prices in kolkhoz markets during 1948–50, of particular significance is the much greater decline in prices of potatoes and grain products from 1947 to 1948 and 1949, obviously indicating a particularly high price level of these primary necessities in 1947 and also in the preceding years.

The prices in kolkhoz trade continued their decline also in 1950, but this was but small (4 per cent) and, most important, much smaller than that in official trade. The year 1950 definitely was a turning point. After this, and until 1955, the prices in official and kolkhoz trade parted ways. While the prices in official trade continued to decline rather rapidly, or, as in 1955, remained stable, the prices in kolkhoz trade reversed their course and became stable, or rose slightly. Thus, with the exception of 1950, when the prices in both markets were about equal, a discrepancy between the two forms of trade in every postwar year could be observed. In all years, except 1949, the prices in kolkhoz trade were the higher.

[36] (Moscow, 1957), p. 116.
[37] Dr. Franklin Holzman (in an unpublished speech) was ahead of this writer in establishing this fact.

The official index of postwar prices in total kolkhoz trade is limited to the years since 1950. It is as follows (1940 equals 100):[38]

1950	104
1951	105
1952	104
1953	97
1954	107
1955	107
1956	97
1957	94
1958	98

At first, the official index of prices in kolkhoz trade, indicating that in 1950, for example, the prices in this trade were only 4 per cent above those in 1940, seems improbable, but gradually one realizes that one has not visualized how high were the prices in kolkhoz trade in 1940.

If the price index in kolkhoz trade in 1950 exceeded that in 1940 by 4 per cent, while for the official trade the index was 186, this implies that if the prices in kolkhoz and official trade were the same in 1950, the 1940 prices in kolkhoz trade exceeded those in official trade by 78.[39] The difference was even greater for food. For food other than hard liquor, the 1940 prices in kolkhoz trade are assumed to have exceeded those in official trade by 85 per cent. In Chart 20 the price indices of kolkhoz trade were calculated on this assumption.

From data in Chart 20, the percentage differentials between the prices in kolkhoz trade and in official trade in food other than hard liquor in 1945–58 were calculated as follows (kolkhoz prices higher by per cent):

1940	85	1952	31
1945	518	1953	42
1947	252	1954	60
1948	111	1955	60
1949	−15	1956	44
1950	4	1957	37
1951	19	1958	44

The precipitous decline of the margin between the prices in kolkhoz and official trade in the first post–World War II years is described on page 273 above. In 1949 the prices in kolkhoz markets were already the lower (see Chart 20).

As the data in the above tabulation stands, in 1950 the prices in kolkhoz trade were again about the same as those of food other than hard liquor in official trade. But after this the different trends in both

[38] *Soviet Trade*, stat. handb., 1956, p. 182, and *Economy of the USSR in 1956*, p. 237. Data for 1956 to 1958 from *Economy of the USSR in 1958*, p. 789.
[39] See also chapter 9.

CHART 20

PRICES IN OFFICIAL AND KOLKHOZ TRADE, 1945–58 *

(1940 prices in official trade = 100)

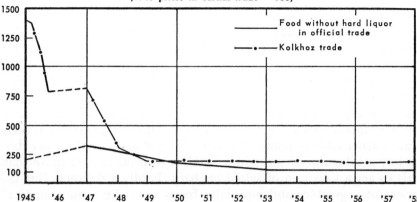

Food without hard liquor
in official trade

————•———— Kolkhoz trade

* Data for official trade from Chart 18. Data for kolkhoz trade from the indices discussed in the text. The prices in kolkhoz trade in 1940 were assumed to have been 85 per cent higher than in official trade (see p. 274, above). In chapter 9 an index of 178 (official trade equals 100) was used for the 1940 prices in kolkhoz trade, but there we operated with the total official trade rather than official trade in food other than hard liquor.

forms of trade brought a disparity, which continued to grow rapidly until a peak was reached with an excess for the prices in kolkhoz trade of about 70 per cent in the first half of 1955. A narrowing of the gap began in the second half of 1955 and lasted until the end of 1957. In 1957, the excess of the prices in kolkhoz trade was already down to about 37 per cent. Then followed a renewed setback.

While the data in the tabulation above show very disturbed conditions in most postwar years, this is only the beginning of the story. The prices of the products more important for kolkhoz trade exceeded those in official trade in the first and fourth quarters of 1955 by the following percentages:[40]

Product	First Quarter	Fourth Quarter
Whole-wheat flour	53	44
Wheat flour other than whole-grain flour	60	66
Groats	108	61
Potatoes	258	145
Vegetables	321	166
Apples	306	204
Beef	95	55
Mutton	117	74
Pork	37	25
Milk	86	45
Butter	108	73
Vegetable oil	53	30
Eggs	86	60

[40] Implied in data in *Soviet Trade*, stat. handb., 1956, pp. 133–34.

Excesses of prices in kolkhoz trade of 25 to 30 per cent over those in official trade look like trifles, although under normal conditions the average prices in kolkhoz trade are likely to be lower than those in official trade.[41] The fact that as recently as 1955 the kolkhoz-trade prices of potatoes, vegetables, and fruits were 2.5 to 4.0 times higher than the prices in official trade, clearly indicates very disorganized conditions.

The prices in plain rubles continued to be concealed, but they could be calculated with approximate exactness from official data (see Table 22). A glance at the table shows that the concealment is understandable. In 1955 it took about a full day's pay of an average wage earner (this is assumed to have been about 24 rubles per day) to buy a kilogram of meat in a kolkhoz market. It took more than this to get a kilogram of salted fat back, hardly a delicacy. But the prices of vegetables and especially fruits were the most abnormal. Prices for vegetables, except cabbage, of over 5 rubles per kilogram and for fruits of about 12 rubles were simply prohibitive. A kilogram of groats or grits (rice, but mostly buckwheat and millet) at a price of 9 rubles also was not exactly a bargain.[42]

Concerning development of prices of individual products in kolkhoz trade during 1950–55, rises all along the line can be observed, with the exception of eggs and vegetable oil, which were less important,[43] and grain products. These price rises reflected enhanced ability to buy even at seemingly prohibitive prices. Considering the small amounts sold in kolkhoz trade, not many people would have been needed to clean out the markets even at the very high prices.

A rather important feature of prices in Soviet trade are the low prices in eating places relative to those in official trade proper. This phenomenon is brought about by the small retail margin,[44] which in its turn is caused by the combination of high prices of the goods sold,

[41] Soviet analysts of prices in kolkhoz trade have repeatedly insisted on a phenomenon to be expected, that the kolkhoz-market prices were higher in larger than in smaller cities. L. Mazel, for example, showed that on October 25, 1954, and October 25, 1955, the prices in kolkhoz markets in republican and oblast centers were on an average higher than in district centers by perhaps 20 per cent. There was only one case (onions, on October 25, 1955) when the prices in district centers were higher by 4.2 per cent (see *Soviet Trade* [monthly], 1956, No. 9, p. 13). But there is no reason for the prices in the kolkhoz markets of large cities to be higher under normal conditions than those in official trade.

[42] It should be noted that whatever inexactnesses caused by the method of calculation are in the data in Table 22, overestimations, or underestimations, in the case of some products are offset by underestimations, or overestimations, in the case of other products. The total value of sales and the amounts of products sold are as officially given.

[43] Both products are classed as less important because of the small amounts sold.

[44] *Soviet Trade*, stat. handb., 1956, p. 118.

TABLE 22

Prices in Kolkhoz Markets in 1950 and 1955*

Product	Price Change in 1940–50 (1940 = 100) Official	Average Price in 1950 (rubles per kilogram or unit) Calculated	Price Change in 1950–55 (1950 = 100) Official	Average Price in 1955 (rubles per kilogram or unit) Calculated
Meat....................	102	...	116	...
Beef....................	99	18.8	132	24.7
Mutton.................	...	23.3	...	24.5
Pork....................	108	23.4	103	22.7
Fat back................	...	32.9	...	33.3
Poultry.................	97	19.4	124	24.6
Milk....................	100	4.1	105	4.2
Butter..................	84	32.3	119	41.5
Eggs (unit)..............	110	1.3	98	1.3
Grain and grain products....	102	...	81	...
Grains..................	108	2.3	76	2.3
Flour...................	107	5.2	70	2.8
Groats..................	98	9.95	86	8.8
Potatoes................	69	2.0	125	2.4
Vegetables..............	95	...	133	...
Cabbage................	58	1.9	143	2.6
Onions.................	112	4.2	133	5.6
Cucumbers..............	...	4.3	...	5.1
Tomatoes, beets, etc.......	...	4.2	...	5.6
Fruits...................	110	10.1	117	11.9
Vegetable oil.............	104	24.8	97	23.4

* *Soviet Trade*, stat. handb., 1956 (p. 190) gives the composition of the returns from the sales of the various products in kolkhoz markets of 71 large cities in 1955 in percentages of the total. But the amounts sold in these markets are not stated for this coverage. There seems, therefore, to be no other choice but to use the total returns from the sales in kolkhoz markets of 251 cities (*ibid.*, p. 185) in conjunction with the percentages of returns from the individual products in 71 cities. This yields the money returns from the individual products in 251 cities. These returns in conjunction with the data on the amounts sold in the kolkhoz markets of the same cities (*ibid.*, p. 188) yield the average realized prices shown here. Owing to the nature of available evidence, these calculations are possible only for 1950 and 1955. In view of the uncertainties involved, the figures have been rounded off to the nearest tenth of a ruble. As a check, the index of price changes during the period 1950–55 in 71 cities from *ibid.*, p. 183, is used. A similar index for the price changes in 1940–50 (1940 = 100) permits the formation of an idea of the kolkhoz-market prices of individual products in 1940.

Soviet Trade, *RSFSR*, stat. handb., 1958, contains data similar to those utilized for Table 20 for the years 1956 and 1957. In some respects these data would be even better, but the figure for the total return in kolkhoz markets in 138 cities, indispensable for our calculations, was withheld. Calculations like those in Table 22 would have been impossible without this figure. The possibility of using the data in *Soviet Trade*, stat. handb., 1956, the way it is used in Table 22 was probably realized, so such material was eliminated in subsequent handbooks. (After Table 22 had been completed, this writer saw a similar calculation made by Alexander Nove of the London School of Economics in, I believe, an unpublished document.)

low rent and wages of the personnel, and large proportion of sales in eating places of goods not produced by them.

The trade margin in eating places was equivalent to 14.76 per cent of the turnover in 1955.[45] As was shown above, the price differential between official and kolkhoz trade was smaller than this only in 1948 and 1950 (in 1949 the prices in official trade were the higher). In other postwar years the price differential was higher to

[45] *Ibid.*

much higher than the retail margin of eating places. This implies that the consumers prefer eating at home to public eating places, taking into the bargain all the trouble of buying the food (frequently standing in line), preparing it, and washing the dishes, even to the extent of bearing higher to much higher costs. In 1955, when the prices in kolkhoz markets were about 60 per cent higher than those in official trade, sales in eating places were only a little larger than in kolkhoz trade, including the commission trade of the Tsentrosoyuz (58.8 billion rubles as against 53.8 billion rubles).* This is particularly noteworthy because most wives have full-time jobs.

One of the reasons for shunning the public eating places, believed by the rulers the only proper form of consumption in a socialist state, is recognized officially. This is the poor quality of the food served in the eating places. But one seriously suspects that the very reason which makes the rulers foster the public eating places above all, weighs heavily among the reasons which lead to their avoidance by the population. People want privacy. They want to get away from the incessant propaganda, from having to hear innumerable times per day about the concern of the Party for the well-being of the population. Both the objections to the poor quality of the served food and the wish for privacy have limits, of course, and the price differential between kolkhoz and official trade has a great effect on the turnover of the eating places (see chapter 16).

Producers' goods.—After having been boosted sharply on January 1, 1949, the prices of producers' goods were reduced substantially in 1950, the very next year. A large part of the cut, effective January 1, 1950, was simply elimination of the excessive rise in 1949. Another partial price cut followed later in 1950 and two more general ones in 1951 and 1952, respectively. Kondrashev (*Price Formation in Industry of the USSR,* Moscow, 1956, p. 145) gave the following wholesale-price index for all industrial goods (1949 equals 100):

$$1950................. \quad 79.7$$
$$1951................. \quad 77.5$$
$$1952................. \quad 70.1$$

A price index specifically for producers' goods for this period seems unfortunately unavailable. Zverev's statement quoted below indicates that the decline of prices specifically of producers' goods in those years was larger than that of all wholesale prices.

---

* Eating places do a large sale in products which are not scarce (beverages, grain products, etc.). The sales of scarce products in them are much smaller than the sales in kolkhoz and commission trade.

The deflationary activity in the field of producers' goods was crowned with a price reduction effective July 1, 1955.[46] The reduction was referred to as drastic in Soviet sources. According to *Economic Survey of Europe in 1956* (I, 4), it was equivalent to 12.5 per cent on the average of all industrial goods.

According to Finance Minister A. G. Zverev, the prices of producers' goods introduced on July 1, 1955, were 8 to 10 per cent below those in 1948,[47] and hence the spectacular boost in prices of these goods in 1949 was more than eliminated. The excessiveness of this boost has become even more obvious than it seemed at the time of the announcement of the new prices.[48]

In conjunction with the estimate of the prices of producers' goods in 1948 in terms of those in 1926/27 in *Essay III* (p. 15), a price rise for all producers' goods is indicated for the time from 1926/27 to July 1, 1955, equivalent to 3.0–3.5 times its initial level.

The prices of machinery, an important component of investment, were slashed drastically after 1949, especially on July 1, 1955. According to Zverev, the prices of machinery on July 1, 1955, were about 40 per cent below those in 1948.[49] The price declines separately of civilian machinery and of armaments remain unknown. According to this writer's calculations, the prices of civilian machinery in 1948 were only about 120 per cent above those in 1926/27[50] Hence, if the price reduction for civilian machinery in 1949 was about the same as for all machinery, and if Zverev's and this writer's estimates are in any way correct, an amazingly low price level of only about 40 per cent above that in 1926/27 can be inferred for the prices of civilian machinery in 1955.[51]

[46] Kondrashev, *op. cit.*, pp. 145–46, designated this price decline as the fifth.

[47] *Planned Economy*, 1956, No. 1, p. 21.

[48] After the 1949 price raise had become history, its excessiveness was discussed frankly (see, for example, Kondrashev, *op. cit.*, pp. 139–48). The prices introduced on January 1, 1949, were calculated by ministries. The Gosplan USSR and the Ministry of Finance, which had to supervise this work, proved powerless to combat the tendency toward excessiveness on the part of the ministries. No great harm occurred, however. The results were not so harmless, though, when soon thereafter the ministries embarked on a policy of having many more construction projects than could have been completed within a reasonable time (see pp. 242–43).

[49] *Planned Economy*, 1956, No. 1, p. 21.

[50] *Essay III*, pp. 15, 20.

[51] According to Kondrashev (*op. cit.*, p. 145), the index of machinery prices is questionable in view of the frequent changes in models. Under Soviet conditions this probably leads to a considerable exaggeration of the reduction in prices. It may be significant that in his later publication, Zverev (*op. cit.*, p. 213) did not repeat his statement that the prices of machinery had become 40 per cent lower than those of 1948. Rather he said: "The wholesale prices of machinery [had become] lower, in many cases much lower, than in 1948."

With all the uncertainty in regard to the price index of civilian machinery,[52] the fact that the increase of its prices from 1928 to 1955 was relatively small is of immense importance. An agricultural country with a particularly weak machinery industry operating at very high costs was transformed in a short space of time into an industrial country with a particularly strong machinery industry operating at very low costs.

The only relatively small increase in prices of machinery from 1928 to 1955 is very relevant for the appraisal of Soviet military expenditure as well. The prices of armaments are not apt to have increased more than the prices of civilian machinery. If there was a divergence, armaments may have shown a smaller price rise than civilian machinery. The relatively small increase in prices of armaments since 1928 compares with a rise in the budgetary appropriation for the military ministries from about 0.8 billion rubles in 1928 to about 100 billion rubles in 1955.

While the prices of all producers' goods were lower on July 1, 1955, than in 1948 by 8 to 10 per cent, the prices of all producers' goods other than machinery still remained above this level. According to Kondrashev (*op. cit.*, p. 148) the excess was even equal to about 20 per cent.

Railway freight rates and costs.—The deflation of railway freight rates ran parallel to that of prices of producers' goods. A cut of almost 11 per cent was ordered effective January 1, 1950. Major reductions also became effective January 1, 1952, and the largest was that of July 1, 1955. The total decline from 1949 to 1956 was equal to 28.6 per cent. The detailed data on the average unit rate and average unit cost and on profits from the transportation of freight on railways are of considerable interest:[53]

Year	Average Unit Rate (kopeks per ton-kilometer)	Average Unit Cost (kopeks per ton-kilometer)	Profit (per cent of cost)
1949	6.012	5.053	+18.9
1950	5.387	4.861	+10.8
1951	5.294	4.505	+17.5
1952	4.832	4.302	+12.3
1953	4.798	4.056	+18.3
1954	4.960	3.929	+25.6
1955	4.631	3.542	+30.0
1956	4.298	3.316	+29.6

The unit cost of freight transportation on railways went down from 1949 to 1956 (because of the reduction in prices of materials

[52] The relatively great lowering of machinery prices remains fully apparent even if Zverev's evidence is on the optimistic side.

[53] Arkhangelskii and Kreinin in *Questions of Economics*, 1957, No. 11, pp. 113.

and equipment, but also because of savings effected through the great increases in performance per man and the better utilization of equipment and materials) even more than the unit rate (by 34.4 per cent as against 28.6 per cent for the average unit freight rate), and the average profit ultimately reached 30 per cent of the cost, a level recognized as excessive in the USSR. By 1956, the transportation of those goods which traditionally entailed a loss either started to return a profit (coal), or at least just about covered costs (timber). Only the transportation of coke remained in the loss category.[54]

Construction costs.—The official index of construction costs, which obviously covers only the cost of building materials, transportation of building materials and machinery, as well as labor, shows the following development after it reached its high point in 1949:[55]

Year	1940 = 100	In Per Cent of Previous Year
1949	178	131
1950	160	90
1951	149	93
1952	142	95
1953	142	100
1954	140	99
1955	132	95
1956	131	99

The index figures for all years starting with 1949, given in terms of 1940, are impossibly low. For the time being, there seems to be no good reason to revise the index calculated for 1949 (1940 equals 100) in *Essay III* (p. 20) at 258. The index figures for the declines in construction costs, shown in the tabulation above, may be correct so far as the changes since 1949 are concerned (it seems difficult to check them, however).

The Soviets never published an index of construction costs covering the whole period of the Great Industrialization Drive. The same is, of course, true for all other types of costs and prices. But an official, though crude, index of costs involved in investment is clearly implied in the official calculations of the investment of the state in terms of prices in effect since July 1, 1955, for the whole period since 1914. This implied index minimizes to a large degree the increase in costs involved in investment and along with this the costs involved in construction. From 1928/29–1932 to July 1, 1955, the costs involved in investment increased by less than 20 per cent according to

[54] *Ibid.*, p. 114.
[55] *Economy of the USSR in 1956*, p. 184.

these data.[56] The welcome outcome of this minimizing of the costs of investment (welcome from the viewpoint of the Soviets) was a corresponding exaggeration of the growth of investment over the stated period.

Calculations in *Essay III* (p. 20) yielded an index of construction costs for 1949 (1926/27 equals 100) of 585. With use of the official index for 1949–56, indicating a decline of 26.4 per cent, the index of construction costs of 1956 (1926/27 equals 100) turns out 431. The increase in costs since 1928 was about fourfold.[57]

Nominal Wages

The "all-citizen statistical ration" [58] does not include the *average* nominal wage in postwar years. Scattered statements for single years are found in sources which may be considered as good as official.

There were large raises in nominal wages during World War II, but almost exclusively to workers and employees believed indispensable to the war effort. These included mainly workers in heavy industry, construction, and transportation. In September of 1946, the so-called "bread supplement" to wages was effected simultaneously with a very large boost in the prices of rationed food.

The "bread supplement" amounted to 110 rubles per month for workers earning less than 300 rubles per month, and declined to nothing for those earning more than 900 rubles per month. While the great raising of the prices of consumers' goods, necessitating compensation by wage boosts (for many, however, this was only partial) was a doubtful proposition, the measure had the advantage that it benefited most those groups of wage earners who were earning

[56] See *Commentary*, p. 141. The changes in construction costs implied in the estimates of investment in construction, given along with the estimates for total investment of the state in the source quoted in the preceding note, cannot be estimated; but the difference between the changes in them and the changes in costs involved in total investment could not have been very large.

[57] This index appears much more sensible than that implied in the official estimates of investment at prices of July 1, 1955. The rate charged on freight by railways increased 3.03 times from 1928 to 1956 (see data above as well as in *Essay III*, p. 39), and the increase in the costs of this transportation was only little less than this. There seems to be no doubt that for various reasons the growth in construction costs over the stated period was substantially larger than that in the costs of transportation by railways calculated per ton-kilometer.

[58] The "all-citizen statistical ration" is a magnificent characterization of the statistics released by the Central Statistical Office, made by academician V. Nemchinov, one of the leading Soviet economists, in *Questions of Economics,* the journal of the Academy of Sciences of the USSR, 1959, No. 4, p. 34. I wish Nemchinov had made the statement two years earlier: I would have used it as a title or motto for my *Commentary.* Nemchinov argues that complicated economic problems cannot be treated with the help of the "all-citizen statistical ration."

the lowest wages before World War II and who did not get any substantial raises during the war. By the end of 1946 the average nominal wage of all wage earners seems to have exceeded that of 1940 by close to 75 per cent. The average nominal wage continued to rise in 1947 and 1948, but only slowly.

The great cuts in prices of consumers' goods which had started in 1949 could not have been effected if the nominal wage had not been nearly stabilized. This would, however, have been a difficult task in itself; it was particularly so at the specific time when the policy of deflation was undertaken. Payment of hired labor was, and still is, to a very large extent based on piece work in the USSR, and fulfilment and overfulfilment of norms was redeemed at high rates in relation to the basic pay. Performances were, moreover, low in 1948, the initial year of the price-cutting campaign. Without drastic countermeasures, the rise in output per man in subsequent years would have led to more than proportionate increases in the yearly earnings. A further complicating factor was that the whole wage structure between industries and occupations was greatly disorganized as a result of the very uneven wage increases since the start of World War II.

The policy of holding nominal wages as nearly stable as possible proved highly effective. Between 1950 and 1955 the average yearly increase in average nominal earnings was only about 2 per cent.[59] In connection with the 1952 International Trade Conference in Moscow, Soviet representatives in conversations with British economists spoke of stability of wages for several years past.

It may be safely assumed that the yearly increase in average nominal earnings would not have been much smaller than 2 per cent, even if the wage rises had been entirely limited to such automatic factors as greater expansion of the labor force in branches with higher average wages, higher payment of workers with a greater number of years of service, and the like, but not increased output per man.[60]

It was, of course, relatively simple not to permit any wage increases of those paid on a time basis. There is no doubt that when new jobs were created, these were frequently, maybe regularly,

---

[59] Various semiofficial sources.

[60] Unfortunately, the problem was not subjected to a thorough study. The pay of truck. automobile. and bus drivers, for example, rises with the increase in the size of the vehicle operated. The rates paid to the drivers of vehicles of a given size remained unchanged, at least from 1948 to 1954, but the average size of the vehicles increased. Thus, there was also an increase in the average pay of this group of wage earners caused by the factor stated.

graded lower than they would have been previously. Performance norms had to be raised about as much as the rise in output per man, the latter having been very large in those years.

In the part of chapter 15 dealing with the output per man in industry, only the change from 1940 to 1950 is discussed. Let us digress to bring here evidence of the large rates of growth in output per man in industry in the postwar years themselves. These large rates can, of course, be shown on the data on output and the labor force. But, for a change, evidence will be brought up which, while good, has not been otherwise used. We have in mind the official calculations of production costs in industry, which should have been reasonably correct. The share of wages and social insurance payments in total production costs of industry amounted to 21.2 per cent in 1955.[61] In 1950–55, an average of 0.73 per cent of total production costs, or 3.5 per cent of labor costs, could have been saved per year by raising output per man. A decline of this size, in spite of a great reduction in total production cost of 23.6 per cent during the five-year period,[62] and the increase, although moderate, in the average nominal wage, testify to a large growth in output per man, several times that of the rise in nominal wages.

The Soviets ended a twelve- to thirteen-year silence on nominal wages when the new, as good as official, text on economics revealed that the average wage of all workers and employees in 1953 exceeded that of 1940 by 101 per cent.[63] Of all Western analysts, Harry Schwartz was possibly closest to the facts with his estimate of the average wage at the end of rationing.[64]

The official figure indicates about 8,150 rubles as the average 1953 nominal wage. Since the average wage is supposed to have increased by 2 per cent in 1953,[65] it was about 8,000 rubles in 1952. Mrs. Janet Chapman had 7,800 rubles for this year, and this figure was presumably also that of Harry Schwartz. The present writer's latest printed figure was "about 7,500 rubles" for 1951, with 150 rubles as the yearly increment.[66]

[61] *Industry of the USSR*, 1957, p. 30.

[62] *Ibid.*, p. 29.

[63] *Political Economy*, p. 462. It still was not a strictly official source. The form of statement also is not exactly straight.

[64] For details see *Essay II*, pp. 29–30.

[65] Report on the Fulfilment of the 1953 Plan.

[66] *Essay III*, p. 10. It should not be concealed that, after publication of *Essay III*, the writer made (and circulated in unpublished form) somewhat lower estimates. Those estimates were based on various data and procedures, but to a large extent on analysis of retail trade. In conjunction with the nominal wages like those released later, the data on this trade pointed to such an immense decline since 1940 in purchases of the population other than the wage earners from the official trade that the present writer did not dare accept it as true before the publication of the data on wages.

In connection with the setting of the target of the seven-year plan for 1965, the average wage in 1958 of 9,430 rubles per year was disclosed.[67] This implies a growth of 16 per cent in the five years since 1953. Part of the additional expenditure on wages was utilized to raise the pay of the worst-paid categories much more than the average.

An average wage of 9,430 per year in 1958 implies a level 13.5 times the 1928 wage. This is roughly the rate by which retail prices grew over the same period (exactness is difficult to attain).

The approximate changes in the average nominal earnings of all wage earners in rubles per year in a few years were:[68] *

1928.................	703
1940.................	4,054
End of 1946...........	Close to 7,000
1948.................	7,500
1952.................	8,000
1953.................	8,150
1958.................	9,430

The Price Structure

In *Essay II,* published in 1952, this writer described the Soviet price system as chaotic. While the description met with objections in this country, it found strong support from Soviet authors after the relatively recent, at least partial, relaxation of the strangulation of Soviet analytical work. Indeed, a whole literature on the Soviet price system, concentrating on means for its improvement, grew up during this short period of time.[69]

The Soviet price system is characterized by absence of co-ordina-

[67] Khrushchev said in one of his speeches that the seven-year plan scheduled an average wage of 990 rubles per month in 1965. The speech was not published in the USSR but was heard on the radio in Britain. Since the seven-year plan programs an increase of the average nominal wage from 1958 to 1965 by 26 per cent, the figure stated in the text is implied.

[68] Includes some revisions as compared with *Essay II,* p. 23. The data are approximations, except for those for 1940, 1952, 1953, and 1958, which are official or nearly official.

* A source not available at the completion of the manuscript (S. Figurnov, in *Labor and Wages,* December, 1959, p. 48) gives an index of nominal wages, which by itself and together with other evidence, yields moderately different data than those quoted in the text. According to Figurnov, the rise from 1953 to 1958 was equal to 13 per cent rather than 16 per cent as stated in the text. Figurnov's index indicates an average yearly wage in 1953 of about 8,400 rubles rather than 8,150 rubles shown in the text. The figures for the preceding years in the tabulation would turn out correspondingly higher, if Figurnov's index is accepted. While Figurnov's evidence must be about official, this writer did not study the material sufficiently to pass judgment. The differences are after all not large. (Thanks are due to Mrs. Luba Richter of the U.S. Department of State for drawing my attention to this relatively rare source.)

[69] See Alfred Zauberman's paper in the symposium at Berkeley, California, in 1958.

tion between the two great groups of prices of industrial products (producers' and consumers' goods). For decades there was also a great discrepancy between the prices paid by the state for farm products and the prices the farm population had to pay for industrial goods it needed. Lack of co-ordination existed and still exists also between prices of similar goods, for example, between different fuels, and for the same goods (regional and quality differentials). Until 1958 the Soviet price system even included multiplicity of prices of the same products as an important feature. Duplicity, to some extent even multiplicity, of prices indeed still exists (higher prices in kolkhoz than official trade and some others).

The chaotic state which the Soviet price system had been in for many years certainly caused many difficulties and waste even under the extremely centralized form of organization that existed during Stalin's day. It became even more difficult to bear after the decentralization of direction of industry, construction, planning, and indeed, of most of the economy which was effected in 1957 and 1958, modest as the extent of this decentralization may be. Transfer of farm machinery from MTS to the kolkhozy in 1958 had a similar effect.

Only a few years ago even the principle that prices must cover costs was not generally accepted. In the last Stalin years some important producers' goods, not to speak of farm products, still sold at prices below costs. The needed subsidies were but small though, as compared with such periods as 1931–35 or 1941–48. By now the principle that the price must cover cost and return a profit seems to have only very small exceptions.

The production costs on which the prices of industrial goods are to be based are the average costs in present-day practice. The production costs show, however, a great deal of differentiation. Differences in natural resources, location, size, and efficiency of the individual enterprises are the principal factors causing differentiation in production costs. The large proportion of enterprises operating at a loss was, and still is, a great handicap to efficiency. This situation, of course, poses the question how to deal with enterprises with lower or higher than average costs.

So long as the enterprises were under the ministries, the problem of production costs departing from the average was settled by averaging the high and low costs of different enterprises of the same ministry. The problem had become still more complicated after the enterprises passed to the *sovnarkhozy*. Those *sovnarkhozy* which have a particularly large proportion of high-cost enterprises, are getting subsidies from the Treasury. Thus the subsidies from the Treasury, which the Soviets have been trying to get rid of since 1936, expanded in scope.

A very important, although by no means the only, reason for the distorted price system of the USSR has been the absence of a charge for use of capital. Since the Revolution, to charge interest for the use of capital has been taboo, allegedly according to Marx. The most important adverse effect of absence of a charge for use of capital was the impossibility of a sensible choice between investment projects, namely, the favoring of projects with the largest investment and the smallest operating costs.

The mistaken investment policies caused by absence of a charge for use of capital were apparent in every branch of the economy. Lenin's enchantment with hydroelectric power, retained for almost forty years, had its origin in this erroneous economic philosophy. The admiration which the Soviets had, and still have, or pretend to have, for electric rather than diesel traction on railways also stems from the same source.

Favored furthermore by the neglect of a charge for use of capital were producers' goods at the expense of consumers' goods, the latter requiring much less fixed capital than the former. Disturbances were introduced by this factor also within the broad group of producers' and consumers' goods.

Absence of a charge for use of capital as well as relative cheapness of fuel, other materials, and especially machinery, led to low costs and rates incurred and charged by means of transportation—with manifold important results. Significant among these was the effect on location of agriculture and industry, specifically their favorable effect on the development of the East, with its long distances.

Such important price-fixing factors as land rent (for agriculture and extracting industries), so far as they were considered at all, were handled in the most haphazard manner.

Immensely varying sales taxes (turnover taxes as they are called in the USSR, and also in Britain) were another factor greatly disturbing the price system. They helped to balance demand and supply in some cases, though. Difficulties of planning contributed their share to the price disturbances. Last but not least came the effect of red tape and simply helplessness.

The disorganization of the price system was particularly pronounced in agriculture. The prices paid by the state on obligatory deliveries of farm products by the producers were very low and some of them almost nominal.[70] These prices were largely retained, when after Stalin's death it was decided to do something for agriculture. But at the same time, up to 14 times more was paid for the same product on the so-called *zakupka* (purchases) in excess of obligatory deliveries. The unhealthy situation with farm prices lasted for not less than thirty years, becoming ever more pronounced and confused until it was eliminated in one stroke, effective July 1, 1958. New disparities arose though, which cannot be gone into here.

An illuminating picture of the unhealthiness of the Soviet price system in the non-farm economy is supplied by a calculation of the surplus value in 1954 made by D. D. Kondrashev in *Questions of Socialist Economy* (p. 262). Surplus value, or, as Kondrashev called it, money accumulations, are everything above production costs, i.e., profit and sales taxes. His data are: light industry, 231 billion rubles; heavy industry, about 60 billion rubles; construction, 1 billion rubles, etc. (the "etc." is Kondrashev's). The great difference in the produced surplus value between heavy and light industry is, of course, the most significant feature of these data. But the fact that construction yielded only small profits seems also worth attention. It is a feature apparently disregarded by Western students in their calculations. The principal components of investment, especially equipment, are priced low in the USSR anyway, and the practical absence of profits, not to speak of sales taxes, in construction contributes even more to the effect of this phenomenon. These considerations are obviously important in calculating the share of investment in national income in the USSR, which is very large even with this factor disregarded.

Concerning the artificial nature of the then existing price relationship between producers' and consumers' goods, Kondrashev stated:[71]

There is no doubt that the prices of means of production as a rule are substantially below production costs and their principal defect is in that they do not permit one to judge what is expensive and what is cheap, consequently, what is profitable to produce from the point of view of the national economy and what is unprofitable.

[70] To have a semblance of justification for these prices, the idea was conceived and extensively propagandized that the obligatory deliveries represented the differential rent due to the state as the owner of the land. The state allegedly took only part of this rent. The idea seems to have been abandoned in this form, after it had become unnecessary with the abolition of the respective prices. Mikoyan was frank when he said in his oration on the occasion of the forty-first anniversary that the purchases of the state at those low prices were in reality a tax on the producers. Krushchev seconded him a little later.

[71] D. D. Kondrashev, "Problems of Price Formation in the USSR," *Questions of Socialist Economy*, a symposium (Moscow, 1956), pp. 264–65.

At the time of Kondrashev's writing almost the total proceeds of the huge sales taxes were derived from consumers' goods (and it still remains so). Even profits were unevenly distributed. The share of consumers' goods in industrial production was equal to 29.2 per cent in 1956,[72] but these goods were scheduled to yield 46.2 per cent of all profits produced by the industry.[73] The combined effect of the uneven distribution of sales taxes and of profits, as well as the absence of charges for the use of capital, were among the principal reasons for the disparity between the prices of producers' and consumers' goods mentioned above.

The great discrepancies between the prices of producers' and consumers' goods are clearly reflected in the price indices discussed in the preceding part of this chapter. It was shown that the prices of producers' goods in force as of July 1, 1955, were 3.0–3.5 times those in 1926/27. Since the retail price index of consumers' goods was nearly 1,500 (1926/27 equals 100) in 1955, consumers' goods had become almost five times as expensive, relatively, as producers' goods during the thirty years.

This great difference in the rise of prices in about the last thirty years was to a considerable extent brought about by the much greater increase in output per man in heavy than in light industry; but sales taxes, differences in profits, and absence of a charge for the use of capital also were very important.

The price discrepancies were large also within the broad groups of producers' and consumers' goods. Kondrashev, for example, writing in 1956, believed that coal was overpriced in relation to petroleum products.[74] Ivliev argued that the wholesale prices of, and freight rates on, coal, ore, metal, timber, and building materials were still much too high.[75] Kondrashev also listed a number of consumers' goods that were sold at too low prices. He especially singled out automobiles, the greatest luxury good of all in the USSR, among the goods with prices that were too low. The great shortage of relatively cheap passenger cars caused long waiting lists and speculation.[76]

[72] *Economy of the USSR in 1956,* p. 56.

[73] A. Zverev on the 1957 budget in *Planner Economy,* 1957, No. 3, p. 23.

[74] D. D. Kondrashev, "Price Formation in the USSR," *Problems of Socialist Economics* (Moscow, 1956), pp. 268, 276.

[75] I. Ivliev, "Operation with Consideration of Costs on Railway Transport," *Questions of Economics,* 1956, p. 41.

[76] *Op. cit.,* p. 272. The disorganized state of the market for passenger cars was ultimately recognized. Since it was believed that this was not the time for covering the demand for cars at the prices then existing (this is obvious from the Control Figures for 1959–65), the prices of passenger cars were raised drastically in January of 1958. For

A good example of the extent of arbitrariness in establishing the prices of a producers' good is the prices of petroleum products. In 1956, these were as follows (in rubles per ton and in percentage of 1937 prices):[77]

Product	Rubles	Per Cent of 1937
Naphtha.............................	403	48.6
Gasoline, automobile, first grade........	673	65.3
Kerosene (lighting)....................	393	57.3
Diesel fuel, heavy.....................	287	274.4
Residual fuel oil, heavy................	271	312.6

In 1937 gasoline was about 10 times as expensive as diesel fuel. In 1956 it was less than 2.5 times as expensive.

An illuminating example of prices which had to be changed in a hurry is the revision of the prices of tractors in 1958. It is of particular interest, because it is connected with a departure from the Soviet practice that producers' goods are allocated to, rather than selected by, the enterprises needing them (before 1958 an exception was made only for building materials going to kolkhozy and the private sector). The law abolishing the MTS and establishing single prices for farm products delivered by the kolkhozy to the state of June, 1958, permitted the kolkhozy themselves to decide on the machinery they wanted to buy—a quite substantial breach in Soviet-type centralized planned economy in favor of market economy.

Before the new measure, all tractor models were overpriced relative to the standard Soviet tractor, the DT-54. (The prices of the DT-54 were relatively low, because of low production costs attained by the huge output of this model.) There seem not to have been great disturbances from these price discrepancies so long as the tractors were allocated. Now, with the new system, it was unlikely that a sensible kolkhoz chairman would have wanted to pay almost twice as much for the C-80 as for the DT-54, especially since the former has only 50 per cent more power than the DT-54 and is less suitable for farming, or to buy a tractor with 37 horsepower for as much as, or more than, the price of a tractor having 54 horsepower. Hence, almost immediately after the decision to let the kolkhozy buy farm machinery, a new price list was issued, effective July 1, 1958. These are the old and new prices for a few tractor models (in rubles):

the cheapest cars the retail price was boosted more than twofold—a capitalist way of adjusting supply to demand, although the drastic extent of the price increase may possibly be "socialistic."

[77] Here quoted from Lynn Turgeon and Abram Bergson, RAND's RM-1919, 1957, p. 47.

	Until July 1, 1958[a]	After July 1, 1958[b]
Crawler S–80[c]	32,200	32,700
Crawler DT–54	16,200	22,000
Crawler KDP–35 (row-crop)	18,250	17,000
Wheel tractor "Belarus'"	22,000	19,800

[a] *Reference Book of Prices of Building Materials and Equipment, Part B, Equipment*, 1957, pp. 884, 909.

[b] "Price List of Tractors and Farm Machinery," *Machine-Tractor Stations*, 1958, No. 8. p. 59.

[c] The symbols stand for the following: *S*, for Stalin, *D* for diesel, *T* for tractor, *K* for Kirovets, and *P* for row-crop (*propashnyui*); the figures show the belt power. The S-80 is also a diesel tractor.

Thus, the wheel tractor "Belarus'" (37-belt horsepower), which cost 13 per cent more than the DT-54, a crawler with 54-belt horsepower, prior to the great event, has become 10 per cent cheaper than the latter. Even the new price relationships still discriminate against the 54-horsepower crawlers.[78]

As recently as the Twenty-first Party Congress, A. N. Kosygin, shortly afterward appointed head of the Gosplan USSR, spoke in a very energetic manner of the great discrepancies in prices of both producers' and consumers' goods.[79]

A certain complication in the realm of prices is the fact that the great increase in prices of farm products without increase in retail prices of the same products in recent years has finally led to the elimination of sales taxes on some farm products or products produced from these. Thus, there are consumers' goods that are heavily taxed, some not taxed at all, and, in exceptional cases, some that are subsidized. (Such discrepancies also existed earlier but they were relatively minor.) The system does not look very healthy, but there seems no reason why it should not become a permanent feature of the Soviet price system.*

[78] Since the DT-54 far predominates in production, the new price list implies a certain price increase for all tractors—even in the midst of a deflation. The kolkhozy are made to pay for the right to own farm machinery.

[79] *Pravda*, January 29, 1959.

* Material which mostly became available after the completion of this volume shows a state of price disorganization which exceeds everything this writer imagined. Ample material is found, for example, in Sh. Ya. Turetskii, *Essays on Planned Price Formation in the USSR* (Moscow, 1959), which became available in the United States only in 1960. Turetskii shows, for example, that iron ore with a low content of iron is not sufficiently cheap to make profitable its amelioration, indispensable for efficient utilization of blast furnaces (p. 112); that lime costs several times more than the price which would make its utilization advisable (p. 205); that the differentiation of prices of round timber and sawn lumber is not such as to encourage the desirable practice that round timber be cut at or near the forest. Rather than this, great amounts of round timber are shipped with great waste over distances up to thousands of miles. It was known before that the fixed selling prices of gas, very cheap to produce, are so high as to make it difficult for it to compete with coal, very expensive to produce. The examples of poor price setting could be lengthened almost indefinitely. And all this pertains to 1959, when substantial improvements since Stalin's day had already been made.

As stated above, the problem of needed reforms of the price system is discussed in the USSR extensively. There is general agreement that the prices must cover costs (in general, average costs). But the analysts disagree on the problem of how the surplus value or the so-called accumulations, i.e., profits and sales taxes, are to be distributed among the produced goods. (The proceeds of sales taxes are also treated as profits in the USSR.)

The still influential Strumilin advocates that the surplus value be distributed in proportion to wages.[80] This system obviously would operate against any improvements, tending to reduce the labor input.

Kondrashev[81] argued in favor of distribution of the accumulations among all goods, producers' and consumers' alike, at equal rates in proportion to production costs. This procedure would obviously have led to an over-all increase in prices of producers' goods and a decline in prices of consumers' goods. However, the prices so calculated would not have adequately reflected differences in invested capital. And the failure to consider this is, as has been mentioned, a very important factor causing disparity among the prices of various goods in the USSR.

I. Malyshev was, it seems, the first to advocate re-establishing the invested capital as the basis of distributing the surplus value. He did not find it difficult to prove the economic justification for this measure. Malyshev even used the old established example of hydroelectric power, with its very large fixed capital in relation to the small operating costs, as a situation in which disregard of profit on the capital led to distortion in price formation.[82]

Malyshev was recently supported by the influential V. Nemchinov, who suggested that the proceeds of sales taxes be reduced by one-third and that this one-third be paid by the state enterprises as *rent* proportionally to the funds they manage.[83] Nemchinov's proposal was thus equivalent to making the charge for use of capital a part of production costs.

The ideas leading to acceptance of interest on invested capital (under another name, of course), as a component of the value of goods, seems to be rapidly gaining momentum. They soon were passed along by economists to statistical technicians. I. Shchadilov wrote in an article entitled "The Most Important Tasks of Statistics of Fixed Investment" (*Courier of Statistics*, 1959, No. 3, p. 30): "The higher the profitableness of the enterprise put in operation,

[80] S. G. Strumilin, in *Planned Economy*, 1957, No. 2, pp. 40–44.
[81] *Price Formation in Industry in the USSR*, pp. 48–57.
[82] *Questions of Economics*, 1957, No. 3, pp. 101–4.
[83] See his "Some Problems of Planning National Economy," *Communist*, 1959, No. 1, p. 82.

relative to the funds spent on its construction, the higher is the effectiveness of the fixed investment." The author also stated that this effectiveness is the most important indicator in appraising the operation of an enterprise. The interest rate obviously is the best, the natural, index of profitableness.

Even if the interest rate is soon accepted as a component of production costs or the invested capital is used as the basis for calculating profits, this would mean that some forty-five years of the "space age" were needed to overcome the wrong—and very harmful—concept.[84]

While the approach to price setting from the end of production costs, that is, from the supply end, may be correct in general, a workable system of prices seems impossible without serious consideration of the value of the goods to the consumers, that is, of the demand end. But the concept of marginal utility is for the Soviet Marxists even more taboo than the concept of interest on the capital. If the concept is introduced in Soviet literature, this occurs only in a very clandestine way.

The neglect of the demand end can continue only so long as the goods are allocated (producers' goods are mainly involved in all discussions; with reference to consumers' goods equilibrium—a very imperfect one—is attained with the help of sales taxes and the operations of kolkhoz trade). The example presented above with prices of farm machinery, which had to be changed in a hurry from prices based on production costs to those considering the utility of the machinery, demonstrates this situation clearly.

While the concept of marginal utility has continued to be ostracized, marginal costs are treated more benevolently. An idea which seems to get ever more adherents is that the prices in agriculture and extracting industries must be set at the costs on the poorest lands and at those of the enterprises working in the worst natural conditions. If and when this idea is accepted, only differences in production costs caused by differences in the efficiency of the individual enterprises will remain. (The incomes obtained by the better enterprises are referred to in the USSR as differential incomes. The losses incurred by the less efficient enterprises should logically be called differential losses, but this seems not to be the case.)

All these discussions are very recent. This is especially true of the problem of differential rent which has attracted considerable atten-

[84] The idea that rational investment policy is impossible without interest on the capital was advocated by V. A. Bazarov, one of the most prominent planners of the time, but a non-Communist, as far back as 1927. See his "On Our Perspectives and Perspective Plans," *Economic Review*, 1927, No. 3, p. 46. Bazarov disappeared in 1930, probably exiled. He died in 1938, presumably one of the victims of the purges.

tion only since about 1958. In September of that year, a special conference on this topic was held.[85] In the center of the discussion was,
however, not the problem how to handle land rent in price setting,
but the very problem whether land rent does exist under socialism.
Quite a few denied this. Some, while acknowledging the existence of
land rent in agriculture or only in kolkhoz farming, denied it for the
extracting industries and/or the sovkhozy. The discussion testified to
the confused state in which the whole problem of price setting continues to be in the USSR.

So far as investment specifically is concerned, the measurement of
its profitableness fared somewhat better than the price setting in
general. In 1956, the number of years during which savings on
production costs cover the cost of new investment, or the cost of the
additional investment in cases of two, or more, competing investment
projects, was accepted as the measure of profitableness of the investment. It was established temporarily by the Gostechnika (State Committee of the Council of Ministers of the USSR for Incorporation
of New Techniques) and restated in 1958 by the All-Union Scientific-
Technical Conference on Problems of Economic Efficiency of Fixed
Investment and New Techniques.[86]

The number of years during which investment is repaid from savings on production costs is a substitute, very inadequate, for the
interest rate. The actual number of years during which the repay-
ment must occur to make investment profitable has apparently not
yet been established either. It has also not been decided whether
the number of years in this use must be the same for all categories
of investment or whether a differentiation should be applied. Only
the principle has been set thus far.

The fact that the price system is going to play a much greater
role in the economy than formerly raises the question of whether
the Soviet Union is heading toward a free-market economy, if not
of the type practiced in Yugoslavia, then of the more mixed type
employed in Poland. This question was extensively discussed in the
symposium at Berkeley in 1958. Peter Wiles, for example, whose
ideas certainly merit attention, apparently believes that decentralization "without a market economy" would be disastrous. The "market
economy" does not need, though, to be of the ordinary type.*

[85] The materials of the conference were released as *Land Rent in Socialist Agriculture*
(Moscow: Gosplan, 1959).

[86] *Economic Effectiveness of Capital Investments and of New Techniques* (Moscow:
Academy of Sciences of the USSR, 1959).

* The volume with the papers, referred to in the text as the symposium at Berkeley,
is now out, but at least this writer got it too late to make the needed use of it. It
carries the title *Value and Plan; Economic Calculation and Organization in Eastern*

The structure of nominal wages was not in good shape before World War II and the uneven wage raises during the war disrupted the structure even more. White-collar workers in administration and elsewhere, workers in the light industries and in trade, and some others, were particularly affected by the wage discrimination. In spite of the fact that the "bread supplement" of 1946 favored the low-paid groups, the average wage of these wage and salary earners has probably increased less since the start of World War II than the average wage of workers and employees in heavy industry, construction, and transportation. The great statification of earnings —a feature which was in evidence already before the Revolution and did not in any case diminish after it—was fully preserved or even strengthened.

The desire of many to be white-collar workers seems to have still been strong enough (the discrimination against white-collar workers also prevailed before World War II) so that the additional discrimination in pay did not cause a shortage of applicants. The going seems not to have been so smooth in light industry, although with the concentration on heavy industry the demand for labor in many light industries did not exceed the prewar level until the end of 1950. The raising of performance norms for piece workers may not have been as large in light as in heavy industry.[87] Serious disturbances were prevented by directing some of the compulsorily mobilized young people into light industries (and more recently also into agriculture).[88] It was disclosed only very recently that serious adjustments in pay to those employed in light industries also were made in the late 1940's.

There were other important defects in the nominal-wage structure (mainly too-high pay for exceeding the norm, coupled with too small a share of the total wage coming from just fulfilling the norm) which it is impossible to go into now.

The discrepancies in the wage structure were recognized, and very

---

Europe, edited by G. Grossman (Berkeley: University of California Press, 1960). Alfred Zauberman's paper with a wealth of material on the topics discussed in this section of the book (the paper is quoted in note 69 above) carries the title "The Soviet Debate on the Law of Value and Price Formation" and is found on pp. 17–35 of the volume. Peter Wiles's thought-provoking paper is entitled "Rationality, the Market, Decentralization and the Territorial Principle" and is on pp. 184–203. There are also illuminating contributions, by Rudolf Bićanić, a Yugoslavian, on the peculiar form of organization and planning in his country, still regarded as socialistic, by John Matias on Polish price setting, and a lot of other interesting material.

[87] This writer has no evidence on this point.

[88] The institution of the compulsory drafting of young people, introduced late in 1940, was aimed at providing heavy industry and transportation with labor. See *Planned Economy,* 1940, No. 11, pp. 34–35.

serious measures were ultimately taken. The introduction of a minimum wage in 1957 helped a little to eliminate the extreme stratification of wages, but it is intended to go much further along this line in the seven-year plan for 1959–65. High earnings will in general be held stable and there will be exceptional cases of reductions in these earnings.

The wage system is also being seriously overhauled otherwise. How successful all this will be, the future will show. But substantial progress is definitely present. The greater the needed changes were and still are, the more disorganized seems the situation existing in Stalin's day. This remark is valid for the whole section on price setting.

CHAPTER 12

Investment as a Whole

For reasons not clear to this writer, the Soviets greatly underestimated the rate of postwar inflation of construction costs and thus overestimated postwar investment in relation to prewar investment in real terms. This writer had a great deal of difficulty trying to ascertain the correct data and, as in some other cases, did not go the whole way in correcting the official underestimate and overestimate. The official data imply an increase of 110 per cent from 1940 to 1950 in fixed investment by the state.[1] This writer's calculations indicated an increase of 68.5 per cent for total net investment in those years. It was a pleasant surprise when Strumilin, celebrated in the USSR, smuggled in estimates of the fixed investment in 1940, 1950, and 1955 at constant (1955) prices.[2] According to him, fixed investment of the state in 1950 at 1955 prices was 45 per cent above that in 1940, not 110 per cent as implied in the official statistical handbook published only a few months earlier (see *Stat. Handb.*, 1956, pp. 158–59) and reproduced in *Economy of the USSR in 1956*, which was published shortly after Strumilin's paper.

After some hesitation, it was decided to accept the rate of growth of fixed investment by the state in 1940–50 given by Strumilin as the rate of growth of total net investment in those years and to calculate

[1] *Economy of the USSR in 1956*, pp. 172–73.
[2] S. G. Strumilin, "The Law of Value and Changes in Social Production Costs in a Socialist State," *Planned Economy*, February, 1957, p. 47. The expression "smuggled in" may seem strange. This writer has no doubt that persons of Strumilin's caliber greatly resent being forced to use falsified and manipulated official "statistical" data and are glad occasionally to put in a couple of correct figures.

the net investment in 1945–49 year by year from Strumilin's index for 1950 with the help of the year-to-year percentage rises implied in the official estimates of fixed investment of the state in *Economy of the USSR in 1956* (p. 173).[3] If Strumilin's estimate of growth of fixed investment of the state from 1940 to 1950 is too low, all index figures since 1945 are, of course, too low also. They are likely to be correct, however.

The years 1945 and 1946.—The official estimate of fixed investment of the socialized sector at prices of July 1, 1955, indicates for 1945 (partly a war year and in any case a very bad year) a fixed investment of the socialized sector in the greatly war-damaged country only 9.3 per cent below that in 1940 and higher than in 1936, the last really good prewar year for the Soviets. By 1946, still very close to the end of the war, the same investment is supposed to have exceeded the 1940 level by 8.3 per cent as against a decline of 27.3 per cent accepted here (see Table 23).

TABLE 23

INVESTMENT, 1940 AND 1945–52

YEAR	FIXED INVESTMENT OF THE STATE, OFFICIAL[a]		TOTAL NET INVESTMENT[b] 1940 = 100
	Billion rubles	1940 = 100	
1940............	43.2	100	100
1945............	39.2	90.7	60.9
1946............	46.8	108.3	72.7
1947............	50.8	117.4	79.7
1948............	62.1	143.7	97.6
1949............	76.0	175.9	118.8
1950............	90.8	210.2	145.0
1951............	102.1	236	163.0
1952............	113.8	263	178.0

[a] At prices of July 1, 1955. See *Economy of the USSR in 1956*, pp. 172–73.
[b] Calculated from data of S. G. Strumilin, "The Law of Value and the Measurement of Social Production Expenses in the Socialist Society," *Planned Economy*, 1957, No. 2, p. 47, for 1950 and from official indices for year-to-year rises in fixed investment of the state. All data are at 1955 prices; otherwise see text for comments.

The fixed investment officially claimed for 1945 was possible only if constructions could have been built of air, and guns could have been installed instead of equipment. As Chart 21 shows, the building materials available in 1945 were only a fraction of what was needed for the amount of construction allegedly completed.

[3] These percentage rises differ little from those published for the various years since 1946 in the respective Reports on the Fulfilment of the Plan. The observed small departures may, moreover, be fully justified by differences in the prices used as weights.

CHART 21

**INVESTMENT IN CONSTRUCTION VS. OUTPUT OF BUILDING MATERIALS,
SELECTED YEARS * (1937 = 100)**

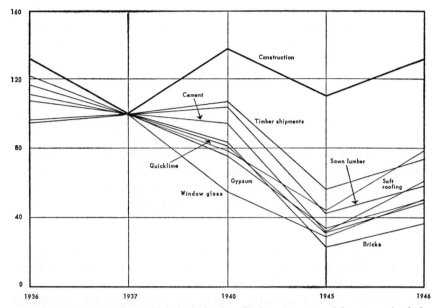

* Data for construction, which includes installation (as part of investment) of the socialized sector, at prices of July 1, 1955, from *Stat. Handb.*, 1956, pp. 158–59. Data for output of building materials from *Industry of the USSR*, 1957, *passim*. The latter data for 1940 were to some extent adjusted to apply to the pre-1939 territory.

Note that the comparison in Chart 21 is not with the total fixed investment of the state but with its construction and installation only, which, according to official data, was much smaller in 1945 and 1946 relative to 1940 than total fixed investment. Still, the amounts of building materials produced in 1945 would hardly have permitted even one-half of the 1940 constructions.[4]

Official data pointing to an amount of construction (including installation) in 1945 only 20 per cent smaller than that of 1940 are odd enough. Even stranger are the official data on investment in equipment for that year. According to these data, investment in equipment (including "other expenses") increased by 29 per cent from 1940 to 1945, although reconversion of the industry from armaments to civilian machinery started in earnest only in the next

[4] It must be considered that in periods of rapid recovery of both construction and output of building materials, less of these materials are available for use in construction during the main construction season in the summer than the output figures for building materials in whole years indicate.

year.[5] The Soviets obtained, it is true, dismantled machinery from the satellites, but could there have been that much of it?

While Strumilin's figure for the rise in fixed investment from 1940 to 1950 leaves one undecided, a decline in investment, implied in Strumilin's data, of 27.3 per cent from 1940 to 1946, the first full year after the end of the destructive war, a year undoubtedly characterized by starvation, strikes one as in no case exaggerated. The same goes for the figure of 60.9 per cent, likewise implied in Strumilin's data as the fixed investment of the state in 1945 in terms of that in 1940.

While the official index figures for 1945 (1940 equals 100) are greatly exaggerated in relation to 1940, the relation between the index figures for this year to that of 1946, indicating a growth in investment of almost 20 per cent, seems to make sense. And hence, different attitudes are necessary toward the relation of the postwar years to 1940 and toward the relation among the individual postwar years, in both cases as officially calculated.

The years 1946–50.—The poor 1946 crops slowed down the growth of investment. Fixed investment of the state rose by 9 per cent in 1947, an increase less than half as large as that in 1946. Taking the whole situation into consideration, however, a 9 per cent rise was still considerable. Then, for 1948, according to official data, we have a growth of fixed investment of the socialized sector of not less than 22 per cent. In this year, total investment seems to have been at about the prewar level (established in *Essay I* and confirmed by Strumilin). The super-rapid growth in investment also continued in 1949 and 1950 (22 and 20 per cent, respectively).

While the official rates of growth of fixed investment of the state in 1946–50 seem to have been more or less reasonable, strange things occurred, on the basis of the official statistics, with the components of this investment—in construction and installation, in equipment, and in other expenses.

These data indicate that construction (always including installation) was growing relatively slowly in 1946–50 and, moreover, in a very irregular manner. In 1947 there was allegedly no increase in construction at all. The share of construction in total fixed investment of the state is supposed to have gone down from 70 per cent in 1946 to 65 per cent in 1947 and to have continued declining until it reached 60 per cent in 1950.

The relatively slow growth of construction and installation in

[5] The Report on the Fulfilment of the 1946 Plan claimed an increase in production of civilian machinery of 18.4 billion rubles (possibly, but not certainly, at current prices) from 1945 to 1946.

1946–50, shown by the official data, does not seem to agree well with the data on the growth in output of building materials. Chart 22 clearly shows that output of building materials was expanding much more rapidly than construction, as officially given, in 1946–50. There was, indeed, no major building material whose output did not display a greater rise than did the officially calculated amount of construction. The output of bricks and cement actually increased more

CHART 22

INVESTMENT IN CONSTRUCTION VS. OUTPUT OF BUILDING MATERIALS,
1936, 1940, 1945–50 * (1940 = 100)

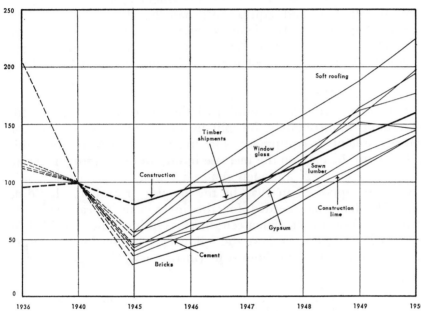

* Construction, which includes installation, of the socialized sector at prices of July 1, 1955, from *Stat. Handb.*, 1956, pp. 158–59. Data on output of building materials from *Industry of the USSR*, 1957, *passim*. Data for 1940 were to some extent adjusted to apply to the pre-1939 territory.

than threefold in those four years. The growth in output of building materials during 1946–50, in relation to the official index of construction, was so large that by 1950 the great discrepancy between them which existed in 1945 and 1946, on the basis of official data, seems to have disappeared.

While investment in construction and installation was increasing relatively slowly in 1946–50, according to official data, there was allegedly a particularly great upswing in investment in equipment.

This form of investment, indeed, is supposed to have jumped from 12.1 billion rubles in 1946 to 30.9 billion in 1950, i.e., slightly more than 150 per cent in only four years.[6] This remains a real mystery, in spite of the fact that the growth of investment in equipment, as officially calculated, is in line with the official index for machinery production, which indicates an increase of 192 per cent in the period analyzed.[7] Contrary to official data on output of building materials, which are in physical terms, the index for output of machinery is calculated in value terms, and such data are less reliable.

Beginning with 1946 official statistics also provide separate data on expenses connected with fixed investment other than construction, installation, and equipment; namely, the so-called "other expenses" (prior to 1946 these expenses were merged with investment in equipment). These "other expenses" are supposed to have increased from 4 per cent of the total investment in 1946 to 6 per cent in 1950. This implies that the "other expenses" were enlarged threefold in 1946–50—another mystery.[8]

The years 1940–50.—Strumilin's index, accepted here for 1940–50, cannot, unfortunately, be split into investment in construction and investment in equipment. The index as a whole is reasonably in line with the data on the increase in output of building materials shown in Chart 22, although somewhat more construction could have been supported in 1950 by the amount of available building materials than that needed for the investment as calculated by Strumilin. As against a 45 per cent increase in investment in 1940–50 shown by this index, we have the following increases for the output of building materials in those years (in per cent):[9]

Bricks	36
Cement	81
Construction lime	38
Gypsum	93
Shipment of industrial timber	37
Sawn lumber	42
Soft roofing	125
Window glass	72

The official 1950 index for output of machinery including other metal processing (1940 equals 100) is 213. Output of armaments undoubtedly grew much less than this during the period and the

[6] Implied in *Stat. Hand.*, 1956, p. 160.

[7] See *ibid.*, p. 74. The figure in the text is for machinery only. Including other metal processing, the growth is supposed to have been equivalent to 150 per cent.

[8] *Ibid.*, p. 160.

[9] *Industry of the USSR*, 1957, pp. 249, 261, 277, 282, 287, 291, 301, 312.

output of civilian machinery would have grown even much more than by the 113 per cent indicated by the official index, if the later were correct.

The years 1951 and 1952.—The official rate of growth of fixed investment of the state showed a great decline from 22, 22, and 20 per cent in 1948, 1949, and 1950, respectively, to 12 and 11 per cent in 1951 and 1952, respectively (data at prices of July 1, 1955). This coincided with the completion of the postwar recovery and with the effect of military preparations in connection with the Korean War. These conditions considered, the claimed rates of growth in investment must be accepted as still large.

The postwar Stalin period as a whole.—If the period from 1945 to 1952 is taken as a whole, it was one of a huge rise in investment. Fixed investment of the state expanded in real terms by not less than 190 per cent during the seven-year period, according to official estimates, and while the rise in total investment may have been smaller than this, it was unlikely to have been very much smaller. The total share of the state (investment, military expenditure, etc.) in national income was not unsubstantially larger in 1952 than in 1940, a year which was intermediate between peace and war as far as the economy is concerned. The excess of the share of the state in national income in 1952 over the respective share in 1936, the last of the *Three "Good" Years,* was even very substantial.

Investment by Sector

The most important feature of the *Stalin Has Everything His Way* period was the immense concentration on heavy industry. This naturally was reflected with particular force in investment. In the 1930's, certainly not a period of neglect of heavy industry, fixed investment in this industry tended to be about one-third of the total (see Table 24). The proportion exceeded two-fifths in 1946–50 and was still larger in 1951 and 1952. Even if it is assumed that the share of heavy industry in total fixed investment of the state in 1951 and 1952 was considerably boosted by the Korean War, the difference in this share as compared with that of the period from 1938 to June, 1941, also largely a period of war preparations, is immense. It was a great record, not to be surpassed. Let us grant Stalin this.

Since so much of the investment funds went into heavy industry, little was left for the other sectors. The share of transportation and communications in total fixed investment of the socialized sector declined by about one-third from the 1930's to the 1940's and by a

TABLE 24

<small>FIXED INVESTMENT OF THE STATE BY SECTOR, FYP PERIODS*</small>
(In per cent of total)

Item	1927/28 to 1932	1933 to 1937	1938 to June 1941	1946 to 1950	1951 to 1955	1956
Industry	42.6	41.8	40.9	48.9	51.1	49.2
Heavy industry	35.8	34.5	34.4	42.9	46.2	43.5
Light industry	6.8	7.3	6.5	6.0	4.9	5.7
Agriculture	13.9	8.1	5.3	7.3	9.6	11.2
Transportation and communications	18.6	21.5	20.4	14.2	10.1	9.3
Housing	11.8	10.2	12.7	12.7	15.5	15.4
All others	13.1	18.4	20.7	16.9	13.7	14.9

<small>* *Attainments*, p. 210. Investments of the state in the variable capital of state enterprises, that of the kolkhozy, and that in private housing are not included. The data reproduced here are preferable to those normally given in the budget and elsewhere because housing, spread over all items in the budget, is here taken out of the individual items and brought together as a separate item. Previously, even if total housing was shown as a separate item, portions of it were included also with the other individual items.</small>

full half to the first half of the 1950's. In 1933–37, this investment was equal to almost two-thirds of the investment in heavy industry, and in 1946–50 to only one-third of it. The Soviets apparently not only learned much in cutting out all investment in the transportation system other than that absolutely necessary to take care of the rapidly expanding traffic, but possibly went below the minimum. No money, to speak of, was allotted for such developments as transportation by pipe, in spite of the great economies this means involved.

Light industry was a neglected child in the allocation of investment funds, but trade and procurements (not shown separately in Table 24) were those squeezed to the greatest extent (among economic pursuits) in postwar years; their share in total investment went down to about one-half of the 1936 level.

Among the economic branches whose share in investment declined from the 1930's, agriculture probably suffered least. Its share in total fixed investment of the state went down very little from 1933–37 to 1946–50. It even increased as compared with 1938–40. But the effect of the niggardliness with investment funds for anything but heavy industry was particularly strong in the case of agriculture, one could say almost disastrous, because the needs of agriculture for investment funds were particularly great.

The share of housing in total investment in 1946–50 was as small as before the war, in spite of the greatly increased need for new housing due to war destruction and to the rapid growth of the urban population. The target of the fourth FYP for new and reconstructed housing was certainly moderate, but it was not fulfilled, and to conceal this, the concept with which housing was measured was watered down a very great deal.[10]

According to official data, there was slightly more urban housing per capita in 1950 than in 1940, but this advantage was probably more than offset by a less favorable regional distribution of the available housing.[11] Moreover, the housing situation was already extremely poor in 1940.

Unfinished Investment

The slowdown of industrial growth in 1956–58 has been adequately explained by the small number of large investment projects completed and the resulting great accumulation of unfinished investment projects in the several years preceding and during the very year named. It is also clear that accumulation of an excessive number of projects in the course of construction started not later than 1951, and possibly even earlier, i.e., in Stalin's day. This was really a fantastic combination: superdictatorship, indeed, despotism of the worst kind and of the greatest strength, and yet a lack right at the top of discipline in the planning of investment and in the execution of investment plans.

The evidence released on unfinished constructions was until recently so amazingly scarce that it was possible to speak of the complete absence of it, but the evidence had certainly been at the disposal of those in power all the time. There undoubtedly were persons in the Gosplan and elsewhere who already in 1951 or 1952 foresaw the bad results of the excessive number of projects in construction, but those making decisions had no understanding and, in any case, no interest in the phenomenon. The absence of reliable data explains why Western analysts not only did not foresee the slowdown but could not explain it after it had already been under way for some time.

Data on unfinished constructions specifically in 1951 and 1952 seem still to be unavailable. In the absence of adequate data on the investment projects in process of construction, which would have permitted timing the development which led to the recent slowdown in industrial growth, one naturally looks for substitutes. The relation between the rate of growth of investment in construction and that in investment in equipment has been helpful in a small way.

In general, first the buildings are constructed and then the

---

[10] See *Commentary*, p. 149.

[11] *Stat. Handb.*, 1956, pp. 163 and 26. The extra housing space was exclusively or mainly in the annexed territories.

machinery is installed. Hence, an increase of the share of equipment in total investment may possibly indicate that the amount of investment nearing completion is being enlarged at the expense of investment which is only in its initial stages. An increase in the proportion of investment going into equipment in total fixed investment may, therefore, be taken as a favorable indicator, and vice versa.

It has been shown above that the increase in investment in equipment in 1946–50 is supposed to have been more than 50 per cent in excess of that in investment in construction (official data). Suddenly a great change occurred:[12]

Year	Construction and Installation	Equipment	Other Expenses	Construction and Installation	Equipment	Other Expenses
	(Billion rubles)			(Per cent of total)		
1950.......	54.7	30.9	5.2	60	34	6
1951.......	64.2	30.6	7.3	63	30	7
1952.......	72.6	31.9	9.3	64	28	8

The almost complete stagnation of investment in equipment in 1950–52 may have been brought about by shortage of civilian machinery resulting from the reconversion to armament production. Also, the Soviets may have started new armament factories and these may have been in a stage during which building materials were primarily needed. All this may have been done without real thought, without real planning. Indeed, no measures were apparently taken to remedy the harm already done, even after the possibility of war had passed. It seems in any case reasonably certain that the inheritance left by the *Stalin Has Everything His Way* period included a substantial excess of unfinished investment projects.

Since the investment in equipment was expanding much more rapidly than investment in construction before 1950 and the opposite was true of 1950–52, the divergent developments partly canceled themselves out and everything seems to have been all right. Over the whole period 1946–52, investment in construction increased by 119 per cent and investment in equipment by 167 per cent. But "other expenses" are supposed to have been enlarged 4.8 times from 1946 to 1952. This writer is unable to explain what this means, although it simply looks like a change in concept made without proper announcement.

Concluding Remarks

This chapter is concluded without the feeling that everything has been settled satisfactorily. The great underestimate of investment

[12] *Industry of the USSR in 1956*, pp. 173–74. Data at prices in effect July 1, 1955.

costs in postwar years relative to those in 1940 implied in the official data is beyond doubt. Correspondingly, the high level of postwar investment relative to that of 1940 in constant values, as shown by official data, must be rejected as greatly exaggerated. On the other hand, the immense growth in investment *during* the postwar years shown by the data seems to be in agreement with the facts. Thus far everything seems clear. Uncertainty enters the picture when one tries to deal with official data on the components of investment. It seems odd to accept the index for the rise in total investment *during* the postwar years and yet to hesitate to accept those for the components. Other analysts, or possibly this writer at a later date, will undoubtedly get better results.

CHAPTER 13

AGRICULTURE I

CONDITIONS

Introduction

Almost since the death of Stalin, Soviet rulers, professors, journalists, indeed everybody, have competed in exposing the harmfulness of the policies pursued toward agriculture before 1953, as though some mysterious force, rather than the Communist Party, was responsible for the misdeeds. Here is only one example, from an editorial in *Economics of Agriculture,* scientific journal of the Ministry of Agriculture of the USSR (1958, No. 4, p. 8):

Distortions and errors existed in the policies of [agricultural] prices in the non-distant past. Procurement prices, in force until 1953 for a number of most important [farm] products, were low; they did not compensate for the input of labor and materials and did not assure the minimum conditions for the development of the socialized economy of the kolkhozy.

For almost a quarter of a century those policies, now condemned, were in agreement with Marxism-Leninism. Now it turns out that "such an incorrect approach to one of the most important problems of the Soviet State contradicts the spirit of Marxism-Leninism" (*ibid.,* p. 9).

The exploitation of agriculture and of the peasants by means of those prices was more and more intensified as the continuing inflation brought the prices nearer and nearer to token prices. Conditions following World War II would have been worse in this respect as a consequence of this factor alone; when such devastating price policies were applied to an agriculture greatly disrupted as a result of the war, disaster or near-disaster was inevitable.

It was difficult to realize the extent of the gravity of the situation in Soviet agriculture so long as its recovery from the great losses it incurred during World War II proceeded, especially since every effort was made to conceal the weaknesses and even to mislead as to the true situation. Only later did it become clear that the recovery harbored features of deterioration or even decay. By 1949 agricultural output started to approach the prewar level. The rapid expansion of the non-farm economy required a proportionate growth of agricultural production beyond that level, but instead the growth of farm output practically, or fully, ceased. Not only did phenomena believed to be war damage emerge as what they really were, decay, but new weaknesses appeared, and old weaknesses were intensified.

As it turned out only much later, deterioration in agriculture in the last years of the *Stalin Has Everything His Way* period was so widespread that it is difficult to select examples. It would be no exaggeration to say that the whole socialized sector of agriculture was in a state of decay. But the deterioration was at its worst where crops and sections of the country least adapted to the "socialist" form of agriculture, Soviet style, were involved.

Data for 1953 on the output of potatoes and vegetables by the socialized sector, supplied by D. D. Brezhnev, vice-president of the All-Union Academy of Agricultural Sciences,[1] in conjunction with official data on acreages,[2] imply the immensely low yields of 4.2 tons per hectare of potatoes and of 5.0 tons per hectare of vegetables. This yield of potatoes was less than double the amount of seed needed to produce it. It was little more than half the yield obtained around 1928 by the individual peasants in a territory potentially less adapted to potato-growing than the present territory of the USSR.[3]

The Northwest, a region particularly unadapted to "socialized agriculture," was clearly in very bad shape. Some territories there yielded less grain per hectare than was harvested 100 years ago. Flax production was especially disorganized. From 1950, its output declined by fully one-third in only three years.[4] And it must be remembered that 1950 production was much less than that of 1940.

[1] *Agriculture* (daily), October 31, 1958.

[2] *Sown Acreages of the USSR*, 1957, p. 192.

[3] *Soc. Agri.*, p. 791. The same phenomenon led to the result that while the socialized sector had almost half (exactly 48.3 per cent of the 1953 total potato acreage, it harvested little more than one-quarter (exactly 27.3 per cent) of all potatoes. In 1950, the same shares were: 44.4 per cent of the total acreage and only 26.4 per cent of the total production (see *Agriculture of the USSR*, a symposium [Moscow, 1958], pp. 257, 260). While the official statistics exaggerated the yields per hectare obtained by the private sector, this sector is still likely to have harvested more than twice as much per hectare as the socialized sector.

[4] *Economy of the USSR in 1956*, p. 107.

The developments in flax clearly show the growing disorganization in agriculture in the last Stalin years even as compared with the late 1930's, which were not too good either.*

Production Factors

Labor.—The number of able-bodied persons, specifically males, lost by the Soviet Union in World War II was staggering. Agriculture's share in this loss was particularly large. The mobilizing of villagers into the armed forces was disproportionately heavy. Furthermore, millions of villagers mobilized, or deported by the Germans, who did not perish, did not return to their villages after the war. The start of agricultural recovery was particularly difficult, because the Soviet government was in no hurry to demobilize its armed forces; and yet in spite of this, rehabilitation of non-farm pursuits, primarily heavy industry, was pushed ahead without consideration for the urgent needs of agriculture for labor, especially male labor.

The non-farm labor force grew from 24,731,000 in 1945 to 35,-782,000 in 1950, i.e., by more than 11 million in five years, so that this sector was provided for amply. Yet the number of those reaching working age was not large during part of the recovery period because among the five years during which the young people who entered the labor force in 1946–50 were born, namely, 1930 through 1934, three years, 1932 through 1934, showed a considerably reduced birth rate. This affected unfavorably the growth in the labor force in the latter part of the period 1946–50. In the early part of the period, on the other hand, the mortality rate was high. To make up the 11-million increase in new non-farm labor in 1946–50, most of those released from the armed forces were needed. Those in the armed forces who returned to agriculture may have been few in number, and part, or all, of these were soon to be lost to non-farm pursuits.

Data published in a rather obscure form in *Stat. Handb.*, 1956 (p. 188), indicate a decline in the number of kolkhozniki engaged in work for the kolkhozy and in their private enterprises and in the number of working individual peasants (including a small number of non-cooperated artisans) from 42.0 million in 1940 to 36.3 million

---

* *Agriculture of the USSR*, 1960, p. 199, contains this series of figures, which reveal at a glance the devastating effect of Stalin's collectivization. The figures are for the yield of flax fiber per hectare (in quintals):

Year	Yield
1909–13	2.8
1933–37	1.7
1949–53	1.4
1953	1.3

One had to wait more than twenty years to know the truth.

in 1950 (see *Commentary*, p. 161). The decline was due to the practical disappearance of individual peasants. The number of kolkhozniki remained about unchanged, in spite of the fact that in the meantime collectivization had been imposed on the peasants in the new territories.[5] * The whole labor force in agriculture, that is,

[5] The official figures for kolkhozniki used here and further on are recalculations. It was assumed in *Commentary* (p. 163) that the figures for working kolkhozniki implied in the data on page 188 of *Stat. Handb.*, 1956, were a recalculation to able-bodied kolkhozniki. A paper of the prominent V. S. Nemchinov, probably based on official data ("Statistics of Social Change in the USSR," *Anglo-American Journal*, Summer, 1957, p. 34) seems to indicate that the assumption was incorrect. Nemchinov splits the 32 million, indicated in *Stat. Handb.* as working kolkhozniki in 1955, into 26 million of kolkhozniki performing kolkhoz work and 6 million of those engaged in work on their private plots.

Assuming that 10 per cent of the 26 million kolkhozniki performing kolkhoz work was the recalculated figure for the old, invalids, and children, 23.4 million remain for the able-bodied kolkhozniki—too small a figure to represent physical persons. It seems more likely that the able-bodied kolkhozniki were also recalculated. To what basis? Was it year-round workers, as in the case of hired workers and employees? or able-bodied male kolkhozniki? One thing is certain, the recalculation was not made on the basis of *trudodni* earned, because the official recalculation of the numbers of working kolkhozniki shows a decline from 34.7 million in 1950 to 32.1 million in 1955 (*Commentary*, p. 161). Yet the number of *trudodni* earned in the kolkhozy increased from 8.3 billion to 10.9 billion in the same years (*Economy of the USSR in 1956*, p. 141). It seems that the recalculation is made with the use of some *constant* coefficients. For example: able-bodied male, one unit; able-bodied female, two-thirds of a unit; old and invalids, one-quarter or one-fifth of a unit; and children, one-eighth of a unit. The figures thus recalculated are then added, a day's work of able-bodied males, able-bodied females, old people, invalids, or children—all being considered equal—the same as in the statistics of hired labor. Individual peasants were presumably recalculated in the same manner as kolkhozniki.

* *Agriculture of the USSR*, stat. handb., 1960, only released in the middle of the year, indicates that the official evidence used in note 5 was revised. According to *ibid.*, p. 450, the kolkhozniki, working for their kolkhozy, numbered only 24.8 million in 1955 (as against 26 million according to Nemchinov), a decline of 4.2 million since 1940 and of 2.8 million since 1950. Moreover, according to *ibid.*, pp. 460-61, the data were obtained from figures for able-bodied kolkhozniki and their family members, who worked even only one day in a given month. (They were included in the labor force of the respective month.) The number of kolkhozniki, workers and employees, working in their own enterprises is given for 1959 (the only year for which this evidence was supplied in the new source) at only 6.8 million. This figure seems to imply a serious downward revision (the older data indicated 9.2 million for the same category in 1955).

Revising the manuscript at this advanced date is impossible. For our analysis it is important that the changes in the number of kolkhozniki over time are not too much different in both sources. According to older data, the number of working kolkhozniki was the same in 1950 as in 1940 and then declined by 2.6 million until 1955 (*Commentary*, p. 161). According to the new data (*Agriculture of the USSR*, stat. handb., 1960, p. 450), the number of kolkhozniki working for their kolkhozy went down by 1.4 million from 1940 to 1950 and declined by a further 2.8 million up to 1955. The supply of labor in agriculture appears to have been even worse in the last Stalin years than on the basis of older data. The unwillingness of the kolkhozniki to work for their kolkhozy was even greater than could be assumed on the basis of previously released data. There should also be implications from the change of data for the output per man, as well as with reference to the numbers of workers who may be released if private farming is discontinued or greatly curtailed, etc.

including the enlarged number of wage earners in state farms and MTS (data on these in *Stat. Handb.*, 1956, p. 190), was reduced by about 11 per cent from 1940 to 1950.

Of the five years 1946–50, the last two years were more unfavorable with reference to total net accession of persons of working age than the first three. Since presumably no new releases from the armed forces took place in 1949 and 1950, it must be assumed with reasonable certainty that the increase in the number of non-farm wage earners of about 4.5 million in these two years occurred to a considerable extent at the expense of the village.

The data in *Stat. Handb.*, 1956 (p. 188), imply a decline in the labor force of the kolkhozy and individual peasants from 36.3 million in 1950 to 32.4 million in 1955.[6] This decline was not fully offset by the increase of 2.8 million in the number of hired workers and employees in agriculture. Moreover, according to *Party Life,* 1957, No. 13, there was a large increase in the number of working kolkhozniki in 1953–56 and, consequently, the decline in the kolkhozniki's labor force in 1950–53 may have been substantially larger than that in 1950–55.*

In addition to the numerical reduction in the labor force on farms since prewar days, there was a great deterioration in its composition. Women are less adapted, or completely unadapted, to certain important operations on the farm. Even in the USSR, where women perform very hard work, mowing of hay by hand is rarely done by them. The Soviet peasant female also proves particularly unsuitable for more skilled work such as that of a mechanic. Yet the proportion of males among able-bodied kolkhozniki is unlikely to have exceeded 35 per cent in 1950.[7] * *

[6] *Commentary*, 1957, p. 161.

* This expectation did not materialize because the information in *Party Life* turned out to be wrong. According to *Agriculture of the USSR*, 1960, p. 450, the number of kolkhozniki working for the kolkhozy declined from 27.6 million in 1950 to 25.6 million in 1953 and to 24.8 million in 1955. Then came an increase to 25.7 million in 1956. The figures for 1953 and 1956 turned out to be equal contrary to the assertion of *Party Life*.

[7] Implied in scattered data, *inter alia*, in the evidence on the number of *trudodni* earned by the various categories of kolkhozniki in the Ukraine. See *Stat. Handb., Ukraine*, 1957, p. 293.

The 1959 census fully confirms the statement; on the new evidence, the estimate in the text may indeed be too favorable. In the USSR as a whole, males made up only 45 per cent of the population in 1959, according to the new census. But there was no disproportion between males and females among those below 32 years of age. The entire deficiency of males was in the age group above 32 years old. Hence, of every 100 persons 32 years old, or older, only about 35 are men. Those 32 years old and older in 1959 were of course 18 years old or older in 1945. Hence, the 35 per cent figure for the number of males in the over-32 group in 1959 applied in 1945 to the

Machinery.—The shortage of labor, especially male labor, in agriculture made it even more imperative to recoup the great losses in, and vigorously to expand, the numbers of farm machinery, particularly because of the loss of, perhaps, 7 million work horses and the need for machinery in the new territories which were fully collectivized during the period. The reality, however, was far from this.

The inadequate provision for investment in agriculture in post-war years has been discussed in chapter 12. As a result, the supply of new farm machinery was far below minimum requirements even at the end of the *Stalin Has Everything His Way* period. This huge country, with "the most mechanized agriculture in the world," had only about 650,000 tractors at the beginning of 1953.[8] These included the almost negligible number of 108,000 row-crop tractors suitable for inter-row cultivation and other jobs requiring little power. Thus, only about one such tractor on the average was available per collective farm, some of which in 1950 (after their amalgamation) averaged more than 10,000 hectares of sown acreages.

The supplies of other farm machinery were even less adequate. Not only cultivating, but seeding of corn and other row crops, and even hay-mowing, was to a large extent done by hand as late as 1955.[9] Ninety per cent of the kolkhoz potato acreage was harvested by hand in 1953.[10]

It is significant that deliveries of machinery to agriculture after World War II—as with everything else not favored by Stalin—were

population 18 years of age or older, or practically to the whole population of working age. The proportion of working males must have been even less in agriculture.

** *The Woman in the USSR,* stat. reference book, 1960, p. 42, gives the proportion of males among kolkhozniki in 1950 at 36 per cent, but the data pertain to able-bodied kolkhozniki who worked for the kolkhozy, and the proportion of able-bodied males not so working is smaller than that of the respective females.

[8] *Stat. Handb.,* 1956, p. 144, gives a somewhat higher figure, but it is for the end of 1953. The official figure usually cited for tractors in the USSR was, and still is, much larger because it was calculated in 15-h.p. units. The number of tractors was reported in these units because of the great power variation of the various tractors. That this reason was not decisive is apparent from the fact that row-crop tractors, whose power is mostly smaller than 15 h.p. per unit, were reported in physical units. Recently output of all tractors has been more frequently given in physical units because the average size of the tractors produced and delivered to agriculture has been declining and hence the increases are larger in numbers than in horsepower.

[9] The order of the Party and government on feed (roughage) preparation in 1954 (*Pravda,* June 3, 1954) was frank in prescribing hay-mowing by hand when no other means were available. Some hay was still cut by hand in 1958 and this practice may continue for some time.

[10] *Stat. Handb.,* 1956, p. 143. A report by Brezhnev was cited at the beginning of this chapter. According to him, only 34 per cent of the acreage in vegetables was seeded by machinery in the kolkhozy in 1957; inter-row cultivation of vegetables was done by machinery on 24 per cent of their acreage in kolkhozy.

timed as though an order had been issued stating that "agriculture, agriculturalists, and the consumers of farm products come last." [11] In 1946, deliveries of farm machinery to agriculture were still nearly non-existent.[12] In the fourth FYP itself, and particularly in the course of its fulfilment, the larger deliveries of machinery were postponed until the end of the FYP period. In *two* years, 1949 and 1950, 330,000 tractors (in 15 h.p. units) and 110,000 combine grain harvesters were delivered to agriculture, compared with only 206,000 tractors and 18,600 combine grain harvesters delivered in the *three* years of 1946–48.

Utilization of commercial fertilizer reached approximately the 1938 level in 1948 and then greatly exceeded it. The significance of this factor was small, however, because the pre–World War II level of utilization of commercial fertilizer was very low.[13]

Prices to producers and the incomes of the kolkhozy.—The Soviets had many occasions to find out that even under their "socialism" better prices to producers of farm products stimulate output. An almost fourfold increase of procurement prices of Central-Asiatic cotton and an almost fivefold increase of these prices in other cotton areas after January 1, 1935, resulted in a jump of 48 per cent in cotton output in that very year. By 1937, cotton production exceeded the 1934 level by 117 per cent.[14] More or less substantial price increases on obligatory deliveries (called *kontraktatsiya* in the case of most technical crops) with corresponding effects on output were also granted in those years on all or most other technical crops. Grain received only a 10 per cent raise in 1935; the other staple crops and animal products were treated in the same fashion. Correspondingly, production of these crops and animal products did not show any favorable developments.

The prewar practice was repeated during the *Stalin Has Every-*

[11] The fact that Voznesenskii's death in 1948 is ascribed to his "crime" of having mentioned the needs of agriculture in the Politbureau (see chapter 10) is of great interest in this connection.

[12] See *Industry of the USSR,* 1957, pp. 226, 232, for the numbers of tractors and grain combines produced in that year. According to *Attainments* (p. 150), the number of tractors (in terms of 15-h.p. units) in agriculture was on January 1, 1946, 28 per cent below that on January 1, 1941. The loss was actually larger than this. Half of the newest and largest tractors disappeared (they were mobilized for the armed forces during the war), a large proportion of the rest was in serious disrepair, and many were simply junk.

[13] The output of commercial fertilizer amounted to 6.4 million tons in 1952, 5.5 million in 1950, and 3.5 million in 1948 as against 3.4 million in 1938 and 3.0 million in 1940. See *Stat. Handb.,* 1956, p. 81. All figures on fertilizer are in terms of bulk. Plant food is little more than 20 per cent of the bulk.

[14] *Soc. Agri.,* pp. 382, 792.

thing His Way period, although from their own experience the Soviets knew that low prices meant small outputs. They took the small outputs into the bargain so far as the staple farm products were concerned. The prices paid on deliveries of cotton, sugar beets, and probably some other technical crops were more or less adjusted to compensate for the great price rise of consumers' and many other goods since prewar days. With reference to cotton, this happened in 1948,[15] the year preceding that when the large reductions in the prices of consumers' goods started. The situation of the growers of these crops should have improved more and more in subsequent years, because growers of cotton and some other technical crops sold little or nothing in kolkhoz trade. Consequently, they were not losing much from the declining trend of prices in this trade, while profiting from a similar trend in the prices of goods they bought in state and co-operative trade. It was largely due to some non-sensical features of the price-setting machinery that the relatively favorable prices for some technical crops failed to increase output very much.[16]

The prices paid on obligatorily delivered grain and most other staple products, on the other hand, remained unchanged or almost unchanged at the 1935 level until 1954 or even 1955.[17] Prior to World War II these prices were very inadequate. The subsequent great inflation made them almost nominal. Can a price in 1952 of 8 kopeks per kilogram for rye delivered on obligatory deliveries to the state be described otherwise? (From September 16, 1946, to December 15, 1947, the state was selling a kilogram of coarse rye bread on *rations* at 3.40 rubles, and this bread still cost, without rations, 1.24 rubles on April 1, 1954, and also on April 1, 1957, in spite of the eight price cuts made since 1947. A meter of calico, the cheapest cotton fabric, cost 8.80 rubles per meter in state stores in 1952.) The prices paid by the state on obligatory deliveries of the main farm products had, indeed, become nominal to such an extent that even the Soviets stopped referring to these deliveries as *sales*. They began to speak of the great underpayment for these products as

[15] See D. D. Kondrashev, *Price Formation in Industry of the USSR* (Moscow, 1956), pp. 67 ff.

[16] Absurdly high premiums were paid for deliveries in excess of targets, or for quality in excess of that treated as standard. The basic price was relatively low, on the other hand. Many of the farms just fulfilling their targets or just failing to fulfil them—and these made up the great majority—could not make enough to pay their kolkhozniki adequately. See Kondrashev, *loc. cit.*

[17] For some products the 1935 price level for obligatory deliveries was the same as the level of 1928/29 or even earlier years.

a differential land rent, part of which was going to the state in the form of procurement at low prices.[18]

In addition to the very low prices paid on the obligatory deliveries of staple products, there were higher prices paid for above-quota deliveries of the same products. But even the higher prices were low, except for meat and milk. The quantities involved were also very small. For grain, the far most important product among those delivered to the state by the kolkhozy, the average price realized for all deliveries by the kolkhozy in 1950 was only about 1 per cent above the almost negligible price paid on obligatory deliveries. (See a compilation of the various types of deliveries of the most important products by the kolkhozy in Nancy Nimitz, "Soviet Agricultural Prices and Costs," Joint Economic Committee of the Congress of the United States, *Comparisons of the United States and Soviet Economics* [Washington, D.C., 1959], I, 282.)

Among other adverse effects of these price policies was that the disproportion between the incomes of the peasants in areas producing grain and other staples and those growing cotton and some other technical crops became much larger than it was before World War II.

Serious improvements in prices paid by the state to the kolkhozy and kolkhozniki did not start until after the end of the *Stalin Has Everything His Way* period.

The money incomes of collective *farms* amounted to 34.2 billion rubles in 1950 and 42.8 billion rubles in 1952 as against 20.7 billion rubles in 1940.[19] Deflated with the retail price index,[20] the 1950 money incomes of the kolkhozy were below the 1940 level, while the 1952 incomes were above the 1940 level. But these average data have little meaning. The money incomes of the kolkhozy growing cotton may have nearly trebled.[21] In the RSFSR as a whole, on the other hand, the money incomes of the kolkhozy grew only from 10.1 billion rubles in 1940 to 10.8 billion in 1950,[22] and in some oblasti there was an actual decline.[23]

[18] That only part of differential rent went to the state was an official idea, but nobody ever computed the total land rent. Also, differential land rent implies that the poorest lands do not return any rent, but there were no farm areas in the USSR without obligatory deliveries of farm products, except possibly for those north of the Arctic Circle.

[19] *Stat. Handb.*, 1956, p. 128.

[20] *Ibid.*, p. 210.

[21] In Turkmenistan, the increase was from 270 million rubles in 1940 to 857 million rubles in 1950. *Stat. Handb., Turkmenistan*, 1957, p. 75.

[22] *Stat. Handb., RSFSR*, 1957, p. 145.

[23] In Stalingrad oblast, for example, the money incomes of the kolkhozy went down from 220 million rubles in 1940 to 123 million rubles in 1950 (see *Stat. Handb., Stalingrad Oblast*, 1957, p. 140). White Russia was expanded by the annexation of

But this is still not all. The money expenditures of the kolkhozy increased greatly from the prewar level, and, consequently, in post-war years a much smaller proportion of the total kolkhoz gross money incomes has been left for distribution to the kolkhozniki. Some kolkhozy in the grain areas distributed only a fraction of the small amounts they had distributed in prewar years.

Enterprises of the Kolkhozniki

Although no adequate steps were taken to provide agriculture with manpower and machinery, and policies with reference to farm prices definitely excluded a sound development of the socialized sector of agriculture, and although the country was indeed at, or near, the starvation point, great vigor was displayed in suppressing the private economy of the kolkhoz peasants. The policy of decimating this economy, initiated in 1938, was only partly relaxed during World War II. The prewar level of encroachment was fully restored by the order of September 19, 1946, and it was greatly exceeded in sub-sequent years. Because the campaign against the private economy of the kolkhoz peasants started after World War II at the time of starvation, or near starvation, the prewar idea that the private economy of the peasants would decline only as the kolkhozy became able to provide for the needs of the kolkhozniki obviously had been fully discarded. Not that the idea should have ever been taken seriously.

The effect of the campaign was relatively small on the kolkhozniki's sown acreages. These showed the following development since 1940 (in millions of hectares):[24]

	1940[a]	1950	1953	1955	1956
All crops:					
USSR	4.50	5.90	5.45	5.79	5.65
RSFSR	2.5	2.6	2.3	2.4	2.3
Potatoes and vegetables:					
USSR	3.12	3.56	3.37	3.70	3.69
RSFSR	1.9	2.0	1.7	1.8	1.8

[a] Prewar boundaries.

Data for the RSFSR, which are more relevant than those for the country as a whole, indicate a small decline in sown acreages of the kolkhozniki from 1940 to 1953. The increases shown by the data for the USSR as a whole are presumably smaller than the respective

---

territory from Poland. If, in consideration of this fact, the money incomes of the kolkhozy are calculated per kolkhoz household, a decline in money incomes of the kolkhozy in this republic also appears (see *Stat. Handb., White Russia,* 1957, p. 190).

[24] *Economy of the USSR in 1956,* pp. 114–15, and *Stat. Handb., RSFSR,* 1957, pp. 131–32.

acreages in the new territories, thus indicating declines also in other pre-1939 territories.

The major losses of the kolkhozniki were in livestock. Already during World War II, the restoration of the herds of the collective farms (and also of the state farms) liberated from the enemy occurred mainly by way of *kontraktatsiya* (compulsory purchase on contract entered into in advance at the price set by the government) of livestock from kolkhoz peasants. This type of "purchase" continued throughout the postwar years. They were particularly large in 1951, the last year of a special three-year plan for enlargement of kolkhoz and sovkhoz livestock. So far as the targets of this plan were even partially reached, fulfilment was achieved to a considerable extent by the requisitioning of livestock from the kolkhozniki.

The evidence on the kolkhozniki's livestock herds in the USSR as a whole is shown in Chart 23. The same evidence for the RSFSR, for which no changes in borderlines need be considered, is presented below (in million head):[25]

	1941	January 1 1951	1953	1953	October 1 1955	1956
Cattle	10.5	8.9	8.0	10.2	11.7	12.9
Cows	7.3	5.7	5.1	5.3	5.9	6.3
Hogs	3.9	1.5	1.8	5.9	6.3	6.6
Sheep	18.9	7.0	6.6	10.8	16.4	19.2
Goats	2.1	3.1	3.8	6.5	5.7	5.1

The number of cows in the kolkhozniki's hands in the RSFSR went down by 30 per cent from 1940 to 1953. Hogs and sheep declined to less than one-half and to a little more than one-third, respectively. An increase, and a large one, is observed only in goats —a good sign of extreme want. The Soviet rulers had every reason to be satisfied that the kolkhozniki's herds were declining in the RSFSR even in the last two years of Stalin's reign. One is unlikely to commit a grave error by assuming that the output of animal products by the kolkhozniki went down from 1940 to 1951 and 1953 about in proportion to the decline in the herds,[26] and that the pos-

[25] *Stat. Handb., RSFSR*, 1957, pp. 137–38.

[26] The claims for total output of potatoes, meat, milk, and eggs in 1953 in conjunction with official data on the output of these products by the kolkhozy and sovkhozy indicate very large to relatively large outputs of these products by the private sector (no data particularly for the kolkhozniki). These claims, not accepted here, will be discussed in greater detail in the monograph dealing with the post-Stalin economy. Right here the question can be posed: Is it possible that the private sector had not much less than 300 million head of adult poultry on January 1, 1953 (this is implied in the claims), and yet the sales in kolkhoz markets of 251 principal cities amounted only to 36,700 tons of poultry (my assumption is that the figure is in terms of live weight) and 485.7 million eggs in that year? (For these data see *Soviet Trade*, stat. handb., 1956, p. 185.)

CHART 23

LIVESTOCK HERDS OF THE PEASANTS, 1938, 1941, 1951, AND 1953 *
(Million heads)

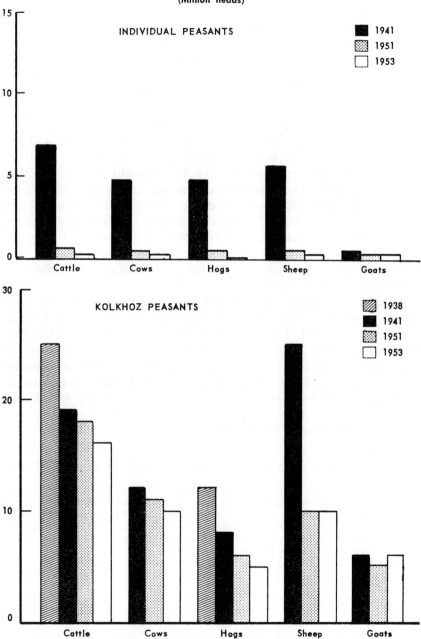

* January 1 of the respective year. Data for 1941–53 from *Stat. Handb.*, 1956, pp. 119–20. Data for 1938 from *Soc. Agri.*, p. 789. The chart for individual peasants represents fast extermination, that for kolkhoz peasants, slower extermination.

sible small increase in output of crops by the kolkhozniki offset only part of the great decline in the output of animal products. "Socialism" was forging ahead, except for food for the population in general and for the incomes of the kolkhozniki, who comprised some 40 per cent of the total population, specifically.

While the kolkhozniki's herds were probably cut in the first place directly by compulsory purchases from them, a very effective measure to force the kolkhoz peasants to curtail their *total* private economy was the continuous raising of the agricultural tax, payable in money by all private owners of farm enterprises, but mainly by the kolkhoz peasants.[27] In 1938, before the upward revisions of the agricultural tax started, the total proceeds from it amounted to 665 million rubles. After the first revision, the tax brought in 1,630 million rubles in 1940.[28] The real pressure on the kolkhozniki came after World War II. In rapid succession the tax rates were raised to such an extent that in 1951/52 a kolkhoz family with a taxable income from its private enterprise of only 5,000 rubles per year had to pay 820 rubles plus 33 per cent of the additional income over 5,000 rubles and up to 6,000 rubles. Above an income of 6,000 rubles the tax became prohibitive.[29]

In spite of the reduction in private farming of the kolkhozniki, the proceeds from the agricultural tax were boosted to 12,400 million rubles in 1952. This was about 25 per cent of the total returns from sales in kolkhoz trade by all sellers. The great effectiveness of the agricultural tax as a means of curtailing the private economy of the kolkhozniki was frankly recognized in the famous orations of Malenkov and Khrushchev in August and September of 1953.[30]

Payments of Kolkhozy to Kolkhozniki

Distributions of the kolkhozy to kolkhozniki in money and kind are discussed together with other sources of peasant incomes in chapter

[27] At first glance such taxation appears not unjustified, in view of the large turnover taxes on the same goods collected in the state and co-operative trade. But the private economy of the kolkhozniki must have compensated them for the grossly inadequate payments of most of the collective farms for the work of the kolkhoz peasants, and moreover the tax in money from the kolkhozniki's enterprises was in addition to their obligatory deliveries in kind at low to nominal prices.

[28] K. N. Plotnikov, *The Budget of the Socialist State* (Moscow, 1948), p. 194.

[29] For details see N. J., "Der Sowietische Staatshaushalt," *Finanzarchiv*, 1954, pp. 145–46.

[30] Speech of Malenkov in *Pravda*, August 9, 1953, and that of Khrushchev in *Pravda*, September 15, 1953. A feature of the agricultural tax worth attention was that kolkhoz peasants of the new territories were paying only about half of the tax levied on the kolkhozniki of the old territories, apparently on the "theory" that one has to be introduced to the great advantages of Soviet socialism only gradually. See N. J., "Der Sowietische Staatshaushalt," *loc. cit.*

16. Here a few words must be said about these payments, because their low level—in conjunction with the small proceeds from their private enterprises—were presumably the principal obstacle to recovery in farm production.

As stated in dealing with production factors, the low money distributions to the kolkhozniki were the result of small gross money incomes of the kolkhozy associated with a small share of the distributions to kolkhozniki in total money incomes of the kolkhozy. The data are beyond the most pessimistic appraisal. According to Khrushchev, the distributions on *trudodni* amounted to 12.4 billion rubles in 1952.[31] The number of *trudodni* earned was equal to 8,847 million.[32] The average earning per *trudoden* was therefore 1.4 rubles. Even this is apparently an exaggeration.[33] It was furthermore an average which included not only the earnings in the advanced kolkhozy throughout the country, but also the amounts earned in areas with much higher than the average earnings.*

M. Solenova bragged (*Communist*, 1956, No. 1, p. 37) that, calculated per working kolkhoznik, the money distributions to the kolkhozniki per *trudoden* in the RSFSR in 1954 were 3.5 times as high as in 1950. The total money incomes of the kolkhozy of the RSFSR amounted to 25.7 billion rubles in 1954, as became known after the publication of Solenova's article.[34] From the data of the same Solenova, it is apparent that in 1954 the distribution to the kolkhozniki in the RSFSR amounted to no more than 35 per cent of the total money incomes of the kolkhozy. Hence, it was equal to about 9 billion rubles in that year. Divided by 3.5, this implies a total distribution of about 2.6 billion rubles in 1950 in the RSFSR as a whole. Small as the figure is, a small discount would need to be made for the fact that Solenova made her calculation in terms of working kolkhozniki, the number of which declined during the four years involved.[35] The total number of *trudodni* worked in the RSFSR in 1950 was 4,366 million,[36] and, therefore, the average

[31] *Pravda*, January 25, 1958.
[32] *Economy of the USSR in 1956*, p. 141.
[33] Data in *Finances and Socialist Construction*, a symposium, 1957, p. 172, make one think so.
* A real record was reported for as recent a year as 1957 in *Selskaya Zhizn* ("Village Life") on June 11, 1960. Mrs. Luba Richter drew my attention to it. In 1958 a "member" of the kolkhoz in the name of Lenin, Voronezh oblast, declared: "Last year I was to be paid 18 kopeks per *trudoden;* even this was not disbursed." For this money, if received, two-fifths of an ounce of meat could be bought in a co-operative store, provided the store had any meat for sale.
[34] *Stat. Handb., RSFSR*, 1957, p. 145.
[35] This very decline in the number of working kolkhozniki after 1950 was the reason that Solenova used these terms in her computation.
[36] *Stat. Handb., RSFSR*, 1957, p. 146.

distribution per *trudoden* was equivalent to only about 60 kopeks in 1950. In official trade coarse rye bread cost 270 kopeks per kilogram in January–March of 1950 and 200 kopeks in April–December of the same year.[37]

Under such conditions the distributions in kind of the kolkhozy to the kolkhozniki, deplorably small as they were, were much more important than the payments in money.[38] But they too have declined drastically since the last prewar years.

It may be useful to mention here that the workers and employees of state farms were likewise paid miserably (the wages of these workers had to be kept in some relation to the earnings of the kolkhozniki). This may have been the major reason for the poor condition of the sovkhoz production and, surprising as this may seem, for their high production costs (see the end of this chapter).

Only the very low pay especially of unskilled labor in urban areas and the severe administrative barricades kept the flight of the kolkhozniki to the cities from being even larger than it apparently was anyway. But those who stayed behind were unwilling to work.[39]

Collectivization in the New Territories

In 1949, the campaign was launched, and practically completed within the same year, to bring the peasants of the new territories into the paradise of collective farming. The victorious course of collectivization in Latvia, for example, is shown in the following data in terms of both households and sown acreages collectivized (in per cent of total number of households and total peasants' sown acreages of the kolkhozy and kolkhozniki as of each year):[40]

[37] The calculated distribution is, of course, still an average for a huge republic. In the RSFSR as a whole the kolkhozy earned, in 1950, 1,080 rubles per household and per year, but in Orel, Tambov, and Voronezh oblasti (all of these in central European Russia), the money earnings of the kolkhozy amounted only to the really astounding 722, 584, 865 rubles, respectively, per household and year (all data from the respective statistical handbooks, published in 1957). In White Russia the money incomes of the kolkhozy made up only 429 rubles per household in 1950 (*Stat. Handb., White Russia,* 1957, p. 190). There must obviously have been many kolkhozy in many oblasti which did not distribute even a token money income in 1950.

[38] Officially, the distributions in kind amounted in 1952 to 35.1 billion rubles as against 12.4 billion rubles distributed in money (see Khrushchev's speech before the plenary session of the Central Committee of the Party on December 15, 1958). While Khrushchev did not state the prices in terms of which his figure had been expressed, it can be proved that the calculation was made at retail prices in official trade or prices close to them.

[39] In no less a place than *Izvestiya* (July 3, 1955) a kolkhoz chairman in Bryansk oblast was reported to have exclaimed: "A really historical event—the people [kolkhozniki] themselves are asking for work. . . ." He added that in preceding years the small distributions per *trudoden* discouraged the people substantially.

[40] *Stat. Handb., Latvia,* 1957, p. 67.

Year	Households	Sown Acreages
1947............	0.1	0.03
1948............	2.4	2.4
1949............	76.7	80.9
1950............	90.7	94.7
1951............	97.7	99.5

The effectiveness of the collectivization campaign was even more pronounced in livestock holdings. In the USSR as a whole, cattle in the hands of all individual peasants went down precipitously from 6,733,000 head at the beginning of 1941 to 433,000 head at the beginning of 1951 (Chart 23). Only mopping-up remained to be done. This brought the number of cattle in the hands of individual peasants down to 114,000 by the end of 1952.

The negative effect of the "glorious" campaign did not fail to show up in farm output. Official data display the serious plight of farming in the Baltic States and White Russia. In yields of grain per acre, some of these territories were thrown back by at least one hundred years. The same situation existed also in the Northwest and the North of the RSFSR collectivized much earlier. The pernicious effect of the sudden collectivization of the new territories did not differ much from the effect of collectivization in similar older areas many years earlier. The particularly unfavorable conditions for collectivization, intensified by not providing suitable machinery and adequate supplies of commercial fertilizer, led to the decay of agriculture in the whole of northwestern and western European Russia. When the great collectivization campaign was conducted in the old territories in the late 1920's and early 1930's, those in power may not have fully realized that, especially in the poorer areas, the campaign would lead to detrimental results for the farm output and the incomes of the peasants, or they at least could have pretended not to realize this. But when in the 1940's they decided to extend collectivization to the new territories with similar soil and climatic conditions, those very results were staring them in the eye in the adjacent territories. They knew exactly the price and they were willing to pay it.

Amalgamation Campaign

In 1950, the very next year after the collectivization campaign in the new territories, the untiring Khrushchev started his great campaign for amalgamation of the kolkhozy into larger units (the kolkhozy once before had been compulsorily amalgamated during the great initial drive in the late 1920's and early 1930's). In addition to the amalgamation of the kolkhozy, the Khrushchev plan included the creation of single centers for each amalgamated kolkhoz. This meant resettlement of uncounted millions of kolkhoz peasants.[41] He went so far as to advocate the replacement of individual houses by city-type blocks of homes. This was not clearly stated, but a cut in private plots of the kolkhozniki, apparently to 0.25 hectare each, was also a component of the Khrushchev plan.[42]

The amalgamation campaign proved an immediate and complete "success." The number of kolkhozy was reduced to less than one-half in a matter of months, possibly weeks. The mergers were also continued later without interruption, although at a much slower pace. The number of kolkhozy, which was 235,500 in 1940 and grew to perhaps 260,000 in 1949 because of the collectivization of farming in the new territories, declined thereafter to 121,400 by the end of 1950 and to 83,000 in 1956.[43] The Report of the Fulfilment of the 1958 Plan implies about 68,000 agricultural kolkhozy.

According to *Economy of the USSR in 1956* (p. 143), in 1956 the kolkhozy were distributed according to sown acreages as follows (per cent of total):

Hectares per Kolkhoz	Per cent of Total
Below 500	17.8
From 501 to 1,000	24.7
From 1,001 to 2,000	29.0
From 2,001 to 5,000	22.5
Over 5,000	6.0

Many of the new collective farms were huge enterprises, each comprising more than 10,000 hectares of sown acreages and more than 1,000 able-bodied kolkhozniki.[44] Some of them, indeed, greatly exceed in size those state farms which proved unmanageable, and were, therefore, split up, in the middle 1930's.[45] There have been, of course, manifold changes since the middle 1930's but hardly sufficiently strong ones to justify the huge size of many present-day kolkhozy.

The measures in Khrushchev's plan other than amalgamation

[41] These centers of the amalgamated kolkhozy were first referred to as "agro-cities" or "agro-towns." Later the name was replaced by the more modest "kolkhoz settlement."

[42] The typical size prior to that had been somewhat below 0.50 hectare.

[43] *Economy of the USSR in 1956*, p. 140.

[44] In Krasnodar krai and Stavropol oblast 62.9 and 58.5 per cent, respectively, of all kolkhozy had over 500 households in 1956. In Stavropol oblast the average number of households per kolkhoz exceeded 1,000. See *Stat. Handb., RSFSR,* 1957, pp. 164, 204.

[45] *Soc. Agri.*, pp. 254–56. But in recent years the Party leaders have also been dissatisfied with the size of the state farms and a relatively mild amalgamation campaign has been in progress in this section as well (see data for the RSFSR in *Stat. Handb., RSFSR,* 1957, p. 149).

were soon declared to have been only his suggestions for discussion, but actually an open and fast attack was replaced by a slow secret drive. There is no doubt that a number of peasants were forced to give up parts of their private plots, but the number of households involved in such cuts and the exact total amount of land lost by the kolkhozniki in this way remains unknown.[46] A certain number of kolkhoz settlements with a limited amount of resettlement also was apparently organized. The secrecy on this point seems impenetrable.[47] All this "socializing" went on, it should be remembered, when the "socialist" kolkhozy of the RSFSR were distributing some 60 kopeks per *trudoden*.

The mergers may have seemed a wise move considering that the kolkhoz peasants were to be made to work for rewards like a ruble per day, but the effect on output was, at the least, doubtful. The fact that mergers continued to take place in later years, after the idea of basing industrial expansion on extreme exploitation of the farm population had been modified, seems to indicate that such Leviathan-like organizations fit in well with the Soviet kind of socialism and communism. The democracy assured by the Kolkhoz Statute of 1935, specifically the deciding powers of the full assembly of the members of the kolkhozy, etc.—all this existed only on paper for a long time prior to the mergers. So the situation could not have been much worsened by the new measures.

[46] P. Fedoseev, a very influential spokesman of the Party, acknowledged in 1954 in *Communist,* the theoretical and political journal of the Party, that the campaign for the diminution of the kolkhozniki's private economic activity had gone so far that in some kolkhozy this activity had been liquidated entirely (see *Communist,* 1954, No. 11, p. 23). Interestingly, Fedoseev did not treat the campaign harshly, but was satisfied with designating it as forestalling the future. As was shown, the total private acreage of the kolkhozniki declined from 5.90 million hectares in 1950 to 5.69 million hectares in 1954, but it was 5.79 million hectares in 1955 (*Stat. Handb.,* 1956, p. 108). The acreage may have been even lower in 1951 than in 1954.

A campaign was going on in 1957 and probably earlier in White Russia, and probably in all other annexed territories, of resettlement of kolkhoz homesteads (*khutora*) from houses located on their former land to the villages. The campaign was proceeding in complete accord with the plans advocated by Khrushchev in 1950 for all kolkhozy. The settlements were to be large, similar to Khrushchev's *agrogoroda.* The houses were to be built to accommodate at least two families each. The land under the apartment, including the adjacent garden, was not to exceed 0.15–0.20 hectare. The balance of the private plot, if any, was to be in the field. The campaign was also to be conducted in the Khrushchev "hurrah" manner so far as speed was concerned (see *Soviet White Russia,* June 25, 1957).

[47] As to the havoc connected with both amalgamation and disamalgamation (there was also this to some extent) as late as 1955, see the illuminating remarks by Valentin Ovechkin in "A Difficult Spring" in the journal *Novy Mir* ("*New World*"), 1956. Those unfamiliar with Russian may use the translation in *Soviet Studies* (Glasgow), January, 1957. Specifically, amalgamation is dealt with on pages 286–87 of this source, but the rest is also of the greatest interest.

But with the size they were brought to, many kolkhozy turned out to be simply unmanageable after the merger. It took quite a while to find a certain remedy for these defects. In the 1930's, the organization of the super-large state farms made necessary either complete splitting or subdivision of the large sovkhozy into more or less independent sections. In a similar way, a tendency developed to subdivide the super-large kolkhozy which embraced more than one village into as many sections as there were villages. The organization of such sections apparently started only in the last few years. A detailed report seems available only from Siberia, but there this development apparently proceeded on a large scale.[48] The previous smaller kolkhozy were frequently reborn under the name "complex brigade." The full extent of such splitting in the country as a whole remains unknown, though.

The Picture As a Whole

Thus, in the post–World War II years under Stalin, Soviet agriculture emerged as having been largely based on the labor of women, ill-fed and ill-clothed: a labor force immensely disgruntled by the small distributions from the kolkhozy for the compulsory work, by compulsory purchases of livestock from them at requisition prices, by enormous taxation in money of the output from their private tiny enterprises (in addition to taxation in kind), and by the huge sales taxes on what little the peasants bought in the co-operative stores.

In October of 1952, Stalin, not in the least restrained by the deplorable state of farm production or, in particular, by the adverse effect of Khrushchev's scheme for farm organization, released his plan of further action for leading agriculture from socialism into communism. The limited free market for farm products was to be partly replaced by "commodity exchange." [49] The collective farms were to deliver the small amounts of farm products then sold by them in kolkhoz trade to the state in exchange for consumers' goods which were to be distributed among the kolkhozniki according to some undisclosed principles.[50]

---

[48] M. Tikhomirov, "New Developments in the Organization of Management of the Kolkhozy," *Economics of Agriculture,* 1957, No. 3, pp. 64–69.

[49] "Economic Problems of Socialism in the USSR," *Bolshevik,* 1952, No. 18, p. 9.

[50] Those interested in Communist theory may ponder the problem of how such a clumsy institution as the commodity exchange, in which money itself was not to be used but the farm products delivered and the goods obtained in exchange were to be evaluated in money (the commodities obtained by the kolkhoz in exchange for the products delivered possibly may have been expected to be later revaluated in

It would be, however, incorrect to say that Stalin did not do anything for agriculture except devise ways by which the existing "socialist" form of organization could ascend to a Communist form. At the very time when the Stalin regime failed to supply kolkhoz farming with the simplest means of production and kept the kolkhozniki's incomes at near-starvation levels, these same kolkhozniki, the rest of the Soviet population, and the whole world were informed that Stalin was engaged in a huge program of changing the climate of Russia. In a matter of only ten to twenty years, belts of trees like huge walls were to eliminate the pernicious effects of the dry winds coming from the desert that affected and still affect the vast semiarid territory of European USSR.[51] An important component of the same program was crop rotations according to the recommendations of Professor Williams, the essence of which was to have a large proportion of the arable land in perennial grasses everywhere, even in the driest areas. (The favorable effect of such rotations in more humid areas was known to our grandfathers.) Connected with the shelterbelts and Williams' crop rotation was a vast program of providing irrigation water, accepted soon after the shelterbelt program. In a matter of only five to seven years, Russia was to have 6.05 million hectares of additional irrigated land (this implied that its irrigated land was to be more than doubled), and in addition an area of near-desert land measuring 22 million hectares, an area bigger than several foreign states combined, was to be supplied with water for drinking purposes and for growing insurance feed.[52] This irrigation and "watering" was to be part of the five Great Stalin Constructions of Communism.[53]

With the death of Stalin, Russia will have to bear with its bad climate, which incidentally deteriorated substantially under

---

trudodni), was expected to bring the state closer to communism. But after all, if Lenin could see communism in the distribution on rations of bread compulsorily obtained from the individual peasants, Stalin's commodity exchange may have been considered a step on the road to communism.

[51] The law of October 24, 1948, provided for a total of nearly 15 million acres of tree planting; of these, 10.3 million were to be field shelterbelts in areas with inadequate precipitation. The plantings were to take place during a period of eighteen years. An immense propaganda campaign was launched. *Literaturnaya Gazeta* (October 27, 1948) wrote: "The landscape is changing. Where there were naked steppes will be forests. The devastating *sukhovei* [scorching dry eastern winds] will be shattered against these." The yearly planting plans of the first few years were fulfilled with immense success, it was claimed.

[52] The provision of such limited supplies of water is called "watering" in the Russian language.

[53] Each of these projects was announced separately by orders issued between August and December of 1950.

Stalin through mass deforestation, specifically at river sheds.* The
government failed to supply the information on how many (or
better, how few) of the planted trees survived, how large (or better,
how small) are the territories which are irrigated and "watered"
or will be irrigated and "watered," in the foreseeable future
by the water obtained in conjunction with the former five Great
Stalin Constructions of Communism.[54] The Williams' rotations
were given up in many areas as impractical. A mountain was
made into a molehill.[55]

Malenkov's report of August, 1953,[56] and Khrushchev's report of

---

* It came as a great surprise when suddenly evidence started to pour out in the
Soviet press of strong dust bowls (called "black storms" in the USSR) in the south of
European Russia, mainly in the southeast, in the spring of 1960. (Evidence of such
storms in Kazakhstan as a quite regular phenomenon was available also previously.)
Large stretches of arable land, which include such in winter grains, are reported to have
been annihilated either by their topsoil having been blown away or by being covered
by dust blown in.

These big losses could have been caused by exceptionally strong winds, by wide
stretches of soil being in a loose form, or both. This writer is not sure that the 1960
spring winds in southeastern Russia were of very rarely occurring strength. It seems that
the phenomenon has occurred frequently also in previous years, but it was just not allowed to be reported. It would need confirmation, but this writer grants the possibility
or even probability that the resistance of wide stretches of land, from eastern European
Russia to eastern Kazakhstan, to blowing was considerably reduced by improper soil
cultivation.

Fall plowing is the rule in the USSR, although on light soils exposure of the naked
soil to the winter winds is likely to be detrimental. Excessive plowing, which is
quite regular, has similar results, except probably on heavy soils. Square cultivating of
row crops, strongly advocated from Moscow, is certainly hard on the land. Last but
not least, millions of hectares of land have been taken in cultivation in semiarid,
indeed near-desert, areas, which was absolutely unadapted for this purpose (this
cultivation incidentally involves also big financial losses).

It would be surprising if the directing of the Party secretaries from the Union to the
raion (district) level, mostly ignorant in agriculture, did not have such results. Even
if they are familiar with agriculture, all the *raion* secretaries are held to is: fulfil and
even overfulfil the plan for deliveries, acreages, herds, and output, regardless of
anything else.

[54] The silence on the shelterbelts was broken by an official in charge of the plantings
in the Ministry of Agriculture (see *Agriculture,* daily paper of the Ministry of
Agriculture of the USSR, November 16, 1954), but he did not dare to disclose information on how many of the new forest sowings had been lost. It is, however, obvious
from his presentation that the strips saved did not amount to more than a small
part of those planted. Dead silence continues on the irrigation projects or irrigation
portions associated with the five Great Stalin Constructions of Communism. It seems
pretty definite that not more than 10 per cent, and probably much less, of the area
announced for irrigation in connection with those constructions has been made
available.

[55] The hydroelectric plants at Kuibyshev and Stalingrad are the only important part
of the huge program, launched in 1948–50, which was realized. In 1958 these plants
were declared, by implication, a misinvestment. In the seven-year plan for 1959–65 the
USSR shifted from hydroelectric to fuel-burning electric power plants.

[56] *Pravda,* August 9, 1953.

September of the same year[57] launched a wave of disclosures of such a large amount of disorganization and waste as to surpass the most pessimistic appraisals of the Soviet economy by serious Western analysts. Khrushchev spoke of a great number of unbred cows, and an immense mortality of livestock, especially of mass deaths of whatever calves were born in whole oblasti and even in a whole republic (White Russia).[58] P. Lobanov, next to Khrushchev among the rulers of Soviet agriculture at that time, in his speech to the conference on southeastern agriculture in Voronezh in 1955, revealed that in eight oblasti of this region the number of fruit trees had declined by 40 per cent since 1940. While winter-killing may have played an important role in the loss of the trees, it is unlikely to have been the only cause. Failure to restore the trees must in any case be traced to the regime.

In the flood of evidence on the disorganization and miserably low output of farm products which has poured out since Malenkov's and Khrushchev's reports, the prize certainly goes to the data disclosed only in October of 1958 that in 1953 the socialized sector had harvested less than double the potatoes sown (see introduction to this chapter). Next, possibly, comes the evidence on the amazingly low grain yields in a wide area, embracing the north-northwest and the north-center of the RSFSR, White Russia, and the Baltic States, contained in the Appeal of the Party and Government to the Farm Producers of January, 1957. The data definitely refer to the *Post-Stalin* period. But the situation hardly could have been any worse previously.

Output data for the USSR as a whole, released only after this volume was completed, confirmed that the extremely low yields of grain in the northeast, and many other unpleasant details, were not exceptions. Agriculture was in a deplorable state in the whole of the USSR, when the collective leadership replaced Stalin early in 1953. (These data are briefly dealt with in the next chapter.)

All this was just the operation of the vicious circle embodied in the system of paying token prices to kolkhozy. After fulfilling all their obligations, many a kolkhoz had nothing, or as good as nothing, to distribute among its kolkhozniki. The kolkhozniki, whether they had run away or not, did not work at all, or did not work properly,

[57] *Pravda,* September 15, 1933.
[58] No data on the death of young (or other) animals are at hand. But only 59 calves were born per 100 cows and 55 lambs and kids were born per 100 ewes and she-goats in White Russia in 1952/53 (see *Stat. Handb., White Russia,* 1957, p. 184). The number of lambs and kids born was only about half of what may be considered normal for these types of animals.

and the following year the kolkhoz frequently was in even poorer shape.[59] As has already been mentioned, one is actually surprised that under the conditions existing in the late 1940's and early 1950's, so many kolkhozniki still remained in the villages and so much recovery in output was effected by Soviet agriculture as seems to have been the case. The remarkable power of the dictatorship! The long-suffering Russian peasant!

[59] A kolkhoz chairman referred to the operation of this vicious circle as late as November, 1958, as existing at that very time (see *Izvestiya,* November 30, 1958). This was after the great improvements in farming, claimed by Khrushchev, had already occurred. When the circle was particularly vicious, discussion of it was prohibited.

CHAPTER 14

AGRICULTURE II:

OUTPUT; MARKETINGS

Output

The policy of holding back evidence on agricultural output pursued during postwar years was relaxed only very gradually. Some data were not released before 1959. So far as evidence exists, it is still in a somewhat chaotic state. Even at this writing not all products have been covered, and for some items the data pertain only to individual widely scattered years. Not a single output series is available covering at least all postwar years. Only scattered official data are available for poultry numbers and the respective data for the output of potatoes, meat, milk, and eggs seem doubtful. The estimates of grain production in the most recent years also are likely to be exaggerated.

War years.—Livestock Herds of the USSR, 1957, for the first time published the data on the herds during the war years (Chart 24). Owing to occupation of the Soviet territory by the enemy it is difficult to associate the herds as stated for the various years with definite territories. In any case, this writer is unable to undertake this job.

The same difficulty would have been faced if it had been finally decided to publish the data on the sown acreages during the war years. The Soviets, of course, have plentiful usable data but they keep them to themselves.

*1945.—*In "Close-up" (p. 160) the 1945 farm production was estimated at 60 per cent of that of 1940 (postwar boundaries in both cases). While the estimate was largely a guess, one does not see how one could do much better now. Data for acreages and livestock herds are available (see Table 25 and Chart 24), but no data were released on the yields of crops per hectare and very few data are available

TABLE 25

Sown Acreages: 1940 and Selected Postwar Years*
(In millions of hectares)

Crop	1940	1945	1950	1953
Total.................	150.4	113.8	146.3	157.2
Grain....................	110.5	85.3	102.9	106.7
Wheat...................	40.3	24.9	38.5	48.3
Corn...................	3.6	4.2	4.8	3.5
Technical crops............	11.8	7.7	12.2	11.5
Cotton.................	2.08	1.21	2.32	1.88
Flax for fiber............	2.10	1.04	1.90	1.24ᵃ
Sunflower seed...........	3.54	2.89	3.59	3.90
Sugar beets.............	1.23	0.83	1.31	1.57
Potatoes..................	7.7	8.3	8.6	8.3
Vegetables...............	1.5	1.8	1.3	1.3
Feed crops...............	18.1	10.2	20.7	28.7

* The data are from *Economy of the USSR in 1956*, pp. 112–13, supplemented by such from other official sources.
ᵃ The acreage in flax fiber was 1.11 million hectares in 1954, according to *Stat. Handb.*, 1956, p. 106.

on the yields per animal. Yet the yields of both types deteriorated owing to war conditions.

The sown acreages and livestock herds showed the following declines from 1940 to 1945 (in per cent):[1]

All crops............................	−24.3
Grain........................	−22.8
Technical crops....................	−34.7
Potato and vegetables...............	+6.0
Feed crops........................	−43.6
Livestock (end of year):	
Cattle............................	−12.7
Cows...........................	−18.0
Hogs.............................	−61.5
Sheep and goats....................	−23.6

The decline in sown acreage in the valuable technical crops was balanced to some extent by the increase in the acreage in potatoes and vegetables, and the all-around decline in acreages (weighted by the value of the crops) may be considered to have been moderately less than by 25 per cent. Animals depending on roughage for their feed (cattle and sheep) declined much less in numbers than hogs, which need concentrated feed. The decline from the end of 1940

[1] *Sown Acreages in the USSR*, 1957, I, 6–9, and *Livestock Herds of the USSR* (Moscow, 1957), p. 6.

CHART 24

LIVESTOCK HERDS, 1941–54 *
(Million heads)

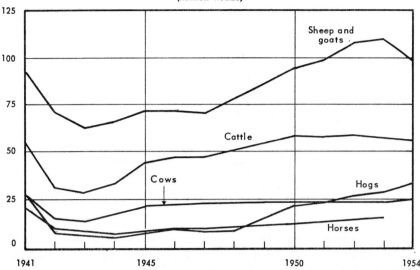

* January 1 data from *Livestock Herds of the USSR*, 1957, p. 6. Territory for the 1941–45 data not stated. Data for 1954 from *Courier of Statistics*, 1958, No. 4, p. 92.

to the end of 1945 indeed varied from 23.6 per cent for sheep and goats and only 12.7 per cent for cattle to as much as 61.5 per cent for hogs. Thus meat supplies must have been depressed considerably more than milk supplies.

The previous estimate of this writer of the 1945 grain crop, which was also not much more than a guess,[2] implied an average yield of 6.7 quintals per hectare, or about 20 per cent below the prewar level of something like 8.5 quintals per hectare. If the other crops showed different declines, these were likely to have been even larger on the average. The sugar-beet acreage went down by almost exactly one-third from 1940 to 1945. The output of crystal sugar, however, declined by not less than 78.5 per cent. Granted that not all harvested sugar beets reached the factories and that the extraction of sugar from the beets also may have gone down because of disorganization, there still was room for a more than 50 per cent reduction in the yield of the sugar beets per hectare.

The declines in the yields per animal from 1940 to 1945 need not have been as large as those for crops. Still, kolkhoz and sovkhoz

[2] The 1945 grain crop was estimated by this writer at 56.7 million tons (*International Affairs*, 1952, p. 459). A decline of fully one-third as compared with the average prewar crop in postwar borderlines was indicated by the estimate.

cows showed reductions in the yield of milk per cow of 7.1 and 19.9 per cent, respectively. The output of wool per sheep went down by 20 per cent in the kolkhozy and by 17.3 per cent in the sovkhozy.[3] Part of the declines in yields as established statistically must have been theft on a larger scale than usual.

An idea about the decline in farm output from 1940 to 1945 also may be formed from the reductions in marketings (see Table 32 at the end of this chapter). The declines for the various items were as follows (in per cent):

Grain	39.4
Potatoes	8.5
Vegetables	21.3
Seed cotton	48.2
Sugar beet[a]	73.0
Slaughter animals	42.9
Milk	50.0
Wool[a]	39.2

[a] Procurements.

An interesting comparison is that of the declines in acreages and herds with the declines in industrial output of processed goods from the respective products (data in per cent):[4]

Sugar beets, acreage	32.5
Crystal sugar, output	78.5
Sunflower seed, acreage	17.2
Vegetable oil, output	63.4
Cotton, acreage	41.3
Cotton yarn, output	53.4
Flax, acreage	51.4
Flax yarn, output	62.2
Sheep herds	13.1
Wool yarn, output	51.7

The data again point to a decline in per hectare yields of all crops for which data are given, as well as in wool obtained per sheep.

All the assembled data make probable that the previous estimate of the decline in farm output from 1940 to 1945 of 40 per cent was too cautious. The destruction and disorganization apparently had an even larger adverse effect than was assumed in making the estimate. However, it may be best to allow the previous estimate to stand.

The recovery.—In "Close-up" (p. 163) the 1950 farm output was

[3] *Attainments*, pp. 162, 183.

[4] Acreages from *Sown Acreages of the USSR*, 1957, I, 6–9. Industrial output from *Industry of the USSR*, 1957, pp. 323, 372. Sheep numbers from *Livestock Herds of the USSR*, 1957, p. 6.

estimated at 95 per cent of that in 1940 (postwar boundaries in both years).[5] The most recent official data on output per man (presumably in terms of 1951 prices) support the writer's estimate of farm output in 1950 in terms of 1940 and may even point to a still lower figure.[6] Together with the official claim of an average rise in farm output of 1.6 per cent in four years 1950–53,[7] the estimate for 1950 brings us by 1953 approximately to the prewar level.

Absence of data at least on acreages in 1946–49 makes it difficult to trace the course of the recovery. The 1946 crops suffered from the drought. This writer estimated the 1946 grain crop at the same figure as the 1945 crop (*International Affairs*, 1952, p. 459). The livestock data in Chart 24 point to an only very slow recovery until the end of 1946 (none for hogs) and only a small advance in 1947. The advance in farm output also was snail-like in the four years 1950–53 (1.6 per cent per year on the average is claimed officially).[8] The increase in output was small even in 1949, as implied in official claims (3 to 4 per cent; weather conditions seem to have been unfavorable in this year, though).[9]

[5] While the estimate was described and probably meant as one for gross farm output, it is preferable to think of it as an estimate of the volume available for sale and consumption in the farm home. There is no evidence for estimating the output of feed (the value of feed makes up the principal item in the difference between gross farm output and the volume available for sale and consumption in the farm home). There is, moreover, no reason to adhere necessarily to a Soviet concept of gross farm production which is highly incorrect. It is an indication of the poor state Soviet statistics have been during the past three decades, that this immature concept has undergone only a minor change during the last forty or more years.

The ECE in its 1951 *Survey* (p. 135) estimated the 1950 Soviet farm output at 7 per cent above that of 1940, while a Soviet writer had an excess of 14 per cent for the same year (N. Shabalin, "The Role of Modern Techniques in the Growth of Farm Output in the USSR," *Questions of Economics*, 1953, No. 8, p. 55).

[6] According to *Attainments* (p. 189) output per man declined (presumably in terms of 1951 prices) from 1940 to 1950 in the kolkhozy (only socialized output) by 1 per cent and in state farms, including subsidiary farming enterprises of the state, by 7 per cent. The number of working kolkhozniki remained unchanged during the period (*Commentary*, p. 161), and increased slightly if the wage earners of the MTS are added. All in all, a very small increase in output of the kolkhozy is implied for those years. On the basis of the official data, there was also an increase in the output of the state farms and of subsidiary state farming enterprises. The decline in the output of the kolkhozniki and the almost complete disappearance of individual peasants must have overcompensated for those increases.

[7] *USSR in Figures*, 1958, p. 175.

[8] *Planned Economy*, 1959, No. 3, p. 7.

[9] The stated percentage is implied in the official claim of a 1.6 per cent rise on the average during the four years of 1950–53 and an average rise of 1.8 per cent in five years, 1949–53 (see *Planned Economy*, 1959, No. 3, p. 7). Frankly, this writer does not trust too much those official averages for increase in farm output: 1.6 per cent in 1950–53 and 1.8 per cent in 1949–53 and some others pertaining to these years. Khrushchev may have wanted to paint a beautiful picture for the time after 1953 and did not mind if the estimates for the years prior to 1953 were on the low side.

Thus, at the end of the *Stalin Has Everything His Way* period farm output was at about the 1940 level. With the 1946 farm production having been in any case not much above 60 per cent of that in 1940 and the increase in 1949 having been small, a jump of almost 50 per cent in only two years, 1947 and 1948, is implied. The picture then was as follows:

Hostilities came to an end in 1945. In 1946 recovery could not get under way owing to the slow demobilization from the armed forces and the drought. But then in quick order farming activities could have been brought to a level not far below that in the last prewar years. It was of course no great achievement to reach this miserable level. By 1949 the course of recovery had already slowed down greatly. For growth beyond this low level, no stimuli were present.

1940–53.—As finally spelled out, all that grain, the most important crop of the USSR, yielded was 80.9 million tons on the average in 1949–53 and 82.5 billion tons specifically in 1953 (see Table 26). This compares with the astronomical output figures, claimed previously "in biological terms" (for example, 124.5 million tons in 1950 or 121.3 million tons in 1951). The probability is very great that the grain output in a comparable territory in the years immediately prior to World War II was not reached.

The 1940 acreages in the postwar territories were probably somewhat larger, at least for some crops, than the figures shown in Table 25. Yet the grain acreage in 1950 and 1953 was still a little below that of 1940, even according to official statistics, although grain is the crop most needed under Soviet conditions and most easily produced under the conditions of the Soviet agricultural setup.[10] It was in line with the existing precarious conditions that the acreage in feed grain went down quite substantially (by 5.1 million hectares), indeed somewhat more than the decline in the total grain acreage in those years. The acreage in food grain was slightly enlarged.

The official calculations of the grain crops in 1949–53 and 1953 are based on average yields of 7.7 quintals per hectare in 1949–53 and 7.8 quintals in 1953.[11] This is about 10 per cent below this writer's estimate of about 8.5 quintals per hectare in the last prewar years (this estimate seemed almost ridiculously low when published in 1949).

Table 25 shows a larger acreage in potatoes and vegetables in 1950 than in 1940, but there was a certain decline in this acreage

[10] The evidence on the grain yields in the non-blacksoil zone makes it clear that the statement in the text is true only with reference to the steppe areas.

[11] *Courier of Statistics*, 1959, No. 3, p. 90.

by 1953. The acreage in potatoes and vegetables was, moreover, particularly small in 1940, both within the pre-1939 boundaries and in the added territories. The detrimental yields of potatoes and vegetables obtained by the socialized sector in 1953 have already been cited. (See note * to Table 26 for remarks on the great increase in output of potatoes shown in official data for the postwar years.)

TABLE 26

OUTPUT OF MAJOR FARM PRODUCTS:
PRE–WORLD WAR II AND SELECTED POSTWAR YEARS*
(In millions of tons or, for eggs, billions of units)

Product	Prewar Average[a]	Average 1949–53	1950	1953
Grain.................................	77.9	80.9	81.2	82.5
Seed cotton..........................	2.51	3.49	3.54	3.85
Flax.................................	0.32	0.23	0.26	0.16
Sugar beets..........................	15.8	21.1	20.8	23.2
Sunflower seed.......................	2.03	2.05	1.80	2.63
Potatoes.............................	47.9[b]	75.7	88.6	72.6
Vegetables...........................	13.7	. . .	9.3	11.4
Meat including pork fat,[c] live weight......	7.2	. . .	8.1	9.4
The same including increase in herds......	7.1	. . .	8.2	9.8
Meat, dead weight....................	4.5	. . .	4.9	5.8
Milk[d]...............................	27.6	. . .	35.3	36.5
Eggs.................................	10.8	. . .	11.7	16.1
Wool[e]..............................	0.15	. . .	0.18	0.24

* This table has been fully reworked on basis of most recent official material. Data from *Economy of the USSR in 1958, passim,* and *Agriculture of the USSR,* 1960, *passim.* Postwar data are believed still to be exaggerated as compared with pre–World War II data not only because of the territorial factor but because of the exaggeration of the output of the kolkhozniki and probably workers and employees in postwar years. For milk still another factor is that a considerable shift occurred from letting calves suck the milk from the cows directly (this milk is not included in the output) to feeding the calves with milk already milked and included in the output.

An increase in output of potatoes in a comparable territory seems not very probable. The output of vegetables went down as compared to prewar years, even on the basis of official data.

ᵃ Average of 1938–40 for all products except vegetables. Data for vegetables pertain to 1940. All data except for vegetables are for the pre–1939 territory. Data for vegetables are for the 1940 boundaries.

ᵇ The 1940 crop in the border lines of the respective year is given at 75.9 million tons.

ᶜ Beef, veal, pork, lamb, kid, poultry, and also horse, camel, rabbits, and reindeer. Edible and non-edible offal is also included.

ᵈ Cow, sheep, and goat milk.

ᵉ Not washed; includes goat and camel hair.

The 1953 output of flax fiber was little more than half that on the average of 1949–53 and, considering the output of the annexed territories, much less than one-half of the pre–World War II level.

Most of the large increase in feed-crop acreages from 18.1 million in 1940 to 28.7 million hectares in 1953 occurred in the last three Stalin years, 1951 through 1953, which were particularly unfavorable for agriculture as a whole,[12] and this is an indication that the increase was not a real improvement. Two-thirds of the increase in

[12] *Economy of the USSR in 1956,* p. 113.

feed-crop acreages was indeed made up of perennial grasses (an increase of 6.8 million hectares during 1950–53),[13] a large part of which was located in semiarid areas and produced only small or token yields. (A large part of this additional acreage disappeared soon after Stalin's death.) The increase in annual grasses from 4.2 million hectares in 1940 to 7.8 million hectares in 1953 may have been more valuable. Suspicious seem the claims of an expansion of the acreage in mowed meadows from 59.2 million hectares in 1940 to 67.6 million hectares in 1953 in the publication on the occasion of the fortieth anniversary, in spite of the fact that the source felt it necessary to add the qualifying word "mowed" before "meadows." [14]

While a larger acreage in wild hay was claimed as harvested in 1953 than in 1940, a decline in total output of hay as compared to the prewar output seems beyond doubt. Meadows and pastures had indeed been permitted to deteriorate considerably.[15] Almost the only favorable factor with reference to feed was the increase in output of silage from 16.0 million tons in 1940 to 27.7 million tons in 1953 (*Attainments,* p. 184); but even 27.7 million tons was very little, especially since a great deal of exaggeration in the reports on this item from the producers to the statistical offices is acknowledged officially.

[13] *Ibid.*

[14] *Attainments,* p. 184.

[15] In a paper, "The Ways of Strengthening the Feed Basis in the Non-Blacksoil Zone" (*Socialist Agriculture* (Monthly), 1954, No. 12, p. 40), M. Elsukov wrote, "From way back meadows and pastures were the basic foundation of the feed supplies of the kolkhozy and sovkhozy for their cattle. At the present time a great part of the meadows and pastures produces very low yields." According to Fotiev, backward kolkhozy are harvesting only 6 to 8 quintals of hay per hectare (see *Communist,* 1957, No. 12, p. 68). Writing in 1958, P. Lobanov, president of the Academy of Agricultural Sciences, said: "In the non-blacksoil belt of the RSFSR, White Russia, the Baltic States and some other regions there are up to 28 million hectares of natural meadows and pastures. But they produce low yields of grass of poor quality (about half of these lands are swamps, or are covered with brush and hillocks)" (see *Economics of Agriculture,* 1958, No. 3, p. 29).

According to S. Fotiev (*Communist,* 1957, No. 12, p. 69), 10 million hectares of meadows were permitted to become swamps or brush. These meadows were yielding only 3 to 3.5 quintals of hay per hectare. Incidentally, Fotiev gave the total area in natural meadows at 51.7 million hectares (apparently in 1956). This is the same figure which was given for them in the pre-1939 territory in 1938. The political boss of White Russia, in a report published in *Soviet White Russia,* April 11, 1957, mentioned that 1.5 million hectares of drained land had been permitted to become swamps. The non-blacksoil zone comprises almost half of European Russia, and the situation as to meadows in the blacksoil zone was not fundamentally different from that in the non-blacksoil zone. Khrushchev, in his speech published in *Pravda,* May 24, 1957, said that there were demands from kolkhozy to write off land which had become unusable. The kolkhozy were obviously interested in freeing themselves from obligatory deliveries and "purchases" by the state from such land.

Attainments, the anniversary publication (p. 179), gave the acreage in fruits and berries at 2.18 million hectares in 1952 as against 1.53 million hectares in 1940 (pre-1939 territory for this year). There was no subdivision into bearing and non-bearing trees. Although the situation with fruits was deplorable in 1940, it certainly was considerably worse in 1952 and 1953. While the source cited did not acknowledge this, it stated, and the statement was made, it should be noted, in 1957, i.e., after a certain improvement in 1953–56: "Fruit and grape growing are the most backward branches of Soviet agriculture," and this means a lot, of course.

Output of sunflower seed shows an unchanged output since pre–World War II on the basis of the 1949–53 output, but a notable advance on the basis of the 1953 crop.

Only sugar beets and seed cotton displayed a definite substantial improvement. The 1953 cotton crop exceeded that of the last prewar years by fully 50 per cent.

Whatever increases in output of certain technical crops in a comparable territory have taken place since the last prewar years and until 1953, they were unlikely to have offset the declines in the output of grain, potatoes, vegetables, flax, and certainly some other crops.

As far as livestock numbers are concerned (Chart 24), the most significant phenomenon was that the number of cows was still 13 per cent below that at the end of 1940 both on January 1, 1951, and January 1, 1953. The increases from the prewar level were limited to sheep and goats. The providing of evidence on the number of poultry was carefully avoided.[16] *

Official data indicate moderate increases in output of all animal products from 1940 to 1953 (see Table 26). The claimed increase in output of eggs during the stated period is even equivalent to as much as 35 per cent. (On the probable incomparability of the prewar and postwar data for output of animal production see note * to Table 26.)

All in all, the 1953 output of all farm products seems to have

---

[16] Evidence for subsequent years, disclosed only in 1956 and 1957, indicates satisfactory numbers for poultry in 1953 as well, but it is difficult to accept in view of the very low marketings of poultry and eggs by the producers.

* At long last *Agriculture of the USSR,* 1960, p. 322, gave the poultry numbers both in a total and separately for the minor holders, the kolkhozy and sovkhozy. There is a seemingly unsolvable contradiction between such large figures as 321.9 million head of poultry allegedly owned by the private sector (including the flocks of the state subsidiary enterprises) at the end of 1953 and the sales of only 485.7 million eggs and 27,300 tons of poultry in kolkhoz markets of 251 cities in the same year (*Soviet Trade,* stat. handb., 1956, p. 185). One will just have to wait until the Soviets publish something more sensible.

been about the size of the corresponding output before World War II (postwar boundaries). It may even have been somewhat smaller than this. The margin of doubt is small in any case, it would seem, and does not really matter.

1953 versus 1913.—They finally pulled it out. This "finally" occurred in 1959. A. Lisenkov, commenting on the official data published for the first time in *Courier of Statistics*, 1959, No. 3 (see Table 26), writes:[17]

In 1949–53, in acreages, yields, and harvests of grain the country remained practically at the 1910–14 level, although the population, especially of the industrial centers and cities, and requirements for grain have grown substantially.

To make possible the use of the word "practically," the 1909–14 data needed to be manipulated downward. This started long ago. Out of the latest downward revision the average grain crop in 1910–14 emerged with 71.8 million tons.[18] In *Soc. Agri.* (p. 726) it was stated: "Our analysis of the disposition of the crops in 1909–13 in Appendix Note J leads to the conclusion that the average 1909–13 grain crop was at least as large as this [81.6 million tons]."

The cited official estimate for 1910–14 is for the present boundaries; mine was for the smaller, pre-1939 boundaries. Thirty-five to forty years of immense, of "immeasurable," progress, but the grain crops in the last Stalin years were substantially smaller than in the backward tsarist Russia.

The same data in *Courier of Statistics*, 1959, No. 3, which make possible the comparison of the 1949–53 grain acreages and outputs with those of 1910–14, contained similar data for only two other crops, sugar beets and, of course, the indispensable seed cotton, far the most successful crop of the Soviets. The acreage in sugar beets became almost 2.5 times larger, increasing from 671,000 hectares on the average of 1909–13 to 1,570,000 hectares in 1953. The average yield did not show any improvement and output was expanded exactly in proportion to the increase in acreage.

The acreages in seed cotton were enlarged not quite fourfold, the average yield per hectare grew from 12.9 quintals per hectare in 1909–13 to 20.5 quintals in 1953, and the total output was enlarged about 6 times over the period.

The official data, prepared to permit a comparison of the present output of animal products with those before the revolution, are certainly such that nobody would be willing to take an oath on their

---

[17] *Planned Economy*, 1959, No. 3, p. 53.
[18] *Courier of Statistics*, 1959, No. 3, p. 88.

accuracy (the data for eggs are again the most doubtful), but even those data show gains which are anything but overwhelming for a forty-year period. The claimed increases from 1913 to 1953 were as follows (in per cent):[19]

Meat (slaughter weight)	17.5
Milk	23.9
Eggs	34.7
Wool	22.4

It hardly is necessary to stress that with the substantial increase in total population and with the trebling of the urban population with its much greater per capita consumption of animal products, the above outputs of animal products, even if they were correctly computed, imply a very high price paid by the population for "socialism" and, specifically, for peasant collectivization.

Stalin's adieu.—Under normal conditions there would not have been any important reason for the rapid growth of farm output in 1947 through 1949, or only in 1947 and 1948, suddenly coming to an almost complete standstill afterward. Actually, with the great scarcity of farm machinery on farms in the early postwar years, the relatively heavy deliveries of it since 1949[20] should have acted against even a strong slowdown in the upward trend of output, which could otherwise have been expected as farm production was approaching the prewar level.

There were, however, too many counteracting factors at work— extremely low incomes of peasants greatly aggravated by the growing disproportion between their incomes and those of the wage earners; the continually decreasing agricultural labor force which resulted from this disproportion; and, last but not least, Khrushchev, the expert in agriculture[21] and his campaign for the amalgamation of the kolkhozy. The combination of all these factors revealed itself with full strength after the more or less automatic postwar recovery brought farm output almost to the prewar level. This automatic growth was concealing the fact that the organism was actually in a state of decay.

The number of cattle declined by 2.2 million head during 1952, a better than normal year as regards weather. The resolution of the Party on Khrushchev's report (September, 1953)[22] stated that "ow-

[19] *Ibid.*, p. 93. The data from 1913 on which the calculation is based, are supposed to pertain to the present territory.

[20] The number of usable combine grain harvesters on farms was about doubled in one year, 1950, and increased again by nearly one-third in 1951.

[21] He called himself this in an interview with an American. See *Collier's*, March 19, 1954.

[22] *Pravda*, September 13, 1953.

ing to poor care, the productivity of animal husbandry remains very low. In recent times milk yields, weight of the wool clip, and a number of other quality indicators have shown declines."

The decay of Soviet agriculture was most pronounced in flax fiber. And what a decay it was! In the fall of 1955 the information was casually dropped that in 1953 in Smolensk oblast—part of the main Soviet flax belt—flax returned 105 quintal of fiber and 0.76 quintal of seed per hectare. The improvement in the subsequent years was ascribed to the immense inflow of technicians into the kolkhozy in accordance with the salutary decisions of the Party.[23] There were no agricultural technicians to speak of before the collectivization, yet on the average during 1925–28 the peasants harvested 2.1 quintals of flax fiber and 3.6 quintals of linseed per hectare in the Western area, of which Smolensk oblast was part.[24] It was the disorganizing result of the collectivization, and specifically of the conditions during the *Stalin Has Everything His Way* period, which brought about in Smolensk oblast the decline in yield per hectare to one-half (flax fiber) and to one-fifth (linseed). The yield of linseed in Smolensk and many other oblasti in 1953 was indeed so small that there was not even enough seed to maintain the greatly reduced acreage. In 1954, the acreage in flax fiber in the RSFSR went down an additional 22 per cent, to less than half of the 1950 acreage.[25]

Terrific as the evidence on flax is, the yield of potatoes of 4.3 tons per hectare of the socialized sector in 1953 is even more appalling.

While the picture of decay in agriculture in the last Stalin years is clear, this very interesting question is difficult to answer: Did the decay go so far as to cause the farm output actually to have a declining trend, or did it permit some slight growth?

Official evidence actually implies that the decay of the Soviet socialized agriculture in the last Stalin years had led to a reversal of the upward trend in farm production. In his report to the Central Committee of the Party (*Pravda,* September 15, 1953), Khrushchev stated that the 1952 agricultural output was 10 per cent above that of 1940. Shabalin's estimate of the 1950 farm output of 14 per cent above that of 1940 has been cited above. Both estimates were exaggerations but they were likely to have been obtained by the same method and may have been comparable. The implication, of course, is that there was a decline in farm output of about 4 per cent from 1950 to 1952. Farm output in 1953 is unlikely to have been larger than that in 1952.

[23] *Socialist Agriculture,* October 30, 1955.
[24] *Statistical Reference Handbook of the USSR, 1928,* pp. 214–15.
[25] *Stat. Handb., RSFSR,* 1957, pp. 128–29.

There are, however, also other data. Data by Shabalin, quoted above, imply an increase in gross farm production in the year of 1949 of 7.8 per cent. With the already cited official calculation that gross farm output increased on the average during the five years 1949–53 by 1.8 per cent, Shabalin's statement allows for no rises in the four years 1950–53, but it does not point to a decline.

According to still other official data, output per man increased from 1950 to 1953 by 16 per cent in kolkhozy and by 15 per cent in state farms including other state farming enterprises.[26] A large part of this increase was offset (in its effect on farm output) by the decline in the labor force on farms. But a small increase in farm output seems not to be excluded.

While in his calculations (see Chart 3 in chapter 1) this writer assumes that there was an increase in farm output of 5 per cent in the three years 1951 through 1953, a full stagnation during those years was quite possible. And such stagnation or decline certainly seemed likely for the future if farm policies remained unchanged.

The most recent official estimates.—While the picture of Soviet agriculture during *Stalin Has Everything His Way,* as implied in the estimates made by this writer over the years, had been gruesome and had not been believed by many, the most recent official estimates in *Economy of the USSR in 1958* (especially p. 350), have fully substantiated it.

The estimates of the official statistical handbook show the following output of farm products in the years 1945–53 (1940 equals 100):

Year	Gross Agricultural Production	Crops	Animal Husbandry
1945	61	60	63
1946	67	65	76
1947	87	90	78
1948	96	102	84
1949	99	106	96
1950	99	97	103
1951	92	86	111
1952	101	95	113
1953	104	95	124

Thus the official estimates indicate for 1945 a decline in gross agricultural production since 1940 of 39 per cent as against 40 per cent estimated by this writer;[*] correspondingly, for 1950 a decline of 1 per cent rather than the 5 per cent given by this writer is indicated. The overestimations of the outputs of the kolkhozniki (and probably

[26] *Attainments,* p. 189.

[*] *Agriculture of the USSR,* 1960, p. 21, corrected the 39 to 40 per cent.

workers and employees) in postwar years relative to 1940 may well account for at least most of the difference of 4 percentage points. Not that the difference matters much.

The new official series for gross agricultural production indicates that the enlarged territory produced in 1952, the last Stalin year, 15 per cent more than the smaller territory produced in 1928. With consideration of the changes in boundaries this estimate implies no increase in output whatever or even a small decline over the period which is only one year short of a quarter of a century. With the skimpy evidence at hand, this writer never dared to go quite that low in estimating the change in gross agricultural production from 1928 to the last Stalin year.

The new official calculations indicate an increase in gross agricultural production of 42 per cent from 1913 to 1952. While even this would not be an exorbitant attainment for a period of almost half a century, the official estimate of gross farm production in 1913 is an underestimate, while the 1952 output may be an exaggeration. In addition to this a downward adjustment for the territorial factor is needed. (The figure for 1913 pertains to the pre-1939 territory.) Comparable data would make a quite different showing.

The Various Producers

Tables 27 and 28 give an idea of the distribution of the sown acreages and livestock herds among the various producers. In 1956, the only year for which such data seem to be available, the acreage in fruits and berries, and vineyards, was distributed among the various producers' groups as follows (in thousand hectares) (see *Agriculture of the USSR,* a symposium [Moscow: State Publishing Office of Agricultural Literature, 1958], p. 288) :

Type of Producer	Fruits and Berries	Vineyards
Total	2,795	445
Kolkhozy	910	302
State farms, including subsidiary farming enterprises	252	72
Kolkhozniki	1,241	62
Workers and employees	392	9

The livestock herds of the various producers show great and important variations by sex and age. These variations cannot be discussed here.

The probable large decline in the private farm output of the kolkhoz peasants from 1940 to the last Stalin year has been discussed. On the first glance it seems that a great deal of labor must have been released, because the labor input per unit of output is

TABLE 27

<small>Sown Acreages, by Type of Producer, 1940, 1945, 1950, and 1953*</small>
(In millions of hectares)

Crop	1940	1945	1950	1953
All crops..	150.4	113.8	146.3	157.2
Kolkhozy..............................	117.7	83.9	121.0	132.0
State farms including subsidiary enterprises...	13.3	...	15.9	18.2
Kolkhozniki.............................	4.5	...	5.9	5.4
Workers and employees...................	0.8	...	1.6	1.4
Individual peasants.......................	14.1	...	1.9	0.1
Grain crops..............................	110.6	85.3	102.9	106.7
Kolkhozy..............................	91.0	67.8	90.1	95.5
State farms including subsidiary enterprises...	8.6	...	9.2	9.3
Kolkhozniki.............................	0.9	...	2.0	1.7
Workers and employees...................	0.2	...	0.3	0.2
Individual peasants.......................	9.9	...	1.4	0.0
Technical crops...........................	11.8	7.7	12.2	11.5
Kolkhozy..............................	10.5	6.7	11.6	10.9
State farms including subsidiary enterprises...	0.3	...	0.4	0.4
Kolkhozniki.............................	0.2	...	0.1	0.1
Workers and employees...................	0.0	...	0.0	0.0
Individual peasants.......................	0.7	...	0.1	0.0
Potatoes and vegetables....................	10.0	10.6	10.5	10.3
Kolkhozy..............................	4.3	3.7	4.7	5.0
State farms including subsidiary enterprises...	0.5	...	0.6	0.6
Kolkhozniki.............................	3.1	...	3.6	3.4
Workers and employees...................	0.6	...	1.3	1.2
Individual peasants.......................	1.5	...	0.3	0.0
Feed crops..............................	18.1	10.2	20.7	28.7
Kolkhozy..............................	11.9	5.7	14.6	20.5
State farms including subsidiary enterprises...	3.9	...	5.7	7.9
Kolkhozniki.............................	0.4	...	0.3	0.3
Workers and employees...................	0.0	...	0.0	0.0
Individual peasants.......................	2.0	...	0.0	0.0

* Data for 1945 from *Sown Acreages of the USSR*, 1957, pp. 6–13. Data for other years from *Economy of the USSR in 1956*, pp. 114–15. Small discrepancies in totals are the result of rounding.

very large in this type of farming. However, most of this labor (married women with many children, old people, invalids, children) is of a kind which would not be fully available for utilization in kolkhoz and sovkhoz work. The principal gain which the socialized agriculture could have had from the curtailment of the private economy of the kolkhozniki was that the reduction of incomes from their private enterprises compelled the kolkhozniki to work for the kolkhozy for any reward, however small.

The output of individual peasants, still substantial in 1940, prac-

TABLE 28

LIVESTOCK: 1941 AND SELECTED POSTWAR YEARS BY TYPE OF PRODUCER*
(In millions of head)

Type	January 1		
	1941	1951	1953
Cattle, all:			
Total	54.5	57.1	56.6
Collective farms	20.1	28.1	30.3
State farms	3.1	3.9	4.2
Kolkhozniki	19.2	18.3	16.3
Wage earners	4.9	6.1	5.3
Rural	3.2	3.8	3.3
Urban	1.7	2.3	2.0
Individual peasants and other owners	6.7	0.4	0.1
Cows:			
Total	27.8	24.3	24.3
Collective farms	5.7	7.0	8.5
State farms	1.2	1.2	1.3
Kolkhozniki	12.7	11.5	10.4
Wage earners	3.5	4.2	3.9
Rural	2.2	2.4	2.3
Urban	1.3	1.8	1.6
Individual peasants and other owners	4.7	0.3	0.1
Hogs:			
Total	27.5	24.4	28.5
Collective farms	8.2	12.3	16.1
State farms	2.9	3.4	4.0
Kolkhozniki	8.6	6.3	5.8
Wage earners	2.7	1.9	2.1
Rural	1.2	0.8	0.8
Urban	1.5	1.1	1.3
Individual peasants and other owners	4.7	0.3	0.0
Sheep:			
Total	79.9	82.6	94.3
Collective farms	39.1	60.8	71.9
State farms	6.7	8.6	10.2
Kolkhozniki	25.4	10.8	10.1
Wage earners	2.6	1.8	1.7
Rural	2.0	1.4	1.2
Urban	0.6	0.4	0.5
Individual peasants and other owners	5.6	0.3	0.1
Goats:			
Total	11.7	16.4	15.7
Collective farms	2.8	7.6	5.3
State farms	0.1	0.1	0.1
Kolkhozniki	6.2	5.4	6.4
Wage earners	2.2	3.1	3.7
Rural	0.9	1.7	2.0
Urban	1.3	1.4	1.7
Individual peasants and other owners	0.3	0.1	0.1

* *Economy of the USSR in 1956*, pp. 129–30, and *Livestock Herds of the USSR*, 1957, *passim*. State farms include other state farming enterprises.

tically disappeared after agriculture had been collectivized in the new territories. Thus, the output of all peasants declined drastically from 1940 to 1953.

While the peasants' farm production with its small output per man went down considerably, the other two secondary forms of farm output, or types of farm producers, likewise characterized by low labor productivity, made considerable progress during the *Stalin Has Everything His Way* period. These two types of farm production were (*a*) the production of farm products by wage and salary earners and their families and (*b*) the production by the subsidiary farms of state enterprises and organizations of every kind. The enlargement of both these types of farm production was necessitated by scarcity of food, by the pressure to have food at any cost. The same factor also operated in the case of the kolkhozniki, but these were forced to curtail their output for ideological reasons.

It may be doubted that the increases in farm output by the wage earners and the subsidiary farming of state enterprises compensated for the great decline in output of kolkhoz and individual peasants. With the assumption of a total farm output in 1953 as large as that in 1940, the assumption just made would imply an increase, albeit very small, in the output of collective and state farms. Whatever expansion occurred in this sector may have been confined to state farms, with the output of the collectives not having offset anything formerly produced by the individual peasants in the new territories in 1940.

Wage earners.[27]—The farming of the wage earners had expanded considerably since 1940, but only in crop production. Shortage of feed proved an obstacle to increasing the output of animal products.

The sown acreages of the wage earners almost doubled from 1940 to 1953, having been enlarged from 0.82 million to 1.43 million hectares. Their most important acreage, namely that in potatoes and vegetables, displayed a similar change (an increase from 0.63 million to 1.22 million hectares during the period).[28] While the share of the wage earners in total sown acreage was little more than 1 per cent in 1953; it was about 12 per cent in total acreage of potatoes and vegetables in that year.

Table 28 shows small increases in cattle (specifically in cows) as well as a large increase in goats in the hands of the wage earners in 1940–53, but their holdings of hogs and sheep declined. The reduction in hogs was certainly a phenomenon that did not occur because of the wishes of the persons involved. A pig and some chickens were

---

[27] Wage earners always include salary earners.
[28] *Economy of the USSR in 1956*, pp. 114–15.

most suitable for the wage earners as a sideline. The decline in hogs owned by the wage earners was presumably caused by an even greater difficulty in obtaining the concentrates needed for this type of livestock than had been the case before World War II.[29] Opportunities for pasturing the cattle, sheep, and especially goats seem not to have been so limited.

The enterprises of the wage earners specifically in urban areas are, of course, the most wasteful in labor owing to the small size of the individual enterprises and the long distances from the homes to the plots; yet the farming enterprises of the wage earners in urban areas were apparently those which had expanded the most since prewar years. Official evidence does not separate sown acreages of wage earners in urban areas from those in rural areas. The increases in herds were larger, and the declines smaller, in the holdings of urban as compared to rural wage earners during the period analyzed, although the differences were not pronounced.[30]

According to calculations of the Scientific Research Institute of Trade and Public Eating of the USSR Ministry of Trade, an average of 44 kilograms of potatoes (after deducting feed and seed use) per capita was produced by the urban population in 1954. The respective output of vegetables was 11 kilograms; of milk, 27 liters (again after deducting the feed use); and of meat (without poultry), 5 kilograms per capita.[31]

The urban population alone produced, according to those data, about 4.5 million tons of potatoes and vegetables in 1954 (net of seed and feed). This is about as much as the official retail trade supplied in 1950,[32] and the output of potatoes and vegetables by the

---

[29] The absolute absence of evidence on the poultry holdings of the workers and employees (even where there should have been such evidence) made this writer certain until 1956 that those holdings had declined since prewar years. Data for post-Stalin years for the whole private sector, disclosed in 1956 and later, indicate at least unchanged poultry holdings by the workers and employees since the prewar years and until 1953. But this is very uncertain. The official evidence implies a large decline in the number of hogs in the hands of wage earners since 1940. Thus, on the basis of this evidence, the trends in these two types of livestock holdings of the wage earners were in the opposite direction—a development one hesitates to believe. There are likewise other and more weighty considerations for rejecting the official data on the poultry numbers of the private sector, which includes also the wage and salary earners, and on the output of eggs and poultry meat by it.

[30] *Livestock Herds of the USSR*, 1957, pp. 175–244.

[31] *Soviet Trade*, 1956, No. 6, p. 11. This source, which dealt with the output of farm products by the urban population, should have also presented evidence on the output of eggs and poultry by the wage earners, but it did not. The source did not, however, state that data are unavailable.

[32] This trade amounted to less than 2.5 million tons of potatoes (a return of 2,070 million rubles at 0.925 rubles per kilogram) and little more than 2 million tons of vegetables (a return of 2,511 million rubles at a price of perhaps 1.30 rubles per

rural non-farm population was, of course, also large. The net milk output of the urban population amounted to about 2.2 million tons in 1954.[33] In 1950, official trade sold little more than half that much milk, including all dairy products other than butter, recalculated to milk.

The data of the Scientific Research Institute of Trade and Public Eating (*ibid.*) also contain calculations of increase in output of farm products by the urban population since the prewar years (an almost threefold increase in potatoes, a more than doubling of the output of vegetables, and an eightfold increase in output of meat). But the respective claims for the changes in output of animal products by the city population cannot possibly be brought into agreement with the data on the changes in livestock herds in the hands of urban wage earners.

An interesting phenomenon is that the enlargement of farm activities of the wage earners was fully or almost fully concentrated in the RSFSR. This is obvious from the following data:[34]

	1940	1950	1953
Sown acreages (million hectares):			
USSR	0.82	1.56	1.43
RSFSR	0.40	1.00	1.00
Other areas	0.42	0.56	0.43
Cows (thousands):			
USSR	3,538	4,248	3,885
RSFSR	2,195	2,804	2,555
Other areas	1,343	1,444	1,330
Sows (thousands):			
USSR	2,705	1,897	2,099
RSFSR	1,305	983	1,133
Other areas	1,400	914	966

Considering that the areas combined under "other areas" include practically all new territories, there must have even been declines in the farming of wage earners in the old territories other than the RSFSR.[35] It seems rather improbable that wage earners in these

---

kilogram). The data on sales in official trade are from *Soviet Trade*, 1956, p. 41; the prices used for this trade were Moscow prices from official sources, with small downward adjustments.

[33] Since urban wage and salary earners owned 1,552,000 cows on October 1, 1954 (*Livestock Herds of the USSR*, 1957, p. 217), a net yield of 1,410 kilograms per cow is implied for this category of owners—not impossible, but not low either in view of the practical absence of concentrates for private owners.

[34] Data for the USSR from the *Stat. Handb.*, 1956, pp. 108, 121–22. Data for the RSFSR from *Stat. Handb., RSFSR*, 1957, pp. 131, 137–38. Livestock data for end of year, except for 1953, which are for the beginning of the year.

[35] Data for White Russia, which was greatly expanded through annexation, show a moderate increase in potato acreage of the wage and salary earners from 1940 to 1950, unchanged total sown acreages and numbers of cows, and a precipitous decline in the number of hogs.

areas did not want to enlarge their farm output. There must have been, at the top level, some differences in policies toward the various nationalities in this respect, in spite of the proclaimed equality of nationalities in the "socialist" state. This writer was actually disinclined to accept such differences, but data are data, unless, of course, the data are wrong.

Subsidiary farming of states enterprises.—The number of such enterprises jumped in a spectacular manner from 45,836 in 1940 (pre-1939 boundaries) to 124,536 in 1950, to drop moderately (to 112,633) in 1952.[36] Most of these enterprises were small. In 1952 they averaged 28.4 hectares of sown acreages, of which only 2.8 hectares were in potatoes and vegetables; also, they averaged 2.9 cows and 7.6 hogs. It is a mystery how these enterprises worked their land, seeing that all of them had only 43,000 tractors in 1952, of which only 5,000 were row-crop tractors. It is unlikely that these enterprises had many horses (no evidence), and they must have relied heavily on hand labor.[37]

While the number of farms of this type grew by 143 per cent from 1940 to 1953, their labor force increased from 1940 to 1952 by only 94 per cent (production workers, by 83 per cent) and the scope of their activities grew even less. Sown acreages were enlarged by 88 per cent, of which those in potatoes and vegetables increased by 69 per cent; the number of cows grew by 30 per cent, and there were fewer hogs in these enterprises to the extent of 13 per cent. Thus the average subsidiary farm had become smaller since 1940, and a great decline in labor productivity must have been involved in them (but not according to the official statistics).[38]

While raising labor productivity in state and collective farms had become the topic of the day, for years hardly anybody brought up the obviously very small output per man in the subsidiary farming of state enterprises. These enterprises must have had sufficient political pull to prevent any meddling, even from the side of N. Khrushchev.[39] A change in this attitude occurred only after Khrushchev's victory in June of 1957.[40]

[36] Implied in data in *Stat. Handb.*, 1956, pp. 146–47.

[37] This is indicated by the large number of wage earners relative to the acreage in crops and to the livestock holdings. For the small acreages and herds stated, the average was 4.9 full-year workers in 1952.

[38] Data in *Attainments* (p. 189) on output per man in state farms, exclusive and inclusive of subsidiary farming enterprises of the state, indicate for the latter about as low an output per man in 1950 as in 1940 and an increase in it of about 10 per cent from 1950 to 1953. But these calculations cannot be trusted fully.

[39] The only allusion to the low labor productivity in subsidiary farming enterprises this writer came across was in a statement by I. Benediktov in *Communist*, 1956, No. 18, p. 81.

[40] Abolition or merging of dwarf subsidiary enterprises was then demanded in an article published in *Izvestiya*, August 27, 1957.

It is constantly advocated that the task of statistics is to draw the attention of the Party and government to possible improvements. In *Stat. Handb.*, 1956 (pp. 134–35), the data on the subsidiary farming of state enterprises are deliberately veiled by giving evidence only for state farms, both separately and together with the subsidiary farming of the state enterprises. It would not have required any additional space and would have been much more meaningful to have presented the data for the latter separately. But the picture disclosed by the data on the subsidiary enterprises had been so unfavorable that clearness was undesirable.

TABLE 29

Kolkhozy, 1940 and 1950–53*

Item	1940	1950	1952	1953
Number at end of year (thousand)ᵃ...........	235.5	121.4	94.8	91.2
Number of on-hand households (million).......	18.7	20.5	19.9	19.7
Sown acreage (million hectares)...............	117.7	121.0	130.6	132.0
Grain..................................	91.0	90.1	95.5	95.6
Technical crops.........................	10.5	11.6	12.2	10.9
Potatoes and vegetables...................	4.3	4.7	4.8	5.0
Feed...................................	11.9	14.6	18.1	20.5
Trucks (thousand).........................	107.	87.	129.	165.
Money incomes (billion rubles)..............	20.7	34.2	42.8	49.8
Trudodni earned (billion)....................	9.3	8.3	8.8	9.0

* *Economy of the USSR in 1956*, pp. 140–41. For data on kolkhoz livestock herds, see Table 27, p. 345.
ᵃ Exclusive of fishing co-operatives.

Collective farms.—It would be natural for the output of the collective farms (kolkhozy) to expand from 1940 to 1950 and 1953, at least to the extent of the decline in output of the individual and kolkhoz peasants. Yet the available evidence indicates that if any gains were made by the collective farms in those years at all, they were very small. The absence, or the smallness, of the advances made by the kolkhozy is fully explained by the small supplies of machinery and fertilizer, by the inadequate supply of labor (relative to available machinery), and primarily by the low prices paid to them and consequently the small payments of the kolkhozy to the kolkhozniki. Even the labor, which was available to kolkhozy, was unwilling to work at all adequately for the token payments made to it.

Official data imply almost complete stagnation in the output of the kolkhozy specifically in 1950–53.[41] The stagnation may indeed

[41] According to *Economy of the USSR in 1956*, p. 108, the output per man in the kolkhozy increased by 16 per cent in 1950–53. But the number of working kolkhozniki declined quite substantially in those years and this decline was presumably compensated

have been complete. In any case the particularly obvious signs of decay, examples of which were given in the introduction to chapter 13 and in this chapter (the catastrophically low yields of potatoes and vegetables in 1953, the prostration of agriculture in the Northwest, especially the precipitous decline in flax production), all involved in the first place the kolkhozy. The disastrous effects of this decay may have been compensated or even slightly overcompensated by expansions, attained with the help of the MTS, which probably operated better than the kolkhozy themselves, by obtaining livestock from their kolkhozniki and owing to the relatively good prices paid for cotton and sugar beets.

Of the individual crops, grown by the kolkhozy, potatoes and vegetables were probably in the worst shape, because the amount and quality of labor available to the kolkhozy played a particularly great role here. And help from the MTS was at a minimum.

The yield of milk per cow in the kolkhozy was the same in 1953 as in 1940 and, since cows in the new territories are likely to have yielded more milk than those in the old territories on an average before annexation, it must be assumed that the prewar yield of milk per kolkhoz cow in a comparable territory had not been restored even by 1953.

The development of the kolkhoz economy since 1940 is much more clearly reflected in the data for the RSFSR, where no consideration needs to be given to changes in territory (see Table 30). The great decline in the number of kolkhozy seems to have been the only "success." In spite of all pushing, sown acreages were not larger in 1952 than in 1940; this is specifically true of the acreages in potatoes and vegetables. With what is known of the low grain yields in the North and Northwest of the republic and of the very low output of potatoes and vegetables around 1953, it is obvious that crop production of the RSFSR kolkhozy was considerably smaller in the last Stalin days than in 1940.

There has been an enlargement in livestock herds in the kolkhozy of the RSFSR since 1940, but the size of the increase must be considered a failure (except for the insignificant poultry holdings) vis-à-vis the successful efforts to cut the livestock herds of the kolkhozniki in favor of the kolkhozy and the complete annihilation of the individual peasants as producers of farm products. (The number of cows in the hands of kolkhozy and kolkhozniki together

---

only partly by the increase of the MTS personnel. The official calculations of the output per man in agriculture may also be too favorable. Specifically, crops showing increases in output, such as cotton, probably have too great a weight in the calculation owing to the relatively high prices paid for it by the state.

TABLE 30

Kolkhozy and MTS, RSFSR, 1940, 1950, and 1952*

A. Kolkhozy			
Item	1940	1950	1952
Number at end of year (thousand)[a]........	167	68	55
Number of households (million).............	11.0	10.0	9.4
Sown acreages (million hectares).............	79.7	74.6	80.3
Grain...................................	63.5	57.9	61.4
Technical crops.........................	6.0	6.0	6.0
Potatoes and vegetables..................	2.6	2.7	2.6
Feed[b].................................	7.6	8.0	10.3
Livestock (million), end of year:			
Cattle.................................	12.1	14.6	15.1
Cows...............................	3.8	4.0	4.7
Hogs.................................	4.7	7.0	8.6
Sheep.................................	22.5	27.3	33.7
Poultry, adult.........................	15.3	32.0	48.5
Horses................................	9.4	5.5	6.3
Trucks (thousand units)...................	59	42	65
Money incomes (billion rubles).............	10.1	10.8	14.4
Trudodni earned (billion)...................	5.7	4.4	4.4
B. MTS			
Number (thousand).......................	4,532	5,294	5,473
Tractors (thousand 15 h.p. units)............	380	485	588
Row-crop tractors (thousand).............	39	30	37
Combined grain harvesters (thousand)........	110	127	170

* *Stat. Handb.*, *RSFSR*, 1957, pp. 144–46, 151.
[a] Exclusive of fishing and hunting co-operatives.
[b] Includes corn for silage and green fodder.

in the RSFSR declined from 11.1 million at the end of 1940 to 9.7 million at the end of 1952; this decline was not offset by the increase in the number of hogs from 9.0 million to 10.4 million.)[42] The evidence on the yields of milk per cow in kolkhozy of the USSR makes probable its decline from 1940 to 1952 in the RSFSR (although evidence specifically for the RSFSR was not provided). Altogether, a decrease in farm output of the kolkhozy in the RSFSR during this period seems to be certain.

State farms proper.—The official index for gross farm production of the state farms (sovkhozy) (1934 equals 1) shows a decline from 1.5 in 1940 to 0.7 in 1945, i.e., by more than 50 per cent.[43] The decline in their output during World War II years was presumably greater than that of farm production as a whole. The course of recovery of

[42] *Stat. Handb.*, *RSFSR*, 1957, pp. 137–38.
[43] *USSR in Figures*, 1958, p. 191. The selection of the base year and the use of "one" as the base—all this is official.

the output of state farms is difficult to ascertain. But if the official index is correct, sovkhoz output moderately exceeded the prewar level in 1950. Contrary to the farm output as a whole, expansion of sovkhoz output continued also beyond 1950, indeed briskly. For 1953 an excess over 1940 of 47 per cent is claimed. Livestock herds seem to have been enlarged, as compared with 1940, more than acreages. As usual, the increase in livestock herds probably occurred to a large extent by acquisition of animals from the private sector.

TABLE 31

STATE FARMS, 1940 AND SELECTED POSTWAR YEARS*

Item	1940	1950	1952	1953
Number (thousand)................	4,159	4,988	4,742	4,857
Gross production (1934 = 100).......	1.5	106	...	2.2
Wage earners (thousand).............	1,373	1,665	1,784	1,844
Occupied in production............	1,186	1,509	1,640	1,708
Sown acreage (million hectares).......	11.6	12.9	14.7	15.2
Grain.........................	7.7	7.5	8.1	7.8
Potatoes and vegetables...........	0.3	0.3	0.3	0.3
Feed..........................	3.3	4.7	6.0	6.6
Livestock at end of year (thousand):				
Cows.........................	952	848	1,018	1,119
Hogs.........................	1,910	2,494	3,119	4,474
Tractors (thousand 15-h.p. units)......	100	130	153	165
Combine grain harvesters (thousand)..	27	33	41	42

* *Economy of the USSR in 1956*, pp. 146–47. The index for gross production from *USSR in Figures*, 1958, p. 191. The figures cover state farms only, i.e., they do not include subsidiary state farming enterprises and institutions.

The average grain yield in state farms was claimed to have been 9.5 quintals per hectare in 1953.[44] This yield, if correct, was moderately higher than the average in the last prewar years.[45] However, the state farms delivered to the state in 1953 exactly as much grain as in 1940 (see *USSR in Figures,* 1958, p. 191) from a moderately larger acreage (9.3 million hectares in 1953 as against 8.6 million hectares in 1940; see *Economy of the USSR in 1956,* p. 146). No evidence seems to have been released on the yields of crops per hectare other than for the one year for grain.

The average yield of milk in the sovkhozy increased from 1,803 kilograms per cow in 1940 to 2,256 kilograms in 1950;[46] but the yield of wool per sheep declined from 2.9 to 2.7 kilograms in those years (*Attainments,* p. 162).

[44] I. Benediktov, *Ways of Reducing Production Costs of Farm Products in Sovkhozy* (Moscow, 1957), p. 8.

[45] See *Soc. Agri.,* pp. 740–42.

[46] There is no certainty that the prewar and postwar figures are comparable.

A very important feature of sovkhoz operations was their high production costs in spite, or perhaps because of, the very low wages.[47] These high production costs make it clear that the enlargement of sovkhoz output in 1950–53 was not caused by any advantages on their part. The reason more probably was that the need for farm products had become so urgent that it was believed imperative to disregard the high production costs of this type of farm.

Also, whatever the reasons for the poor operation of the sovkhozy, the high production costs of the state farms explain why under Stalin the Soviets shunned the idea of converting the kolkhozy into sovkhozy, although otherwise this would have been fully in line with the political philosophy then held.

Marketings

Marketings of farm products naturally went down greatly during World War II. Their low level in 1945 has been discussed at the beginning of the section on output. Data on procurements in that year were not disclosed for most products. The data on marketings in 1945 are also incomplete.

Although marketings and procurements increased considerably from 1945 to 1950 and 1953, the situation remained very unsatisfactory.

For many years, interpretation of the evidence on procurements and state purchases involved the difficulty that the terms in which the official statistical data on the procurements of farm products were expressed were not definitely known. The *Dictionary-Handbook of Social Economic Statistics* (1st ed.; Moscow, 1944, pp. 179–80; 2d ed.; Moscow, 1948, pp. 332–33) obviously by-passed the answer to the question deliberately. Only recently did official sources confirm what this writer had suspected for a long time, namely, that the weight shown in the statistics of procurements has in many cases been the so-called accounting weight (the weight on the basis of which payment is made by the state for the farm products delivered or sold to

---

[47] Possibly in connection with the need of an enlarged sovkhoz output, the high production costs on state farms have become a matter of more or less permanent concern. See for example the speech of N. Khrushchev in *Pravda*, March 21, 1954. See also the article by I. Novikov, "To Reduce Production Costs, To Ensure Profitable Operation of the Sovkhozy," in *Questions of Economics*, 1954, No. 9, pp. 31–39. This author said, *inter alia:* "Production costs are particularly high in the non-blacksoil areas, where they frequently exceed the state retail prices" (*ibid.*, p. 31). The same phenomenon was then specifically emphasized by the author with reference to pork and eggs (*ibid.*, p. 32). Detailed material on the high to fantastic production costs in the sovkhozy is supplied by I. Benediktov, Minister of Agriculture of the RSFSR, in *Ways of Reducing Production Costs of Farm Products in the Sovkhozy, cited above.*

TABLE 32

MARKETINGS AND STATE PROCUREMENTS OF FARM PRODUCTS: SELECTED YEARS*

Product		1937ᵃ	1940ᵇ	1945	1950	1953
Grain (million tons)	M	...	38.3	23.2	...	35.8
	P	31.8	...	...	35.5	31.4
Wheat	M	...	16.2	7.6	...	21.8
Potatoes (million tons)	M	...	12.9	11.8	...	12.1
	P	7.0	8.5	...	6.9	5.4
Vegetables (million tons)	M	...	6.1	4.8	...	5.1
	P	1.5	3.0	...	2.0	2.5
Sunflower seed (million tons)	M	...	1.87	0.62	...	2.07
	P	1.08	1.50	...	1.08	1.80
Seed cotton (million tons)	Mᵉ	2.58	2.24	1.16	3.54	3.85
Flax (thousand tons)	P	275	245	...	174	145
Sugar beets (million tons)	P	21.4	17.4	4.7ᵈ	19.8	22.9
Slaughter animals, live weight (million tons)	M	...	4.2	2.4	...	5.4
	P	1.3	2.0	...	2.1	3.4ᵉ
Milk (million tons)ᶠ	M	...	10.8	5.4	...	13.7
	P	5.0	6.5	...	8.5	10.6
Eggs (billion units)	P	1.44	2.68	...	1.91	2.62
Wool, unwashed (thousand tons)	P	79	120	73	136	197

* M = Marketings; P = Procurements.

Data on marketings from *Attainments*, p. 154. Data on procurements from *Courier of Statistics*, 1957, No. 6, p. 78. (The cynicism of publishing all those data on procurements, but not supplying data on grain, the far most important farm product marketed and even more than that procured by the state.) Data on grain in the table are from *Economic Survey of Europe in 1953*, p. 268, supplemented by data from *Communist*, 1957, No. 10, p. 38. Data on fruits are likewise missing. Data on flax fiber, the crop which suffered most, was suppressed in part. The weight in the procurements is the so-called accounted weight (see text for comments). The same must be true of marketings, so far as these consist of procurements.

The concepts "marketings" and "state procurements" are stretched considerably. The feed needs of the state farms are apparently included in the state procurements. The supplies used by them for their workers are certainly included in marketings. In a similar way, the feeding by the kolkhozy of their workers is considered marketing (see S. V. Sholts, *Agricultural Statistics* [Moscow, 1956] p. 160). It seems, moreover, that the dates of the changes in the stated concepts are not readily ascertainable.

ᵃ Pre-1939 boundaries.

ᵇ Presumably almost exclusively pre-1939 boundaries.

ᶜ Equivalent to procurements.

ᵈ Total marketings.

ᵉ In addition, 172,000 and 203,000 tons (live weight) respectively were obtained by feeding of the delivered animals after the delivery.

ᶠ While data on deliveries of milk to the state naturally include the milk processed as dairy products, the figures for total deliveries to the state and those for total marketings are unlikely to include butter and other dairy products delivered to the state or sold in kolkhoz markets as such.

it).[48] The effect of this substitution may be not insignificant. For example, according to a 1939 order, cattle, sheep, and goats of average quality were counted as a unit in meat deliveries to the state, but fat hogs were equal to 1.25 units (apparently to even more in later years) and poultry to 1.43 units.[49]

[48] *Courier of Statistics*, 1957, No. 6, p. 78, directly specified the data on state procurements and purchases of slaughter animals and wool as given in accounting weight. But other evidence definitely indicates the same for grain and possibly for some other products. Data on procurements in straight (not accounting) weight are certainly available, but are withheld to cause confusion.

[49] *The Most Important Decisions on Agriculture for 1938–46* (Moscow, 1948), p. 614.

Furthermore, one product was delivered to the state instead of another, and it was not always clear whether the stated figure, for example, for the delivered grain included only grain or also other products in terms of grain. There may even have been duplications involved.[50]

While it is certain that procurements were in accounting weight, the question remains unsolved about the weights in which marketings were expressed.

Another difficulty involved in handling statistics of marketings of farm products is that the marketings in the new territories in 1940 are unknown, and it is unknown to what extent they are included in the totals for that year (they possibly are not included at all). It is therefore commendable that the ECE gave in its survey for 1953 the marketings in 1937 along with those of later years.

It is suspected that the products used by the collective farms to feed their workers were classed as marketings.[51] The sovkhozy count all food given or sold to the personnel as marketings.

The catastrophic or near-catastrophic situation in the year of Stalin's death is clearly revealed by the fact that in spite of the greatly increased need for marketed grain, the latter was actually smaller in 1953 than in 1940.

The potatoes procured in 1953 (5.4 million tons) were, of course, a disaster, especially if it is remembered that the state used the procured potatoes in the first place for processing into alcohol, starch, etc. The procurements of vegetables in 1950 and 1953 also were below the 1940 level—for much the greater number of prospective customers.

Procurements of cotton, which in 1953 were more than 50 per cent above those in 1937, were the bright spot. There was also a notable increase in procurements of sugar beets since the prewar years. Procurements of sunflower seed and possibly some other technical crops were higher in 1953 too. The statement that procurements of technical crops displayed a relatively favorable picture does not extend to flax, procurements of which showed a precipitous decline.

The "success" with reference to procurements to be "proud of" was the substantial increase in milk procurements from 1940 to

[50] In the fall of 1956 Khrushchev himself gave the grain deliveries in that year in a figure, which, as it turned out later, included a few million tons of substitutes. The practice of including the substitutes in the statistics of procurements seems to have been discontinued sometime around 1956.

[51] S. V. Sholz, *Agricultural Statistics*, 1956, p. 160.

1950–53, in spite of the decline in total milk output.[52] State procurements of meat are supposed to have grown much more than meat output. The growth in total marketings of meat was also larger than that in output, but here the difference was not large.

While procurements were greatly inadequate to cover even the most urgent needs, the measures taken to increase them went so far as to be per se a handicap to expansion of output and with this, of procurements.

[52] The official estimate indicating an increase in milk output from 33.6 million tons in 1940 to 36.5 million tons in 1953 (*USSR in Figures,* 1958, p. 217) is not accepted here. Nancy Nimitz of the RAND Corporation estimates the 1953 milk output at 27.8 million tons as against 28.2 million tons for 1940. Taking into consideration the enlargement in territory would make the decline even greater.

CHAPTER 15

INDUSTRY; TRANSPORTATION; OUTPUT PER MAN

Industry

Stalin's efforts to industrialize were certainly redeemed by the developments after World War II. For a much longer period than could be observed before, industry was expanding at high rates all during the *Stalin Has Everything His Way* period. In spite of considerable destruction of industrial capacities during World War II and the great complications associated with reconversion from war to peacetime production, the prewar level of industrial output was regained in only three years and far exceeded that level thereafter. The speed of expansion seems almost miraculous until all factors are considered. All Stalin's dictatorial power was needed to start a recovery in industry at high rates, while the population was starving and so many were dying of starvation that deaths greatly exceeded births.

Although total investment of the state, and specifically that in industry, after the war was not nearly as large as claimed, it was immense. The investment was particularly large, relative to total economic power, in the first years after the end of the destructive war. It has been established that the Soviet economy, with its high investment quota and low personal incomes, is geared to rapid expansion rates, if those in power do not embark on such growth-retarding actions as the violent *All-out Drive* of the early 1930's or the *Purge Era* of the late 1930's. The *Stalin Has Everything His Way* period displayed the aforesaid feature of the Soviet economy to the highest degree; moreover, it profited from the *Purge Era*. Utilization of capacities declined considerably during the *Purge Era*, and the expansion in the postwar Stalin period consisted in part in the utilization of capacities dormant in 1940. In comparison with 1940, we should also keep in mind the fact that not only were capacities lost in the West and South during World War II, but considerable capacities were added, especially in the East. In addition to internal resources two important factors contributed much to postwar expansion. Help coming in the form of the payments of the satellites and the work of great numbers of German war prisoners lasted for many years (see the discussion in chapter 10).

It is certainly very significant that, fully in agreement with Stalin's wishes, output of producers' goods (which at the end of World War II was on a level about twice as high in relation to 1940 as the output of consumers' goods) grew at greater rates than the output of consumers' goods from 1946 to 1949. Thereafter, producers' goods maintained their large share in total industrial growth; hence, in view of the large rates of growth of the whole of industry, the output of producers' goods made more than satisfactory progress. The output of strictly producers' goods—i.e., excluding armaments, in statistics usually included in this category—grew even more rapidly from 1946 on. Output of consumers' goods rose by the same, or almost the same, satisfactory rates, beginning with 1948, as producers' goods, including armaments. But the fact that output of consumers' goods was immensely small in the initial year, say, 1948, explains that, in spite of the great rates of growth, this output was still miserably small in the last Stalin days.

The period 1946–50, or, for that matter, 1946–51, was one of recovery. It was almost completely devoted to the restoration and further expansion of what had already existed before the war. New developments did not receive any attention, and in any case they were postponed to better times. The development of the petroleum industry in eastern European Russia, forced by the decline of Baku,[1] seems to have been the only major exception.

Total.—Let us remind the reader first that through 1950 the official index of industrial production still was in terms of the so-called unchangeable 1926/27 prices; but during its remaining life this index operated not in its customary way of just exaggerating the facts.

According to the official index, industrial output in 1945 was only 8 per cent smaller than in 1940 and growth in output from 1945 to 1950 amounted to 89 per cent. In truth, the 1945 output was much lower in relation to 1940, the official index for 1950 (1940 equals

---

[1] Baku (Azerbaidzhan republic) is the center of the South Caucasian petroleum industry.

100) was also exaggerated but probably less than the 1945 index, and therefore the growth in industrial output in 1945–50 seems to have been even larger than officially calculated.[2]

This writer's previous estimate of gross industrial output in 1945 at 70 per cent of that in 1940[3] was raised—on not too much evidence —to 75 per cent in an unpublished study. Warren Nutter of the National Bureau of Economic Research (NBER) has for 1945 in terms of 1940 an index of only 57.8 (1928 weights) or 46.8 (1955 weights).[4] But the index does not include armaments, the output of which presumably was much larger in 1945 than in 1940, especially in relation to total output. Hence, the non-consideration of armament production tended to minimize 1945 output in relation to that of 1940 in Dr. Nutter's index.

In comparing this writer's index with the official index, it needs to be considered that the output in 1940, on which the official index was based, did not probably cover the entire present territory. The same may be true of the NBER index.

It may be best to stick to the original estimate of 1945 industrial production at 70 per cent of that in 1940 (postwar boundaries for both years) until something more exact has been calculated.

The 1950 industrial output exceeded that of 1940 by 73 per cent, according to official estimates; the same output was estimated at 135 per cent of that in 1940 (postwar boundaries also for 1940) by this writer. Both calculations of the NBER yield an index of 151 (1940 equals 100), while Shimkin *et al.* have one of 148 for this year. The calculations of both the NBER and Shimkin may possibly not cover the 1940 territory fully. In this case their indices indicate greater growth than that which actually occurred. The NBER 1950 index is certainly exaggerated by the disregarding of armaments. This writer's 1950 index (1940 equals 100) may still need an upward correction to 140 or possibly somewhat more.

The estimates of the industrial production of 1945 and 1950, suggested here, imply an increase during the five-year period of possibly

[2] This is a disadvantage of statistical exaggeration. It proves impossible to exaggerate more and more. When, for once, there is a letdown in exaggeration, the situation is presented in a worse, or less favorable, light than it actually deserves.

The Soviet statisticians know well that their indices of industrial production for the period 1945–50 are not in line with their indices for some other periods. The statistical handbook *Economy of the USSR in 1956*, for example, gives for industrial production a series of indices based on 1913, 1928, 1940, and 1950 (pp. 51–53), but there is no series based on 1945, although the development in postwar years was certainly satisfactory and is of great interest. Rather, the growth from 1940 to postwar years is stressed.

[3] *Essay I*, p. 22.

[4] Dr. Warren Nutter's paper was presented to the meeting of the American Economic Association in December of 1957.

100 per cent.[5] This is, however, not the whole story. During 1946, reconversion to something closer to a peacetime economy took place. According to the official index, there was a decline in industrial output of as much as 16 per cent in this year. Here the decline will be assumed to have been equal to 9 per cent.[6]

The greater reduction given in the official index for 1946 as compared with the index calculated here fully eliminates the discrepancy between the rates of growth shown by the official index and that of this writer for the period 1945–50. Both calculations have the immense growth in industrial output of 126 per cent (official) or 127 per cent (this writer) in only four years, 1947 through 1950.

The rates of growth in industrial output in 1945–50 were approximately as follows (in per cent):

YEAR	OFFICIAL		HERE SUGGESTED	
	Year-to-year	Cumulative (1940 = 100)	Year-to-year	Cumulative (1940 = 100)
1945............	92	92	...	70
1946............	−16	77	−9	64
1947............	22	93	18	76
1948............	26	118	26	96
1949............	20	141	23[a]	117
1950............	23	173	20[a]	140

[a] The rise in the two years 1949 and 1950 as here suggested is equal to practically 49 per cent, the percentage calculated by Shimkin *et al.*

[5] As was stated, the increase was equal to 89 per cent according to official calculations (*Industry of the USSR*, 1957, p. 32). The NBER has the following increase in industrial output for the period 1945–50 (in per cent):

1928 weights.................... 161
1955 weights.................... 222

[6] While total industrial production allegedly went down by 16 per cent, civilian industrial production is supposed to have increased by 20 per cent (see Report on the Fulfilment of the 1946 Plan). If the 1945 civilian industrial production is estimated at half the total (the raw materials going into armaments must have been treated as civilian production), the following composition of 1945 and 1946 industrial production of military and civilian goods in per cent of total 1945 industrial production is obtained:

	1945	1946
Military..............	50	24
Civilian..............	50	60
Total............	100	[84

If it is assumed, furthermore, that military goods were overpriced (at "unchangeable 1926/27 prices," not current prices) in relation to civilian goods by 50 per cent in 1945, the tabulation above becomes (in per cent of total 1945 production as officially estimated):

	1945	1946
Military..............	33.3	16
Civilian..............	50.0	60
Total............	83.3	76

Thus the calculated declines are: official, 16 per cent; corrected, 9 per cent. No claims of exactness are made, of course; but the calculation gives, it is hoped, an idea of what went on in reality, and in statistics.

As the tabulation shows, a full stride in industrial expansion could have been made in 1947, although in some other respects the poor 1946 crop kept the growth in 1947 down. Such a large rate of growth as 18 per cent in 1947 in the face of starvation was certainly a great "achievement."

The high rates of industrial growth in 1948, 1949, and 1950 of 26, 23, and 20 per cent, respectively, suggested here are in line with the large increases in fixed investment of the state in those years (22, 22, and 20 per cent, respectively),[7] keeping especially in mind that a very large part of the investment went into repairing war damages rather than the much more expensive new constructions.

The growth in industrial output in 1940–50 turns out to have been not much smaller than that in 1950–55, according to the calculation of Shimkin *et al.,* and the NBER (the latter in 1928 weights). The calculation of the NBER in 1955 weights indicates an even smaller growth in 1950–55 than in 1940–50. We have indeed the following increases (in per cent):

Source	1940–50	1950–55
Official.	73	85
Shimkin *et al.*	48	65
NBER:		
1948 weights	51	64
1955 weights	51	47
N.J.	40	65
N. M. Kaplan and R. H. Moorsteen[a]	40	58

[a] This was added just before going to press. The index ("An Index of Soviet Industrial Production") appeared in the June, 1960, issue of the *American Economic Review*, pp. 295–318. It was made with 1950 data used as weights. Munitions and several other important industries were not covered. This needs to be considered when comparing the new index with most of the older ones.

Even more striking is the fact, if it is a fact, that, according to Shimkin *et al.,* output of machinery and equipment, which is supposed to include "military end-items," increased by 113 per cent in 1940–50, but only by 72 per cent in 1950–55.[8]

This writer is unable to check either the calculations of Shimkin *et al.,* or those of the NBER for both 1940–50 and 1950–55, but whatever errors may be involved in them[9] are unlikely to eliminate

[7] Official data; implied in *Economy of the USSR in 1956*, p. 173.

[8] Steel output grew by 49 per cent in 1940–50 and by 66 per cent in 1950–55, i.e., the relation was the reverse of that in output of machinery and equipment as calculated by Shimkin *et al.*

It is a pity that work on the Soviet industrial index by the Shimkin group was terminated before it was really completed. This writer may be wrong, but this index seems to him the best among the projects undertaken by the agency involved (Foreign Manpower Division of the U.S. Bureau of the Census). More work would be needed to make it really good.

[9] The NBER index is certainly unrepresentative to a large extent; but Shimkin's index for the growth in machinery production in 1940–50 also needs to be looked into carefully.

the fact that while this writer never was too low in estimating the growth in industrial output in 1950–55, he definitely tended to underestimate the growth in 1940–50. It seemed to him that the five years from 1950 to 1955 were practically all very favorable for economic growth (the moderate slowdown in the year of Stalin's death could be disregarded).[10] On the other hand, almost eight of the ten years from 1940 to 1950 were taken up by World War II and the recovery from it.[11] Hence, the conclusion seemed reasonable that the growth in industrial output in 1940–50 could not have been very large and specifically that it must have been much smaller than in 1950–55. It took quite some time to realize that a considerably greater expansion of industry could have been attained in 1940–50 than seemed possible at first.

The principal factor in the rapid recovery of industry and its further growth after World War II was, of course, the concentration of all efforts on this one item to the practical exclusion of everything else; but this was the case to almost the same extent in 1950–55. The substantial payments of the satellite countries helped considerably. These payments tended to be larger in earlier than in later years; and, moreover, owing to the relative smallness of the Soviet Union's own investment funds in the earlier years, every ruble was the more important the nearer the respective year was to the end of World War II. During the last years of the 1950–55 period, on the other hand, Soviet industry had to get along without any help from the satellites.

There were important additional reasons why industrial production in the postwar years made a particularly good showing as compared with that in 1940. The conditions in 1940 were abnormal, and this fact should be given adequate consideration in appraising the industrial growth of 1940–50. The year of 1940 was one in which industrial potential was not fully utilized owing to the specific conditions of the *Purge Era.* In chapter 10, the evidence of Malenkov was cited according to which the productive capacity for cement was increased by 22 per cent from 1936 to 1940, and, in spite of this, the output of cement declined by a few percentage points in the same years. The evidence released near the end of 1957 threw much more light on this phenomenon. The steel capacity put in operation in

---

[10] To be very exact, the slowing-down effect of the military preparations in connection with the Korean War in 1951 and 1952 would need consideration.

[11] The USSR was not yet in the war in the first half of 1941, and it may seem that this half-year needs to be added to the years 1949 and 1950 considered in calculating the growth in 1940–50. But everything done during the first half-year of 1941 had no permanent value, having been spent for preparations to enter World War II.

three and a half years of the third FYP period was stated as having amounted to 3.5 million tons,[12] but the output of steel only increased by 0.6 million tons in 1937–40. The same was to a greater or lesser extent also the case with many other heavy-industry products. A substantial decline in the utilization of capacities during the *Purge Era* must indeed be accepted for industry as a whole.

The developments during World War II must also be considered among the factors which affected the industrial growth in 1940–50. Data in *Economy of the USSR in 1956* (pp. 172–73) show almost as large a fixed investment of the state at constant prices in the second half of 1941 through 1945 as in the three and a half years of the third FYP (134.8 billion as against 138.7 billion rubles). According to *Attainments* (p. 212), the capacity of plants put into operation for iron metallurgy and some other important industries was even much larger during World War II than in the preceding three and a half years. Most of the new capacities were in the East. Yet, while the loss of capacities in the western portion of the USSR, which needed restoration after World War II, has been emphasized, the increase in capacities in the eastern portion of the country has been neglected in appraising the industrial growth in 1940–50.[13]

The capacities which were idle at the end of the *Purge Era* and the new capacities put in operation during the war years must be added to the actual 1940 industrial output to get the *normal* output which should be used in measuring the attainment during the fourth FYP period in terms of 1940. The 1948 industrial output, which was almost equal to that of 1940, was substantially below this norm, and the 1950 output may have exceeded this level only moderately.

Incidentally, if 1948 had been the year when the previous normal production level was restored, a great slowdown in the rate of industrial growth would probably already have occurred in this year, and, in any case, in 1949. But with the previous *normal* level not having been restored until much later, the year 1948, the first year without acute starvation, rather than showing a slowdown turned out to be the year with the greatest rate of growth in the recovery period after World War II.

Industrial growth continued at great rates for two to three years after 1948 as well. According to Shimkin *et al.*, the rise was equal to 71 per cent in 1949 through 1951. Their calculations imply that

[12] *Attainments*, p. 212.

[13] The statements in the text do not imply that the official estimates of fixed investment of the state during the war years are accepted here as entirely correct. The respective estimates, indeed, seem improbably high. But the fact remains that substantial constructions took place in the eastern territories during World War II.

industrial output was more than doubled in the four years 1948 through 1951.

The year of 1952 was the first to show no recovery features in industry whatsoever. The sharp decline in the rate of growth of industrial output in this year was in line with the large reduction of the rate of growth of investment in 1951 (allowing for a certain lag between them). The decline in the rate of growth in 1952 must, however, also have had something to do with the great enlargement of the military budget in 1952, although it is not clear in what manner this occurred. Armaments, after all, are industrial goods.

Officially, the rate of industrial growth went down from 16 per cent in 1951 to 12 per cent in 1952. Shimkin *et al.* even have a decline from 16 per cent to 7 per cent, but this seems to be excessive.*

Consumers' and producers' goods.—Small as the output of consumers' goods was in 1940, by the end of the war in 1945 it went down to little more than two-fifths of the 1940 level.[14] In that year, output of consumers' goods was indeed little more than 70 per cent of the level of 1932, a year of great starvation and, moreover, a year with an urban population smaller than that of 1945. The responsibility of Stalin and his entourage for the deprivations of World War II may be a matter of dispute. But it was he who set, in the midst of starvation (in February of 1946 to be exact), a long-range target for steel output (60 million tons to be reached in three five-year periods) without even mentioning the need for bread (see "Planning" in chapter 10).

The relation between the output of consumers' and producers' goods necessarily improved in favor of the former in 1946, when the output of consumers' goods increased while the output of producers' goods declined. But the index of output of producers' goods (1940 equals 100) was still about 50 per cent higher than the index of consumers' goods in that year, and yet Stalin continued to order "producers' goods first." Consumers' goods never regained a substantial part of the loss in the share of industrial output they sustained during World War II. A certain improvement occurred from 1948 to 1950 (from 26.0 per cent of the total industrial output in 1948 to 27.1 per cent in 1950, according to Shimkin *et al.*), but half of this increase was lost in the next two years. In 1950, the

---

* Kaplan and Moorsteen, cited earlier, likewise have an increase of only 6.6 per cent in 1952, but the omission of armaments in their index must have had a particularly strong effect in this year.

[14] NBER calculation.

output of consumers' goods was barely at the prewar level.* This estimate, in conjunction with the assumption that total industrial output increased by 40 per cent in 1940–50, indicates a growth in output of producers' goods of about 60 per cent in those years— quite a gain in relation to the status of consumers' goods.

Individual commodities.—The data for 1945 in Table 33 and, even more, the data for this year in *Industry of the USSR*, 1957 (pp. 40–44), permit an interesting study of industry practically 100 per cent concentrated on the war effort. Space necessitates limiting the analysis to a few remarks. Not only was the output of such items as phonographs, cameras, and bicycles eliminated, but the output of farm and road-building machinery and also, for example, that of artificial fiber was discontinued. The output of such indispensable things as socks and stockings was reduced to less than 20 per cent. The output of trucks, badly needed for the war effort, was in 1945 less than half of the very small 1940 output. Of the long list of individual products for which data are given in *Industry of the USSR*, 1957, only one (a type of lathe) showed a moderate increase in output as compared with 1940. The output of many kinds of armaments was, of course, enlarged from 1940 to 1945; but armaments appear in Soviet statistics only in totals for producers' goods and, moreover, only in totals for these goods in value terms.

The growth in output of individual commodities during the five years from 1945 to 1950 must be skipped. Let us analyze the extent to which the 1950 level compares with that of 1940 (see Table 33).

The difference between individual producers' and consumers' goods with reference to the change in output from 1940 to 1950 is conspicuous. Practically all producers' goods made highly satisfactory progress. Steel output, with an increase of 49 per cent from 1940 to 1950, left little to be desired, if the great destruction in the Donbass (the Soviet's principal metallurgic center) during World War II is considered. Cement production showed an enormous rise over 1940 (78 per cent). A great transformation indeed occurred with reference to the supplies of cement. Previously the Soviets had been unable to increase cement output even nearly as much as was urgently needed. The difficulties seem to have been more or less overcome after World War II.[15] While complaints of inadequate output of cement were still heard, cement was used on a much wider scale than prior to World War II.

---

* Kaplan-Moorsteen (*op. cit.*) have an increase of less than 2 per cent.

[15] There are indications that foreign technicians were used on a large scale to help in expanding the cement industry.

TABLE 33

INDUSTRIAL PRODUCTION, 1928, 1932, 1937, 1940, AND 1945–53*

	1928	1932	1937	1940	1945	1946	1947	1948	1949	1950	1951	1952	1953
Producers' Goods													
Coal (million tons)	35.5	64.4	128.0	165.9	149.3	164.0	183.2	208.2	235.5	261.1	281.9	300.9	320.4
Petroleum (million tons)	11.6	21.4	28.5	31.1	19.4	21.7	26.0	29.2	33.4	37.9	42.3	47.3	52.8
Gas (billion cubic meters)	0.3	1.1	2.3	3.4	3.3	...	...	...	...	6.2	...	...	...
Electric power (billion kw-h.)	5.0	13.5	36.2	48.3	43.3	48.6	56.5	66.3	78.3	91.2	104.0	119.1	134.3
Steel (million tons)	4.3	5.9	17.7	18.3	12.3	13.3	14.5	18.6	23.3	27.3	31.4	34.5	38.1
Sulfuric acid (million tons)	0.2	0.6	1.4	1.6	0.8	0.7	1.0	1.5	1.8	2.1	2.4	2.7	2.9
Soda ash (million tons)	0.2	0.3	0.5	0.5	0.2	0.3	0.3	0.5	0.6	0.7	0.8	1.0	1.2
Commercial fertilizer[a] (million tons)	0.1	0.9	3.2	3.2	1.1	1.7	2.4	3.5	4.6	5.5	5.9	6.4	7.0
Automobile casings[b] (million units)	0.1	0.6	2.7	3.0	1.4	2.0	2.9	4.1	5.7	7.4	7.5	7.6	8.1
Metal cutting machines (thousand units)	2.0	19.7	48.5	58.4	38.4	40.3	50.4	64.5	64.7	70.6	71.2	74.6	91.8
Metal working machinery (thousand tons)	...	6.9	18.4	23.7	26.9	...	...	...	...	111.2	109.7	123.5	145.7
Turbines steam and gas (thousand kw.)	35.7	239	1,068	972	189	...	...	...	...	2,381	2,663	2,873	4,036
Turbines hydraulic (thousand kw.)	8.4	59.5	88.3	207.7	40.6	102.2	133.0	197.1	276.0	314.9	478.2	571.5	718.9
Trucks and cars (thousand units)	0.8	23.9	199.9	145.4	74.7	...	...	...	...	362.9	288.7	307.9	354.2
Tractors (in thousand 15-h.p. units)	1.8	50.8	66.5	66.2	14.7	28.4	65.0	132.6	193.8	240.9	204.3	216.2	242.6
Industrial timber, shipments (million cubic meters)	36.0	99.4	114.2	117.9	61.6	80.3	99.0	132.4	151.3	161.0	184.5	184.6	179.9
Sawn lumber (million cubic meters)	13.6	24.4	33.8	34.8	14.7	19.6	24.2	32.7	42.8	49.5	56.0	60.5	66.4
Paper (thousand tons)	284.5	471.2	831.6	812.4	321.1	516.7	647.5	778.6	995.4	1,193.3	1,341.7	1,461.2	1,611.6
Cement (million tons)	1.8	3.5	5.5	5.2	1.8	3.4	4.7	6.5	8.1	10.2	12.1	13.9	16.0
Bricks[b] (billion units)	2.8	4.9	8.7	7.5	2.0	3.2	4.1	6.1	8.1	10.2	12.8	14.9	16.8
Soft roofing (million square meters)	19.2	66.0	161.4	127.1	71.2	125.8	166.3	199.7	237.7	285.5	316.9	360.0	405.4
Window glass (million square meters)	34.2	29.5	79.3	44.7	23.3	39.9	47.8	59.0	71.5	76.9	67.7	62.0	76.0
Consumers' Goods													
Cotton fabrics (million meters)	2,678	2,694	3,448	3,954	1,617	1,901	2,541	3,150	3,601	3,899	4,768	5,044	5,285
"Silken" fabrics[c] (million meters)	9.6	21.5	58.9	76.6	36.4	48.7	65.4	81.7	105.0	129.7	174.3	224.6	400.4
Artificial fiber (thousand tons)	0.2	2.8	8.6	11.1	1.1	...	...	...	...	24.2	...	...	...
Footwear "leather"[d] (million pairs)	58.0	86.9	182.9	211.0	63.1	81.2	112.8	134.0	163.6	203.4	239.4	237.7	239.4
Flour[e] (million tons)	24	...	28	29	15	...	...	...	...	22	...	...	...
Meat[f] (thousand tons)	678	596	1,002	1,501	663	793	815	1,016	1,149	1,556	1,715	1,965	2,212
Fish, catch (thousand tons)	840	1,333	1,609	1,404	1,125	1,208	1,534	1,575	1,953	1,755	2,142	2,107	2,195
Butter (thousand tons)	82	72	185	226	117	186	218	292	317	336	355	371	382
Vegetable oil (thousand tons)	448	490	539	798	292	326	403	549	722	819	919	999	1,160
Canned goods[g] (million cans)	125	692	982	1,113	558	583	669	868	1,162	1,535	1,848	2,064	2,358
Sugar, crystal (thousand tons)	1,283	828	2,421	2,165	465	466	981	1,666	2,042	2,523	2,979	3,067	3,434
Vodka and other hard liquor (million dekaliters)	55.5	72.0	89.5	92.5	44.3	...	...	...	...	62.8	...	...	...
Beer (million dekaliters)	39.1	42.1	89.6	121.3	40.5	...	...	...	...	130.8	...	...	...
Cigarettes (billion units)	49.5	57.9	89.2	100.4	25.0	...	...	...	...	125.1	...	...	...
Makhorka (million cases)	3.2	3.3	5.3	4.6	0.7	...	...	...	...	3.8	...	...	...
Soap[h] (thousand tons)	311	357	495	700	229	...	...	...	...	816	...	...	...

* Industry of the USSR, 1957, passim.
a Bulk rather than plant food.
b Includes other wall material in terms of bricks.
c Except for 1928, almost exclusively from artificial fiber.
d Includes fabric and combination footwear.
e Includes meal used for feed. Only that meal was counted which was produced by mills not engaged exclusively in grinding to feed.
f Since 1956, the statistics of meat production include edible offal as well as meat of animals other than cattle, hogs, sheep, goats, and poultry. In the process of revision, the old official estimates for the previous years were raised and the data for the various years may well be comparable.
g In 400-gram cans; includes other canned goods recalculated to 400-gram cans.
h In terms of soap with 40 per cent fat content.

Both official and private estimates show an enormous machinery output in 1950 relative to that of 1940. The 1950 figures (1940 equals 100) are as follows:

```
Official:
    Machinery........................................  234
    Machinery including other metal processing...........  215
Shimkin et al.........................................  211
NBER:
    1928 weights......................................  285
    1955 weights......................................  239
```

The official data for machinery output seem in agreement with the likewise official evidence on the utilization of equipment in fixed investment of the state. From about 7.5 billion rubles in 1940, fixed investment in equipment is supposed to have grown to 30.9 billion rubles in 1950 (at prices of July 1, 1955).[16] But both the data on machinery output and those on fixed investment in equipment are in drastic contradiction to the data on steel output, which was enlarged by only 49 per cent during the same period.

Another factor which makes one hesitate to accept the official and unofficial estimates for the growth of machinery production in 1940–50 is labor productivity, the index for which is tied in with the index for output. The official index for machinery output, in conjunction with the official figures for the number of workers in this industry, indicates a growth in labor productivity in this industry of not less than 69 per cent in 1940–50[17]—an impossibly high figure for a period which was in large part characterized by war conditions and starvation or near-starvation. A substantial cut in the officially calculated rate of growth in labor productivity of the machinery industry to reasonable proportions would lead to a corresponding reduction of the calculated rate of machinery-output growth and of the likewise official calculation of the rate of growth of industrial production as a whole.

An analysis of the official data on machinery output in 1950–55 (it is undertaken in my volume on the post-Stalin economy, not yet completed), leads to the conclusion that the growth in the output of machinery in this period was exaggerated to a substantial extent. The same factors which brought about this exaggeration may also have operated prior to this period—with even much greater force— although the weights officially used in calculating the index had been changed.

The indices of the NBER for machinery output in 1950 in terms

[16] *Economy of the USSR in 1956*, pp. 173, 174.
[17] *Industry of the USSR*, 1957, p. 27.

of 1940 must greatly exaggerate the rate of growth in it because the share of armaments in total industrial production, which undoubtedly was much larger in 1940 than 1950, is not considered. While Shimkin *et al.* tried to adjust their index for the output of armaments, a really reliable procedure for such an adjustment was hardly developed. Shimkin *et al.* estimated that the output of "military end-items" declined by 22 per cent in 1940–50, while according to them the output of producers' goods and military components was enlarged by 217 per cent. The latter figure may well be much too high.

Contrary to the machinery output, the official data showing a large growth in output of building materials during 1940–50 and 1945–50, discussed in chapter 12, do not raise any doubts.

The very small output of industrial consumers' goods in 1945 and 1950 is treated in chapter 16. Such figures as an output of lump sugar in 1945 equal to little more than one-half pound per capita (4.7 per cent of the 1938 output) make one shudder.

Statistics of output by the meat industry of the Baltic States show how "beneficial" annexation was to the welfare of the populations of these republics. The data below are in thousands of tons:[18]

Republic	1940	1950
Latvia	35.5	13.7
Lithuania	37.1	15.9
Estonia	11.0	8.8

The eastward and other shifts.—The eastward shift in industry was already in progress prior to World War II, indeed prior to the Revolution; but this development was far from pronounced either before or after the Revolution. It was, of course, much easier to expand industrial output in areas where industry had been established for a long time than to start it anew somewhere else; and expansion by any means and wherever possible was the guiding principle of the Great Industrialization Drive. Occupation by the enemy of large territories in the West and South and the accompanying destruction of capacities during World War II speeded up the eastward move considerably. Almost exclusively, goods which were indispensable to the war effort were involved in the move, though. Also, so far as the eastward shift occurred at all, it was largely con-

[18] *Ibid.*, p. 379. The source in general gives the indices for industrial production by region after 1950 in terms of 1940; but for the Baltic States (see *ibid.*, pp. 85, 89, 99) they are in terms of 1950. Advantage is thus taken of the very great declines in 1940–50.

fined to the eastern part of European Russia (the Volga region and the Urals) and western Siberia. The rest of Asiatic Russia remained practically untouched.

It is odd that in 447 pages the volume *Industry of the USSR*, 1957, does not provide a summarized table on the regional distribution of industrial output. The table on page 24 (bottom) of this source gives (in per cent) the distribution of the manual workers in industry by republics in 1950 and 1955 (only these two years); but employment is not output, and, moreover, the data for the RSFSR are in single figures in the table (70.5 and 68.9 per cent of the totals in 1950 and 1955, respectively), and, hence, little enlightenment on the eastern shift is obtained.[19]

In 1950, when total industrial output was larger than in 1940 by 73 per cent (official calculations at "unchangeable 1926/27 prices"), the addition to the output was equal to 163 per cent in the Volga area, 192 per cent in the Urals, and 214 per cent in western Siberia (in all cases as compared with the respective 1940 outputs and calculated at "unchangeable 1926/27 prices"). The South (the Ukraine and Moldavia), on the other hand, could boast an increase of only 16 per cent from 1940 to 1950, according to the official index.[20] The subsequent industrial expansion in 1950–55 was, however, no larger in the East as a whole than in the country as a whole. It is noteworthy that, while the industrial output of the Volga region was enlarged by 99 per cent in 1950–55, the outputs of the Urals and western Siberia showed increases of 77 and 79 per cent, respectively (official indices).

The most interesting feature of the eastern shift was the development of eastern steel production in competition with that of the Donbass in the Ukraine. The Donbass has the disadvantage of the high cost of coking coal at the mine. A certain compensation for this is the nearness of the excellent iron ore in Krivoi Rog, located somewhat to the west of the Donets Basin. Still, the Donbass never was a cheap producer of steel. In the eastern USSR there is good coking coal in the Kuzbass (Kemerovo oblast, western Siberia), which is much cheaper to produce than that of the Donbass. Until a short time ago, the East was believed to have been also amply provided with excellent iron ore in the Urals; but the distance between the

[19] To obtain regional data one has to turn to the statistical handbooks for the individual republics and oblasti, many of which were released recently (apparently all of them published in 1957). The indices for the regions of the RSFSR quoted in subsequent pages are from *Stat. Handb., RSFSR*, 1957, *passim*.

[20] *Industry of the USSR*, 1957, pp. 51–52.

Kuzbass and the Urals (1,400 miles) always was a serious disadvantage.[21]

Overcoming the great distance between the Urals and the Kuzbass by constructing metallurgical plants at both ends of a special super trunk line and thus insuring particularly low transportation costs, especially in view of the possibility of avoiding transporting empty cars (the so-called Urals-Kuzbass Combine), seemed intriguing. The idea dates back to the eighteenth century. In spite of the great economies in railway transportation as such since that time, the arrangement has not worked fully satisfactorily, and strenuous efforts have been made to base the Urals metallurgical industry (to a large extent) on its own coal and the Kuzbass metallurgy on the iron ore of nearby territories.[22]

While progress was made in the development of metallurgy in the eastern USSR, the Donbass retained the dominant role in the production of pig iron until the outbreak of World War II, when it produced almost exactly two-thirds of the total output of the nation's pig iron (see Table 34).

Of the less than one-third of the output—the share of the Urals-Kuzbass Combine in 1940—the Urals (western end) produced about two-thirds. The share of the eastern end of the Combine was equal only to 10 per cent of the total Soviet output of pig iron in that year.

World War II naturally shattered Soviet steel output. The Ukrainian output of pig iron was in 1945 merely one-sixth of that in 1940 and only a small part of this decline could have been offset by enlarged production in the East. Whatever increase the Urals-Kuzbass Combine contributed was limited to the Urals (western end). The output of pig iron of western Siberia grew by less than 10 per cent.

By 1950 the Ukraine had almost restored its 1940 output of pig

[21] The supply of iron ore with a high content of iron in the Urals seems largely exhausted, and even the ore with a medium content of iron has become much less plentiful. The plan is to substitute for it, to a large extent, the ore of adjacent Kustanai oblast in Kazakhstan. For that matter, the supply of ore with a very high content of iron has become much less plentiful in the Krivoi Rog (Donbass) too. But all these developments concerning iron ore lie beyond the period covered in this volume.

[22] For details see Gardner Clark, *The Economics of Soviet Steel* (Cambridge, Mass.: Harvard University Press, 1956) and Franklin D. Holzman, "Soviet Ural-Kuznetsk Combine; A Study in Investment Criteria and Industrialization Policies," *Quarterly Journal of Economics*, August, 1957, pp. 368–405. Kuznetsk is the center of the Kuzbass. Gardner Clark's book is relied on heavily by analysts of iron metallurgy. A valuable supplement to it is *Steel in the Soviet Union: A Report of the American Steel and Iron Ore Delegation's Visit to the Soviet Union in May and June 1958* (New York, 1959), but the present volume had been completed before the appearance of the report. Gardner Clark was one of the members of the delegation.

TABLE 34

OUTPUT OF PIG IRON BY REGION*
(In millions of tons)

Area	1913[a]	1928	1940	1945	1950	1955
USSR...................	4.2	3.3	14.9	8.8	19.2	33.3
RSFSR..................	1.3	0.9	5.3	7.2	10.0	16.3
Urals..................	0.9	0.7	2.7	5.1	7.2	11.9
Western Siberia.........	0.0	0.1	1.5	1.6	1.9	2.4
Ukraine................	2.9	2.4	9.6	1.6	9.2	16.6

* *Industry of the USSR*, 1957, p. 112.
[a] Post–World War II boundaries.

iron, and in subsequent years this expanded about as much as the total output. The not too rapid expansion in the output of the Urals-Kuzbass Combine in 1945–50 was again largely limited to the western end. The share of the Kuzbass in total output of pig iron remained unchanged at the 1940 level.

In 1950–55, the rate of growth in output of pig iron in the Urals lagged behind the growth in total output. The growth in the Kuzbass was even slower. In 1955, output of the latter was only 7 per cent of the total pig-iron production of the USSR, as against 10 per cent in 1940.

All other attempts to break the dominant role of the Donbass in steel output either gave almost negligible results or were absurd. Eastern Siberia, including the Far East and Central Asia, produced only about 1.5 per cent, and about 1 per cent, respectively, of total Soviet steel in 1955.[23] The two metallurgical plants in Georgia, the South Caucasus, and the North (Cherepovets) brought into existence in postwar years (the Cherepovets plant has been only partly completed thus far) are vivid demonstrations of the wastefulness of which there is quite a little in the Soviet planned economy. The plants are reported to have production costs 60 and 100 per cent, respectively, above the average costs in the country.[24]

Another shift which may be more important than the eastward shift of steel was the move of crude petroleum from Azerbaidzhan, at the periphery of the country in the South Caucasus, to the eastern part of European Russia, closer to the heart of the country (Table 35). There were no handicaps in this move similar to those caused by the great distance between Urals ore and Kuzbass coal. The new

[23] The Asiatic territories to the east and south of western Siberia produced 620,500 tons and 445,100 tons of steel, respectively, in 1955.

[24] Georgia and the Northeast produced 581,800 and 877,500 tons of steel, respectively, in 1955.

TABLE 35

OUTPUT OF CRUDE PETROLEUM BY REGION*

AREA	1913		1940		1955	
	Millions of Tons	Per Cent of Total	Millions of Tons	Per Cent of Total	Millions of Tons	Per Cent of Total
USSR....................	10.28	100.0	31.12	100.0	70.79	100.0
RSFSR...................	1.29	12.6	7.04	22.6	49.26	69.6
North..................	...	...	0.07	0.2	0.55	0.8
Center.................	...	...	...	...	0.73	1.0
Volga..................	...	...	0.22	0.7	24.12	34.1
North Caucasus..........	1.29	12.6	4.62	14.9	6.54	9.3
Urals..................	...	...	1.63	5.2	16.37	23.1
Far East...............	...	...	0.50	1.6	0.95	1.3
Ukraine.................	1.05	10.2	0.35	1.1	0.53	0.7
Uzbek..................	0.01	0.1	0.12	0.4	1.00	1.4
Kazakh.................	0.12	1.1	0.70	2.2	1.40	2.0
Georgia................	...	...	0.04	0.1	0.04	0.1
Azerbaidzhan............	7.67	74.6	22.23	71.5	15.30	21.6
Turkmen................	0.13	1.3	0.59	1.9	3.13	4.4

* *Questions of Economics*, 1957, No. 10, p. 75.

petroleum areas have a great advantage in production costs (also specifically in the amount of needed investment) and are also located closer to the consumer areas than Baku, the old center of petroleum production. The late, but meteoric, development of the new petroleum areas is simply a testimonial to the backwardness of tsarist and Bolshevik Russia in the development of its natural resources. As Table 35 shows, in 1913 the Volga region and the Urals did not produce enough petroleum to be included. As late as 1940, their output amounted to less than 2 million tons and not quite 6 per cent of the total. From 1940 to 1955, however, the output of this area was increased about twenty-two fold. In 1955, it produced 40.5 million tons and accounted for almost 60 per cent of the total Soviet production of crude petroleum.

The famous Baku, on the Caspian Sea in the South Caucasus, which was *the* source of Russian petroleum in tsarist and early Bolshevist times, became a distant second with 21.6 per cent of total petroleum production in 1955.[25] Great efforts to restore the output of Baku yielded only inadequate results. Much smaller investments in the Volga area, on the other hand, resulted in a meteoric rise of output.

[25] The petroleum output of Azerbaidzhan, which had never been occupied by the enemy, declined by almost one-half during World War II (from 22.2 million tons in 1940 to 11.5 million tons in 1945; see *Industry of the USSR*, 1957, p. 155). A great deal of negligence, indeed possibly even sabotage, must have been involved.

The development of the petroleum areas east of the Volga was, however, for quite a while only an inadequate substitute for Baku petroleum. Total output of crude petroleum expanded in 1940–50 considerably less (22 per cent) than the total output of fuel (43 per cent). The deadening lack of initiative was revealed even more clearly by the fact that the output of gas, also largely concentrated east of the Volga (of which now Mr. Khrushchev sings and for which a fivefold rise in output is scheduled for 1958–65), was enlarged only by 10 per cent (likewise much less than the growth in total fuel production) in 1951 and 1952, the last two Stalin years. The share of coal, much more expensive to produce than the petroleum of eastern European Russia and even more expensive than gas, in total output of fuel even increased from 59.1 per cent in 1940 to 66.0 per cent in 1950 and 66.1 per cent in 1952.[26]

Where special conditions were not present, the old established industrial areas were retaining their dominance. This was revealed with particular force in the continued large output of cotton yarn in the Center (the area around Moscow), a location which has no particular advantages except for a concentration of labor traditionally engaged in this work. Cotton was supplied by distant Central Asia and fuel by the likewise distant coal or petroleum areas. The Center still produced 73.2 per cent of all cotton yarn in 1955.[27] Its output of cotton fabrics was even 81.4 per cent of the total in this year.

The domination of the old established production areas, even those with great disadvantages so far as raw materials are concerned, remained strongly pronounced also in machinery production. Even Leningrad, with its extremely unfavorable location in relation to raw materials, retained a large share in this output. Summarized data seem not to have been released. Of the total output (117,087) of metal-cutting machines in 1955, 34,462 were produced in the center and 5,161 in the northwest (mostly Leningrad). The Ukraine and the Urals turned out only 14,375 and 12,085 units, respectively.[28] The giant turbines for installation in electric power plants, of which the Soviets are very proud, seem to come from Leningrad.

Still, while the total industrial output increased by 220 per cent in 1940–55, the increase amounted to 183 per cent in the Center and to 133 per cent in Leningrad oblast (official indices showing exaggerated rates in all cases).[29]

[26] *Industry of the USSR*, 1957, p. 133.
[27] *Ibid.*, p. 327.
[28] *Ibid.*, p. 210.
[29] *Ibid.*, p. 52.

Transportation

As in industry, the postwar recovery of transportation consisted almost exclusively of restoration and further expansion of what had already existed before World War II. Development of new, or relatively new, means of transportation, such as by truck, air, and pipe line, was quite limited. Only a few railways were built.

In 1945, when the share of military goods in transported freight was still very large, total freight traffic (ton-kilometers) by the five carriers was at a level 25 per cent below that in 1940 (Table 36). The decline in transportation serving civilian production and consumption purposes must have been very much greater than this. The recovery of *total* traffic in 1946 and 1947 was slow (5.6 and

TABLE 36

FREIGHT TRAFFIC IN 1940 AND 1945–53*

	FIVE CARRIERS		RAILWAYS				
			Ton-kilometers			Tonnage Shipped	
YEAR	Billion Ton-kilometers	Annual Increase in Per Cent	Billion	Annual Increase in Per Cent	Average Length of Haul in Kilometers	Million Tons	Annual Increase in Per Cent
1940ᵃ......	488	...	415	...	700	593	...
1945.......	375	...	314	...	794	396	...
1946.......	395	5.6	335	6.7	745	453	14.4
1947.......	427	8.1	350	4.5	710	491	10.1
1948.......	537	25.8	446	27.4	730	619	26.1
1949.......	630	17.3	524	17.7	725	735	18.7
1950.......	713	13.2	602	14.9	722	834	13.5
1951.......	799	12.1	677	12.5	745	909	9.0
1952.......	878	9.9	741	9.5	744	997	9.7
1953.......	944	7.5	798	7.7	748	1068	7.1

* Official data, by courtesy of Dr. Holland Hunter.
ᵃ New territories partly included.

8.1 per cent, respectively). But traffic other than military must have grown substantially more than total traffic. Then, in 1948, in one big upward swing (an expansion of not less than 26 per cent), the prewar level of freight traffic was not only reached but substantially surpassed. (The year of 1948 was also the high point in the recovery for industry and construction; agriculture and trade had to wait, the former for quite a long time.)

The very large rate of growth of freight traffic in 1948 could not, of course, be maintained for more than one year. The decline in the rates of growth of this traffic after 1948 continued through 1953. But the rates of growth in freight traffic were large per se in 1949 and 1950, and, considering the circumstances, the rate was also large in 1951. Then it slipped back by more than 20 per cent in one year (1952), indicating the complete end of any recovery features. The further large decline in the rate of growth of freight traffic in 1953 was primarily due to the slowing-down effect of Stalin's death on economic growth in general. But difficulties in the transportation system itself may have been a contributing factor.

The existence of these difficulties is indicated by the fact that in 1953 it was felt necessary to release a special order of the government and Party, "On Further Improvement of Railway Freight Traffic, Especially of Goods of Mass Consumption." In May of 1954, a special conference of railway functionaries was called, and L. Kaganovich in person came out with a lengthy, pompous report.[30] Neither he nor B. Beshchev, the Minister of Transportation, was sufficiently specific to disclose the real extent of the trouble. But this seems not to have been very serious.

The growth of railway freight traffic after World War II was only a little smaller than that of total freight traffic (Table 37). Hence the share of that traffic in the total only declined from 85.1 per cent in 1940 to 84.5 per cent in 1953. The almost exclusive use of railways, certainly outmoded, remained fully preserved.

TABLE 37

RATES OF GROWTH OF FREIGHT TRAFFIC BY VARIOUS CARRIERS IN SPECIFIED YEARS*
(1940 = 100)

Year	Total	Railway	Sea	River	Truck[a]	Pipe
1945..............	77	76	144	52	56	71
1946..............	81	81	124	57	84	77
1950..............	146	145	167	128	226	129
1953..............	194	192	203	164	353	200

* In ton-kilometers, *Transport and Communications of the USSR*, 1957, p. 11.
[a] Including means of transportation of individual enterprises and collective farms.

River freight traffic, on the other hand, grew more slowly than transportation by all carriers; and the share of the river carrier in total freight traffic went down from 7.4 per cent in 1940 to 6.4 per cent in 1950 and 6.3 per cent in 1953. The growth in river freight traffic was still large, however, if its weak competitive power is considered. Already in 1950 the average cost per ton-kilometer

[30] *Pravda*, May 19, 1957.

to the river carrier amounted to 78.6 per cent of that on railways, relatively much too high to permit successful competition by river transportation, which was much slower, usually involved longer hauls than those by railways, and had the disadvantage of being interrupted in the winter by freezing. By 1956 the stated cost relationship increased to 92.0 per cent.[31] A large part of the river traffic was of the type which could be maintained only artificially under such an unfavorable cost relationship.

Freight traffic by truck was expanding more rapidly than transportation by other carriers in post–World War II years; but the rate of its growth was greatly inadequate to bring this means of transportation within a reasonable time to the level of expansion it deserved. In 1953, the share of freight traffic by truck was still only 3.3 per cent of all freight traffic.[32]

About as good as nothing was done during the *Stalin Has Everything His Way* period to reduce the great backwardness of the USSR in transportation of petroleum products by pipe lines, recognized to be a much cheaper means of transportation than railways. The share of pipe lines for petroleum products in total freight traffic stood at the almost negligible figure of 0.8 per cent in both 1940 and 1953. The development of pipe lines for gas, an absolute precondition for its utilization, only started several years after Stalin's death. The official statistical handbook on transportation, published in 1957 and repeatedly cited here, does not yet provide any evidence on this score. It was not lack of investment funds which led to the described attitude toward pipe lines, but the deep freeze of thought and initiative of the Stalin regime, to which, I am afraid, not enough attention is given in this book.

Total railway freight traffic, which the fourth FYP scheduled to be 532 billion ton-kilometers in 1950, reached a level of 602 billion

---

[31] Implied in *Transport and Communications of the USSR,* 1957, p. 24. The average cost of transportation on interior waterways appears particularly high in relation to that of railway transportation, if it is taken into consideration that more than 40 per cent of such traffic consisted of timber shipped in floats (this figure is implied in *ibid.,* p. 134). The average per unit cost of transportation on interior waterways given in the statistical handbooks is, however, rather meaningless. Transportation costs of round timber in floats and of petroleum products in tankers are very low. The unit cost of transportation on interior waterways also differs greatly from one waterway to another.

[32] *Transport and Communications of the USSR,* 1957, p. 8. While the share of trucks in total freight traffic is small anyway, one is surprised to find that the official statistics for this means of transportation include traffic by trucks operated by enterprises transporting their own goods. Even traffic by trucks owned by kolkhozy is included (see *Transport and Communications of the USSR,* 1957, p. 7). But then transportation by animal power should also be included (or is transportation by horse not dignified enough for Soviet statisticians?).

in that year. In a similar manner, the Party Directives to the fifth FYP wanted an increase in ton-kilometers transported by railways of 35 to 40 per cent from 1950 to 1955; but the 1950 level was surpassed in 1955 by 60 per cent. Soviet authorities pretended to be quite jubilant on this account; but actually, as in prewar years, failure to fulfil the targets for the elimination of too-long hauls and counterhauls played a substantial role in this phenomenon. Owing at least in part to this, the average haul of freight on railways, which according to the fourth FYP was to amount to 690 kilometers in 1950, reached 722 kilometers in that year. The result of the so-called fifth FYP was disappointing in this respect as well. The Directives to this FYP scheduled a decline in the average haul, but an increase of 7 per cent actually occurred.

TABLE 38

RATES OF GROWTH OF PASSENGER TRAFFIC BY VARIOUS CARRIERS IN SPECIFIED YEARS*
(1940 = 100)

Year	Total	Railway	Sea	River	Bus	Air
1945.	66	67	72	60	15	276
1946.	99	100	160	83	54	566
1950.	92	90	141	71	152	674
1953.	128	121	167	86	308	1400

* In terms of passenger-kilometers. *Transport and Communications of the USSR*, 1957, p. 16.

Passenger traffic in passenger-kilometers by all carriers was large in 1946, apparently in connection with demobilization (fewer passengers, longer distances, as compared with 1940), but in 1950, by which time things had more or less settled down, passenger traffic was below the 1940 level (in passenger-kilometers). Passenger traffic was 15 per cent above the 1940 level in 1952.

The shift from railways to other means of transportation was more pronounced in passenger than in freight traffic. But the share of railways was larger in total passenger traffic than in total freight traffic in 1940 and remained so until 1953 and later.

Passenger traffic on railways declined from 92.2 per cent of the total (in passenger-kilometers) in 1940 to 89.5 per cent in 1950 and then to 87.2 per cent in 1953—still a very high proportion. Passenger traffic on rivers was actually somewhat less in 1953 than in 1940. The share of transportation by bus, increasing rapidly, reached 7.8 per cent of the total (in passenger-kilometers) in 1953. Transportation by air, although growing even more rapidly than transportation by bus, made up only 1.5 per cent of the total in 1953.

Only 4,000 kilometers of new railways were constructed in 1945–50, and an additional 1,700 kilometers were added in 1951 and 1952.[33] The great expansion of transportation by railway was therefore attained by an almost corresponding increase in the density of the traffic from 4.3 million tons of freight per kilometer of track in 1940 to 5.2 million tons in 1950 and 6.7 million tons in 1952.[34]

In the Soviet Union the turnabout of freight cars, measured in days, is considered an important indicator of the efficiency of railway operation. This number (7.37 days in 1940) jumped during the war to no less than 10.84 days in 1945. Then a decline began. Again it is significant that from 1946 to 1947 the number of days needed for the turnabout went down only from 10.07 to 9.61. More than twice this cut in the days needed could have been achieved in 1948. At a slower, but satisfactory, rate, the reduction in days for freight-car turnabout continued in the succeeding years; but the prewar level had not quite been reached by 1950—another indication that efficiency of operation was commanding only a low priority. The turnabout target set for 1950 by the fourth FYP was attained in 1952. The freight-car turnabout in postwar years was as follows (in days):[35]

Year	Days
1940	7.37
1945	10.84
1946	10.07
1947	9.61
1948	8.68
1949	8.14
1950 (target of the 4th FYP)	6.96
1950	7.49
1951	7.13
1952	6.87

Output per Man

Recovery in output per man from the devastation of World War II lagged behind recovery in output proper. This was the natural result of the slow recovery of agriculture and personal consumption and generally of concentration on volume of output rather than quality factors. The disregard for agriculture and for all of its requirements was reflected in the fact that agriculture was possibly the only economic sector where the prewar output per man had not been restored by 1950.

[33] *Transport and Communications of the USSR*, 1957, p. 27.
[34] *Ibid.*, p. 43.
[35] *Ibid.*, p. 48. (Partly Holland Hunter's data.)

The most reliable data on performance per man, as in most other cases, seem to be those for the railways. The composite tonnage[36] carried per operational railway worker and per year in 1945–55 was as follows:[37]

Year	Index (1940 = 100)
1945	66.9
1946	73.3
1947	75.3
1948	87.3
1949	97.3
1950	110.0
1951	119.0
1952	124.0

Thus, performance per man on railways declined by about one-third during World War II—a good showing considering the disorganization and starvation. As was the case with many other indicators, performance per railway worker was recovering only slowly in 1946 and particularly slowly in 1947. Then a period of rapid advance set in which lasted until 1951. The further increase in 1952 was more moderate.

In 1949 the performance per operational railway worker was still slightly below that of 1940 and was 10 per cent above the 1940 level in 1950. The great increase in density of traffic had a substantial share in this favorable development.[38]

Apparently for the first time in published Soviet statistics, *Transport and Communications of the USSR*, 1957 (p. 23), came out with data on performance per man in traffic on sea and river. The data

[36] "Composite" means freight and passenger.

[37] Data from *Transport and Communications of the USSR*, stat. handb., 1957, p. 65, and A. A. Chertkova, *Productivity of Labor on the Railways of the USSR and Ways for Raising It* (Academy of Sciences of the USSR, 1957), p. 104. There is a small contradiction between the two sources. The figures in the text were obtained from the index of 110 for 1950 (1940 equals 100) in the statistical handbook by counting back with the indices given by Chertkova. In this way an index of 73.3 was obtained for 1946. Yet the statistical handbook (*op. cit., loc. cit.*) implies an index of 74.7 for this year.

David Redding's indices for labor productivity on the railways are superior to the official indices; they are based on operational workers *and employees* rather than manual workers only (see *Soviet Studies*, July, 1953, brought up to date by Holland Hunter in *Soviet Transportation Policies*, pp. 383–84). The differences in the yearly rates of growth, as compared with the official sources, are small, however. Incidentally, the Soviets themselves are abandoning the quasi-Marxian idea that only manual workers are producing value and are shifting to indices of labor productivity per worker and *employee*.

[38] An increase in tonnage transported per kilometer of track is a substantial labor-saving factor.

are somewhat strange. Performance per man in transportation on the sea increased, according to these data, by 12.5 per cent from 1940 to 1950, but was not higher in 1950 than in the disastrous year of 1932. The increase in performance per man in river traffic from 1940 to 1950 was even larger than in traffic on the sea (21.7 per cent); but in 1940 it was not larger than in 1937 and exceeded the 1932 level only by 7.5 per cent. Progress with performance per man in these means of transportation did not in any case seem to have been large. In 1950–56, performance per man grew by 34 per cent in sea traffic, but only by 15 per cent in river traffic. The much smaller increase in performance per man in transportation on the water than by railway is the reason that the targets to expand greatly traffic on interior waterways, standard for Soviet plans, largely failed. The slow traffic on interior waterways, interrupted for many months in the winter, does not fit in well in this age of airplanes.

Officially, output per man in industry increased by 37 per cent in 1940–50. The index is based on the exaggerated rate of growth shown by the index for industrial production in terms of "unchangeable 1926/27 prices" in these years. Fortunately, *Industry of the USSR,* 1957, contains detailed data on this score; some of these are at the suspicious "unchangeable 1926/27 prices," but many are in physical terms (Table 39).

What we see in Table 39 is quite an array of figures, and they vividly demonstrate the exaggerating nature of the indices at "unchangeable 1926/27 prices." Such rises in output per man in 1940–50 as 86 (glass), 79 (china), and 69 (machinery including other metal processing) are simply charming! The only industries showing large increases in physical terms were those with specific reasons, such as pig iron or steel ingots.[39] Even in these cases, the gains in output per man were much smaller than in some indices calculated at "unchangeable 1926/27 prices." In such important industries as coal, petroleum, and timber and lumber, output per man even declined in physical terms in 1940–50. The food industry displayed a decline in output per man even in "unchangeable 1926/27 prices."

The official data on labor productivity in industry imply that, while labor productivity in the machinery industry increased in 1940–50 by 69 per cent, in all other industries taken together the increase was only equivalent to 18 per cent (assuming that the out-

---

[39] There was a shift on a large scale to new, much larger, more effective, and also more labor-saving blast furnaces and open hearths during the period (see *Industry of the USSR,* 1957, pp. 120–21, 124). Early in 1941, for example, 30 per cent of the useful capacity was in blast furnaces with dimensions of 1,001 cubic meters or over; early in 1951 blast furnaces with a capacity of 1,001 cubic meters or over already were accounting for 50 per cent of the total useful capacity.

TABLE 39

CHANGES IN OUTPUT PER MAN IN INDUSTRY BY BRANCH, 1940–50 AND 1951 AND 1952*
(Percentage increase or decline)

Commodity	1940–50	1951	1952
Pig iron	33	9	12
Open-hearth steel	43	7	6
Rolled steel	21	4	6
Coal	−2	8	4
Underground	−7	7	3
Petroleum	−18	10	5
Peat[a]	1	37	−5
Electric power	32	8	9
Machinery and other metal processing (prices)	69	14	10
Chemical industry (prices)	76	13	10
Building materials (prices)	18	14	9
Cement	22	12	12
Glass (prices)	86	7	8
China (prices)	79	12	14
Procurements of timber	−10	6	1
Sawing mills	−11	9	3
Furniture (prices)	12	8	7
Matches	−7	6	5
Paper	7	6	9
Cotton:			
Thread	−7	12	4
Weaving	−10	10	4
Wool:			
Thread	0	8	4
Weaving	3	6	5
Linen:			
Thread	−23	−8	−3
Weaving	−12	1	−7
Silk, mostly artificial:			
Thread and weaving	4	8	9
All food industries (prices)	−3	9	8

* *Industry of the USSR*, 1957, pp. 26–27, 137, 244, 276, 338 and 340–42. The data are calculated in physical terms, except where marked "prices." The prices used were the "unchangeable 1926/27 prices," for the data for 1940–50 and presumably the prices of 1952 for the data for 1951 and 1952.

a Enterprises of the Ministry of Electric Stations only.

put of machinery made up 38 per cent of total industrial production). Thus, the rate of growth of labor productivity in machinery output allegedly was almost exactly four times the increase in labor productivity of the other industries. Does a difference of this size make sense? Is it not much more likely that the bias of the "unchangeable 1926/27 prices" operated with particularly great force in the case of machinery output?

The estimate of a 40 per cent increase in industrial output in 1940–50 in conjunction with the official data on the number of wage earners in industry (this shows a growth of 29 per cent in those years) implies an increase in output per man in total industry of less than 10 per cent in 1940–50 (possibly by somewhat more, because the estimate for output is made for the present territory, while the official estimate of the labor force in industry in 1940, used in the calculation, is unlikely to have included much of the labor in the new territories).[40] *

According to official data, investment in construction and installation, calculated at prices of July 1, 1955, increased from 1940 to 1950 by 59 per cent,[41] while the number of wage earners grew by 64 per cent.[42] This, of course, implies a decline in performance per man. Yet the official index for performance per man in construction in 1950 (1940 equals 100) is 123. The fact that some construction work is done which is not fixed investment cannot matter much; it had, after all, occurred in both the initial and the final year of the period.

The official estimate of a 23 per cent increase in performance per man in construction and installation in 1940–50 is not accepted here. The official estimate of a 59 per cent increase in investment in construction, closely connected in official statistics with the fantastic— more than fourfold—increase in investment in equipment (including other expenses) during the same period is an odd proposition, impossible to accept although impossible to check. The official index for performance per man in construction is most likely a deliberate exaggeration—in order not to make apparent the large exaggeration in the increase in output per man in industry, calculated at "unchangeable 1926/27 prices."

On the occasion of their fortieth anniversary, the "all-citizen statistical ration" was supplemented by estimates of labor productivity in socialized agriculture (kolkhozy and sovkhozy) in several postwar years in terms of 1940.[43] In terms of 1950 the data were

---

[40] Galenson (*op. cit.*, p. 246) estimated the increase in output per man in industry during 1940–50 at 5 to 10 per cent. Shimkin *et al.* have an increase in it of 20 per cent in those years, but the labor productivity in industry as calculated by them for 1940 is particularly low.

* Kaplan and Moorsteen (*op. cit.*, p. 314) do not have a figure for output per man in the industry as a whole. For producers' goods other than machinery, and for consumers' goods together they calculated a decline in output per man of 2.4 per cent from 1940 to 1950.

[41] *Stat. Handb.*, 1956, pp. 159–60.

[42] *Ibid.*, p. 190.

[43] The calculations for the kolkhozy embrace only the socialized sectors. With reference to the private economy of the kolkhozniki, the policy is to disclose as little as possible. In this case the peculiar situation may have existed that the official data on their farm output, wrong for postwar years as they are, would have probably shown a more favorable picture with reference to the changes in output per man since 1940 than the economy of the kolkhozy.

published a year earlier. In 1950 and 1953, labor productivity in agriculture was as follows as compared with 1940, according to the official data:[44]

Ownership	1950	1953
Kolkhozy[a]	99	115
Sovkhozy, including subsidiary farming of State enterprises and organizations	93	106
Sovkhozy proper	91	104

[a] Socialized output only.

It is officially recognized that the Soviet price system of farm products, at least during the time prior to 1958, did not permit their reliable use for the analysis of such items as production costs and labor productivity. Hence, the figures in the tabulation above must be used with great restraint. But they seem close to the mark. While the kolkhozy, according to those calculations, had almost reached the prewar level in labor productivity by 1950, the sovkhozy were measurably behind. It is of interest that the state farms proper made the worst showing.

As the tabulation shows, sizable rises in labor productivity in agriculture were claimed for 1950–53. The principal reason was the decline in the agricultural labor force. Improved deliveries of farm machinery in the later Stalin years also helped. The increasing unwillingness to work on the part of the kolkhozniki was a handicap, it is true, and the official figure on the rise in labor productivity of the kolkhozy from 1950 to 1953 would probably be worth probing, if this were possible. But, after all, the 1953 indices of labor productivity in agriculture, even as they stand, are nothing to brag about.

The kolkhozy, deplorable as their situation was, made a better showing than the sovkhozy in 1953. For a few products produced by sovkhozy proper, the anniversary publication provided data on the changes in output per man from 1940 to certain postwar years in somewhat greater detail. The tabulation below reproduces the respective data for 1950 and 1953 (1940 equals 100):[45]

	1950	1953
Grain	70	95
Milk	104	121
Wool	85	115
Finishing cattle	81	100
Finishing hogs	128	156

[44] *Attainments*, p. 189.

[45] *Ibid.*, p. 164. The series are given in the source in terms of 1934—obviously owing to the particularly small outputs per man in this year. Who is to be deceived?

There is nothing in these data to be happy about. In grain, the principal item of production of the sovkhozy, productivity of labor was far below the prewar level in 1950; it had not regained the prewar level even by 1953.

Strange as it may seem at first glance, official retail trade shows the most favorable development of performance per man in 1940–50. According to official data, this performance calculated at 1940 prices is supposed to have grown in these years by 19 per cent in official retail trade proper and by 29 per cent in eating places.[46]

The relatively large increase in sales per man in retail trade proper since 1940 was a reflection of peculiar developments in that year. Sales per man in retail trade proper declined from 1937 to 1940 by 2 per cent (official data),[47] but increases most probably took place in 1938 and 1939. The decline in sales per man from 1939 to 1940 is indeed likely to have been quite substantial. It seems reasonable under these conditions to assume only a very small increase in sales per man in retail trade proper from prewar years (not necessarily 1940) to 1950.

A further, albeit minor, reason for the increase in sales per man in retail trade proper in 1940–50 was that even Soviet writers were complaining that there were not enough retail establishments after World War II in relation to their number in 1940.[48] The number of stores even declined from 307,100 in the smaller territory of 1940 to 298,400 within the enlarged borders of 1950, and the decline was barely offset by the increase in the number of counters.[49]

With reference to performance per man in eating places, the fact was of great importance that the proportion of food prepared by these places themselves, in the total turnover of these places, went down to less than one-half of the former levels in money terms from 1940 to 1950 (from 56 per cent to 27 per cent).[50]

It will be shown in the next chapter that sales of vodka in eating places in money terms increased greatly over the period, and it did not require a great deal of labor to hand over to the customer a bottle of vodka costing a few times the daily wage of the salesman.

[46] *Soviet Trade,* stat. handb., p. 114.
[47] *Ibid.*
[48] See for example S. Partigul in *Courier of Statistics,* 1957, No. 1, pp. 26–27.
[49] *Soviet Trade,* stat, handb., 1956, p. 137.
[50] *Ibid.,* p. 72.

CHAPTER 16

Introduction

Retail trade naturally showed immense variations during the period 1940–52. The volume of state and co-operative trade (here for brevity referred to as official trade), which had already started to decline before the entrance of the USSR into World War II, continued along this line thereafter, and in a precipitous manner. In the territory substantially reduced by the occupation it may have been equal in 1942, at constant prices, to less than one-third of that in the USSR as a whole in 1940. The small subsequent increase by 1945 brought the level of this trade to only 41 per cent of that in 1940.[1] The recovery after 1945 was strong—but only in percentage terms. The low 1940 level of official trade was not restored until 1950.

The volume of kolkhoz trade followed the pattern of official trade; its level in 1942 probably was even lower than that of official trade (in relation to 1940), but the recovery of kolkhoz trade also at first was more rapid. By 1945, the volume of kolkhoz trade was already much ahead, relatively, of that of official trade.[2] Official trade probably overtook the stagnating kolkhoz trade in 1947, with both about 60 to 65 per cent of the 1940 level. In the next three years the growth of both markets proceeded at about the same rate, but after that their paths parted for good. Official trade continued to expand, while kolkhoz trade stagnated or even declined in real terms.

[1] A large part of the increase from 1942 to 1945, or possibly all of it, was due to the liberation of territory occupied by the enemy.

[2] The turnover in official trade would have made a less unfavorable showing as compared with kolkhoz trade, if only official trade in food had been considered.

Official evidence.—Stat. Handb., 1956, and, even more, *Soviet Trade,* stat. handb., 1956, lifted a large part of the veil from retail operations during World War II and the postwar years. But much remains concealed and confused.

The data of the sources cited consist first of all of those, in current prices, for official trade subdivided into food (beverages, even hard liquor, are treated as food) and non-food goods for all years starting with 1924.[3] For selected years beginning with 1928 the data were, furthermore, presented, likewise at current prices, for a relatively large list of commodities (with important omissions, however). *Soviet Trade,* stat. handb., 1956 (pp. 9–11), also gave indices of turnover in official trade at constant prices by "most important commodities" from 1950 through 1955 (data for official trade as a whole can be reconstructed for a few of the preceding years). Finally, the same source contains some data on kolkhoz trade at current and constant prices, but the effort not to disclose too much was particularly great with reference to this trade. The one figure pertaining to retail trade, definitely rejected here, also involves kolkhoz trade.

A misleading feature of the official indices for the volume of retail trade is that they are based on 1940, "the prewar year," or "the peace year," although in many respects, and particularly with regard to retail trade and private consumption, this was an abnormal year. As shown in chapter 9, the situation in 1940 was actually the reverse of the conditions described by those adjectives, which are standard in the USSR, indeed, almost obligatory, in connection with this year. While agriculture and industrial output of consumers' goods were more or less stagnant in 1940, an unusually large part of the produced goods was diverted from channels leading to the private consumer in order to supply the greatly enlarged armed forces and especially to build up stockpiles. The supplies turned over to be retailed were reduced by not much less than 20 per cent as compared with 1939 (and much more for some important goods). But the price raises more than compensated for this.[4]

Although alcoholic beverages were the largest single item sold in official trade in postwar years, they are not found among the goods for which separate retail-trade data are provided in the official statistical handbook devoted to trade.

[3] Prior to publication of this material, private analysts were compelled to calculate the volume of the official retail trade from scattered evidence. The most successful attempt was that of Peter Wiles, "Retail Trade, Retail Prices and Real Wages in the USSR," *Bulletin of the Oxford Institute of Statistics,* XVI (1954), 376–77.

[4] In spite of a substantial boosting of prices, retail trade at current prices in 1940 was only 6 per cent above that in the preceding year.

TABLE 40

RETAIL TRADE, 1940–55*

A. OFFICIAL TRADE

YEAR	AT CURRENT PRICES (In billions of rubles)					AT CONSTANT PRICES (1940 = 100)		
	Total	Retail Trade Proper	Eating Places	Urban	Rural	Total	Food	Non-food
1940.....	175.1	152.2	22.9	123.5	51.6	100	100	100
1941.....	152.8	131.4	21.4	...	...	...	...	...
1942.....	77.8	59.6	18.2	...	...	...	...	...
1943.....	84.0	63.3	20.7	...	...	...	...	...
1944.....	119.3	90.8	28.5	...	...	...	...	...
1945.....	160.1	127.0	33.1	118.4	47.7	41	...	...
1946.....	247.2	198.4	48.8	191.1	56.1	53	...	...
1947.....	330.8	262.7	68.1	272.0	58.8	62	...	...
1948.....	310.2	264.7	45.5	246.7	63.5	70	...	...
1949.....	335.1	289.6	45.5	259.7	75.4	85	...	...
1950.....	359.6	312.2	47.4	273.0	86.6	110	94	140
1951.....	379.8	329.6	50.2	285.3	94.5	127	110	158
1952.....	393.6	340.2	53.4	295.9	97.7	139	123	167
1953.....	430.7	373.6	57.1	332.9	107.8	169	147	207
1954.....	481.9	421.9	61.0	355.8	126.1	200	169	254
1955.....	501.9	443.1	58.8	368.7	133.2	208	177	263

B. KOLKHOZ TRADE

YEAR	AT CURRENT PRICES (In billions of rubles)	AT CONSTANT PRICES[a] (1940 = 100)	SHARE OF KOLKHOZ TRADE IN TOTAL TURNOVER (In per cent)	
			At Current Prices	At Constant Prices
1940.....	42.1[b]	100	19	11
1948.....	51[c]	...	14	...
1949.....	46[d]	...	12	...
1950.....	49.2	115	12.0	11.5
1951.....	50.8	118	11.8	...
1952.....	53.7	125	12.0	...
1953.....	48.8	121	10.2	...
1954.....	49.0	115	9.2	...
1955.....	48.9	118	8.9	5.6

* Except as noted, the data are from *Soviet Trade*, stat. handb., 1956, pp. 11, 20, 21, 180. The data for official trade include sales of the Tsentrosoyuz on a commission basis (0.07 billion rubles in 1953, 2.2 billion rubles in 1954, and 4.9 billion rubles in 1955, *ibid.*, p. 19). The data for sales in kolkhoz trade at current prices do not consider these sales, but, strangely, the index for sales in kolkhoz trade at constant prices does include them (see *ibid.*, p. 179). The same amounts are thus counted twice in the index for the volume of turnover. The only consolation is that the amounts counted twice are small.

a Calculated on the assumption that the prices in kolkhoz trade exceeded those in official trade by 78 per cent in 1940, by 3 per cent in 1950, and by 75 per cent in 1955. These percentage rises were implied in data in *Soviet Trade* stat. handb., pp. 134, 135.

b The revised official figure, disregarded here, is 29.1 billion rubles.

c This writer's most recent estimate is 50.3 billion (see footnote "b" to table on p. 404).

d Implied in L. Rubinstein *et al.*, *The Economics of Soviet Trade* (1950), pp. 235, 317.

A very important weakness of the official data on trade in postwar years is the downward revision of the previous estimate of the 1940 turnover in kolkhoz trade at current prices from 41.2 billion to 29.1 billion rubles. The revision was announced—after the previous estimate had been the standing one for fifteen years—under the pretext that the former estimate included the total sales of farm products by the producers, while the revised estimate covered only sales of farm producers to the non-farm population.[5] The index for the volume of kolkhoz trade in 1950 (1940 equals 100), which is equal to 115 on the basis of the present official estimate of the turnover in kolkhoz trade in 1950 and of the original official estimate of the turnover in 1940, had become 163 (*Soviet Trade*, stat. handb., 1956, p. 180) after the downward revision of the 1940 figure. It is assumed here that the statistical coverage of kolkhoz trade never included the sales of farm producers to farm producers,[6] and that this also applies specifically to the original 1940 estimate.

Official Trade

Official trade at current prices increased from 175.1 billion in 1940 to 359.6 billion rubles in 1950, or by 105 per cent (Table 40). As is obvious from the data in *Soviet Trade,* stat. handb., 1956 (p. 31), the figure of 175.1 billion rubles in 1940 included only very small amounts for the three Baltic States. The 1940 data for the republics, to which portions of new territories were added in 1939, are presumably also incomplete.

The volume of official trade at constant prices is supposed to have been 10 per cent larger in 1950 than in 1940. *Soviet Trade,* stat. handb., 1956 (p. 12), claimed that retail trade of the Baltic republics was adjusted for the purpose of this index to cover the whole year of 1940, but the adjusted figures were not given. The adjustment was probably made in such a manner that the very small official trade in those territories in the months after "liberation" was expanded to cover the whole year. However, private trade obviously continued on a large scale after "liberation," and this trade, as well as the respective trade prior to annexation, is likely to have been neglected. Nothing was said of similar adjustments of the data for the republics with portions of the new territories added. Official retail trade turn-

---

[5] *Soviet Trade,* stat. handb., 1956, p. 179. Even this pretext was not spelled out. It is merely implied in that the new figure for 1940 is described as that covering "ex-village kolkhoz trade."

[6] I. Malyshev ("Problems of Development of Kolkhoz Trade," *Planned Economy,* 1936, No. 4, p. 112) definitely stated that the estimates of kolkhoz trade involved only ex-village trade.

over in 1950 at constant prices, with a proper adjustment for private trade in the new territories, may well have been about the same as that in 1940 *within the same boundaries.*

A comparison of the official retail trade in 1950 is better made with the same trade in 1939, for which the territory to which the official estimate pertains is more certain (the official data for the 1939 trade may be believed to have covered practically only the pre-1939 territory). As calculated in chapter 9, official retail trade in 1939 was about 20 per cent larger at constant prices than was such trade in 1940, and, consequently, the volume of official retail trade within postwar boundaries in 1950 was about 10 per cent smaller than the 1939 turnover within pre-1939 boundaries.

The total population of the USSR in 1950 was only moderately (approximately 6 per cent) above that of the USSR in 1939 within the pre-1939 boundaries, but the urban population with its perhaps threefold per capita purchases from official retail trade as compared with those of the rural population[7] had increased by close to 30 per cent in the meantime. The per capita purchases in the urban and the rural areas in 1950 were thus greatly below those of 1939.

An increase of 26 per cent was claimed in the volume of official trade in 1950–52. With a small discount for the widening of the concept of retail trade,[8] the increase was probably no larger than 22 to 23 per cent. Even in 1952, the last Stalin year, per capita sales in retail trade to the urban and the rural population must have been below the low levels reached by 1939.

For the World War II years, data on official trade were made available only at current prices (Table 40). With a total of 77.8 billion rubles, official retail trade in 1942 was substantially less than half of such trade in 1940 at current prices, although the weighted prices were considerably higher in 1942 than in 1940.[9] However, the

---

[7] If the sales in urban areas are related to the urban population, and the sales in rural areas, to the rural population, the data in *Soviet Trade,* stat. handb., 1956, p. 22, indicate per capita purchases by the urban population 3.7 times higher than those of the rural population; but an allowance should be made for the fact that the rural population effects purchases in urban areas.

[8] This occurred effective January 1, 1951.

[9] The prices at the end of 1940, which presumably were still valid with reference to most products in urban trade in 1942, were not unsubstantially higher than the weighted prices of 1940. Retail prices in official rural trade, the latter very small after the start of war, were doubled in April of 1942. The prices of liquor and tobacco products were raised drastically for the whole population during World War II. The weighted prices in official trade in 1942 seem to have been at least 50 per cent higher than the *average* prices in this trade in 1940. Since the 1942 turnover amounted only to 43.2 per cent of that in 1940, at current prices, the volume of official trade in 1942 may have been less than 30 per cent of that in 1940.

shrinkage in total territory due to occupation by the enemy must be taken into account. The further expansion of official retail trade at current prices, relatively large in 1944, was partly due to price increases (in 1944, the so-called commercial state stores with their fantastic prices started their operation). The regaining of part of the lost territory was another such factor. The increase in the volume of trade in a comparable territory at constant prices from 1942 to 1945, if any, was not large.

In spite of the introduction of "commercial trade," with its extremely high prices,[10] in 1945 official retail trade did not quite reach the 1940 level at current prices. At constant prices it amounted to only 41 per cent of the latter.[11]

The rapid growth of official retail trade at current prices in 1945–47 may easily mislead. One does not suspect a continuation of inflation, and a strong one at that, *after* the end of the war.[12] The stagnation of official retail trade at current prices in 1947–49 is also noteworthy. Actually there was even a not unsubstantial decline in 1948 (from 330.8 to 310.2 billion rubles).[13] This decline was made up in 1949.

Starting with 1945, official estimates (in percentage terms) of the growth in official trade at constant prices from year to year are available.[14] With their help, the volume of official trade in the years 1945 through 1949 can be calculated by counting back from the official index for 1950. We then have (in per cent of 1940):

---

[10] Commercial trade was not large, it is true. It amounted to 6 billion rubles in 1944 and to 16.5 billion rubles in 1945. See F. Ya. Oblovatskii, *Economy and Planning of Soviet Trade* (1949), p. 47.

[11] The procedure used in obtaining this figure is shown in some detail below. It can also be obtained from the data, obviously official, in *Questions of Economics*, 1957, No. 10, p. 131. The latter data are particularly interesting because they indicate that the constant prices, officially used in these calculations, were those of 1940. The data imply that at these prices the 1950 retail trade was 10 per cent above that of 1940, and that in 1945–50 retail trade increased by 120 billion rubles. Since retail trade was equal to 175 billion rubles in 1940, we have at the 1940 prices: 1950, 192 billion rubles; and 1945, 72 billion rubles.

[12] The great boost in ration prices effective September 16, 1946, was, of course, known. But Soviet pronouncements took great pains to emphasize the declines in prices in state commercial as well as in kolkhoz trade.

[13] The phenomenon was connected with derationing, effective December 16, 1947. It may be doubted that the reform, including the great boost of food prices, effective September 16, 1946, was handled to the best advantage even from the Soviet point of view, although the aims pursued were reached.

[14] They are found in the Reports on the Fulfilment of the Plan of the respective years. The 1948 figure for the growth of retail trade at constant prices (13 per cent) was withheld in order to conceal the falsification of the rate of growth of real wages in that year. But it was slipped in or, in any case given, by Sokolov and Nazarov in *Soviet Trade in Postwar Years* (1954), p. 61. (Mr. E. Zaleskii of Paris drew my attention to this figure.)

1949	85
1948	70
1947	62
1946	53
1945	41

Forty-one per cent of the small official trade of 1940, or perhaps one-third of that in 1939 (by volume), indicated for 1945 certainly spells disaster.[15] Together with the data on the starvation rations distributed by the state[16] and the other evidence, the calculated data for retail trade fully support the assumption of a great increase in the death rate of the civilian population, a similar decline in the birth rate, and a conversion of the large rate of net growth of the Soviet population in prewar years into a strongly declining rate.[17] There is a great suspicion that only the ruthless dictatorship (along with the proverbial patience of the Russian people) could have kept the Soviet Union in the war under these extremely adverse conditions. The excess of deaths over births presumably continued at least until the realization of the 1947 crop (farm population) or until derationing on December 16, 1947 (non-farm population).

So far as actual starvation was concerned, the situation in 1946 was even worse than the figure for the rise in total official retail trade at constant prices of 30 per cent indicates. Sales of food specifically increased by only 15 per cent in that year, of which at least part was bought by those demobilized in the meantime from the armed forces; sales of non-food goods increased by 85 per cent in that year.[18]

The data in Table 40 show that after the volume of retail trade in 1946 rose by 30 per cent, only a relatively slow further recovery was permitted or was possible at first. Even in percentage terms, the growth of official retail trade was larger at the end of the five-year period, i.e., in 1949 and 1950, than in 1947 and 1948. Simply in volume, the recovery was much larger in the *two* last years than in the first *three* years of the five-year period. A 1948 volume of official retail trade 70 per cent that of 1940 is still characterized by near-starvation conditions, and yet for this very year the Party and government claimed that real wages and real peasant incomes had exceeded the 1940 level by 11 and 14 per cent, respectively.[19] Even if this were

[15] So far as food alone is concerned, the situation was not quite as tragic as the figure for total trade implies, because in 1945 food made up 78.5 per cent of total retail trade calculated at constant prices. At current prices, the share of food in retail trade was 75.6 per cent in 1945 as against 63.1 per cent in 1940.

[16] *Commentary*, p. 202.

[17] See N. J., "The Soviet Population of 1956," *American Statistician*, February, 1957, pp. 18–20.

[18] Report of the CSO on the Fulfilment of the 1946 Plan, *Pravda*, January 21, 1947.

[19] *Pravda*, January 18, 1950.

the only falsification put in circulation by the Soviet government, the statistics of that country would deserve a much more decisive condemnation than that of classing its defects as methodological deficiencies (Bergson) or describing them as fairy tales (De Witt).

Official trade and sales taxes.—Before the trade data could be expressed in constant prices, their comparison with the proceeds from sales taxes, at a glance, provided a picture, albeit very crude, of the real volume of trade. This crude yardstick is no longer needed. But Soviet sales taxes, which, by their size, represent a phenomenon unique in world history, are of great interest per se (see Table 41).[20]

TABLE 41

Retail Turnover and Sales Taxes, 1940 and 1944–56*

(In billions of rubles)

YEAR	RETAIL TURNOVER	SALES TAXES		SHARE OF SALES TAXES IN RETAIL TRADE (Per cent)
		Total	On Consumers' Goods	
1940........	175.1	105.9	89.0	50.8
1944........	119.3	94.9	80.7	67.5
1945........	160.1	123.1	105.6	66.0
1946........	247.2	190.9	166.3	67.2
1947........	330.8	239.9	203.9	61.7
1948........	310.2	247.3	210.2	67.8
1949........	335.1	245.5	208.7	62.3
1950........	359.6	236.1	200.7	55.8
1951........	379.8	247.3	210.2	55.3
1952........	393.6	246.9	221.2	56.2
1953........	430.6	243.6	207.1	48.1
1954........	479.7	234.3	199.2	41.5
1955........	497.0	242.4	205.9	41.4
1956........	540.0	258.6	219.4	40.6

* Strictly official data. Data for sales taxes from Franklin D. Holzman, *Soviet Taxation* (Cambridge, Mass.: Harvard University Press, 1955), p. 252. Retail turnover in 1953–56 net of sales in commission trade by the Tsentrosoyuz. The share of consumers' goods in total proceeds of sales taxes was assumed to have been 85 per cent of the total.

The comparison of the retail trade turnover with the proceeds from sales taxes in Table 41 is not exact. The proceeds from sales taxes were approximately adjusted for the taxes imposed on producers' goods, which did not in general enter retail-trade channels. On the other hand, no adjustment was made for the sales taxes

[20] Peter Wiles is quite right in insisting that the sales taxes must be related to the price minus sales taxes. Then, of course, a tax of 66⅔ per cent of the price plus tax becomes a tax of 200 per cent. But here the unsavory Soviet practice is followed of calculating the tax in per cent of the price plus tax.

which were paid from consumers' goods not entering retail turnover. To be noted finally is that the retail-turnover figures include, of course, the retail margin.

Table 41 shows the great amounts by which official retail turnover shrinks after the sales taxes are excluded. The turnover of 1945 goes down to about one-third of the total after this operation. The exorbitant share of the sales taxes in retail turnover of about two-thirds of the turnover was maintained through 1948, supporting the conclusion that improvement in well-being did not start seriously before 1949.

The share of sales taxes in 1940 shown in Table 41 at about 51 per cent of the retail turnover is likely to have been given a particularly large boost by the exceptionally large withdrawal of tax-paying consumers' goods for the needs of the armed forces and for stockpiling. It is therefore particularly notable that in postwar years the share of sales taxes in retail turnover went below the 1940 level only after Stalin's death.

Individual commodities in official trade.—Data on the volume of sales of individual commodities in official trade strengthen the conclusion that the situation was still very poor in 1950. Sales of all food products in this year were supposed to have been 6 per cent below 1940, in spite of the smallness of the sales in 1940 and insufficient territorial coverage of the data for that year. The 10 per cent shortfall of sales of bread in 1950 (1940 equals 100) is particularly significant. The transfer of baking from homes to factories may not have made much additional progress in the old territories in the period discussed, but it probably occurred on a large scale in the new territories. Already in 1940, bread sold in individual units represented only about 5 per cent of the total sales of bread.[21] Hence, there was little room here for a shift to cheaper types of bread after 1940. One is forced to the conclusion that even the requirement for bread, however poor, for any bread, was not satisfied in full in 1950.[22] Sales of milk and milk products other than butter also were 6 per cent less in 1950 than in 1940, while sales of eggs declined by 18 per cent.[23] The large increase in sales of butter from 1940 to 1950 (60 per cent) shown by the official index (Table 42),

[21] According to *Soviet Trade* (monthly), 1956, No. 10, p. 25, 1.2 million tons of bread were sold in individual units in 1940. The *1941 Plan* (p. 75) called for a total output of 22.1 million tons of bread.

[22] The same is indicated by the fact that the per capita consumption of grain products by the kolkhozniki in 1952 was only 95 per cent of that in 1940, even according to the official data, obviously tending to show a more favorable picture than that existing in reality (see *Questions of Economics*, 1957, No. 10, p. 94).

TABLE 42

Volume of Official Retail Trade by Commodities in 1950 and 1952*
(1940 = 100)

Item	1950	1952
All goods	110	139
Food products	94	123
Flour and bread	90	107
Meat and meat products	118	147
Fish and fish products	142	182
Butter	160	176
Vegetable oil	109	186
Lard, margarine and other fats	240	381
Eggs	82	107
Milk and dairy products	94	129
Sugar	128	204
Confections	111	148
Non-food goods	140	167
Cotton fabrics	129	140
"Woolen" fabrics	255	201
"Silk" fabrics	220	329
Garments	110	127
Knit garments	116	161
Socks and stockings	122	159
Footwear, "leather"	120	142
Soap, household	109	129
Soap, toilet	72	80
Radios	6.4 times	8 times
Phonographs	115	174
Watches and clocks	3.3 times	4.3 times
Cameras	66	120
Sewing machines	291	4.7 times
Bicycles	3.4 times	8.3 times

* *Soviet Trade*, stat. handb., 1956, p. 11.

presumably had its origin in the fact that most sales in the new territories, especially all sales in the Baltic States, which used to be an important source of commercial butter in pre-revolutionary days, were not included in the 1940 figure.

Sales of vodka during World War II and later would have permitted an interesting study of demand elasticity for strong liquor under conditions of starvation. But the data provided are inadequate for such an examination. Although vodka was the most important single retail item, it was merged with all other alcoholic and non-alcoholic beverages in the statistics of official trade (tea and coffee are not beverages in this sense). Even for the sales of all beverages, the earliest postwar figure provided by the official statistics is that for

[23] Much more important than these percentages is the fact (it is implied in the evidence of *Soviet Trade,* stat. handb., 1956, pp. 11, 41, 71, 133) that all sales of eggs in official trade in 1950 were less than 1.5 billion units or some 15 eggs per year per head of the non-farm population.

1950 (and only at current but not constant prices), when the high prices charged for liquor during World War II had already been considerably reduced.[24] Evidence on the output of *samogon* (bootleg distilling) also would be needed to get a picture of demand conditions for vodka, but the subject was completely barred from the printed material, since the proceeds from the sales of liquor were considered necessary to the economy.

Retail sales of beverages at current prices increased from 1940 to 1950 by 112 per cent as against a rise of 105 per cent for total retail trade. Since the price of vodka in 1950 was almost fourfold that in 1940, the amounts of it sold in 1950 must have been not much more than half of the latter.[25]

The volume of sales of non-food goods in official trade is supposed to have increased by 40 per cent from 1940 to 1950. The possibility of such a relatively large increase may have come partly or greatly from the large withdrawal of industrial goods in 1940 for the needs of the armed forces and for stockpiling, i.e., from the fact that supplies of these goods in official trade were particularly small in 1940.[26] The great increase in sales of producers' goods to the kolkhozy since prewar times via official retail trade must also be taken into consideration.

How comfortable it is to start from near zero. In such a big country as the USSR, 308,000 sewing machines were sold in 1952.[27] Yet related to the 75,000 sold in 1940, a fourfold increase could be boasted of for 1952.

Eating places.—Up to this point the analyzed figures included both official retail trade proper and sales in the respective eating places. The share of eating places in total official trade was 13 per cent in 1940. This share increased greatly during the war. In 1942–44, it was equivalent to 23 to 25 per cent of the total official retail trade.[28] But by 1950 the prewar relationship had been again

[24] Vodka cost 13 rubles per liter until August 12, 1940; 20 rubles for the rest of 1940; 120 rubles on December 16, 1947; 69 rubles in January and February of 1950; and 57.60 rubles for the rest of 1950.

[25] The data on output of hard liquor including vodka by the industry indicate only a decline of one-third from 1940 to 1950. See *Industry of the USSR*, 1957, p. 372.

[26] The turnover in non-food goods increased from 1939 to 1940 at current prices only by the same small percentage as the total turnover, although the price increase in non-food goods was larger than in food.

[27] *Soviet Trade*, stat. handb., 1956, p. 58.

[28] The proportions of sales in eating places in total retail trade are calculated at current prices, which were not necessarily the same in both forms of this trade. One is able to visualize the changes in relative prices in them (unchanged prices of rationed food, and the greatly increased share of eating places in the sales of beverages greatly raised in price) but it would be hazardous to try to weigh the effect of these relative changes.

restored. The break occurred at the end of 1947, with the abolition of rationing. Sales in eating places at current prices went down from 60.1 billion rubles in 1947 to 45.5 billion rubles in 1948, although only the prices of bread and other grain products declined moderately (by 10 to 12 per cent, effective December 16, 1947).[29] Sales in eating places remained about unchanged at current prices in 1948–50, i.e., they were rising in volume in proportion to the drastic cuts in sales prices. Still, the increase in the volume of sales in eating places was smaller than that in retail trade proper in those years. This accounts for the decline in the share of sales in eating places in total official retail trade from 15 per cent in 1948 to 13 per cent in 1950.

The picture as obtained above from data for total sales in eating places changes fundamentally if sales of beverages, included with food, are separated from the sales of food proper.

It has been shown that the returns from the sales of beverages in total retail trade at current prices (no data specifically for vodka) increased in 1940–50 (no data for intermediate years) a little more than the return from total retail trade (112 per cent as compared with 105 per cent for the latter). But there was a huge rise in returns from sales of beverages in eating places (see Chart 25).

More than one-half of the total increase in sales in eating places in 1940–50 at current prices was accounted for by the increase in sales of beverages. The difference in the rise in the return from beverages of 384 per cent and in the return from food of only 62 per cent in those years was certainly staggering.[30] As Chart 25 shows, sales of beverages in 1950 represented more than one-third of total sales in eating places. Part of the huge increase in the sales of beverages in eating places was presumably caused by the transfer of establishments comprising the so-called "small retail net" ("net" in the sense of "system") from statistics of retail trade proper to those of the eating places. But there may also have been a real shift from shops to eating places. At the prevailing exorbitant prices, wives could not possibly have encouraged drinking at home, and the men went to bars (i.e., "eating places" operated by the state or co-operatives). In any case, sales of liquor in eating places at high prices helped to absorb purchasing power at a time when the population could not have been given much of anything else.

In 1950, 15.5 billion rubles' worth of beverages (at retail prices) was sold in eating places (implied in *Soviet Trade,* stat. handb., 1956, pp. 41, 49). In the same year all foodstuffs which went into the

[29] The price of vodka was also reduced, but only in April of 1948. The prices of vegetables and some minor products were raised at derationing.

[30] Beverages are food in Soviet terminology, but in the text here real food is meant.

CHART 25

VODKA HELPS: SALES IN EATING PLACES AT CURRENT PRICES, 1940, 1950, AND 1955 *

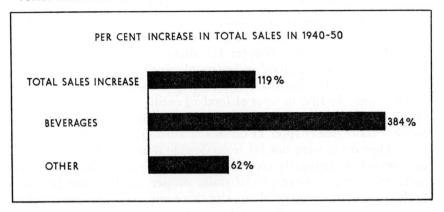

PER CENT INCREASE IN TOTAL SALES IN 1940-50

TOTAL SALES INCREASE   119%

BEVERAGES   384%

OTHER   62%

SHARE OF BEVERAGES IN TOTAL SALES

(IN PER CENT)

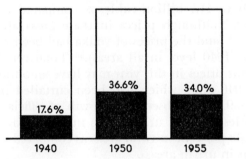

1940	1950	1955
17.6%	36.6%	34.0%

* Implied in *Soviet Trade,* stat. handb., 1956, pp. 20, 41, 49. (The data are for beverages other than tea, coffee, and other hot beverages.) To insure comparability, the margin charged by the eating places in addition to the margin of retail trade proper was excluded in the calculations. "Other" in the chart represents food proper and tobacco products.

preparation of meals (meat and sausage, fish and herring, fats, milk and dairy products including cheese, eggs, groats, dry legumes, macaroni, sugar, potatoes, vegetables, and fruits) had a retail value of only 11.8 billion rubles (*ibid.,* p. 59). The poor composition of the food consumed in the eating places in that year is apparent from the fact that the grain products (other than groats and macaroni) and confections sold had a retail-price value of 7.4 billion rubles. The retail-price value of all foodstuffs—including bread, confections, etc.—was not much larger than the value of beverages (19.2 billion as against 15.5 billion rubles). (We speak of a retail-price value in all cases because the additional margin of the eating places seems not to have been included in the figures stated.)

As has been shown, sales in eating places other than of beverages increased at current prices by only 62 per cent from 1940 to 1950. Since the price index of food other than beverages was equal to 184 in 1950 (see Chart 20 in chapter 11), there actually was a substantial decline in sales of real food in eating places during 1940–50, in spite of the considerable growth in urban population.[31]

This large decline in sales of food in eating places was clearly the outcome of a changed relationship between the prices in official and kolkhoz trade (see chapter 11 on this relationship). In 1940 the prices in kolkhoz trade were not far from double those in official trade and the consumers naturally crowded the eating places where food was more accessible than in official trade proper. In 1950 the prices in both types of trade were about the same and the consumers turned away their noses from the tasteless and generally unappetizing food in state and co-operative eating places.

Official retail trade in rural areas.—Sales in official trade in rural areas naturally declined most during World War II. In 1945 they amounted only to 41.7 billion rubles as compared with 51.6 billion rubles in 1940,[32] although prices in these areas already had been doubled in 1942 (and the prices of vodka had been raised to at least sevenfold their 1940 level in all areas).[33] Total retail sales in rural areas at constant prices in this year may have amounted to only one-third of the 1940 sales, which had been curtailed in turn as compared with 1939. The subsequent growth of official trade in rural areas was also less than in urban areas in some years (in 1945–50 it increased by 108 per cent in rural areas as compared with an increase of 131 per cent in urban areas).

Sales in rural areas were in 1952 not quite one-quarter (exactly 24.6 per cent) of the total official retail trade. Of course, most rural dwellers were themselves producing foodstuffs and a large number of them were also receiving small amounts of it in kind from their kolkhozy. Rural dwellers were, furthermore, also effecting purchases from the official trade in urban areas. But it also must be remembered that the rural population was about 50 per cent larger than the urban population. Altogether, bad as the situation of the urban population

---

[31] This is also indicated by the 21 per cent decrease in the number of courses served in eating places in those years (see *Soviet Trade,* stat. handb., 1956, p. 74). In addition, there may have been some deterioration in the quality of the food served.

[32] *Ibid.,* p. 21.

[33] Commercial state trade with its high prices seems, however, to have operated exclusively in urban areas.

was in the last Stalin years, the data concerning official trade reveal an even more disastrous situation for the rural areas.

The per capita purchases of the rural *non-farm* population from official retail trade were hardly very much smaller than those of the urban population. What then was the share of purchases of the rural *farm* population in the small total sales in rural areas?

Kolkhoz Trade

All efforts to get a reasonably good picture of the kolkhoz trade[34] from 1940 to Stalin's death have so far been only partially successful. The first evidence on the activities in this trade during World War II was not released before the celebration of the fortieth anniversary of the Revolution. The one figure revealed, 136 billion rubles of sales at current prices in 1945,[35] was so high that nobody would have dared to suggest it. Indeed, it is a mystery where so much nominal purchasing power could have come from.[36]

The price indices for the kolkhoz markets reproduced in chapter 11 indicate for 1945 a level about sixfold that in 1940 (although the level was probably somewhat less than this). Hence, total sales in 1945 in kolkhoz trade of possibly not quite 25 billion rubles at 1940 prices is indicated.

The implied volume of 1945 turnover in kolkhoz trade is about 60 per cent (probably somewhat less) of the original estimate of 1940 turnover (41.2 billion rubles); but it is not very much smaller than the officially revised estimate of 29.1 billion rubles for 1940.[37]

Dadugin and Kagarlitskii (*op. cit.,* p. 7) and *Forty Years of Soviet*

---

[34] A short statement on the concept of kolkhoz trade may be found in Appendix C.

[35] According to *Attainments* (p. 338), the turnover in kolkhoz trade was equal to 46 per cent of the total retail turnover in that year. In conjunction with 160 billion rubles given for official trade in 1945, the stated percentage yields the figure for the value of kolkhoz turnover in 1945 that is stated in the text.

[36] To what extent one is helpless on some occasions may be indicated by the fact that Abram Bergson and Hans Heymann, *Soviet National Income and Product, 1940 through 1948* (RAND Corp., 1953, p. 148), estimated the sales in kolkhoz trade in 1944 at 55 billion rubles; and, what is particularly bad from the point of view of this writer, is that he was willing to use this figure before the release of *Attainments.*

[37] The fact that the volume of the 1945 kolkhoz trade turned out to be rather close to the official estimate for 1940 as revised downward is an additional reason for rejecting the revision.

Attainments (p. 154) contains data on marketings of farm products in various years, including 1945, in single figures. It is impossible to separate the sales in kolkhoz trade from the rest of marketings. But total *marketings* of 2.4 million tons of meat (live weight) and 5.4 million tons of milk (including dairy products) in 1945, do not indicate any leftovers at all sizable for the sales of these products in kolkhoz trade. It is true that the totals for potatoes and vegetables shown as marketed in 1945 (11.8 and 4.8 million tons, respectively) may point to enlarged sales in the kolkhoz trade as compared with 1940 for potatoes and only moderately, if at all, reduced sales of vegetables. Kolkhoz trade in 1945 not much smaller than that in 1940 still seems impossible.

Trade, 1957 (p. 114) gave immensely differing rates of growth of turnover in kolkhoz markets from 1942 to 1945. The data of the first source are supposed to have covered the trade in kolkhoz markets of 36 unnamed cities, and those of the second source, the kolkhoz markets of 62 likewise unnamed cities. The data below show the extent ("times") to which kolkhoz trade in 1945 exceeded that of 1942 according to both sources:

Product	Dadugin and Kagarlitskii	Forty Years of Soviet Trade
Meat	3.5	7.7
Butter	4.4	8.5
Vegetable oil	4.9	. . .
Milk	1.38	2.1
Eggs	. . .	2.6
Rye flour	. . .	3.2
Wheat flour	. . .	2.7
Potatoes	2.9	5.8
Vegetables	1.5	3.1
Fruits	2.4	. . .

The data in *Forty Years of Soviet Trade* indicate for 1945 a turnover perhaps fivefold that in 1942. The increase was only 2.5 times the turnover in 1942, or somewhat more, according to Dadugin and Kagarlitskii. The data of *Forty Years of Soviet Trade* imply an unbelievably small kolkhoz trade in 1942. There must have been arbitrary selecting of cities by one or both sources cited. At the risk of being too conservative, the increase in the volume of kolkhoz trade from 1942 to 1945 is assumed to have been not quite three-fold.

The very high prices in kolkhoz markets in 1947[38] and other evidence point to a phenomenon which this writer would not have dared to assume, namely, that the volume of kolkhoz trade hardly increased from 1945 to 1947.

Lifts' statement that the *volume* of kolkhoz trade in 1948 was 22 per cent above that in 1940[39] was highly misleading when made. It seemed impossible to accept the correct use of the term "volume" in this case. Sales in 1948 22 per cent above those in 1940 in physical terms, i.e., double those of 1945, seems to be in too great disproportion to the probable small output by the kolkhozniki, the almost exclusive sellers in the kolkhoz trade, in that year. The great decline of prices in the kolkhoz trade in 1948 was a further factor which made the amount of sales stated by Lifts improbable. Also, Lifts'

---

[38] This high level is indicated by the fact that in 71 large cities, for which data are available, the prices in kolkhoz markets were in 1948 only 36 per cent of those in 1947 (see *Forty Years of Soviet Trade,* p. 116).

[39] *Questions of Economics,* 1951, No. 7, p. 79.

statement for 1948, interpreted literally, would indicate even a small decline in kolkhoz trade in 1948–50.

Refusing the correct interpretation of the term "volume" and, on the other hand, not wanting to dismiss Lifits entirely (he was, after all, Deputy Minister of Trade), nothing is left but to interpret his statement as indicating that his increase in *volume* of 22 per cent occurred simply at current prices. The accepted figure for the real volume of kolkhoz trade indicates a turnover in 1948 of about 80 per cent of that in 1940, a substantial increase over 1947.*

If the calculations of sales in kolkhoz trade at current and constant prices in 1948 and 1950 made here are correct, a fairly rapid growth of the volume of sales in this trade by possibly one-third in two years, 1949 and 1950, is indicated.

All in all, the following picture for the volume of turnover in kolkhoz trade since 1940 is obtained: a precipitous decline in turnover after the start of World War II, with the volume of sales having probably been in 1942 (greatly reduced territory) only about one-fourth of that in 1940, and prices reaching a level about seven times the high prices of 1940.

In 1943, a further large increase in prices of about 100 per cent is supposed to have taken place according to official data. If there also had been an increase in the volume of sales, the turnover would have reached some 200 billion rubles at current prices (not probable). By 1945, the volume of sales in kolkhoz markets approached a level of three-fifths of that in 1940, the prices going down from the 1943 level by perhaps 55 per cent (to close to sixfold the high 1940 level). After an almost unchanged level of kolkhoz trade (or possibly a very slow rise in it) in 1945–47, with the prices declining by about 20 per cent from the average of 1945, in 1948 the turnover in this trade improved to about 80 per cent of that in 1940,* while the prices tumbled to little more than one-third of the 1947 level.

According to Table 40, the 1950 volume of kolkhoz trade exceeded

---

* The last two paragraphs are retained, although this writer does not now hold to the statements made. They are kept as another good indicator of the almost endless, frequently frustrating, groping which is inevitable in analysis based on Soviet "statistics." The situation with the 1948 kolkhoz trade clears up fully if it is assumed that the downward revision of the 1940 kolkhoz trade from 41.2 billion to 29.1 billion rubles, *announced in 1956*, had already been made late in 1948 but was kept secret for eight years. The 22 per cent, by which the volume of 1948 kolkhoz trade exceeded that of 1940 according to Deputy Minister of Trade Lifits, must then be related to the figure as revised downward. Hence 1948 kolkhoz trade was equal to 35.5 billion rubles at 1940 prices, or was below the estimate of the 1940 kolkhoz trade prior to its revision by 13.8 per cent. The topic is handled in greater detail in "The Summit of Falsehood," one of the *Essays on the Soviet Economy*, to be published about the same time as this volume.

* This writer's latest estimate is 86.2 per cent.

the 1940 level by 15 per cent. Even this percentage rise appears quite large in relation to the reduced output of the kolkhozniki in the postwar years. The official claim of an increase of the volume of the 1940 kolkhoz trade of 63 per cent over 1940 does not fit into the picture at all. With a level of 15 per cent over that in 1940, kolkhoz trade was still relatively somewhat larger than official trade. But this was the last such year.

The guess-estimates made above for the development of kolkhoz trade since 1940 are reproduced below (1940 equals 100):

Year	Prices (1940 = 100)	Sales at Current Prices (In billions of rubles)	Volume of Sales at Constant Prices
1940	100	41.2	100
1942	700[a]	75	25
1945	not quite 600	136	not quite 60
1948	150	51[b]	80[b]
1950	100	49.2	115

[a] The yearly average estimated from the four monthly figures given officially assumes an approximately straight rise. The simple average of these figures is only 628.

[b] This writer's latest estimates are 50.3 billion rubles and 86.2 per cent, respectively.

Individual products in kolkhoz trade.—Soviet Trade, stat. handb., 1956 (p. 180), and other recent official sources provide data on the changes in sales in kolkhoz trade from 1940 to 1950 and succeeding years by individual products in percentage terms. The index figures for 1950 and 1952 (1940 equals 100) are as follows:

Product	1950	1952
Grains and grain products............	406	528
Potatoes...........................	295	283
Vegetables........................	105	116
Fruits.............................	141	151
Meat and meat products.............	114	103
Beef and veal....................	152	112
Pork...........................	89	97
Milk and dairy products.............	116	115
Eggs..............................	114	194

The data in the tabulation are not accepted here, as the corresponding figures for total kolkhoz trade are not. The analysis of the official claims for individual products, not reproduced here, is, indeed, one of the reasons for refusing the official revision of the estimate of the kolkhoz trade in 1940. For example, how could the sale of potatoes in kolkhoz trade have increased threefold from 1940 to 1950 (see tabulation above) if potato sales in kolkhoz markets of 251 cities only amounted in 1950 to less than 1 million tons (see tabulation below)? Both figures imply only negligible sales of potatoes in kolkhoz markets or total kolkhoz trade in 1940 and preceding years, although official evidence on this score exists pointing to the reverse. For that matter, the fourfold increase in sales of grain products in kolkhoz trade from 1940 to 1950 shown by the official data seems even more absurd in view of the fact that all sales of grain and grain products in the kolkhoz markets of 251 cities were less than 300,000 tons in 1950 (*Soviet Trade,* stat. handb., 1956, p. 185).

While *Soviet Trade,* stat. handb., 1956, does not in general provide evidence on the sales in official trade in physical terms, it has done so with reference to the sales in the kolkhoz markets of 251 cities for 1950 through 1955 (pp. 185–87).[40] The sales in 1950 and 1952 were as follows (in thousands of tons):[41]

Item	1950	1952
Grain	96.4	190.1
Flour	119.5	226.3
Groats and dry legumes	46.0	61.8
Potatoes	928.9	1,088.5
Vegetables	667.9	565.8
Fruits, berries and melons, fresh	286.5	336.9
Fruits and berries, dried	26.8	43.1
Vegetable oil	23.2	20.4
Meat	292.7	270.4
Milk	243.8	241.9
Butter	15.5	15.2
Eggs (million units)	197.7	365.5
Honey	6.4	8.2

Calculated per capita of the population of the cities involved and per year, such approximate sales are indicated for 1950 as 18 kilograms of potatoes, 13 kilograms of vegetables, 6 kilograms of fresh fruits and berries, 6 kilograms of meat including pork fat, about 5 quarts of milk, and 4 eggs—all this per year!

One is overwhelmed by the smallness of the individual figures, in spite of the information that the 1950 sales in kolkhoz markets of the 251 cities represented only 39.6 per cent of all sales in ex-village kolkhoz trade in that year.[42]

The amount of products sold in 1950 in the kolkhoz markets of the 251 cities, even augmented by 150 per cent,[43] indicates furthermore very small sales per kolkhoznik. There is little doubt that practically every potato and every piece of meat sold by the kolkhozniki was torn from their own or their children's mouths. But the money was needed for the most indispensable purchases, such as

[40] The 251 cities included the bulk of the urban population. It is difficult to locate a large city not included among them, but the data show sales only in *kolkhoz markets* of these cities, rather than total kolkhoz trade in them.

[41] *Soviet Trade,* stat. handb., 1956, p. 185.

[42] *Ibid.,* pp. 19, 188. No such data are available for 1952.

[43] In order to base it on the total turnover of ex-village kolkhoz trade.

salt.[44] Yet the magnitude of these sales disturbed the wise men in the Party more than many other phenomena in the village. Kolkhoz trade, where the kolkhozniki sold these small amounts of produce, was regarded as an obstacle on the path toward communism. In 1952, just before his death, Stalin came out with his plan of "commodity exchange" (see above, chapter 13).

In spite of the smallness of the total supplies in kolkhoz trade in 1950, the official price data indicate only slightly higher prices in them than in official trade in the same year (see chapter 11). This situation was, of course, brought about by the fact that not only the kolkhozniki but the non-farm population also was in bad shape.

In 1952, when Stalin was worried about the large volume of sales in kolkhoz trade, this trade was already on the downgrade. While official trade continued to increase at both current and constant prices after 1950, kolkhoz trade entered a period of stagnation and, after some time, even of decline.

[44] Salt was the only food product for which 1955 sales by the Tsentrosoyuz, which operates almost exclusively in rural areas, were as large as about three-quarters of the total retail sales of this commodity (see *Soviet Trade,* stat. handb., 1956, p. 67).

CHAPTER 17

PERSONAL INCOMES; NATIONAL INCOME

Personal Incomes

Personal incomes of the population and, consequently, its living conditions, were exceptionally bad in 1945. More evidence on these conditions is now available. The situation may not have been much worse in the full-war years, the evidence for which, while leaving no doubts about the great sufferings, is much scarcer than that for 1945. However, conditions not much worse than those existing in 1945 would have been as bad as any that could be imagined.

An exact calculation of personal incomes is impossible for 1945. A level of incomes one-half as high as in 1940 or one-quarter as high as in 1928 in real terms may seem to be a fair estimate of what the urban population was getting in that year.[1] If there was an excess over this level, it was but small. The improvement in 1946 was slight. It was somewhat greater in 1947, mainly in the second half of the year.

Rationing was discontinued as of December 16, 1947, but at very high prices.[2] Not until investment and the output of producers' goods were considerably above the prewar level was a serious start toward improving personal incomes permitted. Moreover, the improvement was largely restricted to wage earners. Real wages, indeed, were climbing rapidly from March 1, 1949, and yet the 1938 level was barely exceeded by the time Stalin's era ended.

The incomes of the peasants may have been slightly better in 1948, relatively, than those of the wage earners (this is uncertain); but the permitted subsequent rise in them was much slower. By

[1] When actually calculated, the index may turn out somewhat more than half, because housing accommodations and most other services probably did not decline measurably from 1940.

[2] A kilogram of coarse rye bread (by far the cheapest kind) cost 3.00 rubles (about one-half of the daily pay of low-wage earners) after derationing.

1951, possibly already by 1950, a substantial disproportion in incomes between wage earners and peasants developed (beyond the great disproportion normally existing in Russia and the USSR), which greatly contributed to the precarious situation in agriculture.

Under these unfavorable conditions, the government resorted to its customary means: blacking out and falsifying statistics on a grand scale. Whatever evidence (factual, not in the form of falsified indices) exists has been released only recently. Every bit of it makes the picture in the early postwar years blacker and blacker. Some of the data on industrial consumers' goods in 1945 (those in 1941–44 remain concealed) indicate an output of these goods lower than anyone would have dared to assume.

Until a short time ago, it was easy to go astray, even with reference to the real situation in 1940; and considerable "advantage" resulted from this for those in power—in the form of indices of real wages and real incomes of the peasants in postwar years expressed in terms of that very year.

With the blacked-out income situation in 1940 appearing better than it really was, the official indices in terms of 1940, even if they had been calculated correctly, would have indicated higher income levels in postwar years than those which actually existed. But the defects of the official income indices for the postwar years were by no means limited to the fact that their basis appeared higher than it really was. By falsification, the real-income indices for the early postwar years were made so high that the purpose of all the tampering was frustrated. No sensible person could have believed the assertion that real wages and real incomes of the peasants were higher in 1948 than in 1940. But the acme of falsification was reached in the claim that real wages had more than doubled in the one year from 1947 to 1948.[3]

Official evidence.—The absence of strictly official evidence (except for 1952) on average nominal wages in the *Stalin Has Everything His Way* period was discussed in chapter 11.[4] Evidence on the incomes of the peasants in postwar years was concealed even more thoroughly. Even the scattered evidence in journals, mostly pertaining only to individual kolkhozy and frequently expressed merely in percentage terms of unknown figures, did not start appearing until about 1956. For many years skimpy evidence on sales in kolkhoz trade was the

[3] Those who advocate the idea that Soviet statistics do not contain falsifications have no choice but to close their eyes to such "indices."

[4] After chapter 11 was finally completed, the average nominal wages in 1945 and in 1947 were disclosed in *Socialist Labor*, 1959, No. 5, pp. 50–51. The nominal wage in 1947 is given as having been one-third higher than that in 1945 and 72 per cent above that in 1940. This implies 5,230 rubles per year for 1945 and 6,973 rubles for 1947. The estimates in *Essay II* (p. 23) were 5,250 rubles for the beginning of 1946 and 6,813 rubles for 1947.

only source from which an idea about one item in the money incomes of the peasants could have been formed. Almost the only figure available, at this writing, on the money distributions (the extremely low figure of 12.4 billion rubles as the total of such distributions in 1952) of the kolkhozy to their kolkhozniki during the period now analyzed was not made public until early in 1958.[5] Nothing was released on the distributions of the kolkhozy in kind.[6] Of the private output of the kolkhozniki, only the acreages and livestock numbers (except for poultry) have been made known in *Stat. Handb.*, 1956, and in later statistical handbooks. The data for poultry for years following the period analyzed here were released in unofficial recent publications. However, the holdings of the kolkhozniki have not been separated from those of other private owners. The evidence seems, moreover, to be incorrect. Discussion of the private economy of the kolkhoz peasants is apparently prohibited in the USSR. Such discussion is completely absent, in any case.

The official statistical data on the incomes of the population during the *Stalin Has Everything His Way* period were almost entirely limited to estimates of the rise of real wages or real incomes of the wage and salary earners and of the real incomes of the peasants (the real-wage index since 1947; the peasant-income index since 1948) relative to 1940 and from one postwar year to another. They have been obtained by undisclosed procedures and published in single figures, with no possibility of verification, which they needed badly. The very concepts were confused; incomes of hired labor were distinguished as follows: (*a*) nominal wages (mostly referred to simply as wages); (*b*) nominal wages with taxes and some other payments subtracted; (*c*) real wages, the same as under (*b*), taking into consideration changes in prices of goods and services; and (*d*) real incomes, the same as under (*c*), taking into consideration gratuitous services of the state. This is simple, but it was not spelled out clearly for a long time. Specifically, no clear distinction was made between real wages

[5] Evidence released at the end of 1957 (*Finances and Socialist Construction in the USSR*, symposium, 1957, p. 172) permits the calculation that the money distributions of the kolkhozy to the kolkhozniki amounted to about 9 billion rubles in 1950. Since the total number of *trudodni* earned was 8.3 billion in that year (*Stat. Handb.*, 1956, p. 129), the average earning was little more than 1 ruble per *trudoden*. But the figure in the first-named source was given in percentage terms and could not have been interpreted then.

[6] After this chapter was written, a figure of 47.5 billion rubles for the distribution to the kolkhozniki in money and kind in 1952 was made available (*Pravda*, December 16, 1958). The prices in which the distributions in kind had been estimated were not announced, so interpretation is not easy. This writer is certain that the prices used were retail rather than the much lower farm prices. Distributions in money and kind worth 47.5 billion rubles at retail prices for over 80 million kolkhozniki, or less than 600 rubles per capita, was very little. Khrushchev gave the figure to stress the big increase to 83.8 billion rubles in 1957. It may be useful to add that the average per capita earning of the wage and salary earners was equal to about 3,800 rubles in 1952.

and real incomes. Indeed, the issue was deliberately confused.[7]

While with reference to hired labor a distinction, albeit difficult to grasp, between *real wages* and *real incomes* was made, no such distinction was made with reference to the peasants. In both cases it was "incomes." When the gratuitous services were not included, the formula was "incomes in money and kind," which was sometimes specified by "at constant prices." The published index figures for real incomes of the peasants (which normally are supposed to include gratuitous services) will be shown below to have harbored the most fantastic exaggerations.

The natural sources for the evidence on personal incomes obviously are the Reports on the Fulfilment of the Plan for each year. But what a poor source this is! In some of the Reports the income of each population group was stated separately, in others both were merged together. For some years the evidence was per working person, but for other years the change in total incomes of each population group or both groups together was stated. In short, this is a very good example of the "all-citizen statistical ration" allowed by the Central Statistical Office. So far as possible, the evidence is compiled in the tabulation below, with some supplementing figures from sources which can be considered as good as official:[8]

	WAGE AND SALARY EARNERS					
YEAR	Real Wages		Real Incomes		Real Peasant Incomes[a]	
	Year-to-year in Per Cent	1940 = 100	Year-to-year	1940 = 100	Year-to-year	1940 = 100
1948[b]	more than double	. . .	. . .	112	. . .	114
1949[c]	. . .	. . .	12	124	14	130
1950[d]	. . .	. . .	(15)[e]	. . .	. . .	. . .
1951[f]	. . .	. . .	(10)[e]	(157)[g]	(10)[e]	(160)[g]
1952[h]	. . .	. . .	7	(168)[i]	8	(173)[i]
1953[j]	12	(165)[k]	13	(189)[k]	. . .[l]	. . .

[a] Including gratuitous services of the state.

[b] *Pravda*, January 20, 1949.

[c] *Pravda*, January 18, 1950.

[d] All incomes of wage and salary earners and peasants (not per worker) grew by 19 per cent. *Pravda*, January 26, 1951.

[e] *Economic Survey of Europe*, 1955, p. 168.

[f] Real incomes of wage and salary earners and of peasants (not per worker) increased by 10 per cent. *Pravda*, January 29, 1952.

[g] *Communist*, 1953, No. 16, p. 47.

[h] *Pravda*, January 23, 1953.

[i] Calculated from the other data in the tabulation.

[j] All real incomes of wage and salary earners and peasants (not per worker) increased by 13 per cent. *Pravda*, January 31, 1954.

[k] *Political Economy*, textbook, 1954, p. 462.

[l] The official source was satisfied merely to claim for the peasants' incomes, a "substantial increase especially in the second half of the year."

[7] See, for example, the comprehensive *Dictionary-Reference Book on Social-Economic Statistics* (Moscow, 1948) or A. I. Gozulov, *Economic Statistics* (Moscow, 1953), pp. 465–68.

[8] Data are per working person, except as noted. All data not in brackets are from the Reports on the Fulfilment of the Plan for the given year.

In addition to the indefiniteness of the concepts and the chaotic state in which the data were presented, there was the peculiar timing in the release of the data.

The index for the real wage (1940 equals 100) in 1953, 24 percentage points below that for the real incomes of the same recipients, published in *Political Economy* (textbook) in 1954, was certainly a great surprise. Until then the Soviet press operated almost exclusively with the indices for real *incomes,* which allegedly rose from 1940 to 1953 by almost 90 per cent for the wage earners and nearly doubled for the peasants. Even the rises since 1948 did not get much attention from it.

The important reason for emphasizing the indices in terms of 1940 has already been mentioned. Hardly anybody realized for a long time how bad the situation was for the population in 1940. That year was chosen by the Soviets as the basis of these and many other indices exactly because of the lack of such knowledge. The year 1940 was the "prewar," the "peace" year. These were the Soviet designations, although so far as real wages and real incomes were concerned, they were grossly inaccurate.

When at long last (it did not occur before 1956) it became possible to form an idea of the prices in kolkhoz trade in 1940 (a component of the calculation of wages in real terms), it turned out that they were substantially higher than anybody in the West dared to assume on the basis of the skimpy evidence available. Somehow one was also unduly impressed by the large receipts of the kolkhozniki from the sales in kolkhoz trade in nominal terms in that year (total sales in this trade were estimated at 41.2 billion rubles) without sufficient evidence on what could have been bought for this amount of money.

As in the case of prices in kolkhoz trade, evidence in reasonably adequate form of sales in official trade in rural areas in 1940 did not become available until 1956. This trade turned out to be in 1940 only as high at current prices as in 1939 in spite of the considerable rise in prices (see chapter 9 for evidence on prices; the data on trade are in chapter 16).

As stated, the announcement of the two indices for wages in 1953 in *Political Economy* in 1954 came as a great surprise. In *Commentary* (pp. 36–45), this writer approached the official claim that the 1953 index for incomes of wage and salary earners (1940 equals 100) was 24 percentage points higher, when in addition to real wages the so-called social wage was considered, as a kind of statistics. Both indexes of that source, taken together, obviously implied an immense rise in the social wage from 1940 to 1953. A suitable explanation seemed to have been that the social wage, allegedly calculated at constant prices, was actually calculated at current prices. The explanation still seems plausible; but an alternative is that they simply were looking for means of getting rid of at least part of the too-high index for the real incomes of the wage and salary earners in terms of 1940, specifically for means of disposing of the fantastic claim that real wages were more than doubled in the one year of 1948 and of the calculation that already in 1948 real incomes of the wage and salary earners exceeded those in 1940 by 12 per cent.

The desire displayed in recent years to make the index for real wages in terms of 1940 as low as possible (or as little improbable as possible) was revealed also by the following minor item: The index given in recent sources for the 1955 paid-out wage is 175 (1940 equals 100). The corresponding index announced in *Political Economy* for 1953—namely, 165—plus the rises of 5 and 3 per cent announced for 1954 and 1955, respectively, in the reports on the fulfilment of the respective annual plans, yield for 1955 an index of 178. The difference of 3 percentage points could, of course, have been brought about by the fact that the percentage rises in 1954 and 1955 were allegedly calculated for the real wage including the socialized wage. But more likely it was just an insignificant cut brought about by the desire to have a smaller figure for the real-wage index (a rounding-off would have made the index 180 rather than 175).

While the attempts at reducing the rises in incomes of wage and salary earners claimed previously, which started in 1954, were going on, nothing happened with reference to the index of real incomes of the peasants, which was even much more absurd than the index for incomes of the wage and salary earners. Indeed, the real peasant incomes in 1953 remained officially equal to nearly twice those in 1940 until the middle of 1958. The reason for the different treatment of the two indices probably was just in the much greater absurdity of the peasant-income index. While with reference to real wages, only the index in terms of 1940 possibly was exaggerated, the index for the real incomes of the peasants also showed a greatly exaggerated growth from, say, 1948 to 1952 and to later years.[9]

Ultimately, the situation with regard to the indices of real wages and real incomes of the wage and salary earners and the real incomes of the peasants became unbearable. Without direct announcement and of course without even a trace of explanation, something like

[9] This extra falsification was aimed at concealing the particularly great discrimination against the peasants in the last Stalin years. The CSO succeeded in that the official index (1940 equals 100) for peasant incomes had been higher than the index for the incomes of wage and salary earners in every postwar year.

new indices turned up for them.[10] Suddenly the 1958 index for total incomes, i.e., real wages and socialized wages, in terms of 1940 was declared to be equal to "close to 200," although the previously released index for this item (189 in 1953), brought up to 1958, would have been not less than 250 and even the index for the real wage alone would have been equal to about 220. The previous index for real incomes of the peasants in terms of 1940 would be 280 or more in 1958. It was now given by the authoritative Volkov at "more than 200."

Since the previous index of real wages of the wage and salary earners in terms of 1940 was now declared to be the index for their real *incomes,* the previously claimed year-to-year percentage rises for these incomes may possibly be applicable to them. We then have approximately the following:

Year	1940 = 100
1953	165
1952	149
1951	139
1950	125
1949	109
1948	98

The real income of the wage and salary earners in 1948 thus becomes somewhat lower than that of 1940 rather than 12 per cent above it, as was officially claimed in 1949 for the real wage.

If an equation sign is set between real wages and real incomes of the labor force, also for 1948, an index of 98 for 1948 (1940 equals 100) in conjunction with the official claim that real wages were more than doubled in 1948, leads to an index of perhaps 45 in 1947. What then would be the official index for real wages for 1945 or the war years? The index of 98, implied for the real incomes of workers and employees in 1948 (1940 equals 100) in the new estimate, while much more sensible than the previous claim, may still be an exaggeration.

Note that the previous index for peasants' real incomes was cut down in recent revisions much more drastically than that of the wage and salary earners. By this additional cut part or all exaggeration in the rise of peasant incomes since 1948 may have been removed, but that from 1940 to 1948 probably remained intact.

[10] The most authoritative statement on this account was made by A. Volkov, chairman of the State Committee of the Council of Ministers of the USSR on Questions of Labor and Wages, *Pravda,* November 25, 1958. For real wages, specifically, the same statement was made prior to Volkov by V. Grishin, chairman of the All-Union Council of Trade Unions, in *Pravda,* November 17, 1958. Both statements were later repeated by Khrushchev in his speech of December 15, 1958.

Again, as in other cases, when important official estimates are "revised" drastically without any explanations, there is no reason to accept the newest estimates without a most thorough examination, and such an examination in this case does not indicate that, at long last, all the exaggerations have been eliminated.

The situation in 1945–47.—Average nominal wages were about one-quarter higher in 1945 than in 1940. The prices of rationed food may have risen somewhat less than this. But the rations were too small to prevent starvation. Still, the underprivileged had at least something at prices they could afford to pay. The prices in kolkhoz trade in 1945 were about tenfold those in official trade in 1940, and the prices in state commercial trade were about as high. Both these markets obviously served only the privileged.

The tragic living conditions in 1945 are adequately revealed by the output and trade data. Farm production was in this year 40 per cent, or more, below that in 1940, in the face of the great need for farm products for the armed forces. Production of grain went down even a little more than total farm production. According to official estimates, the grain crops in 1945 and 1946 were 44 and 43 per cent, respectively, below that in 1940.[11]

Grinding of grain to flour went down about as much as grain production, namely, from 29 million tons of flour in 1940 to only 15 million tons in 1945.[12] The decline in flour production, large as it was, was presumably the smallest among those shown by the data on the processing of crops. Crystal sugar production in 1945 was only 21.5 per cent of that in 1940,[13] that of butter and vegetable oil (by industry) 51.8 and 36.6 per cent, respectively.[14]

Even the items cherished as great sources of state revenue did not in 1945 reach a level of output half as large as that in 1940. The production of vodka and other hard liquor went down by 52.9 per cent, that of cigarettes by 75.1 per cent and of *makhorka* by as much as 84.8 per cent. Only the catch of fish showed in 1945 a relatively favorable level—80.1 per cent of that in 1940.[15]

[11] This writer's calculations indicate a slightly smaller decline from the 1940 level for each of the two years (see *International Affairs,* October, 1952, p. 459). The decline was not as large if calculated to a prewar average as was done in chapter 14, rather than to 1940 as is done here.

[12] *Industry of the USSR,* 1957, p. 372. The data for the grinding of grain include the grinding to feed in mills not engaged exclusively in this operation. The reduction from 1940 to 1945 was presumably somewhat smaller in flour produced for food.

[13] *Ibid.,* p. 371.

[14] *Ibid.,* p. 372.

[15] *Ibid.,* pp. 371–72.

The livestock data for 1945 indicate relatively moderate declines in total cattle, cows, and sheep and goats (12.7, 17.9, and 23.6 per cent, respectively), but the number of hogs went down by 61.6 per cent.[16] The industrial output of meat was reduced by 55.8 per cent.[17]

The dismaying picture disclosed by those output figures is even more intensified if the large requirements of the armed forces are taken into consideration.[18]

The 1945 trade data are about as unfavorable for the private consumer as the output data. Total official trade in 1945, as has been shown, was, at constant prices, only 41 per cent of that in 1940. Sales specifically of food declined to about one-half of the 1940 level (exactly by 49 per cent). The consumers spent the fantastic sum of 136 billion rubles in kolkhoz trade in 1945 (as against 41.2 billion rubles in 1940), obtaining for this mass of money at most 60 per cent as many products as they had purchased in 1940. Total purchases of food in 1945 were thus little more than half of those in 1940. The number of prospective customers in retail trade declined, though.[19]

Sales of non-food goods in official trade almost disappeared by 1945 (a decline of 76.2 per cent since 1940). Only services, consisting largely of house use, went down moderately.

On the basis of the above data, real incomes of the urban population appear to have been in 1945 not very much more than half of those of as poor a year as 1940.

Living conditions of the peasants in 1945 seem impossible to estimate with any degree of precision. The peasants got a lot of money for the greatly curtailed amounts of products sold by them in kolkhoz trade but that was just paper for which almost nothing could be obtained in return. (Some purchases could have been effected in commercial state stores at the enormous prices charged in them.) Most of the paper money had indeed remained unspent until 90 per cent of it was voided by the monetary "reform" of December 16, 1947. The basic problem is: How much did the peasants get to eat

[16] *Stat. Handb.*, 1956, p. 118.

[17] *Industry of the USSR*, 1957, pp. 371–72.

[18] An idea of the magnitude of these withdrawals can be formed from the fact that in 1946, a year of demobilization, output of consumers' goods by industry increased by 13 per cent (at "unchangeable 1926/27 prices"), but the volume of sales in official trade was enlarged by 30 per cent. The about 20 per cent difference may have represented all or part of the former withdrawals for the armed forces.

[19] To estimate the total consumption of the civilian non-farm population in 1945 (or the decline in it since 1940), it would be necessary to add the production of farm products by this population or the difference in this output between the two years mentioned (there was possibly an increase in this type of production during the war).

in 1945 from their own production and the distributions of the kolkhozy minus their sales in kolkhoz trade? The only answer which it seems possible to give is that it could not have been much, what with the farm output (total, not specifically the private output of the peasants) only 60 per cent or less that in 1940, huge armed forces to be fed and clothed at fairly adequate rations and norms, and the non-farm population getting at least some food. This answer is, of course, inadequate, but more exact calculations appear impossible.

It seems, however, probable that the production of their own farm products by the kolkhozniki assured, at least to most of them, a supply of food in 1945 less disastrous than that of the non-farm population. It would be very illuminating to have estimates of mortality rates in that year for the urban and rural population separately, but we do not have such estimates even for the population as a whole.

The situation of the population remained very grave until the realization of the 1947 crop. The 1946 harvest was poor, and the official index for output of industrial consumers' goods grew in this year only by little more than 10 per cent (in "unchangeable 1926/27 prices").

While the official estimate of the 1947 crop may have been too high relative to those for 1945 and 1946, the 1947 farm output was substantially larger than that of 1946 and the realization of the crop of this year may be considered the transition point from the disastrous near-war conditions to a still very precarious situation, but one which at least excluded a greater mortality than birth rate. Output of industrial consumers' goods increased by 21 per cent in 1947 (in terms of "unchangeable 1926/27 prices"), the increases having probably occurred mainly in the second half of 1947 after the new harvest had provided the raw materials for the processing.

In an effort to show the "favorable" situation in 1948, Deputy Minister of Trade Lifts cited the large percentage increases in the retail sales of certain consumers' goods from the first quarter of 1947 to the first quarter of 1948. But since the total retail turnover in official trade in 1948 is now known to have been only about 70 per cent of that in 1940, at constant prices, Lifts' evidence merely underscores the bad situation in the first quarter of 1947 (his evidence included such rises as 72 per cent for bread, 52 per cent for groats and macaroni, 170 per cent for sugar, and 44 per cent for cotton and "silk" fabrics).[20] An increase in sales of bread by 72 per cent in one year describes, of course, a very tragic situation at the time from which the increase is counted, i.e., in this case the first quarter of 1947. This situation was possibly not very much better for the con-

[20] M. M. Lifits, *Soviet Trade*, p. 123.

sumer than that in the year of 1945, or, for that matter, the years of World War II.

The data presented on the situation in 1946 and the first half of 1947 again throw a clearer picture on the incomes of wage earners than on those of the peasants, although the appraisal of the former is complicated by the great raising of ration prices effective September 16, 1946, and the compensating wage boost (see chapter 11). The return to the peasants from sales in kolkhoz trade may have declined moderately in 1946 and 1947 (in paper-money terms), but this loss was of almost no significance. The incomes of peasants in the first place depended on the harvest, although primarily the harvest from their own sowings, which probably were not so badly affected by the 1946 drought as the socialized sowings. The year 1947, with its better harvest, must have brought an improvement also to the kolkhozniki, but all this is very uncertain.

Real wages, 1948–52.—The derationing since December 16, 1947, permits a calculation of the real paid-out wage in 1948 and subsequent years. According to Tables II and III (Appendix B), in 1948 the real wage was only 45 per cent of that in 1928 and 87 per cent of that in the very unfavorable year of 1940.

The establishment of the real wage in 1948 permits a glance backward, to 1947 and even earlier years. As stated, a more than doubling of the average real wage from 1947 to 1948 was claimed officially. With the real wage in 1948 at the low level definitely established, the official claim that real wages were more than doubled from 1947 to 1948 indicates a level of starvation in 1947 which would have wiped out not perhaps the one million, or so, that actually were wiped out, but a substantial proportion of all workers and employees. Analysis in this writer's essay "The Summit of Falsehood" (cited elsewhere) indicates that the average increase in real wages from 1947 to 1948 was equivalent to about 35 per cent; but a statement is made there that even such an increase seems too high on the basis of changes in available supplies. Since the 1948 real wage is here estimated at 87 per cent of that of 1940, a real wage of perhaps 65 per cent of this level is indicated for 1947.

The increase in real wages from 1945 to 1947, difficult to estimate, leads then to a real wage in 1945 half as large as that of 1940 (more likely, somewhat better than this) as a crude approximation.

The level of real wages in 1948 was still so low that it was possible to raise it very strongly in subsequent years without hampering the drastic rate of the growth of industry. The improvement was effected in the first place by the rapid cut in the prices of consumers' goods. According to Tables II and III (Appendix B), real wages jumped by about 33 per cent in 1949 and 1950. Then the last two Stalin years brought a further growth of about 16 per cent.

In spite of the great increase during 1948–52, the real paid-out wage was in 1952, the last Stalin year, only a little more than two-thirds of that in 1928 after twenty-four years of the Great Industrialization Drive (see Appendix B, Table II).[21] The decline in real wages from 1928 to 1952 would have been even much greater than calculated above if the much greater labor productivity in 1952 had been considered. The changes in *composition* of hired labor since 1928 also should have led to a rise in the average wage. On the other hand, the decline in real wages since 1928 was smaller if the calculation is made per capita to include the wage earner and his dependents rather than the wage earner alone (see Appendix B, Table III).

The Soviets make much propaganda of the so-called socialized wage, which supplements the paid-out wage dealt with here. Included in the socialized wage are all expenses of the state on education and medical help, social insurance, pensions, help to married mothers with many children and to unmarried mothers, etc.[22] Even such doubtful items as military schools or atomic research are included with the personal incomes in the process. But even the Soviet method of computing the total real wage, as it stands, boosts the real wage only moderately, if it is properly calculated. If it appears as anything else in Soviet statistics, this is because it is a favorite spot for particular wild manipulations.

The so-called social wage amounted to about 11 to 12 per cent of the total (paid-out and social) wage in 1928.[23] For 1952, the payments comprising the social wage were given at 129 billion rubles (*Stat. Handb.*, 1956, p. 38); but the persons served included in this case the whole population, rather than only the non-farm wage earners. The wages and salaries paid out in 1952 amounted to

[21] Mrs. Chapman's findings are practically the same, so far as she uses the consumption and prices in 1928 as weights. With the 1937 data used as weights, her calculations indicate that the 1928 level of real wages was exceeded in 1952 by 3 per cent (see Janet Chapman, "Real Wages in the Soviet Union, 1928–52," *Review of Economics and Statistics,* May, 1954, pp. 134–35). Detailed analysis leaves no doubt that housing conditions and consumption levels of food and non-food goods were substantially worse in 1952 than in 1928. Per capita data on retail trade indicate indeed that even the very low 1940 level was exceeded only little in 1952 (see chapter 16).

[22] See note on p. 38 of *Stat. Handb.*, 1956.

[23] The basic items of social-cultural service of non-farm workers in 1928 were given at 939.3 million rubles in *Socialist Construction of the USSR*, 1935, p. 322. (The source spoke only of workers, but it is assumed here that workers and employees were implied.) The total wage bill paid out to all non-farm wage and salary earners was equal to 7,481 million rubles in that year (*ibid.*, pp. 318–19).

about 338 billion rubles (42.2 million persons at 8,000 rubles per year). Allowing for the incomes of the residual population, those figures indicate that the social wage of wage and salary earners was equal to less than 20 per cent of their total wages in 1952 and that the total wage, i.e., the paid-out and social wage, calculated per capita, was in this year not above three-quarters of that in 1928.

The great role that the low pay of the labor force had in the Great Industrial Drive was emphasized repeatedly. The wage level was indeed so low in the last days of Stalin that the possibility of improving it represented an important reserve for the rulers who followed him.

Real incomes of the peasants, 1948–52.—The price reductions of consumers' goods in official trade during the *Stalin Has Everything His Way* period were proclaimed as "Stalin's Concern for the Welfare of the Population.[24] The respective announcements included, among the gains made by the population from the reductions in prices, those on purchases from the kolkhoz trade. It was deliberately ignored that what one part of the population (the consumers) was gaining from lower prices in kolkhoz trade, another part (the producers) was losing.[25] The kolkhozniki were not a part of the Soviet population with whose welfare Stalin was concerned.[26]

As far as receipts from their kolkhozy were concerned, the distributions of grain continued to be the principal matter of interest for the kolkhozniki in Stalin's day. Nothing but scattered data is available on this score. In addition, there was the fact that with total grain crops as small as those obtained in those years, and state procurements relatively large, any large distributions to the kolkhozniki were out of the question.

In Krasnodar oblast, the richest agricultural area in the USSR, the 1951–53 distributions of grain, depending on the district, amounted

[24] This was the title of an editorial in *Izvestiya*, March 1, 1950, containing the announcement of the price reductions effective on that date.

[25] The trick of counting reductions in prices in kolkhoz trade as gains of the population was repeated year after year in the announcements on the cuts in retail prices in 1948–53.

[26] Now, in retrospect, everybody is chattering about the neglect of agriculture and the peasants in the days of Stalin. I. Kuzmin, the chairman of the Gosplan USSR, writing in *Pravda*, April 5, 1958, said: "Let us recollect in what a neglected state agriculture was in 1953." The neglect of agriculture obviously included that of the agricultural population. Yet the realization of the severe exploitation of the peasants in Stalin's day did not prevent the Ministry of Finance of the USSR from including a complete list of "gains" of the population coming from the declines in prices in kolkhoz trade (see preceding note) in its anniversary publication *Finances and Socialist Construction* (p. 225).

to 2.01–2.83 kilograms per *trudoden*.[27] Zaporozhie oblast is probably the richest, agriculturally, in the Ukraine; there distributions varied from 2.06 to 2.34 kilograms in the same years. In Moscow oblast, an average of 0.74 kilogram of grain was distributed in 1952.[28] Those areas and years were not picked by this writer. The only other evidence of this kind given in Sergeev's 800-page volume is that for Andizhan oblast (cotton) in Central Asia, where 1.38 to 1.77 kilograms of grain per *trudoden* were distributed in 1953.[29]

Except for Moscow oblast, Sergeev's data certainly described above average conditions. There are quite a number of statements on the conditions in individual kolkhozy depicting immensely deplorable distributions of grain. In *Izvestiya* of February 5, 1957, there is a report on the "For Communism Kolkhoz" in Zhitomir oblast, which states: "Two years ago [presumably in 1954], 20 kopeks and 300 grams of grain were distributed per *trudoden*." Single kolkhozy are not proof, one would say. Yet the kolkhoz system needs possibly to be classed as a failure, if only one such kolkhoz existed. But this is not so. The situation in this specific kolkhoz two years before was disclosed only because the kolkhoz had subsequently made great progress. Those very numerous kolkhozy which were still distributing something like 20 kopeks and 300 grams were not mentioned.[30]

There is no doubt that at the end of Stalin's reign, the average distribution of grain was at least measurably, and possibly substantially, smaller than the 1.6 kilograms distributed in 1936, the worst prewar year in this respect.[31] The average distribution per *trudoden* in 1950–52 was indeed possibly not much larger than one kilogram.[32] The secret would not have been guarded so carefully had the situation not been very bad.

[27] The figures obtained from Sergeev (see n. 28) do not agree well with 1.25 and 1.40 kilograms distributed in Krasnodar oblast in 1950 and 1954, respectively, according to *Questions of Economics,* 1957, No. 8, p. 32. But the author of the paper may have deliberately selected the worst years to make his data for 1956 look better (Sergeev seems to be more reliable).

[28] S. Sergeev, *Questions of Economic-Statistical Analysis of the Kolkhoz Production* (Moscow, 1956), pp. 333, 337, 373.

[29] *Ibid.,* p. 356.

[30] A. Dergachev ("To Enlarge the Labor Resources in Underpopulated Regions," *Socialist Agriculture,* 1955, No. 1, p. 59) mentioned two kolkhozy in White Russia which in 1953 produced a total of 5.2 and 6.0 quintals of grain and earned 240.7 and 204.8 rubles, respectively, per able-bodied person and per year. Both the grain and money figures were gross and obviously the kolkhozy involved not only did not distribute anything to the kolkhozniki for their year's labor, but did not have enough to fulfil their delivery obligations and their payments to the MTS.

[31] *Soc. Agri.,* p. 695.

[32] An official estimate of 47.5 billion rubles as the distribution to the kolkhozniki in money and kind in 1952 has been mentioned above. Since the distributions of money amounted to 12.4 billion rubles in that year (see below), the distributions in kind

The money distribution by the kolkhozy to the kolkhozniki in 1952 of 12.4 billion rubles, mentioned above, was the only such figure revealed for any postwar year until Stalin's death. Even this figure was not disclosed until early in 1958.[33] The number of *trudodni* earned was equal to 8,847 million,[34] and the average receipt for each *trudoden* was consequently 1.40 rubles.[35] In 1940, 1.25 rubles were distributed for each *trudoden*.[36] Yet the retail prices in official trade in 1952 were 61 per cent above those in 1940. The 1952 prices of the main goods purchased by the peasants (coarse bread, salt, soap, cotton fabrics, footwear, and vodka) were at least twice as high as the average prices in 1940. The purchasing power of the total distributions to the kolkhozniki in terms of goods purchased by the peasants, while it had improved since 1950, and especially since 1948, was in 1952 still very unsatisfactory.

One needs patience with Soviet statistics. On the occasion of the fortieth anniversary, one writer[37] jubilantly brought out data on the per capita expenditures by the kolkhozniki at constant prices in 1952 and 1956 as compared with 1940. He commented (enthusiastically) only on the increases in 1940–56, and passed in silence over the fact that, as his data indicated, per capita spending by the kolkhozniki on clothes in 1952 was at constant prices 26 per cent less than in 1940, which, as we know, was a bad year for them. The other data on spending in 1952 in relation to 1940 brought out by the author were as follows: knitted goods, 10 per cent decline; furniture and household goods, 4 per cent increase; cultural goods (books, newspapers, radios, musical instruments, watches, bicycles, motorcycles, etc.), 103 per cent increase. Since the latter purchases

were estimated at 35.1 billion rubles. In calculating the distributions in kind, Sergeev usually counted grain, possibly only wheat, at 2 rubles per kilogram (see, for example, *op. cit.*, p. 337). At this price *all* distributions in kind (including feed) in 1952 would have amounted to 17.5 million tons or 2 kilograms per *trudoden* in terms of grain equivalents. (The total amount of *trudodni* earned in 1952 was equal to 8.8 billion.) Thus the distributions specifically of grain are unlikely to have exceeded 1 kilogram per *trudoden* by much and may not have exceeded this level at all. If the distribution of grain in 1952 was equivalent to 1 kilogram per *trudoden,* some 8 million tons of grain equivalents remained for all distributions other than grain, certainly including feed. This was, of course, very little for a total number of kolkhozniki amounting to some eighty million.

[33] *Pravda,* January 25, 1958.

[34] *Economy of the USSR in 1956,* pp. 140–41.

[35] The distribution of 12.4 billion rubles by the kolkhozy to the kolkhozniki in 1952 implied that only 29.0 per cent of the money incomes of the kolkhozy were so distributed. Such distributions amounted to about 50 per cent of the total kolkhoz money receipts before World War II. The Soviet statisticians could smile when the prewar percentage was applied to postwar years by analysts outside of the USSR.

[36] *Soc. Agri.,* pp. 695–96.

[37] M. Moiseev, "Fundamental Changes in Material and Cultural Life," *Questions of Economics,* 1957, No. 10, p. 95.

have only a very small weight (the same is true of purchases of furniture), the official data leave no doubt that in the last Stalin year the purchases of consumers' non-food goods by the kolkhozniki were not unsubstantially smaller than in 1940. Knowing this full well, the stated author refrained from giving a weighted figure for all purchases of either all consumers' goods or food only.[38]

Only one series of distributions to the kolkhozniki in a whole oblast stretching over several years seems to be available, and, moreover, the series probably is unrepresentative. It pertains to Moscow oblast.

TABLE 43

Distributions to Kolkhozniki per *Trudoden* in Moscow Oblast, 1948–56*
(Rubles or kilograms. 1948 = 100.)

Year	Money	Grain	Potatoes	Vegetables
1948.............	0.61	0.74	3.97	1.53
1949.............	0.62	0.74	3.18	1.35
1950.............	0.55	0.64	1.99	0.96
1951.............	0.51	0.67	1.03	0.34
1952.............	0.57	0.74	1.55	0.46
1953.............	0.92	0.33	1.07	0.98
1954.............	1.81	0.63	0.60	0.80
1955.............	2.73	1.26	0.28	0.87
1956.............	3.48	1.16	1.19	0.80

* The distributions in 1952 are from S. S. Sergeev, *Problems of Economic-Statistical Analysis of Kolkhoz Output* (Moscow, 1956), p. 373. The data are given in the source by small areas. The weighted averages for the oblast as a whole were calculated by use of the number of kolkhozy in each small area as weights. *Questions of Economics*, 1957, No. 6 (p. 77), gave the distributions in all years shown in the table in per cent of those in 1948. The data in the table are obtained by combining those of the two sources.

The first thought is that the distributions in Moscow oblast must have been larger than the average for the country as a whole. Fortunately for the peasants, this was not so. The assumption may have been true of 1948 and adjacent years (even this is uncertain), but it is definitely not true with reference to 1951–53. The great decline shown by the distributions to the kolkhozniki in Moscow oblast from 1948 to 1951–53 in Table 43 probably is likewise unrepresentative. It must have been caused by the same factor which makes one expect a more favorable situation for the kolkhozniki in Moscow oblast than in the country as a whole: proximity to Moscow. This proximity made the effects of the conditions adverse to agri-

[38] Moiseev's data are based on survey material which yielded many an exaggerated figure for the growth in consumption and in the purchases of consumers' goods by the kolkhozniki, as well as by the wage earners, in postwar years as compared with 1940. So the situation discussed by the author in his article may actually have been considerably worse than that he described.

culture at the end of Stalin's years particularly pronounced in this oblast.

While the data for Moscow oblast may not be fully representative, they certainly are worth reproduction. What a picture those figures in Table 43 represent! Here, directly under the eyes of the great leader, the "socialist" kolkhozy are unable to provide even sufficient bread to their kolkhozniki; and Stalin was busy devising means to convert the kolkhozy into an even higher form, the Communist form!

One can hardly visualize a worse situation than a distribution of about 50–60 kopeks per *trudoden* or 70–85 kopeks for a real workday, year in and year out from 1948 to 1952, shown for Moscow oblast in Table 43. The distributions in kind, although limited to small quantities of grain, potatoes, and vegetables, were, of course, much more valuable. But everything obtained for a *trudoden* in kind in 1952 was about as much as an adult may well have eaten himself, and he needed other food to go with the grain, potatoes, and vegetables. The needs of his dependents had to be taken care of, and they all needed a little something besides food.

It has been stated that discussion of the private farming economy of the kolkhozniki is a prohibited subject in the USSR.[39] On the basis of the data on acreages and livestock holdings in the hands of the kolkhozniki (no data on output of crops by the kolkhozniki were released; the recently released data on output of animal products by them are believed to show an exaggerated upward trend), one must conclude that in 1952 the output from the kolkhozniki's private plots and herds was considerably below that in 1940. Yet out of these reduced supplies the kolkhozniki sold in kolkhoz trade around 1952 somewhat more than in 1940 according to this writer's calculations and much more according to official estimates.

The estimates of peasants' real incomes in 1948, 1950, and 1952 in Tables II and III (Appendix B) are guesses, made on the assumption that there was a certain improvement in these incomes between 1948 and 1952, the main item causing the improvement having been the fact that the peasants profited from the reductions in the prices of consumers' goods in official trade.[40] The increase in peasant incomes from 1948 to 1952 as here estimated, though possibly exaggerated, amounted to 20 per cent. This percentage rise compares

[39] There is no doubt, for example, that Sergeev would be all too enthusiastic to include the kolkhozniki's enterprises in his analysis. But all that he has on the kolkhozniki's incomes are the distributions to the kolkhozniki in money and kind, in a few oblasti which are put in as items of the economy of the *kolkhozy*.

[40] In the first two years of the period, the kolkhozniki were losing from the decline in prices in kolkhoz trade.

with the officially calculated increase in real incomes of the peasants of 50 per cent in those years. Quite a difference!

It seems reasonably certain that total per capita peasant incomes in 1952 were smaller than in 1940. If Tables II and III (Appendix B) show the same index for both years, this probably is due to an exaggeration of the 1952 income, caused by the fear of painting an even worse picture than that implied in the stated figures.

The calculations in Tables II and III indicate the extraordinarily low index of 60 for peasant incomes in 1952 in terms of those in 1928, and even this index may be too high. The decline since 1928 would have been moderately smaller if the savings (mostly investment in the farm economy) made by the peasants in 1928 had been excluded. (In 1952, the savings of the peasants were negligible.) Personal consumption by the peasants as such in 1952 was therefore not as disastrously below that of 1928 as is indicated by the calculated index.[41]

The 1952 index of real incomes of the peasants of about 60 per cent of that in 1928 compares with an index of about 70 per cent for the real paid-out wage. The difference is, however, larger, if the calculation of real wages also is made per capita (the calculation of peasant incomes is per capita to begin with). Then the peasants' real income is still 60 per cent of that in 1928, but the real paid-out wage rises to about 75 per cent of the latter. Moreover, the peasant incomes were much lower than those of the wage earners in 1928 (probably at most 60 per cent of the latter, if calculated at equal prices). This great disparity, not unreasonable for a backward agricultural country but unsuitable for an industrial country, should have been reduced over the years. Rather than this, it widened considerably, and this development ultimately brought the situation to near catastrophic dimensions which could not have been tolerated for long. The rather drastic reforms introduced after Stalin's death were overdue.

The rise in incomes in 1948 again.—The claim that real wages were more than doubled from 1947 to 1948 looks quite different upon analysis, which was attempted in "The Summit of Falsehood" (cited above). The lengthy discussion cannot be reproduced here. The summary is as follows:

a) Possibly one-fiftieth of all wage earners, or less than one million, may have had their real wages more than doubled, doubled, or nearly doubled in 1948.

[41] This is discussed in some detail in the essay "Peasant Incomes under Full-scale Collectivization," which is scheduled to be published (together with three other essays) about the same time as this volume.

b) Possibly one-half, the most precarious, had, if any, only negligible to small improvements in their real wages. The lowest wage group definitely lost.

c) The residual approximately 50 per cent of the hired-labor group may have had gains in real wages averaging perhaps 25 to 30 per cent, with a range of from about 10 to perhaps 70 per cent. The higher the wages, the greater unproportionately were the improvements.

d) Total according to the official count: real wages were more than doubled for all wage and salary earners.

A considerable deterioration of peasant incomes from 1947 to 1948 is also a part of this picture.

These conclusions seem to justify the title "The Summit of Falsehood" fully. If something is wrong with it, this is, as it turns out, that falsification of the 1948 data in the Report on the Fulfilment of the 1948 Plan, was preceded by a stupendous deliberate exaggeration of the yields and harvests of three important crops (potatoes, sunflower seed, and flax fiber) in 1933–38, disclosed in *Economy of the USSR in 1958* (pp. 354–55). This manipulation, of which not a hint was given for more than twenty-five years, may possibly be considered on a par with that of the manipulations in the data on 1948 real wages.

National Income

According to Table I (Appendix B), the 1940 national income, calculated at constant prices from the allocation end, had not been quite equaled by 1948. The difference was even greater if it is taken into account that the 1940 estimate for all practical purposes covers only the pre-1939 territory.

Personal incomes in 1948 are estimated to have been below the miserable 1940 level to a greater extent than national income. The 1940 level had not been reached even if the enlarged educational and health expenditures are included with personal incomes proper.

Investment, on the other hand, is believed to have attained the 1940 level in 1948. Investment in 1940, it is true, was at best equal to that of 1937 and was below that of 1936. But 1948 was the first year after the end of the starvation of World War II and of the almost equally bad early postwar years.

The Soviet Union never disarmed properly after World War II. After cutbacks in 1946 and 1947, and specifically after a small additional reduction in 1948, funds earmarked for military expenditures in 1948 dropped to the level of 1940, a year when the Soviet

Union was feverishly preparing for imminent war (the funds earmarked for military expenditures increased at current prices from
23.2 billion rubles in 1938 to 56.7 billion rubles in 1940).[42]

The growth of the national income from 1948 to 1950 and 1952
as estimated in Table I (Appendix B) at 33 and 66 per cent, respectively, seems high. It is, indeed, by no means unthinkable that
the growth in national income in these years, and especially that in
1951 and 1952, estimated at 25 per cent, was somewhat exaggerated.
But it seems inadvisable, after having calculated the individual
components of national income as best one could, to start lowering
them, without a feeling that the corrections are right, only because
the total growth seems too large.

The increase of personal incomes in 1948–52 by about 62 per cent
seems correct, or, in any case, close to correct. The earnings of wage
and salary earners make up the bulk of personal incomes. Yet the
total real wages certainly increased greatly in those years, what with
the substantial cut in prices of consumers' goods and the increase in
the number of wage and salary earners by about 20 per cent. If the
estimate of the increase in total personal incomes in 1948–52 is too
high, this could have occurred only, or mainly, by way of an exaggeration of the increase in the real incomes of the peasants. But this
increase is estimated at only about 20 per cent, and, after all, the
peasants must have profited from the decline in the prices of the
goods they were buying from the official trade, and also possibly from
a certain increase in their own output. There may, furthermore,
have been an increase in the distributions to the kolkhozniki for
trudodni, although this item amounted to very little in those years.
In 1948–50, however, the kolkhozniki were losing because of reductions in prices in kolkhoz trade.

Expenditures on education and health services did not show a
great increase in 1948–52 at current prices; but their value in real
terms necessarily grew considerably, together with the rise in real
wages. The same is true of expenditures on administration.

The growth in expenses earmarked for military purposes in 1948–
52 is estimated at a rate somewhat smaller than that assumed for per-

---

[42] *Essay I*, pp. 46–56. See also the discussion of the paper by Joseph Kershaw of the
RAND Corporation, "The Economic War Potential of the USSR," before the meeting
of the American Economic Association in December, 1950 (*Papers and Proceedings*,
May, 1951, pp. 475–82) by Dr. Edward Ames and this writer (*ibid.*, pp. 486–94). The
essence of Kershaw's paper was that the USA had nothing to worry about. The
attitude of Ames and this writer was not so complacent. It makes this writer extremely
unhappy that his and Ames's analysis elaborated in *Essay I*, was entirely neglected
in the United States until Russia's eye-opening satellites were in orbit.

sonal incomes. Nothing definite, it is true, is known of the prices charged to the military budget for armaments during the period involved. However, it seems improbable that the price development was less favorable for armaments than for civilian machinery, an industry in which a pretty good idea of changes in prices can be formed. The great jump in funds allocated for military purposes in 1951 and 1952 seems beyond doubt. There was an increase in these expenditures at current prices of as much as 31 per cent in only two years at the very time of declining prices of all goods, including machinery. The Soviet Union took its preparations for the Korean War much more seriously than was realized abroad at that time.

The calculated increase in expenditures earmarked for military purposes in 1948–52 may well be an underestimation on the basis of the data for output and utilization of machinery. According to Shimkin *et al.*, the output of machinery and equipment was expanded by not less than 64 per cent in two years, 1949 and 1950. The next two years showed a further increase of 34 per cent according to them,[43] with a total increase of 114 per cent in 1949 through 1952. Equipment used in state investments was officially estimated as having shown a jump of 60 per cent in 1948–50, but an almost unbelievably small increase of only 3 per cent in 1950–52.[44] Thus, almost the entire large increase in output of machinery must have consisted of armaments during the Korean War, according to the official data.[45]

Among the components of national income from allocation, net investment shows the greatest increase, almost 80 per cent, in 1948–52, according to Table I (Appendix B). If anything is exaggerated anywhere in the estimates of national income during this period, investment may be the item. However, fixed investment of the socialized sector grew by 83 per cent at constant prices in the years analyzed, according to official calculations.[46] The exaggeration in the estimate of the rise in total net investment, if any, is unlikely to be large.

The data in Table I imply annual rates of growth in national income of about 14 per cent in 1949 and 1950, and of about 12 per cent in 1951 and 1952.

[43] The official data for output of machinery, including other metal processing, indicate an increase of 37 per cent in these two years (*Industry of the USSR*, 1957, p. 203). No data were released on these items for 1948–50.

[44] Implied in *Economy of the USSR in 1956*, pp. 173–74.

[45] The allocated military expenditures during the period discussed are dealt with in "Der Sowietische Staatshaushalt," pp. 161–63.

[46] *Economy of the USSR in 1956*, p. 173.

A Soviet railway was caught trying to fulfil its targets by shipping empty cars (the Soviet press spoke of shipping of air). It may still be hoped that such occasions do not deprive the statistics concerning railway traffic of their role as the most reliable official Soviet statistical data and therefore as a good check on other data of which one cannot be so certain. Total freight traffic by all carriers (calculated in ton-kilometers) increased in the four years 1948 to 1952 as follows (in per cent):[47]

1949......................	17.3
1950......................	12.7
1951......................	12.0
1952......................	9.9
1948–52...................	62.8

There is, of course, no exact relationship between the growth of national income and the growth of freight traffic. A 66 per cent rise in national income may be somewhat too high vis-à-vis a rise of 63 per cent in freight traffic, but it is also not impossible. A moderately smaller rate of growth in national income would seem more consistent with the growth shown by freight traffic.

If, on the evidence for freight traffic, the estimate for the growth in national income is believed to be somewhat exaggerated, over-estimations are probably involved in the data for 1950 and 1952. But there may have been some specific reasons for the relatively small growth in freight traffic in those two years. Such specific reasons most likely were present, for example, in 1950. Hence only the estimate for 1952 remains in more or less serious doubt. The margin of doubt, however, is unlikely to be large.

On the basis of observation alone, one would have expected the decline in the rate of growth of national income to have been greater from 1948–50 to 1950–52 than from 14 to 12 per cent. An annual growth of 13 per cent in 1949 and 1950, on the average, and of 10 per cent or somewhat more, in 1951 and again in 1952, also on an average, seem reasonably certain.

After the first serious analysis of the data, this writer found very high rates of growth of the Soviet economy in the years following World War II. In *Essay I* (p. 6), published in 1951, he wrote: "Indeed, if the Soviet data on the changes in physical terms can be trusted (and there is too little evidence to distrust them), so large a rate of industrial growth is indicated for the most recent postwar years that there certainly is ground for serious concern." The find-

---

[47] Data for 1951 and 1952 from *Transport and Communications of the USSR*, 1957, p. 18. Data for 1949 and 1950 are those of Dr. Holland Hunter.

ings formulated then were reaffirmed and elaborated repeatedly on subsequent occasions.[48]

At that time and for quite a while thereafter, the findings were not supported by those of others. Gregory Grossman estimated the annual rate of growth of gross national product in 1949 and 1950 at $6.5 \geq 7$? per cent, or only about one-half this writer's estimate.[49] The Legislative Reference Service of the Library of Congress, in a report for the Joint Congressional Committee, *Trends of Economic Growth* (Washington, 1955, p. 71), estimated the average growth in gross national product of the USSR at 10 per cent in 1948–50 and at 6 per cent in 1950–53. If they had separated the indivdual years of the second group, they probably would have reached slightly higher figures for 1951 and 1952 than 6 per cent.

Relatively low estimates of Soviet economic growth were not limited to the United States. The editor of *Konjunkturpolitik,* in a boxed note to this writer's paper (cited in n. 48) welcomed the paper in the expectation that "at long last a more realistic appraisal is established of the substantial real rates of growth [of the Soviet economy]" and "that the habit of the lighthearted underestimating of the [Soviet] attainments will finally end."

Colin Clark is the pioneer in this field of inquiry. His method of calculation necessarily yields relatively low rates of growth. Yet his findings showed considerably higher rates than those of Grossman and the Library of Congress. He had an increase of 14.2 per cent in 1952 and 1953, the two years with substantially lower rates than those of 1949 and 1950.[50]

The findings of Peter Wiles of Oxford and of Alexander Nove of the University of London seem to have been the only ones in line with those of the present writer.

This writer's estimates will apparently find full confirmation when the calculations of Abram Bergson, started as far back as around 1947, are brought to a conclusion, which is expected to occur soon. Data in Table I (Appendix B) indicate an increase in national income from 1950 to 1952 of 26 per cent. RAND Memorandum RM-2101 (April, 1959) by O. Hoeffding and N. Nimitz, part of Bergson's project, calculated the increase in Soviet GNP in those two years *at current prices* at 12 per cent. When this percentage is adjusted for the undoubtedly large monetary deflation in those years,

[48] See, for example, "Die Zuwachsraten der Sowietischen Wirtschaft," *Konjunkturpolitik* (Berlin), 1956, No. 2. The rates of growth of Soviet national income were there estimated at 13 per cent both in 1949 and in 1950 and at 8.5 per cent in each year, 1951–54, on the average (p. 82).

[49] *Soviet Economic Growth,* ed. A. Bergson, p. 9.

[50] See his *The Conditions of Economic Progress* (3d ed.; London, 1957), p. 247.

a figure is likely to be obtained not much different from that cal-culated here.[51]

No calculation of national income was made for 1945. However, it is unlikely to have been larger than two-thirds of that in 1940 and may well have been measurably smaller than this in a comparable territory.

All in all, for 1952 we have an excess of national income of more than 50 per cent over that in 1940 (implied in data in Appen-dix B, Table I) and a rise of little more than 100 per cent since 1945. The rise since 1940 was even larger than this on a per capita basis, because in 1952 the population was smaller than in 1940 by about 8 per cent—again in a comparable territory. All in all a favorable picture, except for the price of this growth: the greatly dis-organized agriculture and the very low level of incomes of wage and salary earners, and especially those of the peasants, at the end of the successful period. It is left to the reader to appraise this price as compared with the attainments. If such an appraisal is made, the decade of the 1930's, consisting largely of the *All-out Drive* with its devastations and the *Purge Era* with its stagnation, should be taken into account.

[51] The cited report does not contain a calculation for 1949. For 1950, it shows a practically unchanged GNP from that for 1949—again at current prices—but that was a year with a particularly large decline in prices of both producers' and consumers' goods. When the GNP index for this year is recalculated to constant prices, it too may turn out to be no smaller than that implied in the calculations made here.

So much has happened in the Soviet economy in the short period of seven years since Stalin's death that I find it difficult to squeeze all the changes into my forthcoming volume devoted to the post-Stalin economy. Yet the Soviet economy is still so much Stalinist in 1960 that the Polish economic organization, also a "socialist" one, seems very liberal by comparison. Stalin's economic organization was indeed unique. He succeeded in putting economic thought, economic initiative, in such a state of deep freeze that defrosting has been a very slow process. Almost nothing happened in this respect for three years, until the Twentieth Party Congress (February, 1956), indeed largely until later than that. The most important developments did not start mainly until the end of 1956 (to name only some: turn to more realistic planning by the decision of the plenary session of the CC of the Party of December 25, 1956; decentralization of industry, whatever there is of it, according to the law of May 10, 1957; abolition of multiple prices paid by the state to the kolkhozy and the sale of farm machinery to kolkhozy according to the decision of the plenary session of the CC of the Party of June 17–18, 1958; fundamental change in the composition of producer fuels; shift away from hydroelectric power. The chief exceptions (the reversal in farm policies and a change in expenditures on the armed forces), which both occurred right after Stalin's death, had special weighty reasons for this. A timid step toward reducing the enormous stratification of wages—another characteristic of Stalin's "socialism"—was taken only in 1956.*

* Upon reconsideration, the conclusion was reached that the plenary session of the CC of the Party of December, 1956, was definitely the point when the period of slow conversion of deep freeze under Stalin was replaced by actual defrosting, definite features of which can be observed in the succeeding years.

431

As shown in chapter 11, the Soviet price system was in a chaotic state under Stalin. This pertains to both price formation and to choice between investment projects. While more or less important improvements were made after Stalin's death, the price system is still in bad shape; specifically, there is no charge for use of the invested capital—a fundamental defect. Reward for land use (in agriculture and extracting industries) and quasi-rents are also not settled properly. A thorough overhauling of the prices of producers' goods is believed necessary. It is to last for two years (1961 and 1962). These new prices will not start operating until almost ten years after Stalin's death. Yet, even for the new price system, the inclusion of interest on capital (in one form or another) and other needed basic improvements have not been announced, probably not yet decided upon.

Measures to insure rational selection among investment possibilities have made better progress, but this issue is also far from settled. The opinion is widespread in the West that the problem of a proper yardstick to insure rational selection among investment projects came up recently because the economy has become more complex; this factor, however, has not been decisive. The reason why this problem was not settled ten or even twenty years ago, was the deep freeze of all thought, of all initiative, under Stalin.

The problem of hydroelectric power versus fuel-burning electric plants did not become more complicated in 1958, when the shift from hydroelectric to fuel-burning power plans was decided, than it was in 1950. The Soviet economy was much more badly in need of investment funds in the earlier than the later year. Yet, in the second half of 1950 the construction of gigantic and very expensive hydroelectric plants was decided upon without any discussion or study. When in 1958 the decision was at long last made that differences in the needed investment and in construction time must be taken into consideration in dealing with the problem of hydroelectric versus fuel-burning plants, it turned out that fuel-burning electric plants had to be given preference before even the Krasnoyarsk hydroelectric plant, per kilowatt of capacity thus far the cheapest such plant to be undertaken in the USSR.

The deep freeze of thought and initiative in Stalin's day can be doubted only if one sees merely the program of space conquest. Even in this field of great Soviet successes it is not certain that much had been done under Stalin. And it is certainly a great exception.

The principal change since Stalin's death is in the attitude toward agriculture. The Stalin period was largely based on severe exploitation of agriculture and the peasants. The harmful effect of these policies was so great and a reversal so badly needed that it might have occurred even under Stalin had he lived a few years longer. The more liberal farm policy was announced by Malenkov as early as August, 1953, five months after Stalin's death, but the reversal proceeded very slowly and partly in a nonsensical way. The decisive step in this area was not made before 1958. The difficulties are far from overcome, however, in particular because the policy of improving the income of the peasants must be brought in conformity with the attempt to get rid of another Stalin inheritance—the immense stratification of wages. The incomes of most peasants, though improved, continue to be so low relative to those of comparable wage earners, that healthy development is seriously impeded.

Along with the shift away from hydroelectric power, several other important improvements have occurred in industry—all of them very recently and none which could not have happened much earlier. The already mentioned decisive shift from the expensive coal to the cheap petroleum and even cheaper gas may be the most important change. Intensification of development of the chemical industry, with increased emphasis on artificial fibers, also is among these changes. The speed-up in the chemical industry was not announced until 1958; the decisions on fuel were made in 1957 and especially in 1958.

The year 1958, that is, five years after Stalin's death, was indeed one of feverish changes, of which some were not well thought out and some completely nonsensical and had to be abandoned in a hurry. As if prolonged stagnation was to be made up by hasty change, by any change.

Stalin was spending immense amounts on the armed forces. Soviet expenditures on the armed forces remain large, but despite all the secrecy surrounding these expenditures, one may venture the assumption that their share in the national income has declined substantially since 1952, Stalin's last year. Yet the Soviet economy has become much stronger, and the present threat is greater. The change in policy toward the armed forces, which, like the change in farm policy, occurred right after Stalin's death, permitted an improvement in peasant incomes, without sacrificing the rate of growth of investment and also with full retention of the great rate of over-all economic growth.

So much for differences. But the similarities are vital too. The exploitation of the agriculturists, i.e., the peasants, under Stalin has already been emphasized. The exploitation of wage and salary earners differed from it only in degree. An industrialized country with personal incomes far below the level of a backward, heavily overpopulated agricultural country—this is the unique phenomenon observed in Stalin's day. Socialism is the name believed appropriate for this arrangement.

It was the drastic exploitation of the whole population that permitted the immense investments, the messy state of prices, misinvestments and, last but not least, the very large expenditures on the armed forces. While there has been a substantial improvement in personal incomes since Stalin's death, real wages did not regain their 1928 level until 1958. Peasants' per capita real incomes were still below that level in 1958, according to the calculations of the writer. The margin of error in these calculations is small as compared with the improvement in real wages and per capita real incomes of the peasants, which would have occurred under any regime but the communist dictatorship during the thirty-year period.

As under Stalin, so under Khrushchev, severe exploitation of the population remains the foundation of the great progress that the Soviet economy is displaying.

VLADIMIR GUSTAVOVICH GROMAN

An important page in the history of the Russian intelligentsia is fading into oblivion through the efforts of the Soviet government and the neglect of the opposing camp.

By the time Lenin's attempt at introducing Communism, by way of obtaining from the peasants a few million tons of grain gratis and distributing it among factories, collapsed in the great famine of 1921–22, or soon thereafter, most political leaders opposing the regime were abroad. Most of those interested in the economy, however, remained in the USSR. Indeed, at least two prominent men, N. P. Makarov and A. N. Chelintsev, came back (Makarov from the United States) to participate in the reconstruction of Russia from the ruins.

The Narodniki faction, or, as they were called, the neo-Narodniki, naturally concentrated on research in agriculture. Under the very able leadership of N. D. Kondradiev, the Narodniki almost monopolized research and planning in the Commissariat of Agriculture. N. P. Makarov, A. V. Chayanov, A. N. Chelintsev, Albert Weinstein, and A. A. Rybnikov were among the other important names. Kondratiev was also director of the Institute of Current Economics of the Commissariat of Finance and editor of its very important *Bulletins*. On its staff the Institute had also a number of first-rate mathematical statisticians, who upheld the great reputation Russia had enjoyed in this field.

The Mensheviks turned their eyes to the industry and economy as a whole. They played a considerable role in the field of theory, and had a very great influence in practical economics. Now, in retrospect, the Russia of the NEP certainly does not look like the realization of the ideal of democratic socialism. It was far from this even to the contemporaries. Yet almost all large-scale industry was in the hands of the state, and so was

Reprinted by permission from the *Russian Review*, January, 1954.

435

all banking and foreign trade, and almost all wholesale trade. A large part of the retail trade was operated by the state or the co-operatives. There certainly was a vast field for work, especially until Stalin could get rid of all his enemies inside the Party and could pay more attention to "operating" the entire national economy.

The Menshevik A. M. Ginzburg directed the planning work in the Supreme Council of National Economy. But the great stronghold of the Menshevik forces was the Gosplan, with V. G. Groman as a leading light. From 1923 to 1927, inclusive, this group dominated the current planning and had a profound influence also on the preparation of the first Five-Year Plan. The extremely important milestones of Soviet planning, *The Control Figures of the National Economy of the USSR* for 1925–26, 1926–27, and 1927–28, were almost entirely the work of the Groman group.

V. A. Bazarov, a follower of A. A. Bogdanov,* but in agreement with Groman in practical problems, was Groman's closest collaborator. Among the others may be mentioned B. A. Gukhman, N. M. Vishnevsky, G. V. Shub, and V. I. Zeilinger—all Mensheviks.

V. P. Milyutin, a leading Communist, in his report "On Counter-revolutionary Wrecking in Agriculture" at the meeting of the Agrarian Institute of the Communist Academy, October 1, 1930, thus described this group of non-Communist intelligentsia:

> Those agents of world capitalism and of the domestic bourgeoisie among us selected specific methods of fighting. They occupied responsible positions, many of them top positions in our central governmental organizations. Groman was a member of the Presidium of the Gosplan; Kondratiev played an important role in the Commissariats of Finance and Agriculture for a long time; Makarov held a responsible position in the Commissariat of Agriculture for a long time; Sukhanov did responsible work in the Commissariat of Trade and Agriculture; Sadyrin was a member of the Central Executive Committee; Yurovsky played a dominant role in the Commissariat of Finance and was a member of its Presidium. . . .[1]

In 1928, with the NEP drawing to an end, Groman was dropped from the Gosplan, Kondratiev was deprived of the control of his Institute, Yurovsky (apparently in 1929) was fired from the Commissariat of Fi-

---

* The fate of Bogdenov is possibly the greatest tragedy in Soviet Communist history. Naturally, except in such sources as encyclopedias, the regime keeps mum, and they certainly succeed in concealing the very interesting truth. In the early years of the Party, especially the 1890's, Bogdanov, a highly talented philosopher and economist, was first in the Bolshevist ranks after Lenin. Then he began to drift away from strict Marxian philosophy. But he did not leave the Party. He wanted Bolshevism to be founded on another philosophy. It was Lenin who did not want to permit anything of this kind. When the Bolshevist Party grasped power in 1917, there was no place for Bogdanov. He felt compelled to leave political life and turned to medicine (he graduated as a medical doctor in his early years). In 1928, Bogdanov died of poisoning while experimenting on himself. Suicide? Possibly. Deep desperation in any case.

[1] The Agrarian Institute of the Communist Academy, *Kondratievshchina* (Moscow, 1930), p. 7.

nance, and so on. By the end of 1930, almost everybody (only one exception is known to me) was taken off the active list, even those who had accepted the collectivization drive before being put in jail. The Menshevik trial, early in 1931, was the wind-up of a glorious era.

The time for shooting of Stalin's enemies had not yet arrived. If any of the named and unnamed anti-Communists who were active in the economic life of the twenties lost his life, this probably occurred later. But a whole generation of the intelligentsia disappeared without a trace, and the country was deprived of the opportunity to profit from their talents and their experience.[2]

In the late twenties, planning of the national economy implemented through compulsion replaced planning by methods which, with certain exceptions, would have been acceptable in democratic countries. In direct connection with this fundamental change of policy, the Gosplan and other state economic agencies were cleared not only of those opposed to the new methods, but also of those not fully enthusiastic about them. While Communists received a mild treatment (Krzhizhanovsky, the president of the Gosplan of the USSR and a personal friend of Lenin, and Strumilin, primarily responsible for the first Five-Year Plan, were relegated to the Academy of Sciences of the USSR); non-Communists, with only one exception known to me, L. B. Kafengaus, simply disappeared.

Vladimir Gustavovich Groman, member of the Presidium of the Gosplan and "Distinguished Worker of Science" (this was the highest title bestowed upon Soviet scholars then) was the one most abused. The extreme viciousness of the attacks upon him only shows how high he stood as a planner, fighter, and man.

It may be thought that I am prejudiced in favor of Groman. Hence, rather than speaking myself, I will quote the editors of *Courier of Statistics,* a scientific journal of the Central Statistical Office of the USSR. The occasion was the thirtieth anniversary of the statistical and scientific work of V. G. Groman (he was fifty-two years old then). Only relatively short extracts from the lengthy eulogy can be reproduced here.[3]

Russian statistics, whether in the field of statistical practice or that of statistical theory, includes many great names. One of the most prominent is that of Vladimir Gustavovich, who is renowned not only as an original scholar but as a remarkable person as well. One may disagree with V. G. Groman, one may fight with him on this or that issue, but even in extreme disagreement one cannot help but fall under the spell of his exceptional charm and his brilliant mind. The most striking characteristics of Vladimir Gustavovich are his boundless, bursting vitality and the breadth of his national-economic approach to all

[2] Other urgent tasks prevent this writer from undertaking a history of this important period. For some time he has been working on a monograph on Soviet planning, in which the activities of the Groman-Bazarov group are to be given their due. In this article the author is happy to have an opportunity to publish a short statement on Groman.

[3] *Courier of Statistics,* 1927, No. 2, pp. i–viii.

the problems which he attacks. Vladimir Gustavovich is incapable of thinking piecemeal, in scraps; such thinking is organically alien to him. His thought is always synthetic, his analysis always grasps the aggregate of a whole number of isolated factors. . . .

. . . When the uproar of Civil War started to subside and the Soviet society turned from revolutionary wars to revolutionary construction, the ideas of V. G. Groman began to attract attention and to make progress toward realization in life. When, shortly after the organization of the Gosplan, V. G. Groman had become one of its foremost workers, he at once started to develop statistical methods which would throw light on the national economy as a whole with all its manifestations. Thus came to life the statistics of current economic observations, thus developed *The Control Figures of the National Economy of the USSR,* and thus became visible the ways of planned statistical work, which now forms the basis of our economic policies. Undoubtedly, the idea of the balance of national economy is also his. Everybody who worked with him at this time or in later periods, knows well his ability to produce in all his collaborators that special enthusiasm which is the characteristic feature of all working units organized by Groman. . . .

In the Gosplan he organized the Council for Current Economic Observation and started to assemble scattered statistical studies of departmental and state statistics into something that makes sense. Thus came to life the first surveys of current economic observation and the first reports to the Soviet of Labor and Defense [STO] on the national economy. As is usual, many tried to imitate Groman. Bureaus for current economic observation were organized in each Commissariat; everybody who had leisure started to manufacture surveys of current economic observation. Groman himself made a further step and took an active part in the preparations of Control Figures, which now are the basis of all our planning. . . .

In this synthesis of planning and statistical work, for which Groman strove all his life, but which he could realize only after the October Revolution, in the epoch of active socialist construction, is the best characterization of V. G. Groman as a social scientist and thinker. Let us hope that now, when conditions for fruitful work in this field are at hand, V. G. Groman will start a new brilliant page in the history of his activities and will help to develop what he calls statistics of a national-economic total.

This fully deserved eulogy may be supplemented and modified to a certain extent. The idea of Groman as a thinker is, perhaps, over-emphasized. Let us quote V. A. Bazarov, Groman's closest collaborator in the last and most important decade of his active life. The very title of Bazarov's article "Groman's Concept of the National-Economic Total and the Planning Principle" [4] shows that on the vital point of handling the economy as a unit, Bazarov's appraisal was exactly the same as that of the editors of *Courier of Statistics.* But in the following characteristic, Bazarov introduces a note different from that of these editors and, in my opinion, more to the point: "V. G. Groman, as a brilliant artist in the sphere of economics, possesses a spark of mysterious insight which by its very essence is untranslatable into the language of our economic discussion of scientific-methodological perception."

[4] *Planned Economy,* 1927, No. 6, pp. 162–65.

When, in 1916, Groman attacked the Constitutional-Democratic Party and its spokesman A. I. Shingarev for their ineffective ways of fighting inflation, it was not so much Groman's better knowledge or greater wisdom as that "mysterious insight" of which Bazarov spoke.

The picture of Groman would be incomplete without emphasizing his quite extraordinary scientific truthfulness. When Groman committed an error, he would not try to close his eyes to facts, or look for excuses. For him facts, the truth, were supreme. Once he realized his error, he would speak of it freely, would look for an opportunity to acknowledge his error to the person who may have pointed out to him the correct interpretation. Without this crowning feature he would never have commanded the prestige, the adoration, which he enjoyed, especially among his collaborators.

Groman was the son of a German father and a Russian mother. I always thought his buoyant energy came from his father. His lack of restraint, on the other hand, was certainly from his Russian mother.

The thirtieth anniversary of Groman's activities was in May, 1927. The "brilliant page," which the editors of the *Courier of Statistics* had wished him, lasted only about a year. He continued to fight for another year. When the all-out war against the peasants was on, Groman had the great courage to address an open letter to the Council of People's Commissars and the Council of Labor and Defense (the Gosplan, the center of Groman's activities, was a committee of the latter council) in the Moscow papers of October 10, 1929, in which he referred to himself as a "socialist who does not share the point of view of the Communist Party." Gorbunov (secretary to Rykov, who was then chairman of the Council of People's Commissars and chairman of the Council of Labor and Defense) answered the letter on Rykov's orders. He correctly interpreted Groman's position as that of an adherent of the Second International.[5]

Groman's arrest followed. He was broken and was made the chief performer at the so-called Menshevik trial, March 1–9, 1931, with N. D. Kondratiev, the leader of the Narodniki opposition, as the star witness for the prosecution.[6] I wonder how many planning enthusiasts in this and other countries have ever heard of this trial. Yet this was not a trial of men, but the triumphal burial of planning without force, of planning combined with freedom for the worker to take and leave his job, of planning which allowed for the small-scale enterprise and, to some degree, freedom of thought and expression, in short, the kind of planning which many Western enthusiasts visualize and want for their own countries.

One feature of the trial, minor on the surface, may be mentioned here.

[5] P. E. Vaisberg, "Bourgeois Distortions in the Realm of Planning," *Planned Economy*, 1930, No. 1, p. 19. I could not find either Groman's letter or Gorbunov's reply in Moscow papers of all-Russian circulation. It is possible that they were printed in a local paper such as *Moskovskaya Pravda*. But Vaisberg had a responsible position in the Gosplan and *Planned Economy* was the Gosplan's journal, so the authenticity of the letter itself and of the reply are beyond any doubt.

[6] *The Trial of the Counterrevolutionary Organization of the Mensheviks* (Moscow, 1931)—the official stenographic report of the trial.

Throughout the trial, the court and the prosecutor addressed the accused by their last names. The accused themselves and the prosecution witnesses (there were no others) mostly called one another by the first name and the patronymic, the usual polite form of address among Russians. At first it apparently occurred spontaneously. But as the trial proceeded, it seems to have become a deliberate policy. The persistence in referring to Groman as Vladimir Gustavovich Groman by the chief prosecution witness, Kondratiev, was indeed so great that it must have had the effect of a deliberate demonstration.

In his final summing-up of the individual characteristics of the accused, Krylenko, the prosecutor, described Groman as "the leader," "the authority," "the organizer," "the man who enjoyed the greatest confidence." [7] Krylenko was right; Groman was indeed a leader, an organizer, a man who enjoyed great confidence.

Several reasons combined to make it understandable that such a fearless fighter as Groman was forced to repeat the foolish "confessions" dictated to him by Stalin's henchmen. Prolonged angina pectoris (in 1923 a Berlin specialist gave him a year to live) and excessive addiction to liquor had much to do with this. More than thirty years of uninterrupted fighting for something, against somebody, not infrequently against everybody, also contributed. Furthermore, almost all the Narodniki of the opposition confessed and gave up the unequal fight when still not in jail. (I am far from blaming anybody; I have nothing but pity for them.) But the decisive factor in Groman's surrender may have been the hopelessness of seeing planning, his cherished child, being put to use for the oppression of the whole Russian people, and especially of the hundred million peasants, for aims, exactly the reverse of what he wanted it to serve. Now, there was no more sense to living, to fighting; nothing made any great difference; one might as well comply with the henchmen's demands if this would bring the liquor which had become practically indispensable to him.

I may add that I was happy to work under Groman in the short time from July, 1916, to mid-March, 1917. In 1923, 1925, and 1927, Groman made trips to Germany where I lived at that time, and we spent much time together. The interruptions made it easier for me to realize the changes. In 1917, when I tore myself away from Groman, he was a planning maniac, the more dangerous the bigger his abilities, the stronger his drive. Long before 1928, the end of his career, he was a wise statesman, of great value to Russia because of his superhuman energy, his infectious enthusiasm, and, last but not least, his honesty.

An editor, to whom I submitted a note on Groman, suggested that I censure him for having "confessed" at the trial. My answer is this: "I am proud that Groman adhered to the same social-economic philosophy that I do; I am proud that I had the opportunity to work under him; I am proud that I have the right to call myself a friend of Vladimir Gustavovich Groman."

[7] *Ibid.*, p. 355

A Further Note on Groman

The idea of linear programming, with input-output analysis as its important component, attracts considerable attention now. The idea of input-output analysis of course dates back to Quesnay, but its rebirth in recent times and its practical application go back to Groman under the designation "balance of national economy." Early in 1923, Groman reported on the balance to the economic-statistical section of the Gosplan (*Bulletin of the Gosplan,* 1923, No. 3–4, p. 73). In November, 1923, he read a paper on it before an extraordinary meeting of the chief board of the Gosplan (*ibid.,* No. 11–12, pp. 120–22). On the urging of the Gosplan, STO (Council of Work and Defense, a small Sovnarkhom) ordered the CSO to prepare a balance of national economy. The result was the monumental volume: CSO, *Balance of National Economy of the USSR of 1923–24* (Moscow, 1926). An early release of the balance was discussed by Wasilii Leontiev of Harvard, then still in Leningrad, in *Welwirtschaftliches Archiv,* 1925. With the name of Groman not rehabilitated, unjustified claims of authorship of the idea have been made. Under Soviet conditions regarding freedom of speech, they may be confident that nobody will quote the statement from an editorial in the *Courier of Statistics,* the journal of the Central Statistical Office, 1927, No. 2, p. ii, cited above: "To him [Groman] undoubtedly belongs also the idea of the balance of national economy." The West also is misled on this point.

TABLE I

USSR Net National Product or Income, Selected Years*
(In billions of rubles, at real 1926/27 prices)

Item	1928	1937	1940[a]	1948	1950	1952	1955
Total with some duplication	32.6	54.0	60.1	59.0	78.0	96.4	118.6
Administration, MVD and communal services[b]	0.8	1.5	2.2	2.8	3.5	3.7	3.7*
Military purposes, earmarked[d]	0.8	5.7	13.3	13.3	14.6[e]	20.6[e]	23.3
Net investment[f]	5.1	18.0	18.0	18.0	26.1	32.3	39.9
(subtotal)	5.9	23.7	31.3	31.3	40.7	52.9	63.2
Personal incomes[g]	24.3	24.1	22.3	19.3	25.8	31.4	39.9
Education and health services	1.6	4.7	4.3	5.6	8.0	8.4[h]	11.8[i]
(subtotal)	25.9	28.8	26.6	24.9	33.8	39.8	51.7
Duplication[j]	2.8	2.9	3.7	4.3	5.2	5.7	7.1
Total, less duplication	29.8	51.1	56.4	54.7	72.8	90.7	111.5

* Exactness seems impossible of course. Only orders of magnitude are aimed at. No conclusions will be found in the volume which would be incorrect, if one or another figure in Tables I and III and elsewhere turned out moderately inexact.

The original manuscript included four rather lengthy Appendix Notes, explaining the details of some of the calculations, but these had to be omitted owing to technical reasons. In calculating incomes of wage (wage always includes salary) earners only wages were considered. Pensions and social-insurance payments received were not included. This was a minor item before 1956 (see Tables II and III below). A major item is that the incomes of the residual non-farm population had to be assumed to have changed in the same proportion as that of those at work (on a per capita basis). The calculation of the incomes of farm population is necessarily as crude as that of the non-farm population.

It is hoped that investment is covered fully, but investments, which were financed out of the non-specified balance of budgetary appropriations for the national economy and from the "surplus" of budgetary incomes over expenditures may possibly need to be added to the totals here calculated. Inadequately considered are possibly such forms of investment as the costs connected with putting new plants in operation, industrial migration, etc. All those omissions and inaccuracies do not necessarily affect the calculation of rates of growth. If expenditures earmarked for military purposes appear also under other items, mainly investment, they cannot be excluded there. For various reasons, national income in postwar years may be moderately underestimated relative to prewar years. But on the other hand, depreciation charges are inadequate, the losses caused by wars, misinvestment, and technological obsolescence are not properly written off. On balance, the rates of growth implied in the calculations may be moderately exaggerated. This pertains specifically to the postwar period.

a Strictly pre-1939 territory, so far as private consumption is concerned. Practically the same territory for the other items.

b This item was omitted in Essay I, p. 85, owing to the difficulties involved in converting the values at current rubles into those in real 1926/27 prices. The values in current prices until 1948, inclusive, were taken from Oleg Hoeffding, Soviet National Income and Product, 1928 (Columbia University Press, 1954), p. 19, and Abram Bergson and Hans Heymann, National Income and Product, 1940 through 1953 (RAND, 1953), Table 4. The data for later years in nominal terms are official, so far as these are available; otherwise they are estimated. The same percentage composition of the expenses on administration, into "personnel" and "other expenditures" and the same conversion factors were used for the years since 1937, which were applied in the case of education and health services (see Essay I, p. 80).

c The expenditure on administration in nominal terms in 1955 was 12.5 billion rubles as against 14.4 or 14.5 billion in 1952. An expenditure at constant prices unchanged since 1952 was assumed in view of the increase in real wages and reduced prices of all goods.

d The estimates of expenditures on the armed forces follow the estimates in Essay I, p. 85, except for 1928. The expenditure planned for 1927/28 was equal to 800 million rubles. This figure is used here for 1928. Hoeffding (op. cit., p. 19) gives 760 million as the fulfilment figure.

e The increase in the funds earmarked for military expenditures from 1948 to 1949 was presumably small. From 1949 to 1952 funds earmarked for military expenditures were enlarged in nominal terms by 44 per cent, from 1950 to 1952 by 37 per cent. The increase from 1948 to 1952 is assumed to have been equivalent to 55 per cent in real terms. Of this increase 11 per cent is assigned to 1948–50 and 40 per cent to 1950–52.

f The estimate for 1928 is explained in chapter 4. The increase in the fixed capital of the private sector in 1927/28 is excluded further down in the column as duplication. Such duplication occurs also in the estimates of the subsequent years, but it is unimportant quantitatively. The figure for 1937 is a downward revision of the estimate in *Essay I*, p. 85, errata sheet, with a further discount of 10 per cent. The estimates for the subsequent years are explained in the portions dealing with investment in the various periods.

g From Table II below. The figures for 1927/28 in that table were computed by dividing the total income of the farm and the non-farm population as estimated by the Gosplan by the respective populations. Gosplan's estimates must have included all forms of income, inclusive of compensation of unemployed, pensions, etc. It included also all kinds of savings, including that invested in the fixed and variable capital and this involves a certain duplication (see below).

The figures for 1937 and later years for the non-farm population are computed under the assumption that the per capita incomes of this population changes proportionately with the real wage of the wage-earning families. However, unemployment benefits, pensions, other social insurance benefits, stipends of students, etc., increased (in nominal terms) more than wages proper. According to Hoeffding (*op. cit.*, p. 14) and Bergson-Heymann (*op. cit.*, pp. 20–23), they rose from 790 million rubles in 1928 to 29.1 billion rubles in 1948, or 36.8 times the 1928 level, while total incomes of households of wage earners and employees increased from 25,770 million rubles to 531.4 billion rubles, or 20.6 times the 1928 level. The share of those income items advanced from 3.0 to 5.5 per cent and the incomes of the non-farm population since 1937 may be underestimated to a somewhat smaller extent than these 2.5 percentage points. But the share of incomes other than wages and the enumerated benefits in the total incomes of the non-farm population presumably declined over time even on a per capita basis.

The incomes of the farm population are calculated to include incomes in money and kind.

The 1927/28 data are applied to 1928 (the same is true of some other items). No recomputation from 1927/28 prices to 1926/27 prices has been made. The official living cost index based on workers' budgets was the same in 1926/27 and in 1927/28 prices (*Control Figures for 1929/30*, p. 578). Farm prices and consequently the value of farm income in kind rose by 4.8 per cent in the same year. Hence a small reduction of the figures expressed in 1927/28 prices would actually be needed.

h Computed by the procedure used in *Essay I*, p. 80; see also errata sheet. Real wages are assumed to have grown by 49 per cent from 1948 to 1952. The conversion factor for "other expenditures" is assumed to have remained almost unchanged over the period 1948–52.

i The expenditures increased by 27.2 per cent in nominal terms from 1952 to 1955. Ten per cent has been added for the increase in the purchasing power of money.

j The wages of personnel in administration, etc., have been deducted.

ADDENDUM.—I am extremely sorry to have missed the valuable work by Raymond P. Powell (*A Materials-Input of Soviet Construction, Revised and Extended*, RAND Corporation, September, 1959, processed), which represents an index of Soviet construction in 1927/28 to 1958 based on the amounts of building materials used. Exact agreement on the rates of growth in materials used in construction calculated by Powell and those of net investment calculated in this book cannot, of course, be expected. With this consideration, the findings of the two sources are very close, almost too close. According to official sources, construction (including installation) of the socialized sector increased close to twenty fold in 1928–55; Powell's index (1927/28 equals 100) is 721, this writer's (1928 equals 100) is 784.

This writer's estimates for 1932–37 and 1937–40 coincide exactly with those of Powell. For 1927/28 to 1932 Powell has an increase of 74 per cent as against 130 per cent in 1928–32 of this writer. This relatively great difference was to be expected on the basis of the discussion on pages 87–88. The fact that Powell has a higher rate of growth for 1940–50 than this writer (54 per cent rather than 45 per cent) is not too surprising in view of the discussion on page 302. This writer is also somewhat lower than Powell for 1950–55.

TABLE II

REAL WAGES AND REAL INCOMES OF THE PEASANTS, SPECIFIED YEARS*
(1928 = 100)

Year	Real Wage[a]	Real Income of Peasants
1932/33........	49	53
1936..........	55	...
1937..........	60	81
1940..........	52	60
1948..........	45	50
1950..........	60	55
1952..........	70	60
1955..........	80	75

* The indices for wages cover only paid-out wages minus taxes and bond purchases; wage earners include salary earners. The incomes of the peasants are calculated in a similar manner.

This writer calculated real wages in *Essay I*, but he has here utilized extensively Mrs. Janet Chapman's very valuable material, published later. He strongly hopes, however, that Mrs. Chapman will fundamentally revise her real-wage index with 1937 prices as weights. The peasant incomes are worked out in a special essay, to be published about the same time as the present volume.

There are some small revisions in the above table as compared with the estimates in *Commentary*, p. 41.

[a] The calculation in *Commentary* still subdivided the real wage into that before taxes and bond purchases and that after these. After payments on all bonds were discontinued beginning with 1958, bonds purchased in previous years were equivalent to payment of taxes.

TABLE III

PERSONAL INCOMES IN SPECIFIED YEARS*

| YEAR (1) | POPULATION (in millions) | | REAL NON-FARM WAGE^a (1928 = 100) (4) | DEPENDENTS PER WAGE AND SALARY EARNER (5) | REAL INCOME PER CAPITA | | | | TOTAL REAL INCOME (in billions of rubles) | | |
| | Farm (2) | Non-farm (3) | | | 1928 = 100 | | Rubles | | Farm^c (10) | Non-farm^c (11) | Total (12) |
					Farm^a (6)	Non-fa.m^b (7)	Farm (8)	Non-farm (9)			
1928........	120	31.3	100	1.35	100	100	120^d	320^d	14.4	9.9	24.3
1932........	100	52	49	1.25	53	51	72	163	6.4	8.4	14.8
1937........	92	74	60	1.20	81	64	97	205	8.9	15.2	24.1
1940........	90	85	52	1.10	60	58	72	186	6.5	15.8	22.3
1948........	87	88	45	1.10	50	50	60	160	5.2	14.1	19.3
1950........	87	94	60	1.10	55	67	66	214	5.7	20.1	25.8
1952........	85	101	70	1.10	60	78	72	250	6.1	25.3	31.4
1955........	87	113	80	1.10	75	89^e	90	284	7.8	32.1	39.9

* Rubles of 1927/28 or 1928 purchasing power. The details of calculations were laid down in the Appendix Notes mentioned in the asterisk footnote to Table I above. The distribution of the population in farm and non-farm hardly involves great doubts. More uncertain are the calculations of the changes in the number of dependents per wage and salary earner. (Salary earners are always included with wage earners.) Most uncertain is the assumption that the per capita incomes of the whole non-farm population were changing in proportion to the changes in the paid-out wage. Pensions were not considered (see note "g" to Table I).

   ^a From Table II.

   ^b Obtained from data in columns 4 and 5.

   ^c Obtained from data in columns 2 and 3, and 8 and 9.

   ^d Implied in data in Control Figures for 1929/30, pp. 470–71.

   ^e Although the figure works out to 89.52, it is rounded to 89.

THE CONCEPT OF KOLKHOZ TRADE

There has hardly been a Soviet concept in such a confused state as "kolkhoz trade"—or possibly this writer went astray. This note has been rewritten several times over a stretch of years. The present version has been written as this volume goes to press. There were, it is true, changes in the USSR itself in the use of terms pertaining to this trade, the justification of which is not clear. Not clear also is the timing of the changes.

In prewar days and up to 1956 the terms "kolkhoz markets," "kolkhoz market," and "kolkhoz trade" were used almost indiscriminately as synonyms. *Stat. Handb.*, 1956 (p. 215), used the term "kolkhoz market" (*rynok*) for total *kolkhoz trade,* the same phrase in the plural meaning sales in special places officially designated as kolkhoz markets. But on page 206 of the source, "kolkhoz market" and "kolkhoz trade" were used for the same thing in the same table. *Soviet Trade,* stat. handb., 1956 (pp. 180–90), gave the same figures as *Stat. Handb.*, 1956, but spoke in the first case of "kolkhoz ex-village market." *Economy of the USSR in 1958* (pp. 774, 787) uses the terms "kolkhoz ex-village market" (*rynok*) and "kolkhoz trade" (*torgovlya*) for total kolkhoz trade. Occasionally the term kolkhoz *bazary,* equivalent to farm markets of the USA, was used to designate kolkhoz markets. This word is, for example, found in the title of the 1949 pamphlet of Dadugin and Kagarlitskii, repeatedly quoted in this volume. But the word *bazar* was replaced by the word *rynok* (both words mean "market") in a late edition of the same pamphlet (see A. P. Dadugin and P. N. Fedorov, *Organization of Kolkhoz Market [Rynok] Trade* [Moscow, 1957]).

The present definition of kolkhoz markets is rather strange. It seems odd that the standard data, those for the kolkhoz markets of 251 cities, do not include sales by producers to the population *in these very cities* other than in places designated as kolkhoz markets, for example, the milk delivered by the peasant women to the homes of city dwellers. It seems even less probable that this definition of kolkhoz markets existed and was followed in statistics all the time since 1932.

In general, this writer must emphasize that he has been unable to wade through the whole mess concerning kolkhoz trade and kolkhoz markets. Every statement on the kolkhoz trade pertaining to the present and past is assumed to refer to the total kolkhoz trade as *now* officially defined as ex-village kolkhoz trade, unless the opposite is definitely obvious from the source.

The situation with *prices* in kolkhoz trade is similar to that involving its volume. For prewar years one is limited to prices calculated from indices for amounts traded in current and constant prices from sources very close to official. If these amounts are accepted as representing the total kolkhoz trade, then the calculated prices also pertain to this trade. For the war years and also for 1948 to 1950, price indices are available only for kolkhoz markets of a limited number of large cities. Even these data had not been released before late in 1957 and this writer was very happy to have them. The prices in 1947 can be calculated from the above data, but the evidence for 1946 is not sufficiently conclusive. Data for the few years (1950 and 1954 through 1958) for which price indices both for the total kolkhoz trade and a number of urban kolkhoz markets are available (*Soviet Trade*, stat. handb., 1956, pp. 182–83, and *Economy of the USSR in 1958*, pp. 789–90) show discrepancies between the two types of price data which should not be disregarded. But the analyst has no choice but to use all available price data as the prices of the kolkhoz trade as a whole, so far as a different treatment is not made possible by the evidence.

It may be useful to add that the official data on the sales in kolkhoz markets are obtained by observation of these markets. The sales in kolkhoz trade, however, are estimated from data obtained from reports of kolkhozy, surveys of incomes and expenditures of the kolkhozniki, and simply by crude estimates. It is not known whether the data on kolkhoz trade and on kolkhoz markets as obtained from the two different sources are comparable. Their comparability seems indeed doubtful. There is, for example, this strange phenomenon: According to data in *Soviet Trade*, stat. handb., 1956 (pp. 19, 188), the sales in kolkhoz markets of 251 cities increased from 19.5 billion rubles in 1950 to 30.2 billion rubles in 1955, while the residual sales of farm products in kolkhoz trade declined from 27.0 to 17.3 billion rubles. Such a large shift in the kolkhoz trade during the relatively short period of only five years does not strike one as very likely.

GLOSSARY AND ABBREVIATIONS

CC	Central Committee of the Communist Party
CSO	Central Statistical Office (had other names during various periods)
FYP	Five-Year Plan
Gosplan USSR (or simply Gosplan)	State Planning Committee of the Council of Ministers of the USSR
Gosplan, RSFSR, etc.	Gosplans of the republics
Kolkhoz (plural: kolkhozy)	Collective farm
Kolkhoznik (plural: kolkhozniki)	Member of collective farm or member of his family
MTS	Machine-Tractor Station
NBER	National Bureau of Economic Research, New York
N. J.	Naum Jasny
Oblast (plural: oblasti)	Political subdivision of the individual republics which compose the USSR
Official trade	State and co-operative trade. Whether official trade is specified as retail trade or not, this is always the case. Wholesale trade is not discussed
Raion (plural: *raiony*)	The term has two meanings. First, a political subdivision of the oblast (see above) corresponding to the county in the United States, here translated "district." Second, an economic subdivision which is up to several hundred times the size of the *raion* as a political subdivision. Possibly it would have been best to

	translate it here as "economic region," but simple transliteration has been used instead.
RSFSR	Russian Socialist Federative Soviet Republic
Sovkhoz	State or, literally, Soviet farm
Sovnarkom	Council of People's Commissars
Sovnarkhoz	Council of the National Economy
SYP	Seven-Year Plan for 1959–65
Trudoden (plural: *trudodni*)	Abbreviation for workday. In the USSR it was until quite recently the exclusive unit of payment by the kolkhozy for the work of the kolkhozniki. Each operation is assigned a value of from 0.5 to several *trudodni* per day. An average *trudoden* is equal to about two-thirds of a workday.
USSR	Union of Soviet Socialist Republics
VSNKh	Supreme Council of the National Economy
VKP (b)	All-Union Communist Party (Bolsheviks)

FREQUENTLY CITED PUBLICATIONS

WITH ABBREVIATIONS

Except for *Pravda* and *Izvestiya* (the Library of Congress transliteration), Russian publications are cited by the English translations of their titles throughout. The translated titles enable the readers who are unfamiliar with Russian to see the character of the publications used by the writer. The reader familiar with Russian will have no difficulty in identifying them.

Periodicals

Courier of Statistics	Central Statistical Office, number of issues varies from year to year
Izvestiya ("News")[1]	Presidium of the Supreme Soviet of the USSR, daily
Planned Economy	Politico-economic journal of the Gosplan of the USSR, number of issues varies from year to year
Pravda ("Truth")[1]	Central Committee of the Communist Party of the USSR, daily
Problems of Economics	Academy of Sciences of the USSR, Institute of Economics, monthly
Questions of Economics	The same as above after World War II
Socialist Agriculture (replaced by *Agriculture;* in 1960, replaced by *Rural Life,* published by the Central Committee)	Ministry of Agriculture, daily

[1] A Russian joke has it: There is no news in *News* (*Izvestiya*), and there is no truth in *Truth* (*Pravda*).

Socialist Agriculture[2] (replaced by *Economics of Agriculture*)	Ministry of Agriculture of the USSR, monthly; lately eight issues a year
Soviet Trade	Ministry of Trade, monthly

Books

1st FYP	*The First Five-Year Plan of National-Economic Construction.* 3 vols. 3d ed. Moscow: Gosplan USSR, 1930.
2d FYP, draft	*Draft of the Second Plan for the Development of the National Economy of the USSR (1933–37).* 2 vols. Moscow: Gosplan USSR, 1934.
2d FYP	*The Second Five-Year Plan for the Development of the National Economy of the USSR (1933–37).* 2 vols. Moscow: Gosplan USSR, 1934.
3d FYP, draft	*The Third Five-Year Plan for the Development of the National Economy of the USSR, Draft.* Moscow: Gosplan USSR, 1939.
4th FYP	*Law on the Five-Year Plan for the Restoration and Development of the National Economy of the USSR for 1946–50.* Moscow: Gosplan USSR, 1946.
Directives to the 5th FYP	*Directives of the Nineteenth Party Congress to the Fifth Five-Year Plan of the Development of the National Economy of the USSR for 1951–55.*
Directives to the 6th FYP	*Directives of the Twentieth Party Congress to the Sixth Five-Year Plan of the Development of the National Economy of the USSR for 1956–60.*
Control Figures for 1925/26, 1926/27, 1927/28, 1928/29, 1929/30	*Control Figures of the National Economy of the USSR,* for the years cited. Moscow, Gosplan USSR.
Control Figures for 1959/65	*Control Figures for the Development of the National Economy of the USSR for 1959–65.*
1935 Plan	*National Economic Plan of the USSR for 1935.* 2d ed. Moscow: Gosplan USSR.
1936 Plan	*National Economic Plan of the USSR for 1936.* 2d ed. Moscow: Gosplan USSR.

[2] In Russian, the titles of the two publications here called *Socialist Agriculture* were not the same. The monthly was called *Sotsialisticheskoe Selskoe Khozyaistvo.* The daily was called *Sotsialisticheskoe Zemledelie.* The confusion was caused by sloppiness in terminology, usual in Russia, and by changes in the meaning of the words over the years. Before 1928, *selskoe khozyaistvo* meant rural economy, in which were included agriculture, forestry, and fishing; *zemledelie* was strictly agriculture. Now the two terms must be considered synonyms, meaning strictly "agriculture."

1937 Plan	*National Economic Plan of the USSR for 1937.* Moscow: Gosplan USSR, 1937.
1941 Plan	*State Plan of Development of the National Economy of the USSR for 1941* (Supplements to the Order of the Sovnarkhom of the USSR and of the Central Committee of the VKP (b), No. 127, January 17, 1941). Released in the USSR with the notation "Not to be disclosed." Photographic reproduction by the American Council of Learned Societies.

(The plans for the years after World War II are cited in the same manner.)

Reports on the Fulfilment of the Plan	"On the Results of Fulfilment of the State Plan of Development of the National Economy of the USSR." A document published twice a year, both in newspapers and separately.
National Economy of the USSR, 1932	*National Economy of the USSR,* statistical handbook, 1932. Moscow: Central Office of National-Economic Accounting, 1932.
Socialist Construction of the USSR, 1936	*Socialist Construction of the USSR,* statistical yearbook. Moscow: Central Office of National-Economic Accounting of the Gosplan USSR, 1936.

(The same publications for 1934, 1935, and for 1933–38 are treated similarly.)

Stat. Handb., 1956[3]	*National Economy of the USSR,* statistical handbook. Moscow: Central Statistical Office, 1956; in the USSR occasionally cited as *National Economy* (1956).
Economy of the USSR in 1956	*National Economy of the USSR in 1956,* statistical handbook. Moscow: Central Statistical Office, 1957.
USSR in Figures, 1958	*USSR in Figures,* statistical handbook. Moscow: Central Statistical Office, 1958.
Stat. Handb., RSFSR, 1957	*National Economy, RSFSR,* statistical handbook, 1957. Moscow: Statistical Office of the RSFSR.

(The numerous statistical handbooks of the individual republics and oblasti released in the same year are cited in the same manner.)

Soviet Trade, stat. handb., 1956	*Soviet Trade,* statistical handbook, 1956. Moscow: Central Statistical Office.

[3] This was the first such publication issued after an interval of seventeen years. Hence the volume was simply called *Stat. Handb.* in the *Commentary.* The abbreviation was not changed when the subsequent volumes appeared.

Industry of the USSR, 1957	*Industry of the USSR,* statistical handbook. Moscow: Central Statistical Office, 1957.
Attainments	*Attainments during Forty Years of Soviet Power in Figures.* Moscow: Central Statistical Office, 1957.
Symposium	*Soviet Economic Growth, Conditions and Perspectives.* Proceedings in more or less revised form of a conference held at Arden House, Harriman, New York, May 23–25. Edited by Abram Bergson. Evanston, Ill.: Row, Peterson & Co., 1953.

By the Present Writer

Economy, 1955.

"Intricacies"	"Intricacies of the Russian National-Income Indexes," *Journal of Political Economy,* August, 1947.
Soc. Agri.	*The Socialized Agriculture of the USSR.* Stanford University, Calif.: Food Research Institute, 1949.
Essay I	*The Soviet Economy during the Plan Era.* Stanford University, Calif.: Food Research Institute, 1951.
Essay II	*The Soviet Price System.* Stanford University, Calif.: Food Research Institute, 1951.
Essay III	*Soviet Prices of Producers' Goods.* Stanford University, Calif.: Food Research Institute, 1952.
"Close-up"	"A Close-up of the Soviet Fourth Five-Year Plan," *Quarterly Journal of Economics* (Harvard University), May, 1952.
Commentary	*The Soviet 1956 Statistical Handbook: A Commentary.* East Lansing: Michigan State University Press, 1957.

(There are a few more Soviet books with no full title in the text and yet not listed here. For example, *Corps in the USSR,* 1939. Many of them are listed in *Soc. Agri.*)

Acreages, sown: collectivization of, 322–23; declines in, 332–33, 334; distribution of, 344–46; of kolkhozniki, 195, 317–18, 423; of kolkhozy, 324, 351, 352, 353; during postwar years, 336–39; of sovkhozy, 354; of state enterprises, 350; targets, of annual plans, 120, of 1st FYP, 96, of 2d FYP, 75; of wage earners, 347, 348, 349

Agriculture, 6, 7, 35, 176, *308–58;* during *All-out Drive,* 83–85, 96–97, 139; investment in, 84–85, 137, 191, 192, 238, 304; labor in, 310–12, 320, 384–86; during NEP, 41–42; during *Post-Stalin,* 329, 432–33; and price system, 287–88, 293; during *Purge Era,* 177, 195–98; during *Stalin Has Everything His Way,* 238, 239, 241–42, 309–10, 343–44; during *Three "Good" Years,* 139–42, 156–58, 176; during *Warming-up,* 55–56; *see also* Acreages, sown; Animal products; Crop production; Farm output; Farm products; Kolkhozy; Livestock; Peasants; Sovkhozy; *and names of individual commodities*

"All-citizen statistical ration," 282, 384, 410

All-out Drive (1929–32), 52, 59, 69, *70–118,* 119, 122, 129, 147, 159, 173, 188, 194, 203, 204, 260, 359; *see also* Stages of Great Industrialization Drive

Amalgamation campaign, 238, 323–26, 341

Andizhan oblast, 420

Andreev, A. A., 236 n.

Animal products: output of, 93, 97, 139, 140–41, 196, 318, 339, 340–41, 343, 423; price of, 314; sale of, 103, 159, 211; and 2d FYP, 127; supply of, 157; yield per animal, 333–34; *see also names of individual products*

Annual plans: functioning of, 27, 125–26; for 1931, 73, 77–79, 120; for 1932 and 1933, 120–21; for 1935 and 1936, 129–32; for 1937, 184–85; for 1947, 254–56; targets of, 120, 130–32, 183; *see also* Control figures

Arden Conference, 178 n.

Armaments: output of, 3, 177, 190, 198, 239, 302, 361, 362 n., 367, 370; price of, 201, 263, 279, 280, 427; subsidies for, 264–65 n.; *see also* Military expenditures

Armed forces, 178, 245, 247, 310, 388, 397

Arteli, 121, 122

Artificial fiber, 248, 367, 433

Automobiles, 213, 255, 289

Azerbaidzhan, 104, 373, 374

Bacchanalian planning, 73–80, 120, 122, 138

Baku, 360, 374, 375

Baltic States, 329, 370, 390, 396

Baran, Paul, 61 n.

Bazarov, V. A., 54, 69, 293 n.

Beer, 143, 270

Bergson, Abram, 37 n., 162, 263 n., 394, 401 n., 429

Berkeley symposium, 294

Beshchev, B., 377

Beverages: price of, 208 n., 210; **sale of,** 102–3, 159, 209, 210, 211, 214, 388, 397, 398, 399; *see also* Beer; Liquor, hard; Vodka; Wine

Bicycles, 213, 367

"Biological" crops, 93, 336

Birth rate, 244, 393, 396

Black market, 226

Blast furnaces, 20, 78, 88, 99, 193, 291 n.

Bootleg distilling, 159, 397

Bread: consumption of, 100, 206; output of, 142, 143, 199, 214; price of, 112 n., 113–14, 151, 152–53, 170, 270, 271, 315, 322; sale of, 159–60, 175, 214, 395, 396, 416; and 2d FYP, 127; supplement to wages, 282

Brezhnev, D. D., 309

Bricks, 129, 189, 301, 302

Brodskii, G., 179

Building materials: investment in, 192; output of, 100, 144–45, 177, 188–89, 200, 298–99, 300–301, 302, 383; sale of, 213; and 2d FYP, 129 n.; *see also* Bricks; Cement; Roofing material; Timber; Window glass

Bukharin, N. I., 59 n., 129

Business depressions, 241–42; *see also* Inflation

Butter: output of, 199, 414; price of, 113, 153, 210, 270, 273, 275, 277; sale of, 210, 211, 222, 395, 396, 402, 405

Cameras, 213, 367, 396

Capital; *see* Investment

Cattle, 84, 92, 96, 341–42, 346, 347–48

Cement, 88, 97, 142, 143, 180, 186, 189, 192, 193, 194, 199, 255, 301, 302, 364, 367

Central Committee; *see* Government or Party agencies, etc.

Chapman, Janet, 158 n., 166, 217 n., 223, 224, 284, 418 n.

Chemical industry, 383, 433

Cherepovets metallurgical plant, 373

Chernyavskii, 213, 214

Chertkova, A. A., 21 n.

China (country), 95

China (ware), 383

Cigarettes, 143, 199

Clark, Colin, 7, 10 n., 34, 198, 429

Clark, Gardner, 372 n.

Clocks and watches, 213, 396

Coal: investment in, 192; output of, 99, 115, 116, 142, 143, 177, 193, 194, 199, 200, 375; output per man, 106, 147, 383; price of, 260, 289; quality of, 202; targets, of annual plans, 120, 255, of 2d FYP, 75, of 3d FYP, 186; transportation of, 281

Coke, 116, 199, 200, 281

Collective farms; *see* Kolkhozy

Collectivization: by force, 235; and industrialization, 71–72; in new territories, 322–23; of peasant farming and households, 41, 51, 52, 63–64, 70–72, 83, 84, 90, 92; results of, 93–95, 118

"Commodity exchange," 326, 406

Communications, 138, 191, 192, 303, 304

Concentration camps, 179–80, 200

Confections, 100, 103, 211, 271, 396

Congresses; *see* Government or Party meetings

Construction: costs, 80, 115, 265, 281–82, 288, 297; and 1st FYP, 61, 80; growth of, 6, 31, 42, 144–46, 176; investment in, 81, 87–88, 106, 136, 145, 188–89, 205, 297–302, 384; output per man, 106, 147–48, 205, 384; unfinished, 84, 88, 305–6

Constructions of Communism; *see* Stalin

Consumers' goods: compared with producers' goods, 42, 182, 260, 286, 287, 288–89, 292, 366–68; investment in, 89, 192, 287; output of, 3, 5, 6, 100, 143–44, 182, 199, 201, 209, 360, 366–67, 368, 370, 416; output per man, 32; prices of, 28, 35, 80, 128, 151–56, 169, 174, 257–63, 267–78, 283, 292, 315; sales of, 213; sales taxes on, 291, 394–95; supply of, 209, 225, 226, 227, 230–31; targets, of annual plans, 66, 120, 130, of 1st FYP, 61, 67, 80–81, of 2d FYP, 124, 127, 130, 138, of 4th FYP, 251, of 5th FYP, 253 n.; *see also names of individual commodities*

Consumption: by farm population, 93, 215; of home-produced vs. commercial goods, 9–10; by kolkhozniki, 206, 416, 421–22; levels, 117, 123, 125, 150, 156, 158, 161–67, 175, 206–7, 230; by nonfarm population, 161–67, 211–12, 224, 415 n.; by peasants, 35, 43, 112, 141, 175, 195, 415–16, 424; private, 3, 176, 181, 206, 225; by rural population, 35–36; and 2d FYP, 74, 76, 127, 156; by urban population, 36, 104, 112–13; 157, 222, 341; by wage and salary earners, 170, 175, 212; by workers and employees, 149, 170, 206

Control Figures: of annual plans, 27, 47, 62, 66, 68, 73, 79–80; for 1959/65, 31, 248

Copper, 199, 255

Cost-of-food index, 167–69

Cost of living, 172; index of, 170, 208; of wage earners, 226–27

Cotton: acreage in, 332, 334; mills in operation, 193; output of, 6, 78, 139, 157–58, 196, 197, 314; price of, 314, 315; procurements of, 357

Cotton fabric: consumption of, 174, 207; output of, 17–18, 19, 99, 143, 144, 199, 201, 240, 270, 375; output per man, 147, 383; price of, 210, 270, 271, 315; sales of, 174–75, 207, 210, 396, 416; targets, of annual plans, 120, 129, 132–33, of 2d FYP, 132

Cotton seed: marketing and procurement of, 356; output of, 97, 334, 337, 339, 340; supply of, 157; targets of 2d FYP, 75, 76

Cows, 41, 346, 349, 352–53

Crop production, 55, 78, 97, 123, 139–40, 156–57, 195, 196, 333–34, 352–53, 354; *see also* Farm output; *and names of individual crops*

Crop rotation, 327–28

Cultural goods, 103, 213, 421

Dadugin, A. P., and Kagarlitskii, P. G., 161, 216, 217 n., 218, 219, 220, 224, 401–2, 448

Dairy products, 46, 112–13; *see also* Butter; Eggs; Milk

Death rate, 243, 393

Decentralization, 286, 294, 431

Defense, 4, 176; *see also* Military expenditures; War preparations

Deflation; *see* Inflation

Demand, 293

Derationing; *see* Rationing and ration prices

Diet, 35, 91, 111

Directives; *see* Five-Year Plans

Dnepr River, 249

Dobb, Maurice, 66 n., 68 n.

Donbass, 104, 240, 256, 367, 371, 372, 373

Dugashvili, Joseph; *see* Stalin

Dulles, Allen, 24

Eating places: number of, 109, 148 n.; performance per man in, 108, 148, 205, 386; prices in, 171 n., 276, 277, 278; quality of food in, 278, 399, 400; sales in, 101–2, 103, 104, 108–9, 161, 208 n., 241, 397–400

Economic equilibrium, idea of, 53 n., 59–60, 66

Education and health services, 2, 89, 91, 238, 426, 444

Eggs: consumption of, 35, 111, 162–63; marketing and procurement of, 356; output of, 97; price of, 210, 273, 275, 277; sale of, 103, 159, 161, 209, 210, 211, 218, 219, 223, 337, 339, 340, 395, 396, 402, 404, 405

Eidelman, M., 216 n.

Electric power: output of, 99, 115, 116, 142, 143, 177, 193, 194, 199, 200; targets, of 2d FYP, 75, of 3d FYP, 186, of 5th FYP, 248, of 1947 Plan, 255; *see also* Hydroelectric power

Electrification, 39, 61

Equipment, investment in, 301–2, 306, 384, 427

"Extinguishing curve," 53–58, 59, 97–98, 101

Fabrics, 103, 104; *see also* Cotton fabric; Linen fabric; Silk; Woolen fabric

Farm output, 34, 331–44; and collectivization, 71, 93; gross, 37, 43, 97, 140, 195–97, 343; growth or decline of, 31, 114, 123, 139, 173, 195–97, 414–16; of kolkhozy, 351–53; of major stages, compared, 18; of sovkhozy, 353–55; targets, of annual plans, 66, 78, 131, 256, of 1st FYP, 60, 61, 64, 67, 94, of 2d FYP, 129 n., 137, of 3d FYP, 185, 186, of 4th FYP, 251, of 5th FYP, 252; *see also* Animal products; Crop production; Farm products; *and names of individual commodities*

Farm products: marketing of, 112–13, 355–58; price of, 64, 80, 113, 257, 258, 291; supplies of, 111, 156–58, 171; *see also* Farm output, Kolkhoz trade; Official trade; Procurements; *and names of individual products*

Fat back, 270, 276

Fedoseev, P., 325

Feed crops, 332, 337–38, 345

Fertilizer, commercial, 143, 314

Fish, 103, 111, 143, 159, 199, 211, 270, 271, 396

Five-Year Plans, 2, 3; compared with stages of Great Industrialization Drive, 21–24; periods of, 12–13, 25–27, 136, 250–54; as propaganda, 12, 65, 68, 79–80, 125–27, 150, 256; first, 56–74, 80, 86, 96–97, 109, 117, 122, 125, 128; second, 74–77, 88, 121, 124, 126–29, 130, 132–33, 137, 138, 149–50, 154–56; third, 149, 178 n., 179, 183–85, 208 n.; fourth, 53, 250–51, 314, 365, 378; fifth, 53, 248, 250–53, 379; *see also* Targets

Flax, 46, 75, 157, 309–10, 332, 334, 337, 342, 356

Flour, 199, 275, 402, 405

Food: consumption of, 161–65, 224; cost index, 167–69; price of, 104, 170, 207–8, 268, 275; sales of, 103, 159–61, 227, 395–96, 398–400, 415; *see also* Consumption; Farm output; *and names of individual commodities*

Footwear: consumption of, 165–67, 207, 224; output of, 99, 143, 165, 192, 193, 194, 199, 201–2; output per man, 106, 147; price of, 35 n., 36, 166–67, 210, 212, 213, 270, 271; quality of, 212, 213; sale of, 103, 165, 174–75, 207, 210, 212–13, 396

Fotiev, S., 338 n.

Freight car turnabout, 256, 380

Freight traffic: costs of, 258, 266–67, 280–81; performance per man, 281, 381–82; rate of growth of, 13, 38, 98 n., 101, 134, 146, 177, 202–3, 376–79, 428; railway rates for, 260, 261, 280, 289; targets, of 1st FYP, 61, of 2d FYP, 128, of 3d FYP, 186, of 4th FYP, 378, of 5th FYP, 379; *see also* Railways; Transportation

Fruits, 103, 272, 273, 277, 339, 344, 402, 404, 405

Furniture, 103, 383, 421

Galenson, Walter, 105–6, 147

Georgia, 373, 374

German war prisoners, 245, 246–47, 360

Germany, 246

Gerschenkron, A., 115, 134

Ginzburg, A. M., 53 n., 56, 97, 98

GOELRO (State Plan for Electrification of Russia), 39

Gosplan, 44, 47, 51, 53, 56, 57, 63, 65, 69, 73, 74, 76–77, 109, 125, 128–29, 149–50, 154–55, 187, 252, 305; *see also* Planning; Groman, V. G.

Government or Party agencies, institutions, etc.: Central Committee, 42, 51, 77, 78, 119, 121, 122, 187, 248, 342; Central Control Commission, 119, 121, 122; Central Statistical Office, 109, 410; Council of Ministers, 251; defense ministries, 176; Gostechnika (State Committee of Council of Ministers for Incorporation of New Techniques), 294; Ministry of Agriculture, 308; Ministry of Building Materials, 254; Ministry for Eastern Areas, 255; Ministry of Finance, 221, 279 n.; Ministries of Metallurgy, 254; Ministry of Tractor and Automotive Transport, 254; Ministry of Trade, 348, 349; Ministry for Western Areas, 255; People's Commissariat of Supplies, 78; Sovnarkom (Council of People's Commissars), 357; Sovnarkoz (Council of the National Economy), 286–87; Supreme Council of National Economy (VSNKh), 56–57, 65, 78, 98

Government or Party meetings: All-Union Scientific-Technical Conference, 294; Party Congresses, (10th) 40, (11th) 40, (12th) 42, (13th) 41, (14th) 42, 45 n., (15th, Congress of Industrialization) 2, 46, 51, 52, 54, 70, 172, (17th) 74, 76, 78, 92, 101, 117, 125, 128, 132, 154, (18th) 149, 185, 186, 253, (19th) 53, 252, (20th) 431, (21st) 291

Grain: acreage in, 332–33, 336, 340, 345; distributions of, 37, 136, 228, 316, 419–20; marketings of, 112, 141, 198, 356–57; output of, 55, 93, 94, 96, 97, 123 n., 139, 309, 329, 334, 336, 337, 340, 354, 386, 414; output per man, 385; price of, 314, 315, 316; procurements of, 356, 357; sale of, 159, 161, 218, 219; and 2d FYP, 75; supply of, 157

Grain products: consumption of, 35, 111; price of, 172, 208 n., 210, 273, 277, 314, 315; sale of, 160, 206, 209, 210, 211, 404, 405, 416; and vodka, 102; *see also* Bread

Granik, David, 23

Great Industrialization Drive: aims of, 2–5, 370; results of, 5–11; *see also* Stages of Great Industrialization Drive

Groman, V. G., 44, 47, 53, 59, 61, 62, 69, 97, 435–41

Gross national product, 24–25, 429

Grossman, Gregory, 198, 429; and Shimkin, D. B., 7

Gukhman, B. A., 69

Handicrafts, 5

Hay, 97, 338

Health services; *see* Education and health services

Hearths; *see* Open hearths

Heymann, Hans, 401 n.

Hodgman, Donald, 22, 98, 114, 134, 142, 147, 178 n.

Hoeffding, O., 429

Hogs, 84, 92, 96, 346, 347

Holzman, F., 273 n.

Horses, 41, 84, 90, 92, 96

Housing, 4, 74, 83, 124, 138, 304–5

Hunter, Holland, 13, 100, 107, 128 n.

Hydroelectric power, 248, 287, 292, 432–33

Income, *407–30*, 444–47; during *All-out Drive*, 109–14, 116, 173; during *Purge*

Era, 181, 186, 223–31; during *Stalin Has Everything His Way,* 238, 303; during *Three "Good" Years,* 126, 167–76; *see also* Income, national; Income, personal; Kolkhozy

Income, national, *425–30,* 444; allocation of, 7, 176, 238; growth of, 2, 3, 5, 13, 30, 31, 114, 176, 231; origin of, 6, 176; real, 34, 116; targets, of annual plans, 78–79, of 1st FYP, 43, 61, 67, of 2d FYP, 126–27, of 3d FYP, 186, of SYP, 31

Income, personal, 223–30, *407–25,* 447; growth of, 1–2, 7, 8–9, 434; money, 181; real, 56, 167–75, 186, 409–14; 446; targets, of 1st FYP, 65–66, 67, of 3d FYP, 186; *see also* Kolkhozniki; Peasants; Wage and salary earners; Wages

Industrial capacities, utilization of, 72, 178, 180, 181, 192–93, 239, 242, 245, 359–60, 364, 365; *see also* Construction

Industrial production: compared to U.S.A., 34; comparison of in various areas, 370–75; costs, 43–44, 55, 60, 264, 266, 286–87, 288, 292–93; gross, 6, 43, 57, 66, 198, 361; indices of, 13, 31–33, 114, 134, 142, 360–63, 366, 369–70, 375; per man, 10, 32–33, 46, 55, 58, 60, 72, 104–9, 115–16, 204, 260, 284, 289, 382–84; quality of, 46, 55, 116, 202; rate of growth of, 5, 16, 37, 38, 42–43, 46, 54–55, 56–57, 97–100, 114, 123, 142–43, 181–82, 198–201, 204, 239, 242, 250, 359–70; targets, of annual plans, 66, 78, 120, 129, 130, 131, 186–87, 255, of 1st FYP, 57, 59, 60, 61, 66, 67, 98–99, of 2d FYP, 121, 128, of 3d FYP, 186; *see also* Consumers' goods; Producers' goods; *and names of individual commodities*

Industrialization, rate of, 4, 5, 51–52, 71–72, 74, 94, 97–100, 176

Industry, *359–75;* during *All-out Drive,* 72, 80, 97–100, 104–6, 114–16, 120; eastward shift in, 370–75; investment in, 89–90, 191–94, 198–202, 204–5, 303–4, 359, 363; labor productivity in, 382–84; during NEP, 40–46; during *Post-Stalin,* 30, 286, 433; private, 40–41, 44, 63, 83; during *Purge Era,* 181–82, 186, 238, 239; during *Stalin Has Everything His Way,* 238, 253–54, 264, 303; during *Three "Good" Years,* 123, 125, 130, 134, 137, 142–44, 147; during *Warming-up,* 53–55, 58, 60, 61, 66–67; *see also* Construction; Industrial capacities; Industrial production; Industry, heavy; Industry, light

Industry, heavy; investment in, 8, 89–90,

137, 191–92, 238–39, 303–4; labor costs in, 104; priority for, 3–4, 125, 191–92, 239, 253, 303–4; and 2d FYP, 124–25; and surplus value, 238; and transportation, 91; *see also* Steel

Industry, light, 4, 63, 137, 138, 288, 295, 304

Inflation, 178, 188, 297; and deflation, 27–28, 80–81, 128, 154–55, *257–95*

International Bank for Reconstruction and Development, 117

International Trade Conference, Moscow (1952), 283

Investment, *297–307;* during *All-out Drive,* 81–93; costs, 294, 307; growth of, 2, 3; private, 82–84; during *Purge Era,* 180–81, 187–94, 231; during *Three "Good" Years,* 121, 123–24, 133–38; during *Stalin Has Everything His Way,* 237–39, 246; use of capital in, 287, 289, 292–93, 432; *see also* Agriculture; Construction; Industry

Investment, fixed: disorganization of, 249, 250; gross, 75, 81–82, 84–85, 89–91, 133–36; net, 82, 85–86, 136–37, 190–91, 231; by sector, 88–91, 137–38, 191–92, 303–5; of socialized sector, 81, 82, 84–85, 89, 91, 133–35, 190, 298, 300; targets, of annual plans, 86, 120, 131, 133, of 1st FYP, 60–61, 72, of 2d FYP, 124, 125, 126

Iron, 99, 106, 115, 116, 147, 192; *see also* Pig iron

Irrigation, 83, 327–28

Ivliev, I. 289

Jewkes, John, 39 n.

Kafengaus, L. B., 43 n.

Kagarlitskii, P. G.; *see* Dadugin, A. P.

Kaganov, I. Z., 55 n.

Kaganovich, Lazar, 138, 377

Kakhovka hydroelectric plant, 249

Kamenev, L., 181

Kaplan, N. M., 178 n., 192, 233 n.; and Moorsteen, R. M., 31, 32, 33, 363

Karcz, Jerzy F., 217 n.

Kats, V., 79

Kautsky, Karl, 94

Kershaw, Edward, 25 n., 94

Khrushchev, N., 76; on agriculture, 93 n., 241, 320, 321, 328–29, 341–42; and amalgamation campaign, 238, 323–26, 341; and industry, 4; on gas output, 375; and state enterprises, 350; on wages, 285 n.

Kirov, murder of, 181 n.

Knitted goods, 143, 144, 271, 396, 421

Kolkhoz markets; *see* Kolkhoz trade
Kolkhoz Statute, 121, 325
Kolkhoz trade, 215–22, 272–78; concept of, 448–49; inflation in, 28, 258; legalization of, 119 n., 151; and peasants, 110, 174, 222–23, 227–29, 415–16; prices in, 113–14, 151–53, 170, 207, 230; prices compared with official trade, 113, 168–69, 220, 224–27, 231, 258, 262–63, 273, 276, 400, 414; sales in, 161, 162–63, 315, 401–6; volume of, 168, 401–6; volume compared with official trade, 227, 229, 387–90
Kolkhozniki: distributions to, 136, 228, 229, 241, 317, 320–22, 329, 409, 419, 421–23; number of, 310–12, 324; per capita expenditures by, 405–6, 421–22; private economy of, 121, 195, 222–23, 317–20, 384 n., 409, 423; private production of, 228, 344–46, 409; *see also* Kolkhozy; Peasants
Kolkhozy (collective farms): amalgamation of, 323–26, 341; distributions by to kolkhozniki, 136, 228, 229, 241, 317, 320–22, 329, 409, 419–23; income of, 314–17, 321, 351; investment of, 83–84, 136, 190; and labor, 311, 343, 384–85; livestock of, 92, 346, 352–53; and marketings, 357; output of, 139, 351–53; sales to, 213, 290; size of, 351, 353; and socialization, 5, 41, 82–83, 92, 94, 121–22, 325; sown acreages of, 324, 344, 345
Kondrashev, D. D., 278, 279 n., 280, 288, 289, 292
Kondratiev, N. K., 44, 45, 69 n.
Kontraktatsiya (obligatory deliveries), 314, 315, 316, 318
Korean War, 303, 364 n., 427
Kosygin, A. N., 291
Kotelnits line, 101
Kovalevskii, N. A., 51
Krasnodar oblast, 419–20
Krasnoyarsk hydroelectric plant, 432
Krzhizhanovskii, G. M., 39 n., 73
Kuibyshev, V. V., 74, 76, 129
Kuibyshev hydroelectric plant, 249, 328 n.
"Kulaks," 13, 35, 51–52, 64, 70–71, 93, 112 n.
Kuzbass, 371, 372, 373

Labor: agricultural, 310–12, 320, 341, 345, 350, 352; costs, 44–45, 46, 260; force, 8, 104, 115, 148, 205, 248, 419; German war prisoners as, 246–47; living standards of, 150, 172; non-farm, 172, 238, 310; productivity of, 10, 105–8, 369, 382–83, 384–86; targets, of 3d FYP, 186, of

4th FYP, 251, of 5th FYP, 248–49, 252; wages of, 172, 283, 322, 409, 410, 413, 419; *see also* Output per man: Wage and salary earners
Land rent, 293, 294
Lange, Oscar, 51
Laspeure method, 223
Latvia, 322
Leedy, F.; *see* Shimkin, D.
Lenin, 34, 37–40, 94, 117, 122, 236, 287
Leningrad, 104, 375
Lifits, M. M., 402–3, 416
Linen fabric, 199, 383
Liquor, hard, 261, 267, 268, 270, 271; *see also* Beverages; Vodka
Lisenkov, A., 340
Livestock: and collectivization, 323; decline in, 84, 96, 332–33, 415; distribution of, 344, 346; of kolkhozniki, 136, 195, 318–20, 423; of kolkhozy, 92, 352–53; of peasants, 82, 319; during postwar years, 331–34, 339; of sovkhozy, 354; value of, 56, 83
Living standards, 5, 36, 41, 47, 52, 123, 150, 407, 414; *see also* Cost of living
Lobanov, P., 329
Lokshin, E., 3
Lorimer, Frank, 72, 157

Machine-tractor stations (MTS), 90, 138, 286, 290, 312, 352, 353
Machinery: farm, 78, 238, 313–14; imports of, 6; output of, 99, 115, 134, 190, 198, 199, 201, 302–3, 367, 369–70, 375, 427; output per man, 147, 204–5, 382–83; prices of, 261 n., 265, 279–80, 427; and 2d FYP, 75; *see also* Equipment
Makarova, M., 218, 119
Makhorka, 143, 144, 199, 414
Malenkov, G. M., 4, 93 n., 180, 241, 252, 253, 320, 328–29, 433
Malyshev, I., 112 n., 292
Manganese ore, 199, 200
Manual workers, 44–45, 171, 206
Marginal utility, 293
Market economy, 294
Marketings, 334, 355–58
Matches, 271, 383
Mazel, L., 276 n.
Meat: consumption of, 35, 55–56, 111, 112–14, 162–64, 207, 222; marketing of, 41, 356, 358; output of, 97, 99, 139, 143, 196, 199, 201, 337, 340, 347, 370, 415; prices of, 113, 153, 208 n., 210, 270, 271, 273, 275, 276, 277; sales of, 103, 113, 159, 161, 207, 210, 211, 218, 219,

396, 402, 404, 405; supply of, 157, 195, 198, 222, 333
Menshevik trial, 69, 97
Mensheviks, 52, 62, 122; *see also* Groman, V. G.
Metal products, 213
Metallurgy, 192, 372, 373
Metals, non-ferrous, 177, 260
Military expenditures, 6, 8, 10, 21, 123, 231, 280, 425–26, 433, 444; *see also* Armaments; Armed forces
Milk: consumption of, 35, 111, 113, 162–64, 195, 222; marketing and procurement of, 141, 356, 357–58; output of, 97, 112 n., 127, 139, 196, 334, 337, 340, 347, 348; output per man, 385; price of, 210, 273, 275, 277; sales of, 103, 162–64, 209, 210, 211, 218, 219, 222, 395, 396, 402, 404, 405; supply of, 157, 333; yield per cow, 352, 353
Milyutin, V. P., 52 n.
Ministries; *see* Government or Party agencies, etc.
Moldavia, 371
Molotov, V. N., 74, 122, 149, 172–73
Moorsteen, R. M.; *see* Kaplan, N. M.
Moscow, 116, 220 n., 221
Moscow oblast, 104, 420, 422, 423
Munitions; *see* Armaments

Nails, 213
National Bureau of Economic Research, 190, 198, 361, 363, 369
National income; *see* Income, national
Natural gas, 248
Nemchinov, V., 292
Neo-Narodniki, 44, 52
New Economic Policy (NEP), 2, 13, 40–42, 47, 51, 52, 79, 236, 242
Nimitz, Nancy, 316, 358 n., 429
NKVD, 179, 185
Non-farm economy, 30, 31, 37, 45, 46, 81, 85, 140, 182, 197, 239, 249–50, 288, 309
Nove, Alexander, 429
Nutter, G. Warren, 25 n., 361

Obligatory deliveries; see *Kontraktatsiya*
Official trade, 207–14, 267–72; performance per man in, 107–8, 148, 205, 386; prices in, 151–53, 231 n., 257, 262, 421; prices compared with kolkhoz trade, 113, 168–69, 220, 224–27, 231, 258, 262–63, 273–76, 400, 414; sales in, 158–61, 162–63, 168, 169, 211–15, 222, 227, 411; and sales taxes, 394–95; volume of, 107–9, 174–75, 206, 387–401; volume compared with kolkhoz trade, 227, 229, 387–90

Open hearths, 19, 20, 88, 99
Ordzhonikidze, S., 78
Output; *see* Farm output; Industrial production; *and names of individual commodities*
Output per man, 33, 283, 284, 289, 343; in *All-out Drive,* 105–9, 115–16; postwar, 380–86; in *Purge Era,* 178, 182, 204–5; targets, of annual plans, 105, 120, of 2d FYP, 128, of 4th FYP, 251, of 5th FYP, 252; in *Three "Good" Years,* 123, 146–48; *see also* Construction; Industrial production

Paasche method, 223
Pakistan, 117
Paper, 99, 143, 199, 383
Party; *see* Government or Party agencies, etc.; Government or Party meetings
Pavlov, Minister of Trade, 212 n.
Passenger transportation, 203–4, 379
Peasant economy, 43, 178–79, 195, 196, 222, 238–39; *see also* Kolkhozniki
Peasants: diet of, 35; force used against, 64, 235; income of, 10, 110, 173–75, 186, 206, 224, 227–31, 240, 316, 341, 407–8, 410, 411, 417, 419–25, 433, 446; individual investments of, 136; and kolkhoz trade, 110, 174, 222–23, 227–29, 415–16; livestock of, 82, 319, 346; output of, 345, 347; prices charged to, 45–46, 151, 156, 269, 270, 308; private enterprises of, 121, 139, 326; purchasing power of, 214; *see also* Collectivization; Consumption; Kolkhozniki
Personal income; *see* Income, personal
Petroleum: industry, eastward shift of, 360, 373–75; investment in, 192; output of, 99, 115, 116, 117, 142, 143, 199, 200, 374; output per man, 106, 147, 383; price of, 271, 289; products, price of, 290; targets, of 1947 Plan, 255, of 2d FYP, 75, 127; transportation of, 378
Pig iron: capacities in operation, 78, 193, 194; output of, 20, 74, 116, 193, 194, 372–73; output per man, 383; targets, of 1947 Plan, 254, of 2d FYP, 75
Pipe lines, 378
Planning, 25–27, 39, 47, 119–22, 125–33, 154, 183–87, 235, 247–56, 431; *see also* Annual plans; Five-Year Plans; Targets
Poland, 294
Population: movements of, 204; rate of growth, 36, 46, 72–73, 111, 157, 174, 197, 243–45, 341, 391, 393, 430, 447; rural and urban compared, 9, 36, 104, 111–13, 213–14, 348–49, 391, 400–401; *see also*

Consumption; Peasants; Purchasing power; Wage and salary earners

Post-Stalin (1953——), 30–31, 248, 329; *see also* Stages of Great Industrialization Drive

Potatoes: acreage in, 332, 336–37, 345, 347; consumption of, 112, 163–64, 195, 224; marketing and procurement of, 141, 334, 356, 357; output of, 97, 139, 196, 197 n., 309, 329, 334, 337, 342, 348; price of, 46, 113, 210, 273, 275, 277; sales of, 103, 161, 210, 211, 218, 219, 223, 402, 404, 405; supply of, 111, 157

Prices: indices of, 43–44, 167–69, 207–8, 210, 265, 268, 270, 271, 272, 273, 274, 278, 281–82, 400; relationship of, 27–28, 45–46, 80–81, 151–56, 167–70, 257–82, 288–89, 314–16; setting of, 293–94, 315; structure of, 285–96, 432; weighted, 152, 154, 156, 168, 169; *see also* Consumers' goods; Inflation; Kolkhoz trade; Official trade; Producers' goods; Rationing and ration prices; Statistics, official Soviet; *and names of individual commodities*

Private enterprise; *see* Industry; Kolkhozniki; Peasants; Trade

Procurements, 64, 141, 173, 191–92, 198, 201

Producers, comparison of, 344–55

Producers' goods: compared with consumers' goods, 42, 182, 260, 286, 288–89, 292, 366–68; investment in, 89, 123–24, 180, 287; output of, 4, 6, 42, 125, 182, 185, 186, 199, 360, 366; output per man, 32; prices of, 28, 257, 258, 260–64, 278–80; targets, of annual plans, 66, 78, 120, 130, of 2d FYP, 124, 130, of 3d FYP, 185

Production costs, 178, 186–87, 293; *see also* Construction; Industry

Productivity; *see* Labor

Prokopovicz, S. N., 113, 150, 167, 168, 169, 170

Purchasing power, 149, 213–14, 221, 225

Purge Era (1937–40), *177–231*, 236, 259, 359; *see also* Stages of Great Industrialization Drive

Purges, 196; effects of, 178–82, 195, 198, 222 n., 236, 239, 241, 259

Quarterly plans, 185, 256
Quiring, E., 63 n.

Radios, 396
Ragolskii, M., 81 n.
Railways: new construction of, 75, 380; operation of, 203, 380; performance per man on, 107, 128, 204, 381; per-kilo-

meter costs to, 266–67, 280–81; *see also* Freight traffic; Passenger transportation

Rationing and ration prices, 65, 102, 113, 148, 151–53, 155–56, 160, 161, 167, 168, 170, 172, 261, 272, 273, 282, 315, 393, 398, 407, 414, 417

Real wages; *see* Wages

Redding, David, 381 n.

Restaurants; *see* Eating places

Retail trade; *see* Trade

River traffic, 377–78, 379, 381–82

Roofing material, 189, 301

Rubles, conversion of 1861, 188 n.

Rural population; *see* Consumption; Population

RSFSR, 317–18, 321–22, 325, 329, 342, 349, 352–53, 371, 373

Saburov, M. Z., 53, 248, 249, 252

Salary earners; *see* Wage and salary earners

Sales taxes, 287, 288, 289, 291, 292, 326, 394–95

Salt, 270, 271, 406

Satellite countries, 245–47, 360, 364

Schlesinger, R., 71, 93 n.

School enrolment, 240–41

Schwartz, Harry, 284

Schwarz, Solomon, 150, 172

Sea traffic; *see* River traffic

"Second revolution," 6, 52, 81

Sergeev, S., 420

Services, 24–25, 169, 409, 415

Seven-Year Plan, 12 n., 26, 31, 248, 249, 285, 328 n.

Sewing machines, 213, 396, 397

Shabalin, 342, 343

Shchadilov, I., 292

Sheep and goats, 84, 92, 96, 334, 346, 347

Shimkin, D. B.: et al., 198, 361, 363, 365, 366, 369, 370, 427; and Grossman, G., 7; and Leedy, F., 32, 190

Shoes; *see* Footwear

Siberia, 326, 371, 373

Silk, 270, 271, 272, 383, 396, 416

Smilga, I., 77

Smolensk oblast, 342

Soap, 199, 396

Social Democrats, 94

Socialization; *see* Collectivization; Kolkhozy

Socks and stockings, 143, 144, 199, 201, 271, 367, 396

Solenova, M., 321

South Caucasus, 373

Sovkhozy (state farms), 137–38, 353–55; investments of, 83; livestock of, 346; output of, 139, 318, 322; output per man, 343, 384–86; size of, 326; sown acreages of, 344–45

Sown acreages; *see* Acreages, sown

Spindles, 194; *see also* Cotton

Spulber, Nicholas, 246

Stages of Great Industrialization Drive, 11–24, 27, 29–31, 33, 235–42; *see also All-out Drive; Post-Stalin; Purge Era; Stalin Has Everything His Way; Three "Good" Years; Warming-up*

Stalin, Joseph: and collectivization, 52, 64, 68, 92–93, 121; and "changing the climate," 237, 249, 327; and Communist ideology, 62, 63, 69, 122; "Constructions of Communism," 249, 327–28; and industrial expansion, 3, 54, 90, 119, 359; and planning, 63, 73, 76, 117, 183, 187, 191, 235–37, 253–54, 326–27; on purges, 181; and workers, 63, 109

Stalin Has Everything His Way (1945–52), *235–56*, 259, 303, 309, 314–15, 343, 378, 419; *see also* Stages of Great Industrialization Drive

Stalingrad hydroelectric plant, 249, 328 n.

Starlinger, Wilhelm, 95

Starovskii, V., 272

Starvation, 71, 72, 93, 100, 118, 119, 122, 173, 222, 300, 317, 393

State enterprises, 190, 350–51

State farms; *see* Sovkhozy

Statistics, official Soviet: on agricultural production, 5, 7 n., 43, 93, 96–97, 123 n., 140–42, 197 n., 323, 329, 331–53; on building materials, 213, 299, 301, 302, 370; on construction, 87–88, 144–46, 147, 188–89, 205, 265, 281, 299, 300–301, 305–6, 384; on consumers' goods, 182 n., 199, 201, 213; on consumption, 111–12, 206–7; falsification of, 129, 174, 297, 394, 408, 412, 424–25; on footwear, 165–66, 201, 212–13; on freight traffic, 266, 376, 378, 428; on housing, 305; on industrial production, 5, 43, 98–99, 116, 127 n., 142–43, 199, 240, 264, 284, 360–62, 368, 371–75; on investment, 81–92, 135–37, 188–90, 246, 265, 297–300, 307; on kolkhoz trade, 215–21, 272–77, 389–90, 401–5, 448–49; on kolkhozniki, 311, 312, 409, 422; on kolkhozy, 322, 324, 351–53; on livestock, 319, 331–33, 346; on machinery, 201, 302, 369; on nominal wages, 284, 408; on official trade, 207–8, 210–11, 214, 267–71, 388–99; on output per man, 105–7, 115, 146–48, 201, 204–5, 335, 343, 381–86; on peasant incomes, 229–30, 409; on personal incomes, 9, 109–10,

408–14; on population, 112, 243–44; on prices, 113–14, 264–66, 267–71; on procurements of farm products, 355–56; on producers' goods, 182 n., 199, 264; on retail trade, 101–4, 107–8, 113, 156, 159, 174, 205, 224, 388–89; on sovkhozy, 353–54; on sown acreages, 309, 332, 335, 337–39, 345, 348; *see also* "All-citizen statistical ration"; Targets

Statistics and politics, 129

Steel: investment in, 200; output of, 17–20, 99, 115, 116, 142–43, 177, 178, 186, 199–200, 240, 371–73; output per man, 106, 147, 383; price of, 261; sale of, 213; and Stalin, 3, 15, 77, 236–37; targets, of annual plans, 77–78, 120, 254–55, of 3d FYP, 178 n., 185–86, 193; utilization of capacities, 19–20, 99, 193–94, 364–65

Strumilin, S. G., 41 n., 56, 63, 65, 73, 292, 297–98, 300, 302

Sugar: consumption of, 35, 111, 164–65, 207, 215; output of, 100, 103, 143, 194, 199, 333, 334, 414; output per man, 147; price of, 153, 208 n., 210, 214, 271; sales of, 207, 210, 211, 214–15, 226, 396, 416

Sugar beets, 46, 75, 76, 78, 96, 97, 139, 157, 196, 315, 332, 333, 334, 337, 339, 340, 356, 357

Sunflower seeds, 97, 139, 157, 196, 197 n., 332, 334, 337, 339, 356, 357

Surplus value, 10, 288, 292

Sweezy, Paul, 35 n., 93, 94–95

Targets: of annual plans, 66, 120, 183, 184, 254–55; of 1st FYP, 56–61, 64–69, 73, 94; of 2d FYP, 74–75, 124–29, 149–50, 154–56; of 3d FYP, 178 n., 185–87, 193, 199, 208 n.; of 4th FYP, 251, 378; of 5th FYP, 248, 252, 379; of SYP, 248, 249, 285; of Stalin's long-range plan, 253–54

Taxes, 5 n., 41, 239, 320, 326; *see also* Sales taxes

Technical crops, 345, 357

Textiles, 36, 138, 158, 165, 224; *see also* Cotton fabric; Silk

Three "Good" Years (1934–36), *119–76*, 177–78, 181, 183, 197, 198, 200, 203, 204, 225, 260; *see also* Stages of Great Industrialization Drive

Timber: output or procurement of, 88, 98, 114, 142, 143, 144, 189, 199, 200–201, 301, 302; output per man, 106, 116, 383; price of, 291 n.; targets, of 2d FYP, 127, of 1947 Plan, 255; transportation of, 281

Tobacco, 207, 208 n., 209, 210, 211, 261, 271

Tractors, 143, 147, 254, 255, 290–91, 313–14, 350, 353, 354

Trade, *387–406;* during *All-out Drive,* 101–4, 107, 112; investment in, 191, 192; postwar, 414, 415; private, 5 n., 40–41, 63, 80, 92, 101, 166, 390; during *Purge Era,* 206–22; targets, of 1st FYP, 61, 67, 80, of 4th FYP, 251; during *Three "Good" Years* 148, 158–67, 174–75; *see also* Consumers' goods; Kolkhoz trade; Official trade; Producers' goods; *and names of individual commodities*

Transportation, 38, 91; during *All-out Drive,* 89, 100–101, 107, 115–16, 123, 147; investment in, 138, 191, 303, 304; passenger, 203–4; postwar, 376–80; during *Purge Era,* 192, 202–4; during *Stalin Has Everything His Way,* 238, 239–40; during *Three "Good" Years,* 138, 146, 147; *see also* Freight traffic; Railways

Trotsky, Leon, 122

Trucks, 75, 213, 353, 367, 378

Trudoden, 241, 311 n., 321–22, 351, 353, 420, 421, 422, 423

Tsentrosoyuz, 214, 278, 406 n.

Tsuryupa, A., 40

Turetskii, Sh., 270, 291 n.

Turkmen, 374

Ukraine, 104, 112, 114, 153, 371, 372–73, 374, 375

United States embassy, 209, 212, 216 n.

Urals, 371, 372, 373, 375

Urban population; *see* Consumption; Population

Uzbek, 374

Vainstein, A., 45

Valentinov, N. V., 39 n.

Vegetable oil: consumption of, 36; output of, 143, 199, 201, 334, 414; price of, 152, 270, 271, 275, 277; sales of, 209, 210, 396, 402, 405

Vegetables: acreage in, 332, 336–37, 345, 347; consumption of, 112; marketing and procurement of, 356, 357; output of, 139, 309, 334; price of, 273, 275, 277; sales of, 103, 161, 218, 219, 223, 402, 404, 405: supply of, 111

Vodka: consumption of, 36, 207; output of, 143, 199, 414; price of, 169, 269, 270, 400; sales of, 102–3, 159, 210, 211, 214, 241, 386, 396–97

Volga region, 104, 112, 371, 374

Volkov, A. 413

Voronezh, 329

Voznesenskii, N. A., 188, 208 n., 209 n., 236 n., 249, 262 n., 314 n.

Wage and salary earners: dependents of, 110, 225; discrimination among, 295–96; farm production of, 347–50; income of, 10, 45, 110, 167, 168, 171–75, 181, 224–25, 226, 230, 341, 407, 408, 410, 413, 417, 418–19, 426, 433–34; livestock of, 346; number of, 204, 383; in official trade, 107–8; prices charged to, 151, 156, 276; restrictions on, 8, 182; sown acreages of, 345, 347, 348; on state farms, 354; *see also* Consumption; Labor

Wage structure, 295–96, 431, 433

Wages: comparison of, 45, 170–71, 295; indices of, 45, 172, 227, 411, 412, 413, 424, 447; nominal, 172, 181, 224–27, 231, 257, 258–59, 260, 282–85, 409, 414; real, 10, 44–45, 72, 110, 172, 223, 224–27, 230, 238, 240, 407, 408, 409–14, 417–19, 424–25, 426, 434, 446, 447; targets, of 1st FYP, 65, 66, 67, 68, 109, of 2d FYP, 149–50, of 3d FYP, 186; *see also* Income, personal; Labor; Wage and salary earners

War Communism, 13, 38, 39, 40, 43, 118, 122

War preparations, 33, 178, 200, 207, 303, 425–26

War prisoners, 245, 246–47, 360

Warming-up (1928–29), *51–69,* 74, 80; *see also* Stages of Great Industrialization Drive

Weather, 61, 114, 122, 131, 196, 263, 327–28

Weighted prices; *see* Prices

Wheat, 46; *see also* Grain

White-collar workers, 295

White Russia, 325 n., 329, 338 n.

Wiles, Peter, 15 n., 30, 247 n., 294, 388 n., 394 n., 429

Williams, Professor, 327–28

Window glass, 88, 144, 189, 255, 301, 302

Wine, 270

Winston, Victor, 246

Women in labor force, 8, 278, 312, 326

Wool, 334, 337, 340, 354, 356, 383, 385, 396

Woolen fabric, 199, 271

Workday, 44, 104, 182; see also *Trudoden*

World War II: agriculture during, 309, 331; effect of on prices, 221, 226, 260–67, 397; industry during, 199, 245, 365, 366; and loss of manpower, 244, 310; recovery after, 237, 245–47, 359, 364;

and steel output, 372; trade during, 391–92, 400, 403; wages during, 282, 295
Wyler, Julius, 10 n.

Yearly plans; *see* Annual plans
Yugoslavia, 294

Yurovskii, L. N., 53 n.

Zaporozhie oblast, 420
Zelenevskii, A., 179, 185 n.
Zinoviev, 122
Zverev, A. G., 191, 261 n., 278, 279